PUBLISHER
DAMIAN A. WASSEL

EDITOR-IN-CHIEF
ADRIAN F. WASSEL

SENIOR ARTIST
NATHAN C. GOODEN

MANAGING EDITOR
DER-SHING HELMER

E.V.P. BRANDING & DESIGN
TIM DANIEL

PRODUCTION MANAGER
IAN BALDESSARI

SENIOR DESIGNER
SONJA SYNAK

VICE PRESIDENT, SALES & MARKETING
DAVID DISSANAYAKE

SALES & MARKETING, BOOK TRADE
SYNDEE BARWICK

COMMERCE & COMMUNICATIONS
DANIEL CRARY

SOCIAL MEDIA COORDINATOR
ALEX SCOLA

SOCIAL MEDIA & COMMUNITY MANAGER
BRITTA BUESCHER

WRITER
DAVID ANDRY

ARTIST ISSUES 1-5
ALE ARAGON

ARTIST ISSUES 6-10
SKYLAR PATRIDGE

COLORIST
JASON WORDIE

LETTERER
DERON BENNETT

RESONANT

FOREWORD

EMBRACE THE WAVES

THE PERIODICAL CICADA EMERGES EVERY SEVENTEEN YEARS AND INFESTS ENTIRE AREAS. YOU KNOW THEY ARE BACK BECAUSE THEY ARE FLYING EVERYWHERE, AND THEY ARE CHIRPING—LOUDLY. NEVER-ENDING. BEYOND ANNOYING. IF ONE WORD COULD DESCRIBE THAT SOUND, IT WOULD BE RESONANT.

WHEN I OPENED THE FIRST ISSUE OF RESONANT, I DIDN'T KNOW WHAT TO EXPECT. WHAT I DISCOVERED AMAZED ME. I IMMEDIATELY KNEW THAT I NEEDED TO BE A PART OF THIS PROJECT AND ADAPT IT INTO A TV SERIES. I NEEDED TO BRING THE STORY OF PAXTON AND HIS CHILDREN TO THE SCREEN.

RESONANT ISN'T YOUR AVERAGE POST-APOCALYPTIC STORY EITHER. THERE ARE SURPRISING LAYERS TO THE WORLD-BUILDING. WHAT BRINGS US TO THE END ISN'T ZOMBIES OR ALIENS OR A VIRUS. IT'S THE WAVES.

THE WAVES PULL OUR DEEPEST, DARKEST IMPULSES TO THE SURFACE. THEY MAKE US ACT ON THOSE IMPULSES AND BETRAY OURSELVES AND OTHERS AROUND US. RESONANT SHOWS US HOW SURVIVORS RESIST THE WAVES, REACT TO THE WAVES, AND USE THE WAVES FOR THEIR OWN BENEFIT. EVERY TWIST AND TURN WILL MAKE YOU QUESTION WHO YOU CAN TRUST WHEN THE NEXT WAVE HITS. A FRIEND CAN BECOME A FOE IN MOMENTS, AND THE ONLY IMPACT WARNING IS THAT ANNOYING CICADA CHIRPING.

THE WAVES REMIND ME OF MY FIRST STUDIO FILM, THE FIRST PURGE, ABOUT A NIGHT WHEN PEOPLE ARE LEGALLY ALLOWED TO ACT OUT THEIR DEEPEST, DARKEST DESIRES. SEEING THIS CONCEPT ON A GLOBAL SCALE FELT FAMILIAR AND NEW TO ME, ALL AT ONCE.

RESONANT ALSO HAS THOSE TRADITIONAL POST-APOCALYPTIC FACETS, TOO. CORRUPT FIGUREHEADS, PEOPLE WHO HAVE BECOME ANIMALISTIC OVER TIME, THE DETERIORATION OF THE WORLD, AND A STRONG LEADER WHO IS GUIDING US THROUGH IT.

ALL OF THIS MEANT I CONNECTED TO RESONANT ON A DEEP LEVEL. I CAN RELATE TO A SINGLE, BLACK FATHER WHO WOULD DO ANYTHING FOR HIS KIDS BECAUSE THAT WASN'T FICTION IN MY CHILDHOOD. I GREW UP IN NEW ORLEANS AND EXPERIENCED THE DISASTER OF HURRICANE KATRINA. I'VE SEEN DESTRUCTION AND ABANDONMENT IN THE REAL WORLD. I'VE LIVED THROUGH A VERSION OF THE WAVE.

I ADMIRE THAT HUMANITY ALWAYS FINDS A WAY TO COME BACK TOGETHER, REBUILD AND HEAL.

FOREWORD.

AND, FRANKLY, WE'RE SEEING SOMETHING NEW BY FOLLOWING A STRONG, BLACK FAMILY, LED BY A SINGLE, BLACK FATHER, THROUGH THE DANGEROUS LANDSCAPES OF THESE GENRES. THIS IS A FAMILY THAT HAS LEARNED TO ADAPT TO THE WORLD AROUND THEM, AND EVEN THOUGH THEY ARE STRUGGLING, THEY ARE SURVIVING.

THAT'S WHAT RESONANT SHOWS US. IT ISN'T JUST WOE, VIOLENCE, AND DEATH, IT IS ALSO ASPIRATIONAL AND HOPEFUL. WE ALL MAY STRUGGLE, BUT THE GOAL IS TO ADAPT AND SURVIVE. THOSE HUMAN TRUTHS ARE WHAT I LOVE ABOUT THIS STORY.

HERE'S WHAT I PROMISE: IN THESE PAGES...

YOU WILL FIND THE STORY OF A MAN WHO DESPERATELY WANTS TO BE THE BEST FATHER HE CAN BE.

YOU WILL FIND HIS CHILDREN, WHO WANT HIS APPROVAL, WHO BICKER AND COOPERATE IN EQUAL MEASURE AS THEY LEARN TO BE BRAVE—AS THEY LEARN HOW TO STAY A FAMILY.

YOU WILL FIND THE TALES OF SO MANY DISPARATE GROUPS DOING WHATEVER THEY CAN, FOR BETTER OR WORSE, TO SURVIVE.

YOU WILL CONFRONT YOURSELF. YOU WILL QUESTION HOW YOU WOULD ACT IN THE SAME SCENARIO.

YOU WILL QUESTION WHAT YOUR IMPULSES WOULD MAKE YOU DO IF THE WAVE HIT TODAY, WHETHER YOU COULD SUPPRESS OR CONTROL THEM LIKE SOME OF OUR CHARACTERS HAVE LEARNED TO DO—WORST OF ALL, WHETHER YOU WOULD WANT TO.

YOU WILL ENCOUNTER HUMANITY AT ITS CORE.

RESONANT IS A FEVER DREAM COME TRUE. AS YOU READ, LIKE I DID THE FIRST TIME, AND THE SECOND TIME, AND MANY MORE TIMES SINCE, YOU WILL DISCOVER THAT THIS IS A STORY THAT MUST BE TOLD. BUT BRACE FOR IMPACT.

I HEAR THEM.

CHIRP. CHIRP. CHIRP.

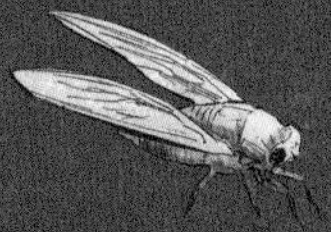

GERARD MCMURRAY
WRITER/DIRECTOR/SHOW-RUNNER
RESONANT
THE FIRST PURGE
BURNING SANDS
FRUITVALE STATION

CHAPTER ONE

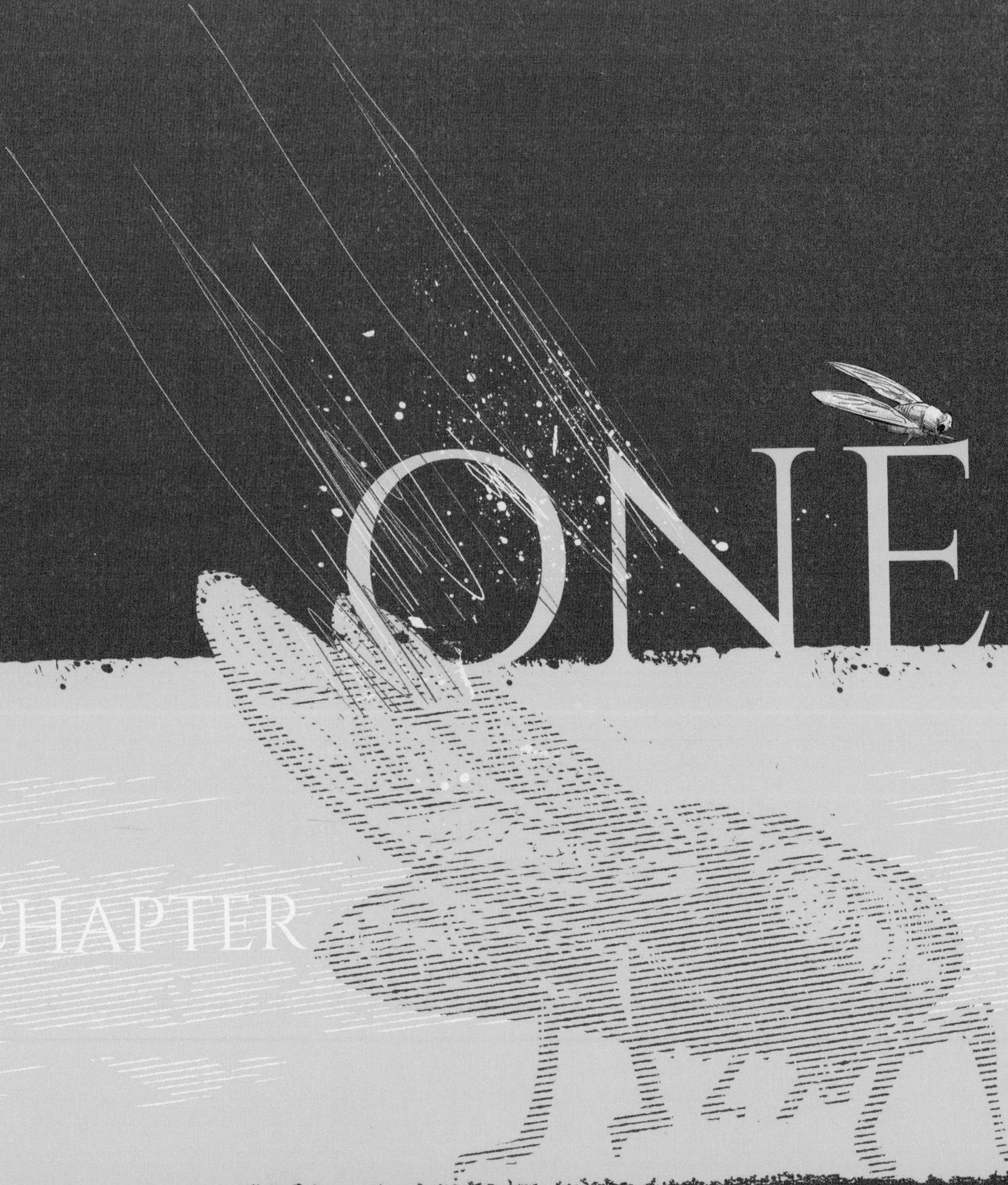

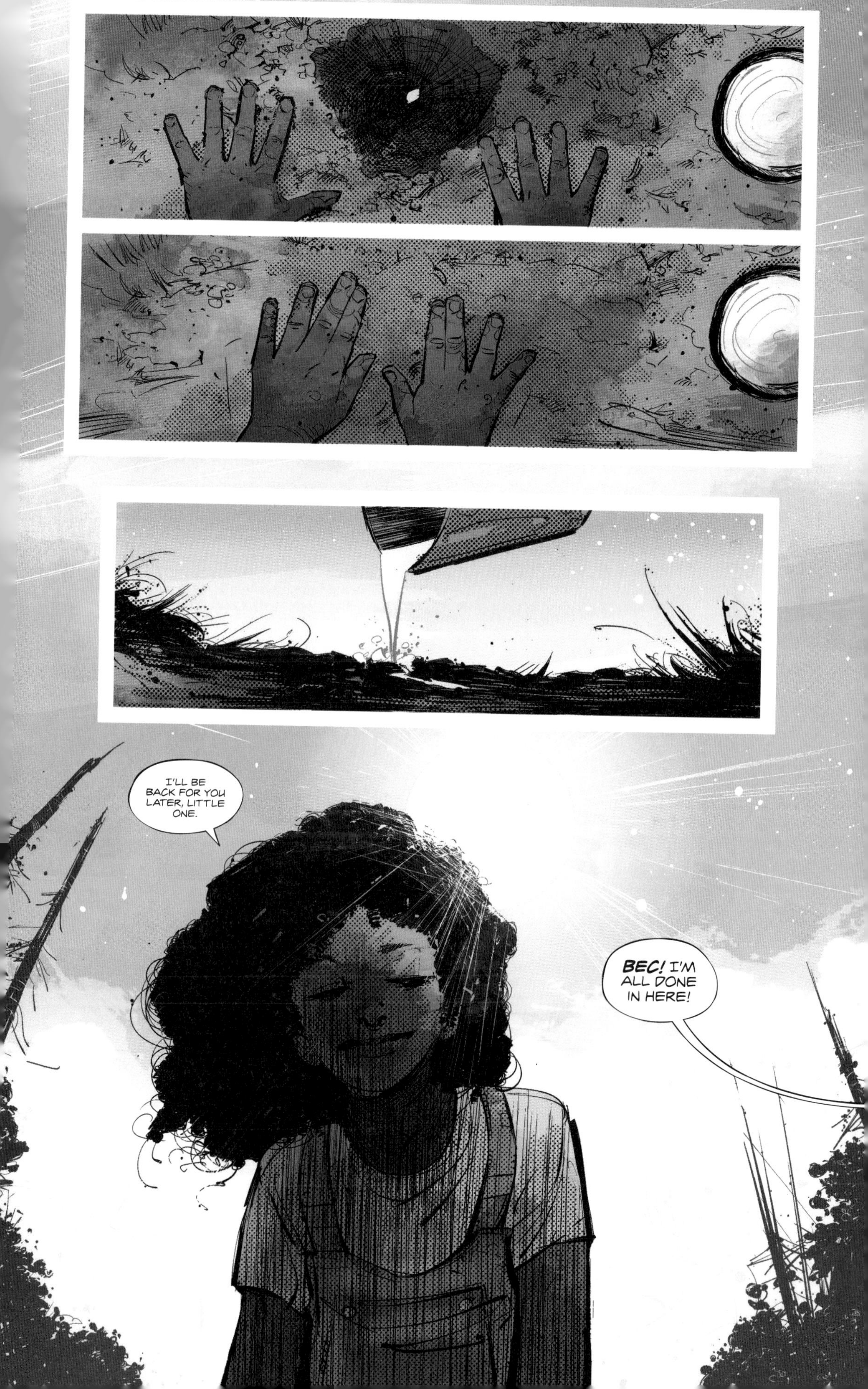
I'LL BE BACK FOR YOU LATER, LITTLE ONE.
BEC! I'M ALL DONE IN HERE!

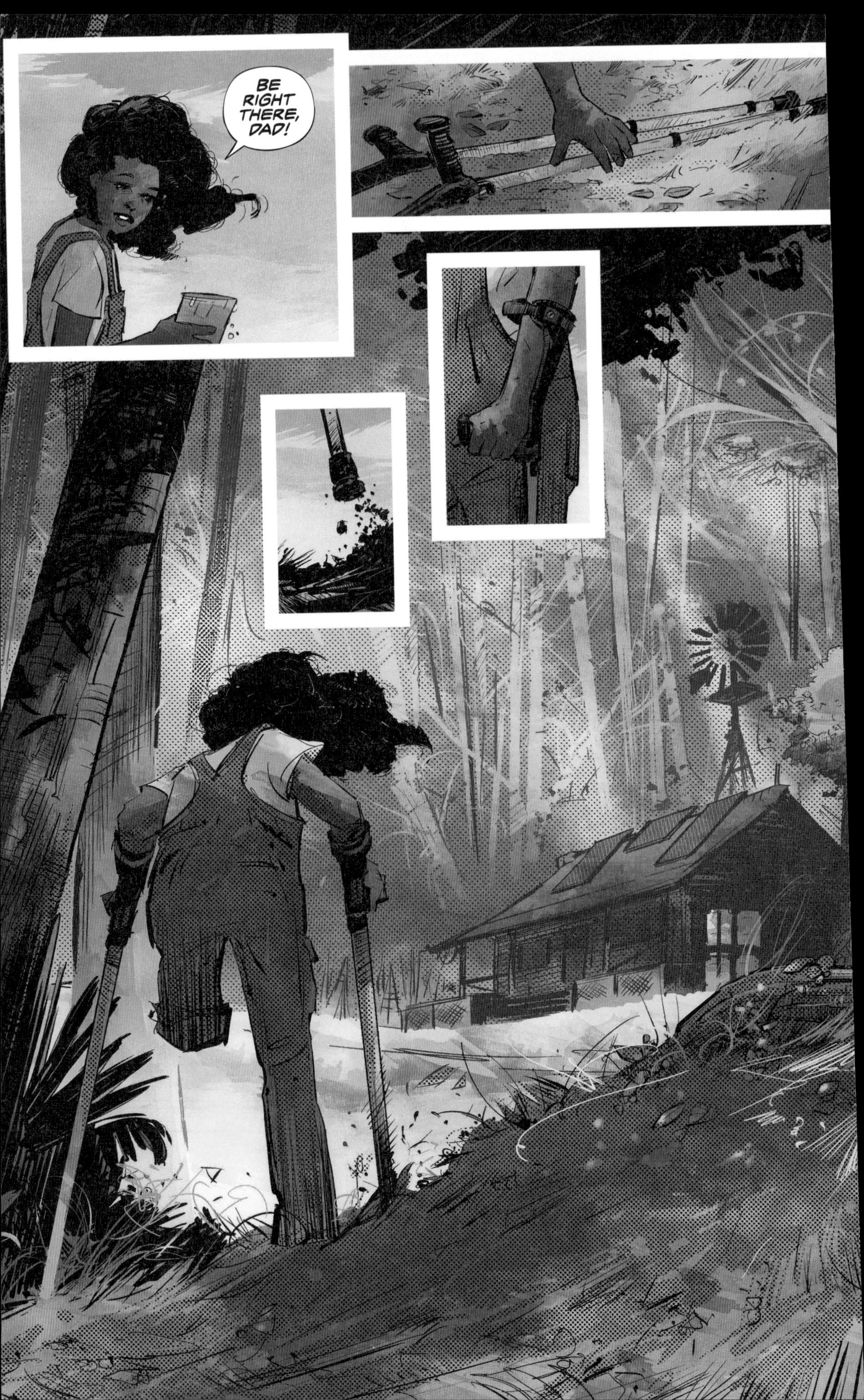
BE RIGHT THERE, DAD!

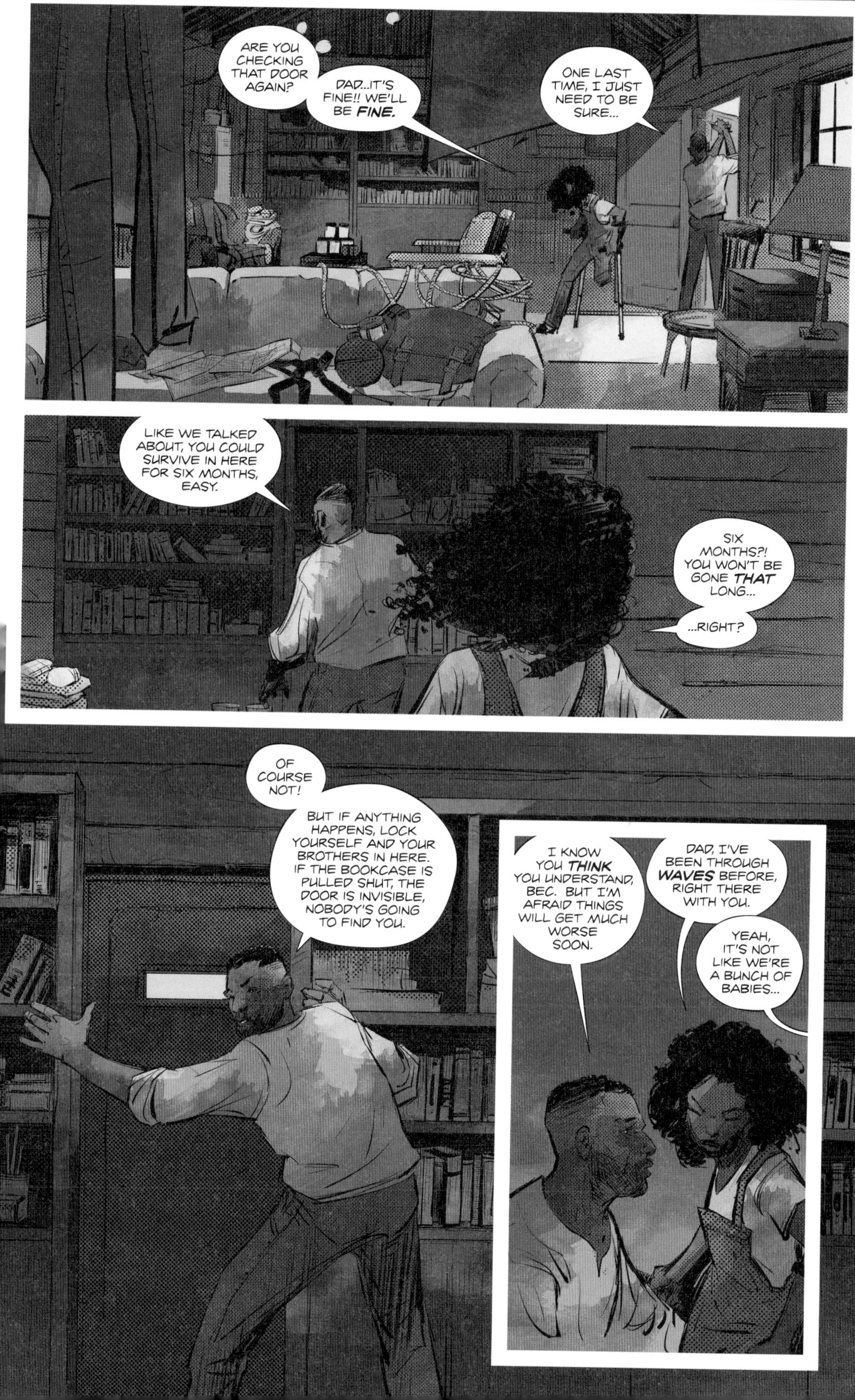
ARE YOU CHECKING THAT DOOR AGAIN?
DAD...IT'S FINE!! WE'LL BE **FINE.**
ONE LAST TIME, I JUST NEED TO BE SURE...
LIKE WE TALKED ABOUT, YOU COULD SURVIVE IN HERE FOR SIX MONTHS, EASY.
SIX MONTHS?! YOU WON'T BE GONE **THAT** LONG...
...RIGHT?
OF COURSE NOT!
BUT IF ANYTHING HAPPENS, LOCK YOURSELF AND YOUR BROTHERS IN HERE. IF THE BOOKCASE IS PULLED SHUT, THE DOOR IS INVISIBLE, NOBODY'S GOING TO FIND YOU.
DAD, I'VE BEEN THROUGH **WAVES** BEFORE, RIGHT THERE WITH YOU.
YEAH, IT'S NOT LIKE WE'RE A BUNCH OF BABIES...
I KNOW YOU **THINK** YOU UNDERSTAND, BEC. BUT I'M AFRAID THINGS WILL GET MUCH WORSE SOON.

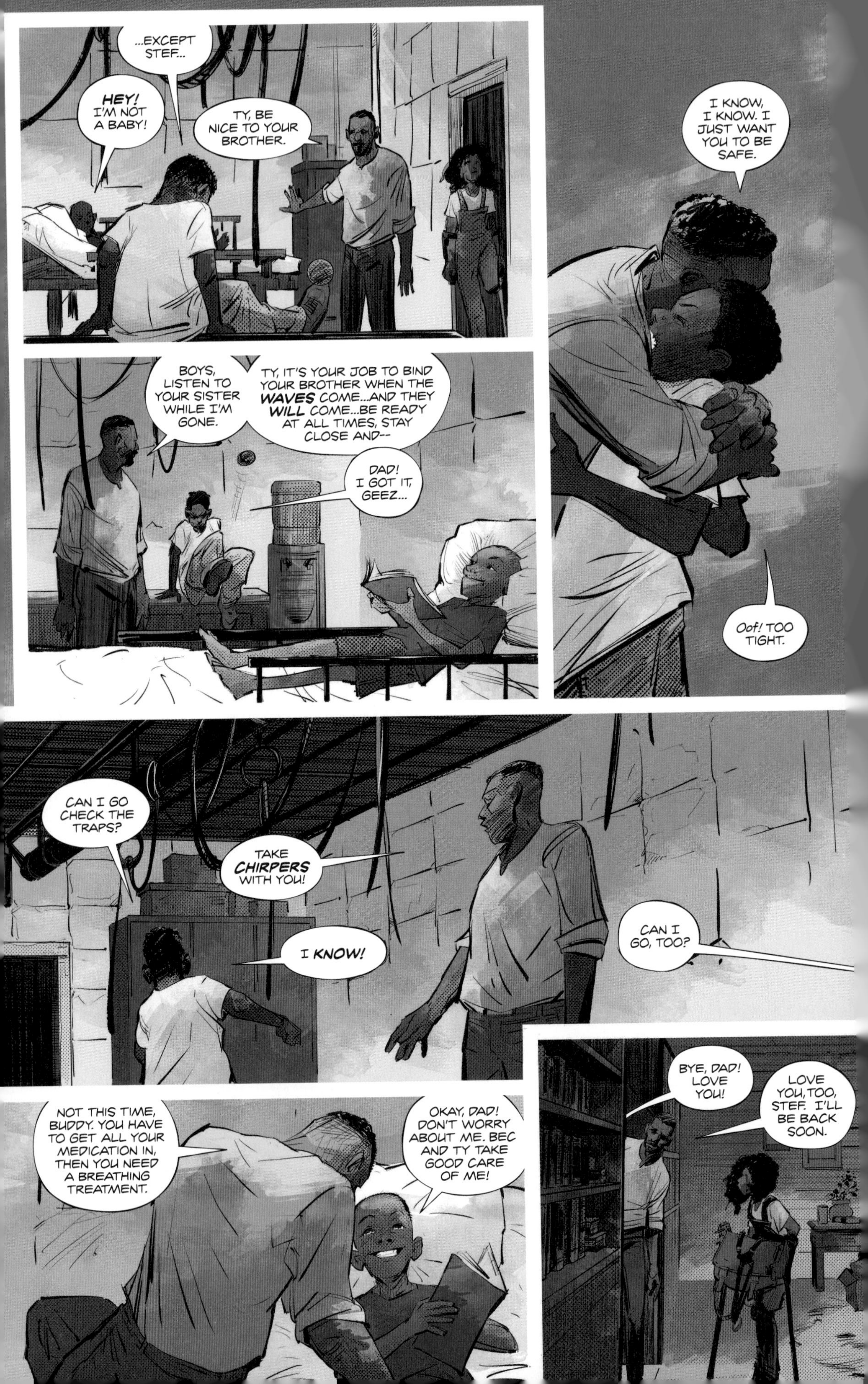
...EXCEPT STEF...
HEY! I'M NOT A BABY!
TY, BE NICE TO YOUR BROTHER.
BOYS, LISTEN TO YOUR SISTER WHILE I'M GONE.
TY, IT'S YOUR JOB TO BIND YOUR BROTHER WHEN THE WAVES COME...AND THEY WILL COME...BE READY AT ALL TIMES, STAY CLOSE AND--
DAD! I GOT IT, GEEZ...
I KNOW, I KNOW. I JUST WANT YOU TO BE SAFE.
Oof! TOO TIGHT.
CAN I GO CHECK THE TRAPS?
TAKE CHIRPERS WITH YOU!
I KNOW!
CAN I GO, TOO?
NOT THIS TIME, BUDDY. YOU HAVE TO GET ALL YOUR MEDICATION IN, THEN YOU NEED A BREATHING TREATMENT.
OKAY, DAD! DON'T WORRY ABOUT ME. BEC AND TY TAKE GOOD CARE OF ME!
BYE, DAD! LOVE YOU!
LOVE YOU, TOO, STEF. I'LL BE BACK SOON.

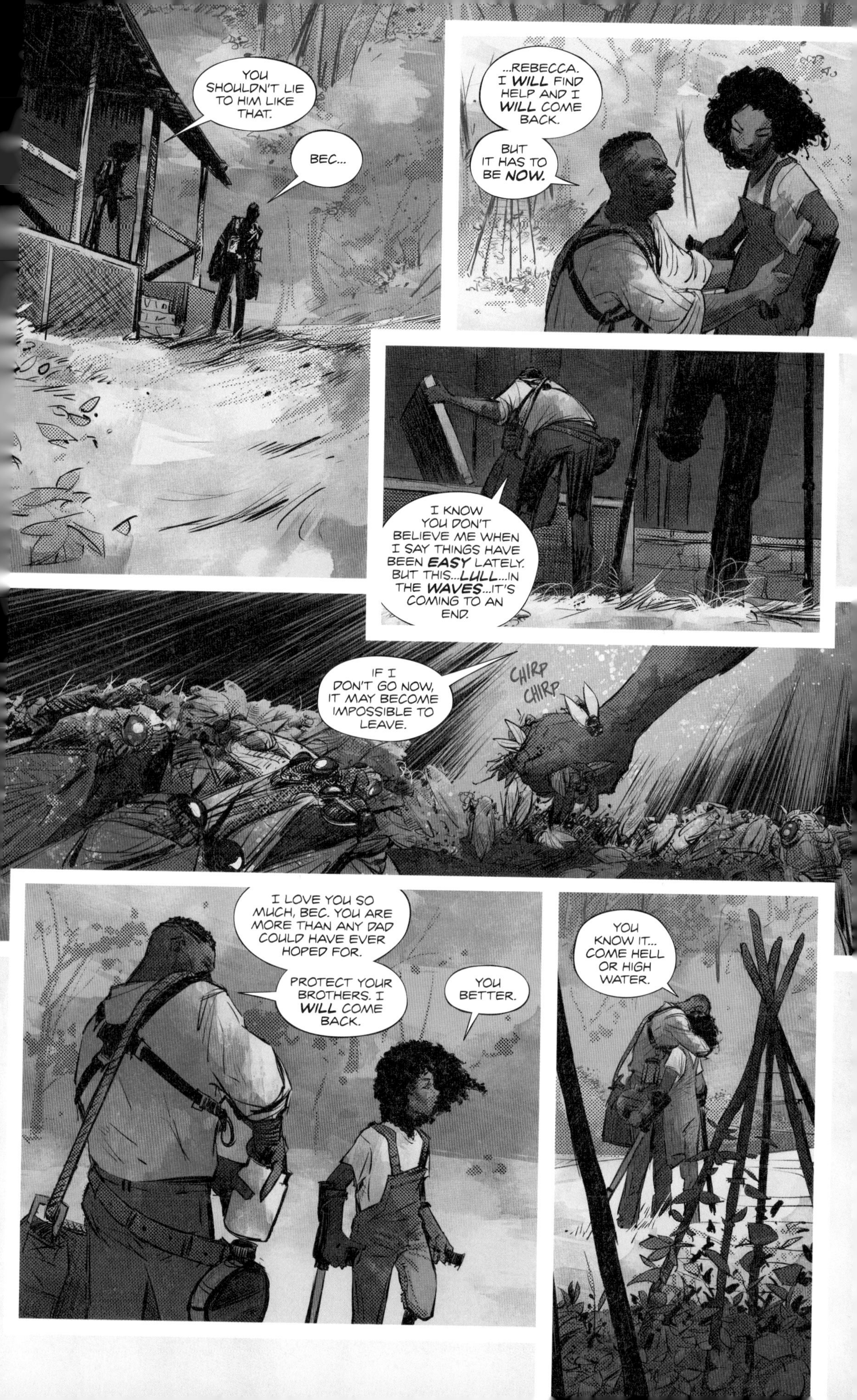
YOU SHOULDN'T LIE TO HIM LIKE THAT.
BEC...
...REBECCA. I WILL FIND HELP AND I WILL COME BACK.
BUT IT HAS TO BE NOW.
I KNOW YOU DON'T BELIEVE ME WHEN I SAY THINGS HAVE BEEN EASY LATELY. BUT THIS...LULL...IN THE WAVES...IT'S COMING TO AN END.
IF I DON'T GO NOW, IT MAY BECOME IMPOSSIBLE TO LEAVE.
CHIRP
CHIRP
I LOVE YOU SO MUCH, BEC. YOU ARE MORE THAN ANY DAD COULD HAVE EVER HOPED FOR.
PROTECT YOUR BROTHERS. I WILL COME BACK.
YOU BETTER.
YOU KNOW IT... COME HELL OR HIGH WATER.

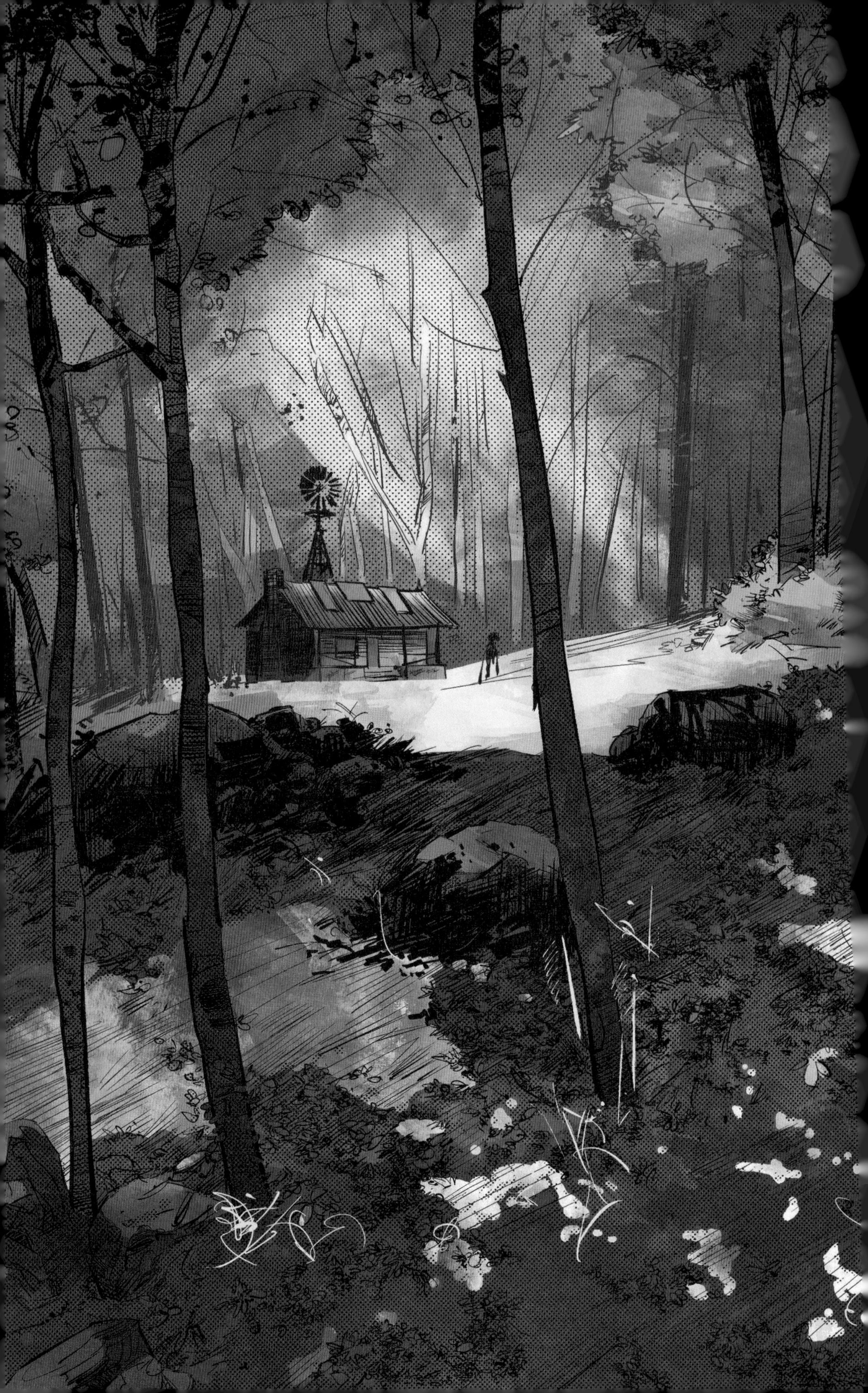

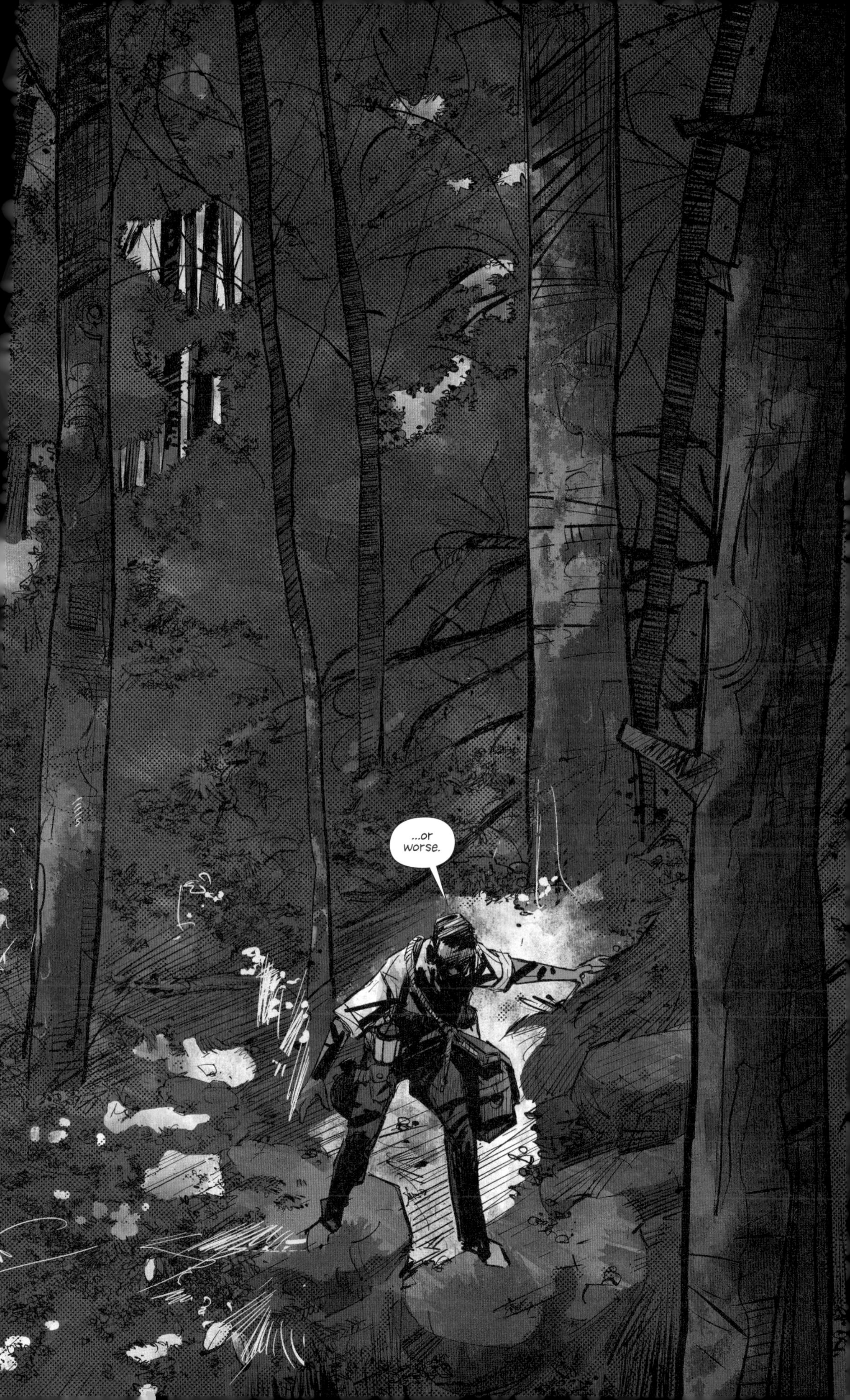
...or worse.

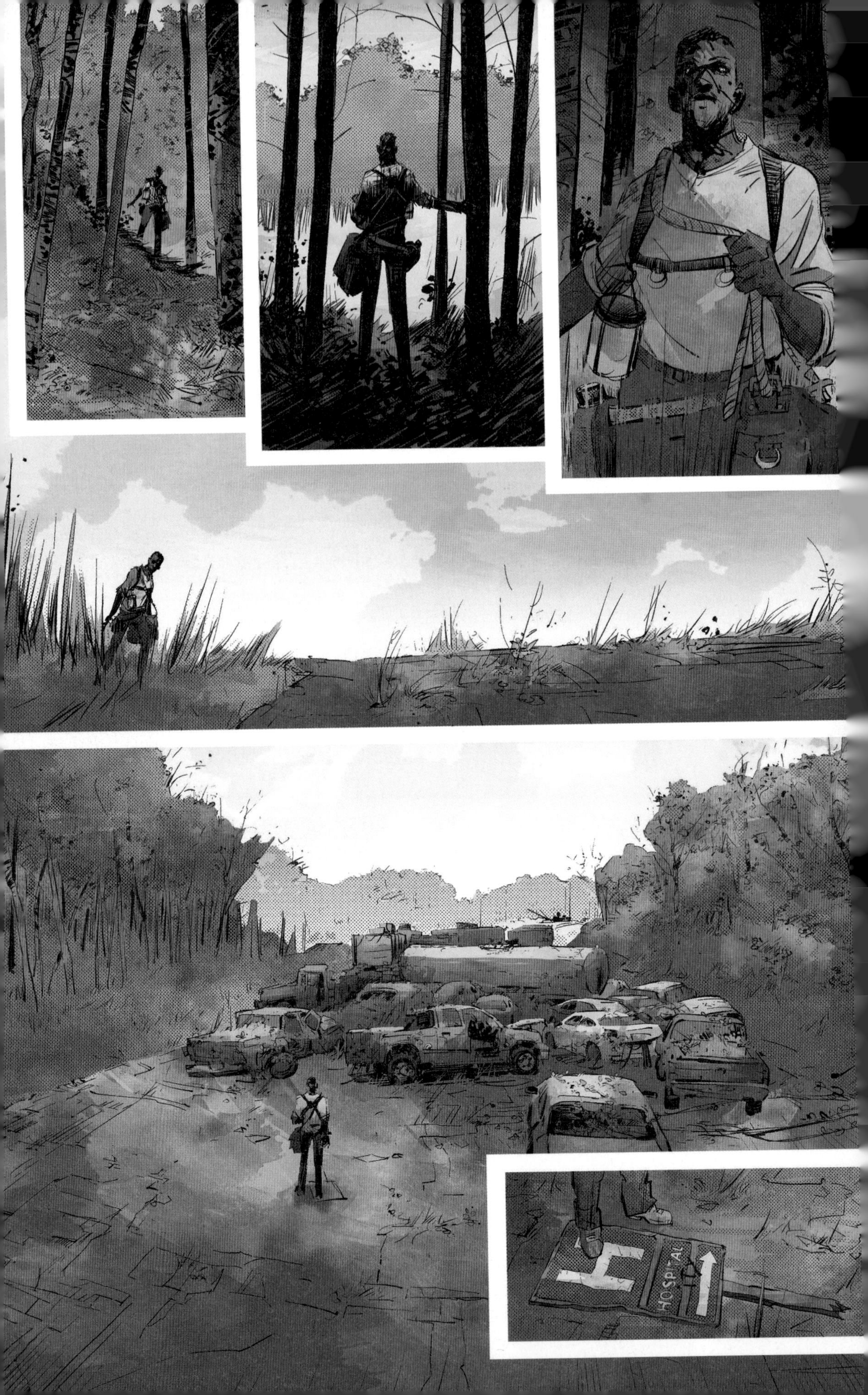
HOSPITAL

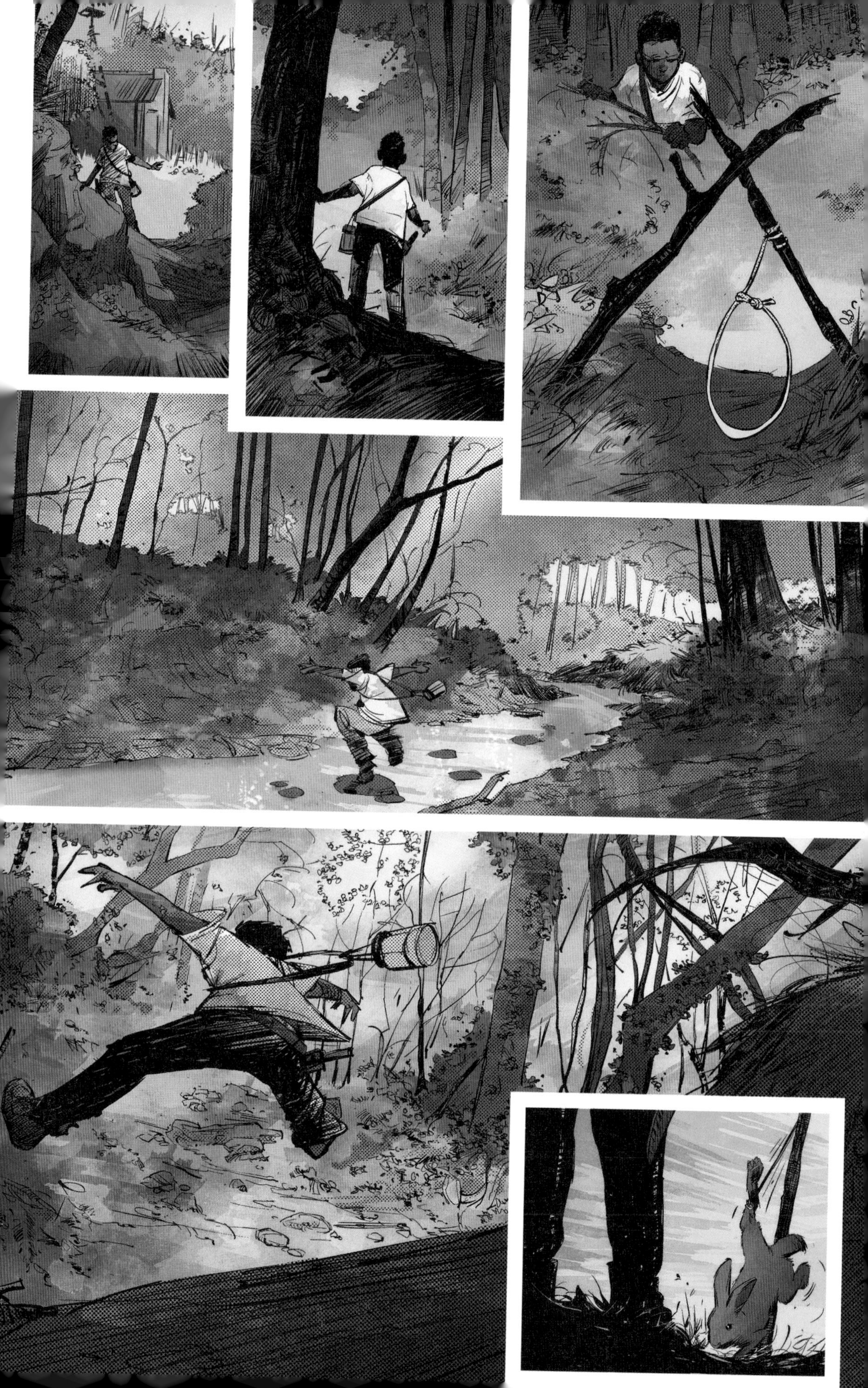

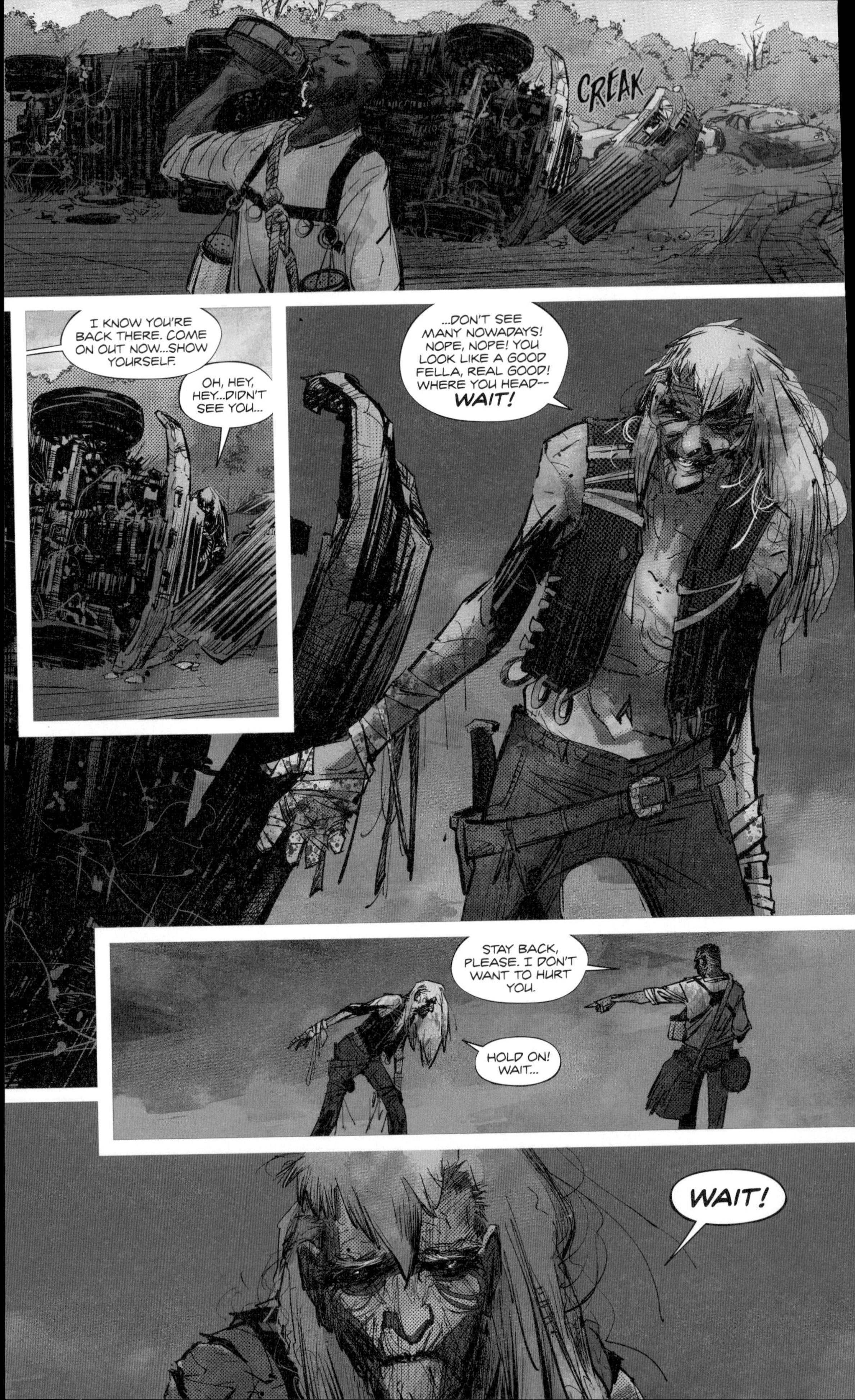
CREAK
I KNOW YOU'RE BACK THERE. COME ON OUT NOW...SHOW YOURSELF.
OH, HEY, HEY...DIDN'T SEE YOU...
...DON'T SEE MANY NOWADAYS! NOPE, NOPE! YOU LOOK LIKE A GOOD FELLA, REAL GOOD! WHERE YOU HEAD-- WAIT!
STAY BACK, PLEASE. I DON'T WANT TO HURT YOU.
HOLD ON! WAIT...
WAIT!

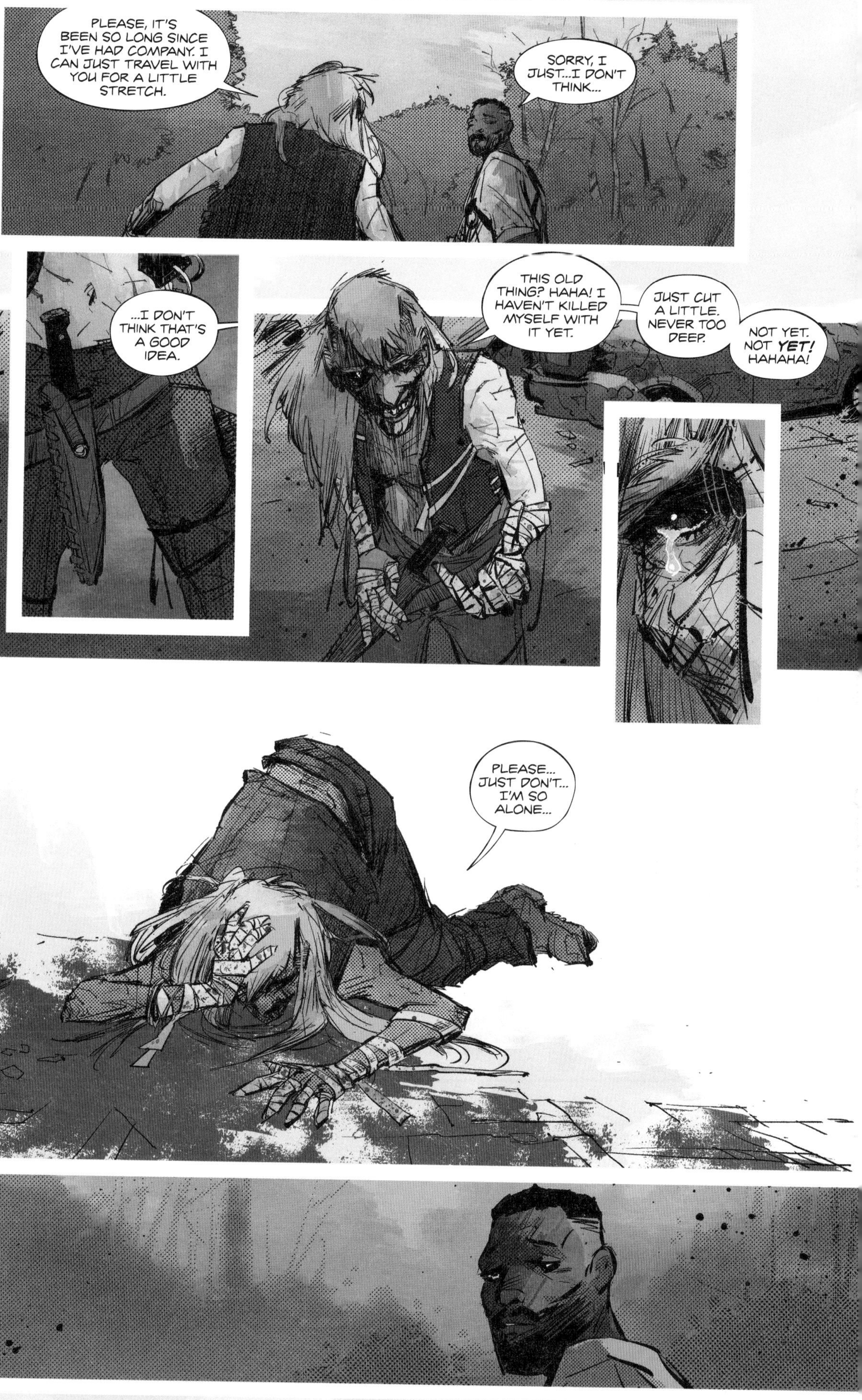
PLEASE, IT'S BEEN SO LONG SINCE I'VE HAD COMPANY. I CAN JUST TRAVEL WITH YOU FOR A LITTLE STRETCH.
SORRY, I JUST...I DON'T THINK...
...I DON'T THINK THAT'S A GOOD IDEA.
THIS OLD THING? HAHA! I HAVEN'T KILLED MYSELF WITH IT YET.
JUST CUT A LITTLE. NEVER TOO DEEP.
NOT YET. NOT ***YET!*** HAHAHA!
PLEASE... JUST DON'T... I'M SO ALONE...

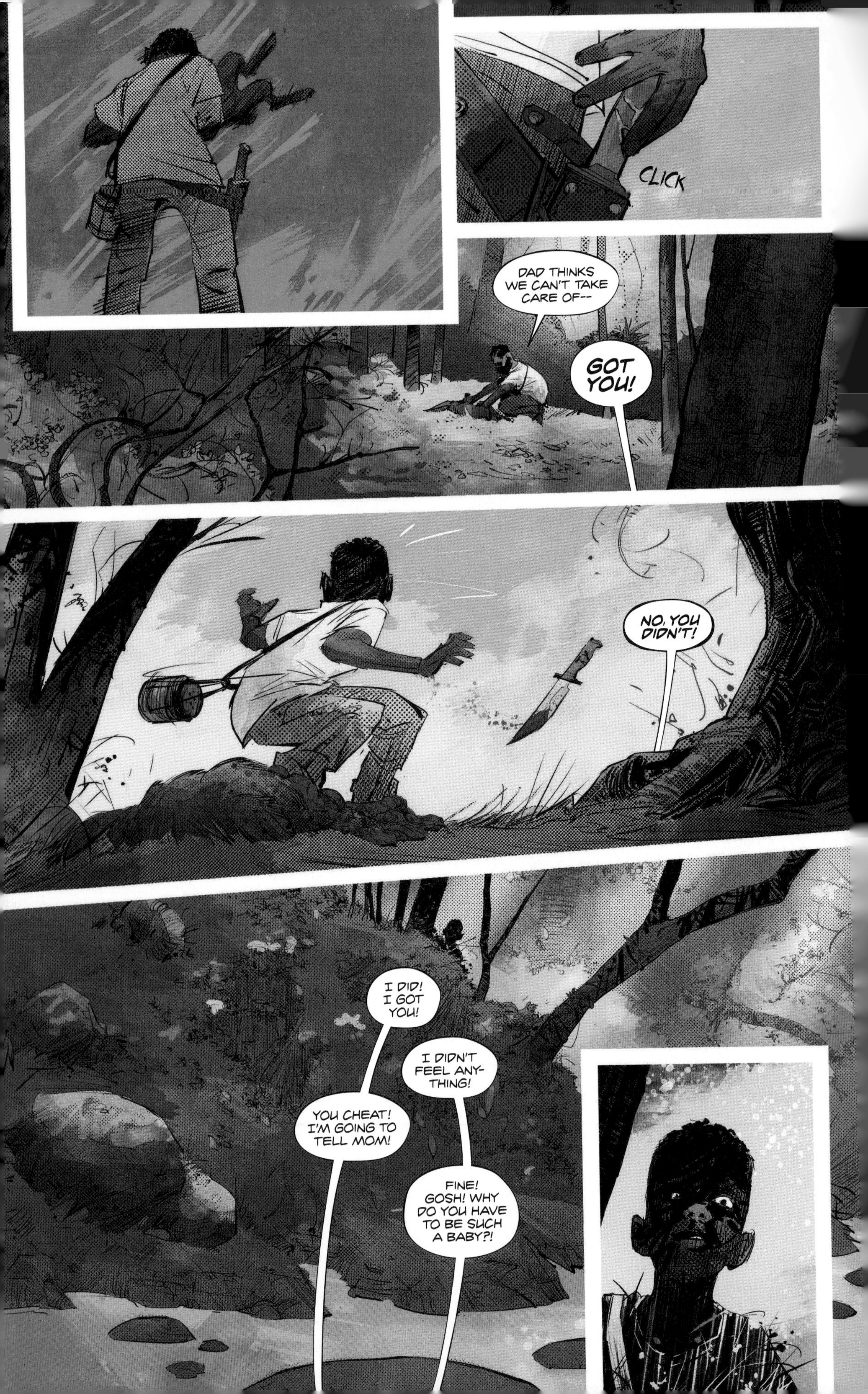
CLICK
DAD THINKS WE CAN'T TAKE CARE OF--
GOT YOU!
NO, YOU DIDN'T!
I DID! I GOT YOU!
I DIDN'T FEEL ANY-THING!
YOU CHEAT! I'M GOING TO TELL MOM!
FINE! GOSH! WHY DO YOU HAVE TO BE SUCH A BABY?!

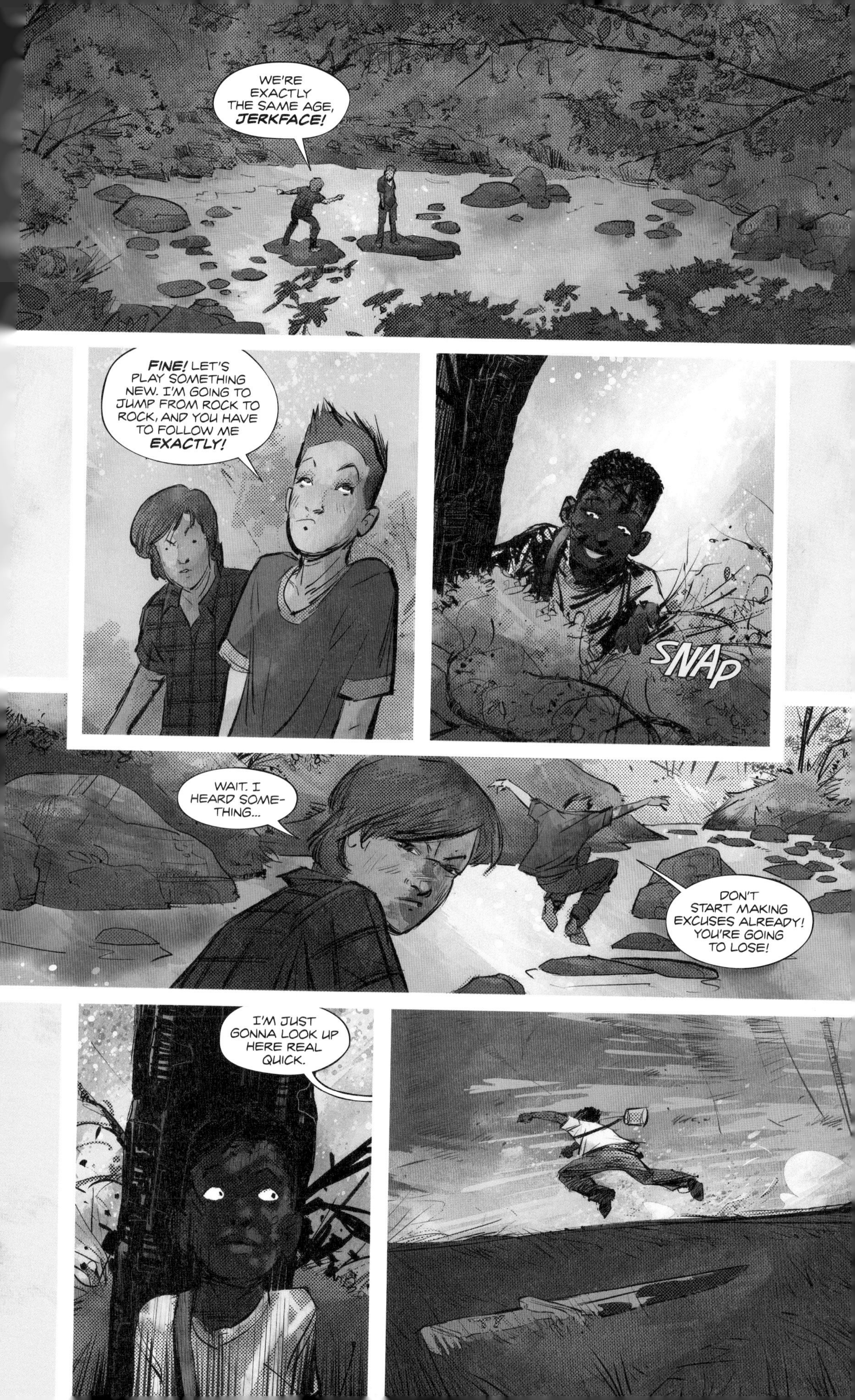
WE'RE EXACTLY THE SAME AGE, **JERKFACE!**
FINE! LET'S PLAY SOMETHING NEW. I'M GOING TO JUMP FROM ROCK TO ROCK, AND YOU HAVE TO FOLLOW ME **EXACTLY!**
SNAP
WAIT. I HEARD SOME-THING...
DON'T START MAKING EXCUSES ALREADY! YOU'RE GOING TO LOSE!
I'M JUST GONNA LOOK UP HERE REAL QUICK.

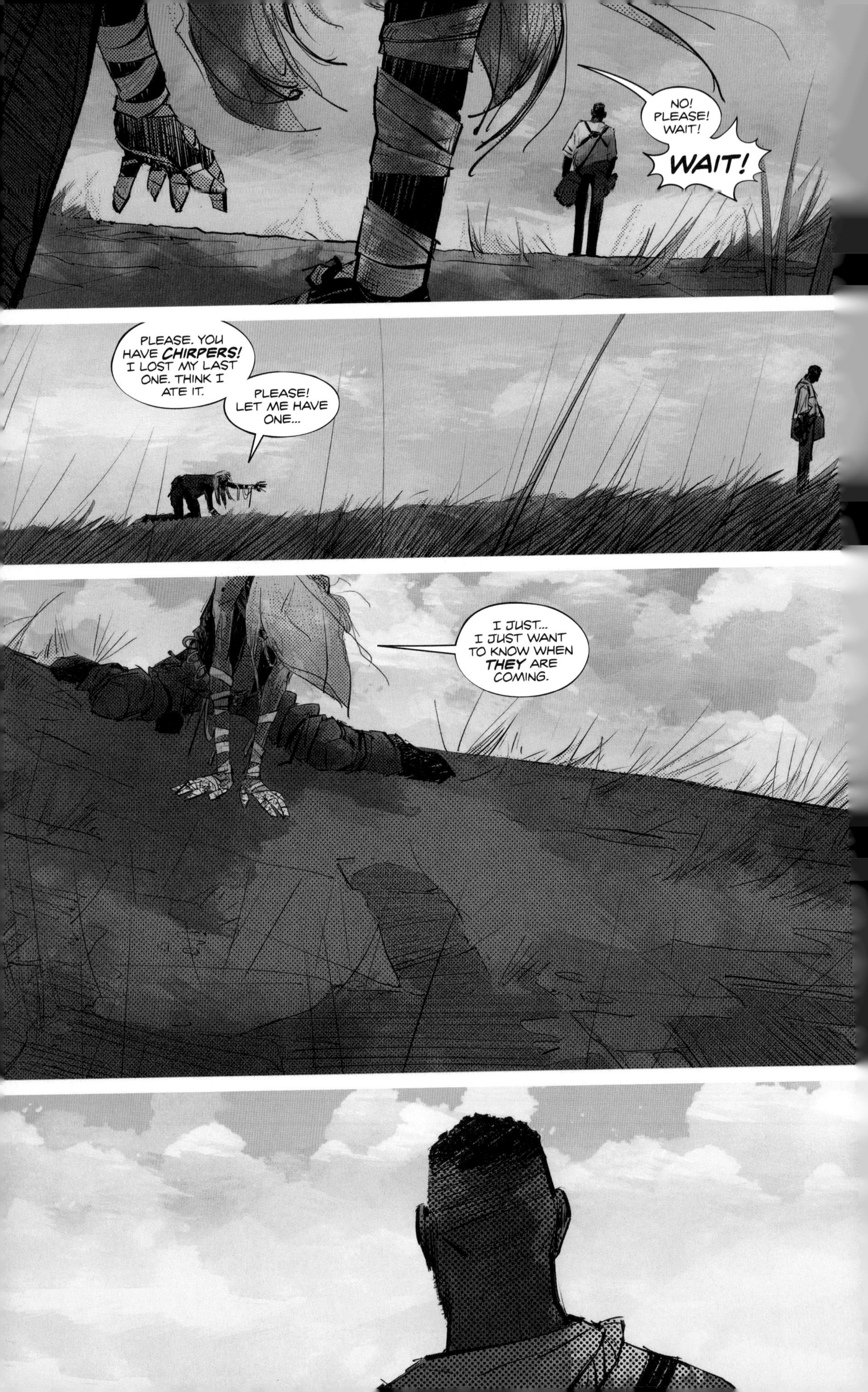
NO! PLEASE! WAIT!
WAIT!
PLEASE. YOU HAVE CHIRPERS! I LOST MY LAST ONE. THINK I ATE IT.
PLEASE! LET ME HAVE ONE...
I JUST... I JUST WANT TO KNOW WHEN THEY ARE COMING.

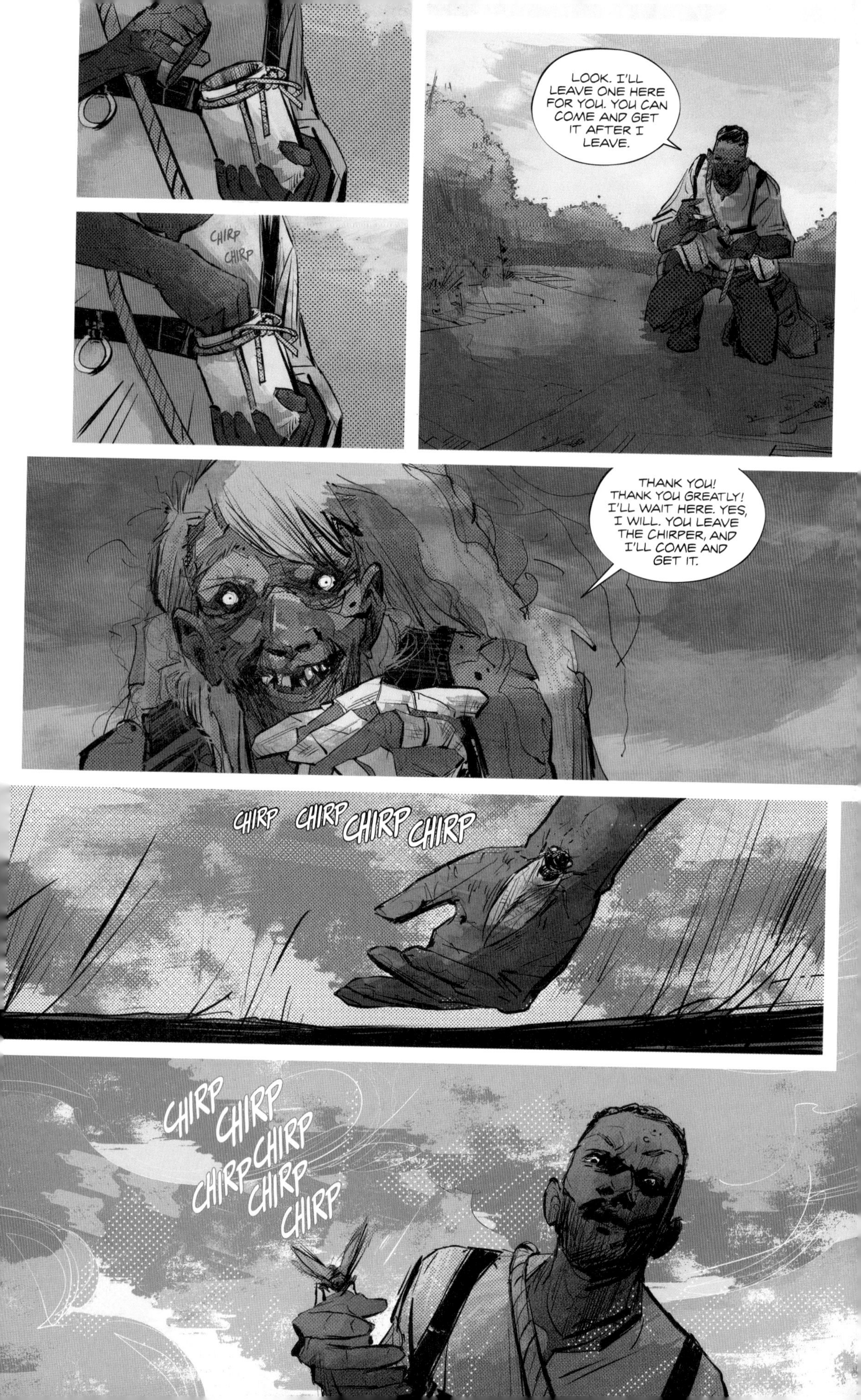
CHIRP
CHIRP
LOOK. I'LL LEAVE ONE HERE FOR YOU. YOU CAN COME AND GET IT AFTER I LEAVE.
THANK YOU! THANK YOU GREATLY! I'LL WAIT HERE. YES, I WILL. YOU LEAVE THE CHIRPER, AND I'LL COME AND GET IT.
CHIRP CHIRP CHIRP CHIRP
CHIRP CHIRP CHIRP CHIRP CHIRP CHIRP

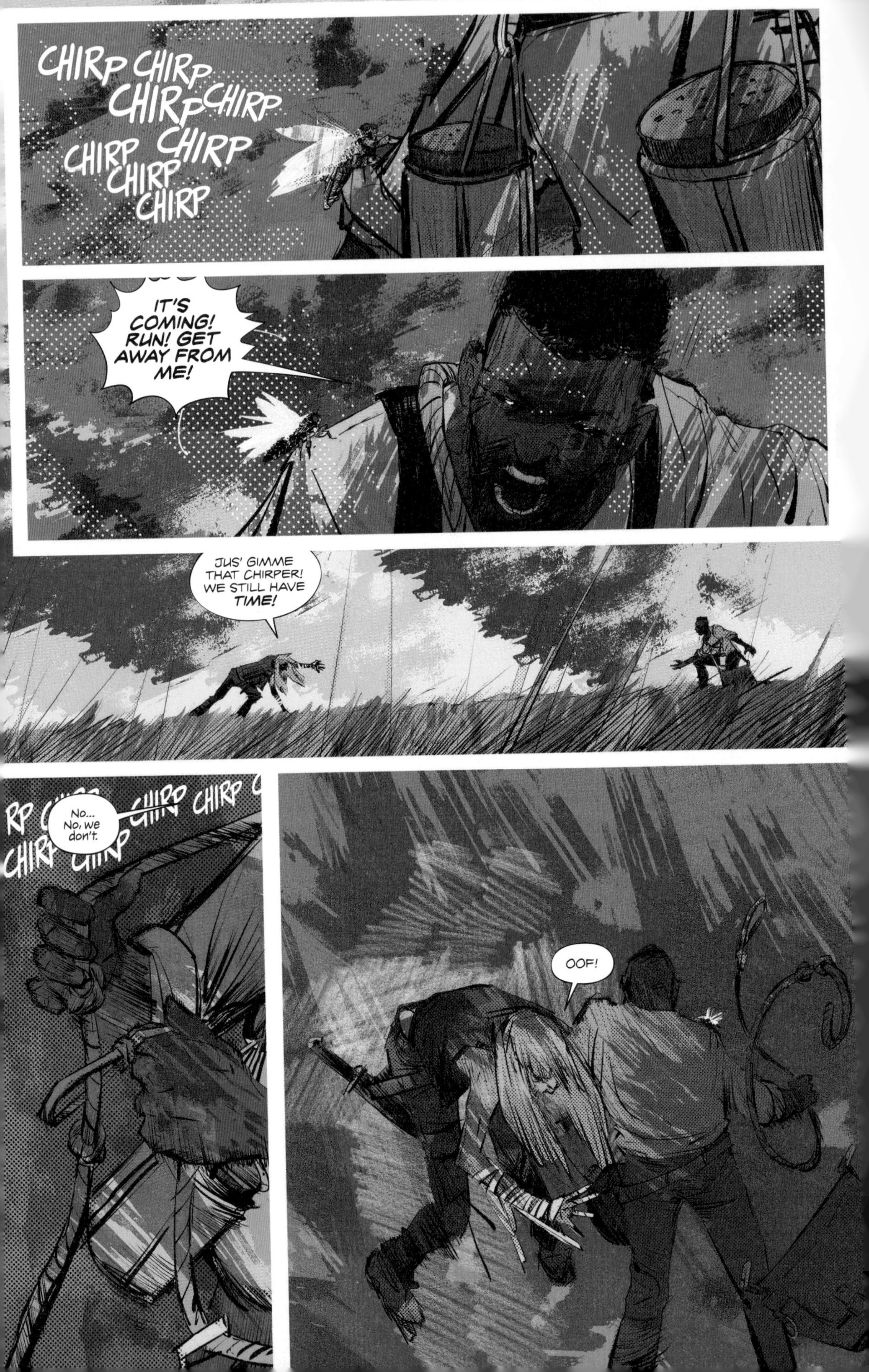
CHIRP CHIRP
CHIRP CHIRP
CHIRP CHIRP
CHIRP
CHIRP
IT'S COMING! RUN! GET AWAY FROM ME!
JUS' GIMME THAT CHIRPER! WE STILL HAVE TIME!
No... No, we don't.
CHIRP
OOF!

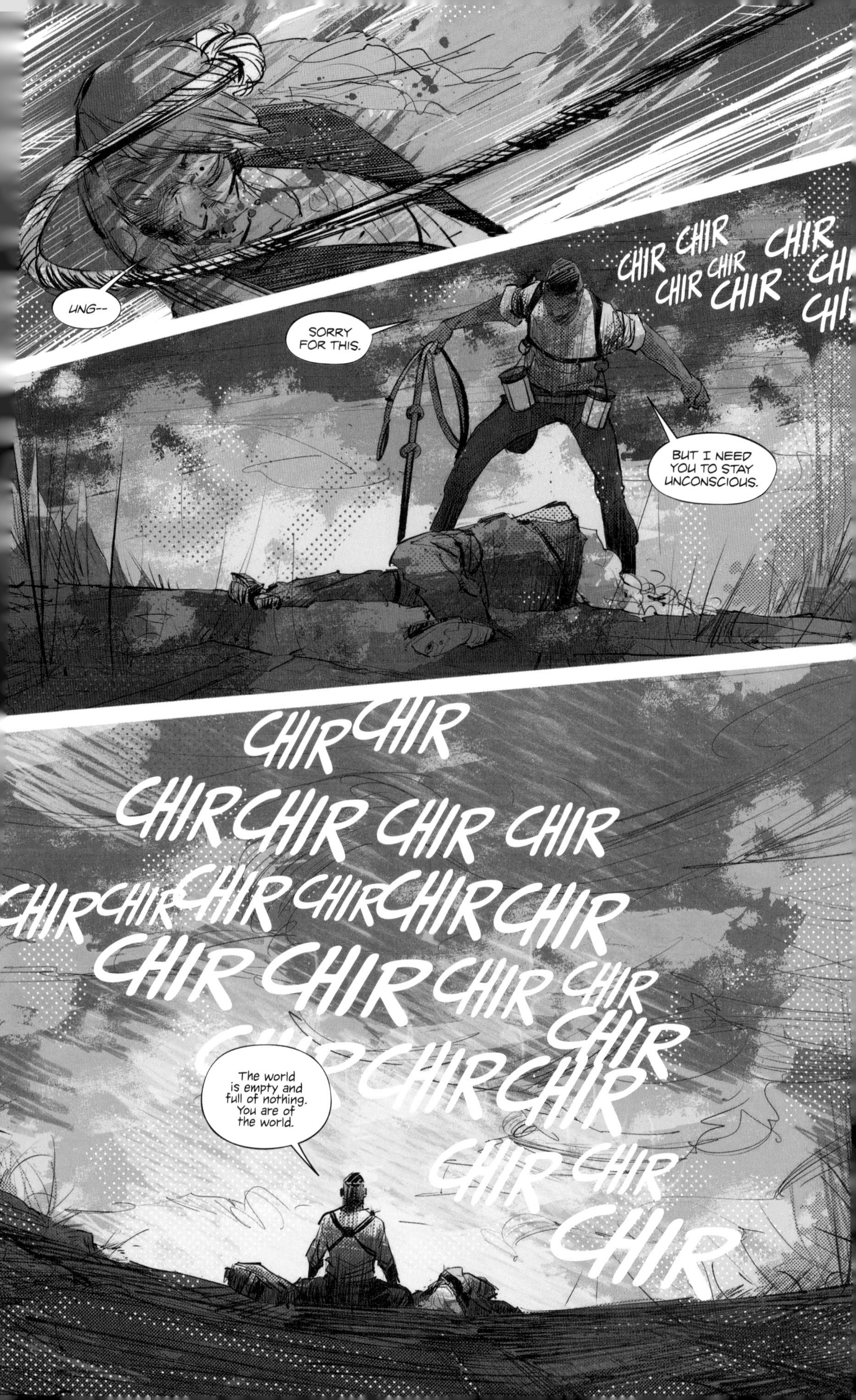
UNG--
CHIR CHIR CHIR CHIR CHIR CHIR CHIR CHIR
SORRY FOR THIS.
BUT I NEED YOU TO STAY UNCONSCIOUS.
CHIR CHIR
CHIR CHIR CHIR CHIR
CHIR CHIR CHIR CHIR CHIR CHIR
CHIR CHIR CHIR CHIR CHIR
CHIR CHIR CHIR
The world is empty and full of nothing. You are of the world.
CHIR CHIR CHIR

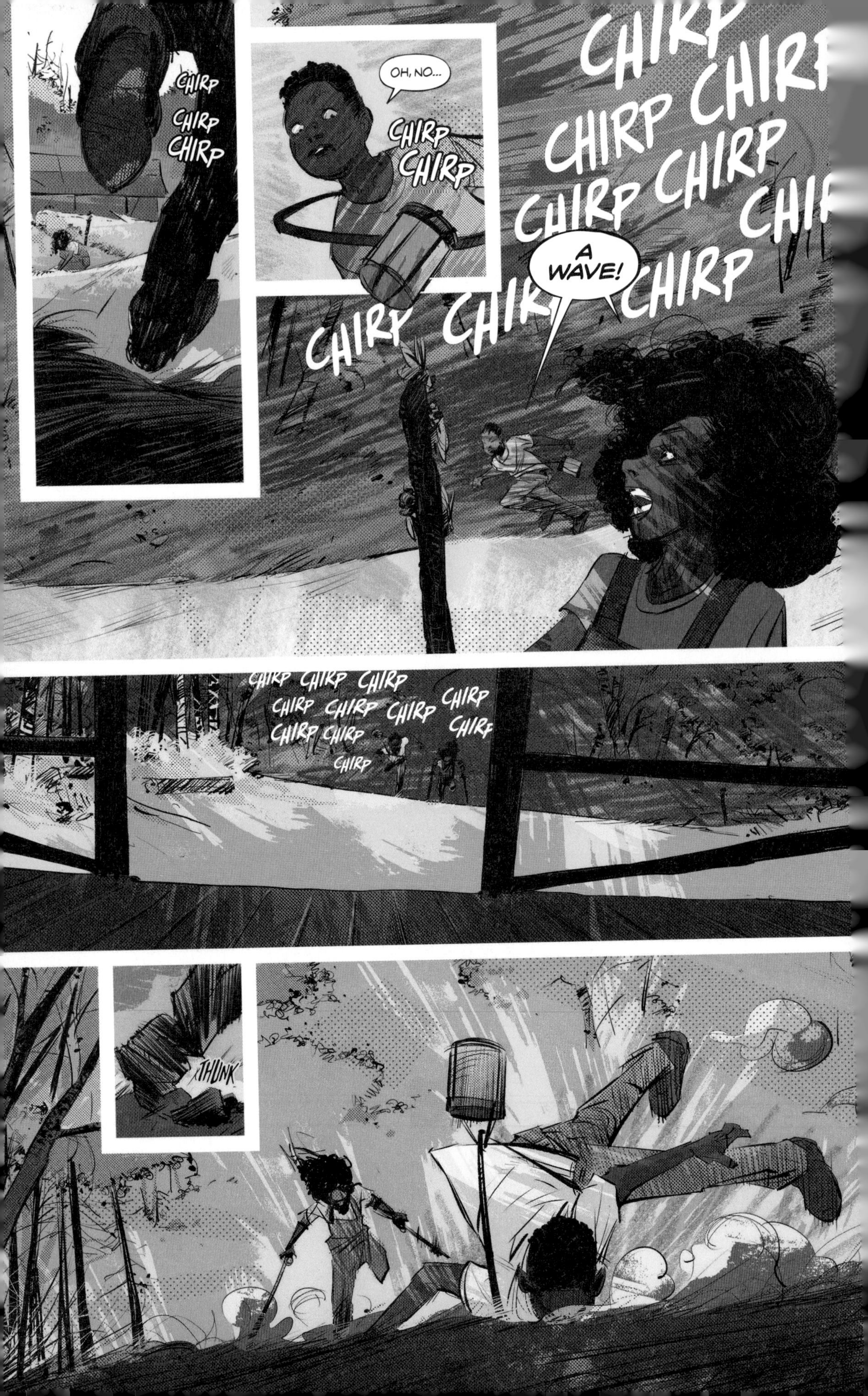
CHIRP
CHIRP
CHIRP
OH, NO...
CHIRP
CHIRP
CHIRP CHIRP CHIRP CHIRP CHIRP CHIRP
A WAVE!
CHIRP CHIRP CHIRP CHIRP
CHIRP CHIRP CHIRP
CHIRP CHIRP CHIRP CHIRP
CHIRP CHIRP CHIRP
CHIRP
THUNK

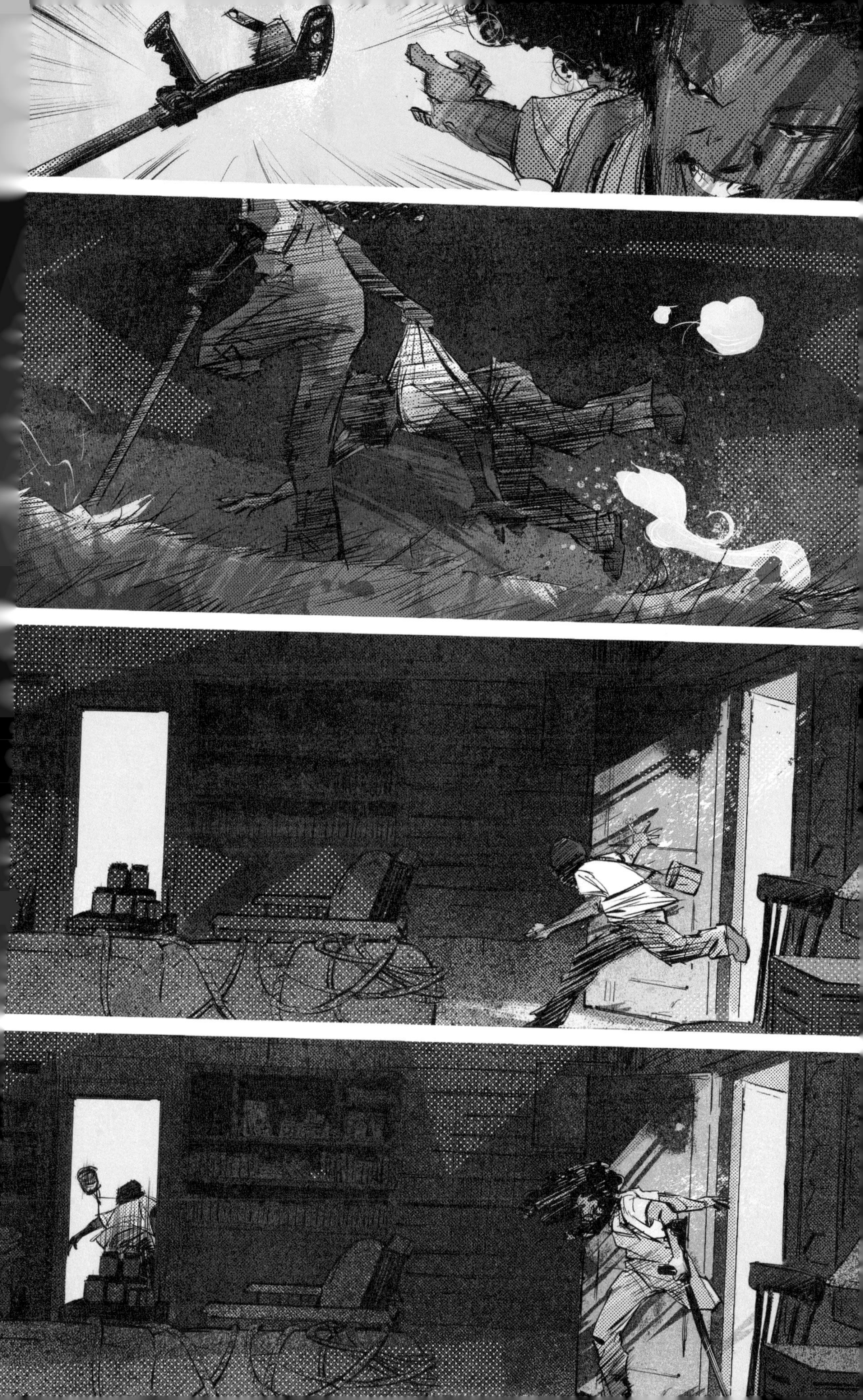

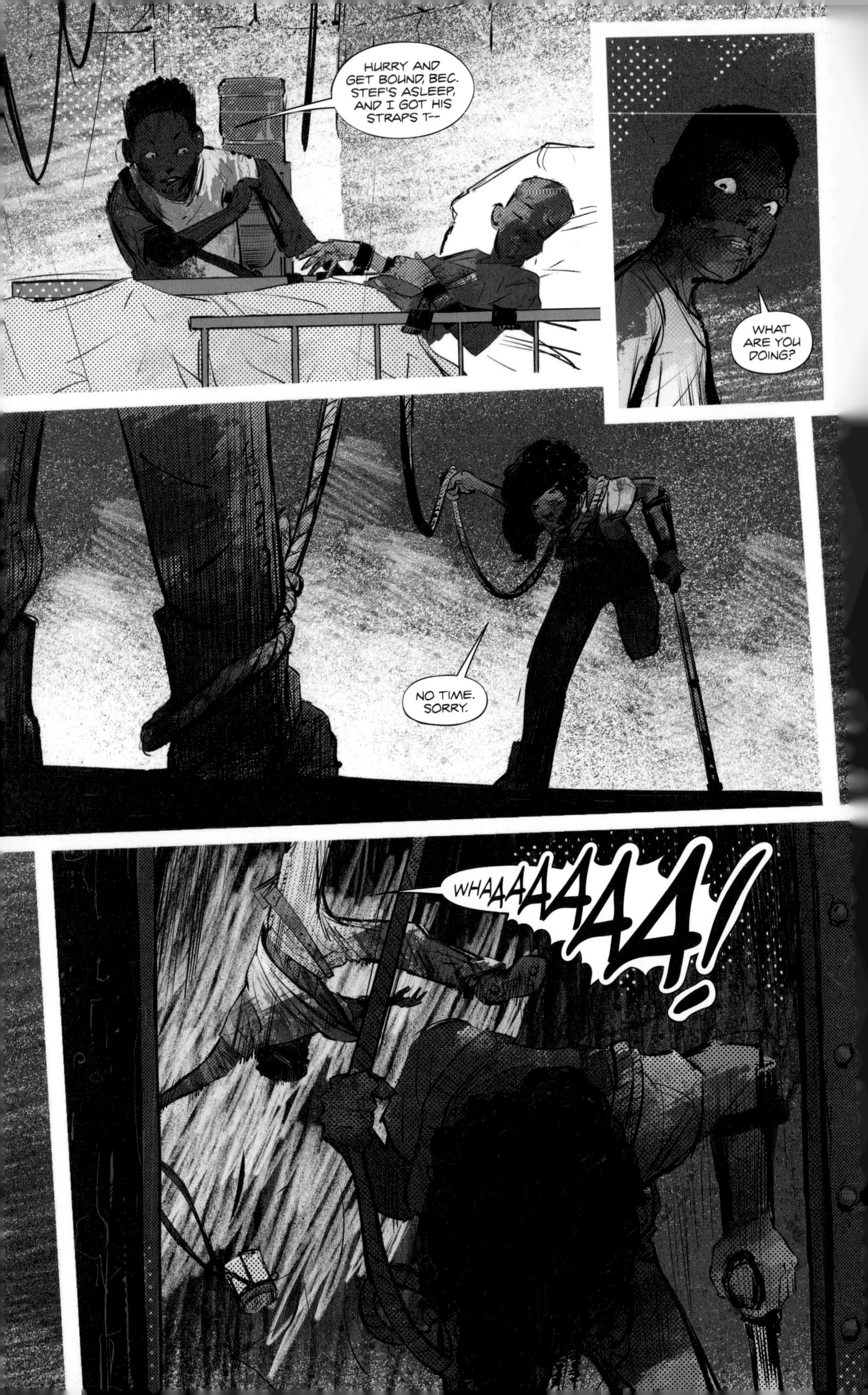
HURRY AND GET BOUND, BEC. STEF'S ASLEEP, AND I GOT HIS STRAPS T--
WHAT ARE YOU DOING?
NO TIME. SORRY.
WHAAAAAAA!

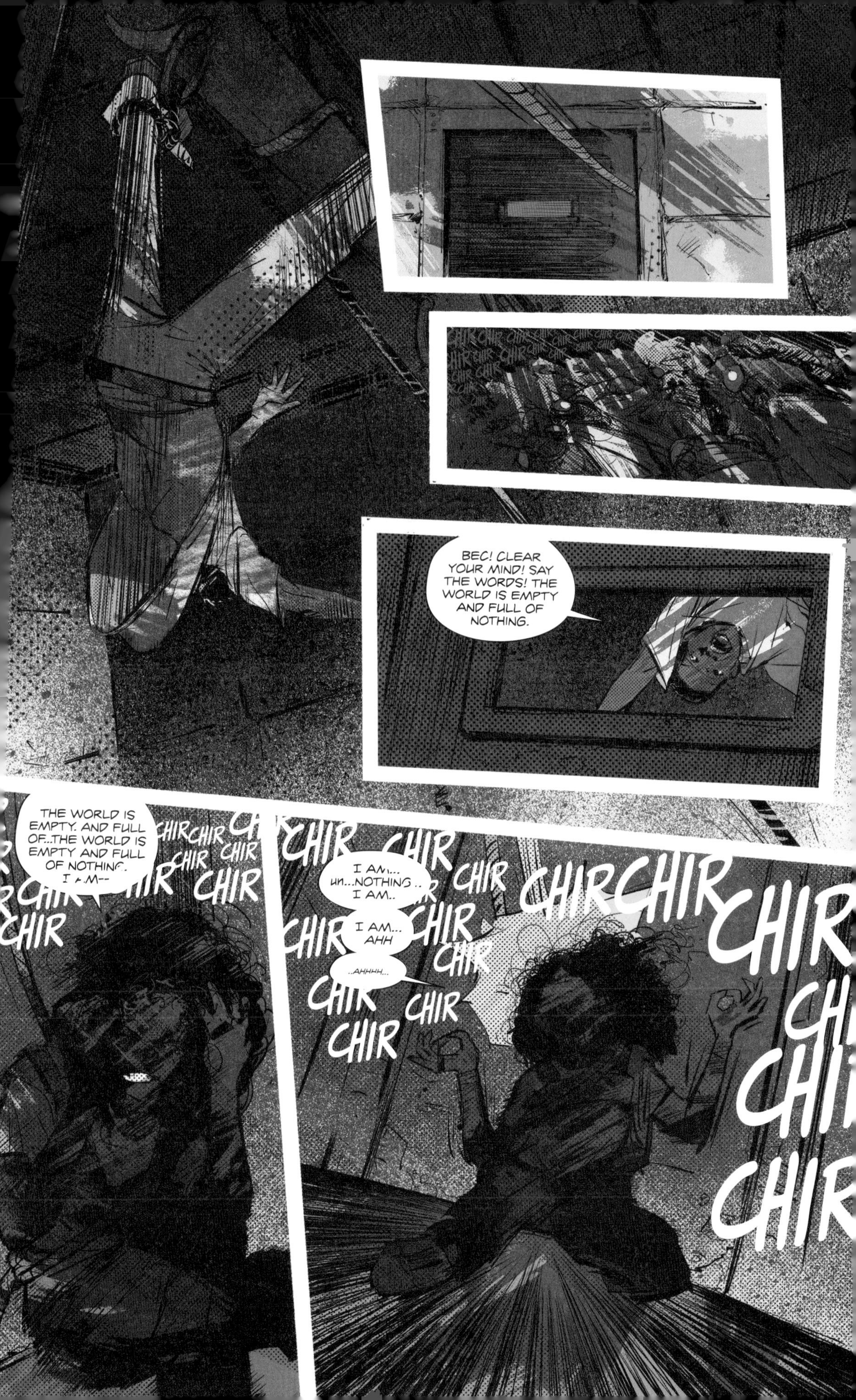
CHIR CHIR CHIR CHIR CHIR CHIR CHIR
BEC! CLEAR YOUR MIND! SAY THE WORDS! THE WORLD IS EMPTY AND FULL OF NOTHING.
THE WORLD IS EMPTY. AND FULL OF...THE WORLD IS EMPTY AND FULL OF NOTHING. I AM--
CHIR CHIR CHIR CHIR CHIR CHIR CHIR
I AM... un...NOTHING.. I AM..
I AM... AHH
..AHHHH...
CHIR CHIR CHIR CHIR CHIR CHIR CHIR CHIR CHIR CHIR CHIR

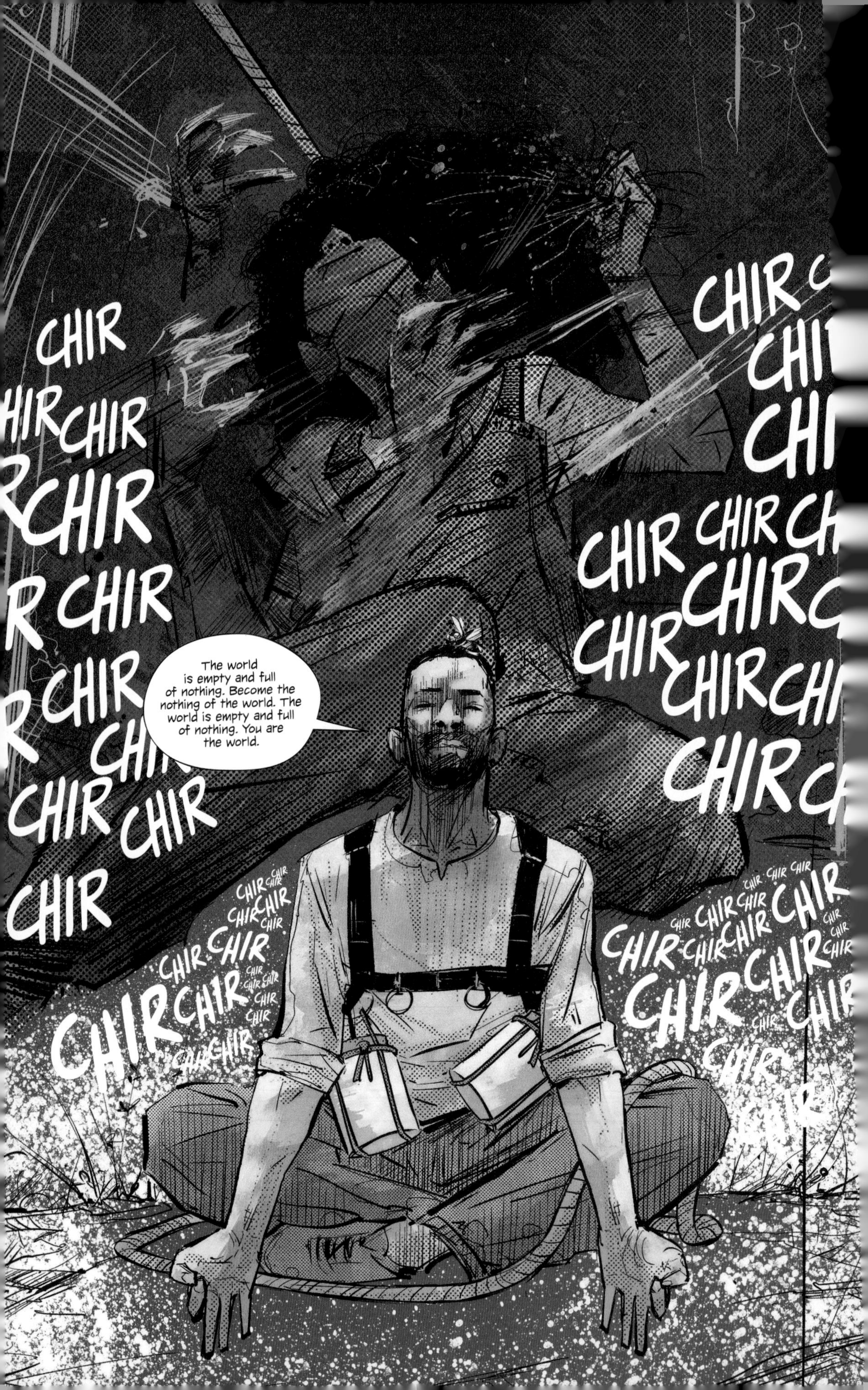
The world is empty and full of nothing. Become the nothing of the world. The world is empty and full of nothing. You are the world.
CHIR CHIR CHIR CHIR CHIR CHIR CHIR CHIR CHIR
CHIR CHIR CHIR CHIR CHIR CHIR CHIR CHIR CHIR

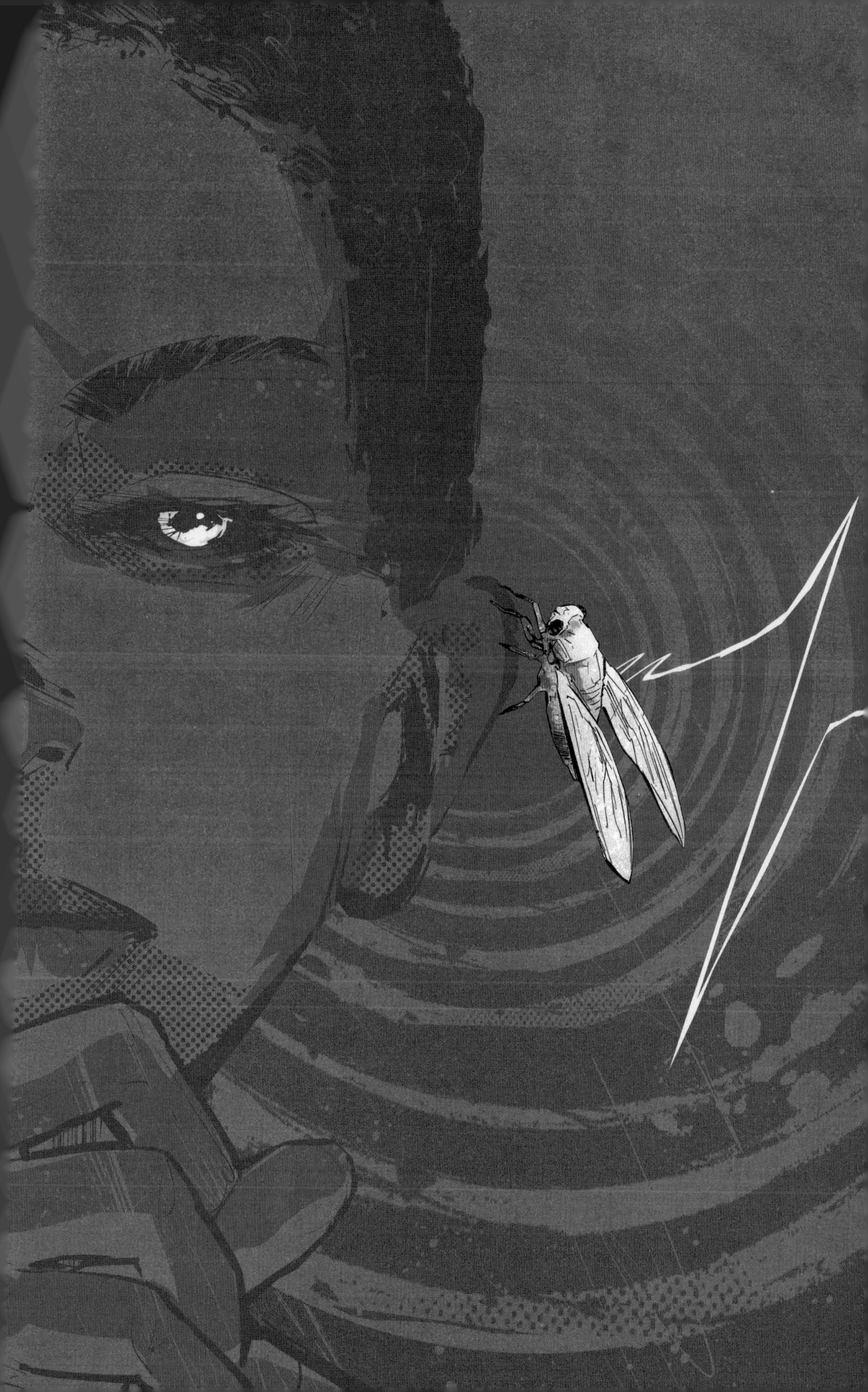

CHAPTER TWO

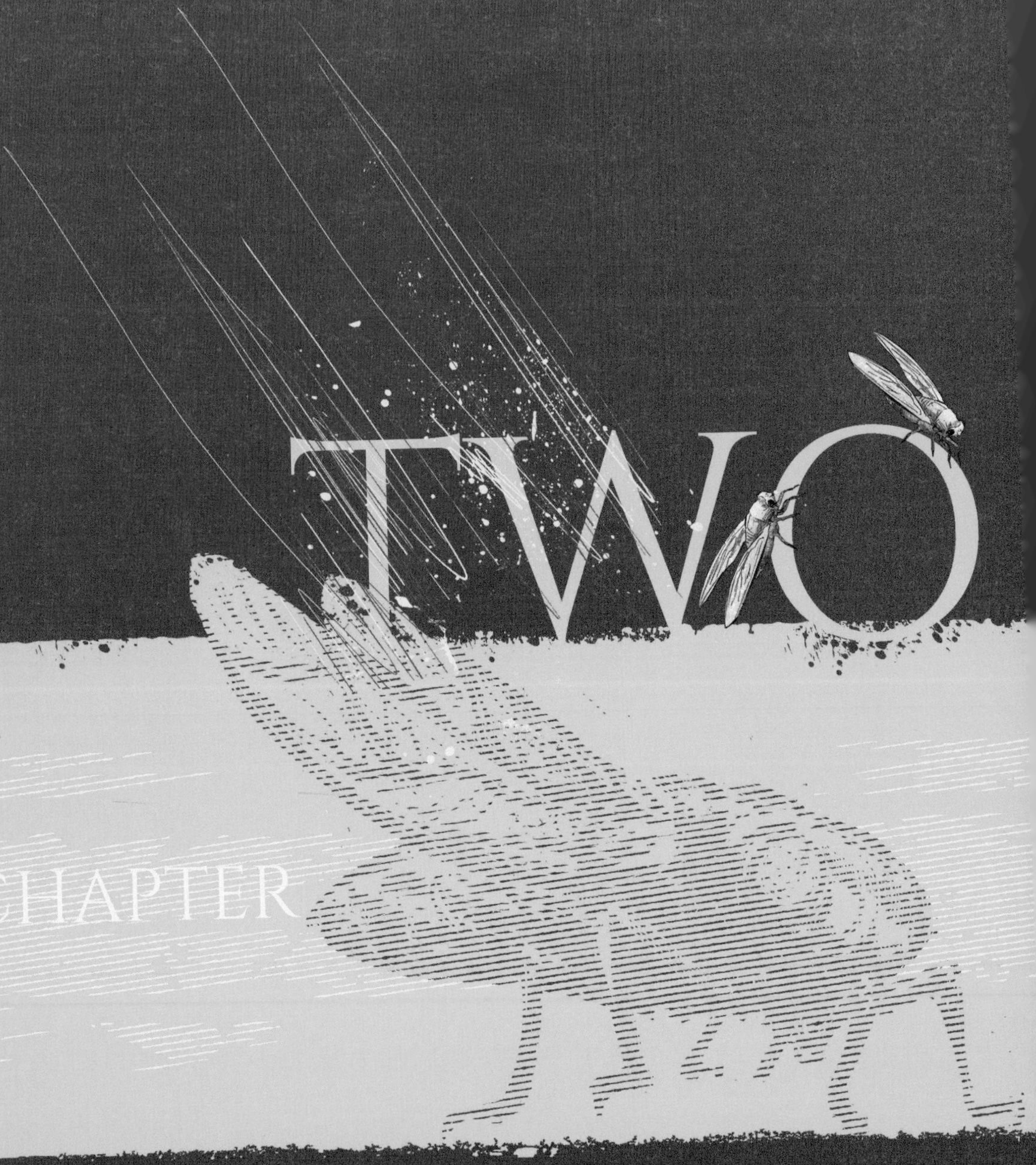

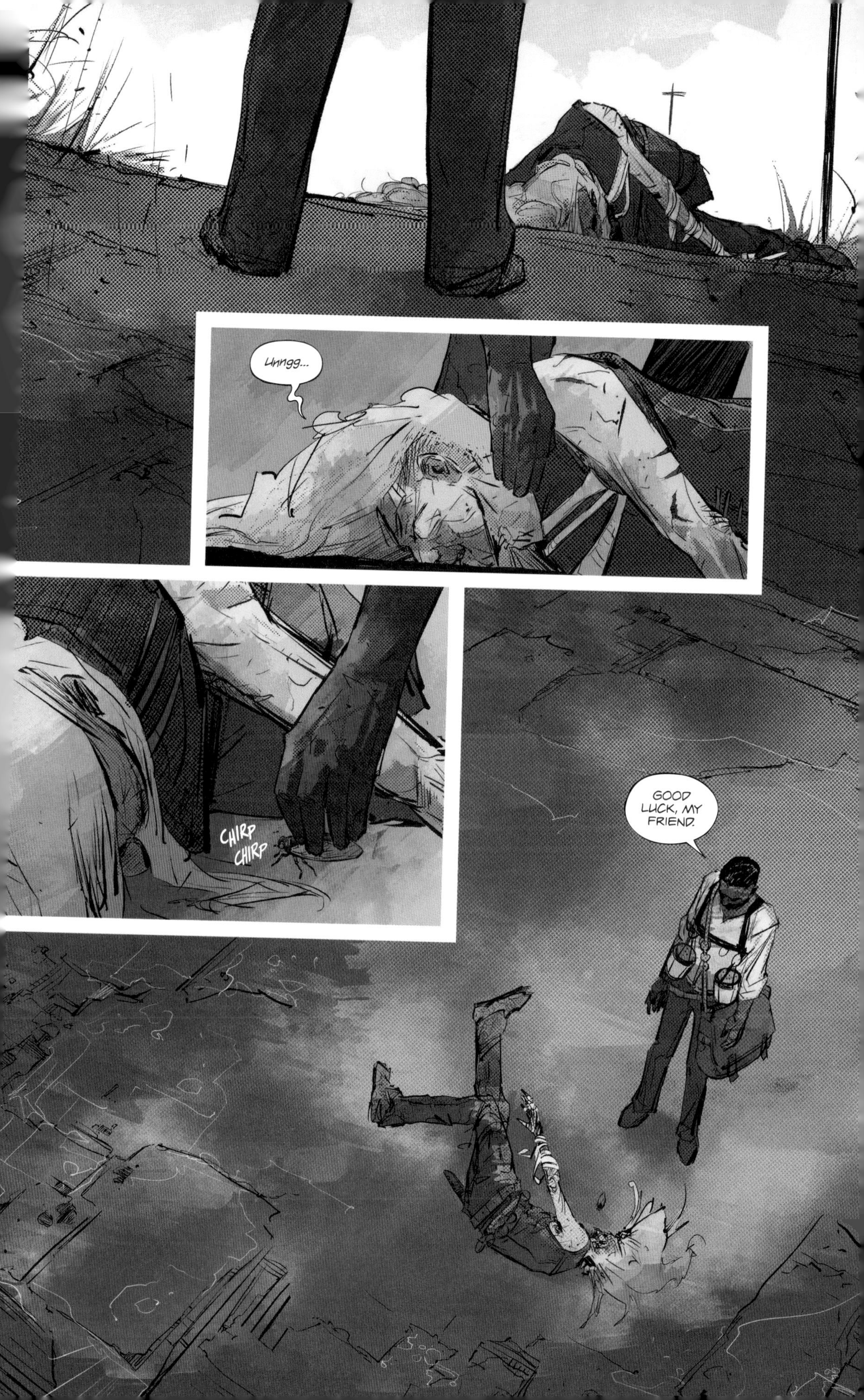
Unngg...
CHIRP CHIRP
GOOD LUCK, MY FRIEND.

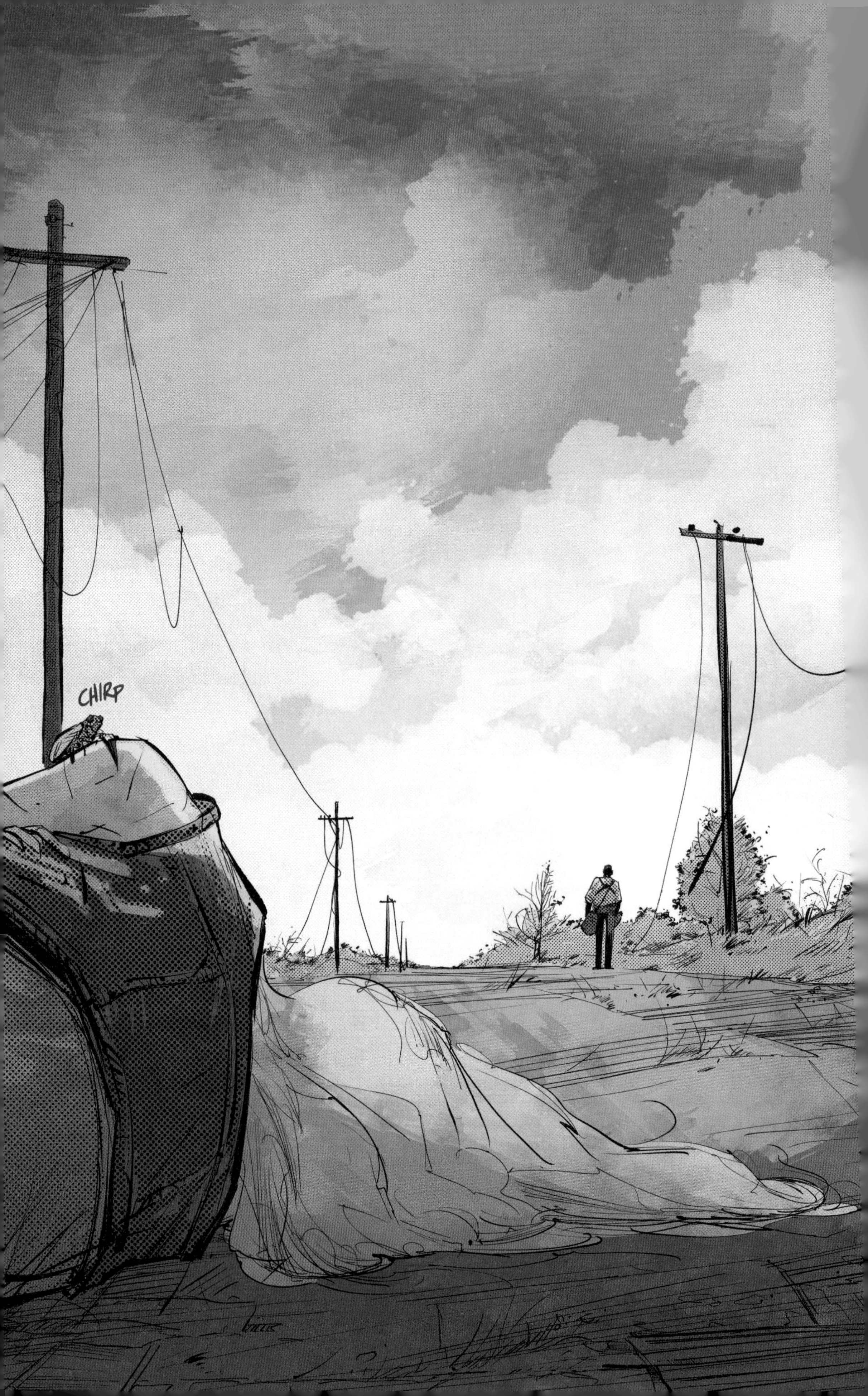
CHIRP

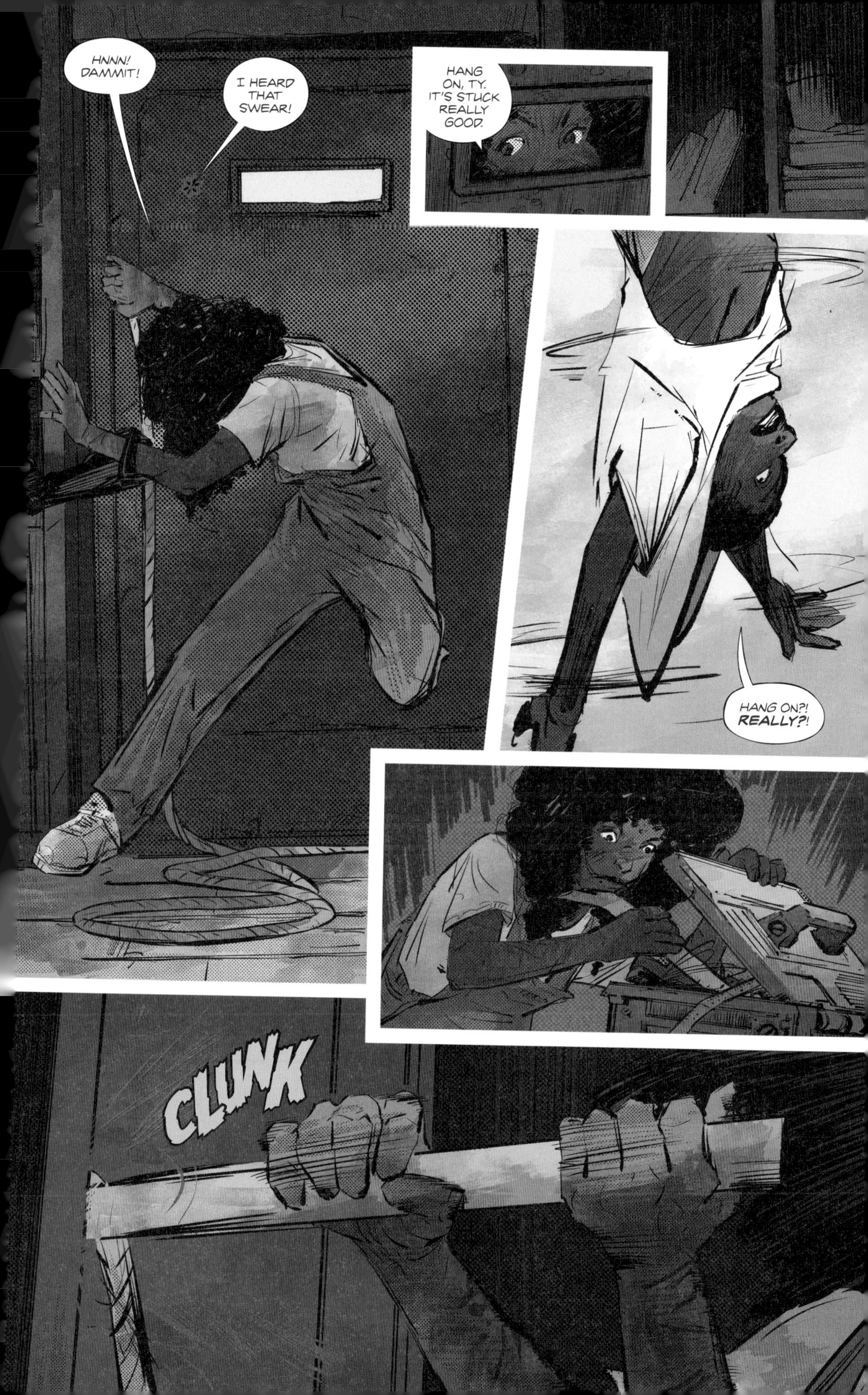
HNNN! DAMMIT!
I HEARD THAT SWEAR!
HANG ON, TY. IT'S STUCK REALLY GOOD.
HANG ON?! REALLY?!
CLUNK

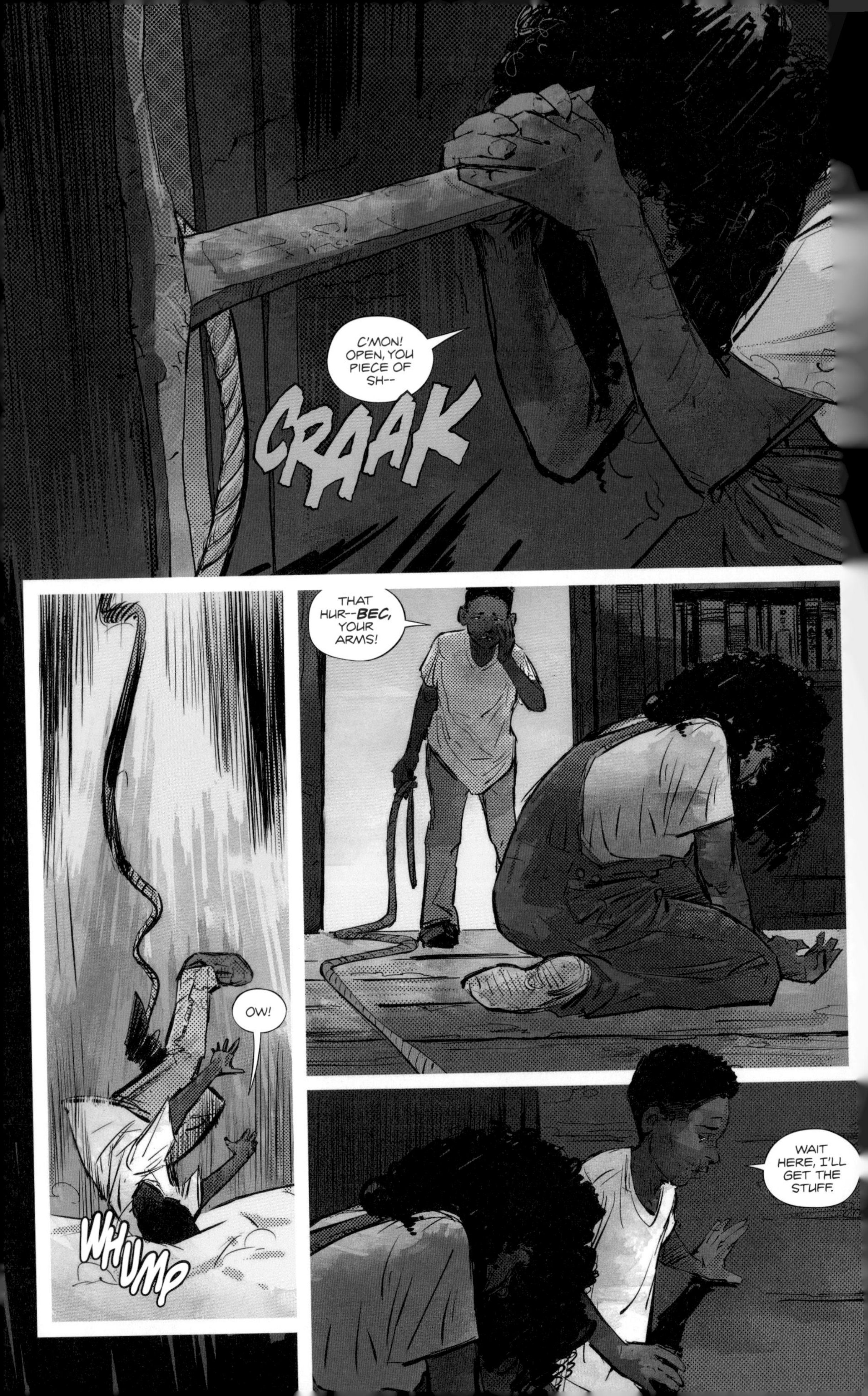
C'MON! OPEN, YOU PIECE OF SH--
CRAAK
OW!
WHUMP
THAT HUR--BEC, YOUR ARMS!
WAIT HERE, I'LL GET THE STUFF.

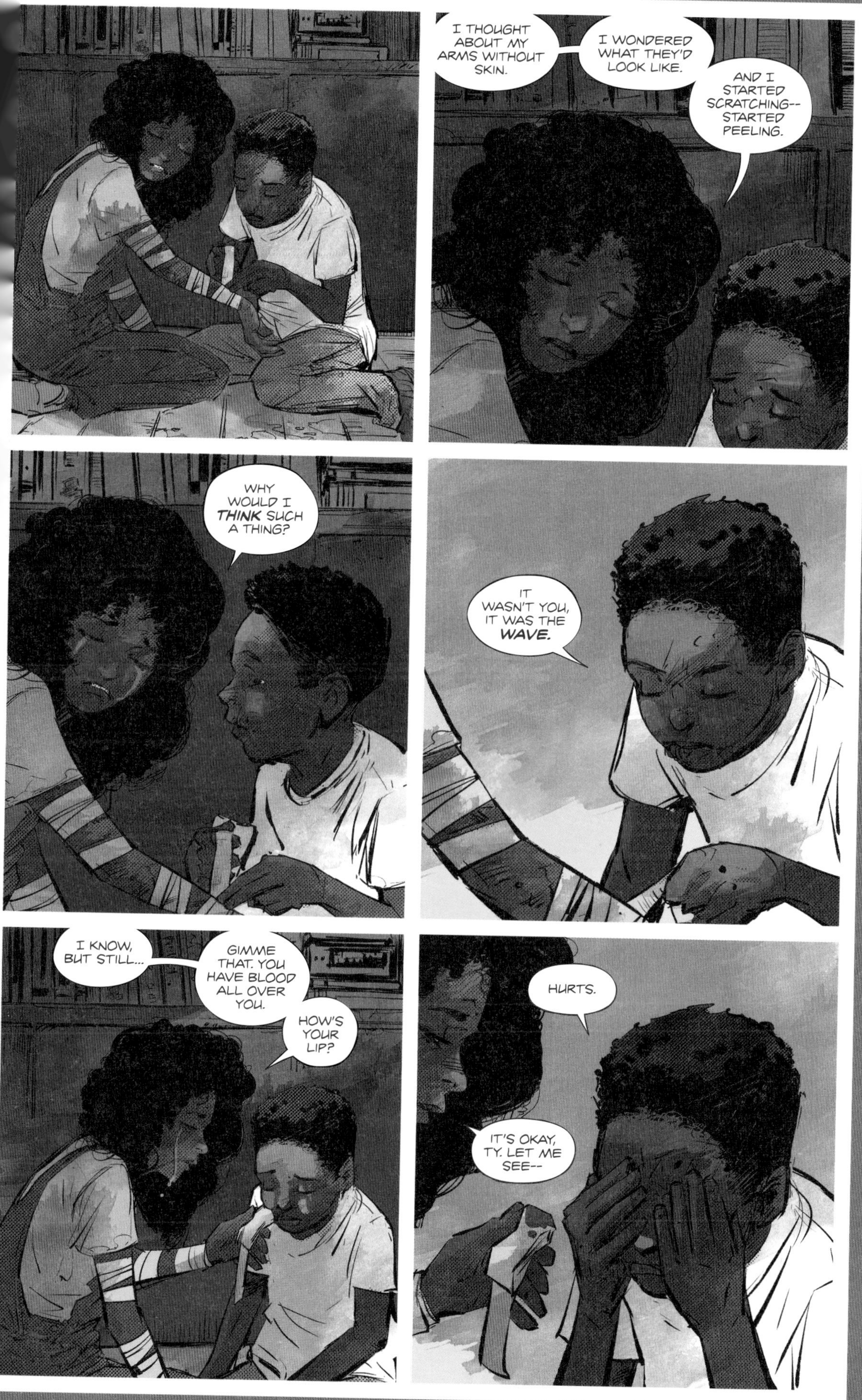
I THOUGHT ABOUT MY ARMS WITHOUT SKIN.
I WONDERED WHAT THEY'D LOOK LIKE.
AND I STARTED SCRATCHING-- STARTED PEELING.
WHY WOULD I THINK SUCH A THING?
IT WASN'T YOU, IT WAS THE WAVE.
I KNOW, BUT STILL...
GIMME THAT. YOU HAVE BLOOD ALL OVER YOU.
HOW'S YOUR LIP?
HURTS.
IT'S OKAY, TY. LET ME SEE--

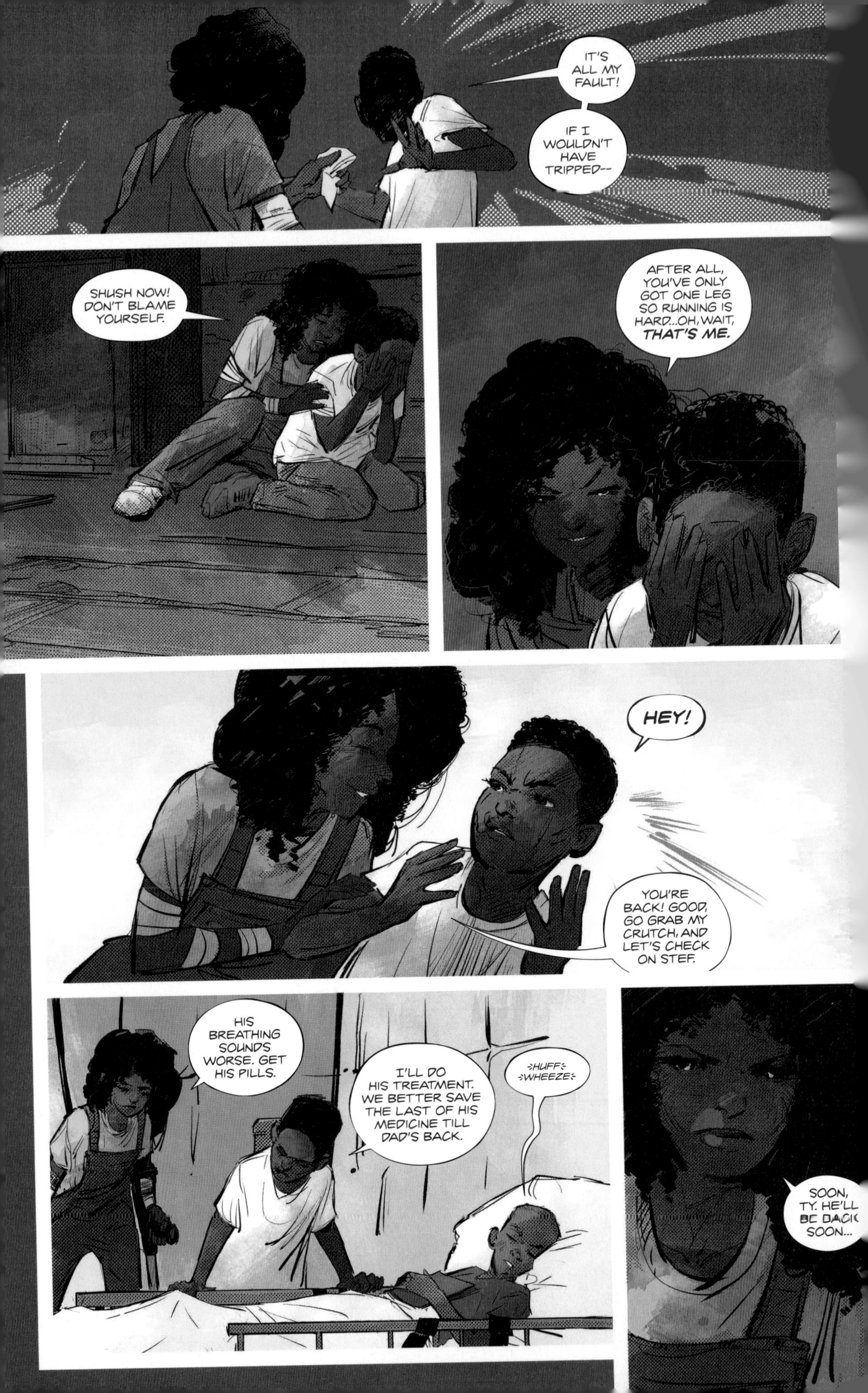
IT'S ALL MY FAULT!
IF I WOULDN'T HAVE TRIPPED--
SHUSH NOW! DON'T BLAME YOURSELF.
AFTER ALL, YOU'VE ONLY GOT ONE LEG SO RUNNING IS HARD...OH, WAIT, THAT'S ME.
HEY!
YOU'RE BACK! GOOD, GO GRAB MY CRUTCH, AND LET'S CHECK ON STEF.
HIS BREATHING SOUNDS WORSE. GET HIS PILLS.
I'LL DO HIS TREATMENT. WE BETTER SAVE THE LAST OF HIS MEDICINE TILL DAD'S BACK.
HUFF WHEEZE
SOON, TY. HE'LL BE BACK SOON...

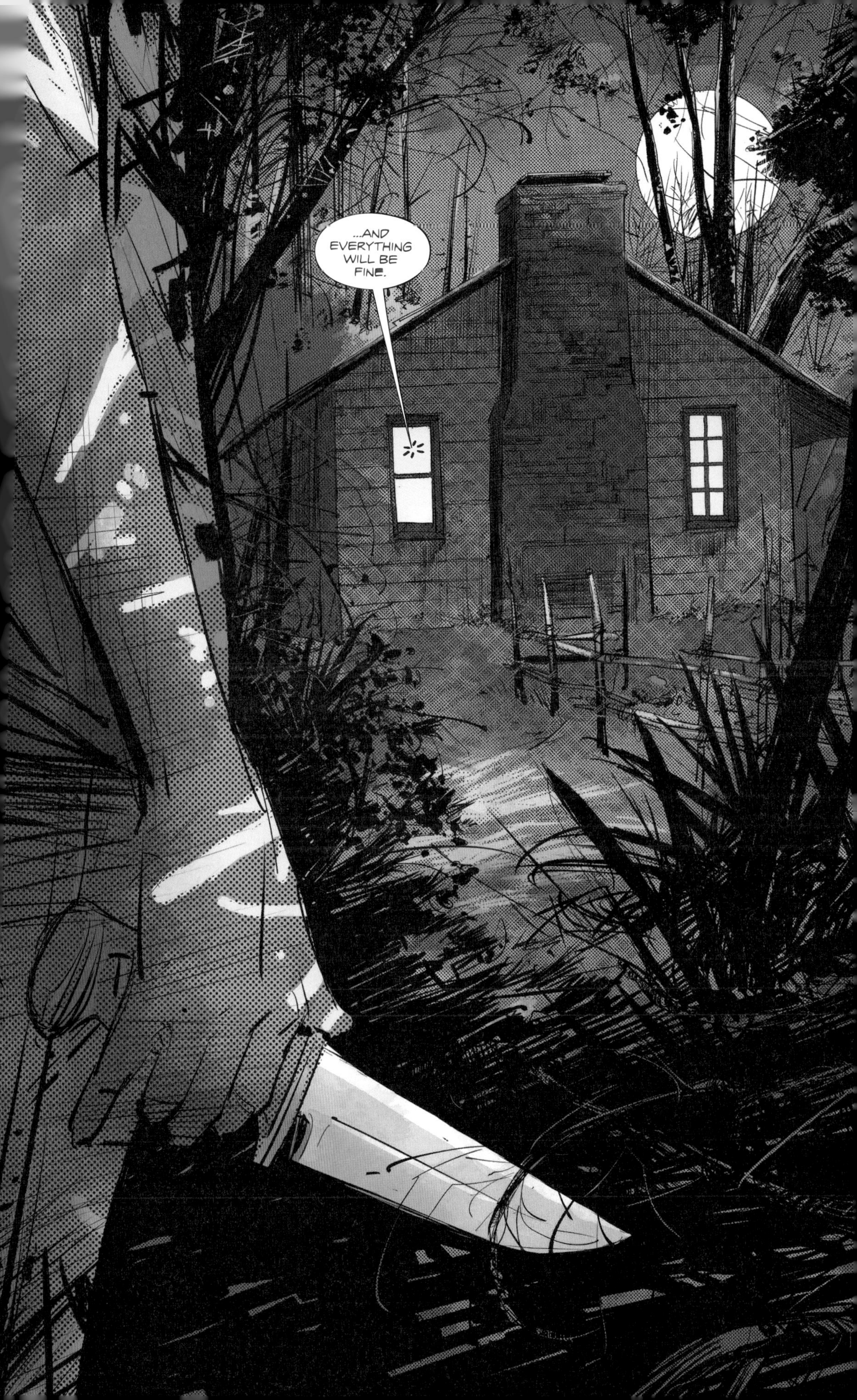
...AND EVERYTHING WILL BE FINE.

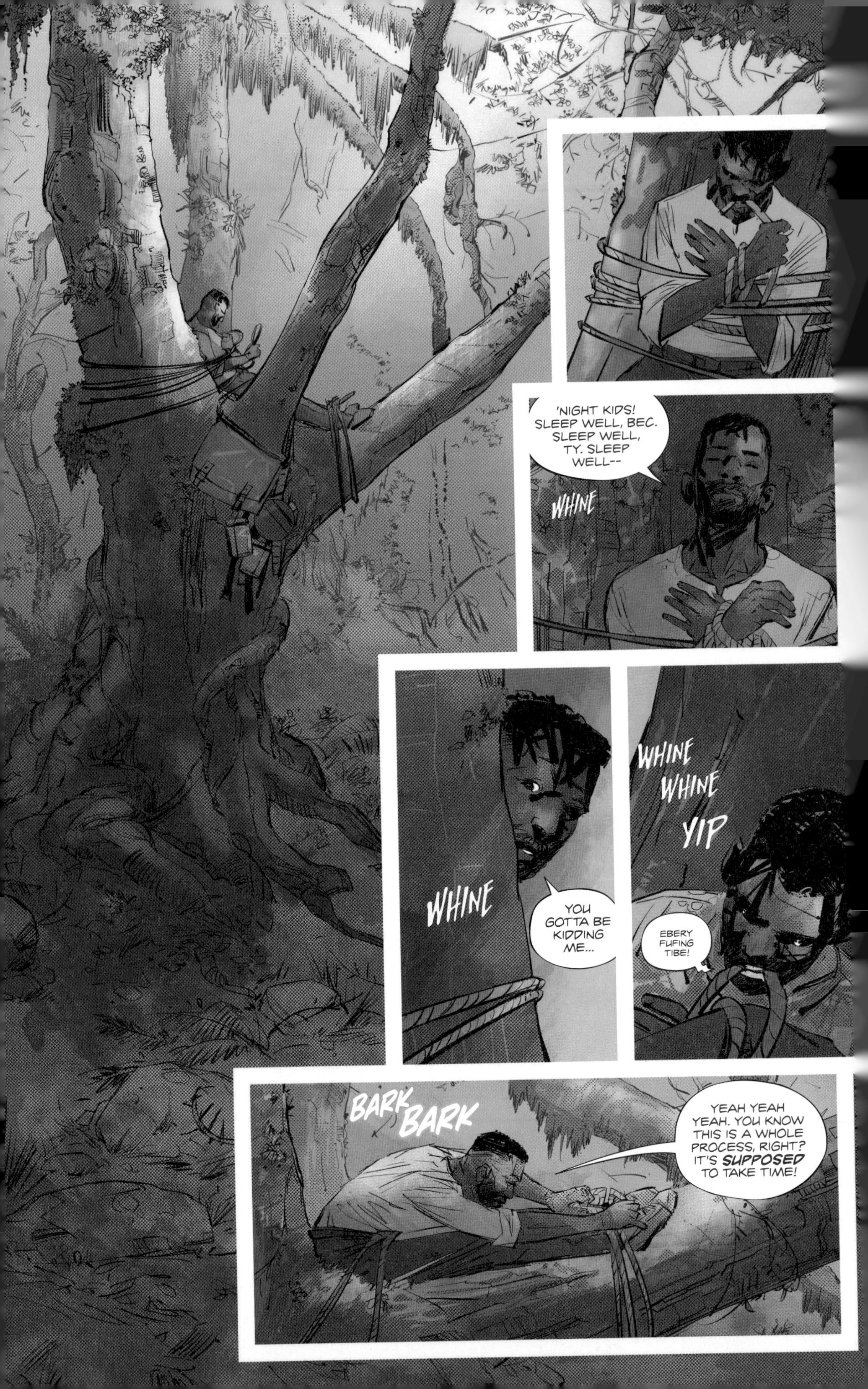
'NIGHT KIDS! SLEEP WELL, BEC. SLEEP WELL, TY. SLEEP WELL--
WHINE
WHINE
YOU GOTTA BE KIDDING ME...
WHINE WHINE YIP
EBERY FUFING TIBE!
BARK BARK
YEAH YEAH YEAH. YOU KNOW THIS IS A WHOLE PROCESS, RIGHT? IT'S SUPPOSED TO TAKE TIME!

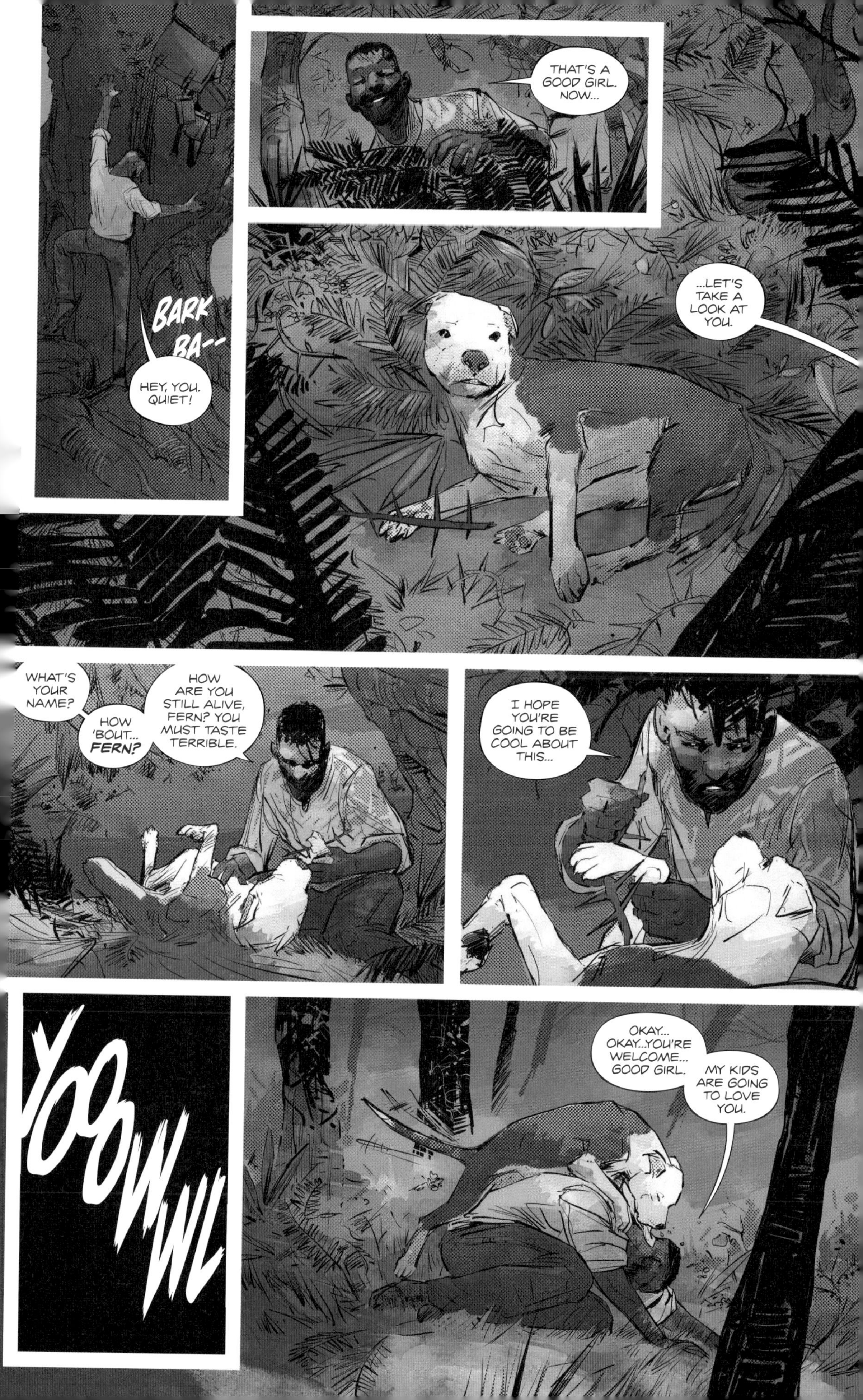
BARK BA--
HEY, YOU. QUIET!
THAT'S A GOOD GIRL. NOW...
...LET'S TAKE A LOOK AT YOU.
WHAT'S YOUR NAME?
HOW 'BOUT... FERN?
HOW ARE YOU STILL ALIVE, FERN? YOU MUST TASTE TERRIBLE.
I HOPE YOU'RE GOING TO BE COOL ABOUT THIS...
YOOOWWL
OKAY... OKAY...YOU'RE WELCOME... GOOD GIRL.
MY KIDS ARE GOING TO LOVE YOU.

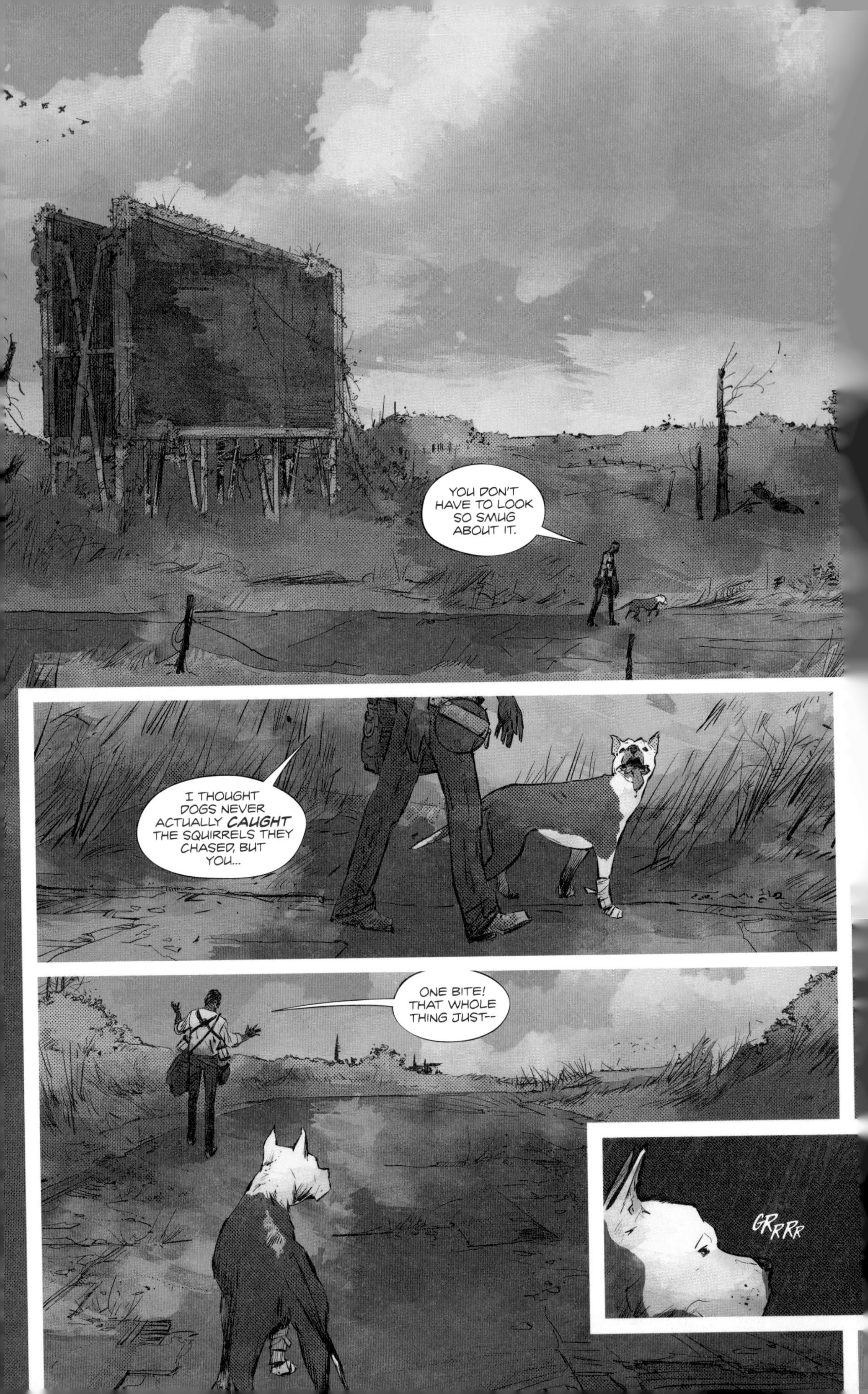
YOU DON'T HAVE TO LOOK SO SMUG ABOUT IT.
I THOUGHT DOGS NEVER ACTUALLY CAUGHT THE SQUIRRELS THEY CHASED, BUT YOU...
ONE BITE! THAT WHOLE THING JUST--
GRRRR

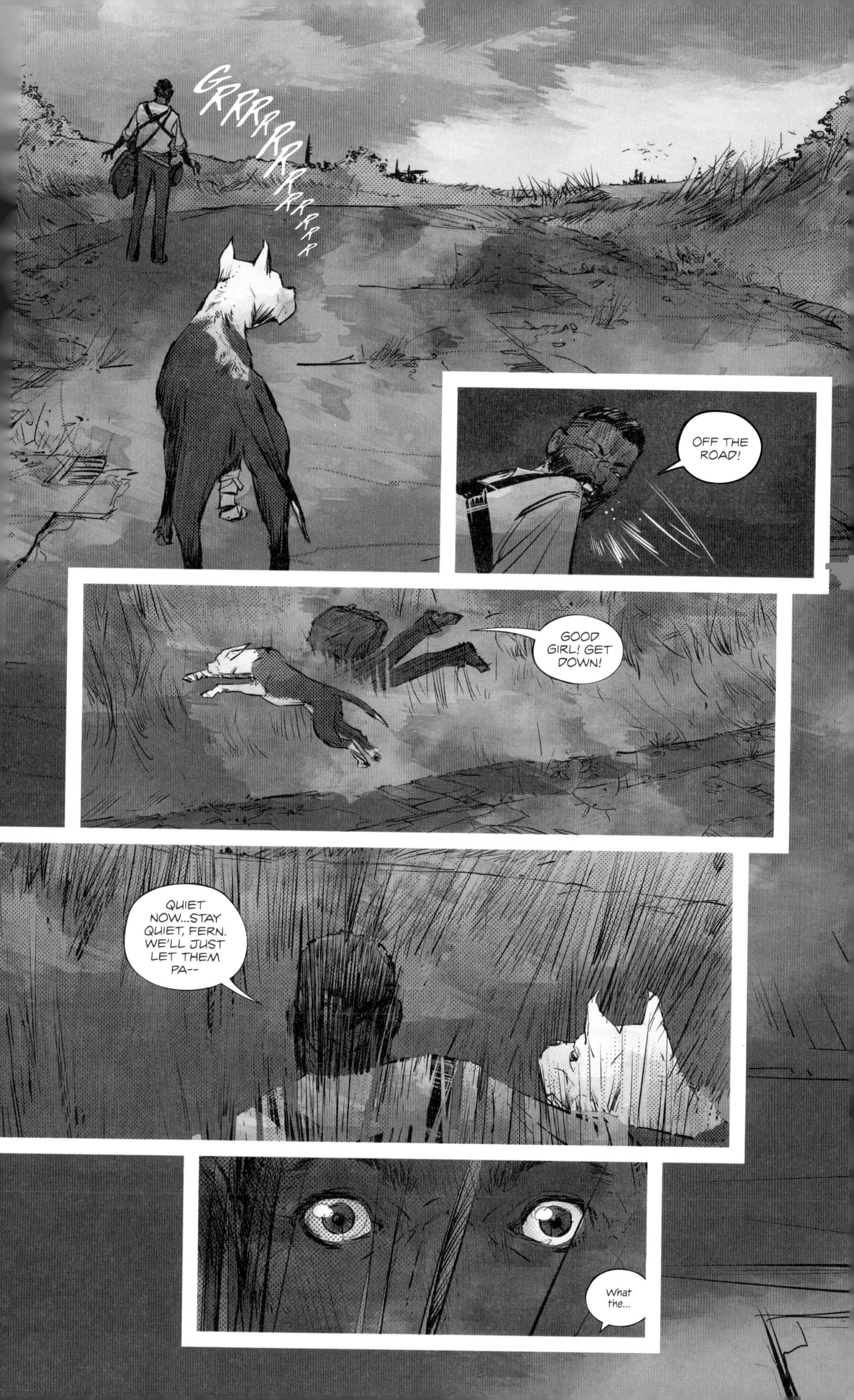
GRRRRRRRRRRR
OFF THE ROAD!
GOOD GIRL! GET DOWN!
QUIET NOW...STAY QUIET, FERN. WE'LL JUST LET THEM PA--
What the...

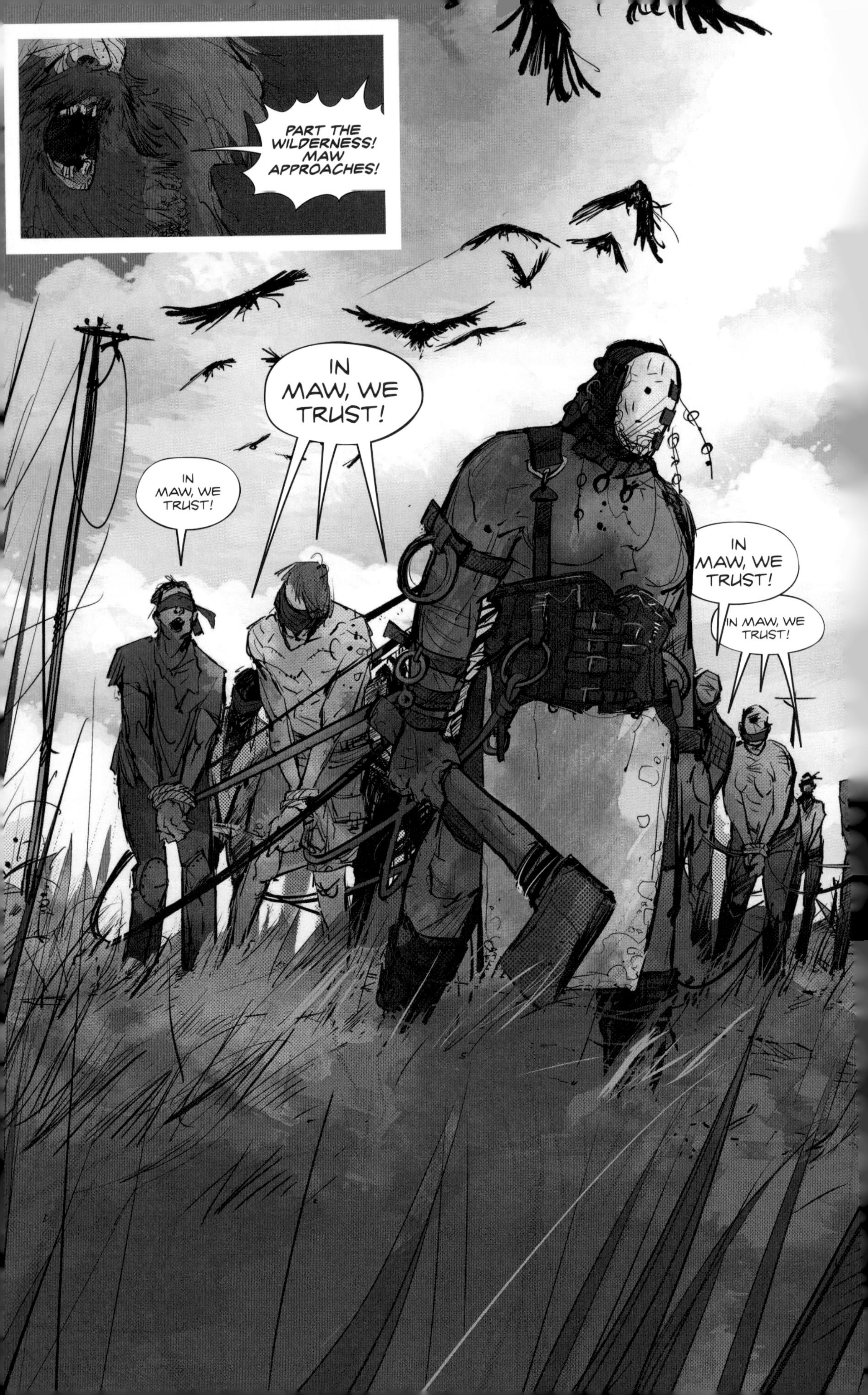
PART THE WILDERNESS! MAW APPROACHES!
IN MAW, WE TRUST!
IN MAW, WE TRUST!
IN MAW, WE TRUST!
IN MAW, WE TRUST!

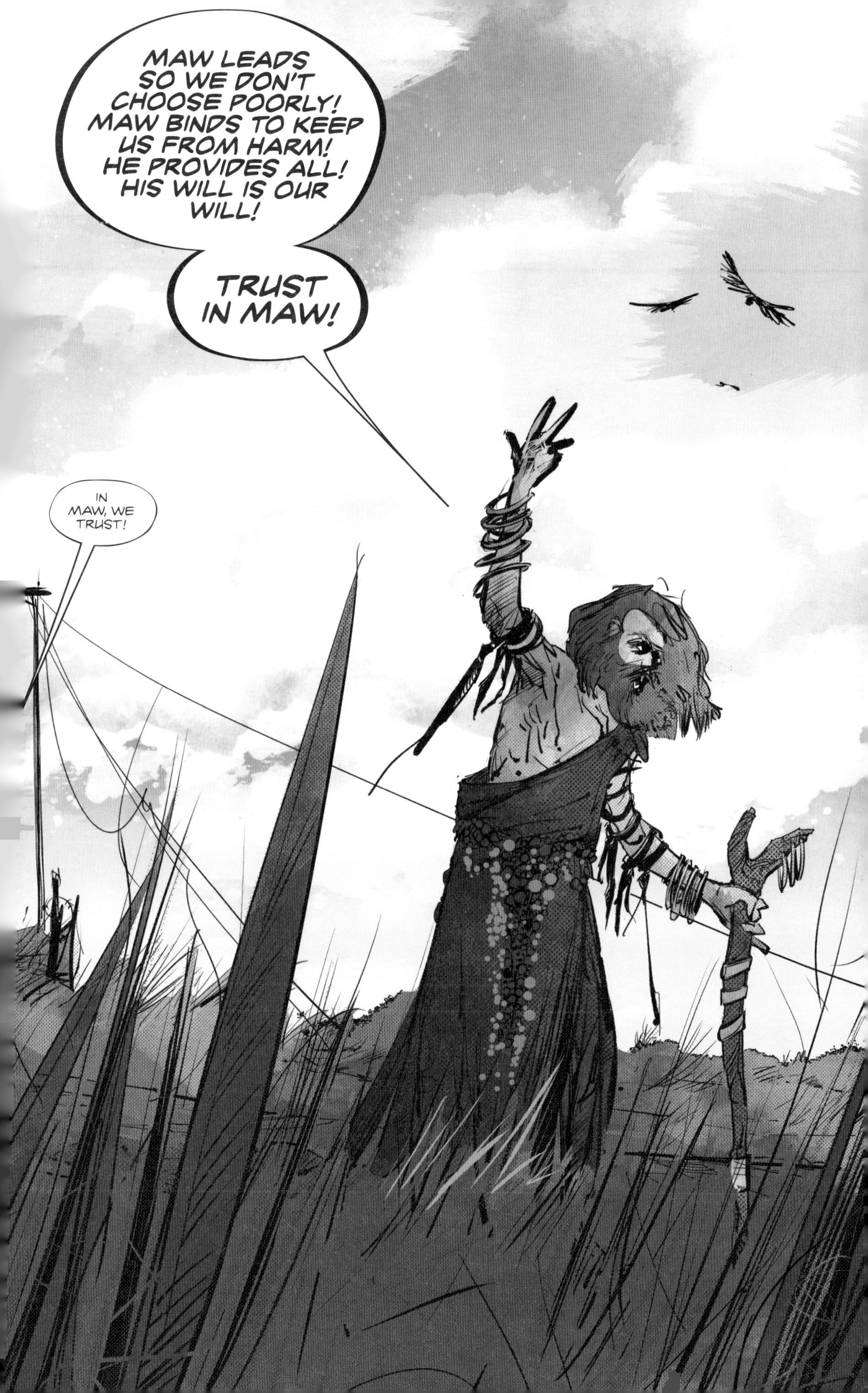
MAW LEADS SO WE DON'T CHOOSE POORLY! MAW BINDS TO KEEP US FROM HARM! HE PROVIDES ALL! HIS WILL IS OUR WILL!
TRUST IN MAW!
IN MAW, WE TRUST!

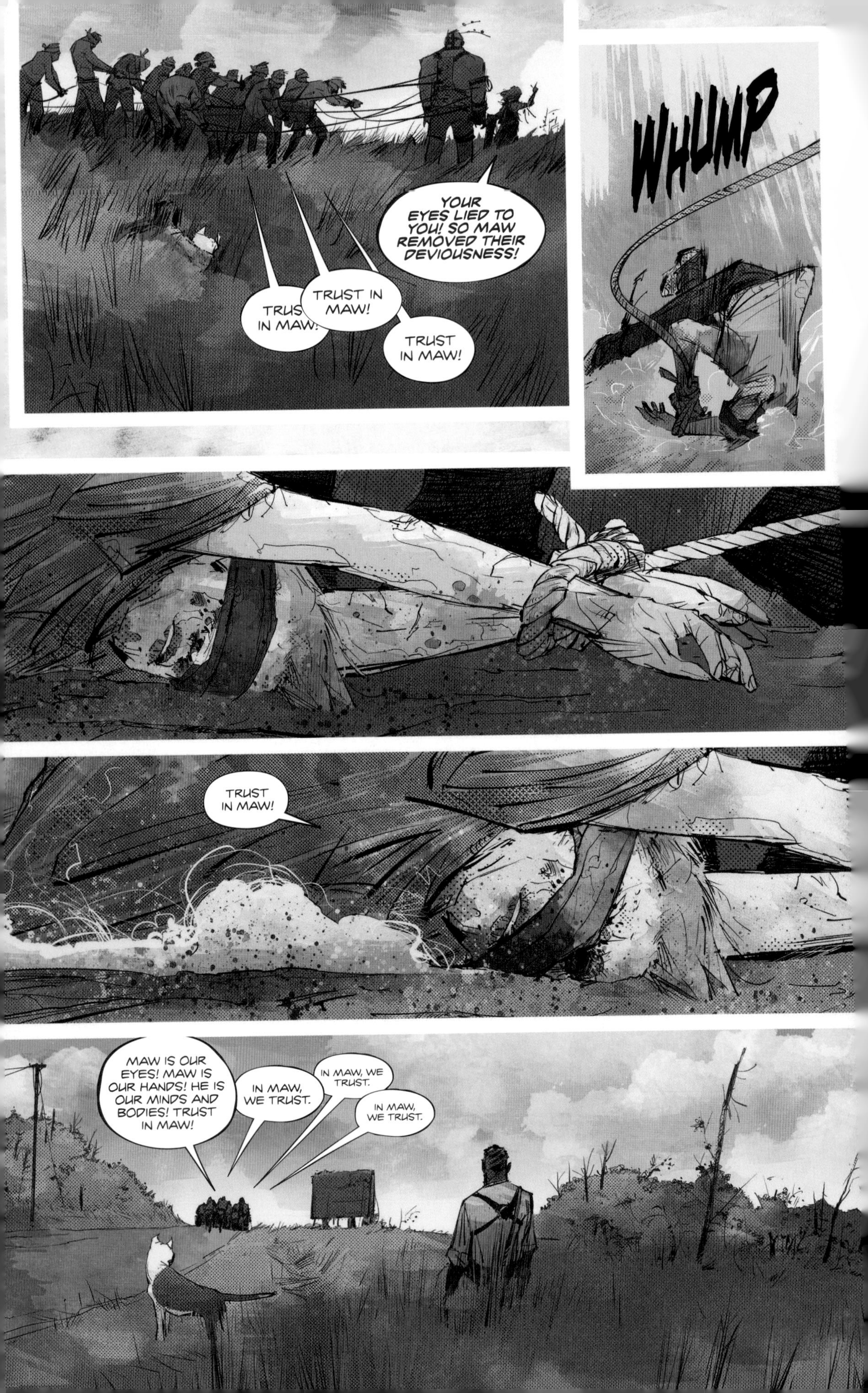
YOUR EYES LIED TO YOU! SO MAW REMOVED THEIR DEVIOUSNESS!
TRUST IN MAW!
TRUST IN MAW!
TRUST IN MAW!
WHUMP
TRUST IN MAW!
MAW IS OUR EYES! MAW IS OUR HANDS! HE IS OUR MINDS AND BODIES! TRUST IN MAW!
IN MAW, WE TRUST.
IN MAW, WE TRUST.
IN MAW, WE TRUST.

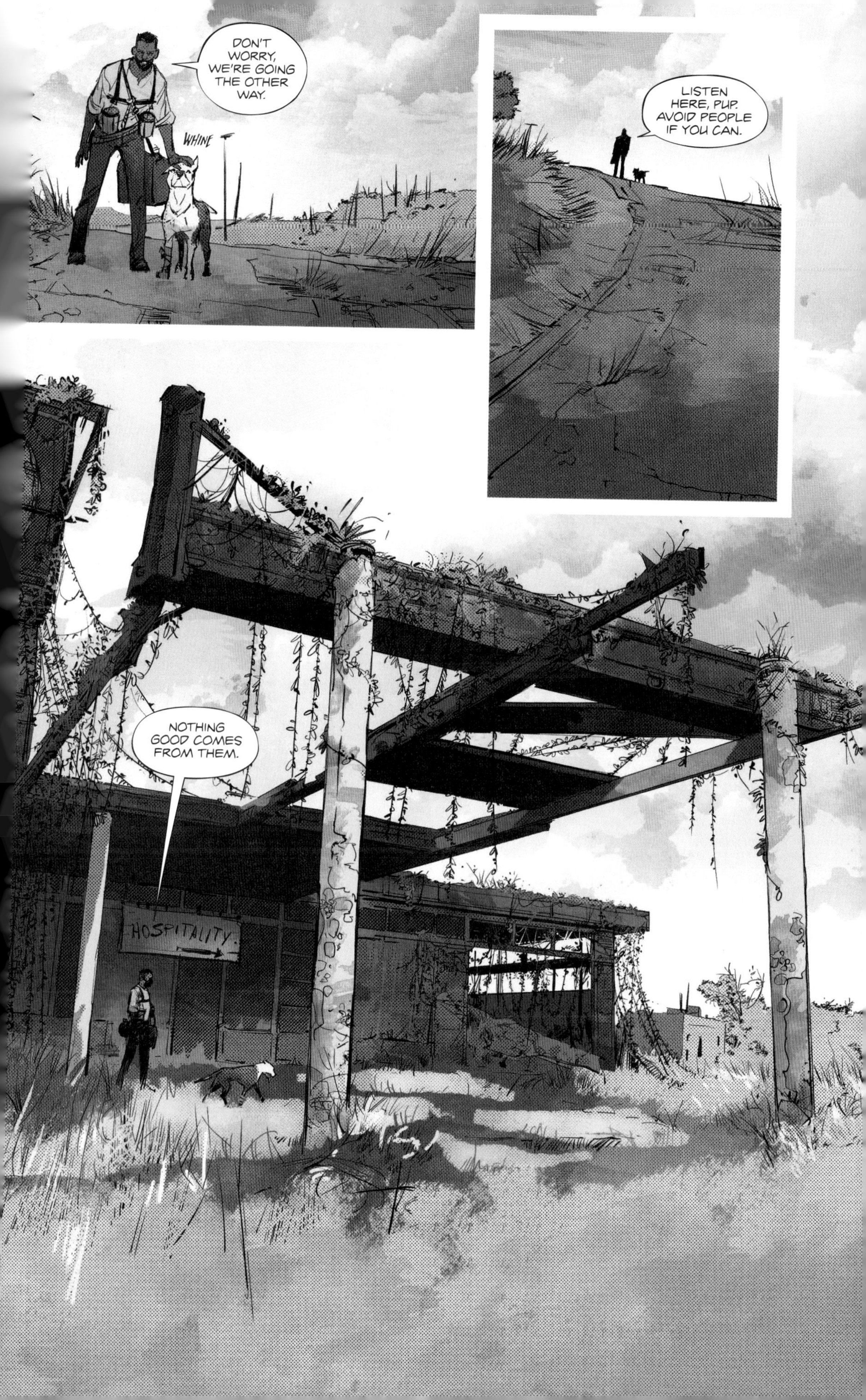
DON'T WORRY, WE'RE GOING THE OTHER WAY.
WHINE
LISTEN HERE, PUP. AVOID PEOPLE IF YOU CAN.
NOTHING GOOD COMES FROM THEM.
HOSPITALITY

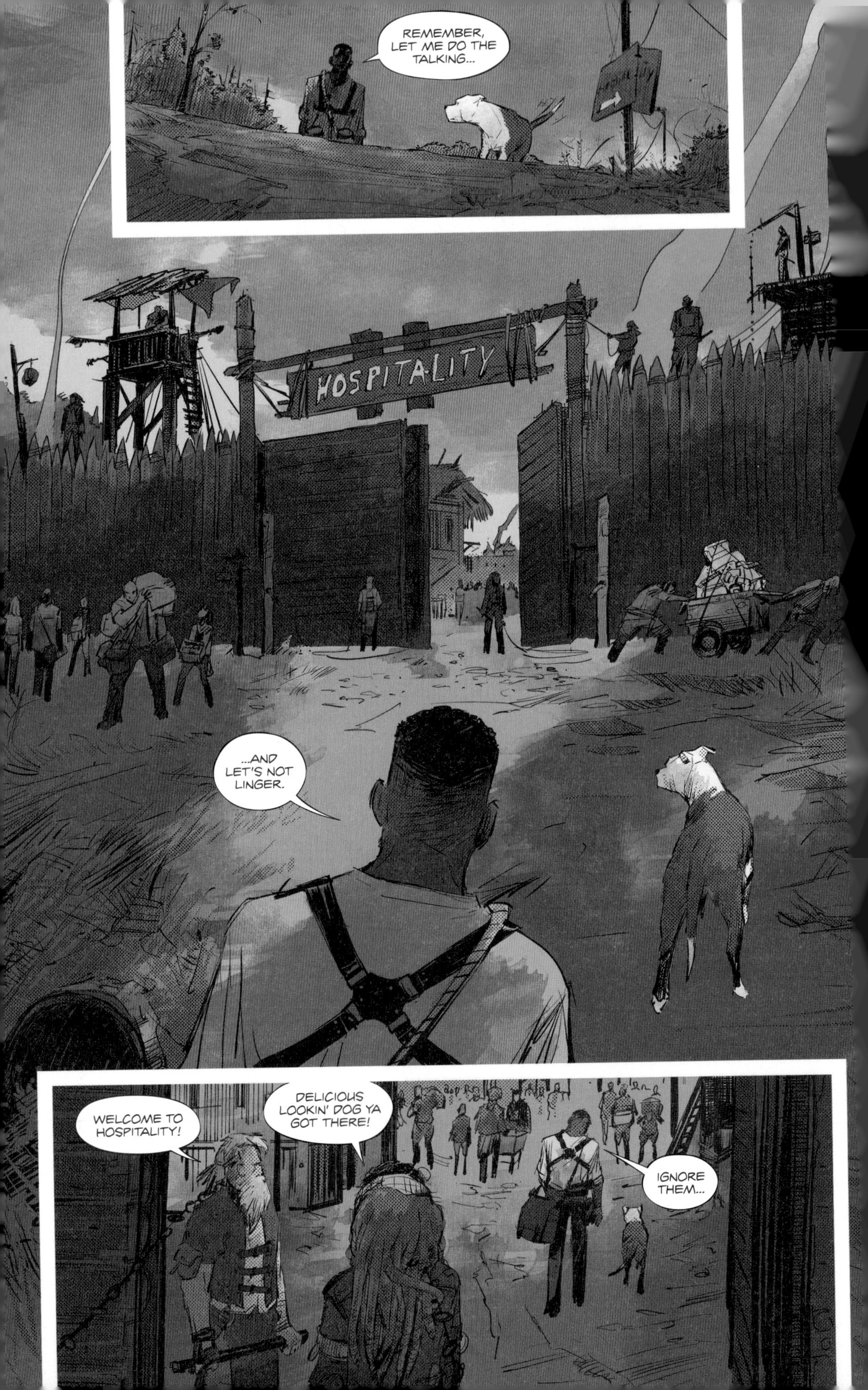

REMEMBER, LET ME DO THE TALKING...
HOSPITALITY
...AND LET'S NOT LINGER.
WELCOME TO HOSPITALITY!
DELICIOUS LOOKIN' DOG YA GOT THERE!
IGNORE THEM...

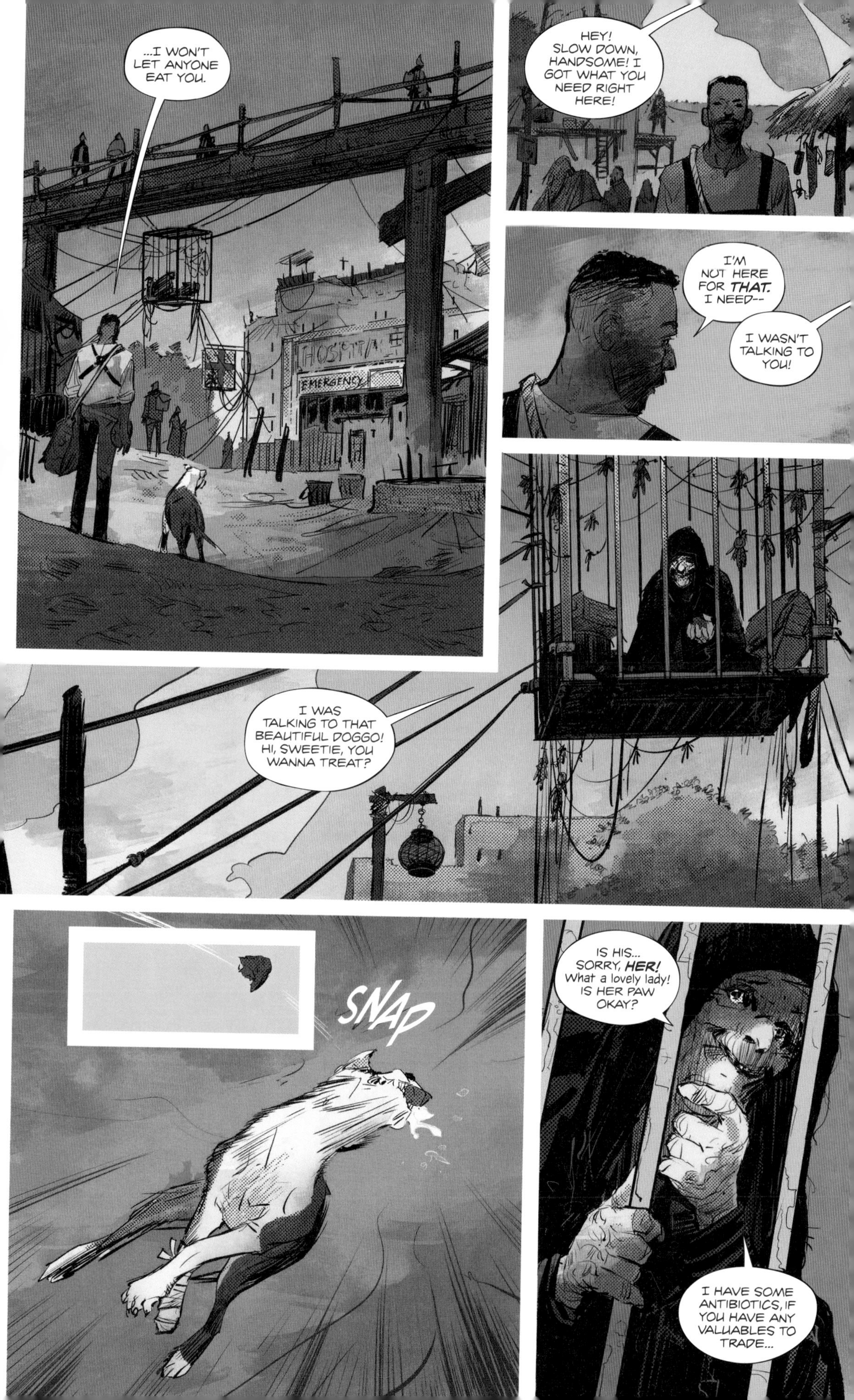
...I WON'T LET ANYONE EAT YOU.
HEY! SLOW DOWN, HANDSOME! I GOT WHAT YOU NEED RIGHT HERE!
HOSPITAL
EMERGENCY
I'M NOT HERE FOR **THAT.** I NEED--
I WASN'T TALKING TO YOU!
I WAS TALKING TO THAT BEAUTIFUL DOGGO! HI, SWEETIE, YOU WANNA TREAT?
SNAP
IS HIS... SORRY, ***HER!*** What a lovely lady! IS HER PAW OKAY?
I HAVE SOME ANTIBIOTICS, IF YOU HAVE ANY VALUABLES TO TRADE...

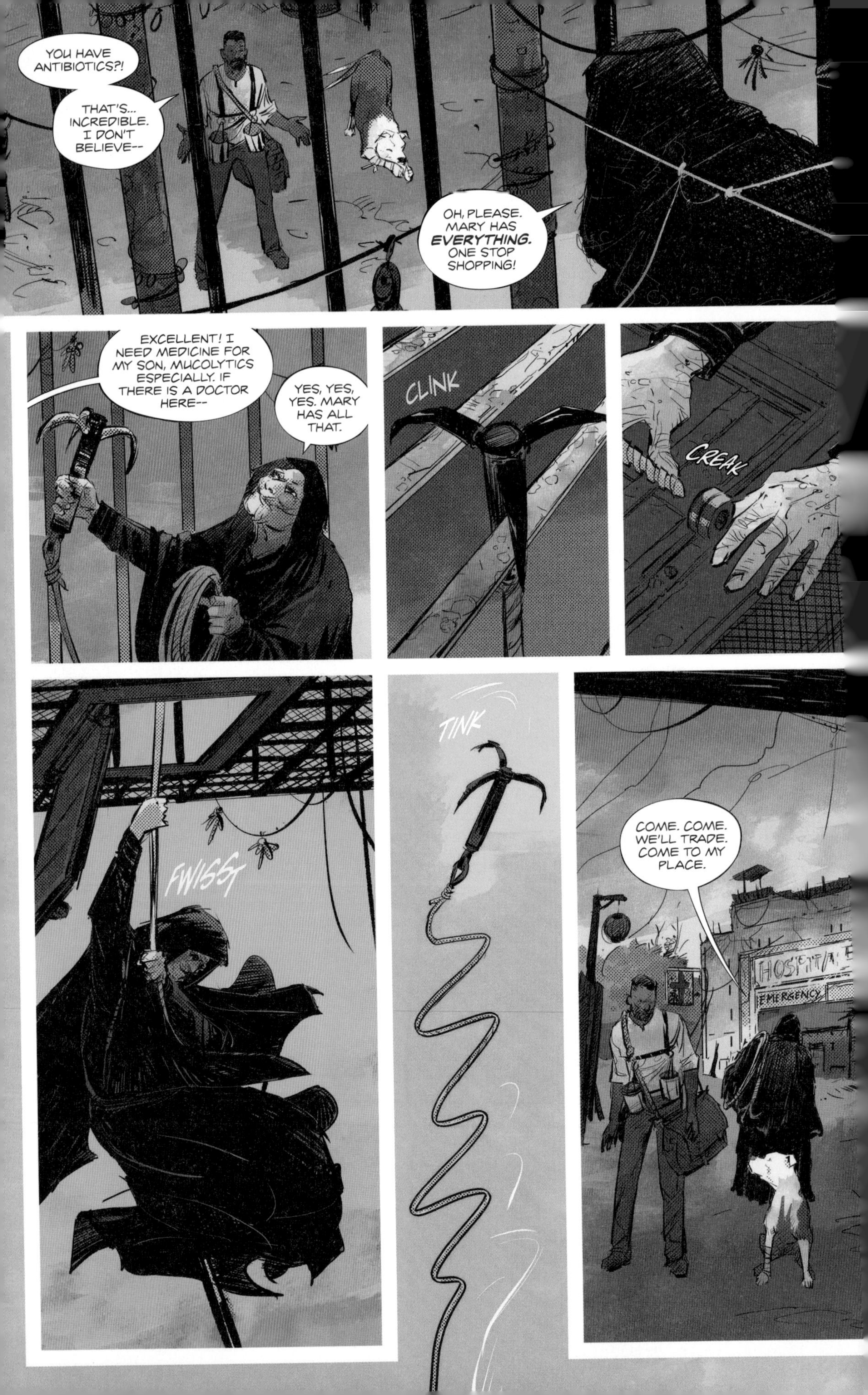
YOU HAVE ANTIBIOTICS?!
THAT'S... INCREDIBLE. I DON'T BELIEVE--
OH, PLEASE. MARY HAS **EVERYTHING.** ONE STOP SHOPPING!
EXCELLENT! I NEED MEDICINE FOR MY SON, MUCOLYTICS ESPECIALLY. IF THERE IS A DOCTOR HERE--
YES, YES, YES. MARY HAS ALL THAT.
CLINK
CREAK
FWISST
TINK
COME. COME. WE'LL TRADE. COME TO MY PLACE.
HOSPITAL
EMERGENCY

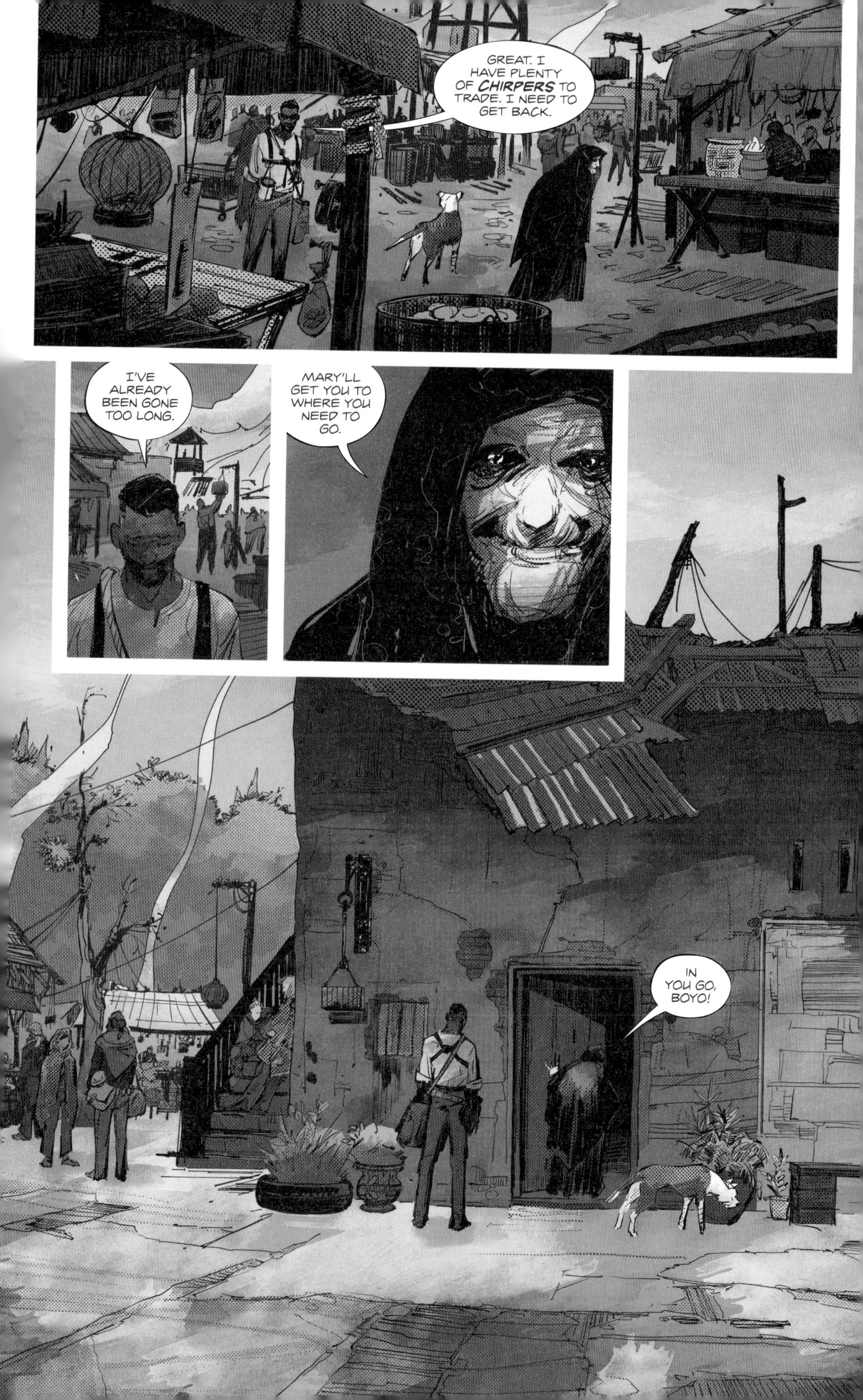
GREAT. I HAVE PLENTY OF CHIRPERS TO TRADE. I NEED TO GET BACK.
I'VE ALREADY BEEN GONE TOO LONG.
MARY'LL GET YOU TO WHERE YOU NEED TO GO.
IN YOU GO, BOYO!

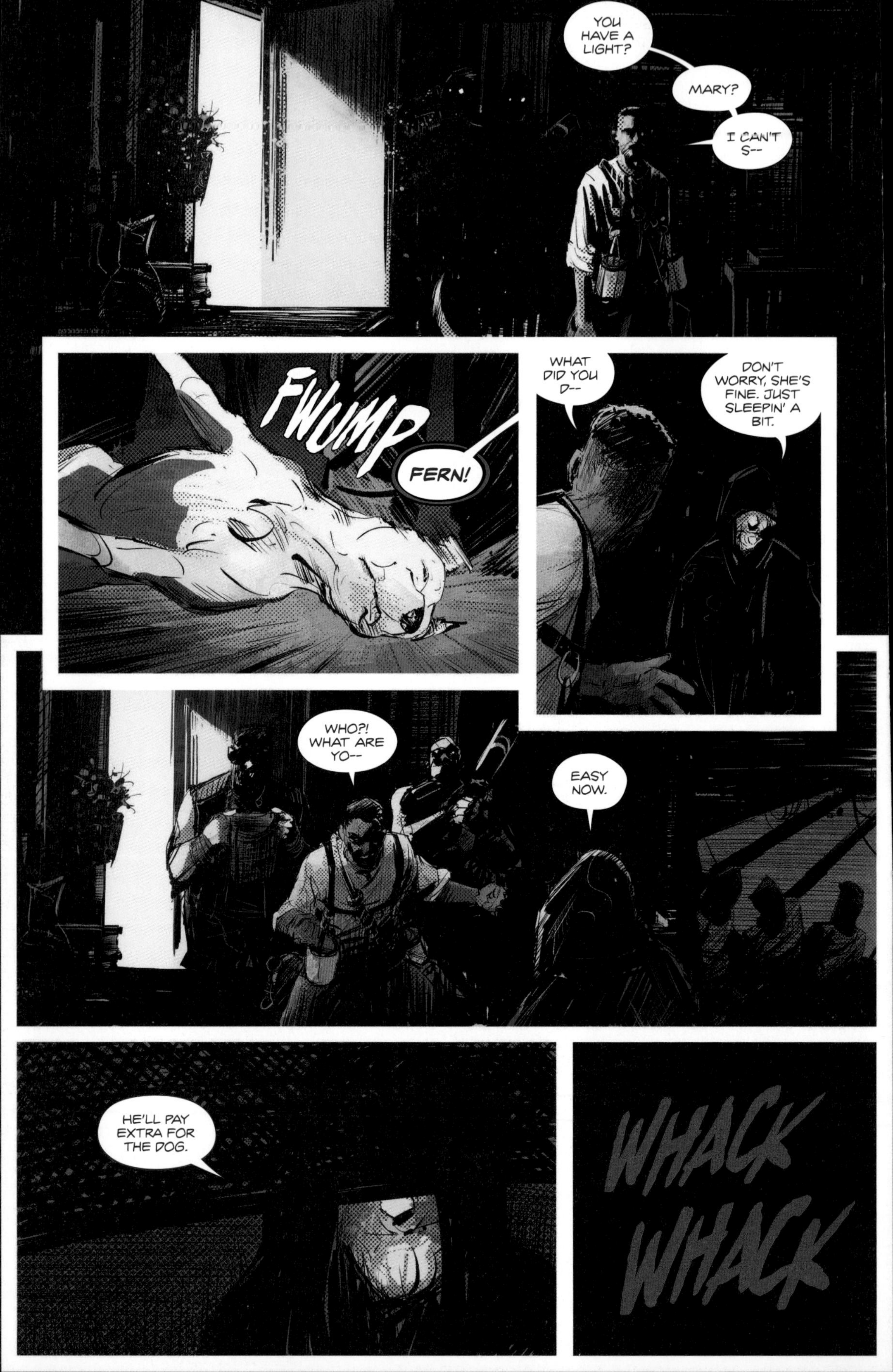
YOU HAVE A LIGHT?
MARY?
I CAN'T S--
FWUMP
FERN!
WHAT DID YOU D--
DON'T WORRY, SHE'S FINE. JUST SLEEPIN' A BIT.
WHO?! WHAT ARE YO--
EASY NOW.
HE'LL PAY EXTRA FOR THE DOG.
WHACK
WHACK

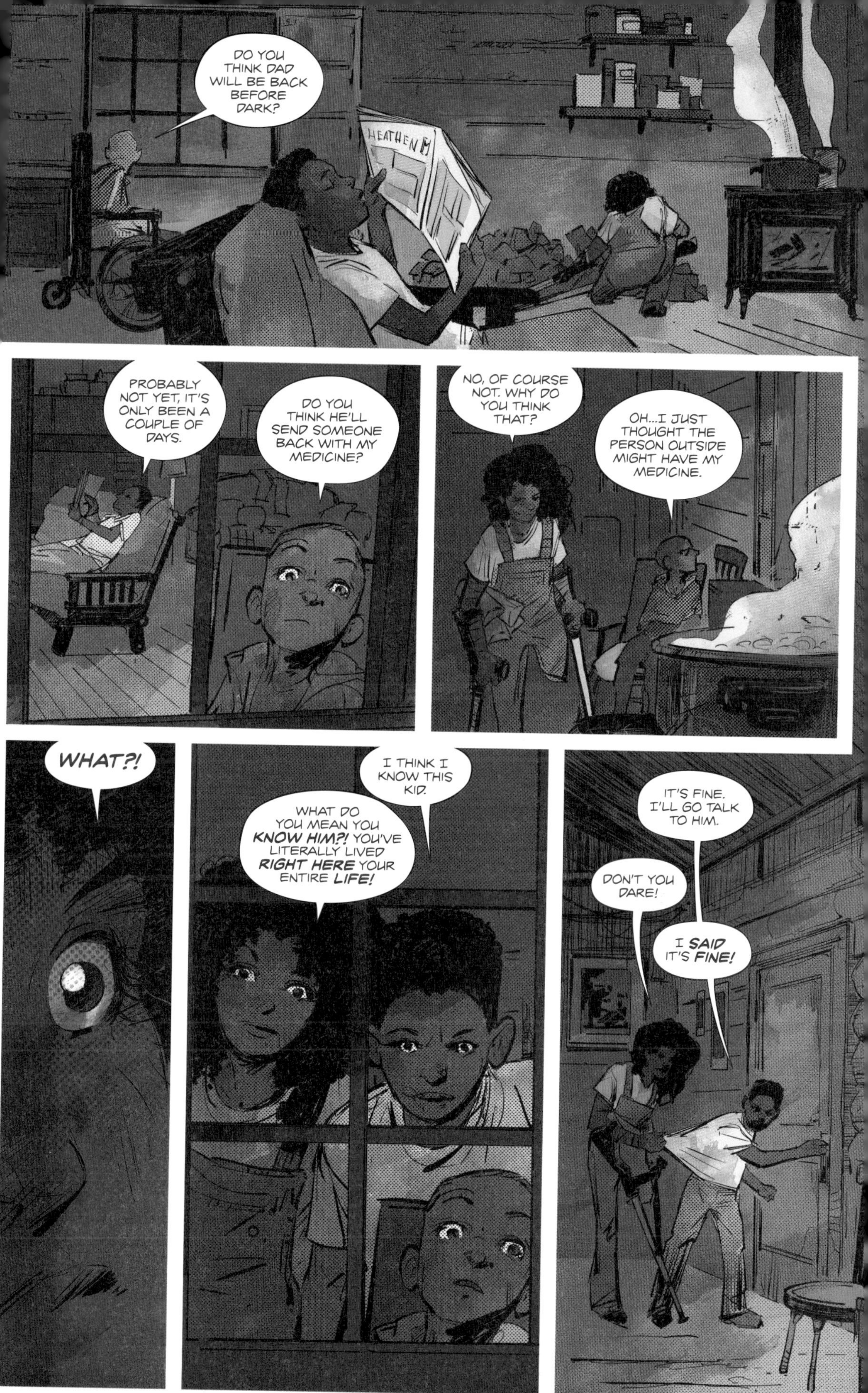
DO YOU THINK DAD WILL BE BACK BEFORE DARK?
HEATHEN
PROBABLY NOT YET, IT'S ONLY BEEN A COUPLE OF DAYS.
DO YOU THINK HE'LL SEND SOMEONE BACK WITH MY MEDICINE?
NO, OF COURSE NOT. WHY DO YOU THINK THAT?
OH...I JUST THOUGHT THE PERSON OUTSIDE MIGHT HAVE MY MEDICINE.
WHAT?!
I THINK I KNOW THIS KID.
WHAT DO YOU MEAN YOU KNOW HIM?! YOU'VE LITERALLY LIVED RIGHT HERE YOUR ENTIRE LIFE!
IT'S FINE. I'LL GO TALK TO HIM.
DON'T YOU DARE!
I SAID IT'S FINE!

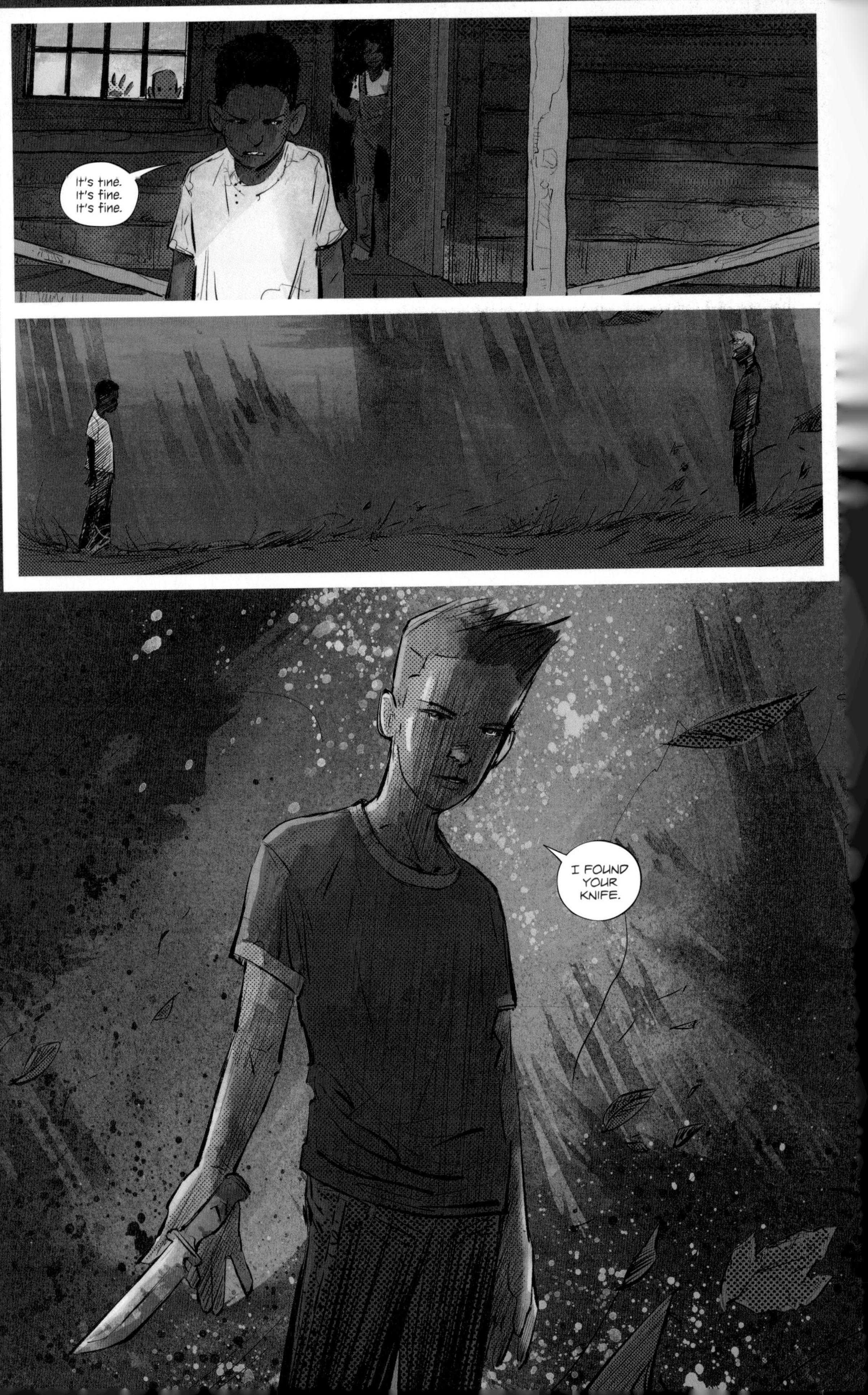
It's fine. It's fine. It's fine.
I FOUND YOUR KNIFE.

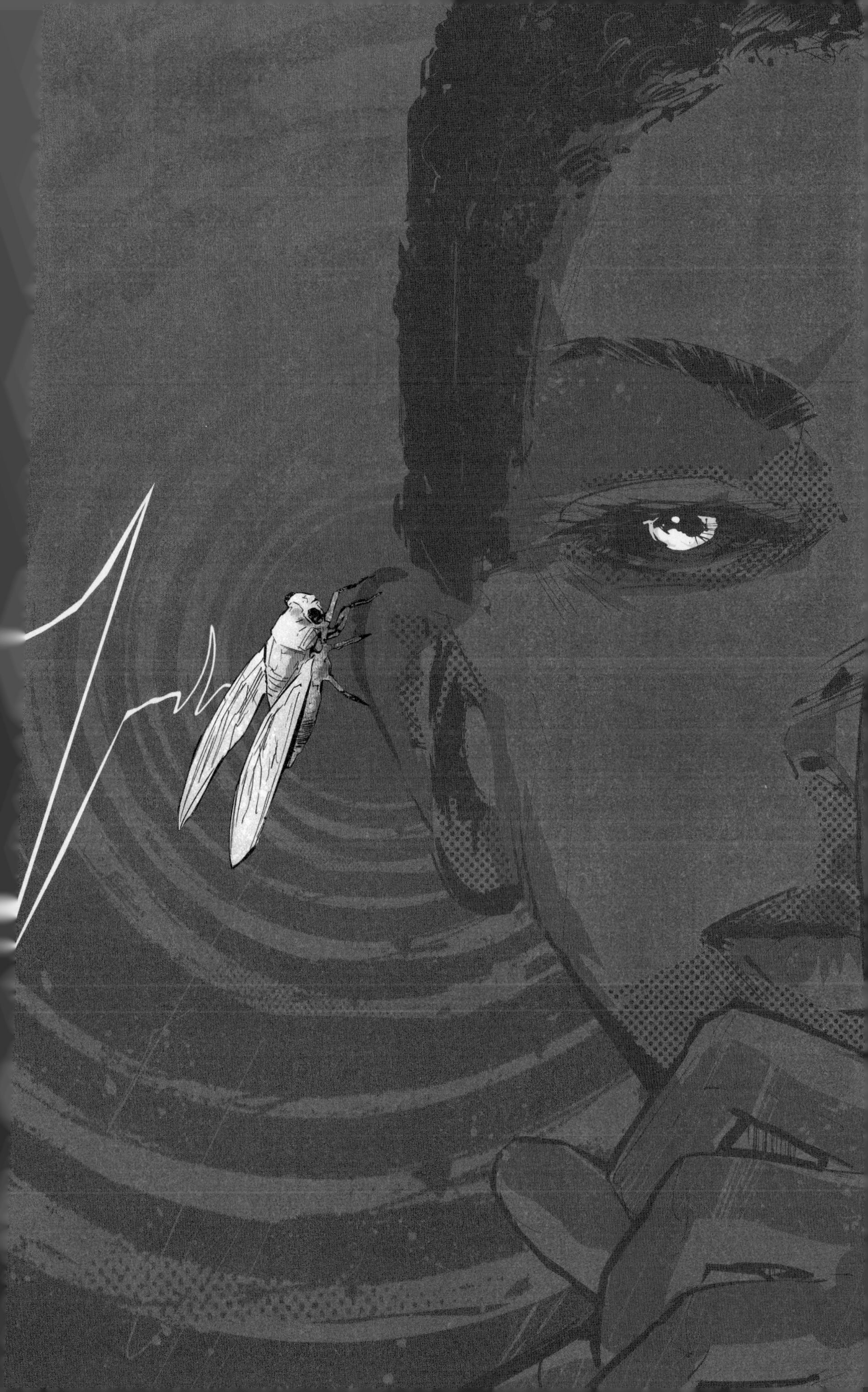

CHAPTER THREE

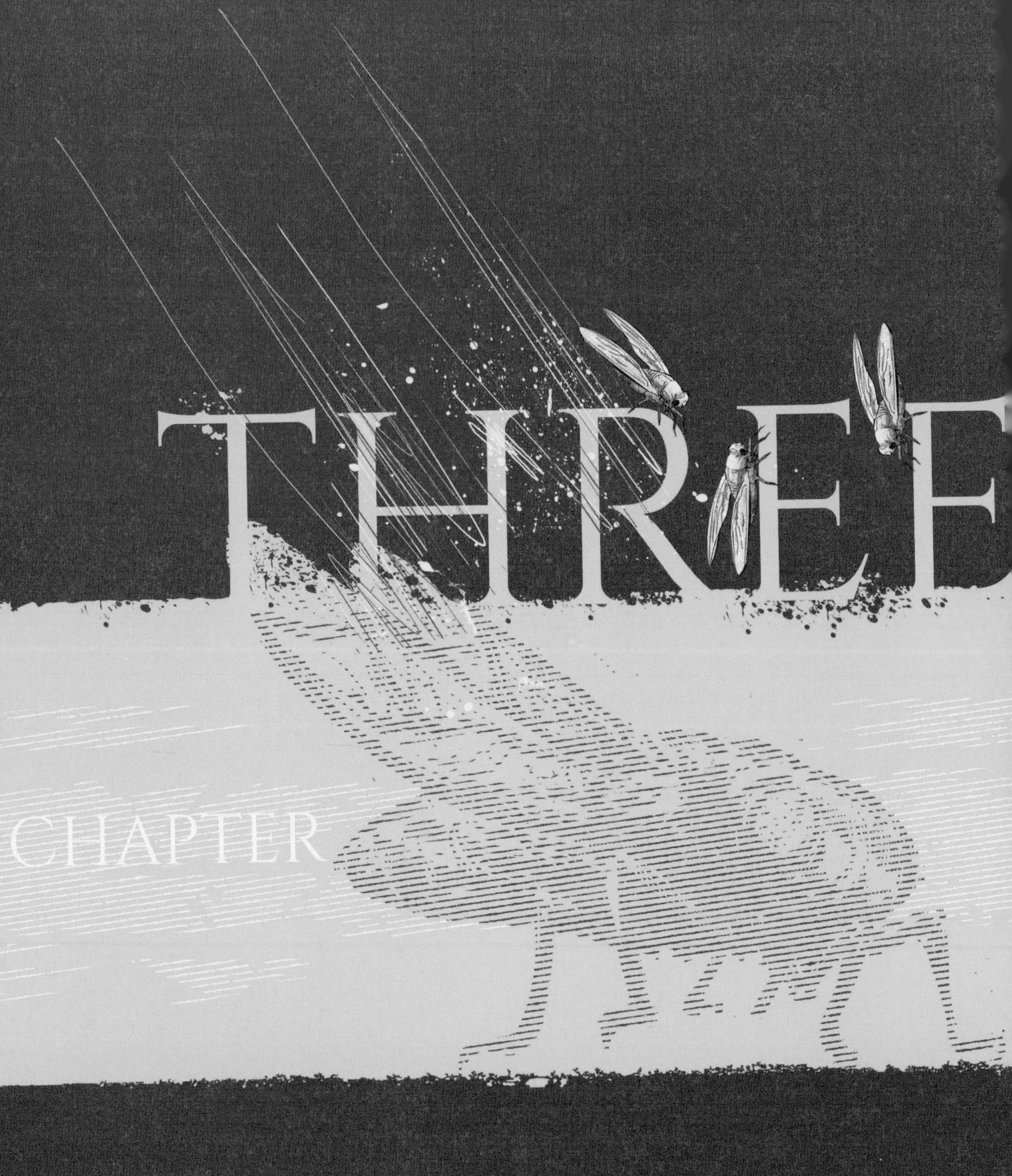

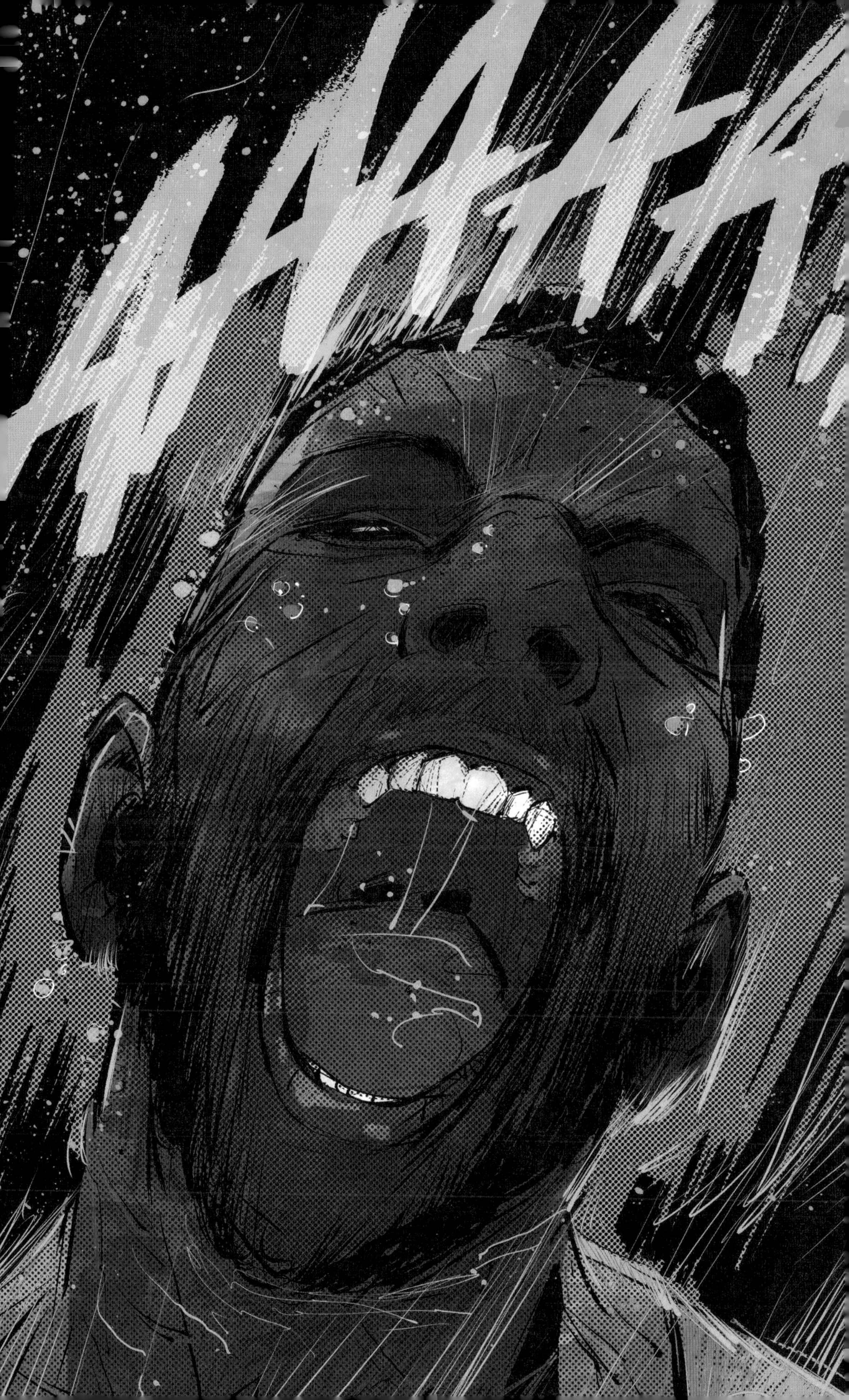
AAAA

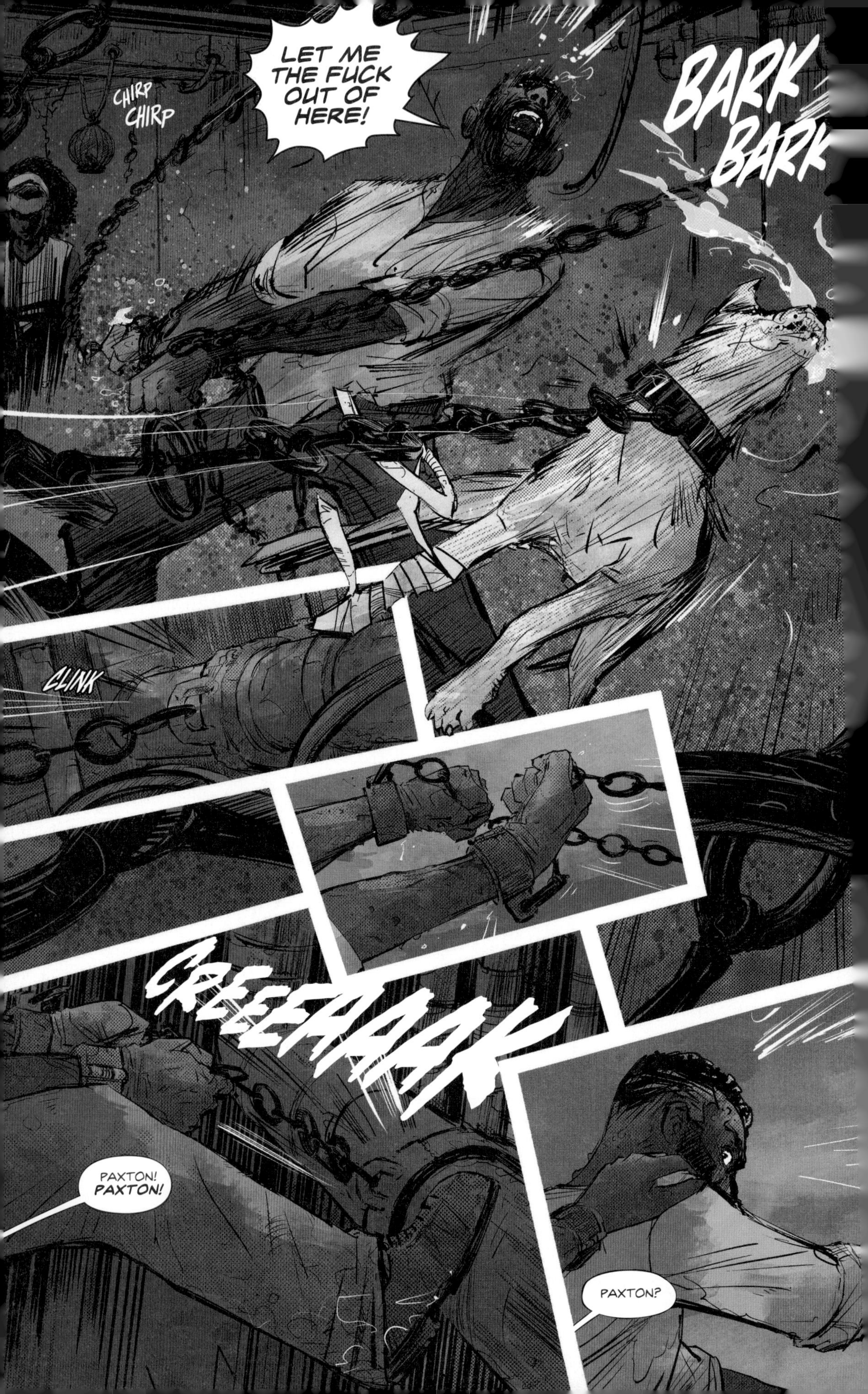
LET ME THE FUCK OUT OF HERE!
CHIRP CHIRP
BARK BARK
CLINK
CREEEAAAK
PAXTON! PAXTON!
PAXTON?

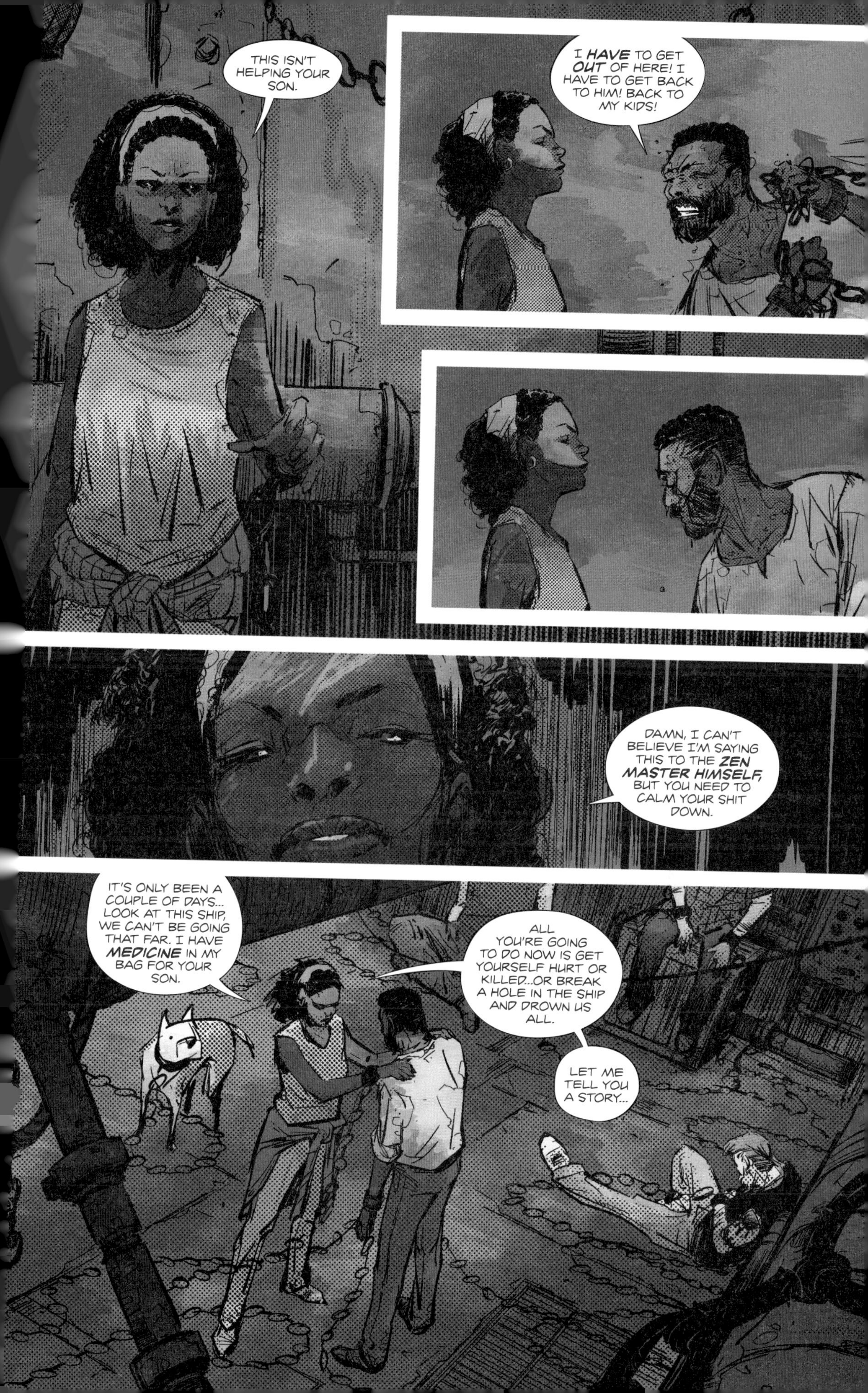
THIS ISN'T HELPING YOUR SON.
I HAVE TO GET OUT OF HERE! I HAVE TO GET BACK TO HIM! BACK TO MY KIDS!
DAMN, I CAN'T BELIEVE I'M SAYING THIS TO THE ZEN MASTER HIMSELF, BUT YOU NEED TO CALM YOUR SHIT DOWN.
IT'S ONLY BEEN A COUPLE OF DAYS... LOOK AT THIS SHIP, WE CAN'T BE GOING THAT FAR. I HAVE MEDICINE IN MY BAG FOR YOUR SON.
ALL YOU'RE GOING TO DO NOW IS GET YOURSELF HURT OR KILLED...OR BREAK A HOLE IN THE SHIP AND DROWN US ALL.
LET ME TELL YOU A STORY...

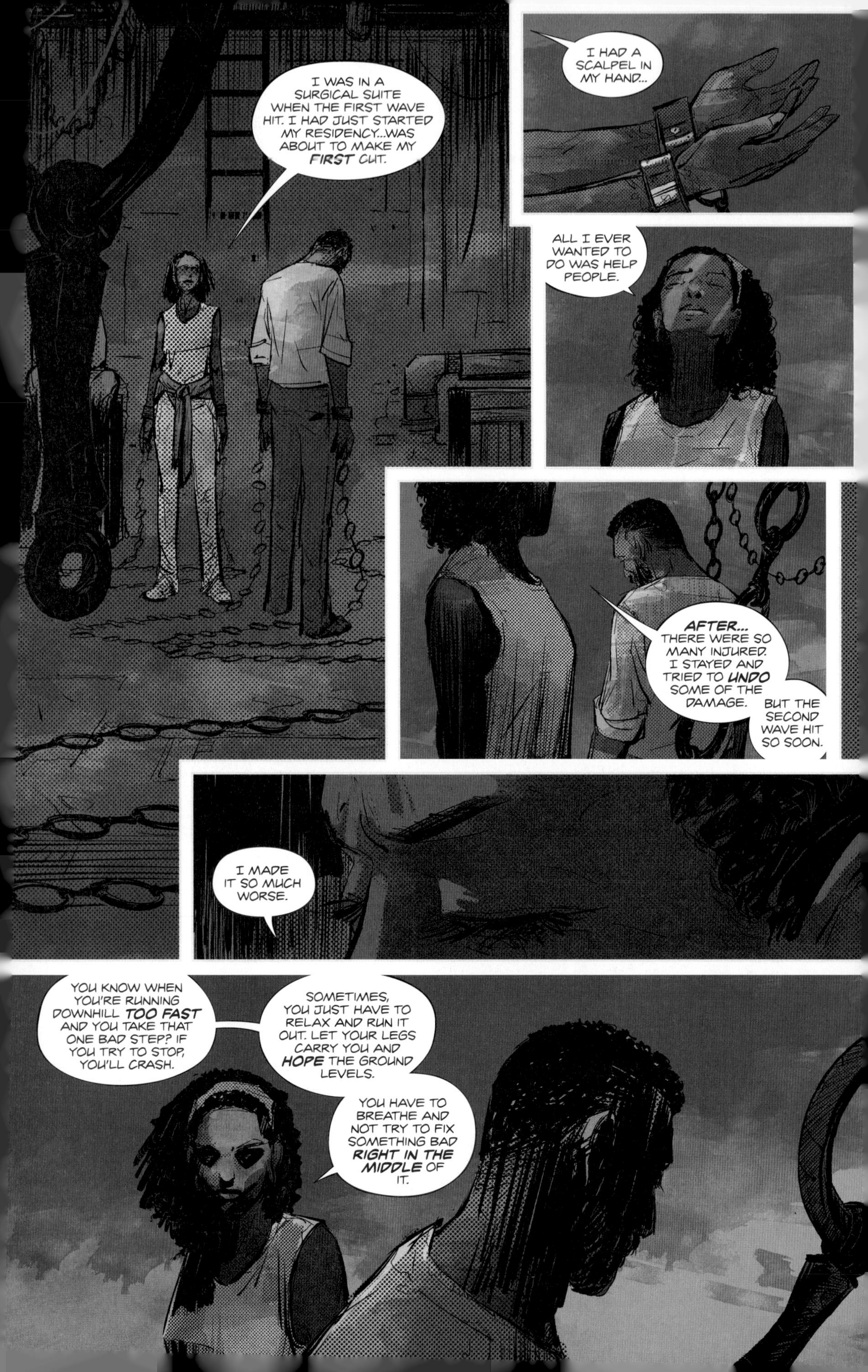

I WAS IN A SURGICAL SUITE WHEN THE FIRST WAVE HIT. I HAD JUST STARTED MY RESIDENCY...WAS ABOUT TO MAKE MY **FIRST** CUT.
I HAD A SCALPEL IN MY HAND...
ALL I EVER WANTED TO DO WAS HELP PEOPLE.
AFTER... THERE WERE SO MANY INJURED. I STAYED AND TRIED TO **UNDO** SOME OF THE DAMAGE.
BUT THE SECOND WAVE HIT SO SOON.
I MADE IT SO MUCH WORSE.
YOU KNOW WHEN YOU'RE RUNNING DOWNHILL **TOO FAST** AND YOU TAKE THAT ONE BAD STEP? IF YOU TRY TO STOP, YOU'LL CRASH.
SOMETIMES, YOU JUST HAVE TO RELAX AND RUN IT OUT. LET YOUR LEGS CARRY YOU AND **HOPE** THE GROUND LEVELS.
YOU HAVE TO BREATHE AND NOT TRY TO FIX SOMETHING BAD **RIGHT IN THE MIDDLE** OF IT.

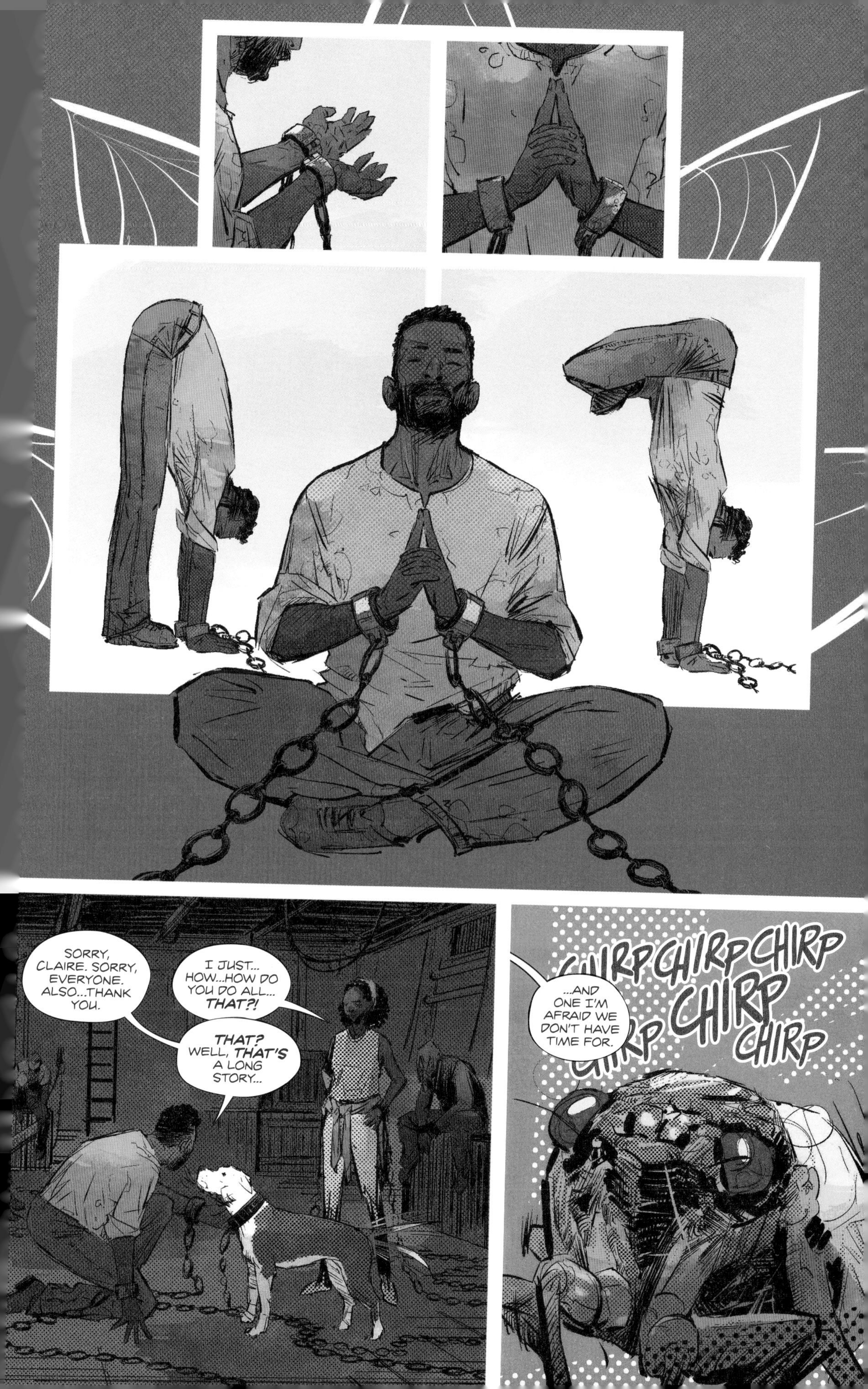
SORRY, CLAIRE. SORRY, EVERYONE. ALSO...THANK YOU.
I JUST... HOW...HOW DO YOU DO ALL... THAT?!
THAT? WELL, THAT'S A LONG STORY...
CHIRP CHIRP CHIRP
...AND ONE I'M AFRAID WE DON'T HAVE TIME FOR.
CHIRP CHIRP
CHIRP

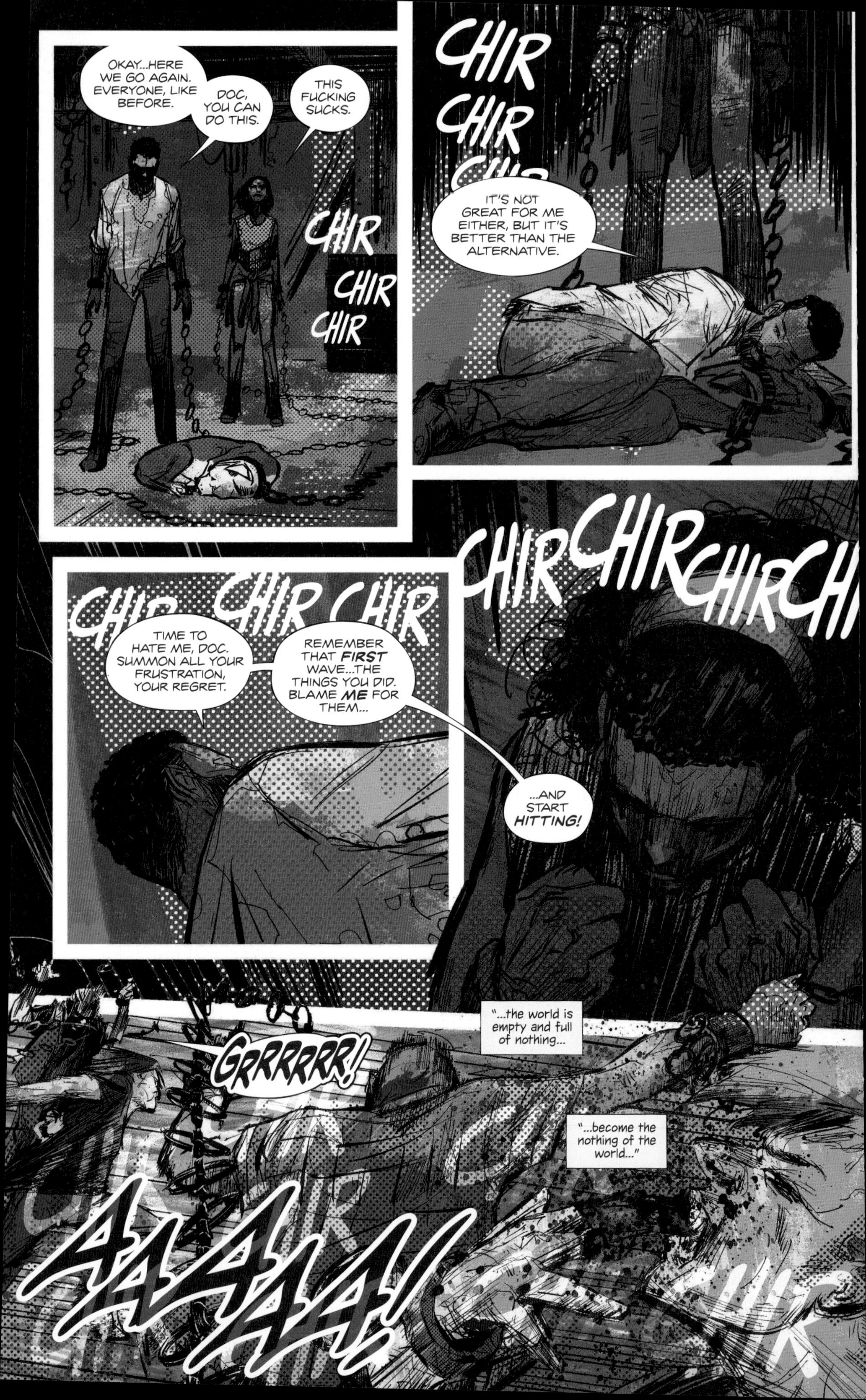
OKAY...HERE WE GO AGAIN. EVERYONE, LIKE BEFORE.
DOC, YOU CAN DO THIS.
THIS FUCKING SUCKS.
CHIR
CHIR
CHIR
CHIR
CHIR
IT'S NOT GREAT FOR ME EITHER, BUT IT'S BETTER THAN THE ALTERNATIVE.
CHIR CHIR CHIR
TIME TO HATE ME, DOC. SUMMON ALL YOUR FRUSTRATION, YOUR REGRET.
REMEMBER THAT **FIRST** WAVE...THE THINGS YOU DID. BLAME **ME** FOR THEM...
CHIR CHIR CHIR
...AND START **HITTING!**
"...the world is empty and full of nothing...
GRRRRRR!
"...become the nothing of the world..."
AAAAA!

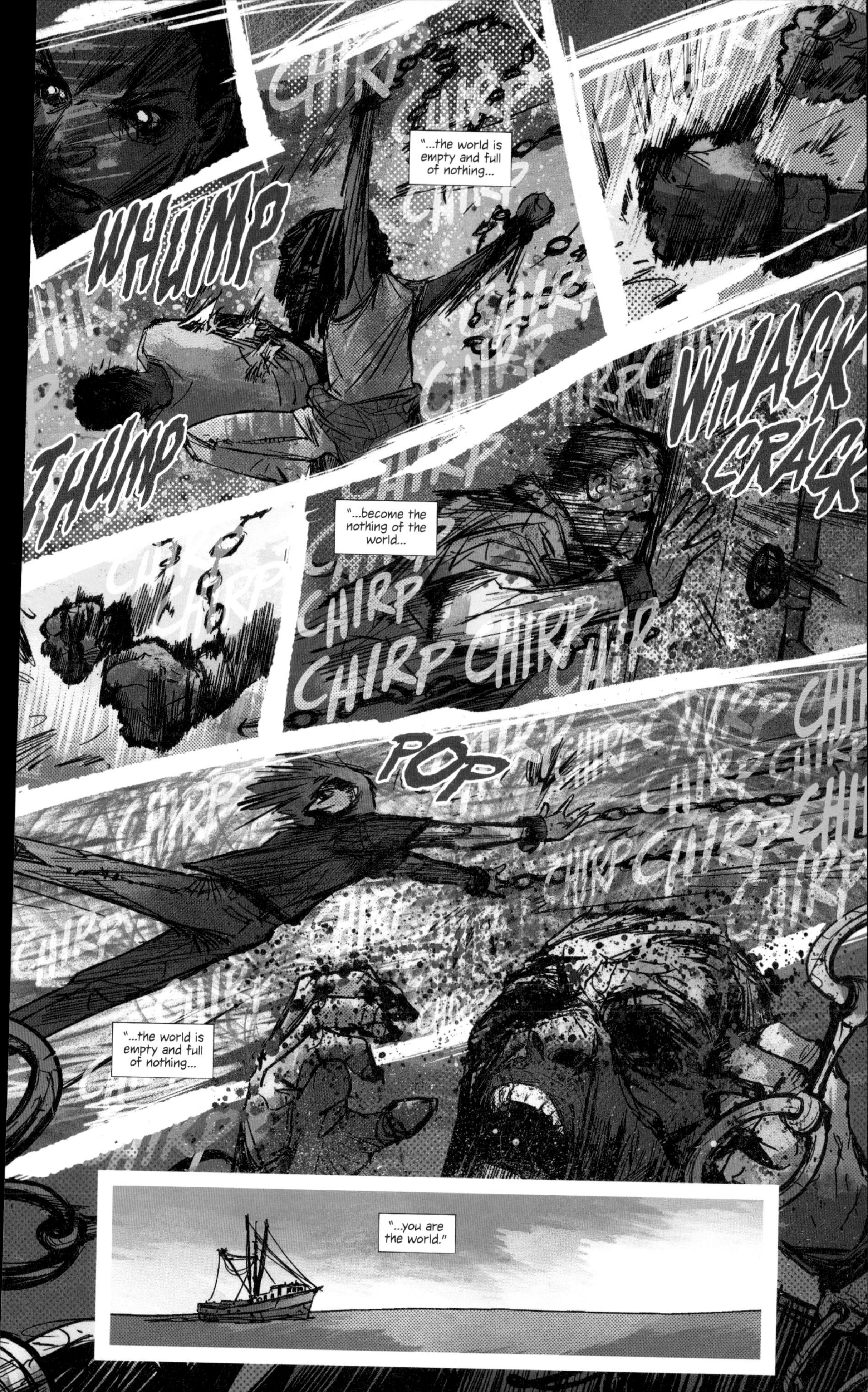
"...the world is empty and full of nothing...
WHUMP
THUMP
WHACK
CRACK
"...become the nothing of the world...
CHIRP CHIRP CHIRP
POP
CHIRP CHIRP
"...the world is empty and full of nothing...
"...you are the world."

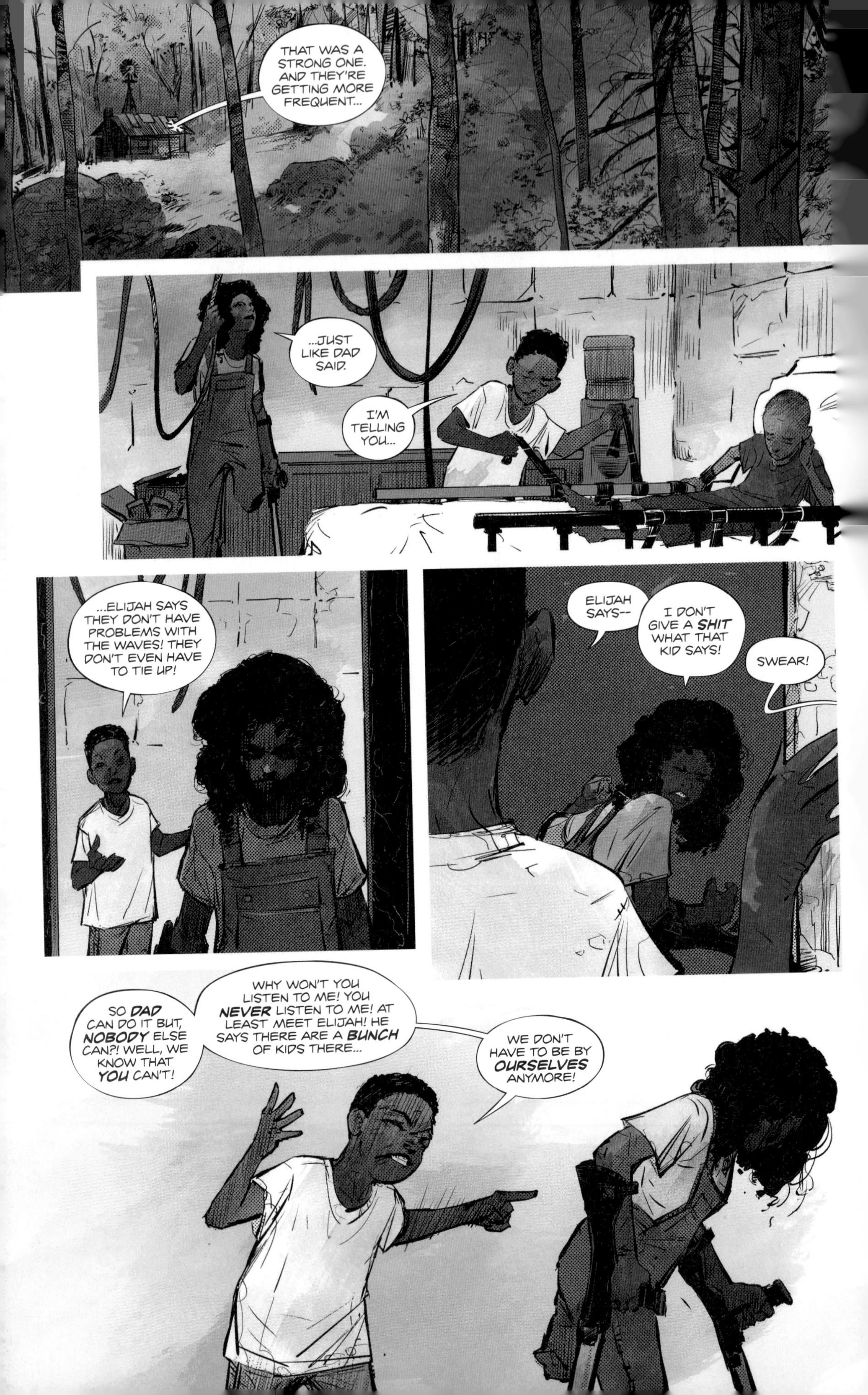
THAT WAS A STRONG ONE. AND THEY'RE GETTING MORE FREQUENT...
...JUST LIKE DAD SAID.
I'M TELLING YOU...
...ELIJAH SAYS THEY DON'T HAVE PROBLEMS WITH THE WAVES! THEY DON'T EVEN HAVE TO TIE UP!
ELIJAH SAYS--
I DON'T GIVE A SHIT WHAT THAT KID SAYS!
SWEAR!
SO DAD CAN DO IT BUT, NOBODY ELSE CAN?! WELL, WE KNOW THAT YOU CAN'T!
WHY WON'T YOU LISTEN TO ME! YOU NEVER LISTEN TO ME! AT LEAST MEET ELIJAH! HE SAYS THERE ARE A BUNCH OF KIDS THERE...
WE DON'T HAVE TO BE BY OURSELVES ANYMORE!

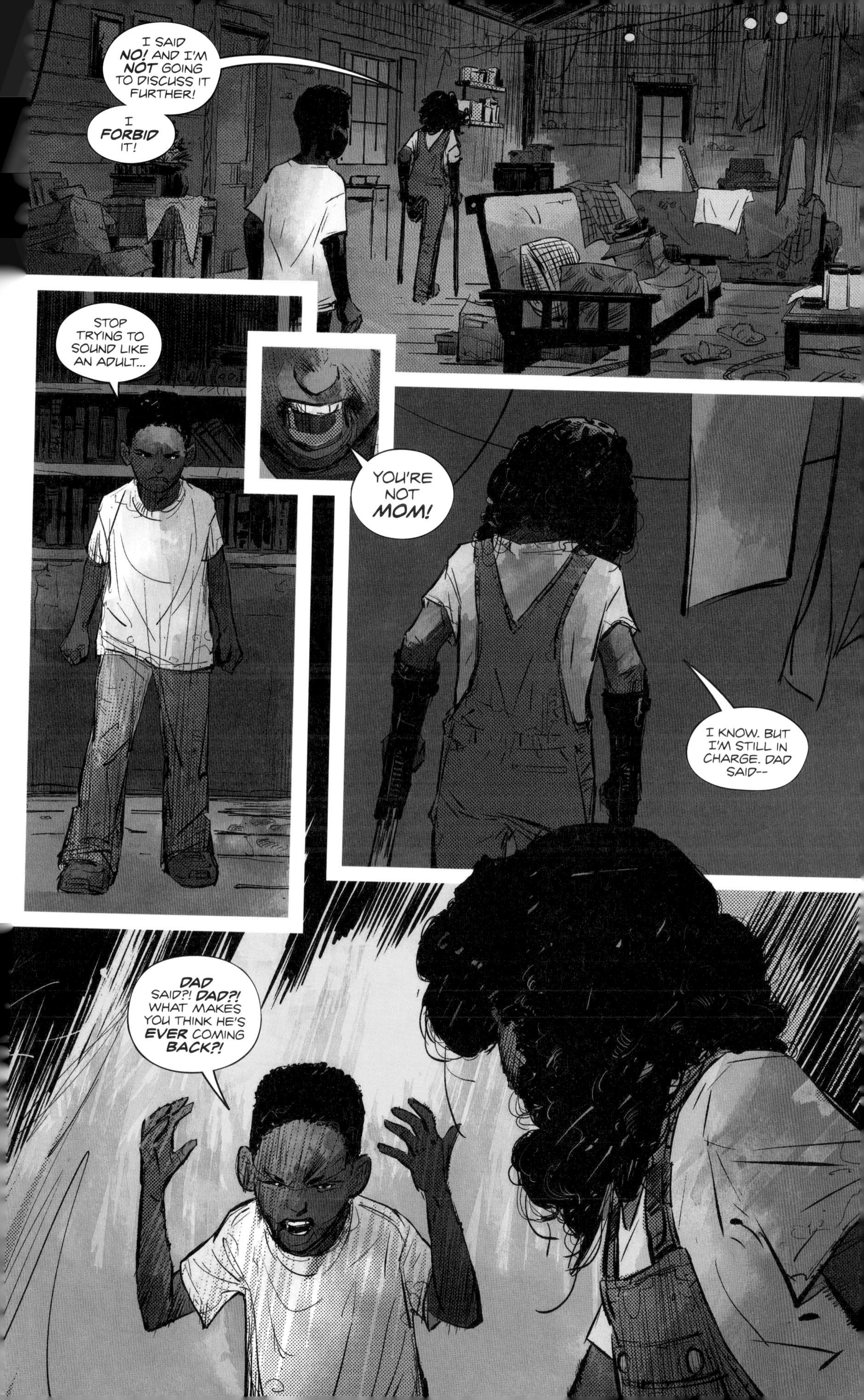
I SAID NO! AND I'M NOT GOING TO DISCUSS IT FURTHER!
I FORBID IT!
STOP TRYING TO SOUND LIKE AN ADULT...
YOU'RE NOT MOM!
I KNOW. BUT I'M STILL IN CHARGE. DAD SAID--
DAD SAID?! DAD?! WHAT MAKES YOU THINK HE'S EVER COMING BACK?!

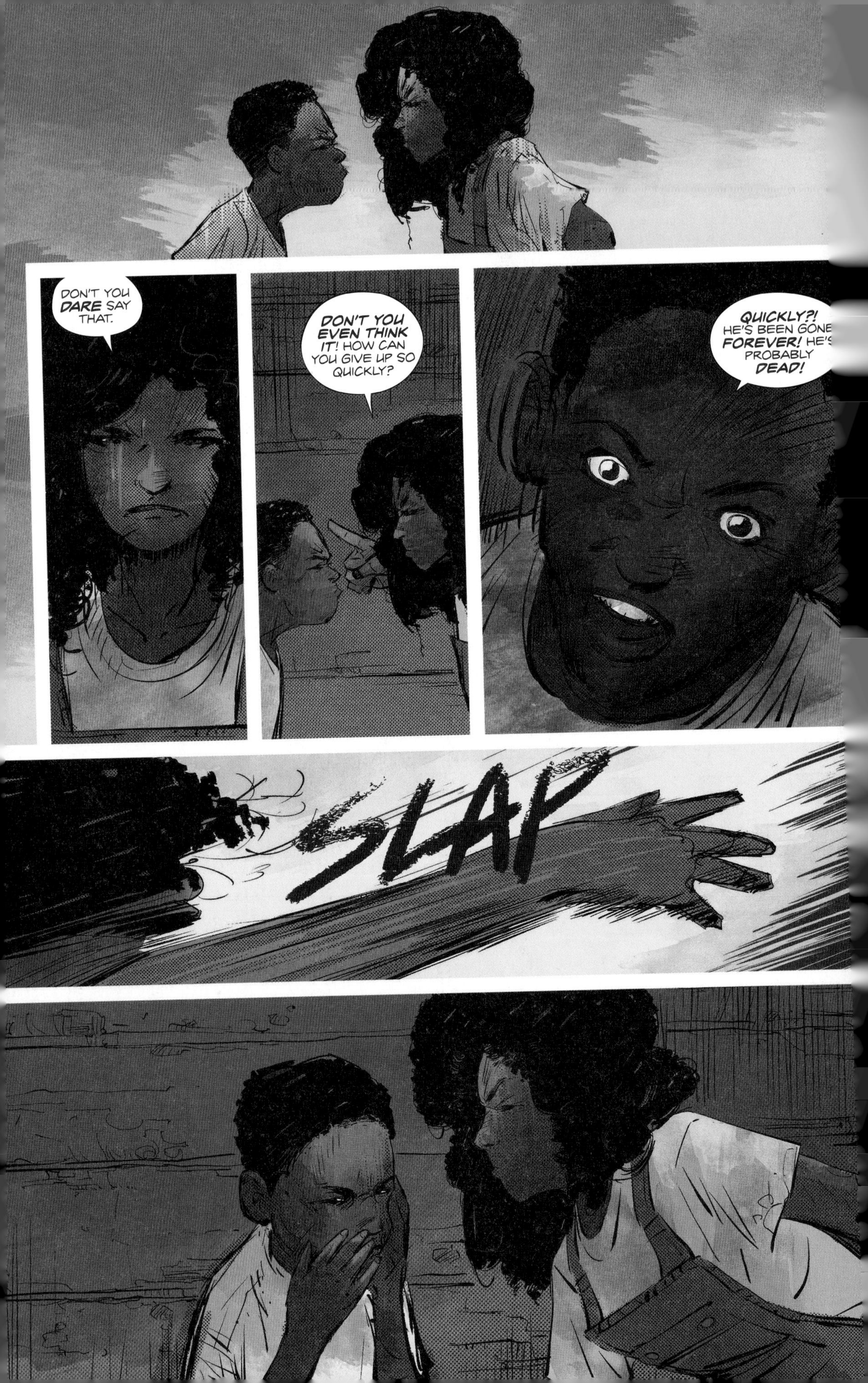
DON'T YOU **DARE** SAY THAT.
DON'T YOU EVEN THINK IT! HOW CAN YOU GIVE UP SO QUICKLY?
QUICKLY?! HE'S BEEN GONE **FOREVER!** HE'S PROBABLY **DEAD!**
SLAP

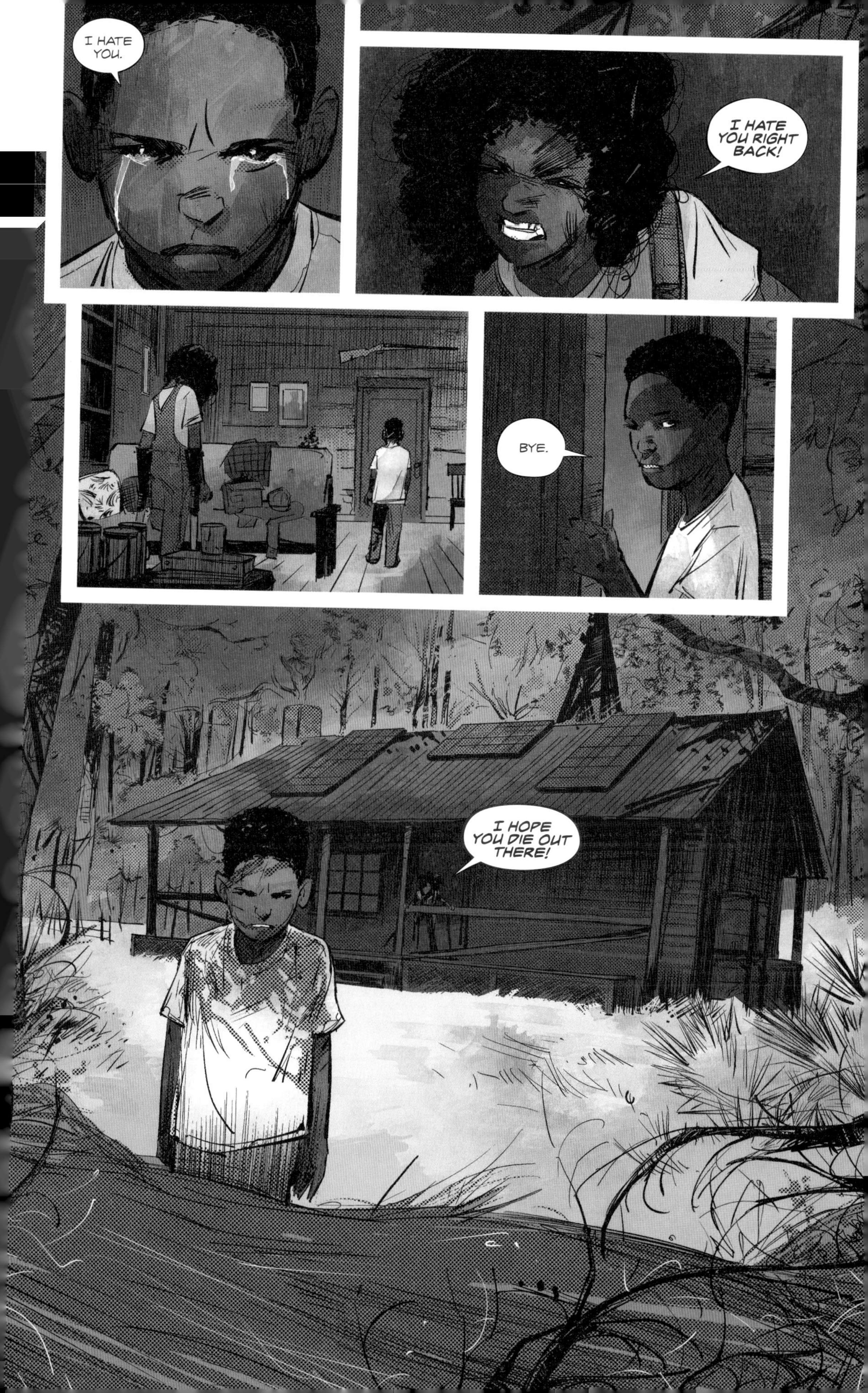
I HATE YOU.
I HATE YOU RIGHT BACK!
BYE.
I HOPE YOU DIE OUT THERE!

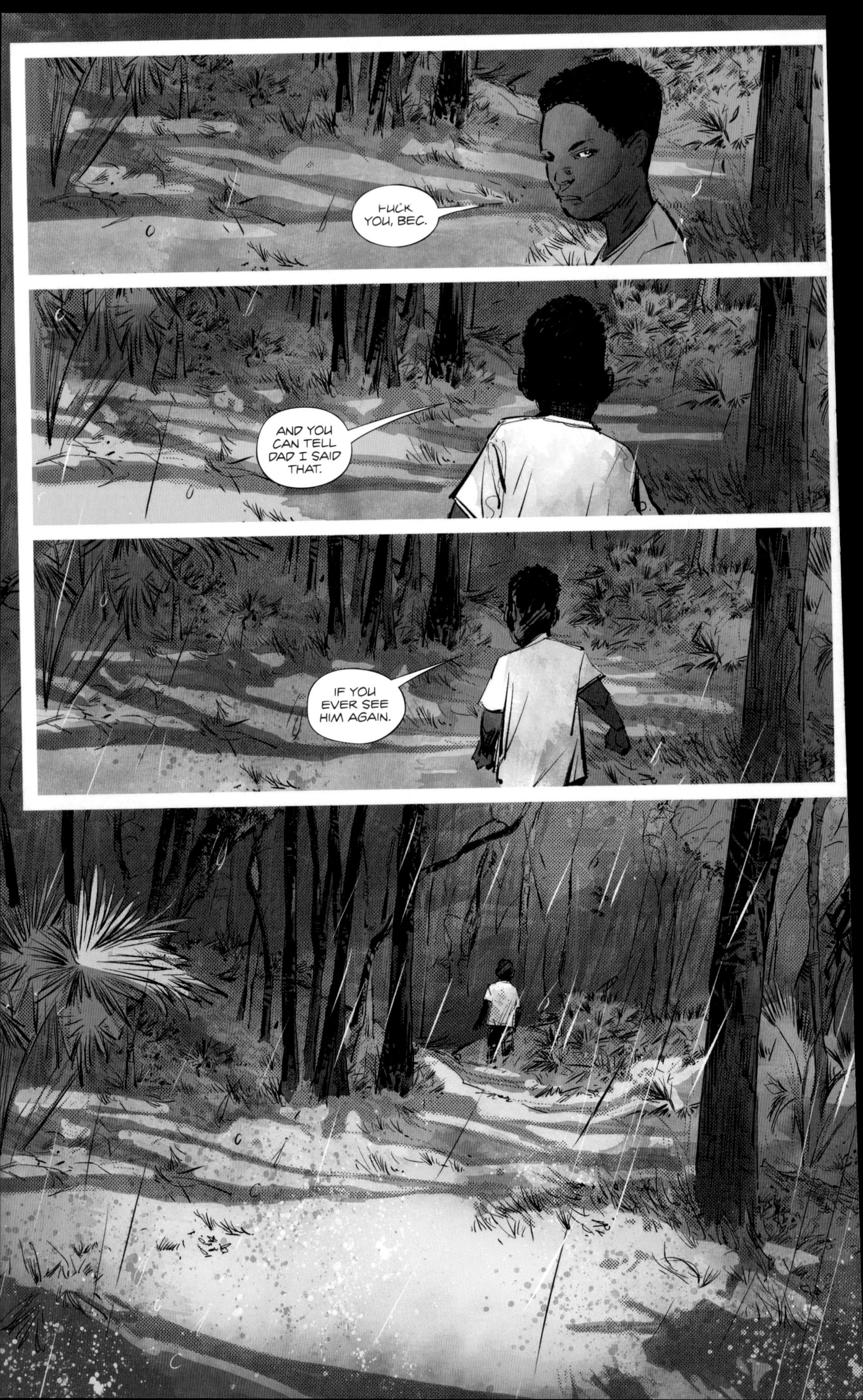
FUCK YOU, BEC.
AND YOU CAN TELL DAD I SAID THAT.
IF YOU EVER SEE HIM AGAIN.

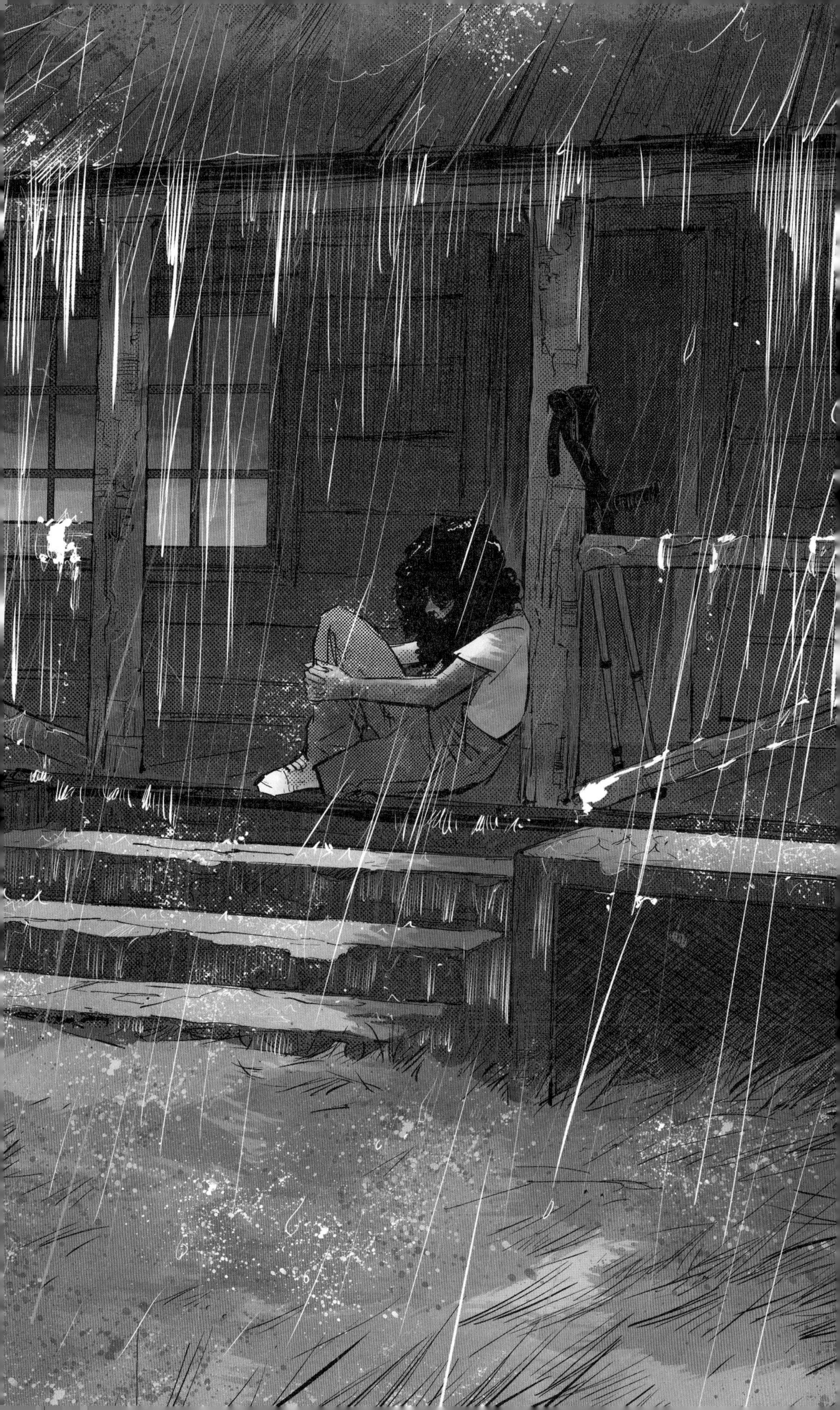

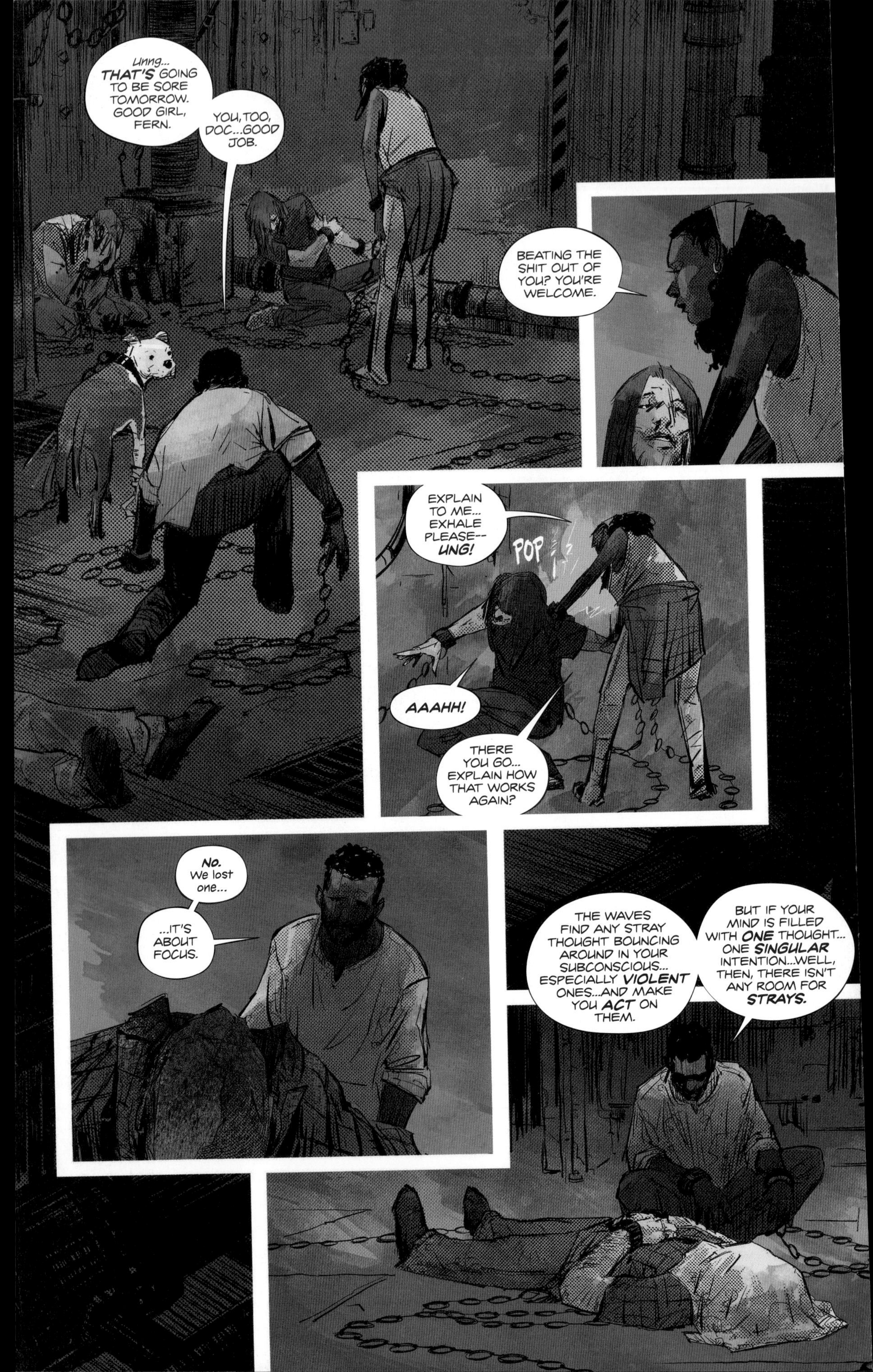
Unng... THAT'S GOING TO BE SORE TOMORROW. GOOD GIRL, FERN.
YOU, TOO, DOC...GOOD JOB.
BEATING THE SHIT OUT OF YOU? YOU'RE WELCOME.
EXPLAIN TO ME... EXHALE PLEASE-- UNG!
POP
AAAHH!
THERE YOU GO... EXPLAIN HOW THAT WORKS AGAIN?
No. We lost one...
...IT'S ABOUT FOCUS.
THE WAVES FIND ANY STRAY THOUGHT BOUNCING AROUND IN YOUR SUBCONSCIOUS... ESPECIALLY VIOLENT ONES...AND MAKE YOU ACT ON THEM.
BUT IF YOUR MIND IS FILLED WITH ONE THOUGHT... ONE SINGULAR INTENTION...WELL, THEN, THERE ISN'T ANY ROOM FOR STRAYS.

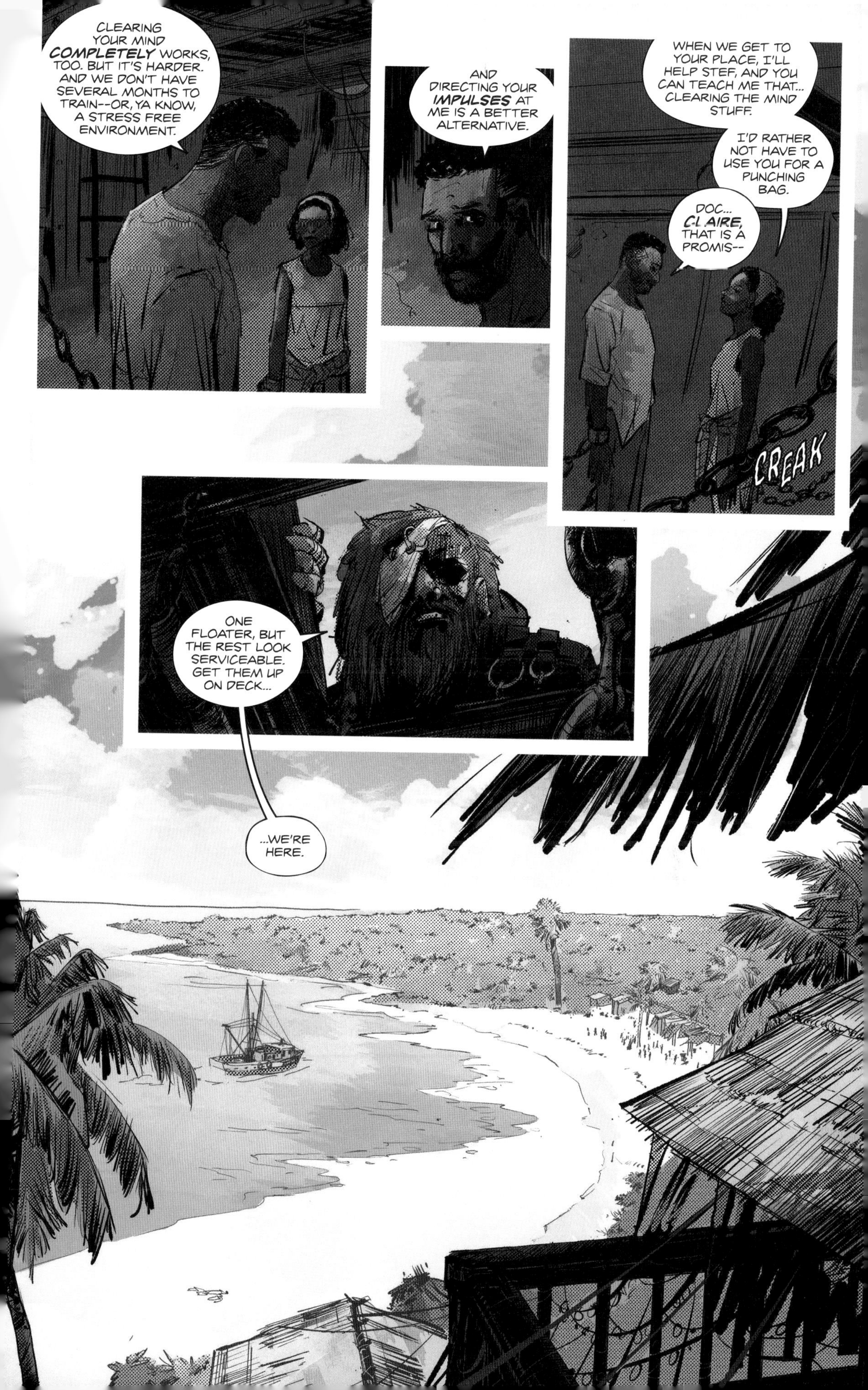
CLEARING YOUR MIND COMPLETELY WORKS, TOO. BUT IT'S HARDER. AND WE DON'T HAVE SEVERAL MONTHS TO TRAIN--OR, YA KNOW, A STRESS FREE ENVIRONMENT.
AND DIRECTING YOUR IMPULSES AT ME IS A BETTER ALTERNATIVE.
WHEN WE GET TO YOUR PLACE, I'LL HELP STEF, AND YOU CAN TEACH ME THAT... CLEARING THE MIND STUFF.
I'D RATHER NOT HAVE TO USE YOU FOR A PUNCHING BAG.
DOC... CLAIRE, THAT IS A PROMIS--
CREAK
ONE FLOATER, BUT THE REST LOOK SERVICEABLE. GET THEM UP ON DECK...
...WE'RE HERE.

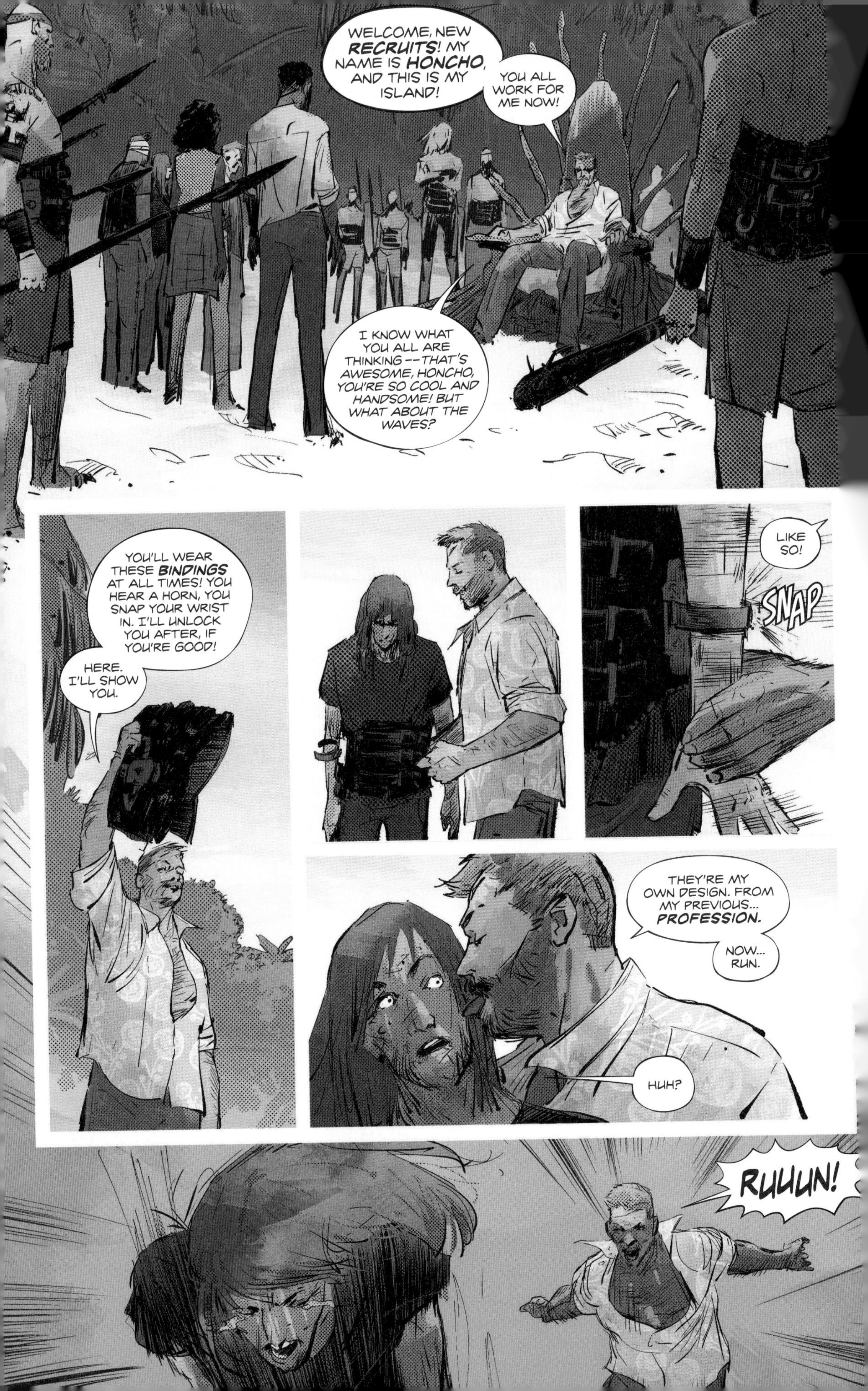
WELCOME, NEW RECRUITS! MY NAME IS HONCHO, AND THIS IS MY ISLAND!
YOU ALL WORK FOR ME NOW!
I KNOW WHAT YOU ALL ARE THINKING--THAT'S AWESOME, HONCHO, YOU'RE SO COOL AND HANDSOME! BUT WHAT ABOUT THE WAVES?
YOU'LL WEAR THESE BINDINGS AT ALL TIMES! YOU HEAR A HORN, YOU SNAP YOUR WRIST IN. I'LL UNLOCK YOU AFTER, IF YOU'RE GOOD!
HERE. I'LL SHOW YOU.
LIKE SO!
SNAP
THEY'RE MY OWN DESIGN. FROM MY PREVIOUS... PROFESSION.
NOW... RUN.
HUH?
RUUUN!

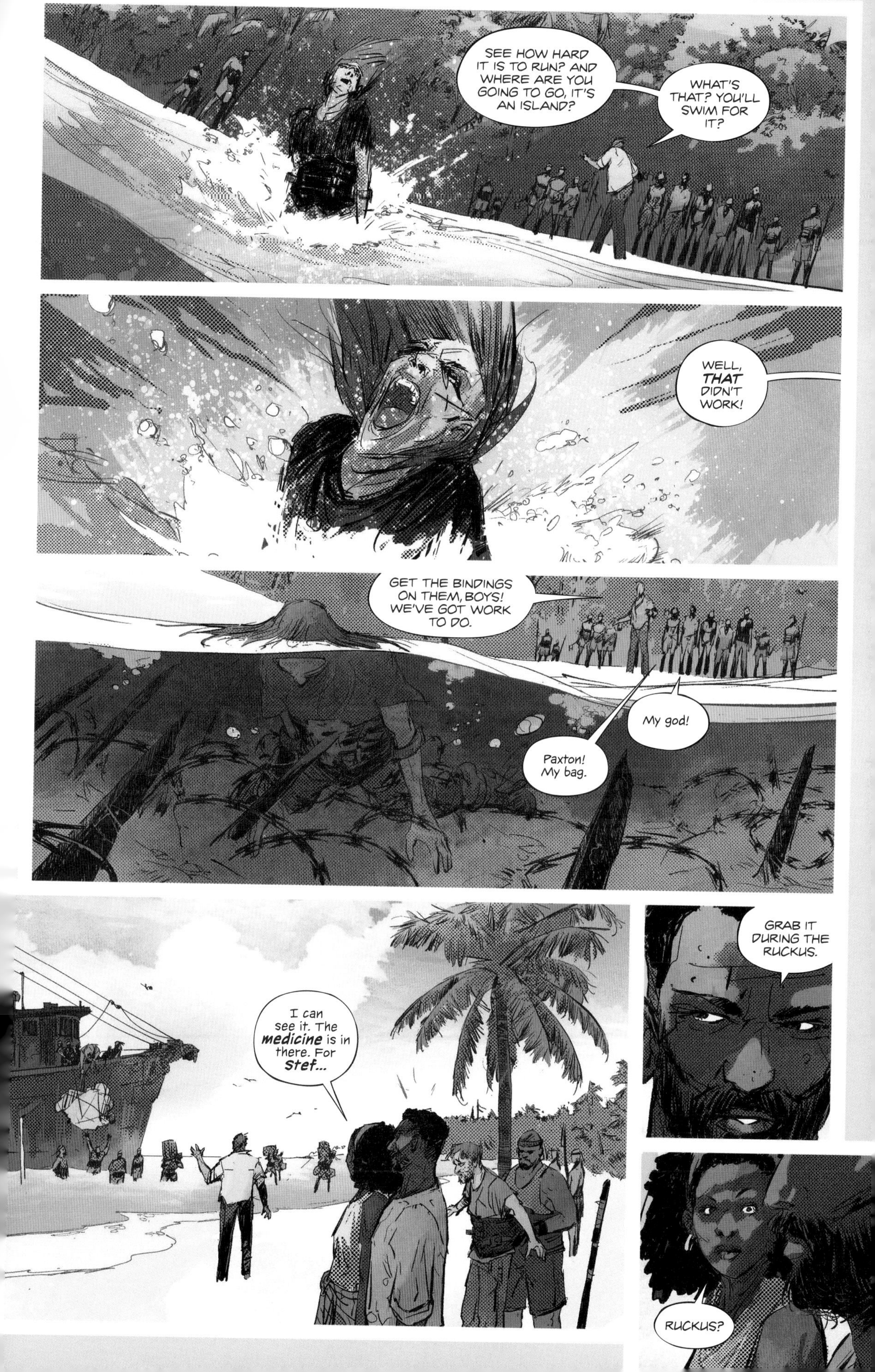
SEE HOW HARD IT IS TO RUN? AND WHERE ARE YOU GOING TO GO, IT'S AN ISLAND?
WHAT'S THAT? YOU'LL SWIM FOR IT?
WELL, ***THAT*** DIDN'T WORK!
GET THE BINDINGS ON THEM, BOYS! WE'VE GOT WORK TO DO.
My god!
Paxton! My bag.
I can see it. The ***medicine*** is in there. For ***Stef...***
GRAB IT DURING THE RUCKUS.
RUCKUS?

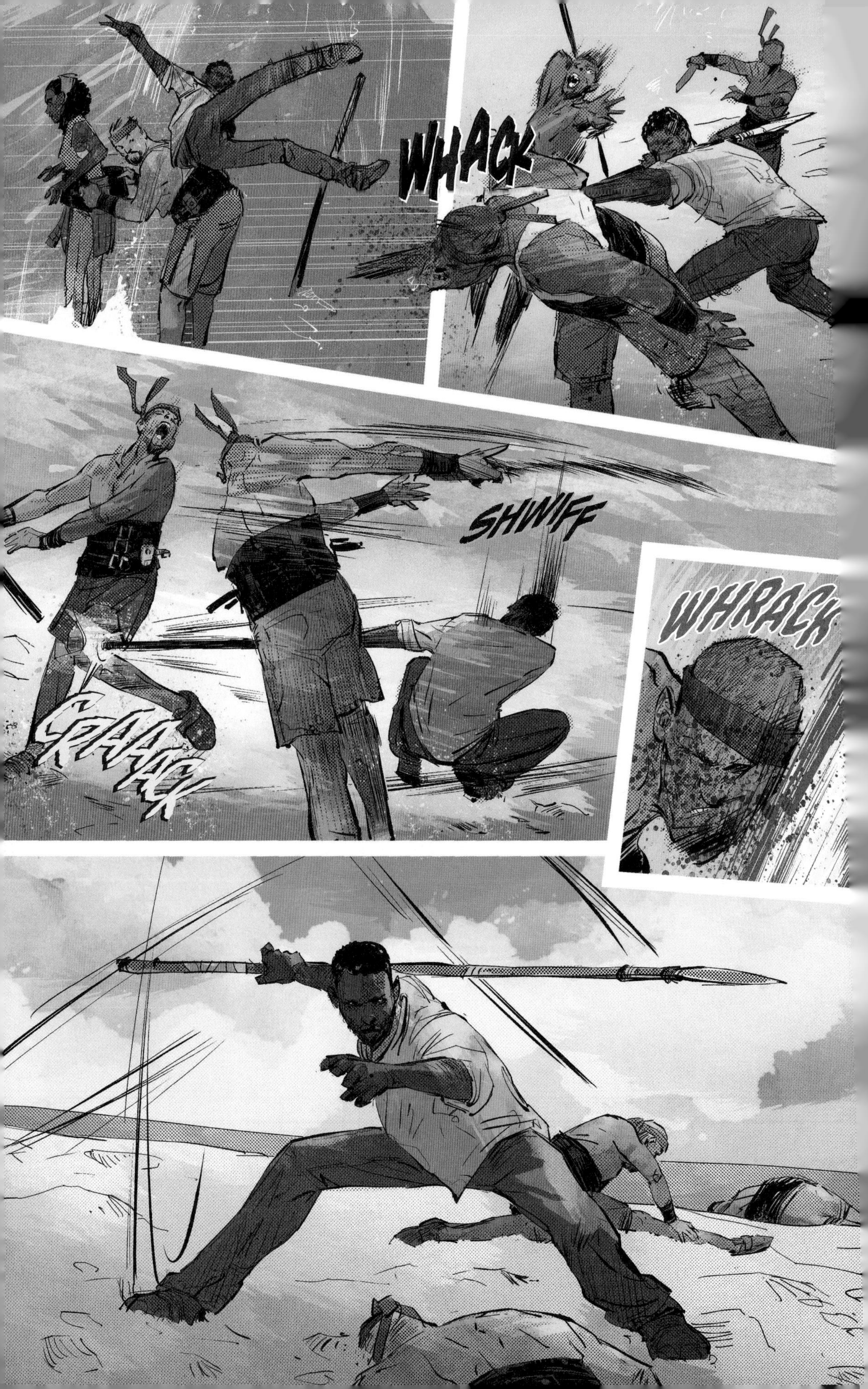
WHACK
SHWIFF
CRAAACK
WHRACK

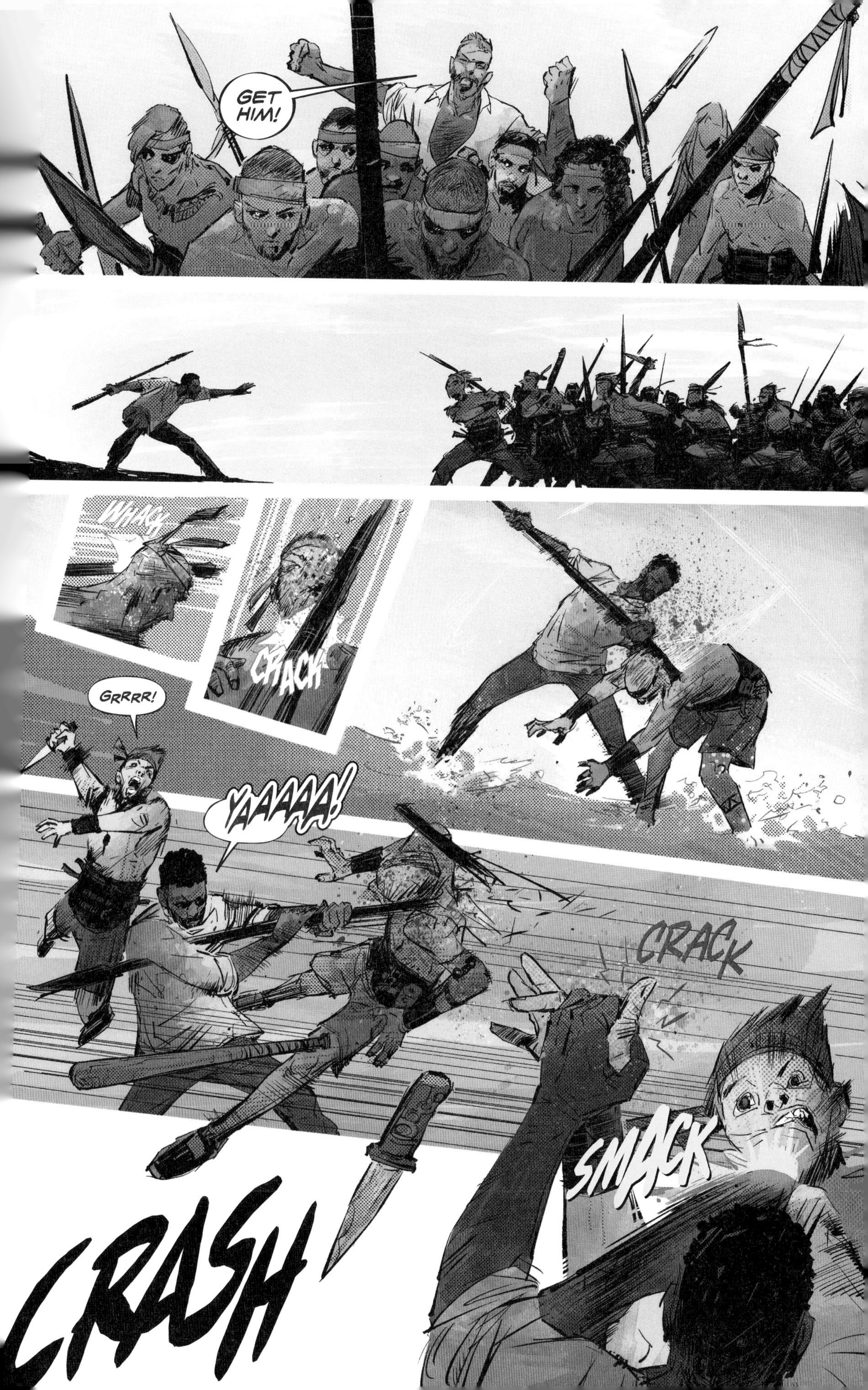
GET HIM!
WHACK
CRACK
GRRRR!
YAAAAA!
CRACK
SMACK
CRASH

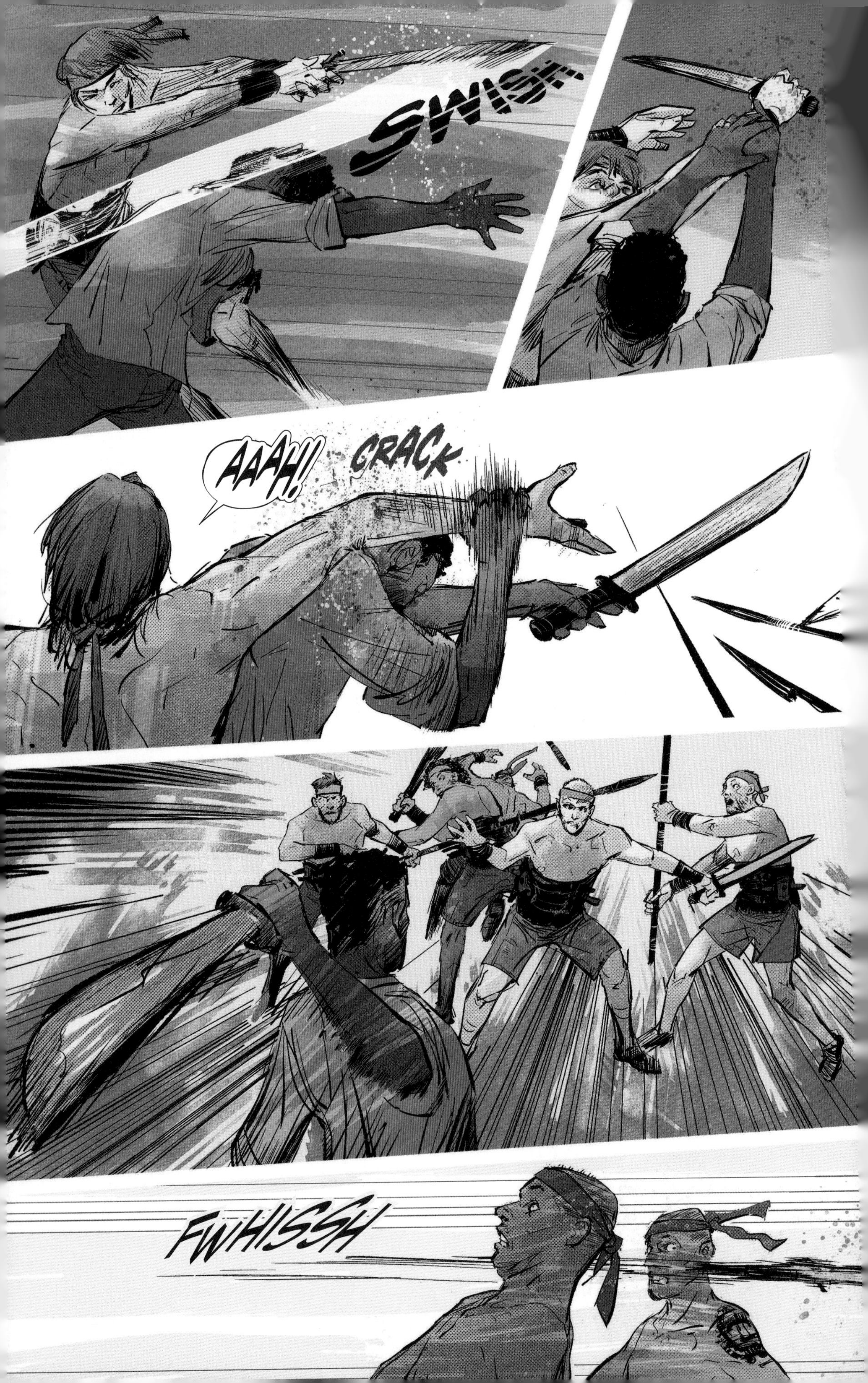
SWISH
AAAH!!
CRACK
FWHISSH

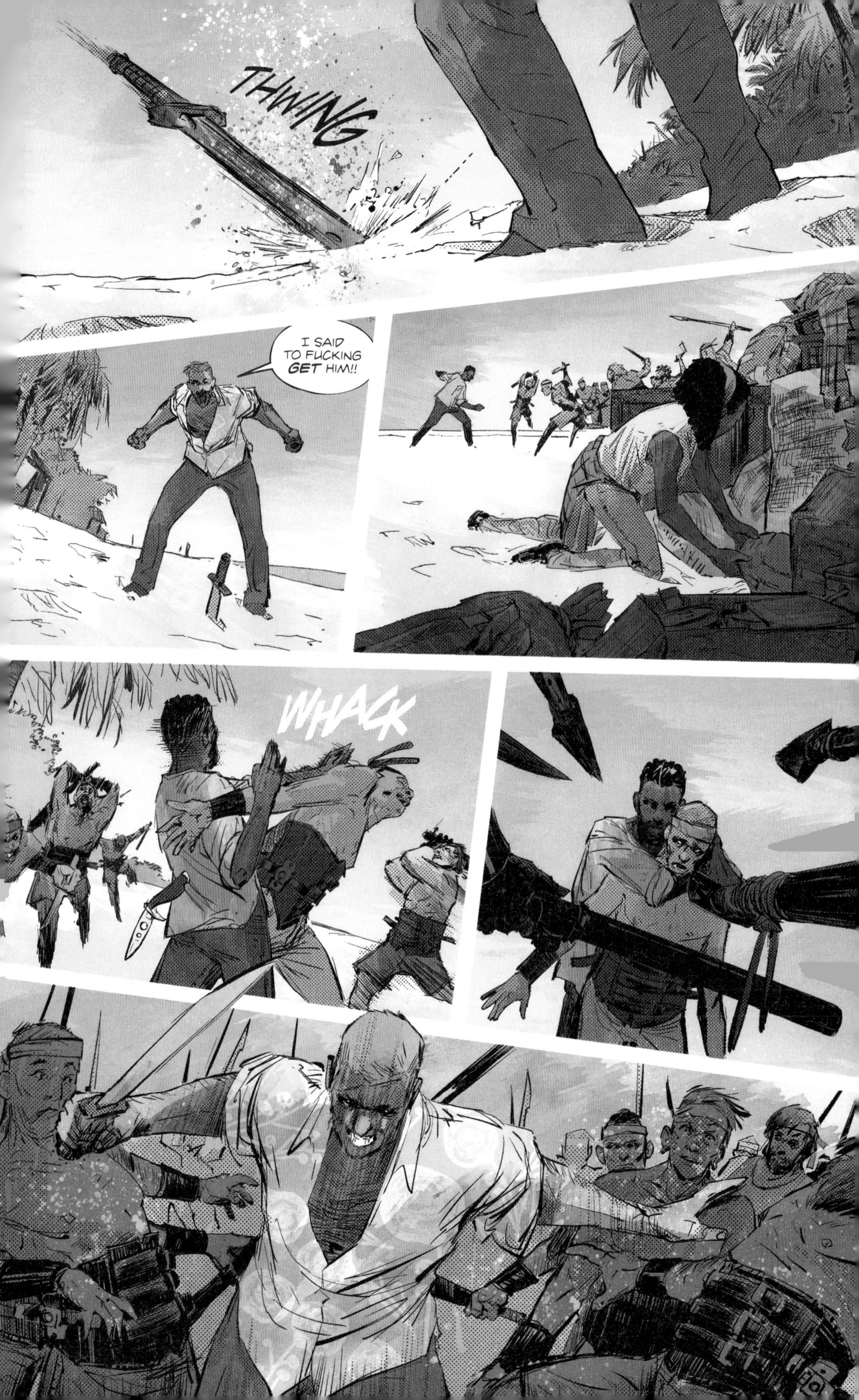
THWING
I SAID TO FUCKING GET HIM!!
WHACK

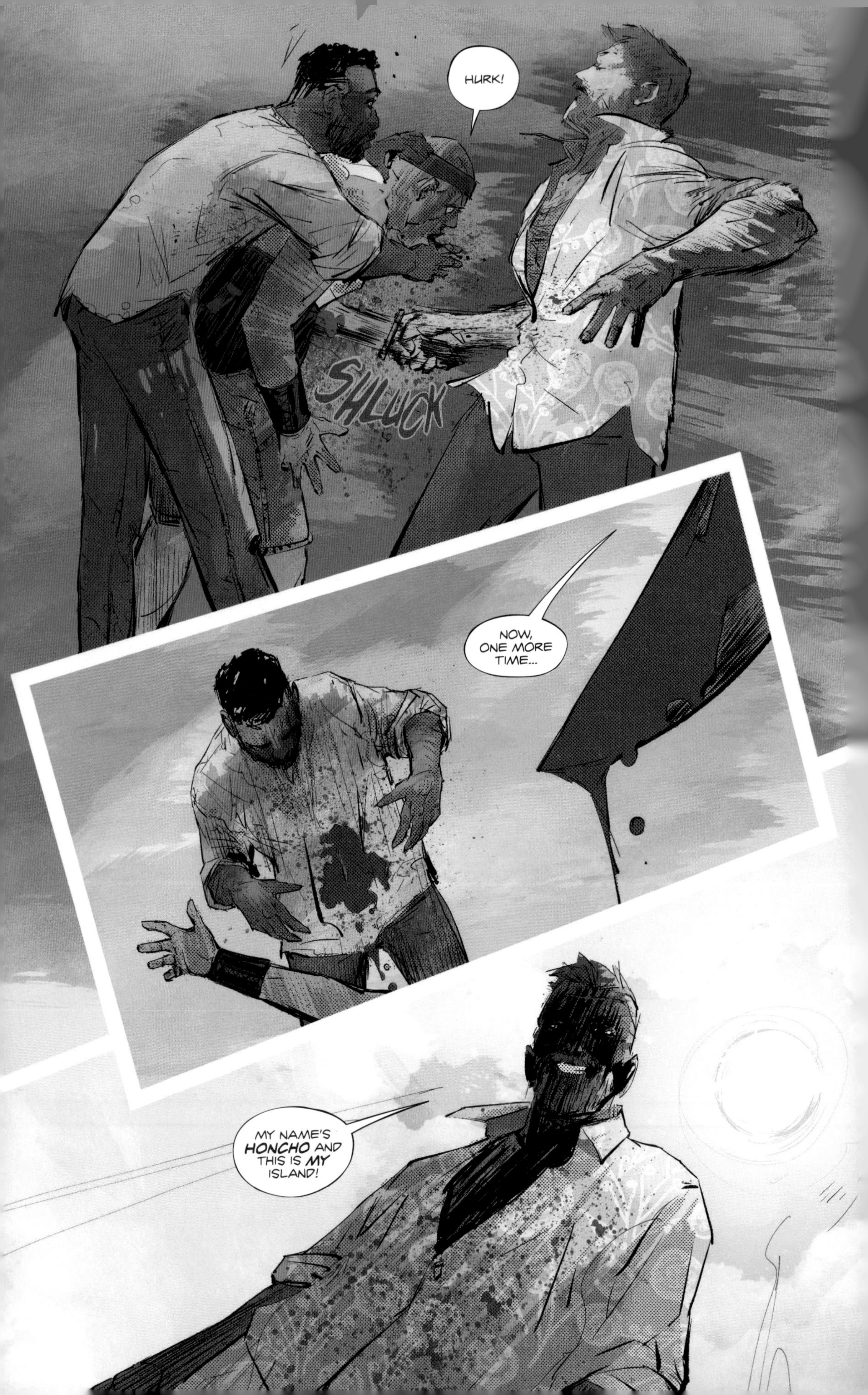
HURK!
SHLUCK
NOW, ONE MORE TIME...
MY NAME'S **HONCHO** AND THIS IS **MY** ISLAND!

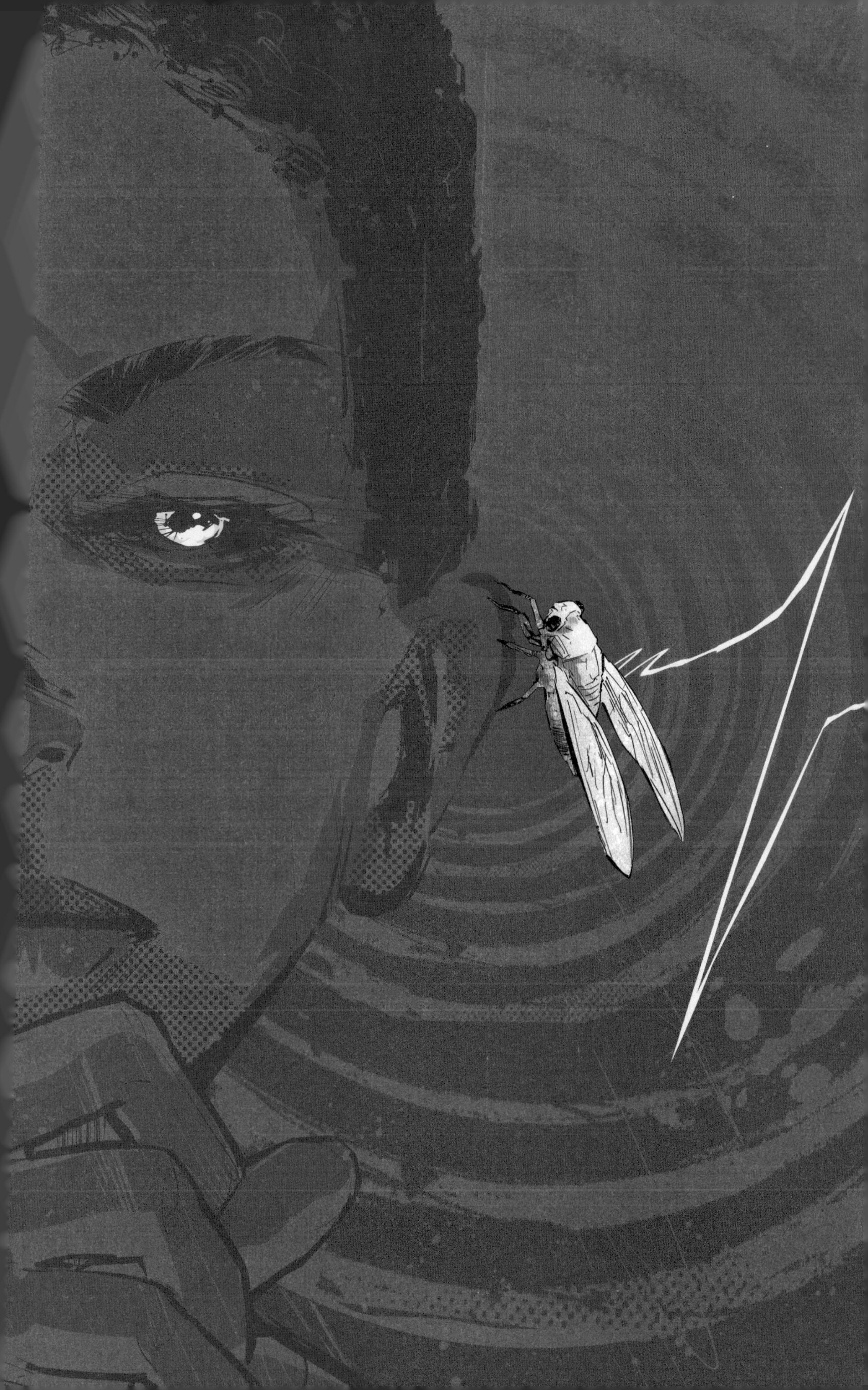

CHAPTER FOUR

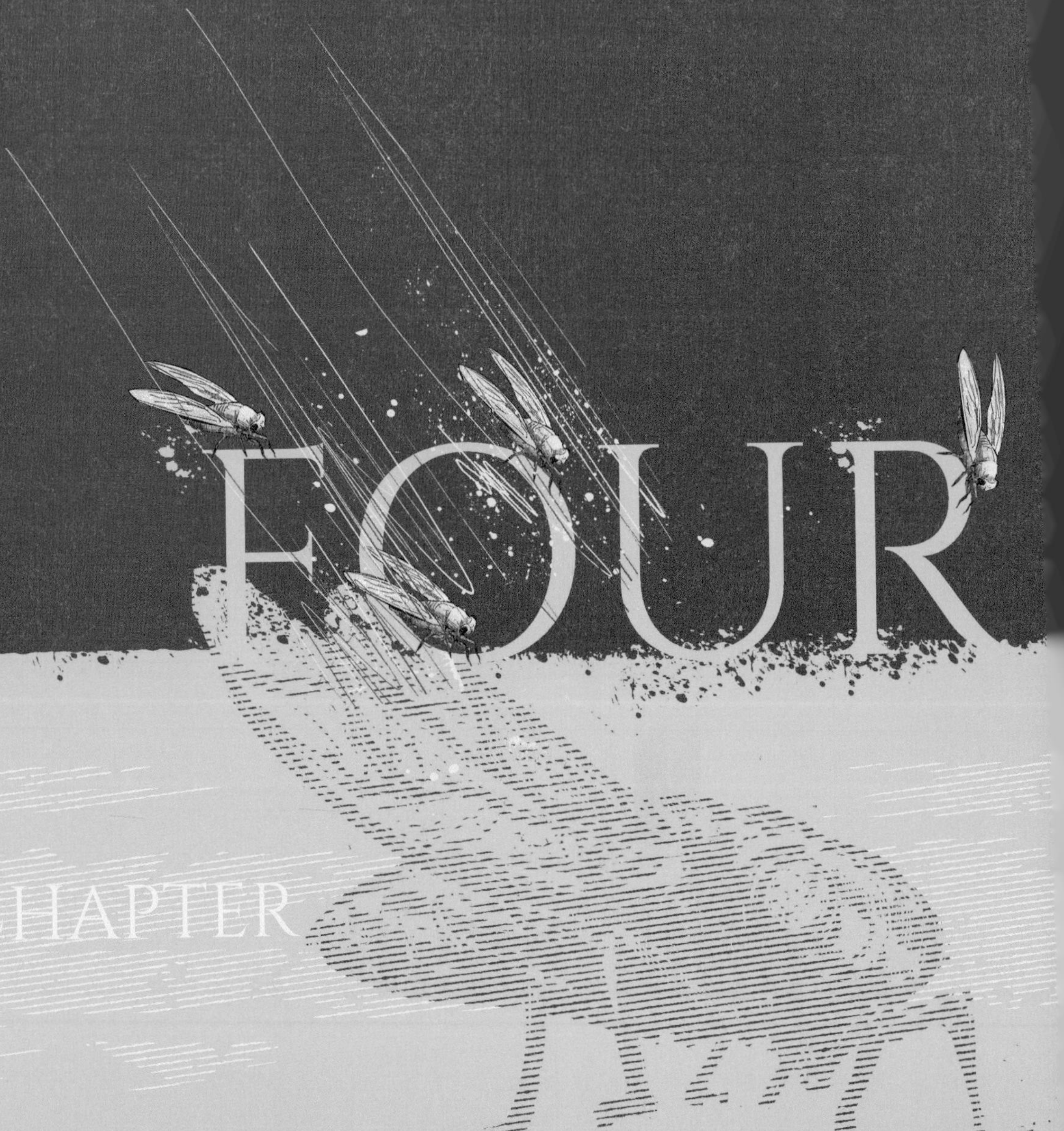

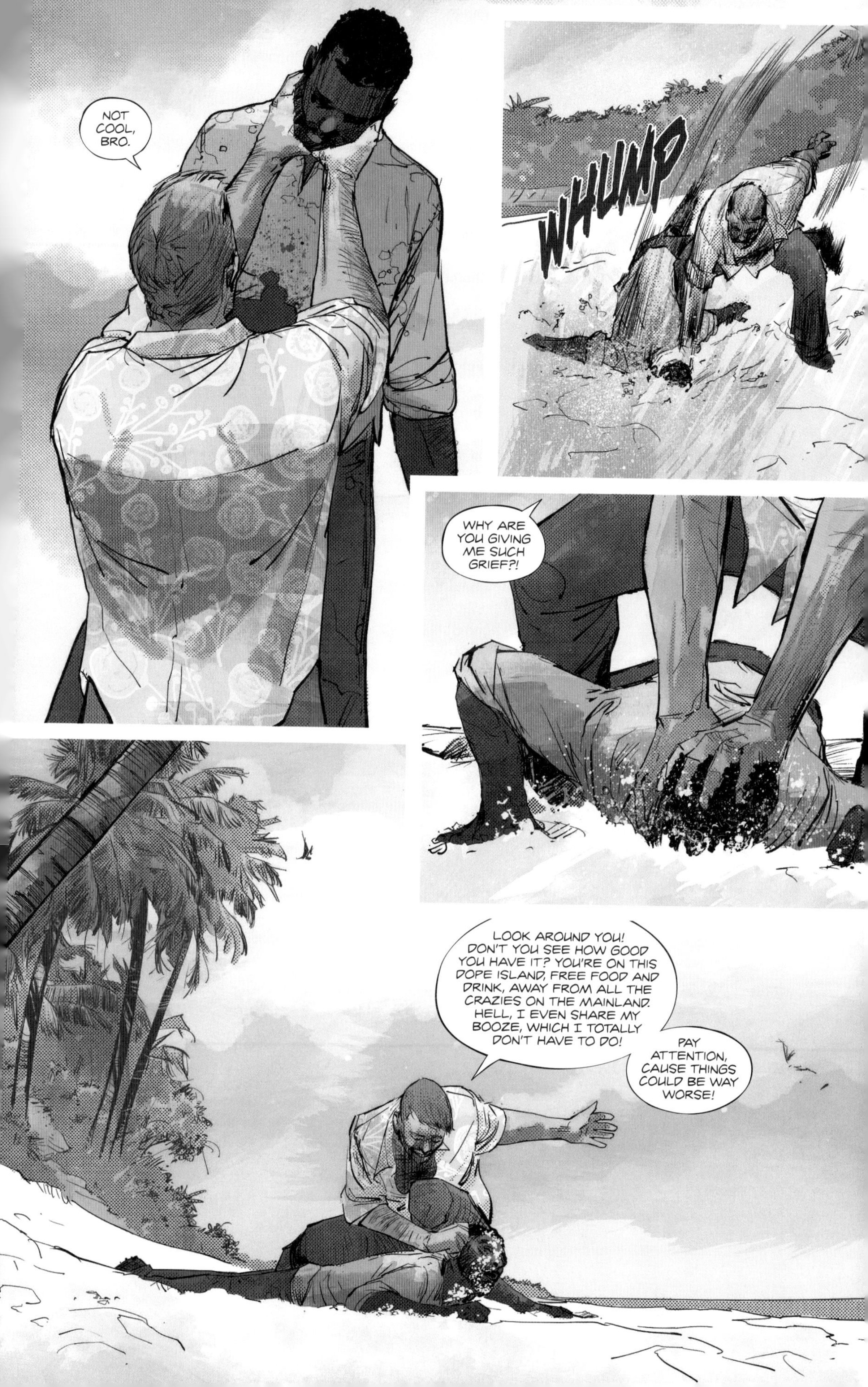
NOT COOL, BRO.
WHUMP
WHY ARE YOU GIVING ME SUCH GRIEF?!
LOOK AROUND YOU! DON'T YOU SEE HOW GOOD YOU HAVE IT? YOU'RE ON THIS DOPE ISLAND, FREE FOOD AND DRINK, AWAY FROM ALL THE CRAZIES ON THE MAINLAND. HELL, I EVEN SHARE MY BOOZE, WHICH I TOTALLY DON'T HAVE TO DO!
PAY ATTENTION, CAUSE THINGS COULD BE WAY WORSE!

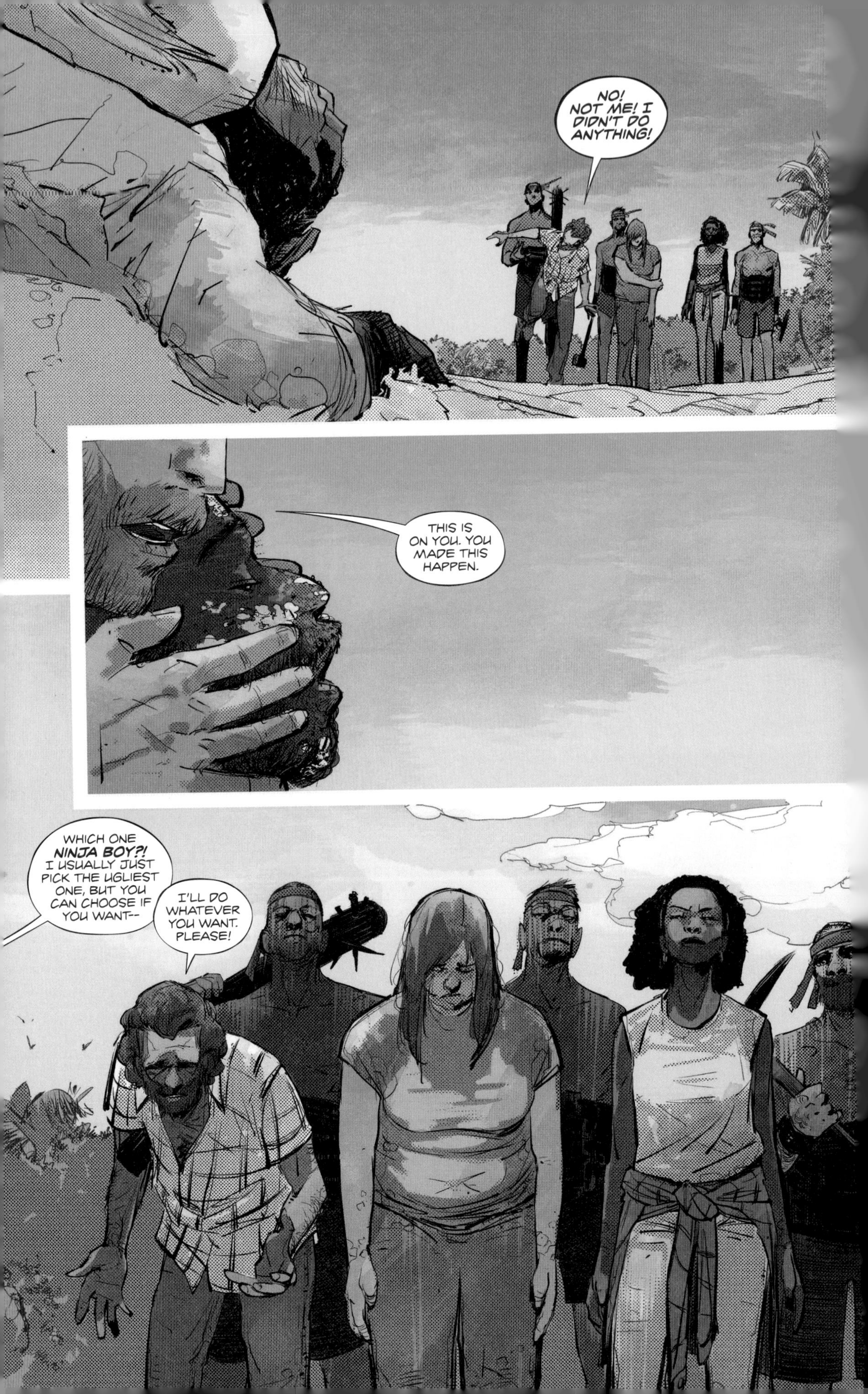
NO! NOT ME! I DIDN'T DO ANYTHING!
THIS IS ON YOU. YOU MADE THIS HAPPEN.
WHICH ONE *NINJA BOY?!* I USUALLY JUST PICK THE UGLIEST ONE, BUT YOU CAN CHOOSE IF YOU WANT--
I'LL DO WHATEVER YOU WANT. PLEASE!

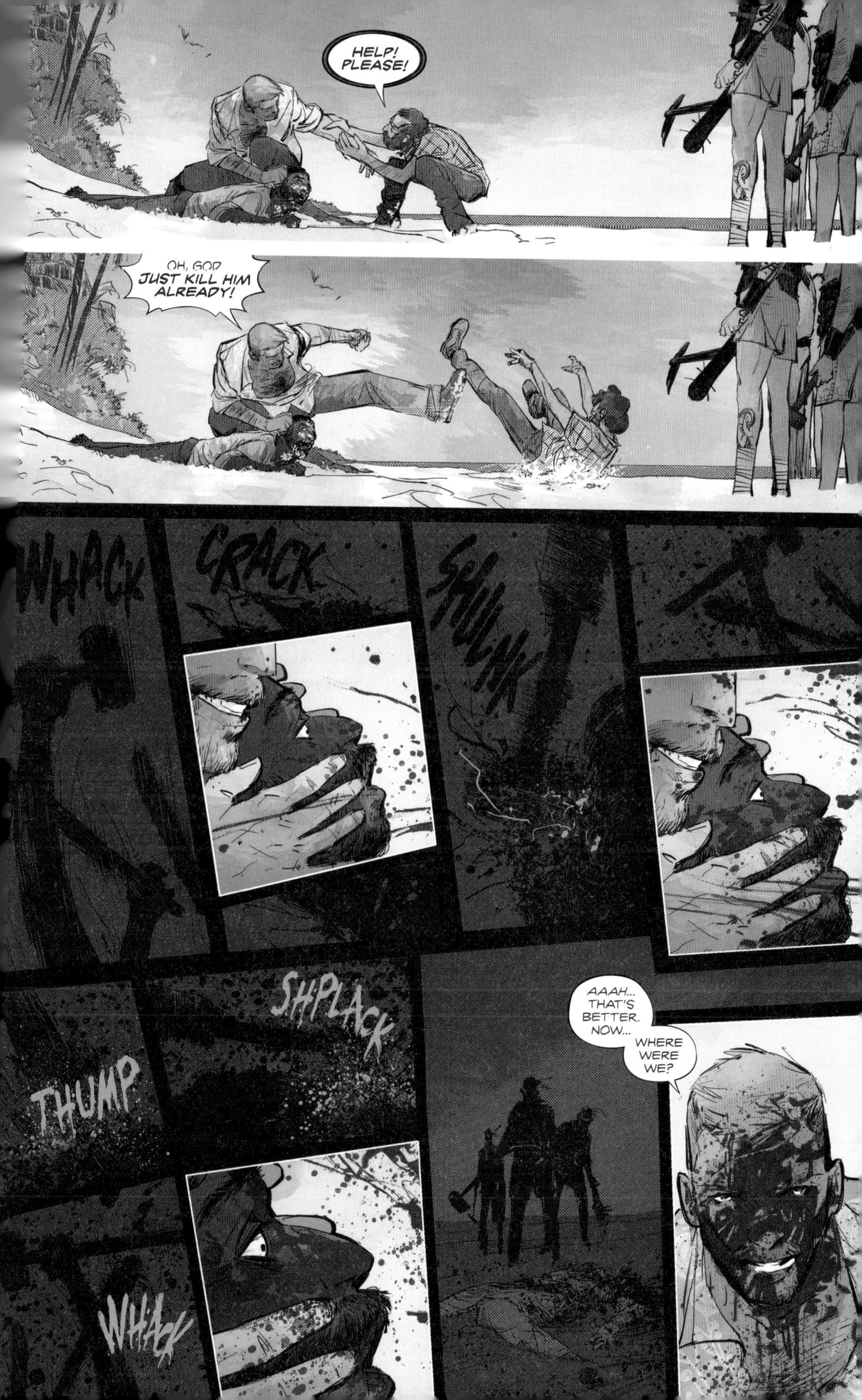
HELP! PLEASE!
OH, GOD
JUST KILL HIM ALREADY!
WHACK
CRACK
SHUNK
SHPLACK
THUMP
WHACK
AAAH... THAT'S BETTER. NOW...
WHERE WERE WE?

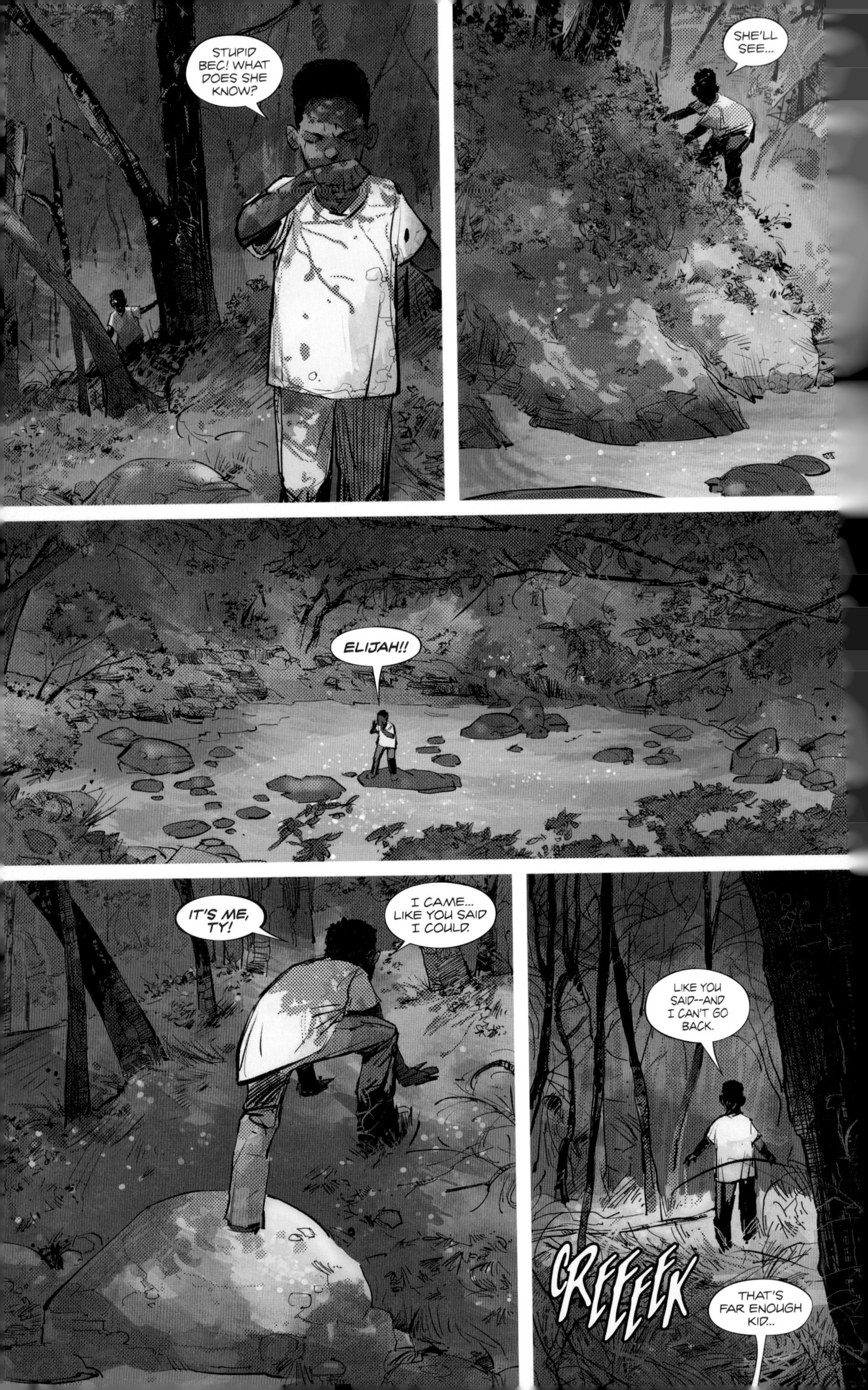
STUPID BEC! WHAT DOES SHE KNOW?
SHE'LL SEE...
ELIJAH!!
IT'S ME, TY!
I CAME... LIKE YOU SAID I COULD.
LIKE YOU SAID--AND I CAN'T GO BACK.
CREEEEK
THAT'S FAR ENOUGH KID...

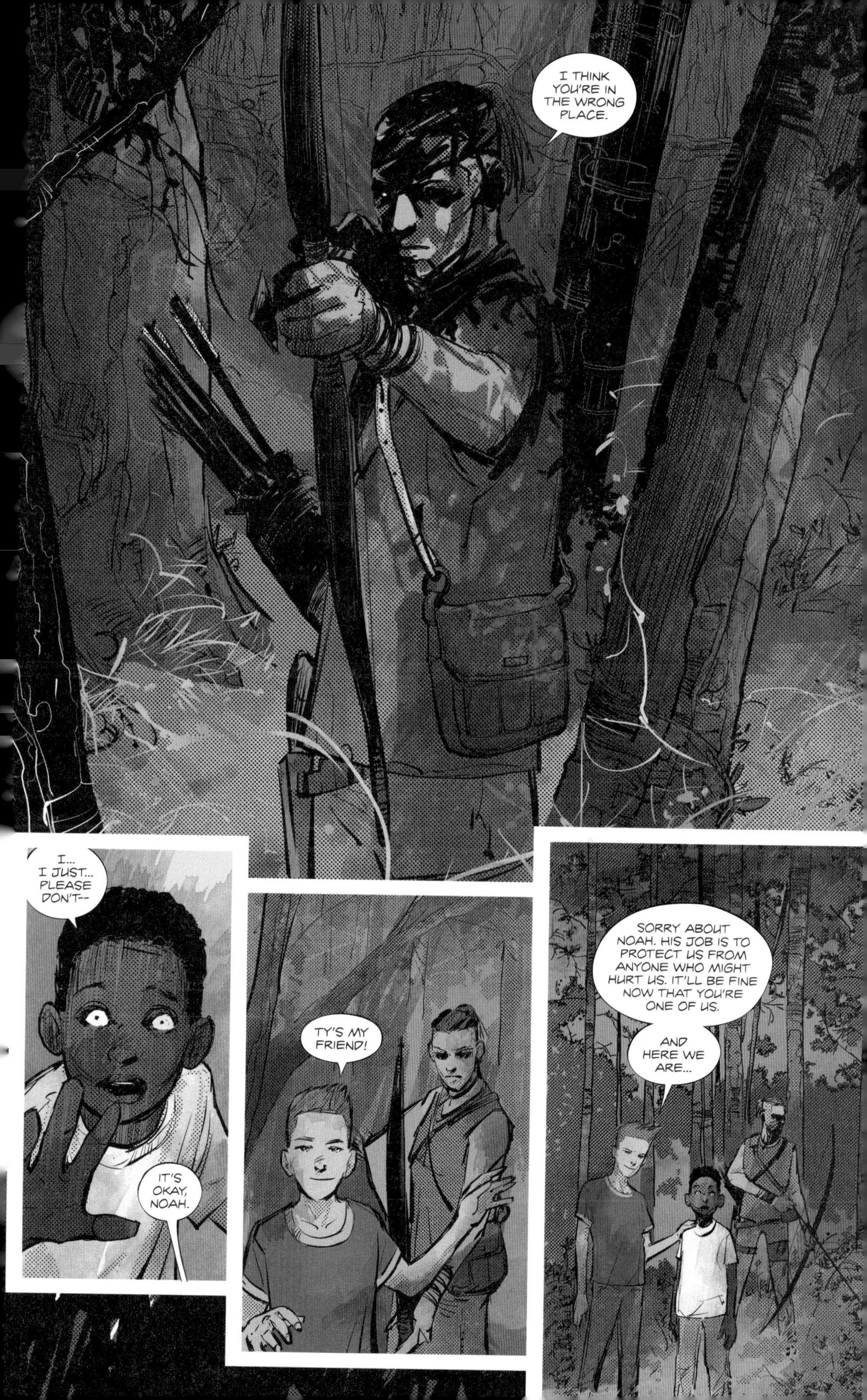
I THINK YOU'RE IN THE WRONG PLACE.
I... I JUST... PLEASE DON'T--
IT'S OKAY, NOAH.
TY'S MY FRIEND!
SORRY ABOUT NOAH. HIS JOB IS TO PROTECT US FROM ANYONE WHO MIGHT HURT US. IT'LL BE FINE NOW THAT YOU'RE ONE OF US.
AND HERE WE ARE...

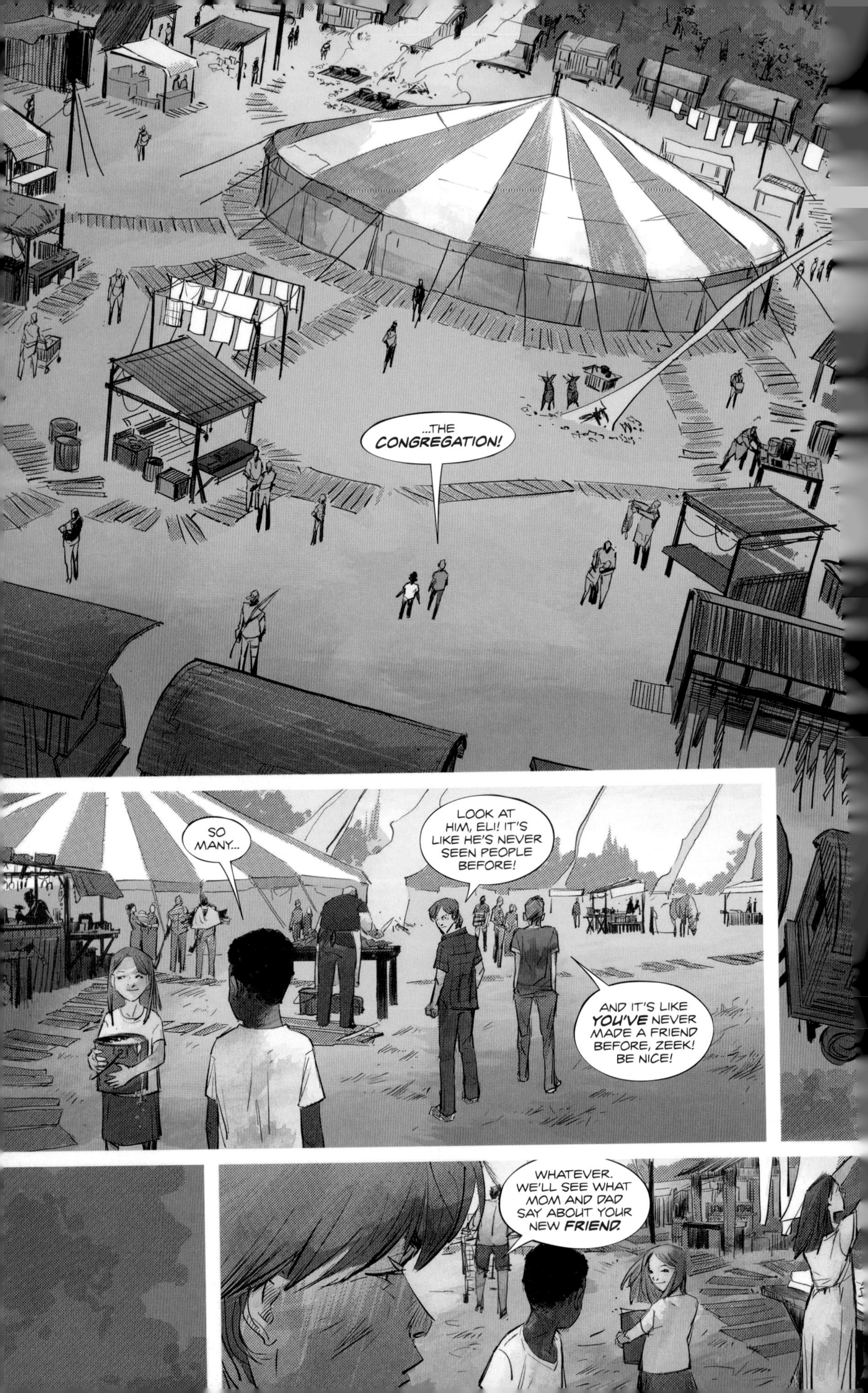
...THE CONGREGATION!
SO MANY...
LOOK AT HIM, ELI! IT'S LIKE HE'S NEVER SEEN PEOPLE BEFORE!
AND IT'S LIKE YOU'VE NEVER MADE A FRIEND BEFORE, ZEEK! BE NICE!
WHATEVER. WE'LL SEE WHAT MOM AND DAD SAY ABOUT YOUR NEW FRIEND.

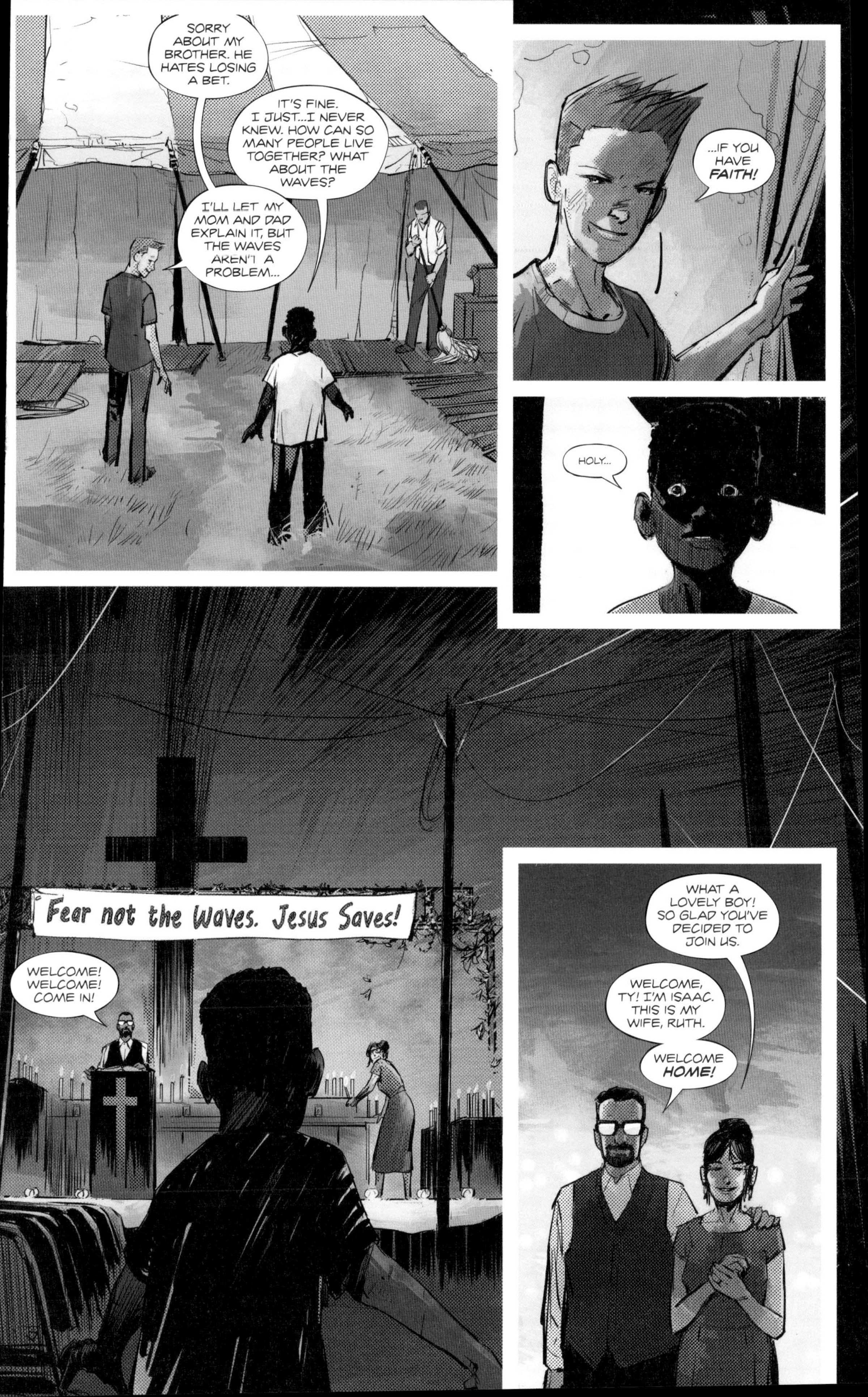
SORRY ABOUT MY BROTHER. HE HATES LOSING A BET.
IT'S FINE. I JUST...I NEVER KNEW. HOW CAN SO MANY PEOPLE LIVE TOGETHER? WHAT ABOUT THE WAVES?
I'LL LET MY MOM AND DAD EXPLAIN IT, BUT THE WAVES AREN'T A PROBLEM...
...IF YOU HAVE *FAITH!*
HOLY...
Fear not the Waves. Jesus Saves!
WELCOME! WELCOME! COME IN!
WHAT A LOVELY BOY! SO GLAD YOU'VE DECIDED TO JOIN US.
WELCOME, TY! I'M ISAAC. THIS IS MY WIFE, RUTH.
WELCOME *HOME!*

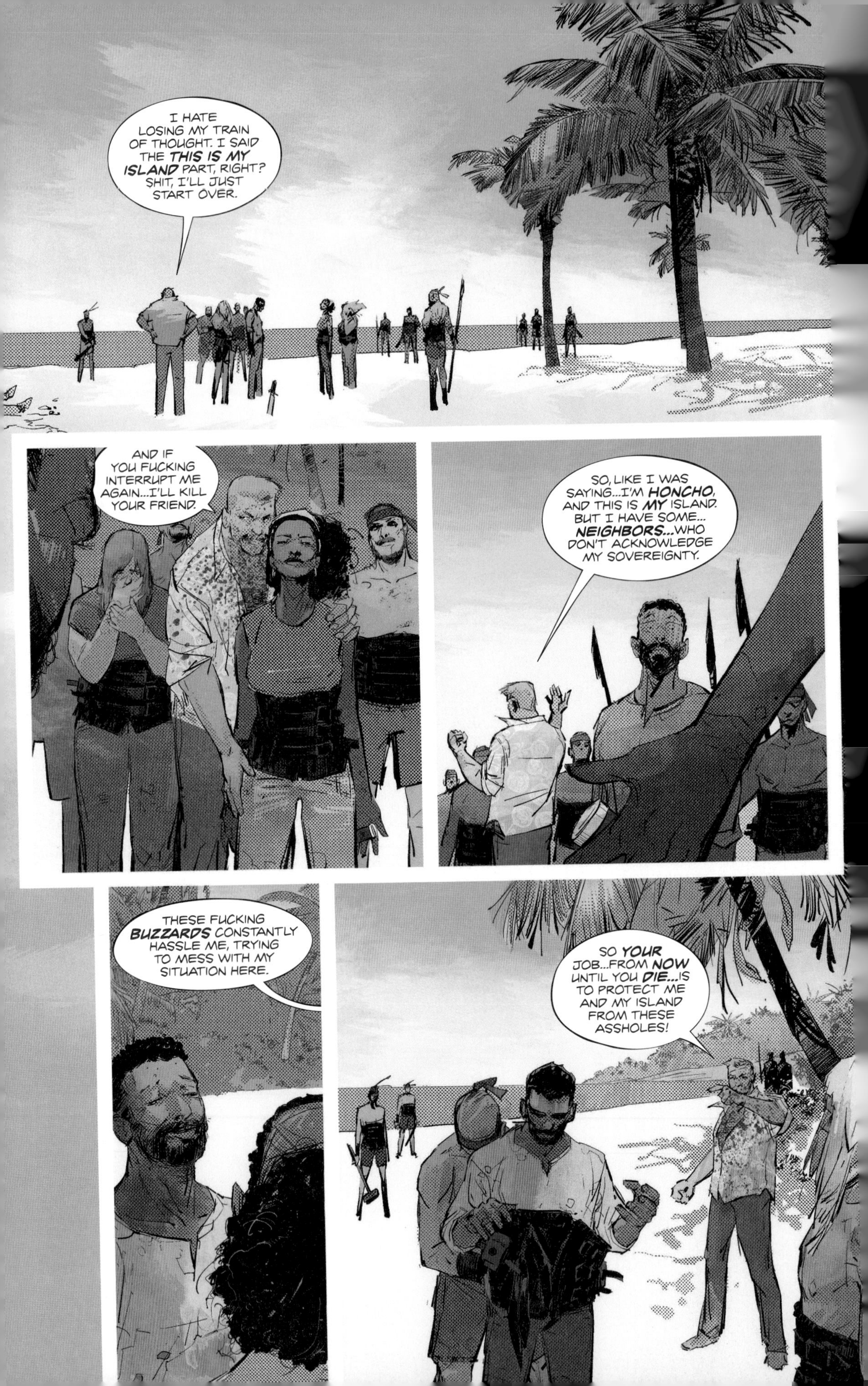
I HATE LOSING MY TRAIN OF THOUGHT. I SAID THE THIS IS MY ISLAND PART, RIGHT? SHIT, I'LL JUST START OVER.
AND IF YOU FUCKING INTERRUPT ME AGAIN...I'LL KILL YOUR FRIEND.
SO, LIKE I WAS SAYING...I'M HONCHO, AND THIS IS MY ISLAND. BUT I HAVE SOME... NEIGHBORS...WHO DON'T ACKNOWLEDGE MY SOVEREIGNTY.
THESE FUCKING BUZZARDS CONSTANTLY HASSLE ME, TRYING TO MESS WITH MY SITUATION HERE.
SO YOUR JOB...FROM NOW UNTIL YOU DIE...IS TO PROTECT ME AND MY ISLAND FROM THESE ASSHOLES!

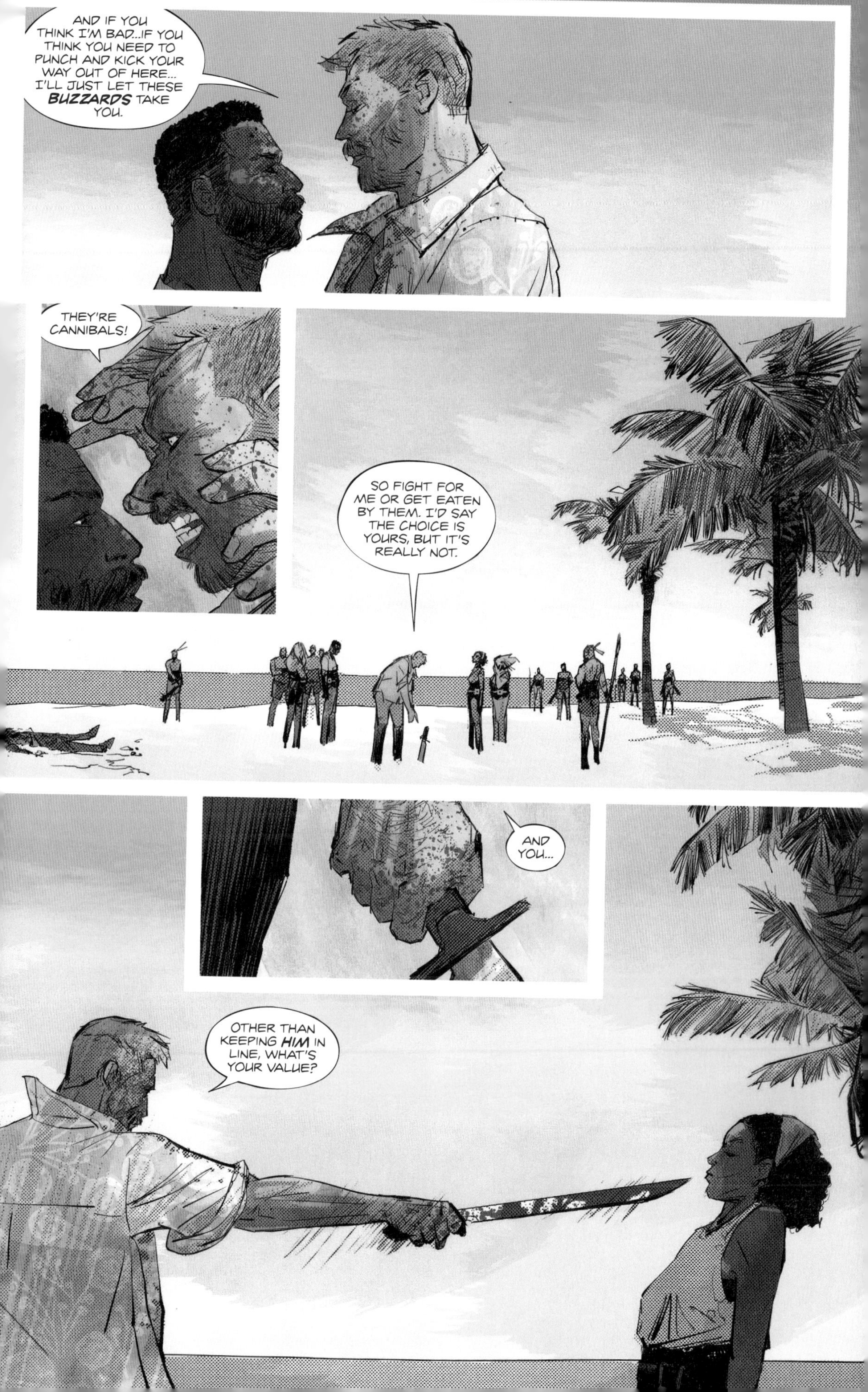
AND IF YOU THINK I'M BAD...IF YOU THINK YOU NEED TO PUNCH AND KICK YOUR WAY OUT OF HERE... I'LL JUST LET THESE **BUZZARDS** TAKE YOU.
THEY'RE CANNIBALS!
SO FIGHT FOR ME OR GET EATEN BY THEM. I'D SAY THE CHOICE IS YOURS, BUT IT'S REALLY NOT.
AND YOU...
OTHER THAN KEEPING **HIM** IN LINE, WHAT'S YOUR VALUE?

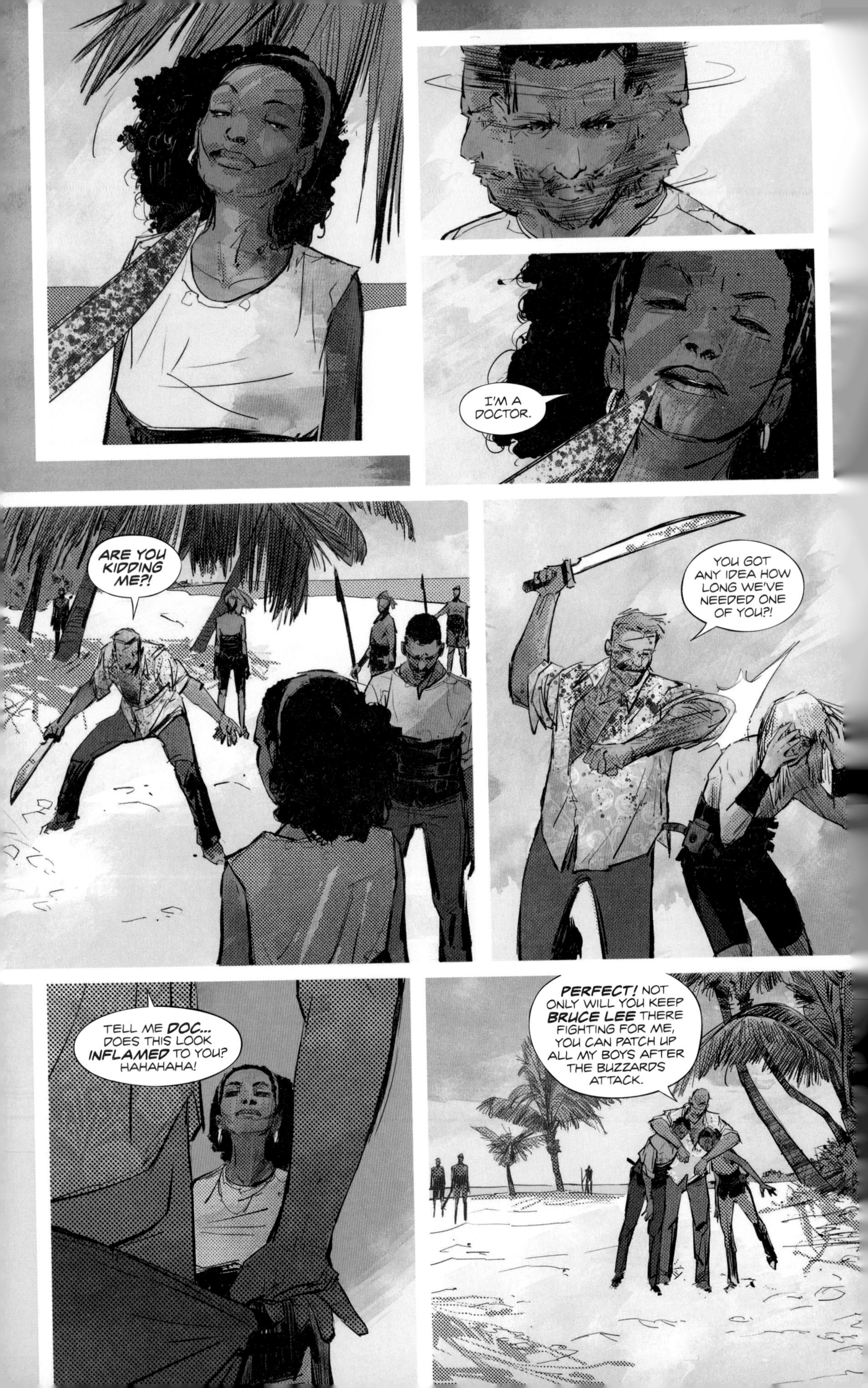
I'M A DOCTOR.
ARE YOU KIDDING ME?!
YOU GOT ANY IDEA HOW LONG WE'VE NEEDED ONE OF YOU?!
TELL ME DOC... DOES THIS LOOK INFLAMED TO YOU? HAHAHAHA!
PERFECT! NOT ONLY WILL YOU KEEP BRUCE LEE THERE FIGHTING FOR ME, YOU CAN PATCH UP ALL MY BOYS AFTER THE BUZZARDS ATTACK.

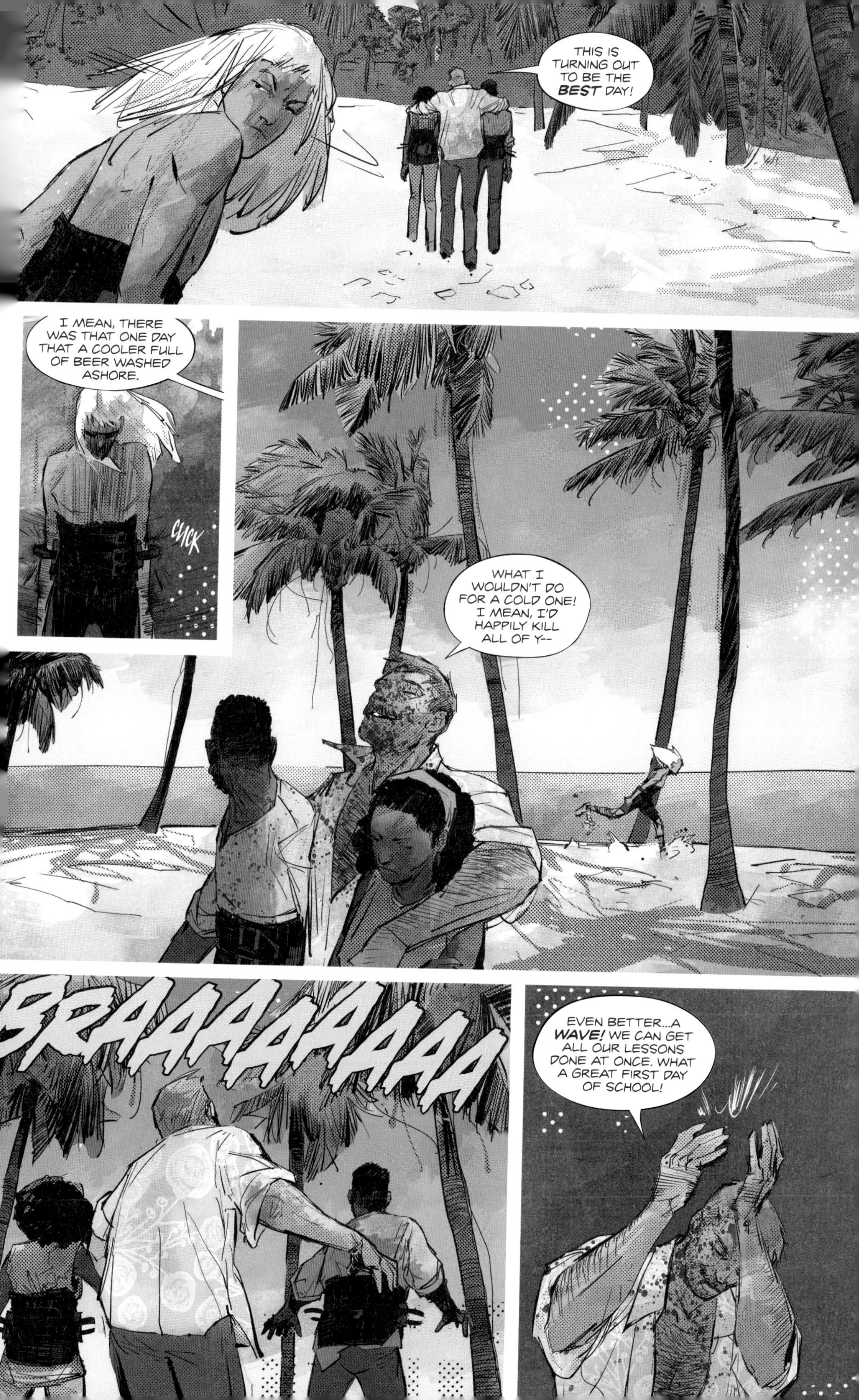
THIS IS TURNING OUT TO BE THE BEST DAY!
I MEAN, THERE WAS THAT ONE DAY THAT A COOLER FULL OF BEER WASHED ASHORE.
CLICK
WHAT I WOULDN'T DO FOR A COLD ONE! I MEAN, I'D HAPPILY KILL ALL OF Y--
BRAAAAAAAAAA
EVEN BETTER...A WAVE! WE CAN GET ALL OUR LESSONS DONE AT ONCE. WHAT A GREAT FIRST DAY OF SCHOOL!

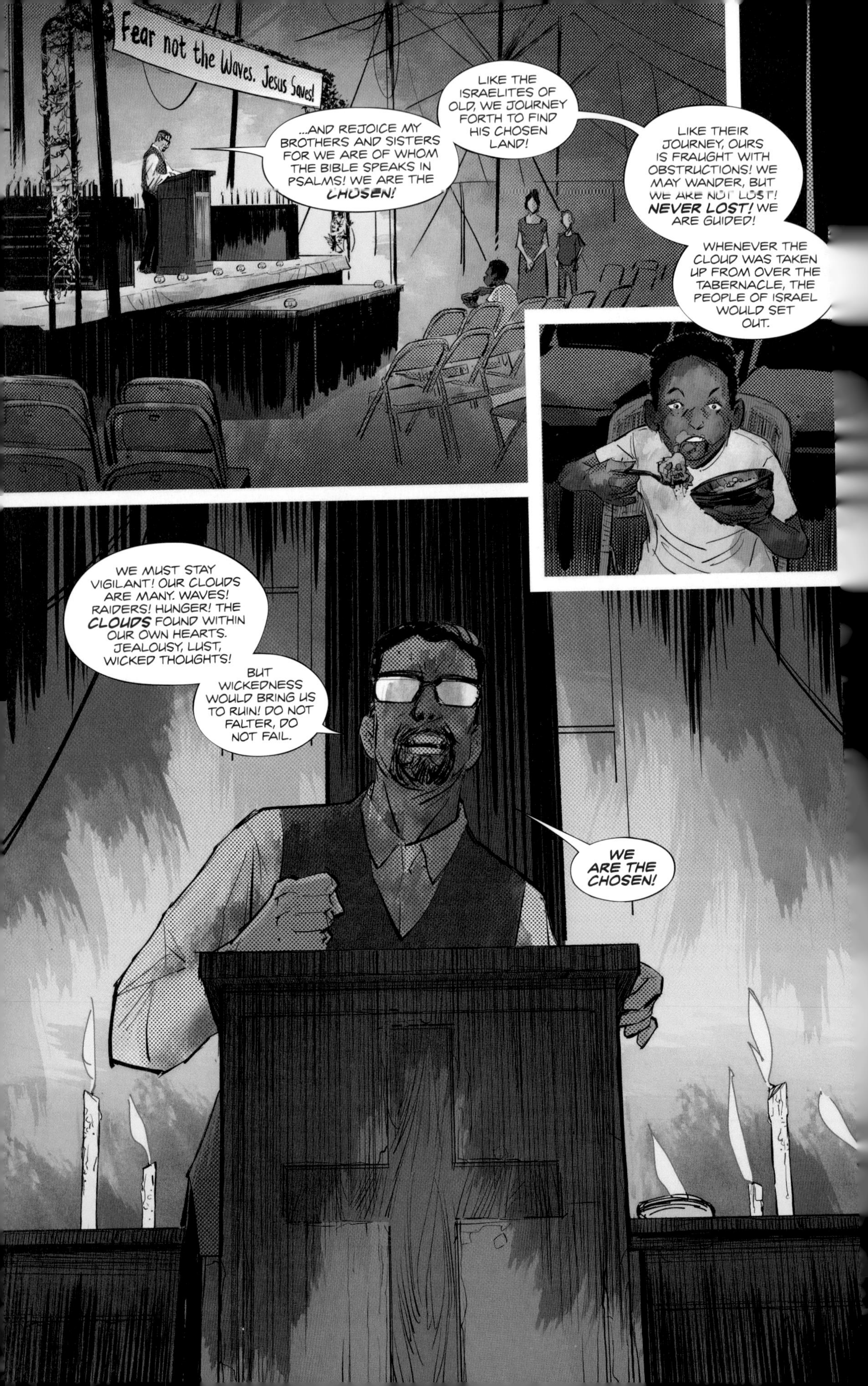
Fear not the Waves. Jesus Saves!
...AND REJOICE MY BROTHERS AND SISTERS FOR WE ARE OF WHOM THE BIBLE SPEAKS IN PSALMS! WE ARE THE CHOSEN!
LIKE THE ISRAELITES OF OLD, WE JOURNEY FORTH TO FIND HIS CHOSEN LAND!
LIKE THEIR JOURNEY, OURS IS FRAUGHT WITH OBSTRUCTIONS! WE MAY WANDER, BUT WE ARE NOT LOST! NEVER LOST! WE ARE GUIDED!
WHENEVER THE CLOUD WAS TAKEN UP FROM OVER THE TABERNACLE, THE PEOPLE OF ISRAEL WOULD SET OUT.
WE MUST STAY VIGILANT! OUR CLOUDS ARE MANY. WAVES! RAIDERS! HUNGER! THE CLOUDS FOUND WITHIN OUR OWN HEARTS. JEALOUSY, LUST, WICKED THOUGHTS!
BUT WICKEDNESS WOULD BRING US TO RUIN! DO NOT FALTER, DO NOT FAIL.
WE ARE THE CHOSEN!

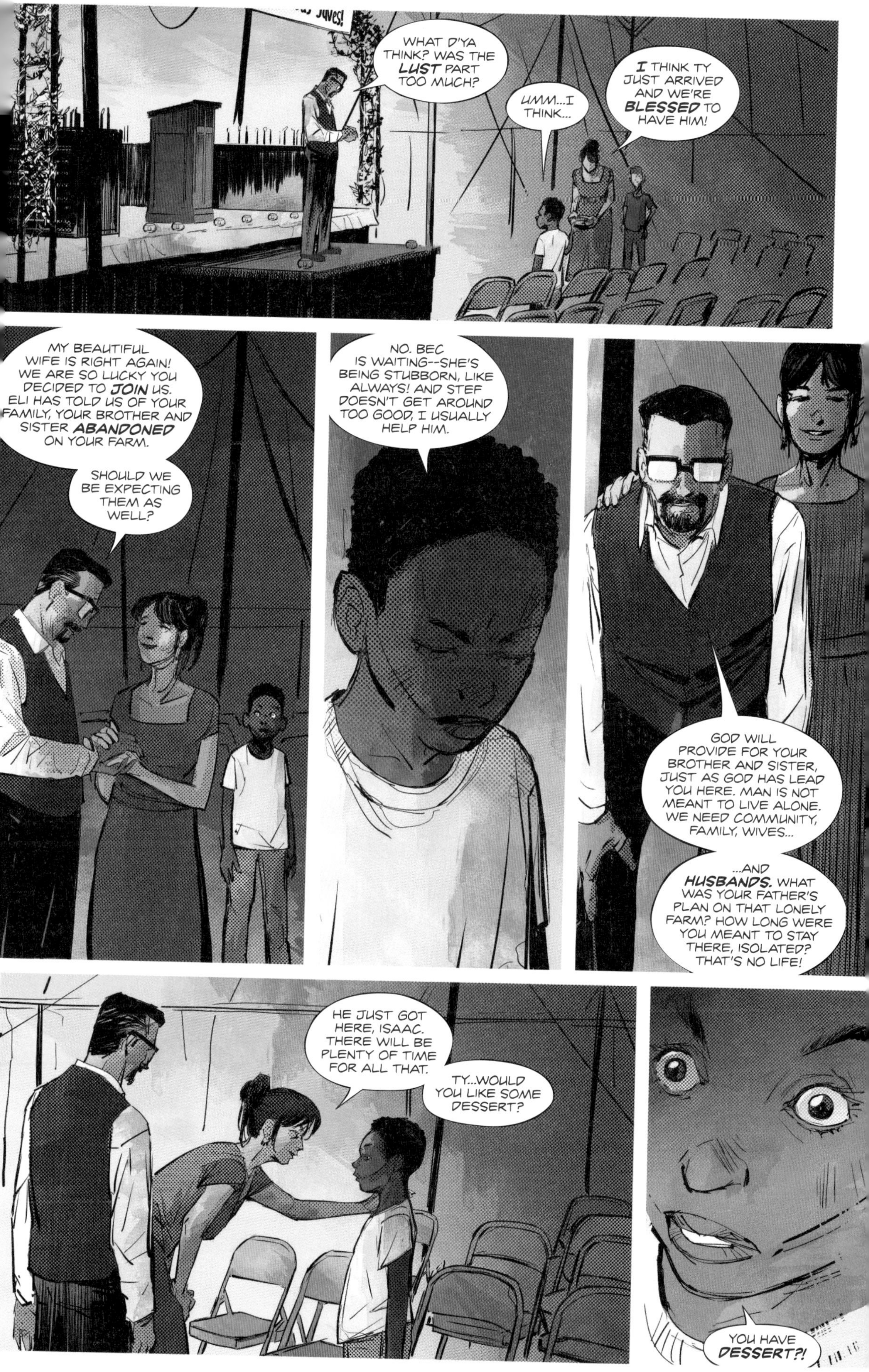
WHAT D'YA THINK? WAS THE LUST PART TOO MUCH?
UMM...I THINK...
I THINK TY JUST ARRIVED AND WE'RE BLESSED TO HAVE HIM!
MY BEAUTIFUL WIFE IS RIGHT AGAIN! WE ARE SO LUCKY YOU DECIDED TO JOIN US. ELI HAS TOLD US OF YOUR FAMILY, YOUR BROTHER AND SISTER ABANDONED ON YOUR FARM.
SHOULD WE BE EXPECTING THEM AS WELL?
NO. BEC IS WAITING--SHE'S BEING STUBBORN, LIKE ALWAYS! AND STEF DOESN'T GET AROUND TOO GOOD, I USUALLY HELP HIM.
GOD WILL PROVIDE FOR YOUR BROTHER AND SISTER, JUST AS GOD HAS LEAD YOU HERE. MAN IS NOT MEANT TO LIVE ALONE. WE NEED COMMUNITY, FAMILY, WIVES...
...AND HUSBANDS. WHAT WAS YOUR FATHER'S PLAN ON THAT LONELY FARM? HOW LONG WERE YOU MEANT TO STAY THERE, ISOLATED? THAT'S NO LIFE!
HE JUST GOT HERE, ISAAC. THERE WILL BE PLENTY OF TIME FOR ALL THAT.
TY...WOULD YOU LIKE SOME DESSERT?
YOU HAVE DESSERT?!

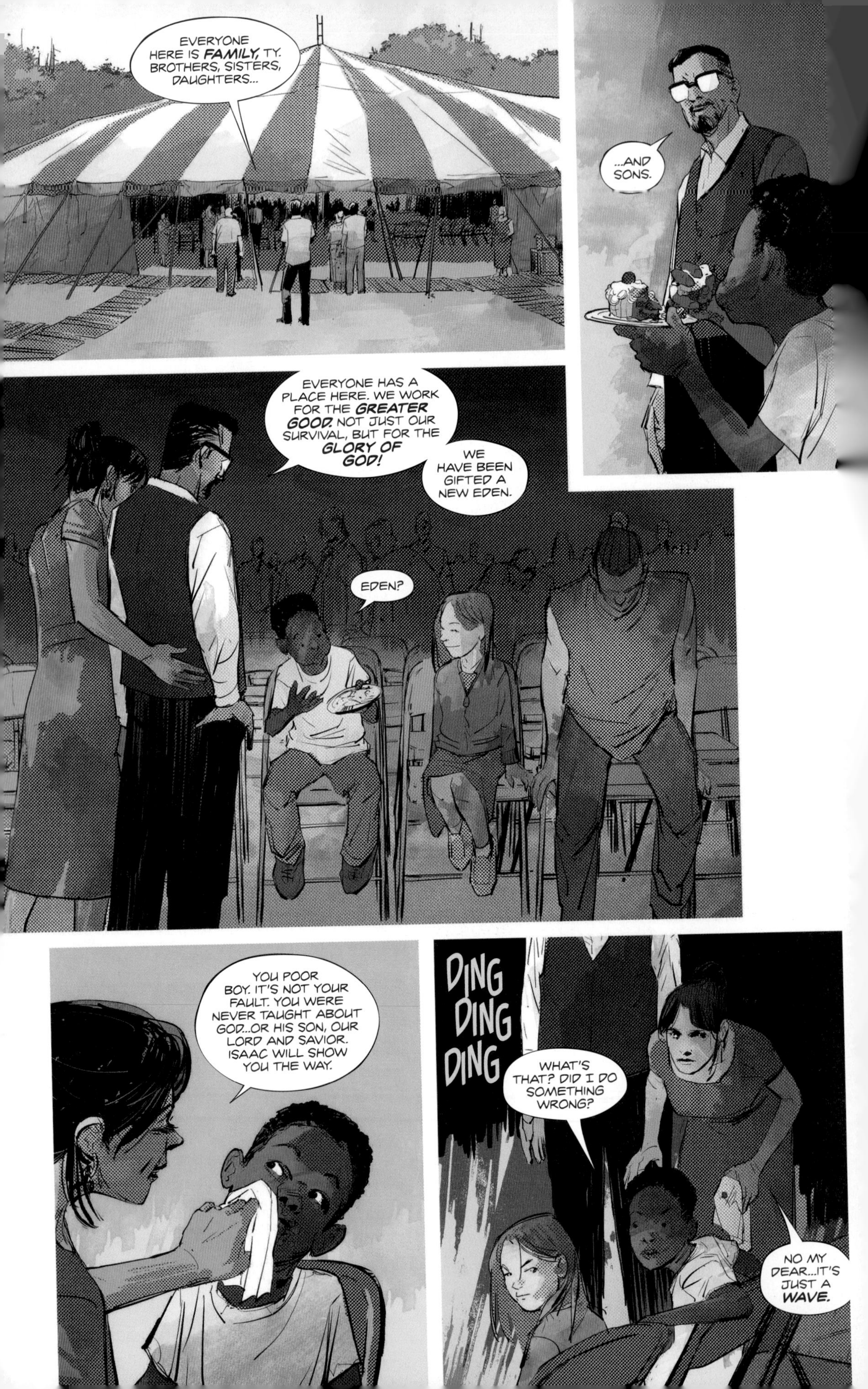
EVERYONE HERE IS FAMILY, TY. BROTHERS, SISTERS, DAUGHTERS...
...AND SONS.
EVERYONE HAS A PLACE HERE. WE WORK FOR THE GREATER GOOD. NOT JUST OUR SURVIVAL, BUT FOR THE GLORY OF GOD!
WE HAVE BEEN GIFTED A NEW EDEN.
EDEN?
YOU POOR BOY. IT'S NOT YOUR FAULT. YOU WERE NEVER TAUGHT ABOUT GOD...OR HIS SON, OUR LORD AND SAVIOR. ISAAC WILL SHOW YOU THE WAY.
DING DING DING
WHAT'S THAT? DID I DO SOMETHING WRONG?
NO MY DEAR...IT'S JUST A WAVE.

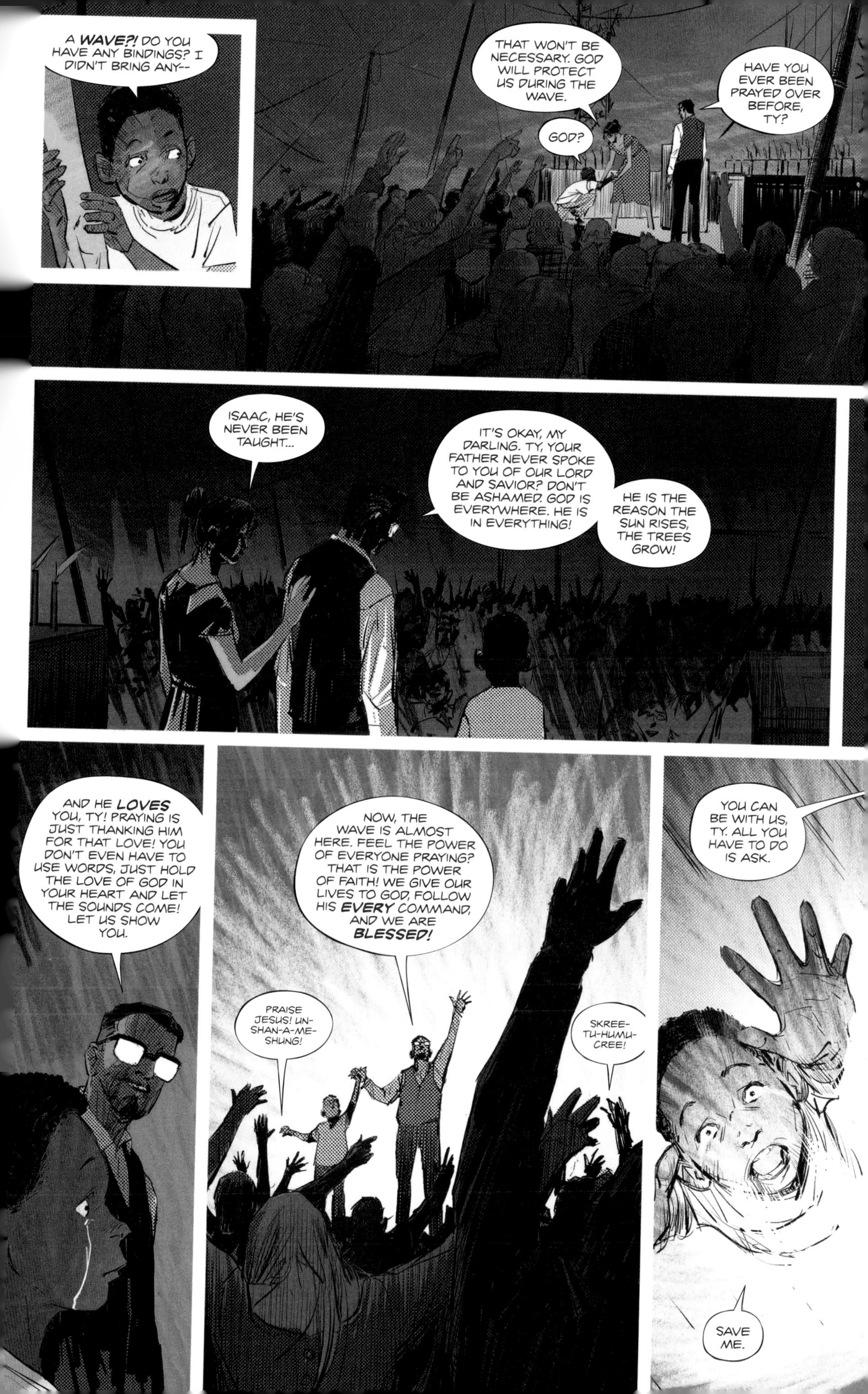
A WAVE?! DO YOU HAVE ANY BINDINGS? I DIDN'T BRING ANY--
THAT WON'T BE NECESSARY. GOD WILL PROTECT US DURING THE WAVE.
GOD?
HAVE YOU EVER BEEN PRAYED OVER BEFORE, TY?
ISAAC, HE'S NEVER BEEN TAUGHT...
IT'S OKAY, MY DARLING. TY, YOUR FATHER NEVER SPOKE TO YOU OF OUR LORD AND SAVIOR? DON'T BE ASHAMED. GOD IS EVERYWHERE. HE IS IN EVERYTHING!
HE IS THE REASON THE SUN RISES, THE TREES GROW!
AND HE LOVES YOU, TY! PRAYING IS JUST THANKING HIM FOR THAT LOVE! YOU DON'T EVEN HAVE TO USE WORDS, JUST HOLD THE LOVE OF GOD IN YOUR HEART AND LET THE SOUNDS COME! LET US SHOW YOU.
NOW, THE WAVE IS ALMOST HERE. FEEL THE POWER OF EVERYONE PRAYING? THAT IS THE POWER OF FAITH! WE GIVE OUR LIVES TO GOD, FOLLOW HIS EVERY COMMAND, AND WE ARE BLESSED!
PRAISE JESUS! UN-SHAN-A-ME-SHUNG!
SKREE-TU-HUMU-CREE!
YOU CAN BE WITH US, TY. ALL YOU HAVE TO DO IS ASK.
SAVE ME.

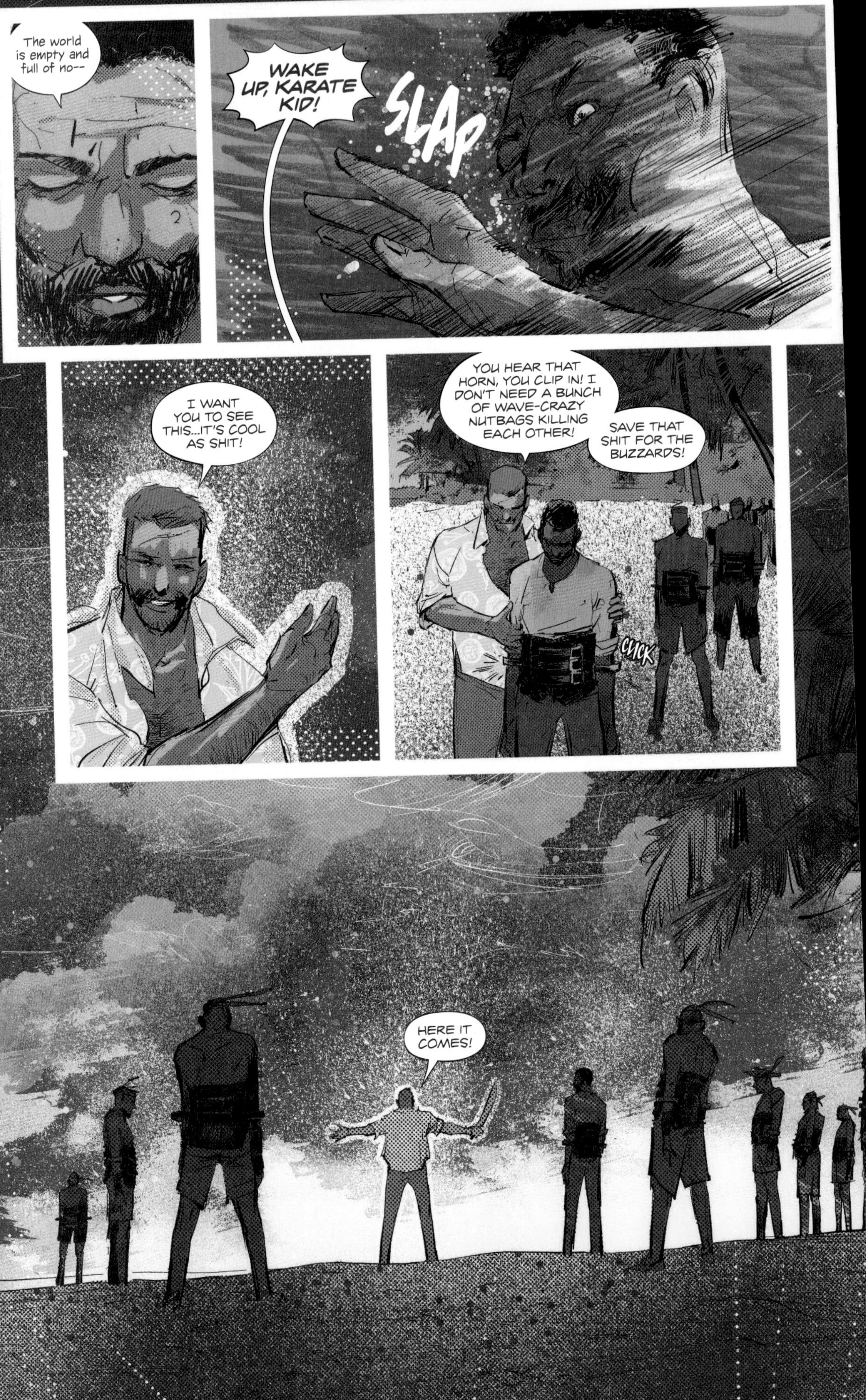
The world is empty and full of no--
WAKE UP, KARATE KID!
SLAP
I WANT YOU TO SEE THIS...IT'S COOL AS SHIT!
YOU HEAR THAT HORN, YOU CLIP IN! I DON'T NEED A BUNCH OF WAVE-CRAZY NUTBAGS KILLING EACH OTHER!
SAVE THAT SHIT FOR THE BUZZARDS!
CLICK
HERE IT COMES!

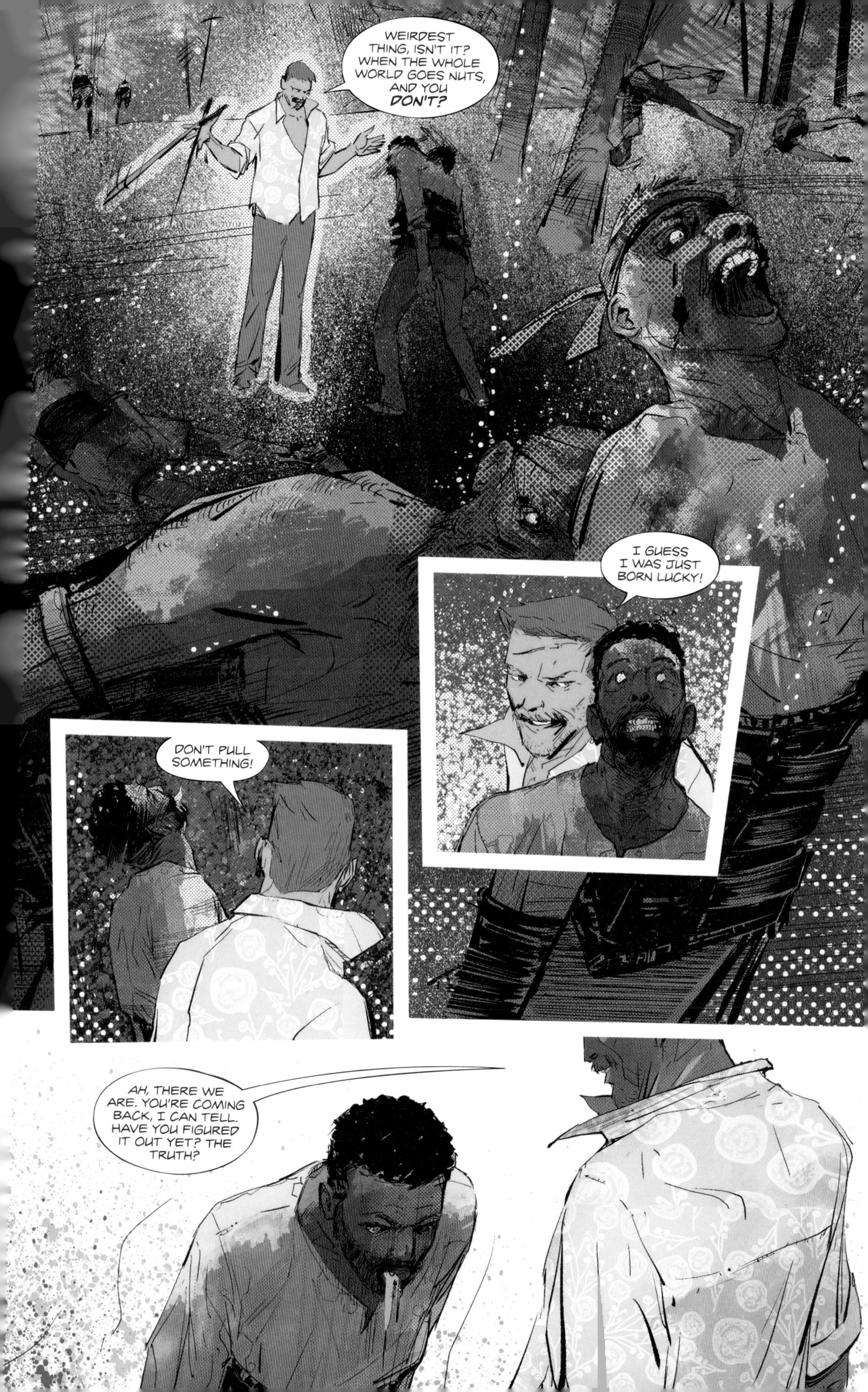
WEIRDEST THING, ISN'T IT? WHEN THE WHOLE WORLD GOES NUTS, AND YOU **DON'T?**
I GUESS I WAS JUST BORN LUCKY!
DON'T PULL SOMETHING!
AH, THERE WE ARE. YOU'RE COMING BACK, I CAN TELL. HAVE YOU FIGURED IT OUT YET? THE TRUTH?

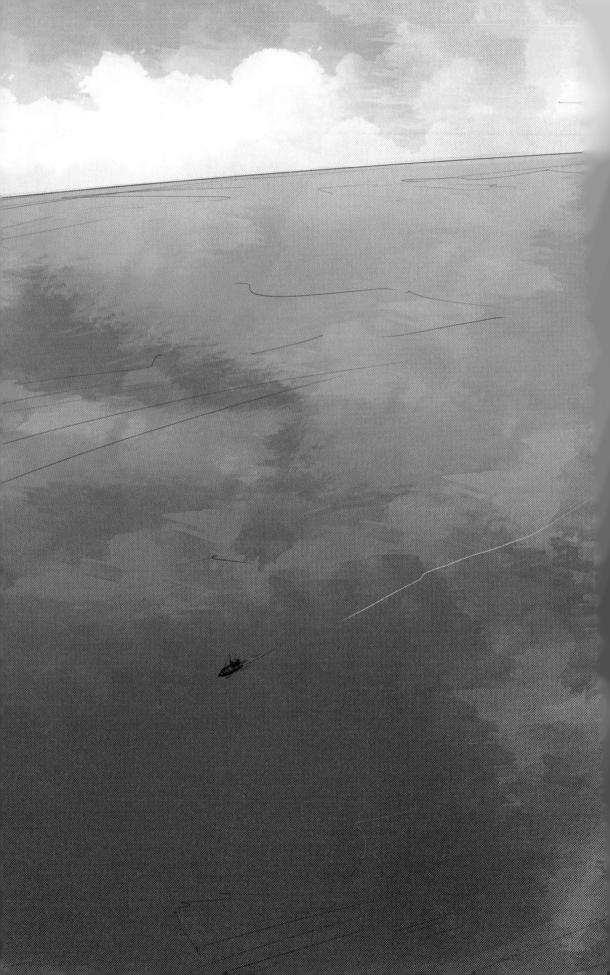

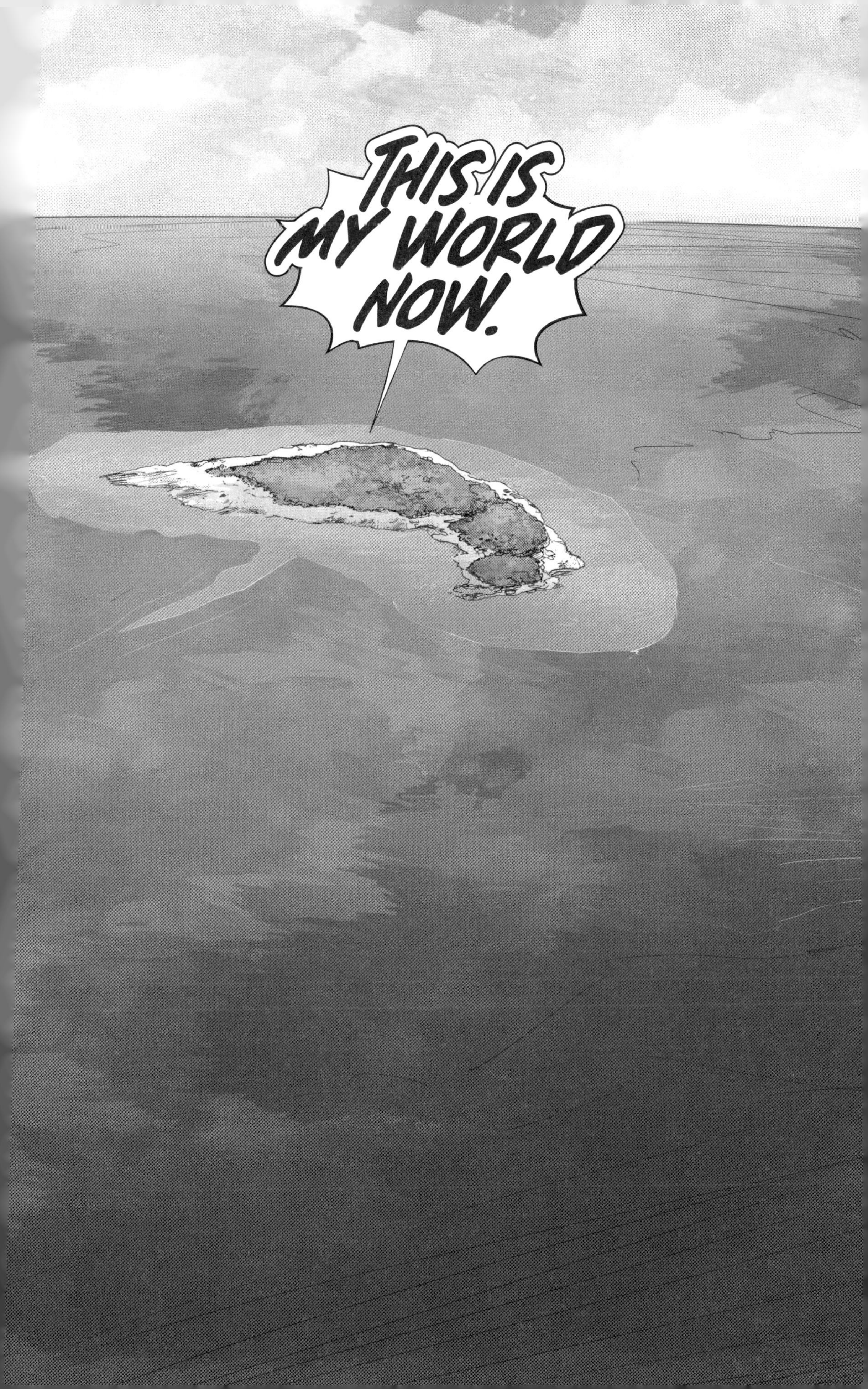
THIS IS MY WORLD NOW.

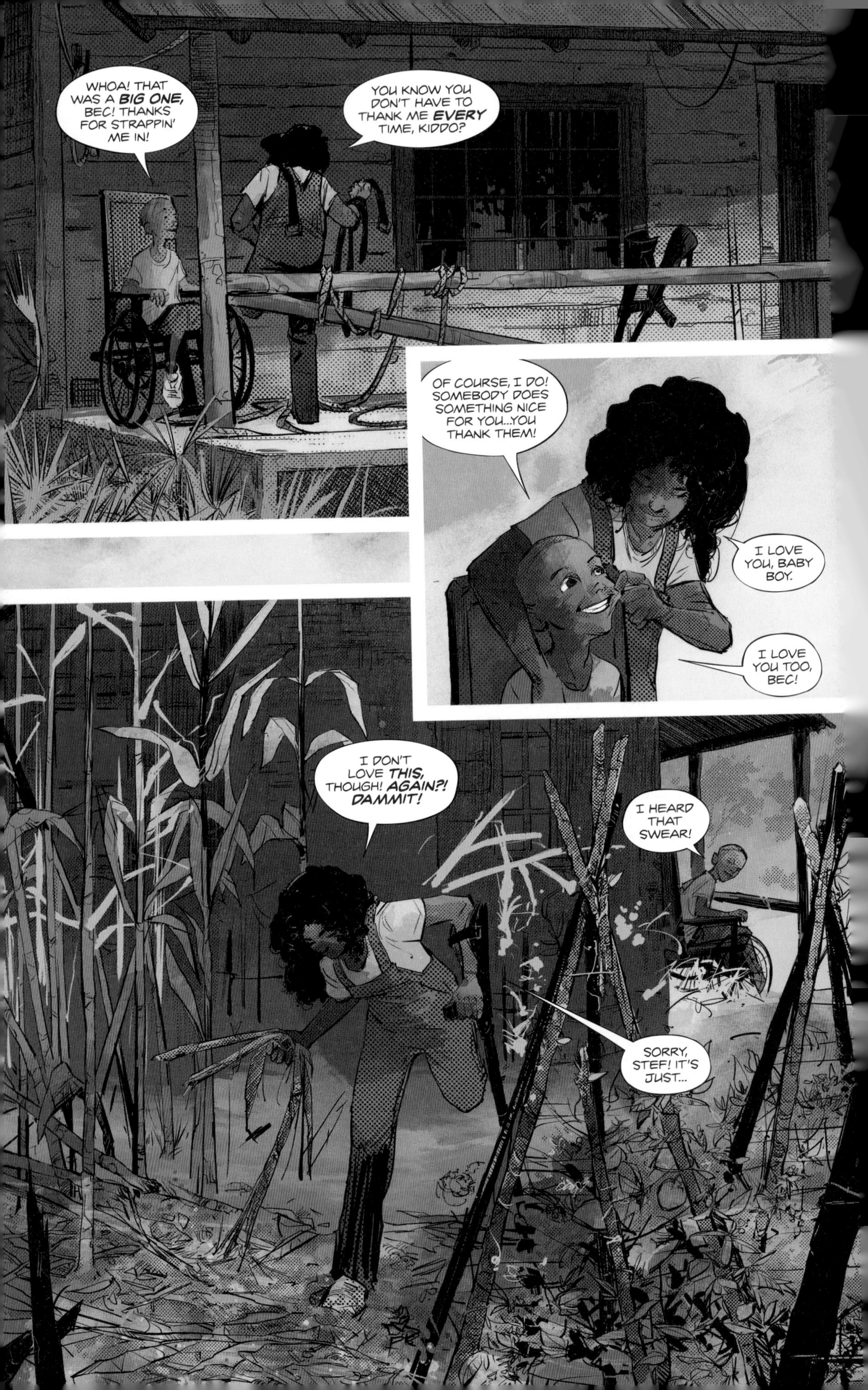
WHOA! THAT WAS A **BIG ONE,** BEC! THANKS FOR STRAPPIN' ME IN!
YOU KNOW YOU DON'T HAVE TO THANK ME **EVERY** TIME, KIDDO?
OF COURSE, I DO! SOMEBODY DOES SOMETHING NICE FOR YOU...YOU THANK THEM!
I LOVE YOU, BABY BOY.
I LOVE YOU TOO, BEC!
I DON'T LOVE **THIS,** THOUGH! **AGAIN?! DAMMIT!**
I HEARD THAT SWEAR!
SORRY, STEF! IT'S JUST...

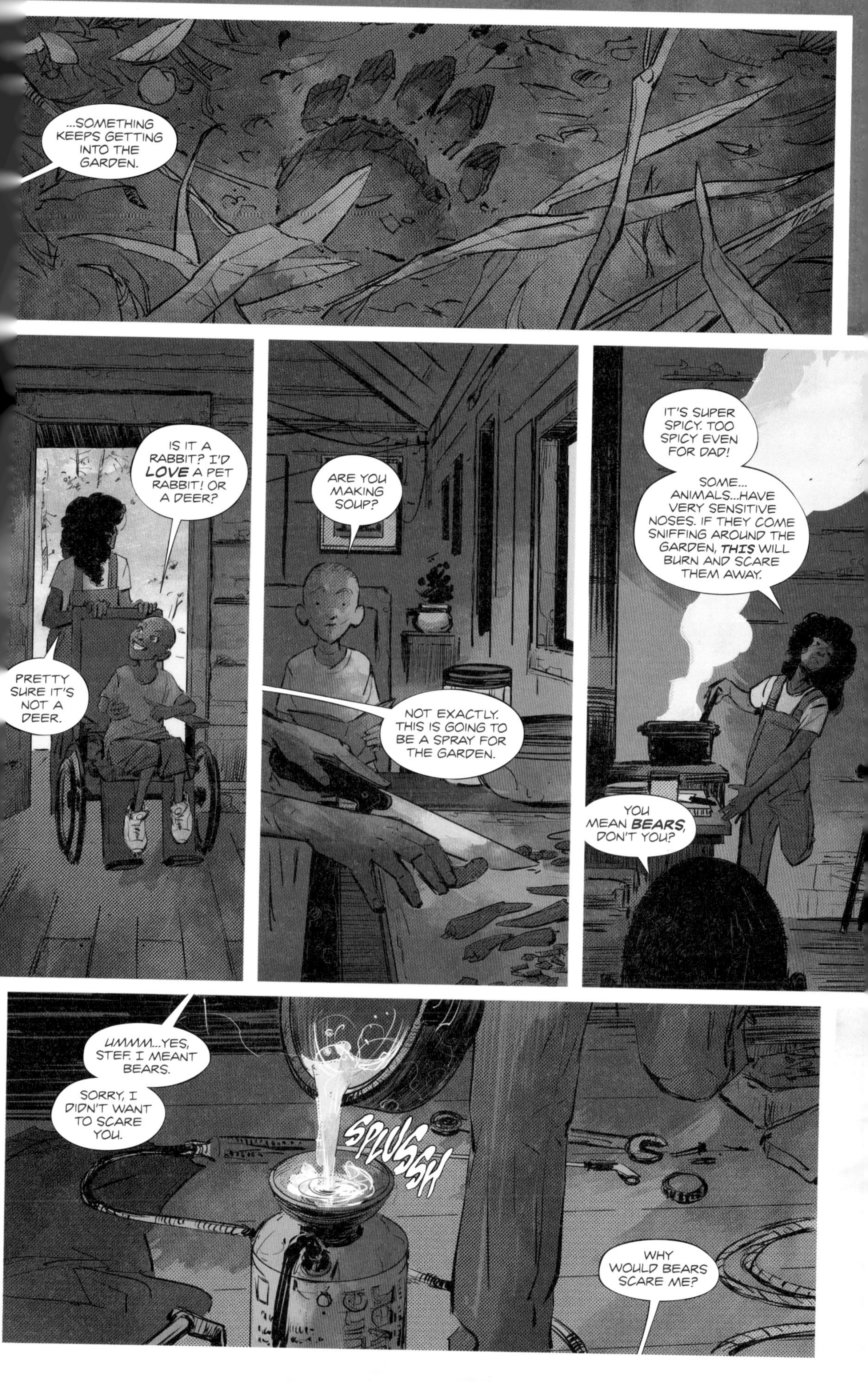
...SOMETHING KEEPS GETTING INTO THE GARDEN.
IS IT A RABBIT? I'D LOVE A PET RABBIT! OR A DEER?
PRETTY SURE IT'S NOT A DEER.
ARE YOU MAKING SOUP?
NOT EXACTLY. THIS IS GOING TO BE A SPRAY FOR THE GARDEN.
IT'S SUPER SPICY. TOO SPICY EVEN FOR DAD!
SOME... ANIMALS...HAVE VERY SENSITIVE NOSES. IF THEY COME SNIFFING AROUND THE GARDEN, THIS WILL BURN AND SCARE THEM AWAY.
YOU MEAN BEARS, DON'T YOU?
UMMM...YES, STEF. I MEANT BEARS.
SORRY, I DIDN'T WANT TO SCARE YOU.
SPLUSSH
WHY WOULD BEARS SCARE ME?

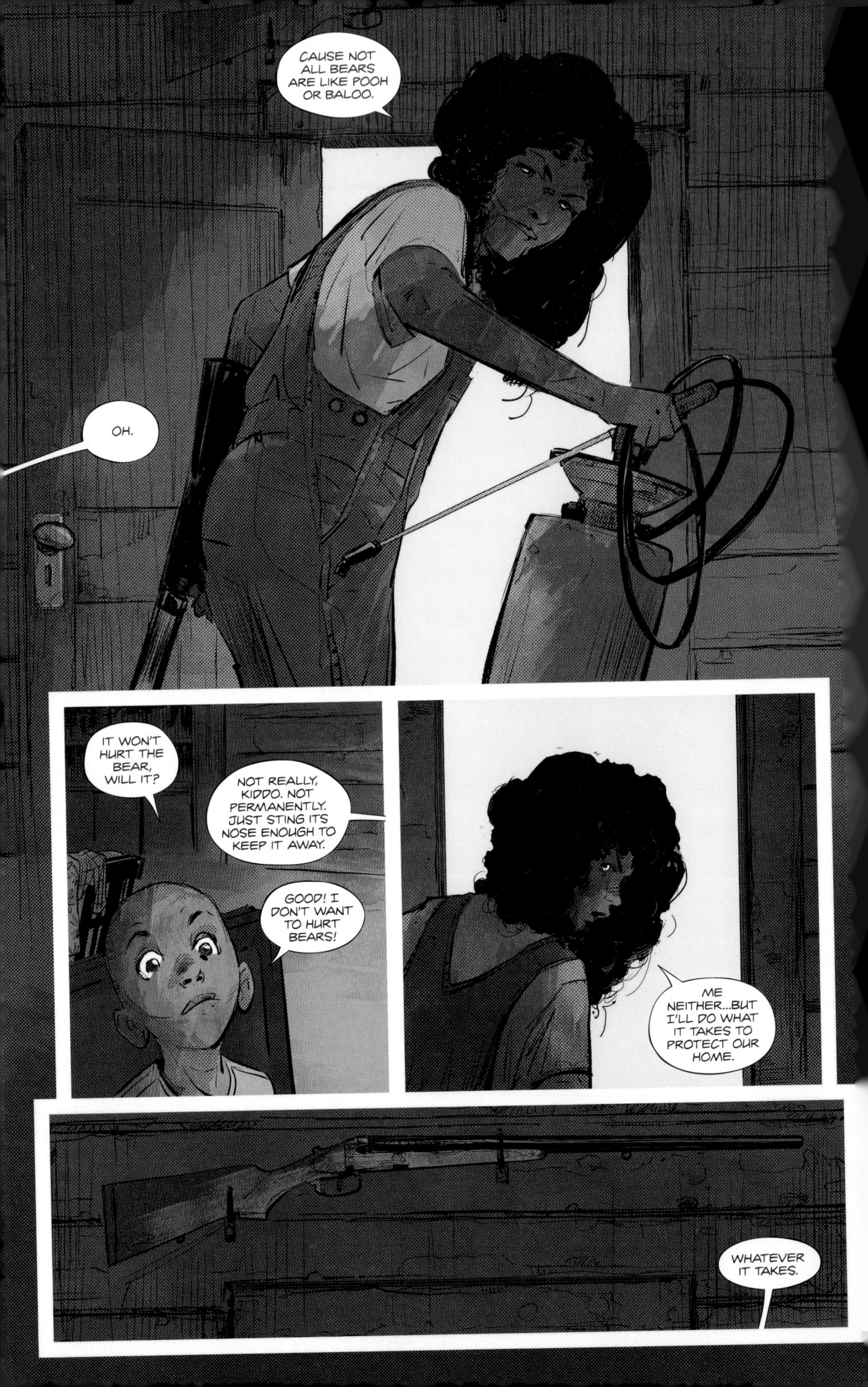
CAUSE NOT ALL BEARS ARE LIKE POOH OR BALOO.
OH.
IT WON'T HURT THE BEAR, WILL IT?
NOT REALLY, KIDDO. NOT PERMANENTLY. JUST STING ITS NOSE ENOUGH TO KEEP IT AWAY.
GOOD! I DON'T WANT TO HURT BEARS!
ME NEITHER...BUT I'LL DO WHAT IT TAKES TO PROTECT OUR HOME.
WHATEVER IT TAKES.

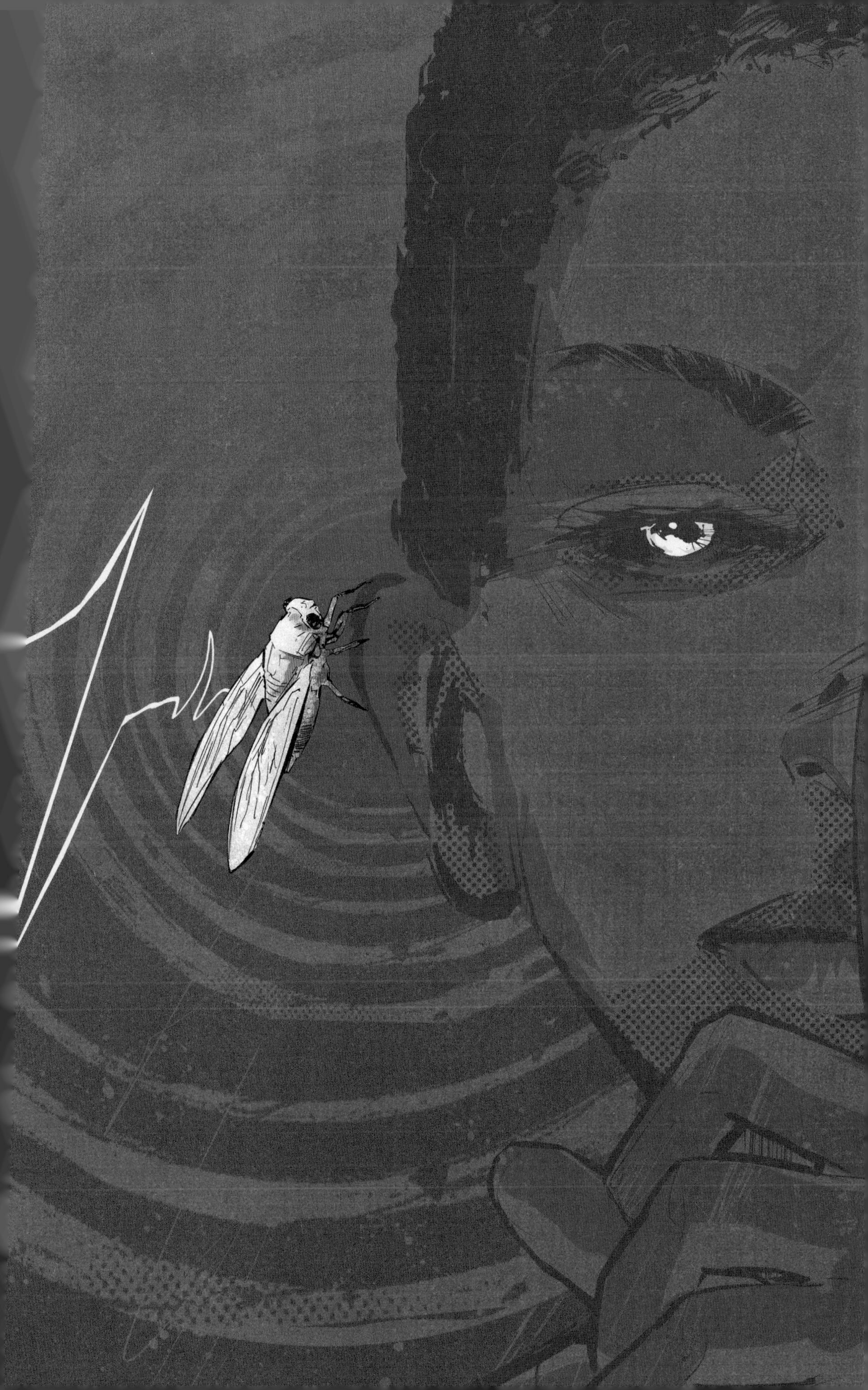

FIVE

CHAPTER

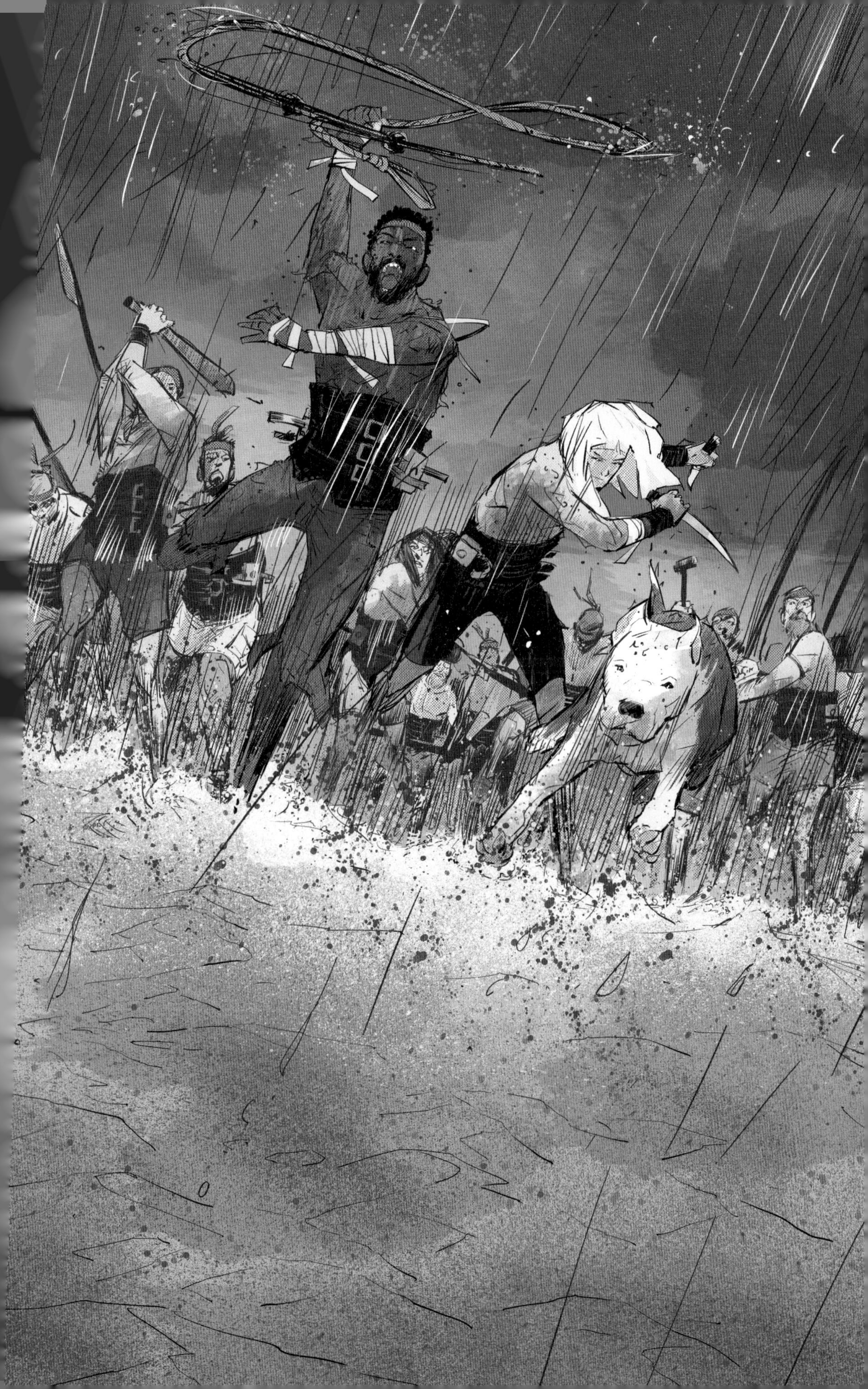

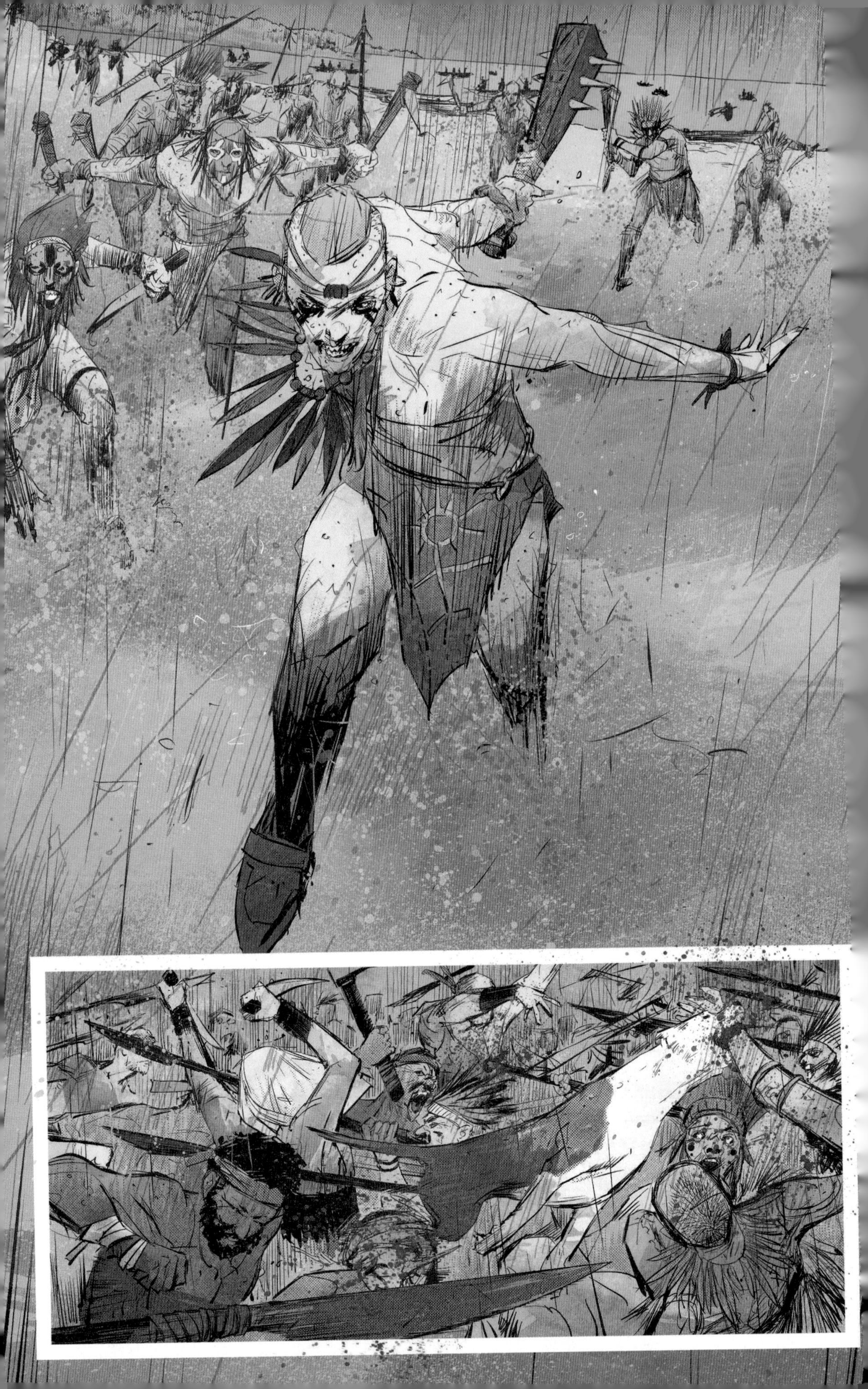

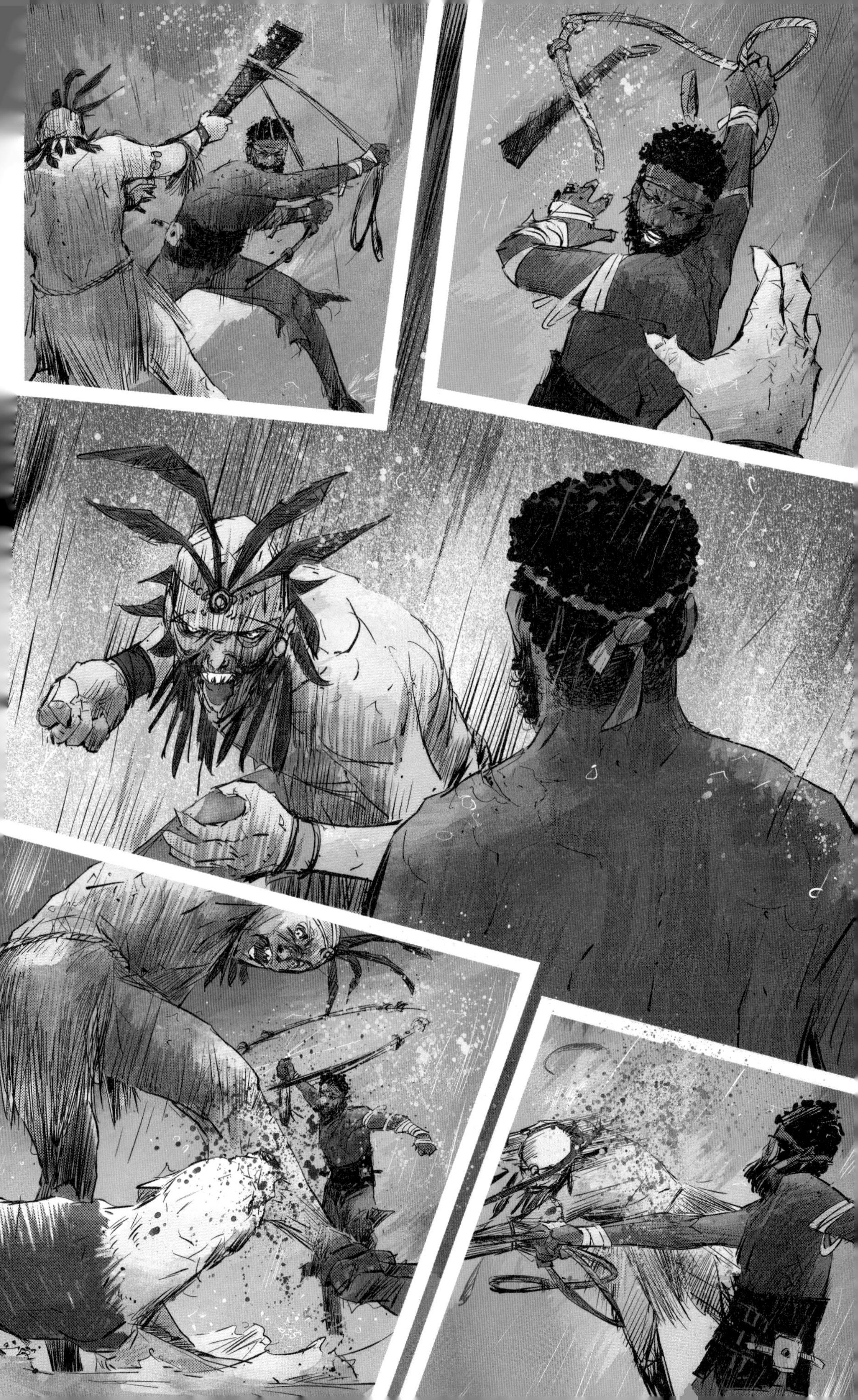

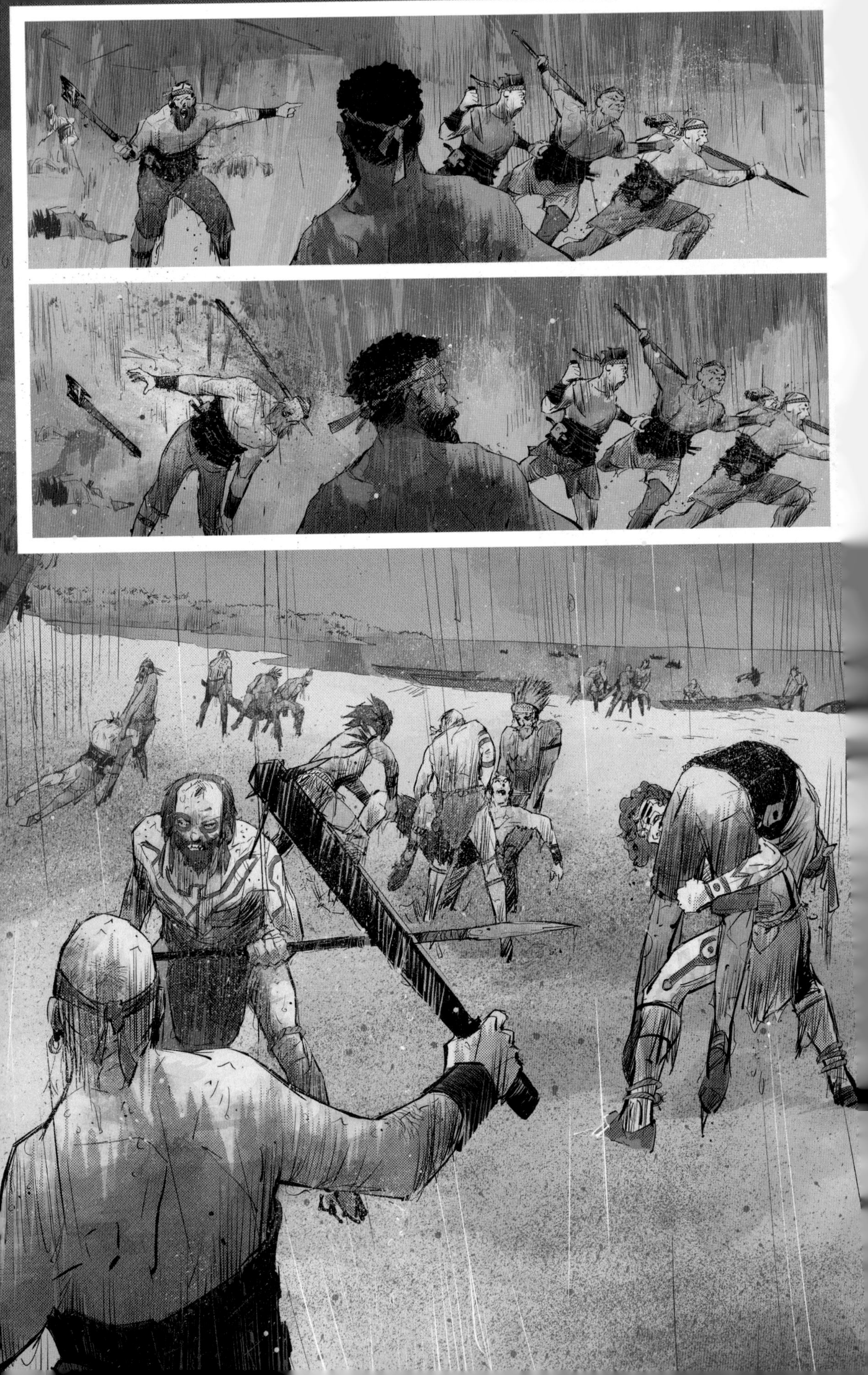

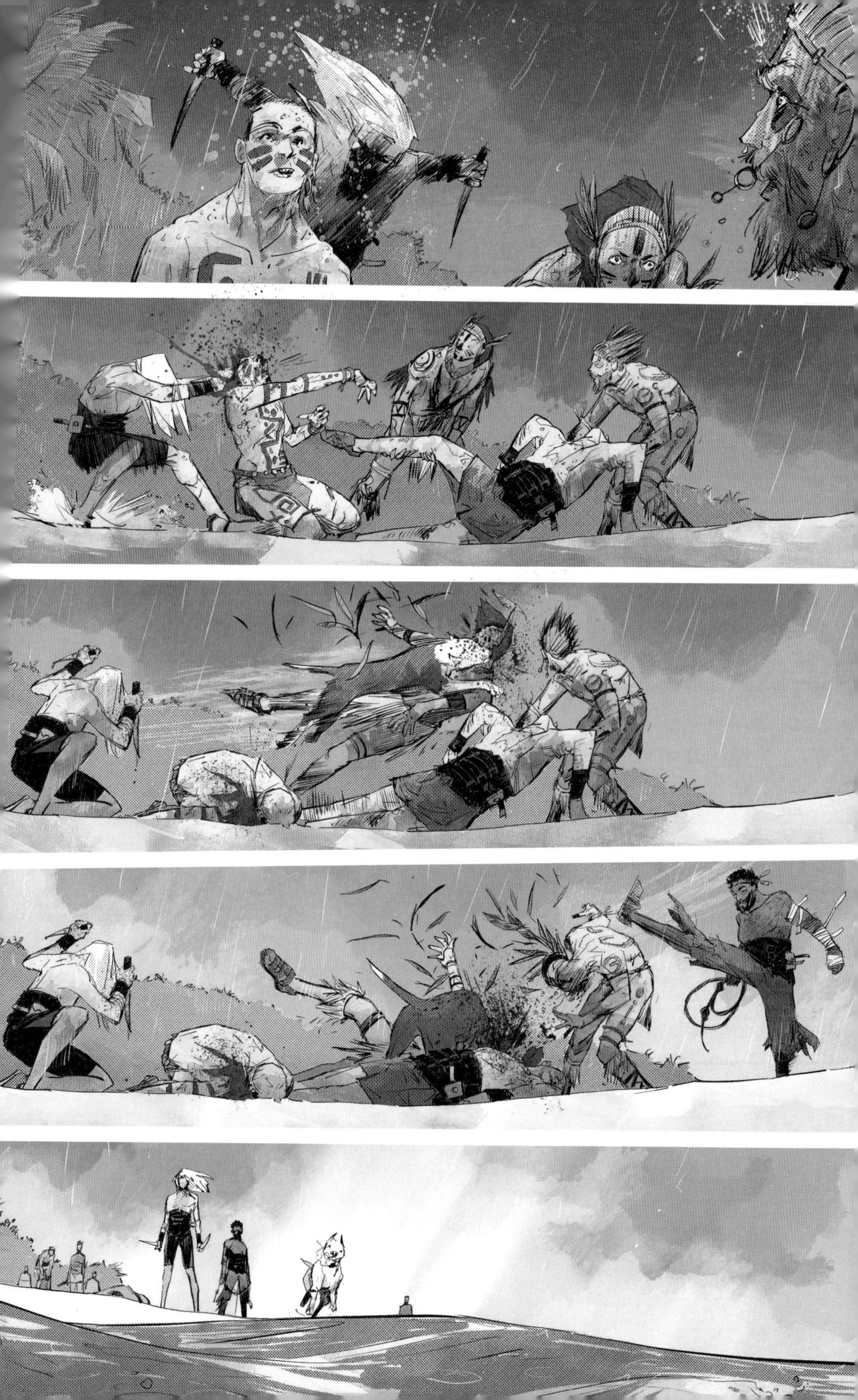

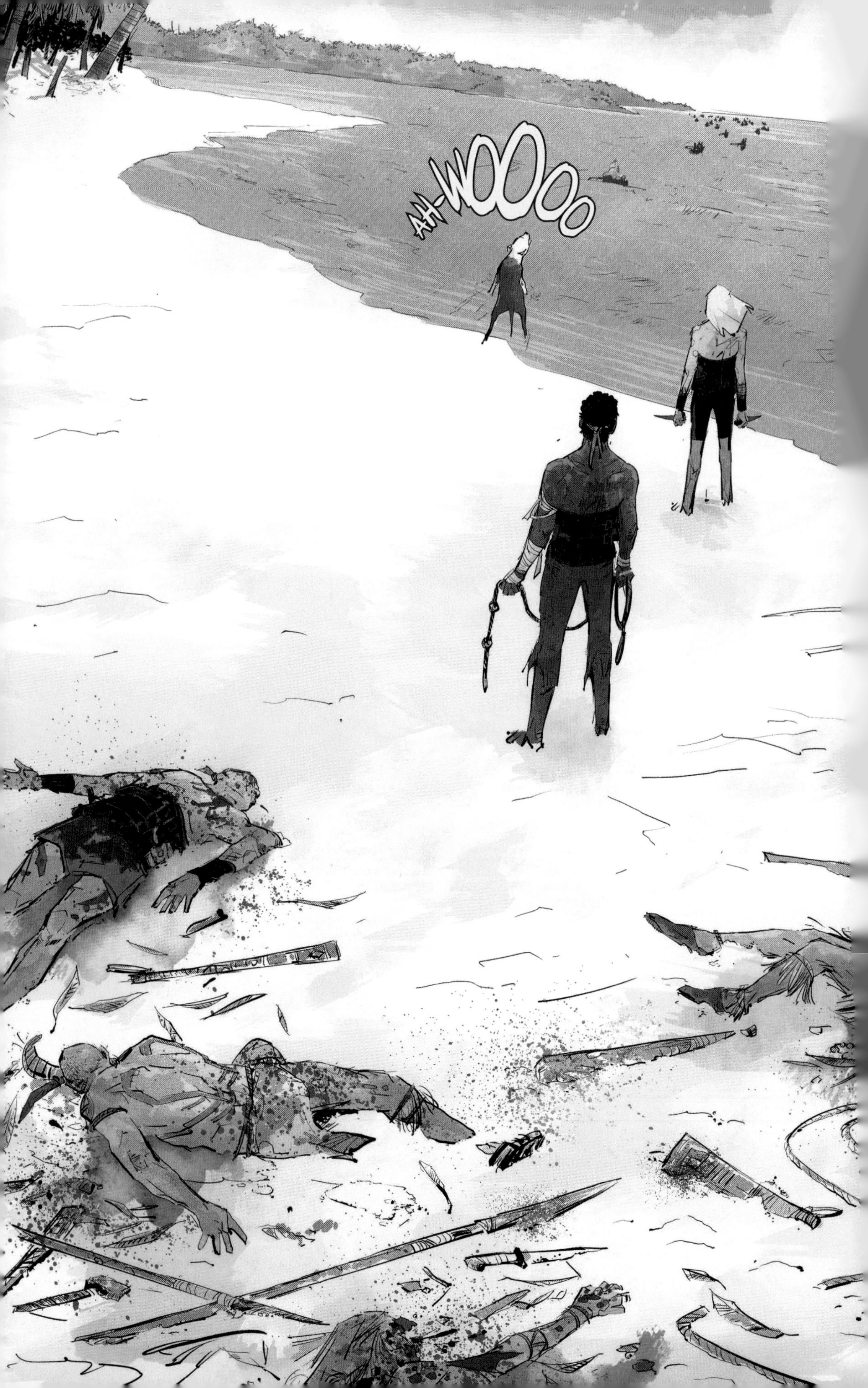
AH-WOOOoo

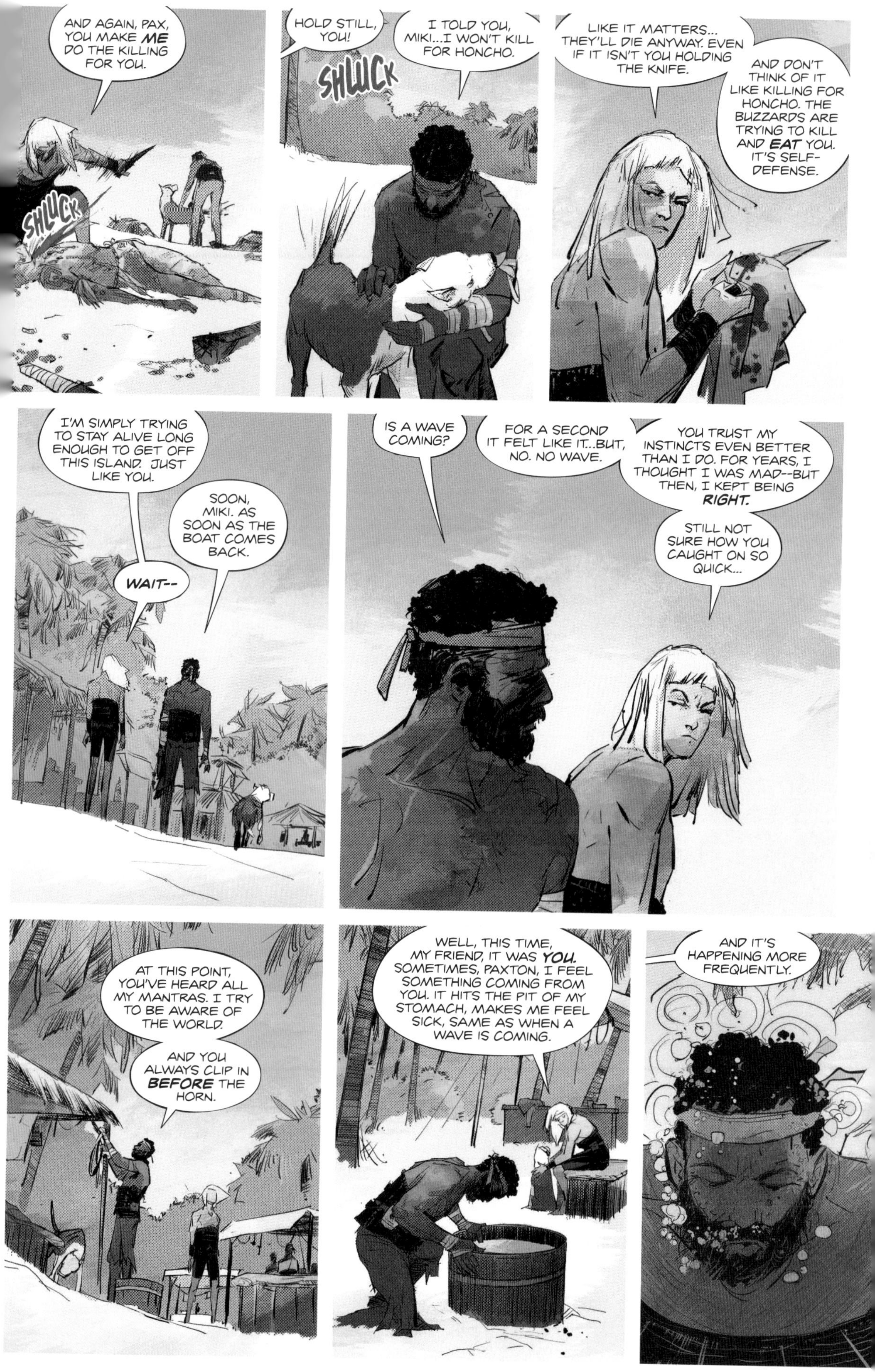
AND AGAIN, PAX, YOU MAKE ME DO THE KILLING FOR YOU.
SHLUCK
HOLD STILL, YOU!
I TOLD YOU, MIKI...I WON'T KILL FOR HONCHO.
SHLUCK
LIKE IT MATTERS... THEY'LL DIE ANYWAY. EVEN IF IT ISN'T YOU HOLDING THE KNIFE.
AND DON'T THINK OF IT LIKE KILLING FOR HONCHO. THE BUZZARDS ARE TRYING TO KILL AND EAT YOU. IT'S SELF-DEFENSE.
I'M SIMPLY TRYING TO STAY ALIVE LONG ENOUGH TO GET OFF THIS ISLAND. JUST LIKE YOU.
SOON, MIKI. AS SOON AS THE BOAT COMES BACK.
WAIT--
IS A WAVE COMING?
FOR A SECOND IT FELT LIKE IT...BUT, NO. NO WAVE.
YOU TRUST MY INSTINCTS EVEN BETTER THAN I DO. FOR YEARS, I THOUGHT I WAS MAD--BUT THEN, I KEPT BEING RIGHT.
STILL NOT SURE HOW YOU CAUGHT ON SO QUICK...
AT THIS POINT, YOU'VE HEARD ALL MY MANTRAS. I TRY TO BE AWARE OF THE WORLD.
AND YOU ALWAYS CLIP IN BEFORE THE HORN.
WELL, THIS TIME, MY FRIEND, IT WAS YOU. SOMETIMES, PAXTON, I FEEL SOMETHING COMING FROM YOU. IT HITS THE PIT OF MY STOMACH, MAKES ME FEEL SICK, SAME AS WHEN A WAVE IS COMING.
AND IT'S HAPPENING MORE FREQUENTLY.

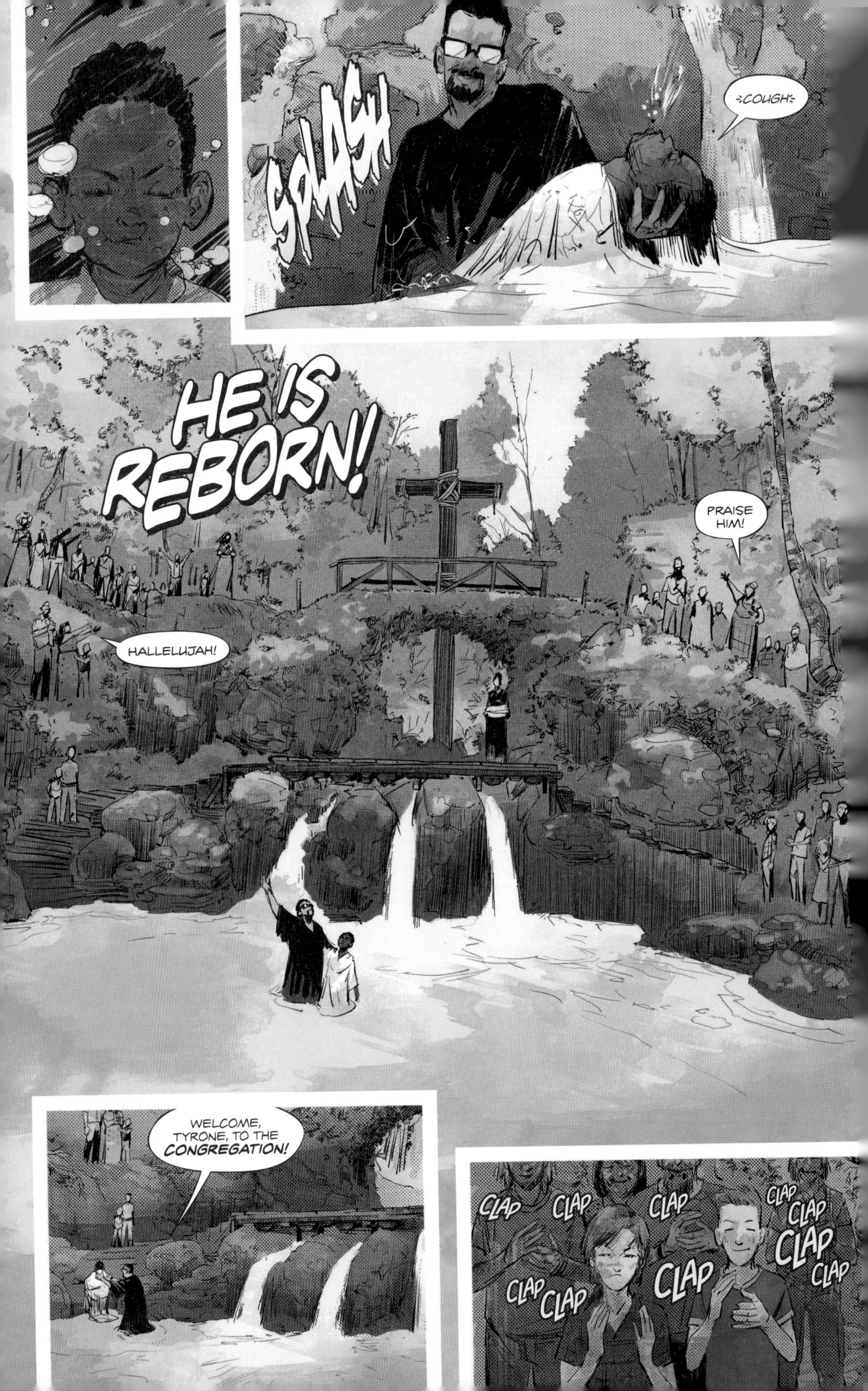
SPLASH
COUGH
HE IS REBORN!
PRAISE HIM!
HALLELUJAH!
WELCOME, TYRONE, TO THE CONGREGATION!
CLAP CLAP CLAP CLAP CLAP CLAP CLAP CLAP CLAP CLAP

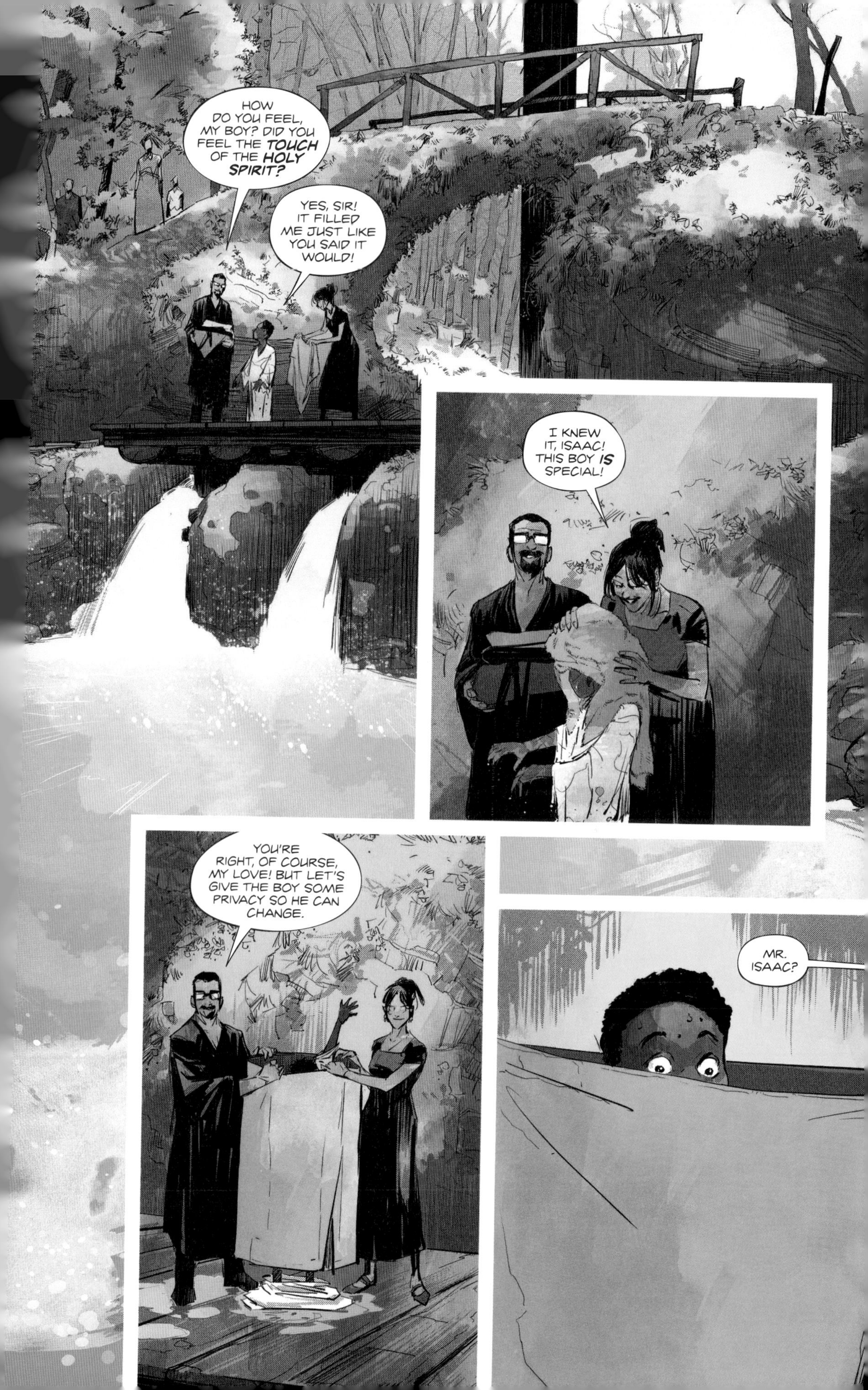
HOW DO YOU FEEL, MY BOY? DID YOU FEEL THE TOUCH OF THE HOLY SPIRIT?
YES, SIR! IT FILLED ME JUST LIKE YOU SAID IT WOULD!
I KNEW IT, ISAAC! THIS BOY IS SPECIAL!
YOU'RE RIGHT, OF COURSE, MY LOVE! BUT LET'S GIVE THE BOY SOME PRIVACY SO HE CAN CHANGE.
MR. ISAAC?

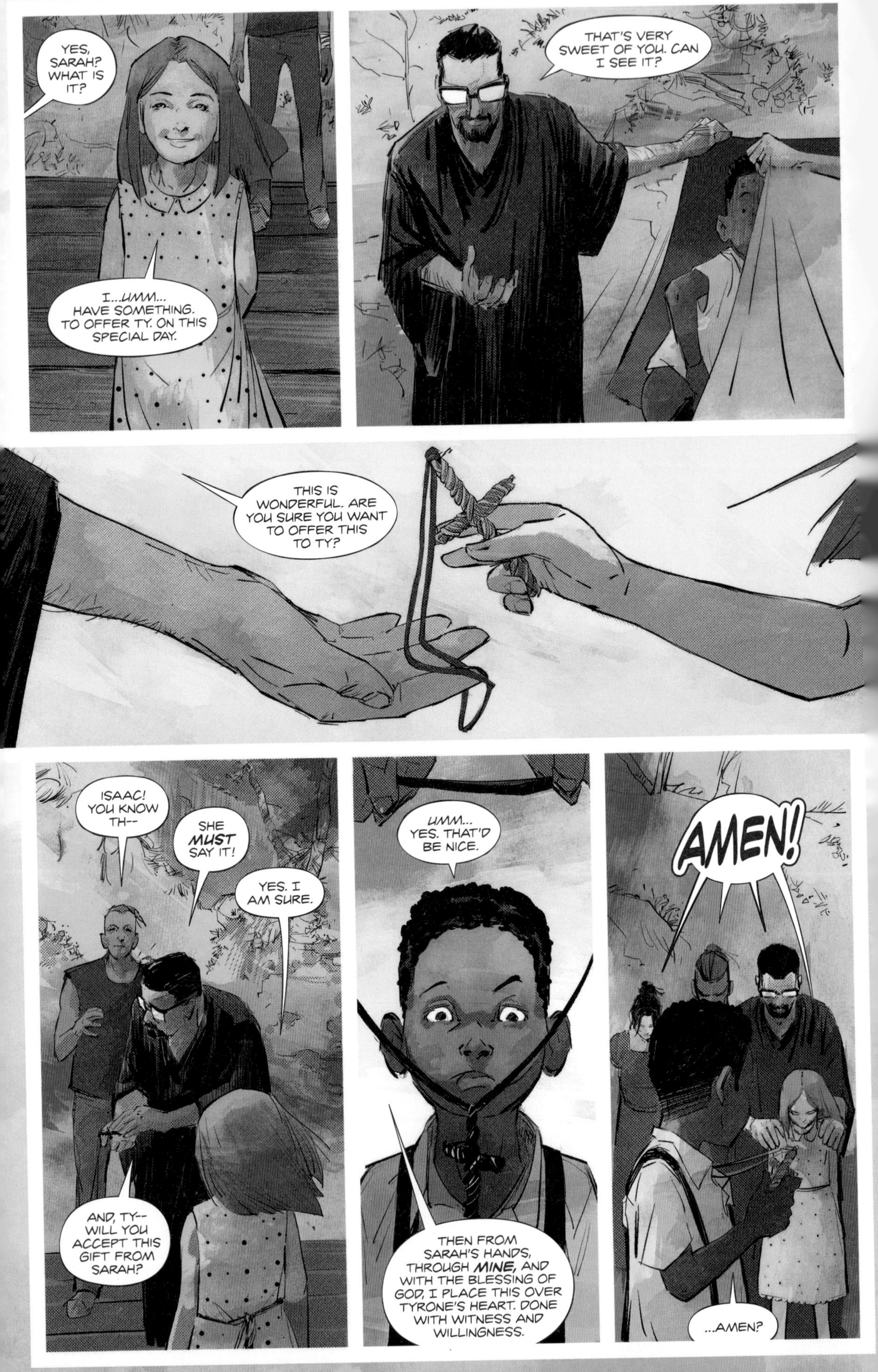
YES, SARAH? WHAT IS IT?
I...UMM... HAVE SOMETHING. TO OFFER TY. ON THIS SPECIAL DAY.
THAT'S VERY SWEET OF YOU. CAN I SEE IT?
THIS IS WONDERFUL. ARE YOU SURE YOU WANT TO OFFER THIS TO TY?
ISAAC! YOU KNOW TH--
SHE MUST SAY IT!
YES. I AM SURE.
AND, TY-- WILL YOU ACCEPT THIS GIFT FROM SARAH?
UMM... YES. THAT'D BE NICE.
THEN FROM SARAH'S HANDS, THROUGH MINE, AND WITH THE BLESSING OF GOD, I PLACE THIS OVER TYRONE'S HEART. DONE WITH WITNESS AND WILLINGNESS.
AMEN!
...AMEN?

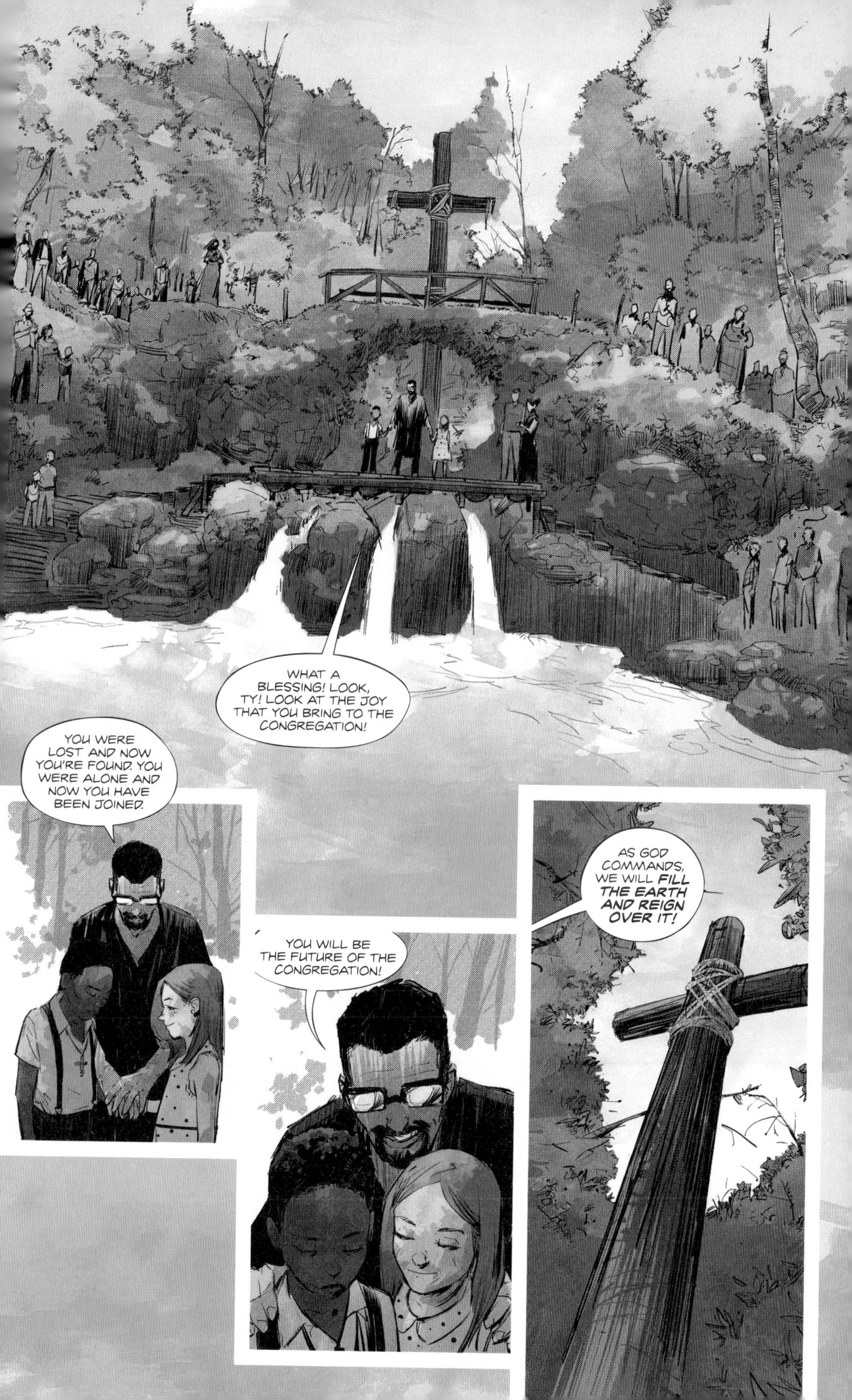
WHAT A BLESSING! LOOK, TY! LOOK AT THE JOY THAT YOU BRING TO THE CONGREGATION!
YOU WERE LOST AND NOW YOU'RE FOUND. YOU WERE ALONE AND NOW YOU HAVE BEEN JOINED.
YOU WILL BE THE FUTURE OF THE CONGREGATION!
AS GOD COMMANDS, WE WILL **FILL THE EARTH AND REIGN OVER** IT!

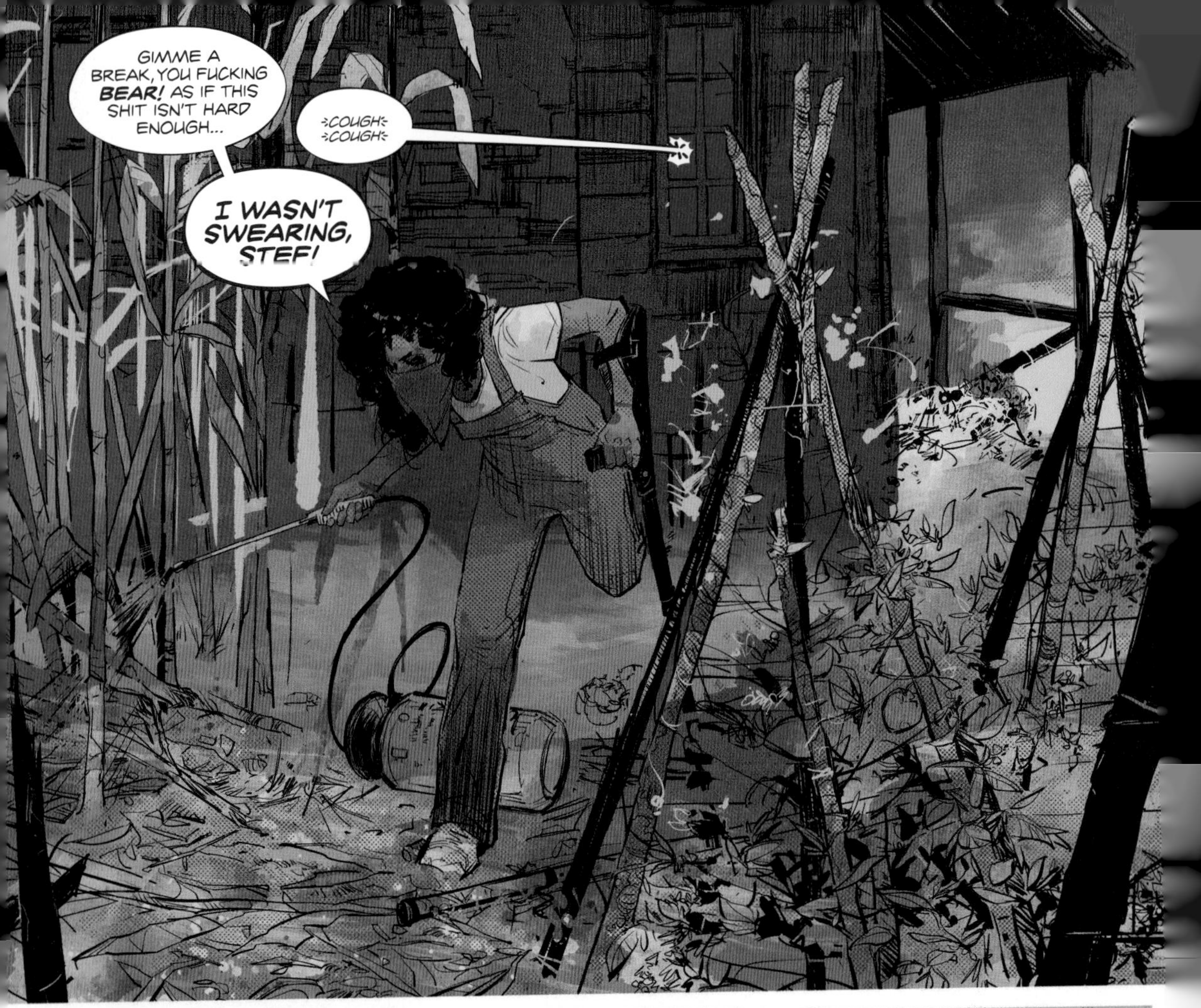
GIMME A BREAK, YOU FUCKING BEAR! AS IF THIS SHIT ISN'T HARD ENOUGH...
COUGH COUGH
I WASN'T SWEARING, STEF!

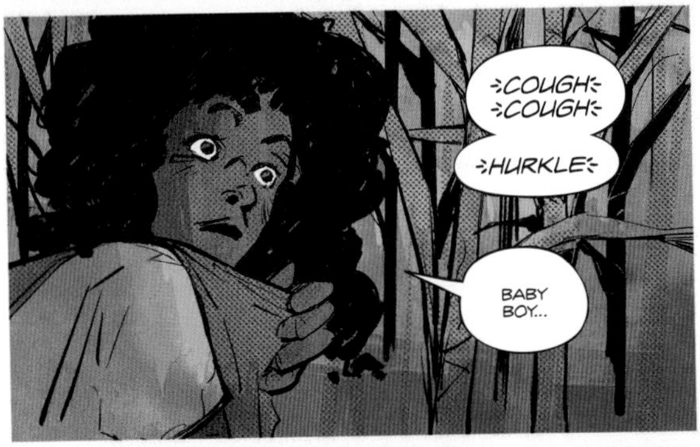
COUGH COUGH
HURKLE
BABY BOY...

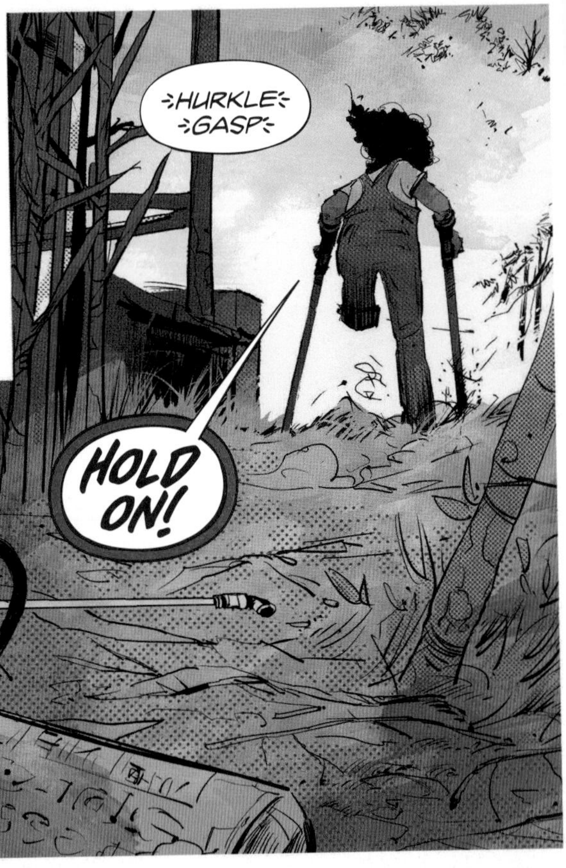
HURKLE GASP
HOLD ON!

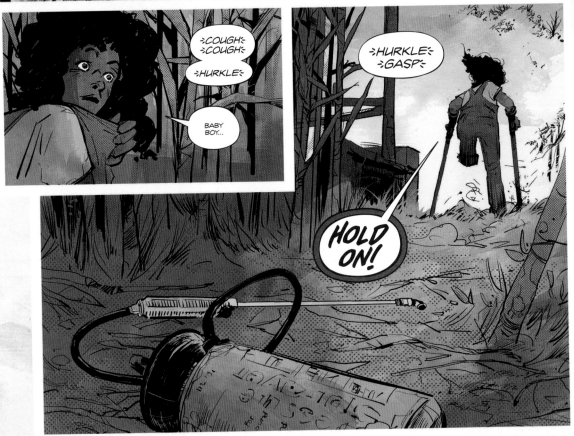

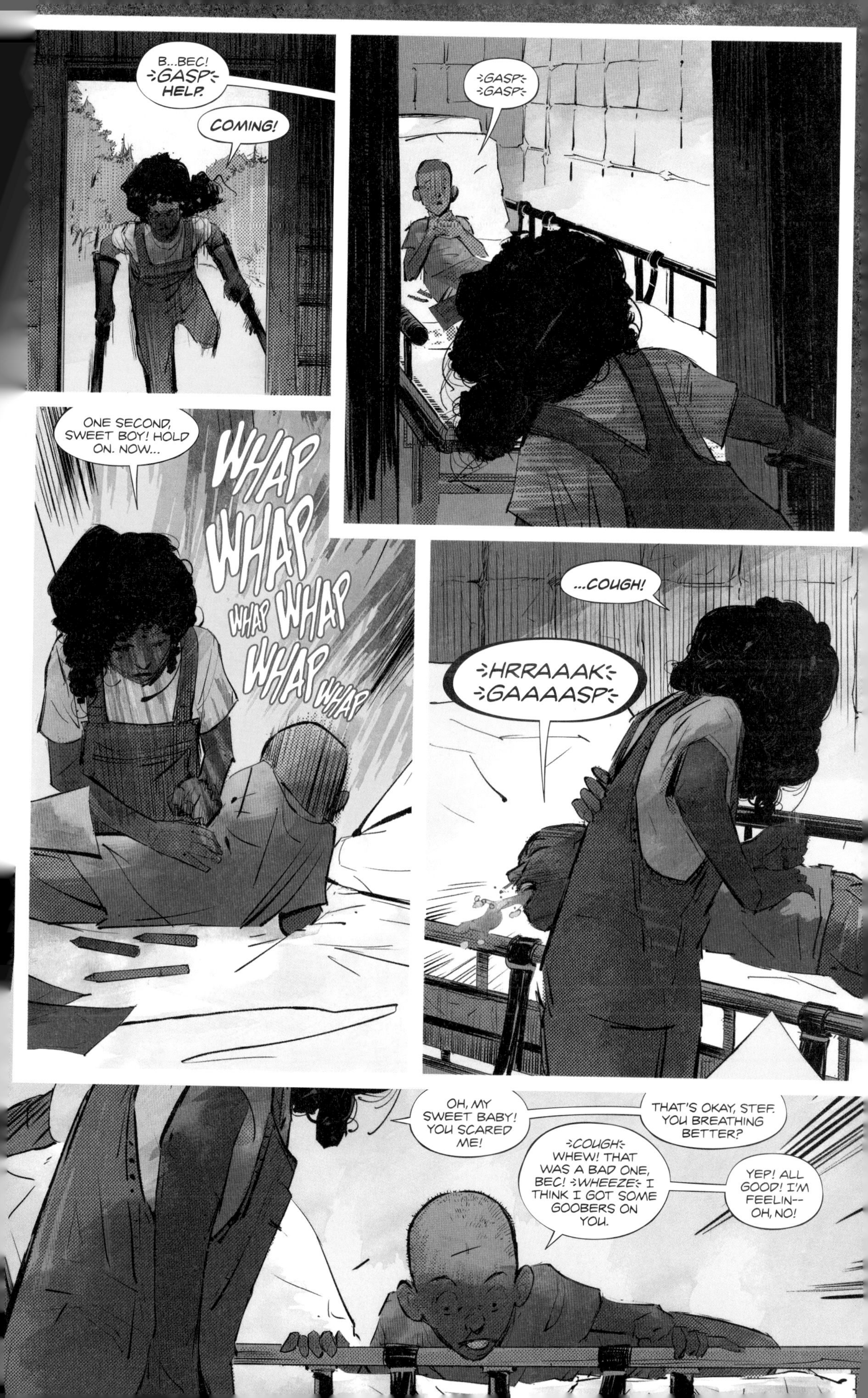
B...BEC! ~GASP~ HELP.
COMING!
~GASP~ ~GASP~
ONE SECOND, SWEET BOY! HOLD ON. NOW...
WHAP WHAP WHAP WHAP WHAP WHAP
...COUGH!
~HRRAAAK~ ~GAAAASP~
OH, MY SWEET BABY! YOU SCARED ME!
THAT'S OKAY, STEF. YOU BREATHING BETTER?
~COUGH~ WHEW! THAT WAS A BAD ONE, BEC! ~WHEEZE~ I THINK I GOT SOME GOOBERS ON YOU.
YEP! ALL GOOD! I'M FEELIN-- OH, NO!

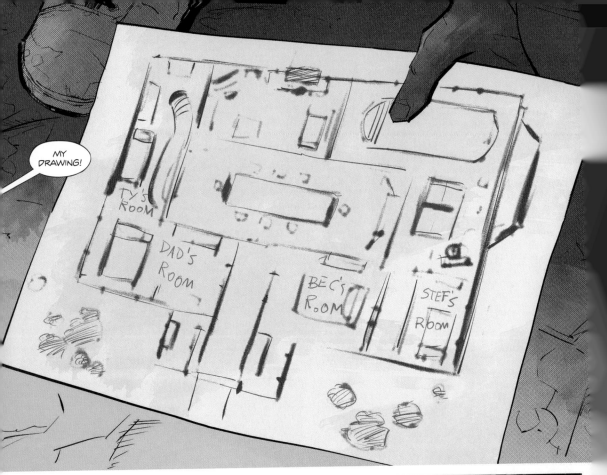

MY DRAWING!

TY'S ROOM

DAD'S ROOM

BEC'S ROOM

STEF'S ROOM

THAT'S OUR HOUSE! SEE...THERE'S YOUR ROOM. TY'S ROOM IS THE ONE WITH THE SLIDE IN IT. DAD GETS A FIREPLACE. AND THERE IS A POOL HERE.

WE CAN ALL LIVE THERE WHEN DAD AND TY GET BACK!

÷SMACK÷

I LOVE YOU, STEF.. DON'T EVER CHANGE.

WHY WOULD I?

CREAK

WHAT NOW...

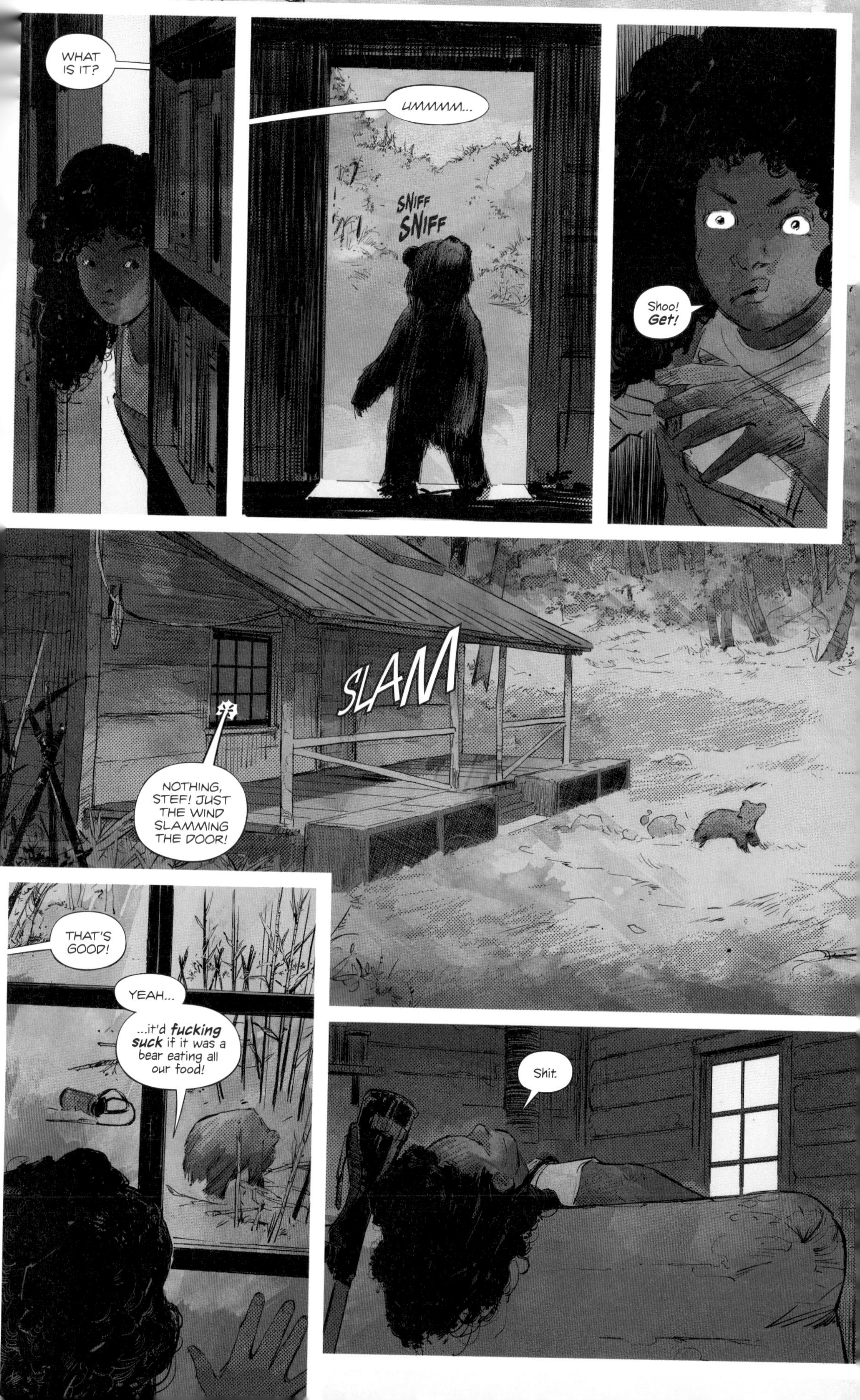
WHAT IS IT?
UMMMM...
SNIFF SNIFF
Shoo! **Get!**
SLAM
NOTHING, STEF! JUST THE WIND SLAMMING THE DOOR!
THAT'S GOOD!
YEAH...
...it'd **fucking suck** if it was a bear eating all our food!
Shit.

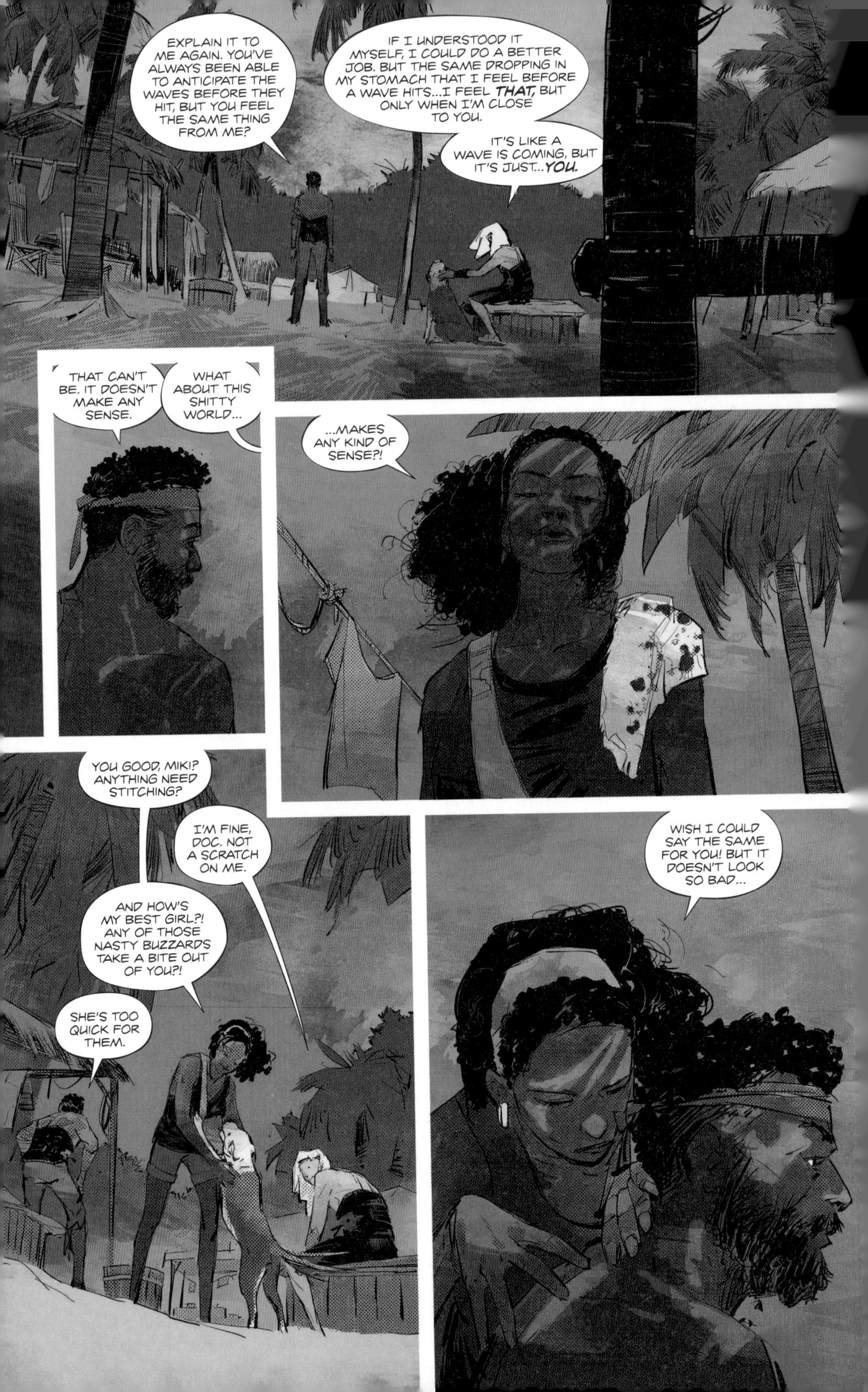
EXPLAIN IT TO ME AGAIN. YOU'VE ALWAYS BEEN ABLE TO ANTICIPATE THE WAVES BEFORE THEY HIT, BUT YOU FEEL THE SAME THING FROM ME?
IF I UNDERSTOOD IT MYSELF, I COULD DO A BETTER JOB. BUT THE SAME DROPPING IN MY STOMACH THAT I FEEL BEFORE A WAVE HITS...I FEEL **THAT,** BUT ONLY WHEN I'M CLOSE TO YOU.
IT'S LIKE A WAVE IS COMING, BUT IT'S JUST...**YOU.**
THAT CAN'T BE. IT DOESN'T MAKE ANY SENSE.
WHAT ABOUT THIS SHITTY WORLD...
...MAKES ANY KIND OF SENSE?!
YOU GOOD, MIKI? ANYTHING NEED STITCHING?
I'M FINE, DOC. NOT A SCRATCH ON ME.
AND HOW'S MY BEST GIRL?! ANY OF THOSE NASTY BUZZARDS TAKE A BITE OUT OF YOU?!
SHE'S TOO QUICK FOR THEM.
WISH I COULD SAY THE SAME FOR YOU! BUT IT DOESN'T LOOK SO BAD...

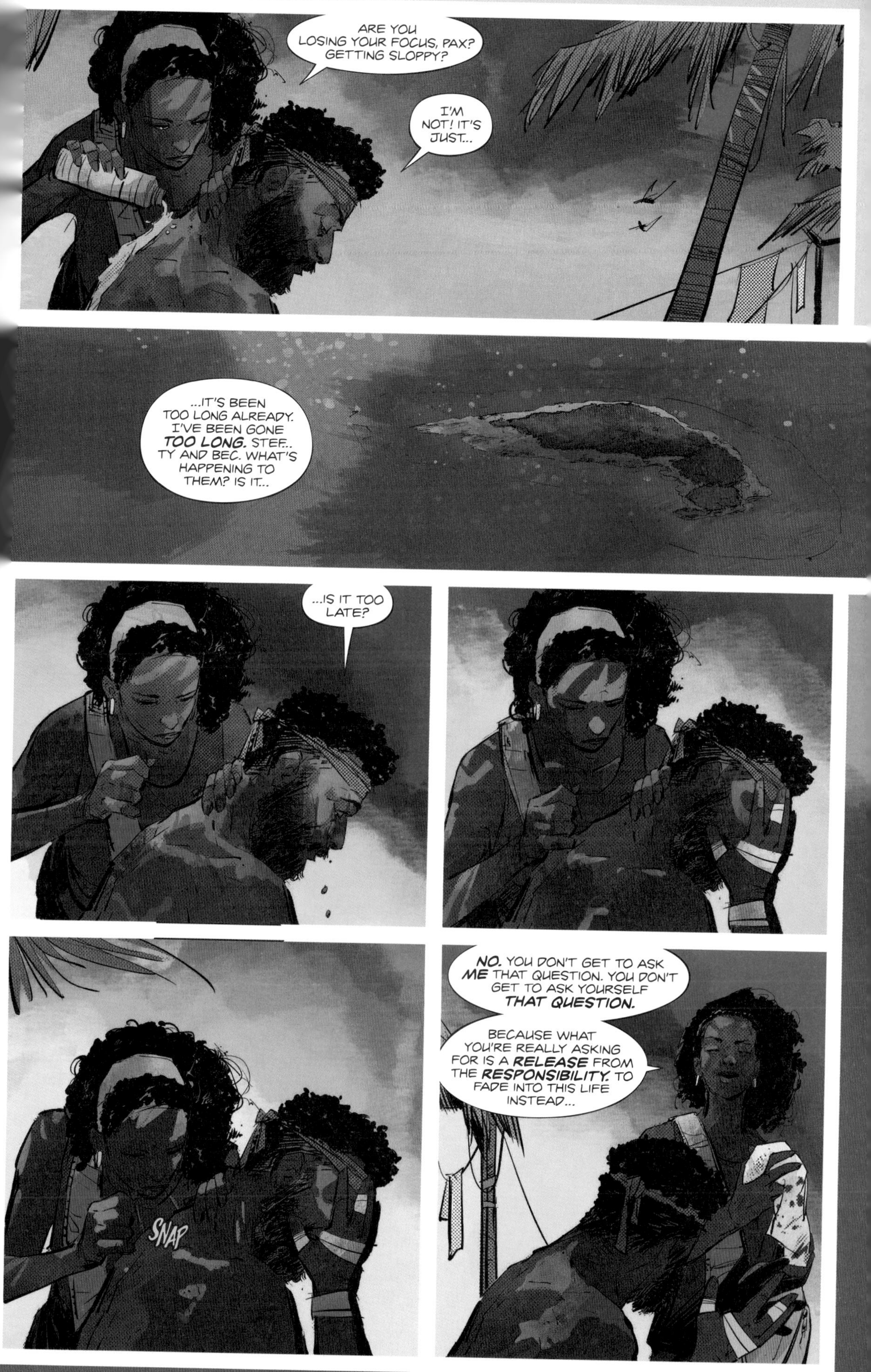

ARE YOU LOSING YOUR FOCUS, PAX? GETTING SLOPPY?
I'M NOT! IT'S JUST...
...IT'S BEEN TOO LONG ALREADY. I'VE BEEN GONE **TOO LONG.** STEF.. TY AND BEC. WHAT'S HAPPENING TO THEM? IS IT...
...IS IT TOO LATE?
SNAP
NO. YOU DON'T GET TO ASK **ME** THAT QUESTION. YOU DON'T GET TO ASK YOURSELF **THAT QUESTION.**
BECAUSE WHAT YOU'RE REALLY ASKING FOR IS A **RELEASE** FROM THE **RESPONSIBILITY.** TO FADE INTO THIS LIFE INSTEAD...

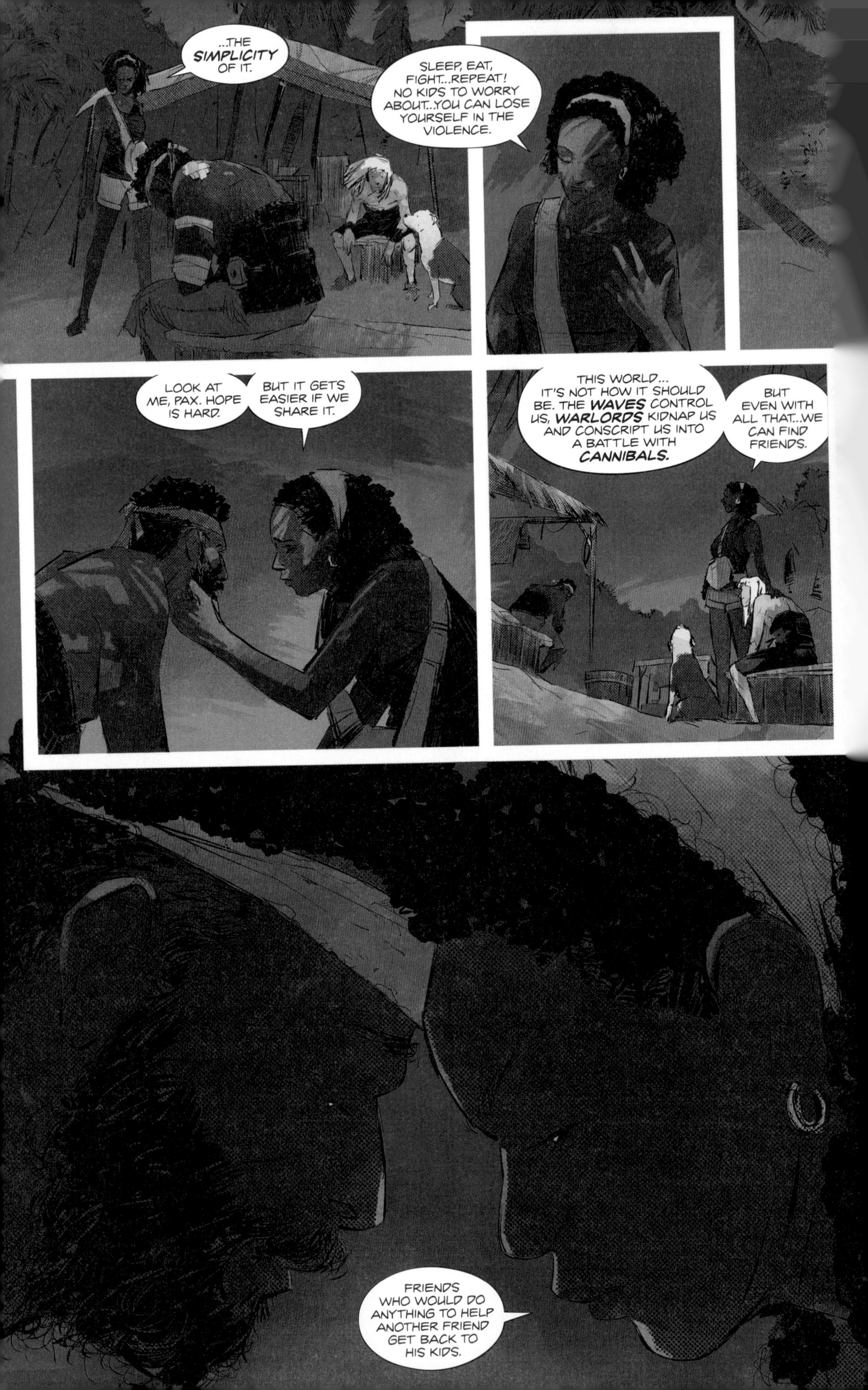
...THE SIMPLICITY OF IT.
SLEEP, EAT, FIGHT...REPEAT! NO KIDS TO WORRY ABOUT...YOU CAN LOSE YOURSELF IN THE VIOLENCE.
LOOK AT ME, PAX. HOPE IS HARD.
BUT IT GETS EASIER IF WE SHARE IT.
THIS WORLD... IT'S NOT HOW IT SHOULD BE. THE WAVES CONTROL US, WARLORDS KIDNAP US AND CONSCRIPT US INTO A BATTLE WITH CANNIBALS.
BUT EVEN WITH ALL THAT...WE CAN FIND FRIENDS.
FRIENDS WHO WOULD DO ANYTHING TO HELP ANOTHER FRIEND GET BACK TO HIS KIDS.

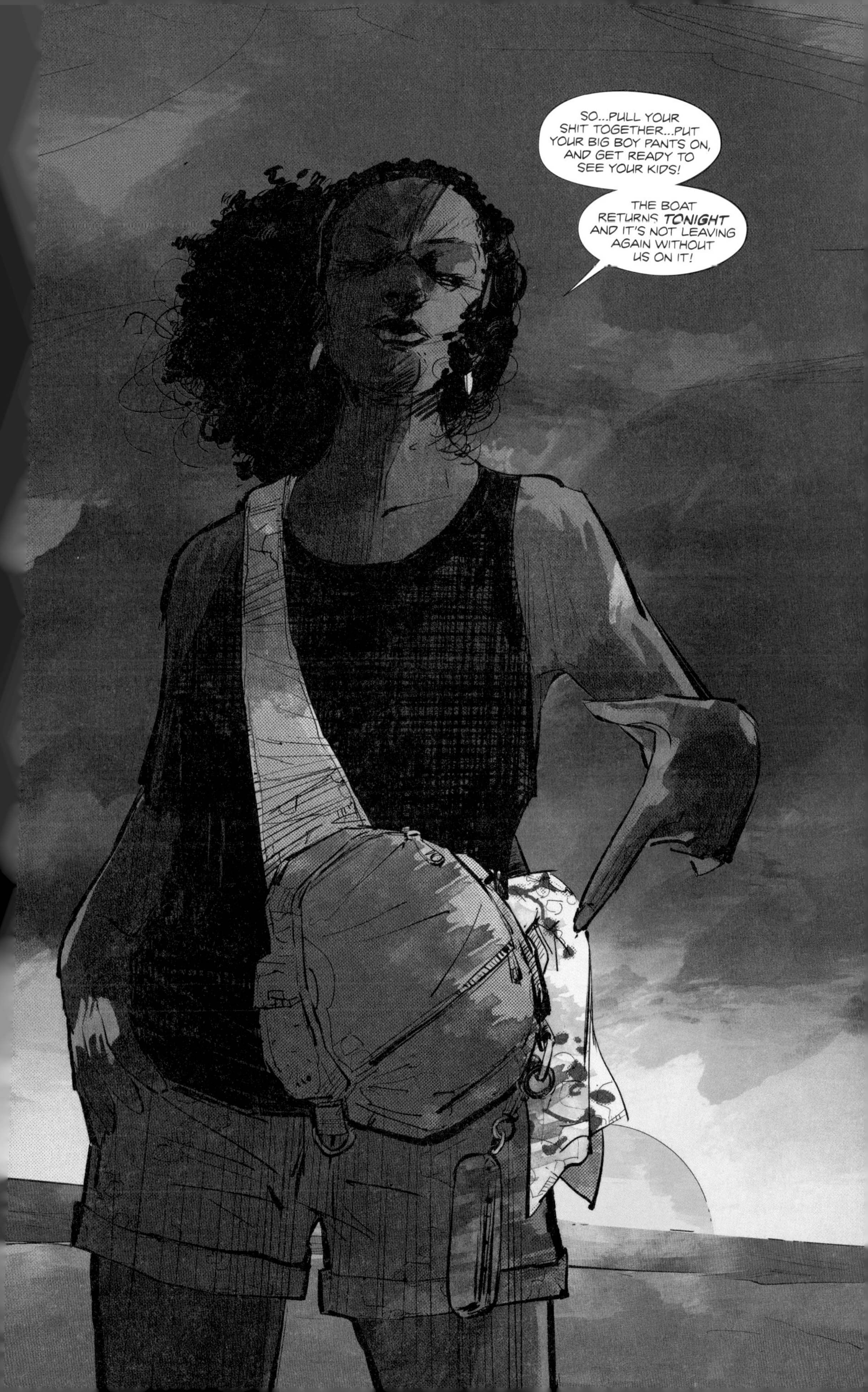
SO...PULL YOUR SHIT TOGETHER...PUT YOUR BIG BOY PANTS ON, AND GET READY TO SEE YOUR KIDS!
THE BOAT RETURNS TONIGHT AND IT'S NOT LEAVING AGAIN WITHOUT US ON IT!

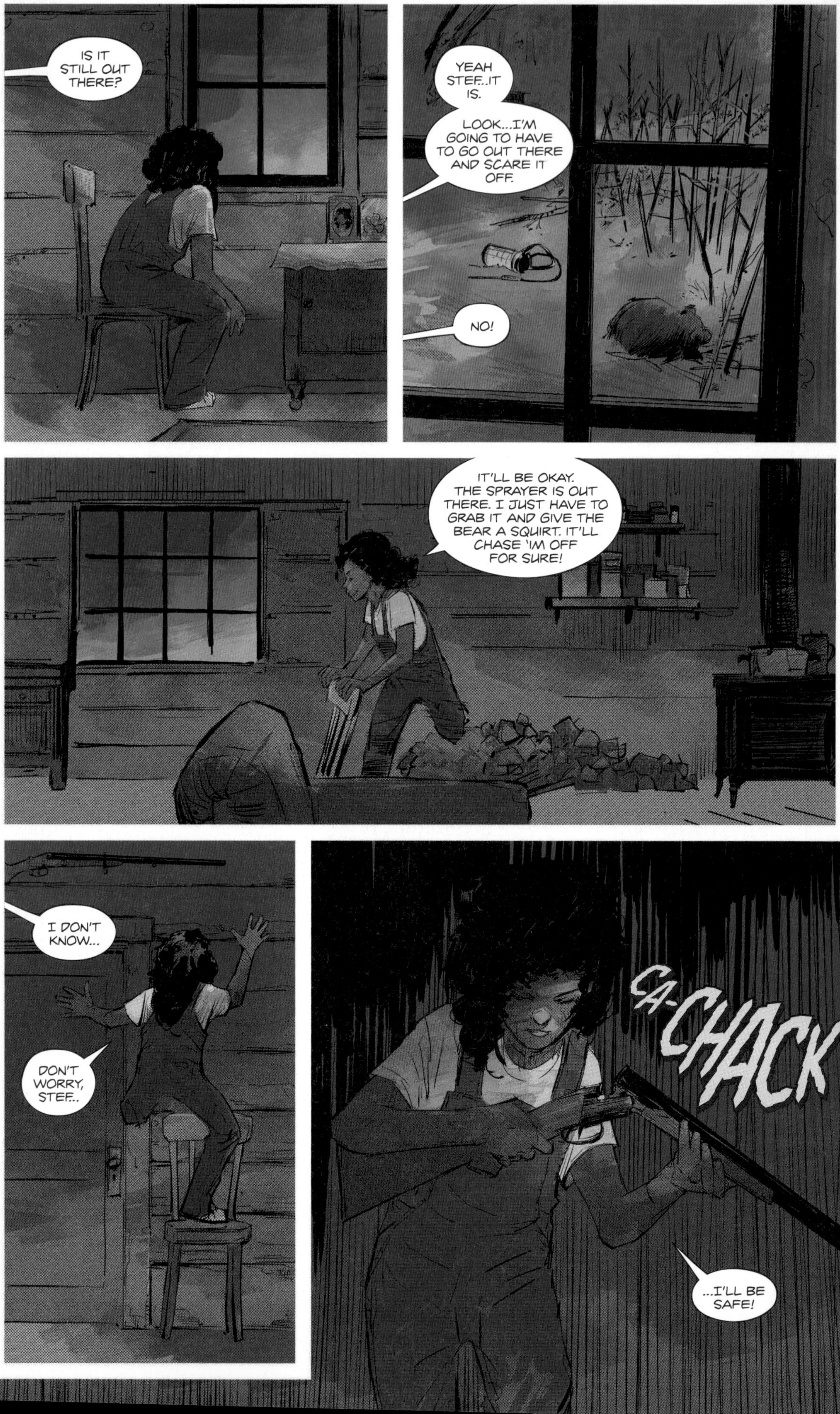
IS IT STILL OUT THERE?
YEAH STEF...IT IS.
LOOK...I'M GOING TO HAVE TO GO OUT THERE AND SCARE IT OFF.
NO!
IT'LL BE OKAY. THE SPRAYER IS OUT THERE. I JUST HAVE TO GRAB IT AND GIVE THE BEAR A SQUIRT. IT'LL CHASE 'IM OFF FOR SURE!
I DON'T KNOW...
DON'T WORRY, STEF...
CA-CHACK
...I'LL BE SAFE!

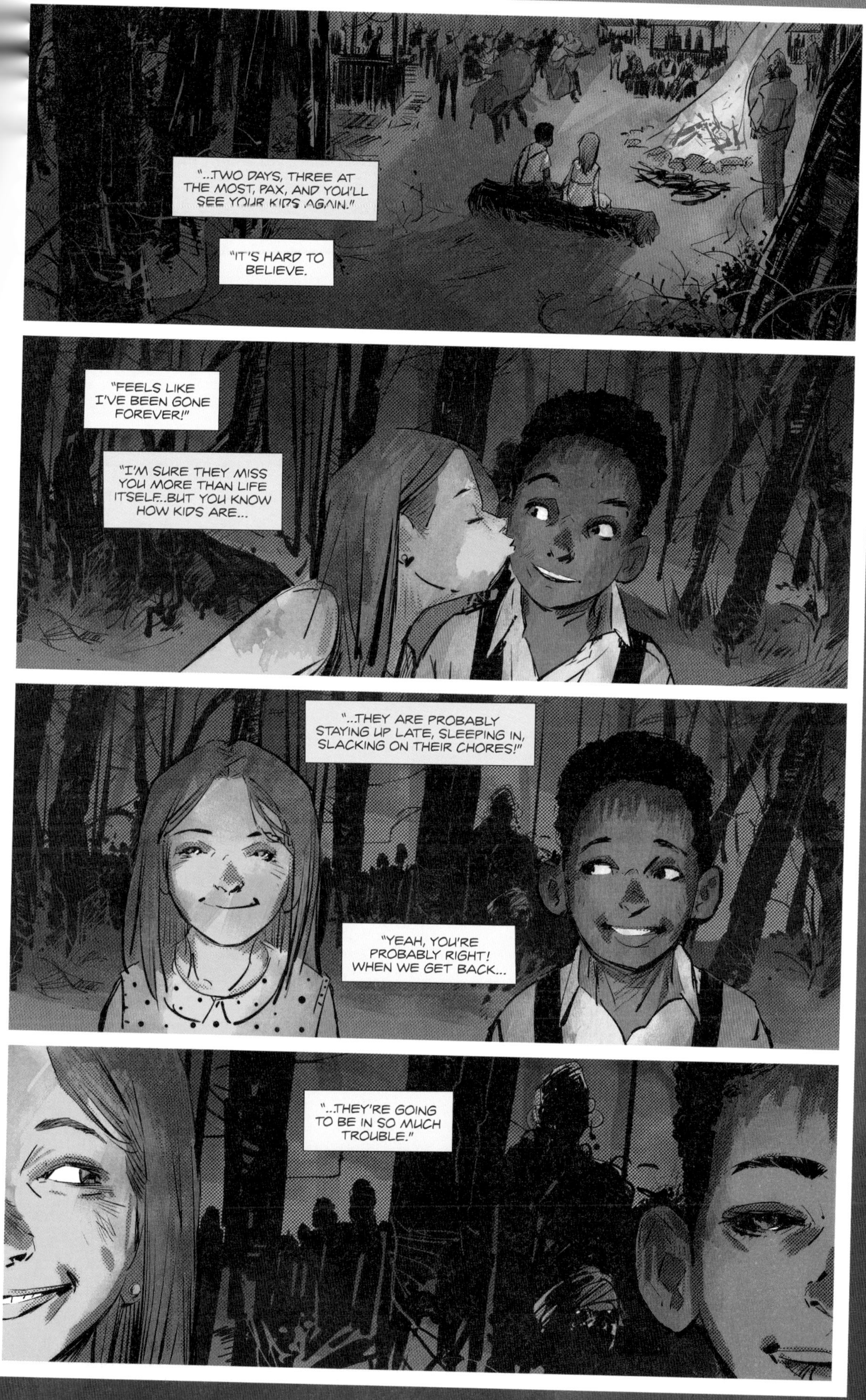
"...TWO DAYS, THREE AT THE MOST, PAX, AND YOU'LL SEE YOUR KIDS AGAIN."
"IT'S HARD TO BELIEVE.
"FEELS LIKE I'VE BEEN GONE FOREVER!"
"I'M SURE THEY MISS YOU MORE THAN LIFE ITSELF...BUT YOU KNOW HOW KIDS ARE...
"...THEY ARE PROBABLY STAYING UP LATE, SLEEPING IN, SLACKING ON THEIR CHORES!"
"YEAH, YOU'RE PROBABLY RIGHT! WHEN WE GET BACK...
"...THEY'RE GOING TO BE IN SO MUCH TROUBLE."

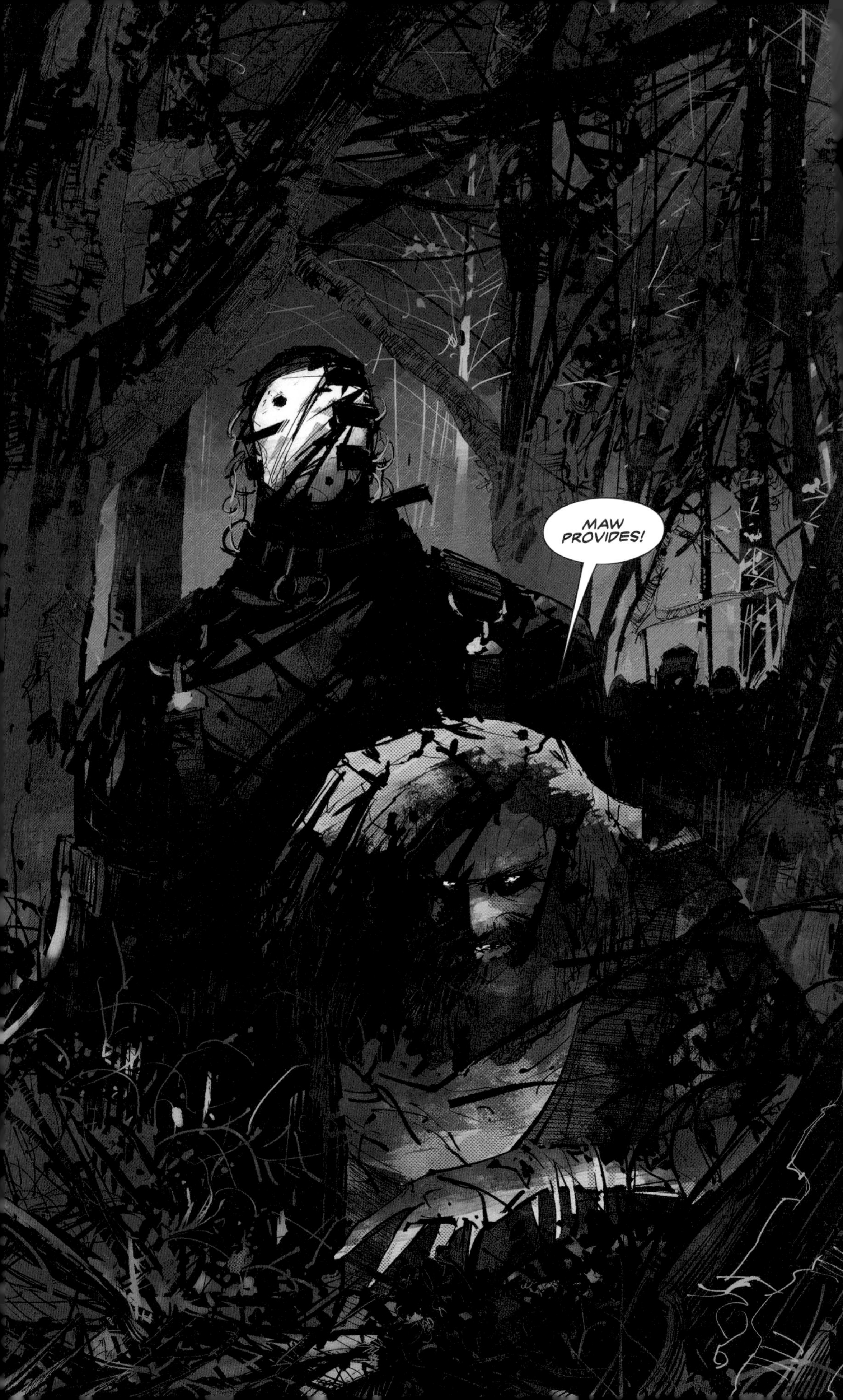
MAW PROVIDES!

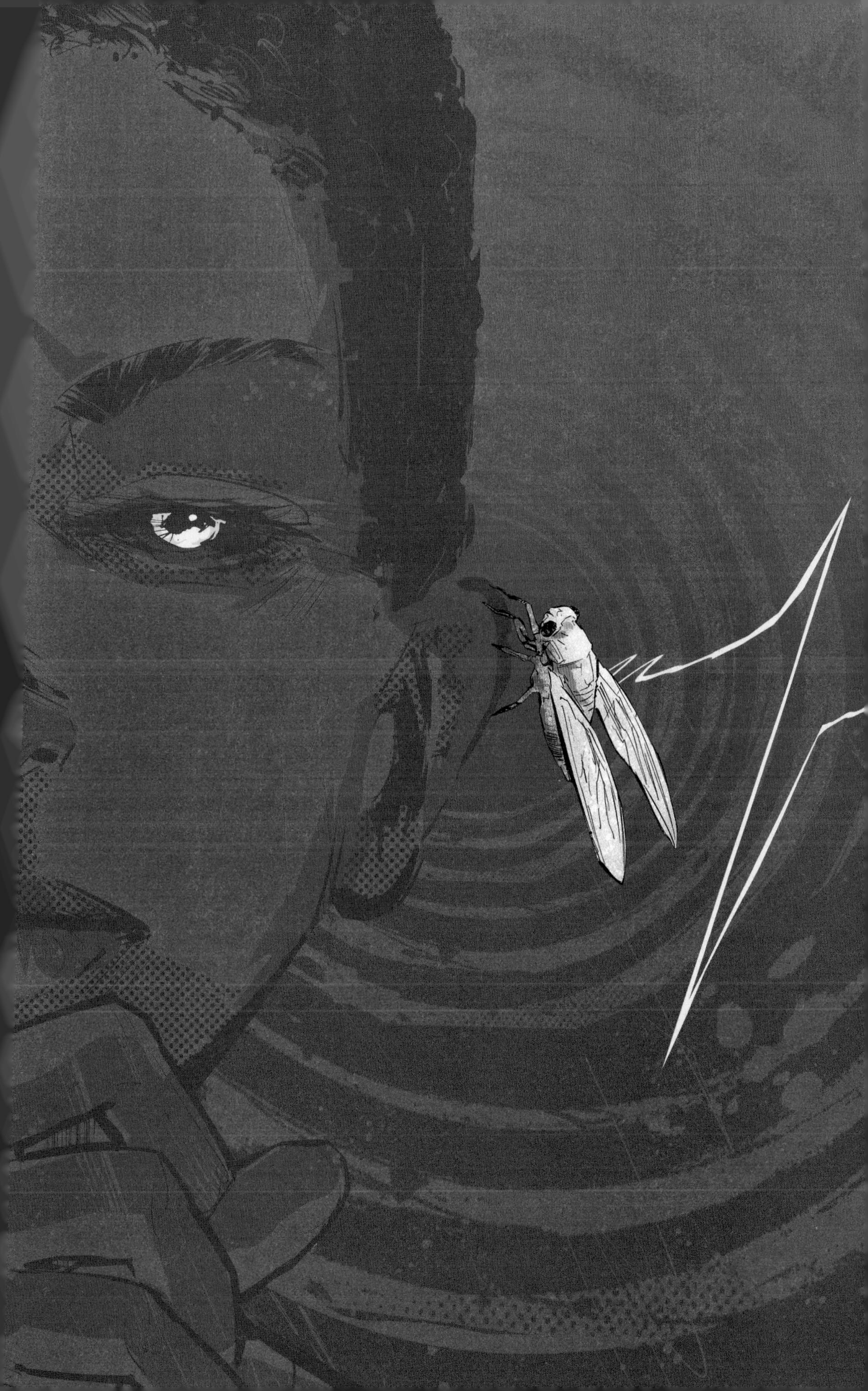

CHAPTER SIX

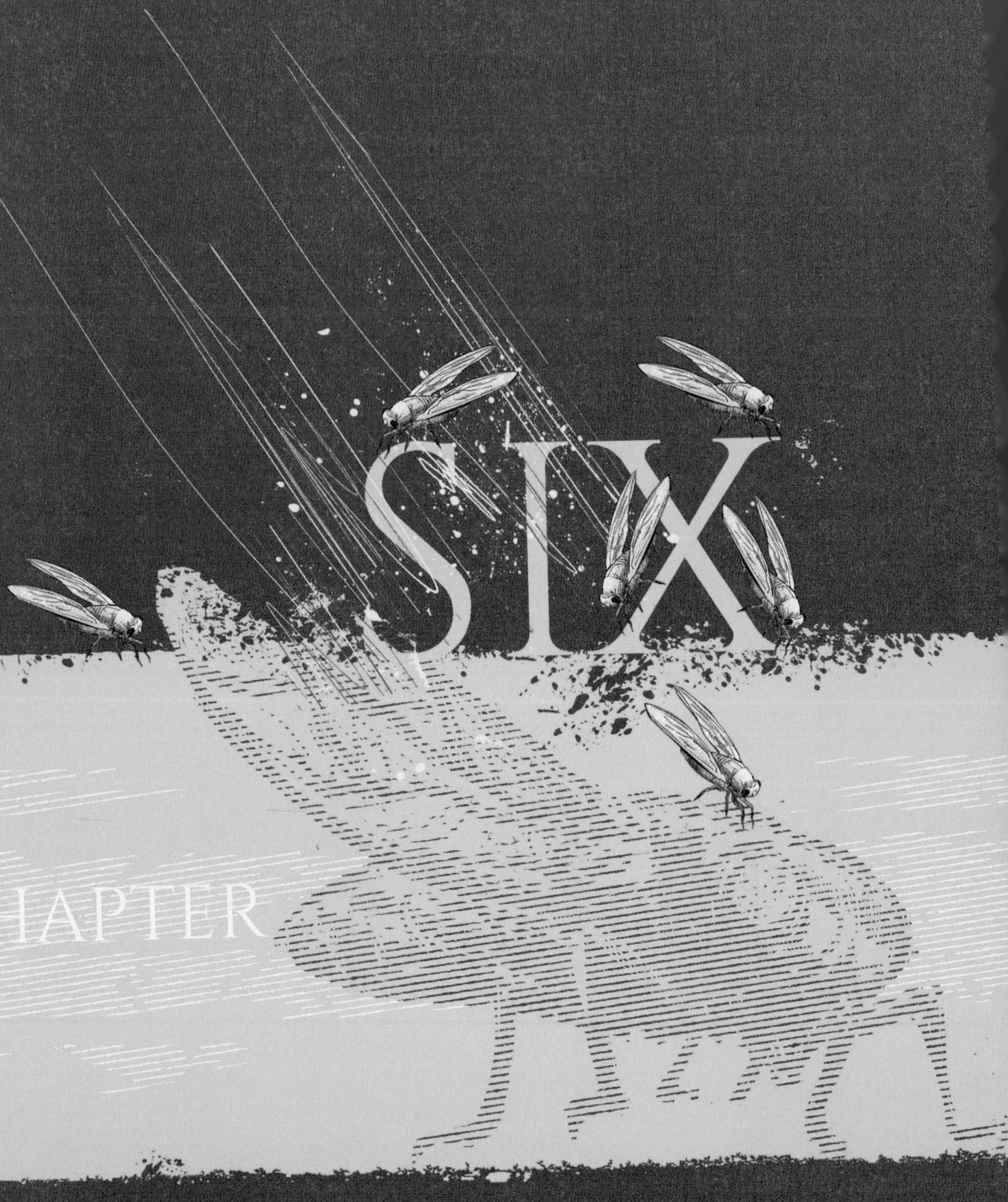

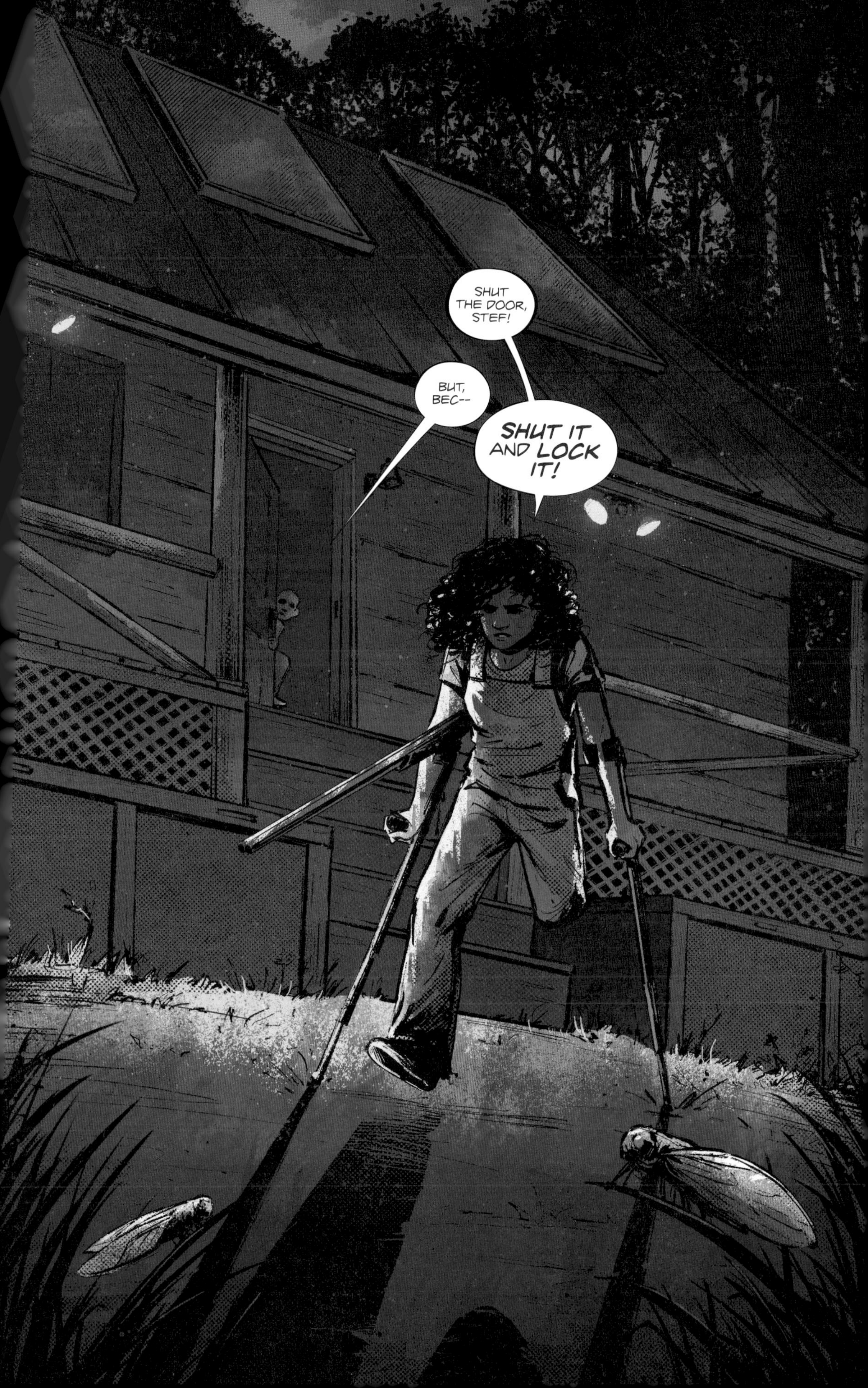
SHUT THE DOOR, STEF!
BUT, BEC--
SHUT IT AND LOCK IT!

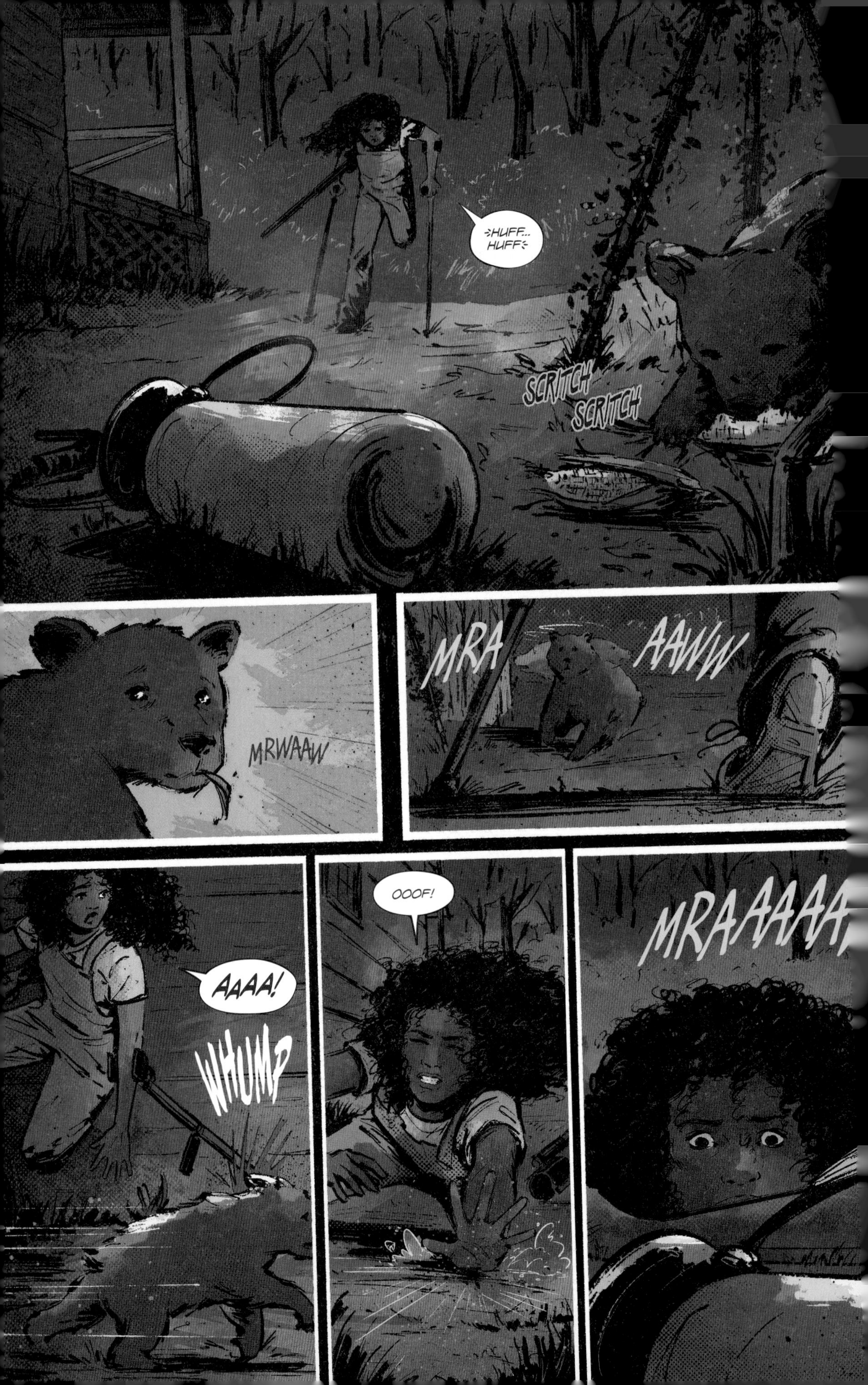

HUFF... HUFF
SCRITCH
SCRITCH
MRWAAW
MRA
AAWW
AAAA!
WHUMP
OOOF!
MRAAAAA

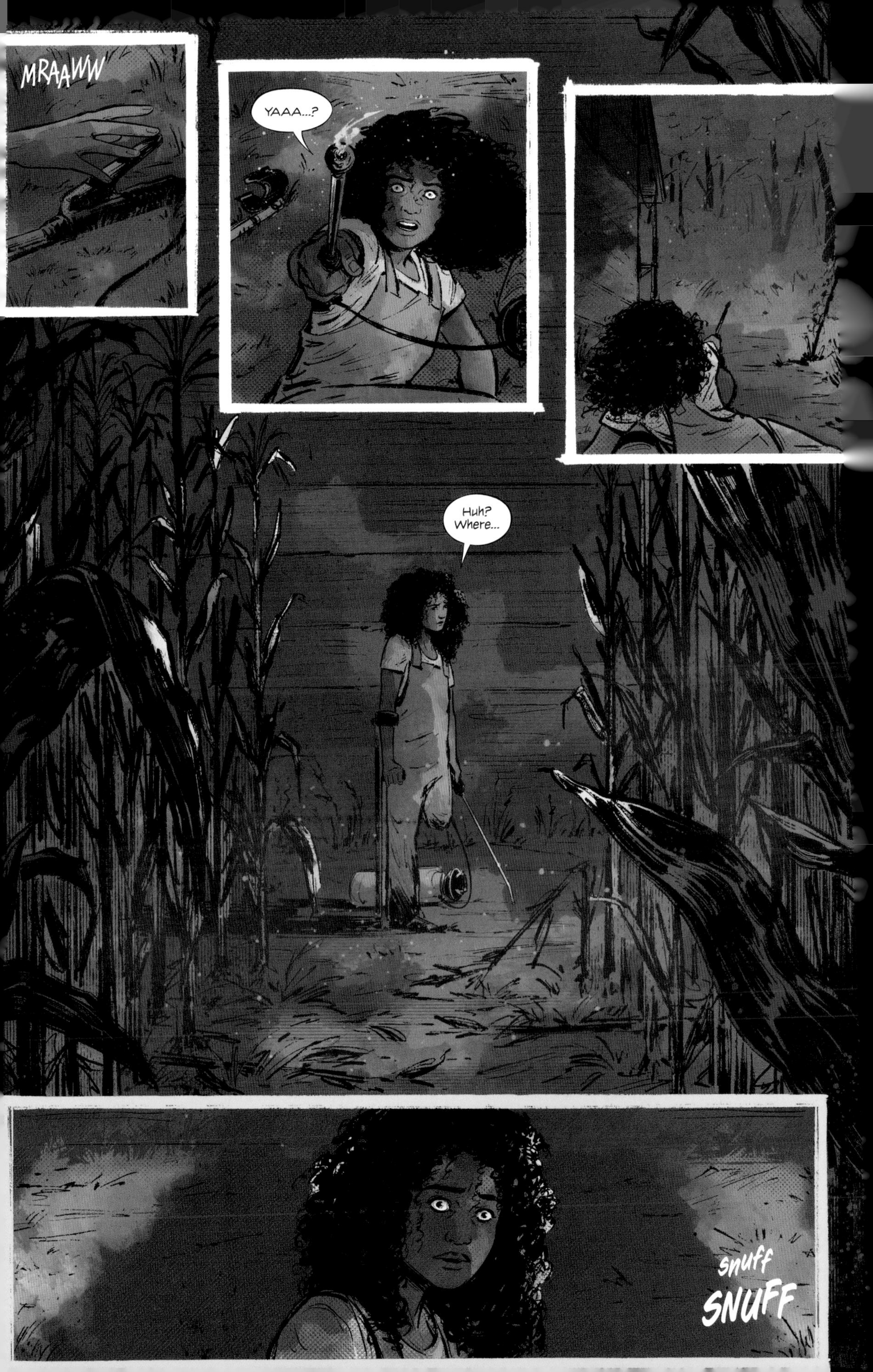
MRAAWW
YAAA...?
Huh? Where...
snuff
SNUFF

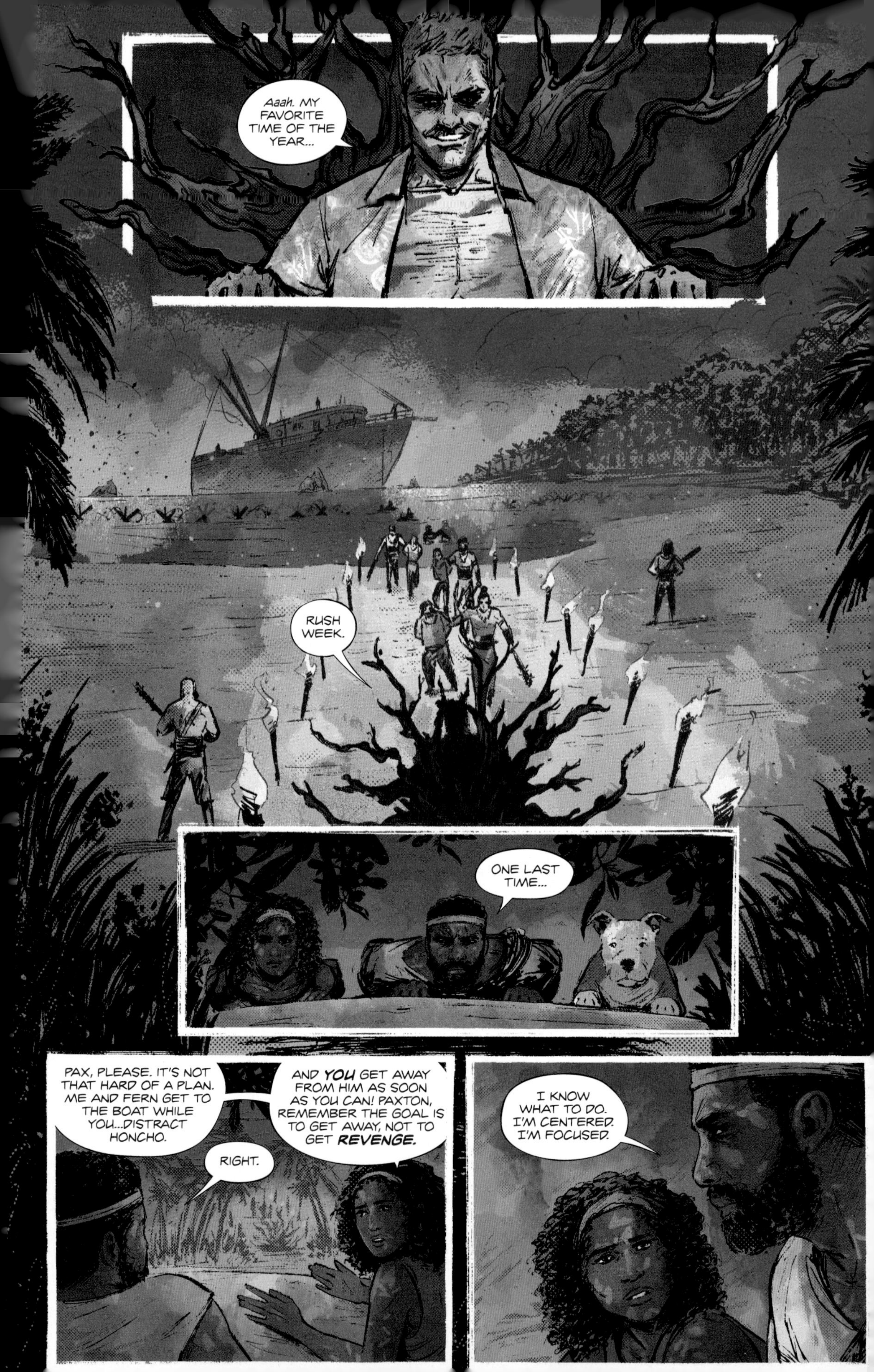

Aaah. MY FAVORITE TIME OF THE YEAR...
RUSH WEEK.
ONE LAST TIME...
PAX, PLEASE. IT'S NOT THAT HARD OF A PLAN. ME AND FERN GET TO THE BOAT WHILE YOU...DISTRACT HONCHO.
RIGHT.
AND YOU GET AWAY FROM HIM AS SOON AS YOU CAN! PAXTON, REMEMBER THE GOAL IS TO GET AWAY, NOT TO GET REVENGE.
I KNOW WHAT TO DO. I'M CENTERED. I'M FOCUSED.

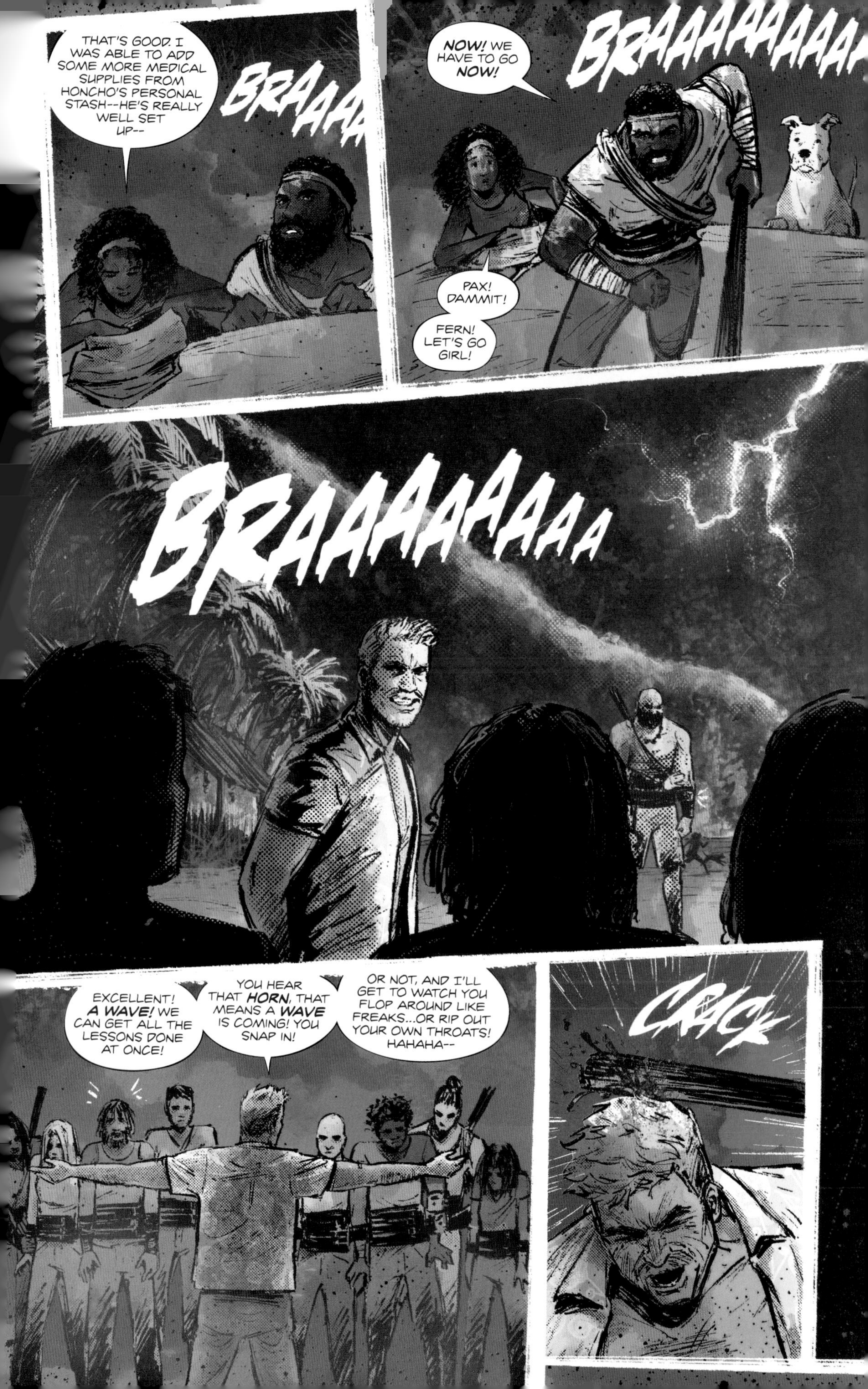
THAT'S GOOD. I WAS ABLE TO ADD SOME MORE MEDICAL SUPPLIES FROM HONCHO'S PERSONAL STASH--HE'S REALLY WELL SET UP--
BRAAAA
NOW! WE HAVE TO GO NOW!
BRAAAAAAAAA
PAX! DAMMIT!
FERN! LET'S GO GIRL!
BRAAAAAAAAA
EXCELLENT! A WAVE! WE CAN GET ALL THE LESSONS DONE AT ONCE!
YOU HEAR THAT HORN, THAT MEANS A WAVE IS COMING! YOU SNAP IN!
OR NOT, AND I'LL GET TO WATCH YOU FLOP AROUND LIKE FREAKS...OR RIP OUT YOUR OWN THROATS! HAHAHA--
CRACK

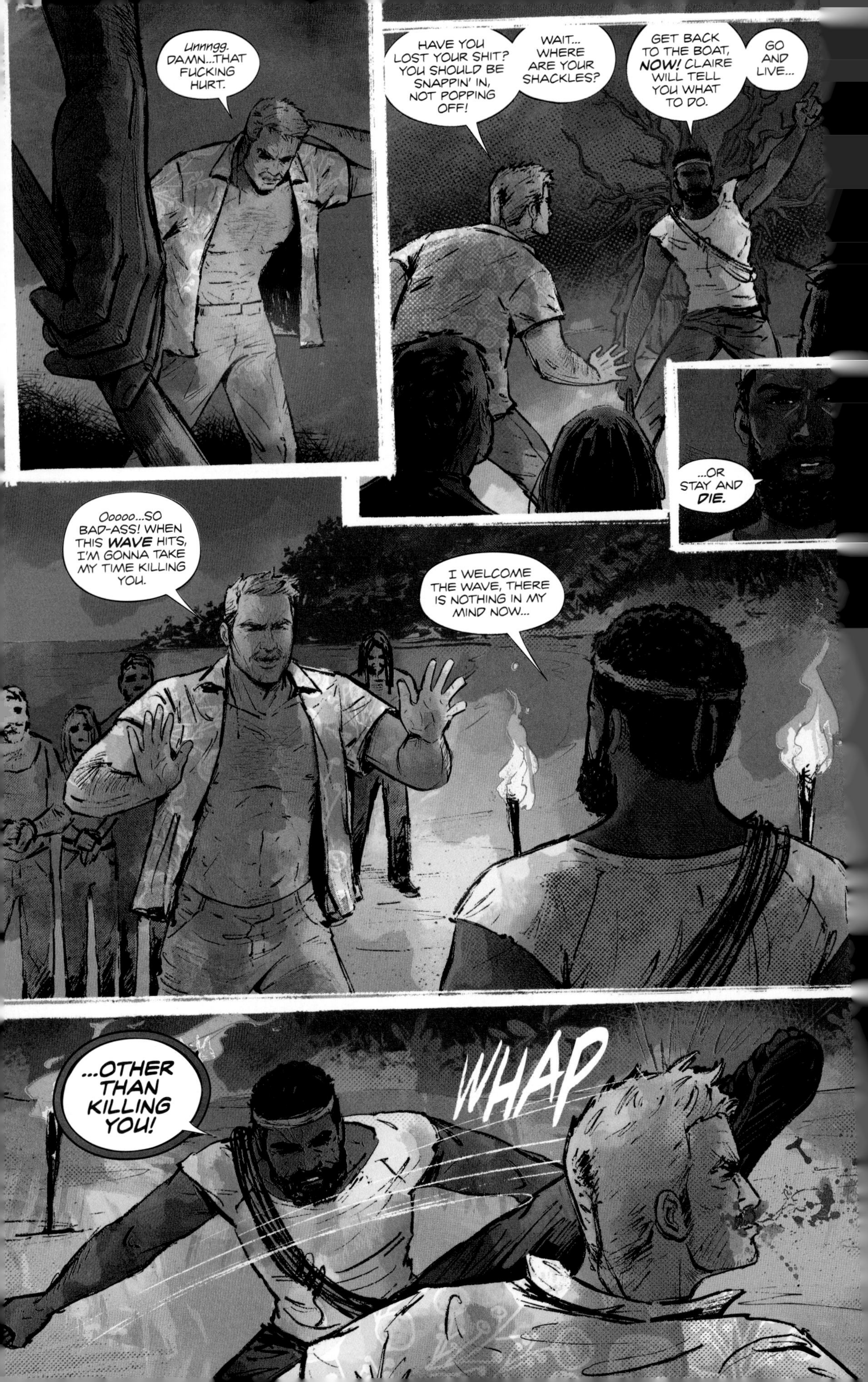
Unnngg. DAMN...THAT FUCKING HURT.
HAVE YOU LOST YOUR SHIT? YOU SHOULD BE SNAPPIN' IN, NOT POPPING OFF!
WAIT... WHERE ARE YOUR SHACKLES?
GET BACK TO THE BOAT, NOW! CLAIRE WILL TELL YOU WHAT TO DO.
GO AND LIVE...
...OR STAY AND DIE.
Ooooo...SO BAD-ASS! WHEN THIS WAVE HITS, I'M GONNA TAKE MY TIME KILLING YOU.
I WELCOME THE WAVE, THERE IS NOTHING IN MY MIND NOW...
...OTHER THAN KILLING YOU!
WHAP

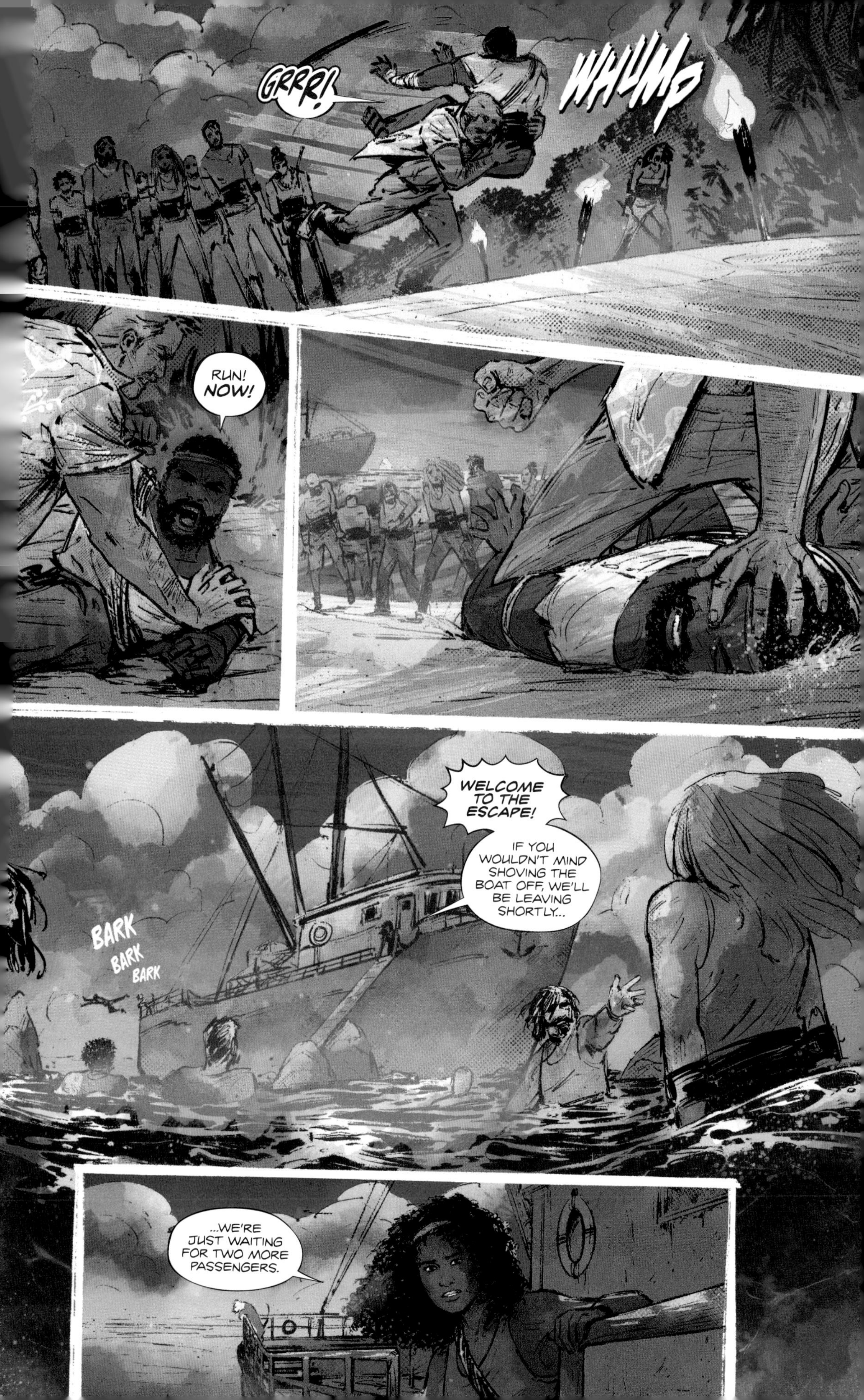
GRRR!
WHUMP
RUN! NOW!
WELCOME TO THE ESCAPE!
IF YOU WOULDN'T MIND SHOVING THE BOAT OFF, WE'LL BE LEAVING SHORTLY...
BARK
BARK
BARK
...WE'RE JUST WAITING FOR TWO MORE PASSENGERS.

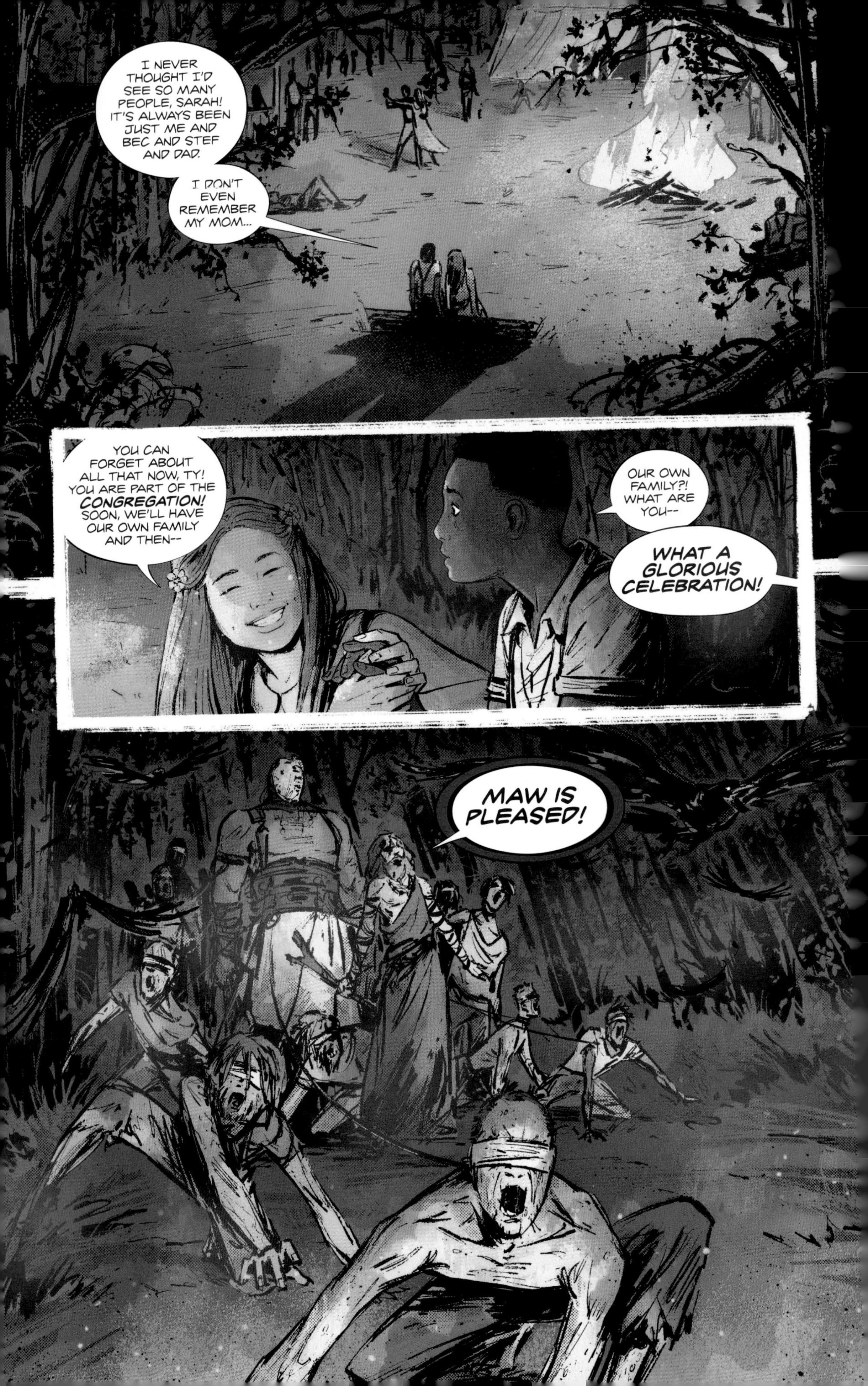
I NEVER THOUGHT I'D SEE SO MANY PEOPLE, SARAH! IT'S ALWAYS BEEN JUST ME AND BEC AND STEF AND DAD.
I DON'T EVEN REMEMBER MY MOM...
YOU CAN FORGET ABOUT ALL THAT NOW, TY! YOU ARE PART OF THE CONGREGATION! SOON, WE'LL HAVE OUR OWN FAMILY AND THEN--
OUR OWN FAMILY?! WHAT ARE YOU--
WHAT A GLORIOUS CELEBRATION!
MAW IS PLEASED!

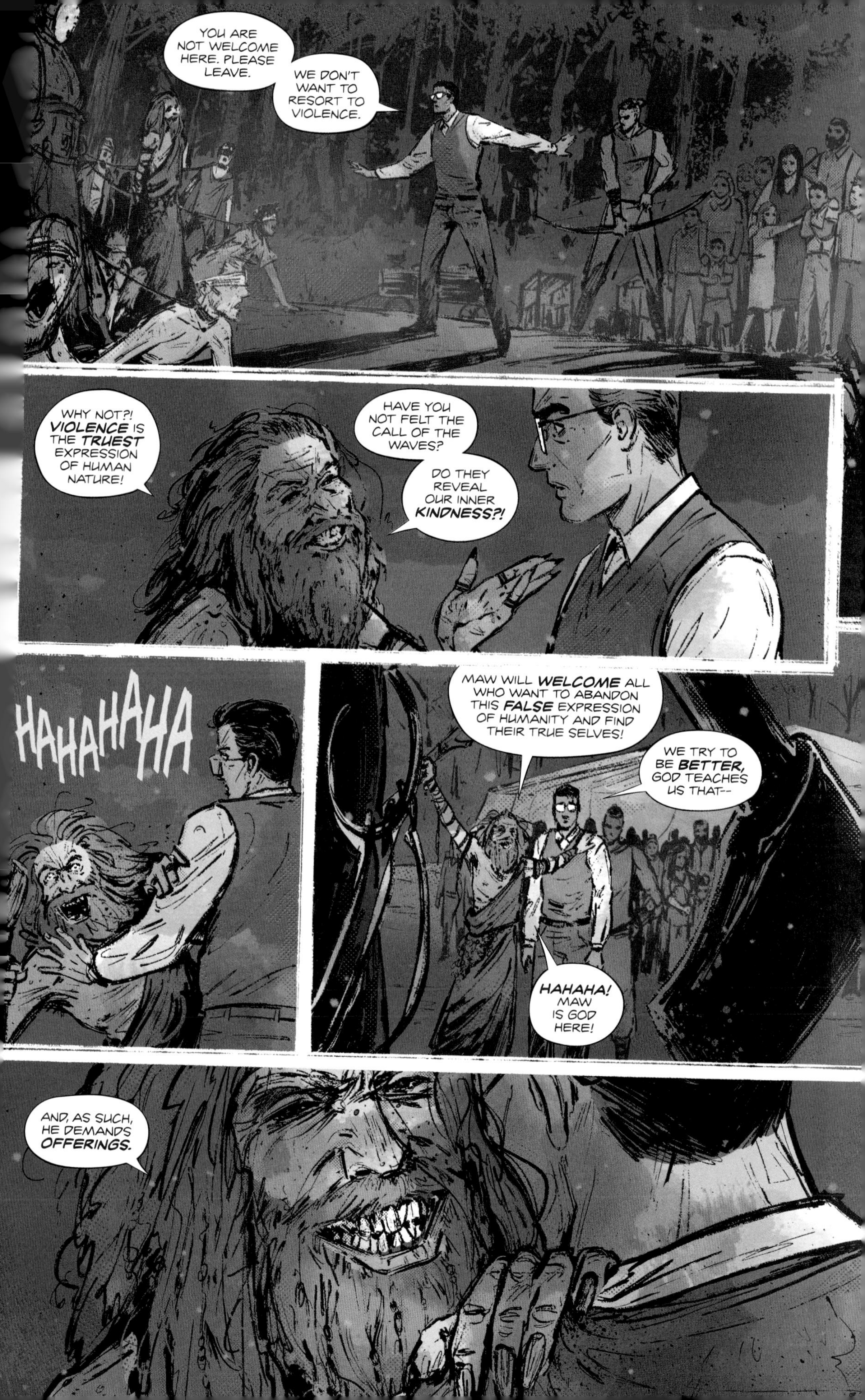

YOU ARE NOT WELCOME HERE. PLEASE LEAVE.
WE DON'T WANT TO RESORT TO VIOLENCE.
WHY NOT?! VIOLENCE IS THE TRUEST EXPRESSION OF HUMAN NATURE!
HAVE YOU NOT FELT THE CALL OF THE WAVES?
DO THEY REVEAL OUR INNER KINDNESS?!
HAHAHAHAHA
MAW WILL WELCOME ALL WHO WANT TO ABANDON THIS FALSE EXPRESSION OF HUMANITY AND FIND THEIR TRUE SELVES!
WE TRY TO BE BETTER, GOD TEACHES US THAT--
HAHAHA! MAW IS GOD HERE!
AND, AS SUCH, HE DEMANDS OFFERINGS.

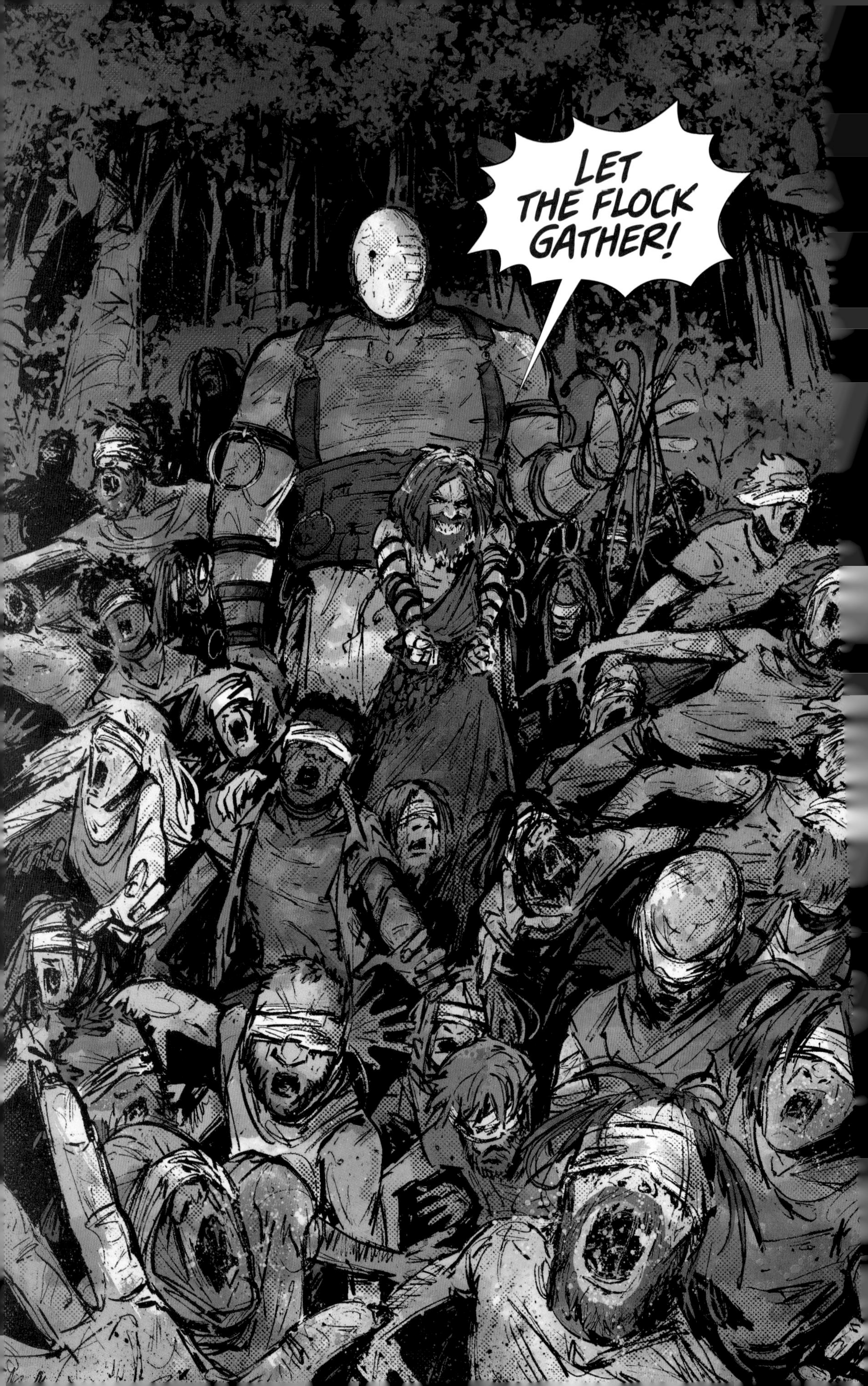
LET THE FLOCK GATHER!

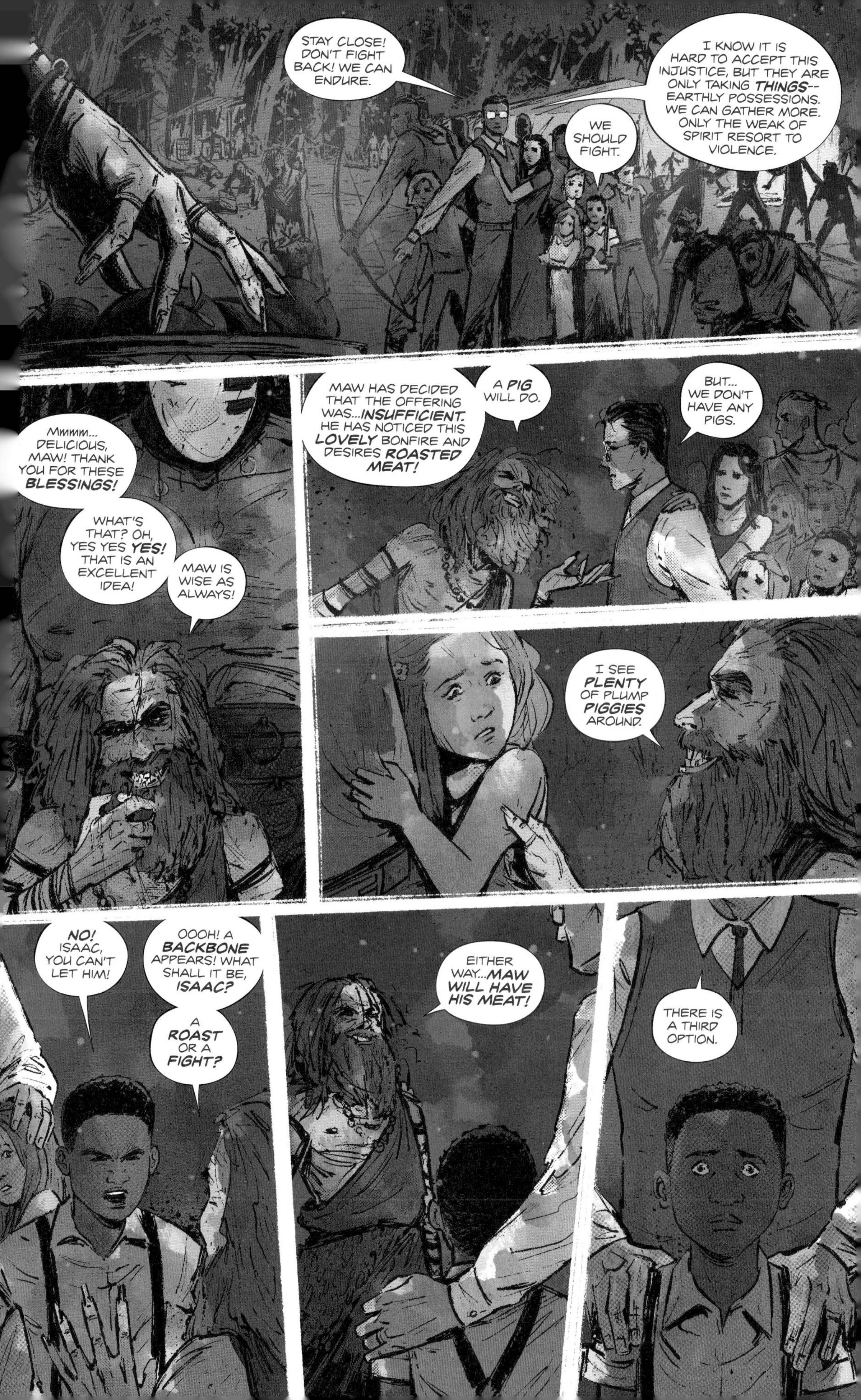
STAY CLOSE! DON'T FIGHT BACK! WE CAN ENDURE.
I KNOW IT IS HARD TO ACCEPT THIS INJUSTICE, BUT THEY ARE ONLY TAKING THINGS-- EARTHLY POSSESSIONS. WE CAN GATHER MORE. ONLY THE WEAK OF SPIRIT RESORT TO VIOLENCE.
WE SHOULD FIGHT.
Mmmm... DELICIOUS, MAW! THANK YOU FOR THESE BLESSINGS!
WHAT'S THAT? OH, YES YES YES! THAT IS AN EXCELLENT IDEA!
MAW IS WISE AS ALWAYS!
MAW HAS DECIDED THAT THE OFFERING WAS...INSUFFICIENT. HE HAS NOTICED THIS LOVELY BONFIRE AND DESIRES ROASTED MEAT!
A PIG WILL DO.
BUT... WE DON'T HAVE ANY PIGS.
I SEE PLENTY OF PLUMP PIGGIES AROUND.
NO! ISAAC, YOU CAN'T LET HIM!
OOOH! A BACKBONE APPEARS! WHAT SHALL IT BE, ISAAC?
A ROAST OR A FIGHT?
EITHER WAY...MAW WILL HAVE HIS MEAT!
THERE IS A THIRD OPTION.

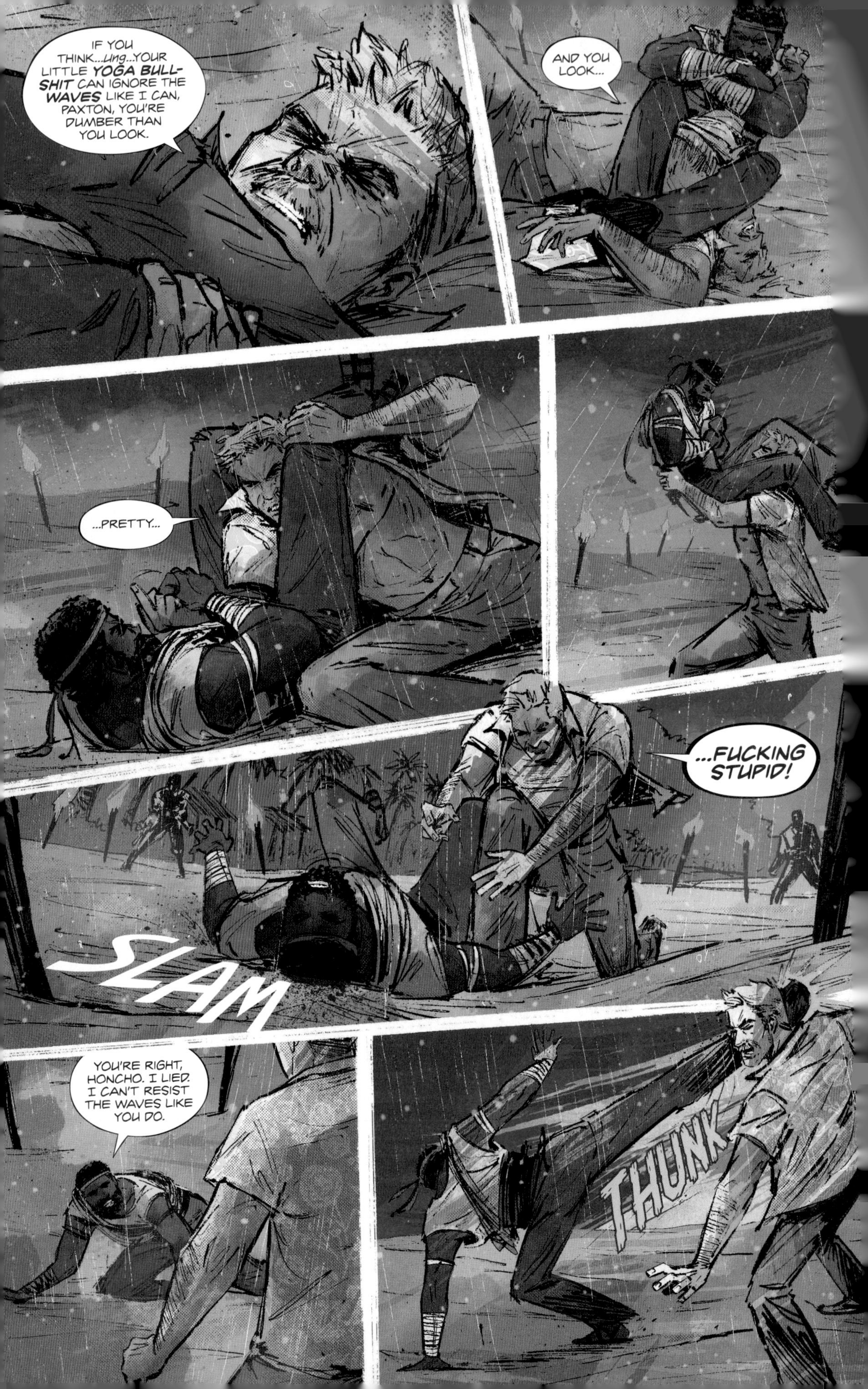
IF YOU THINK...*ung*...YOUR LITTLE **YOGA BULL-SHIT** CAN IGNORE THE **WAVES** LIKE I CAN, PAXTON, YOU'RE DUMBER THAN YOU LOOK.
AND YOU LOOK...
...PRETTY...
...FUCKING STUPID!
SLAM
YOU'RE RIGHT, HONCHO. I LIED. I CAN'T RESIST THE WAVES LIKE YOU DO.
THUNK

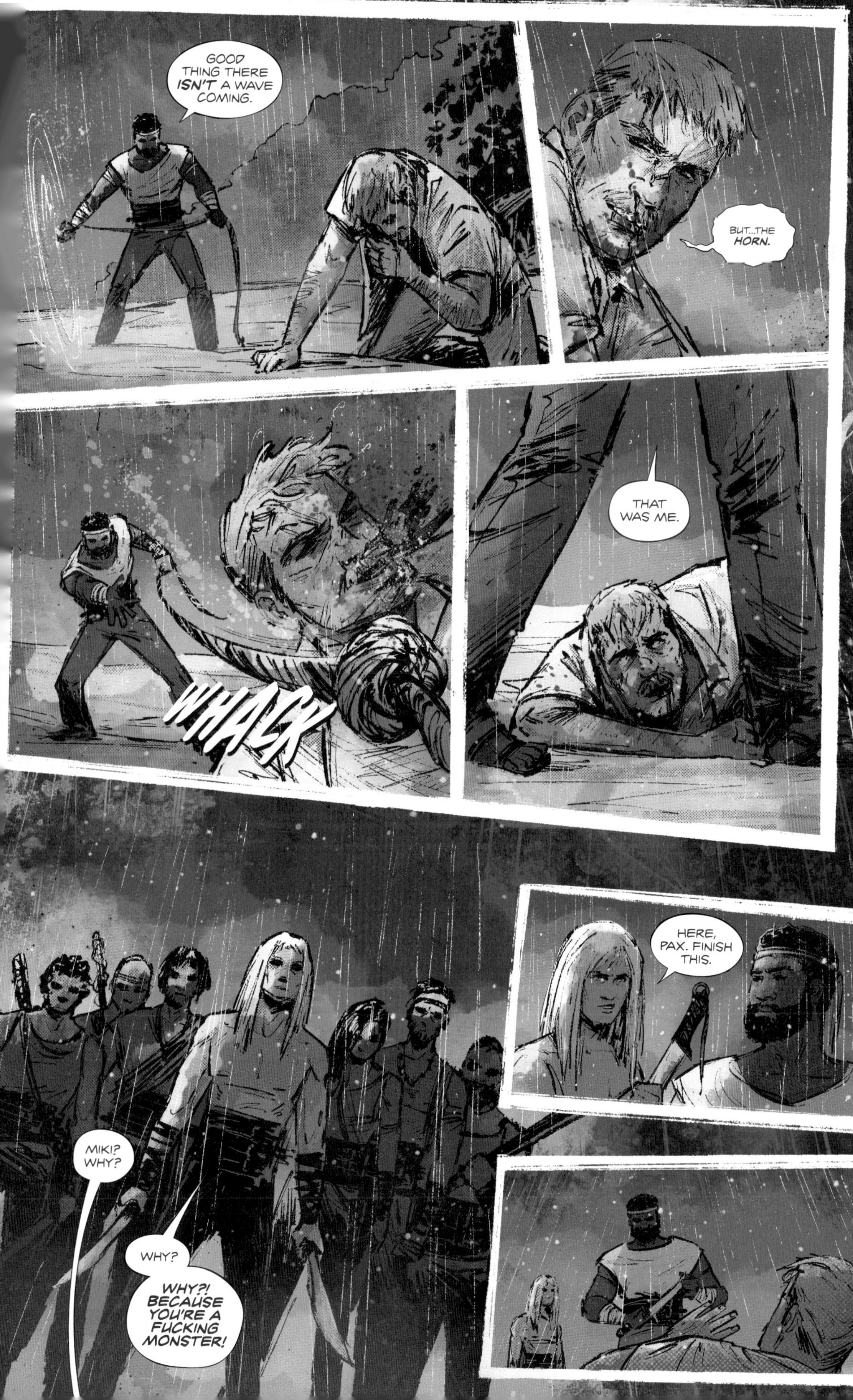
GOOD THING THERE ISN'T A WAVE COMING.
BUT...THE HORN.
WHACK
THAT WAS ME.
MIKI? WHY?
WHY?
WHY?! BECAUSE YOU'RE A FUCKING MONSTER!
HERE, PAX. FINISH THIS.

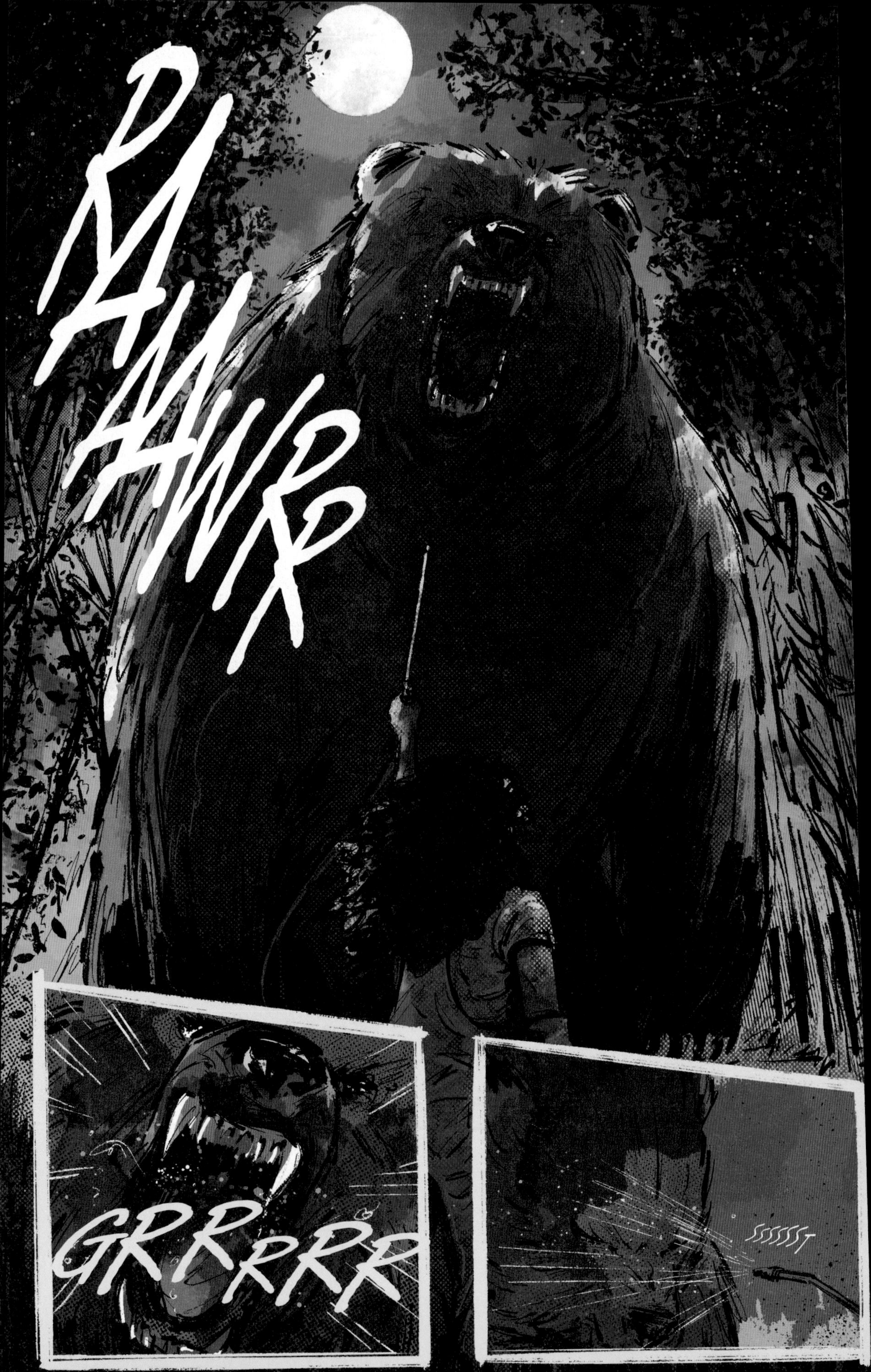
RAAWRR
GRRRRRR
SSSSSST

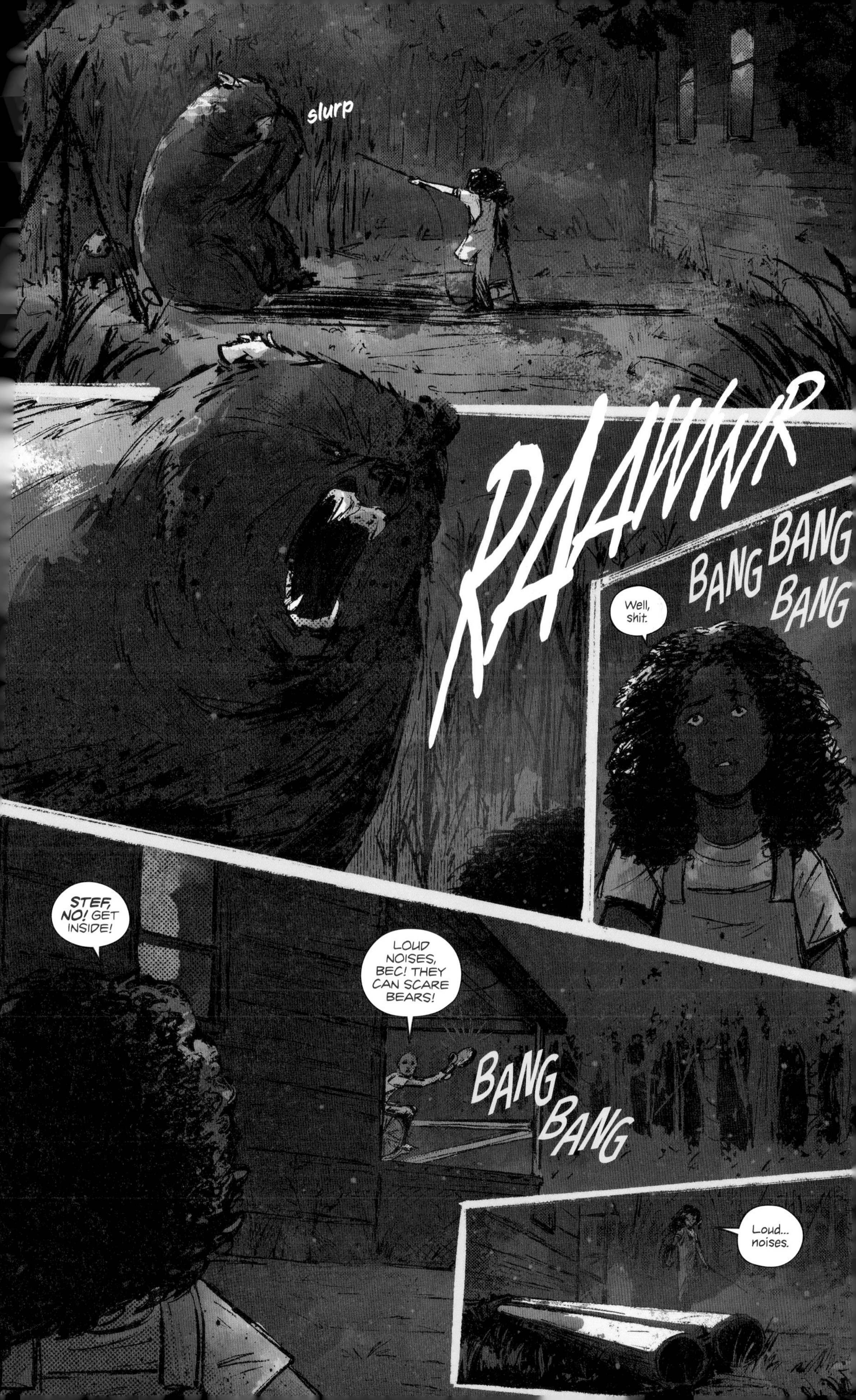
slurp
RAAWWR
BANG BANG BANG
Well, shit.
STEF, NO! GET INSIDE!
LOUD NOISES, BEC! THEY CAN SCARE BEARS!
BANG BANG
Loud... noises.

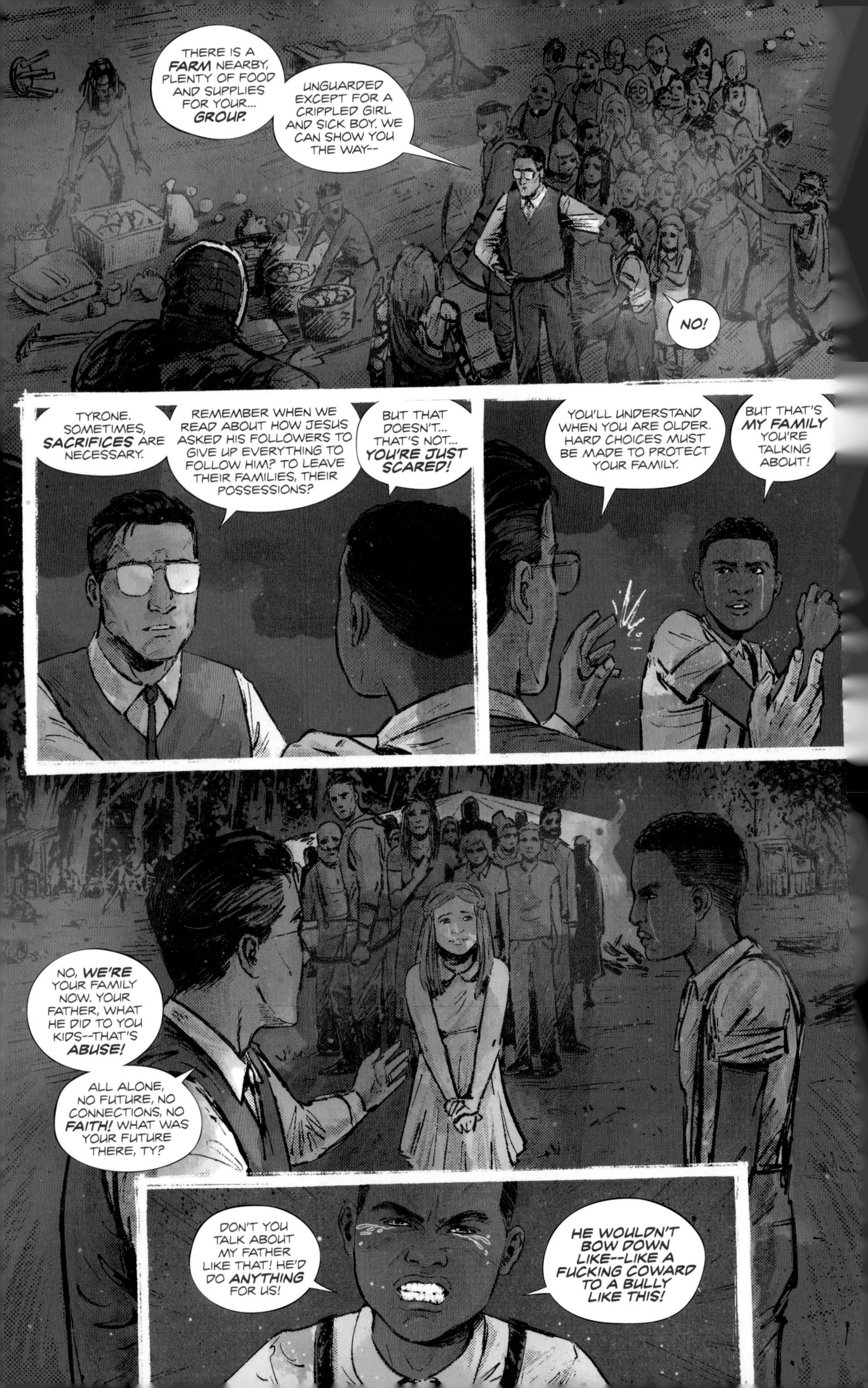

THERE IS A FARM NEARBY, PLENTY OF FOOD AND SUPPLIES FOR YOUR... GROUP.
UNGUARDED EXCEPT FOR A CRIPPLED GIRL AND SICK BOY. WE CAN SHOW YOU THE WAY--
NO!
TYRONE. SOMETIMES, SACRIFICES ARE NECESSARY.
REMEMBER WHEN WE READ ABOUT HOW JESUS ASKED HIS FOLLOWERS TO GIVE UP EVERYTHING TO FOLLOW HIM? TO LEAVE THEIR FAMILIES, THEIR POSSESSIONS?
BUT THAT DOESN'T... THAT'S NOT... YOU'RE JUST SCARED!
YOU'LL UNDERSTAND WHEN YOU ARE OLDER. HARD CHOICES MUST BE MADE TO PROTECT YOUR FAMILY.
BUT THAT'S MY FAMILY YOU'RE TALKING ABOUT!
NO, WE'RE YOUR FAMILY NOW. YOUR FATHER, WHAT HE DID TO YOU KIDS--THAT'S ABUSE!
ALL ALONE, NO FUTURE, NO CONNECTIONS, NO FAITH! WHAT WAS YOUR FUTURE THERE, TY?
DON'T YOU TALK ABOUT MY FATHER LIKE THAT! HE'D DO ANYTHING FOR US!
HE WOULDN'T BOW DOWN LIKE--LIKE A FUCKING COWARD TO A BULLY LIKE THIS!

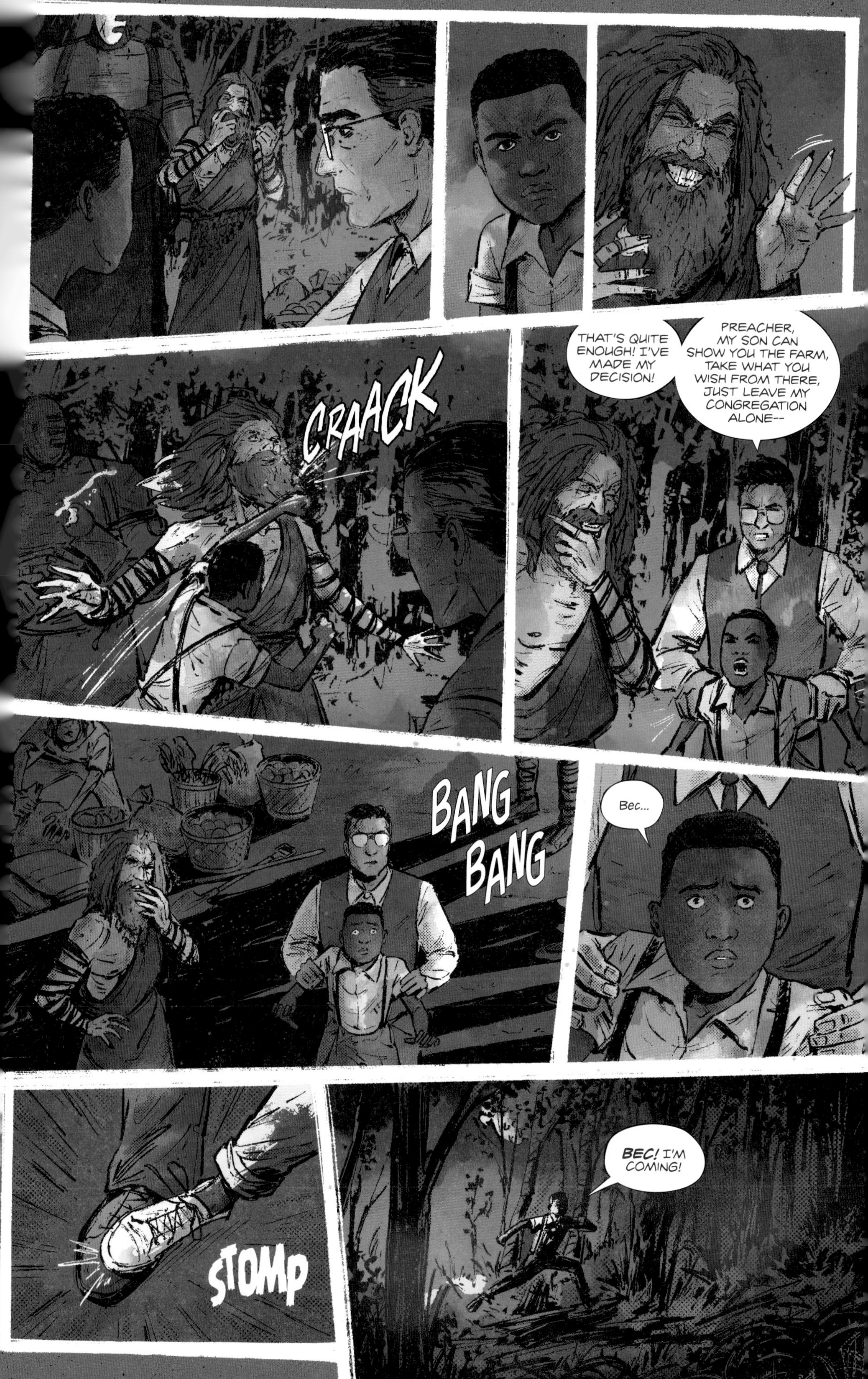
CRAACK
THAT'S QUITE ENOUGH! I'VE MADE MY DECISION!
PREACHER, MY SON CAN SHOW YOU THE FARM, TAKE WHAT YOU WISH FROM THERE, JUST LEAVE MY CONGREGATION ALONE--
BANG BANG
Bec...
STOMP
BEC! I'M COMING!

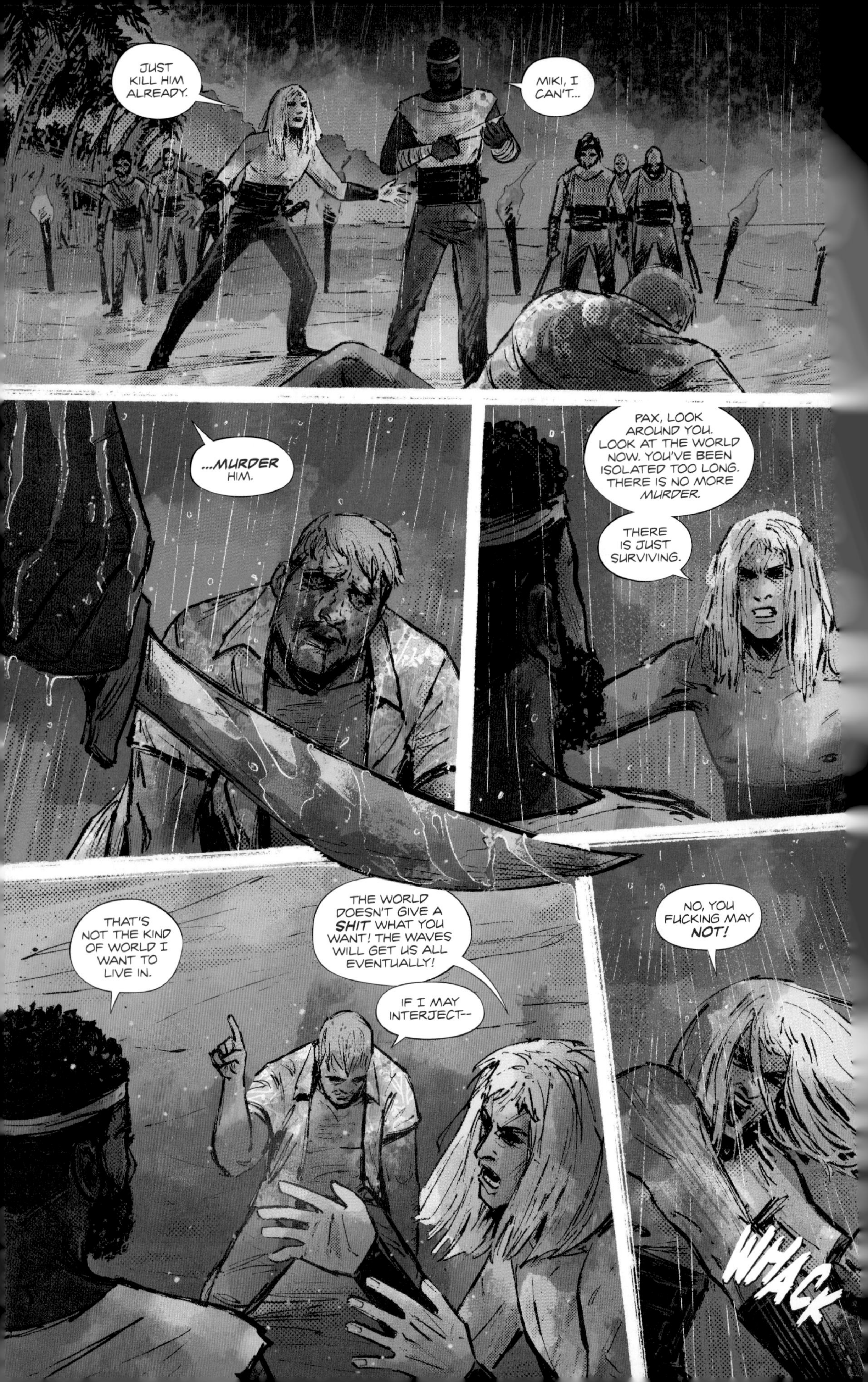
JUST KILL HIM ALREADY.
MIKI, I CAN'T...
...MURDER HIM.
PAX, LOOK AROUND YOU. LOOK AT THE WORLD NOW. YOU'VE BEEN ISOLATED TOO LONG. THERE IS NO MORE MURDER.
THERE IS JUST SURVIVING.
THAT'S NOT THE KIND OF WORLD I WANT TO LIVE IN.
THE WORLD DOESN'T GIVE A SHIT WHAT YOU WANT! THE WAVES WILL GET US ALL EVENTUALLY!
IF I MAY INTERJECT--
NO, YOU FUCKING MAY NOT!
WHACK

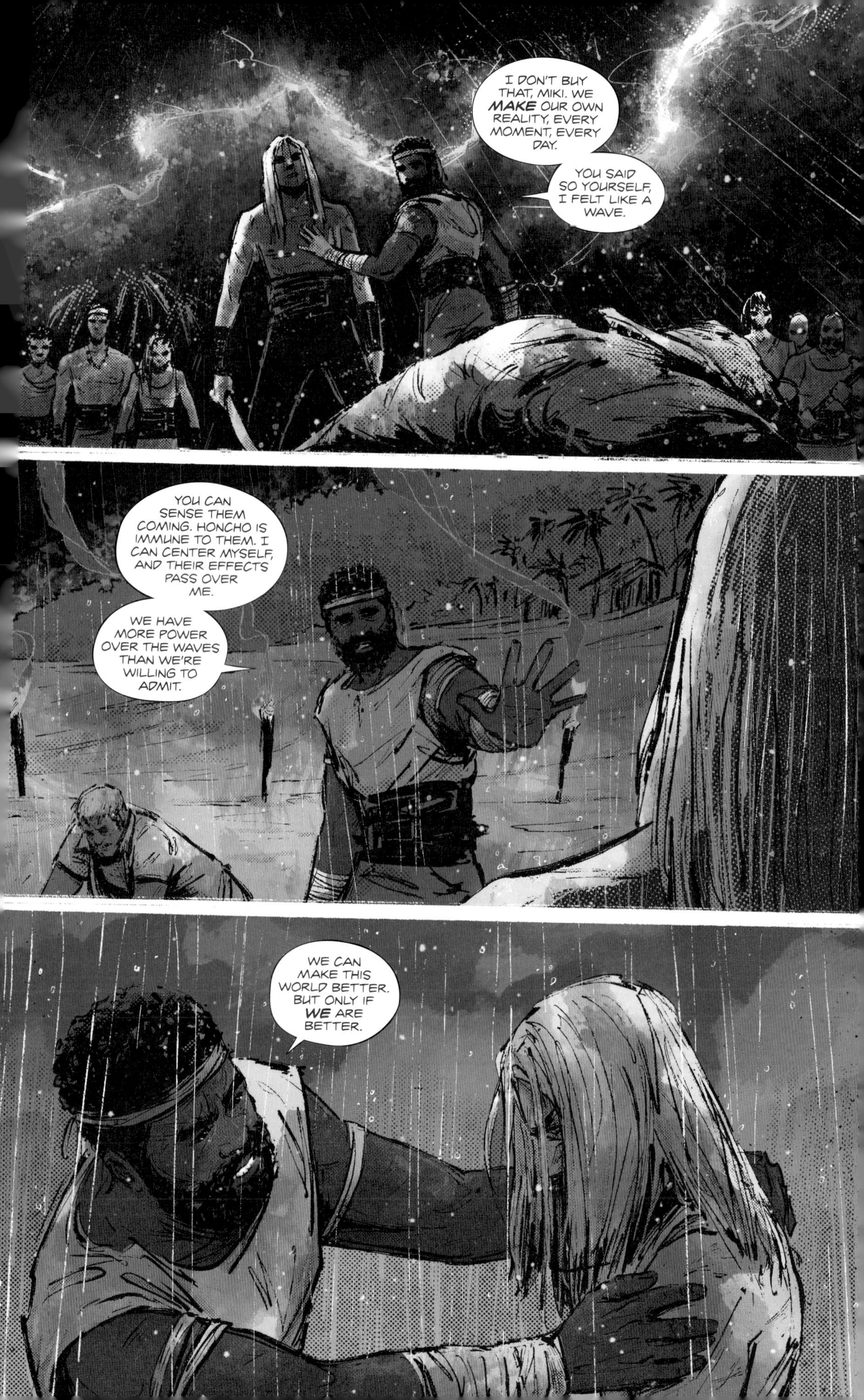
I DON'T BUY THAT, MIKI. WE *MAKE* OUR OWN REALITY, EVERY MOMENT, EVERY DAY.
YOU SAID SO YOURSELF, I FELT LIKE A WAVE.
YOU CAN SENSE THEM COMING. HONCHO IS IMMUNE TO THEM. I CAN CENTER MYSELF, AND THEIR EFFECTS PASS OVER ME.
WE HAVE MORE POWER OVER THE WAVES THAN WE'RE WILLING TO ADMIT.
WE CAN MAKE THIS WORLD BETTER. BUT ONLY IF *WE* ARE BETTER.

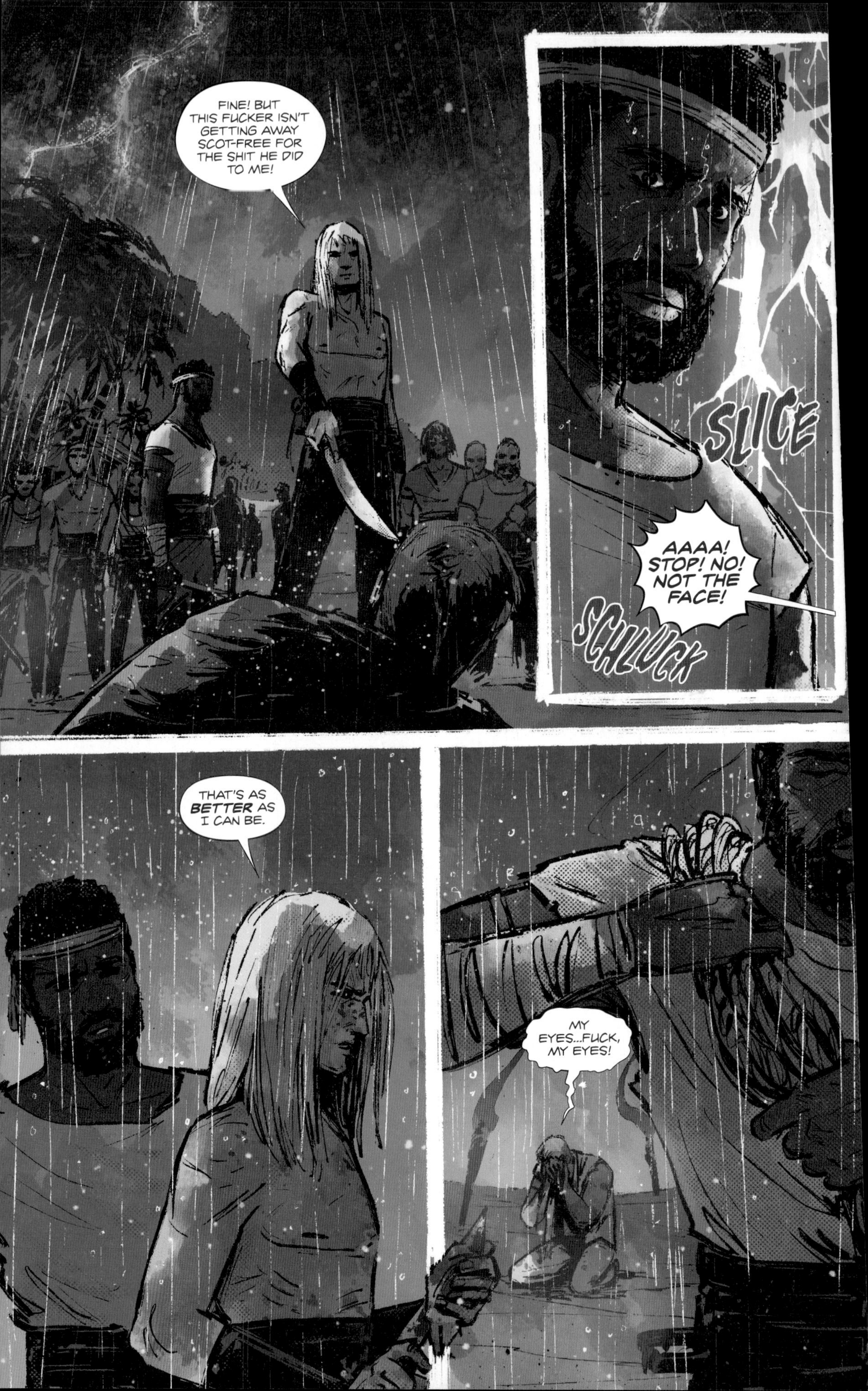
FINE! BUT THIS FUCKER ISN'T GETTING AWAY SCOT-FREE FOR THE SHIT HE DID TO ME!
SLICE
AAAA! STOP! NO! NOT THE FACE!
SCHLUCK
THAT'S AS BETTER AS I CAN BE.
MY EYES...FUCK, MY EYES!

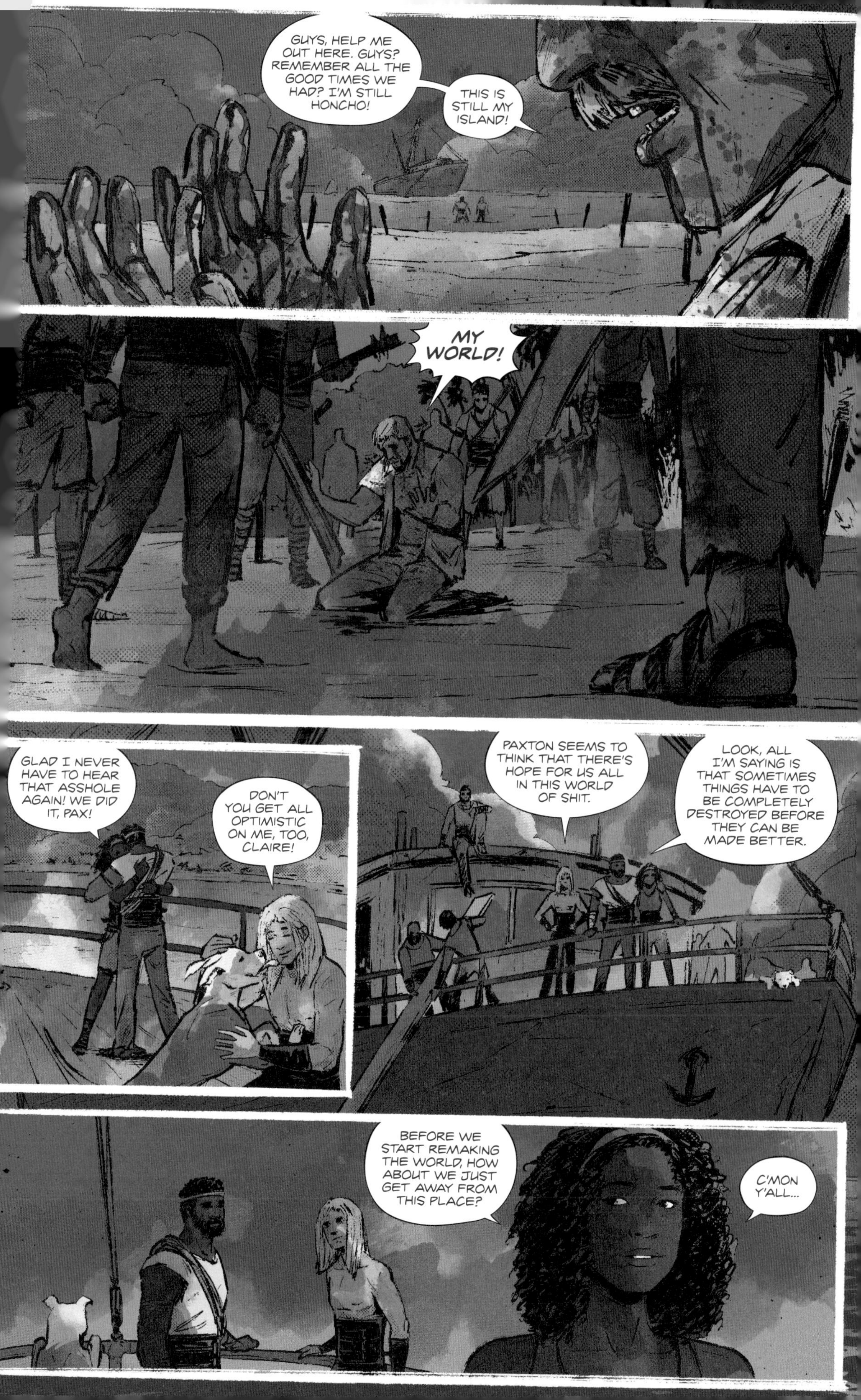
GUYS, HELP ME OUT HERE. GUYS? REMEMBER ALL THE GOOD TIMES WE HAD? I'M STILL HONCHO!
THIS IS STILL MY ISLAND!
MY WORLD!
GLAD I NEVER HAVE TO HEAR THAT ASSHOLE AGAIN! WE DID IT, PAX!
DON'T YOU GET ALL OPTIMISTIC ON ME, TOO, CLAIRE!
PAXTON SEEMS TO THINK THAT THERE'S HOPE FOR US ALL IN THIS WORLD OF SHIT.
LOOK, ALL I'M SAYING IS THAT SOMETIMES THINGS HAVE TO BE COMPLETELY DESTROYED BEFORE THEY CAN BE MADE BETTER.
BEFORE WE START REMAKING THE WORLD, HOW ABOUT WE JUST GET AWAY FROM THIS PLACE?
C'MON Y'ALL...

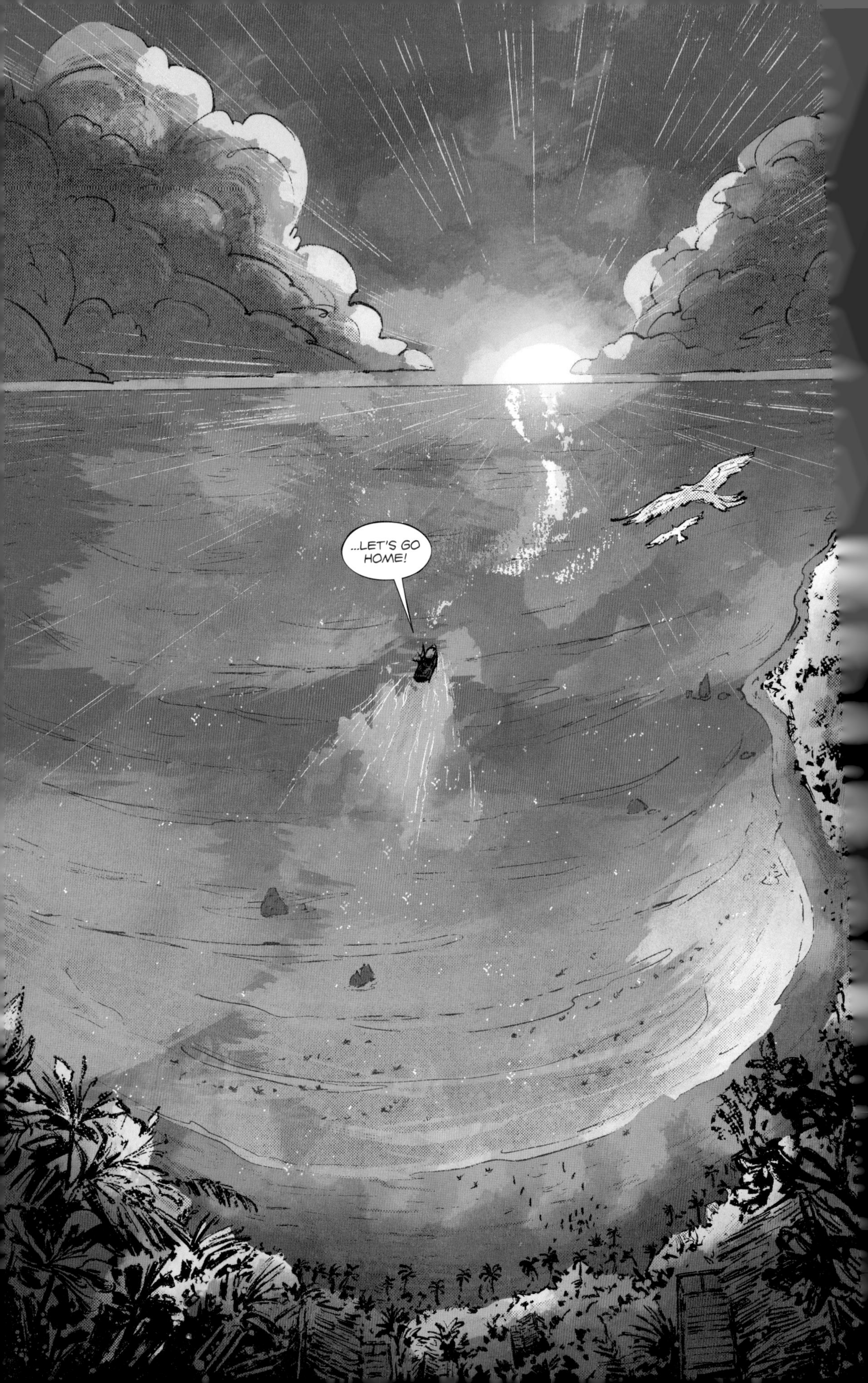
...LET'S GO HOME!

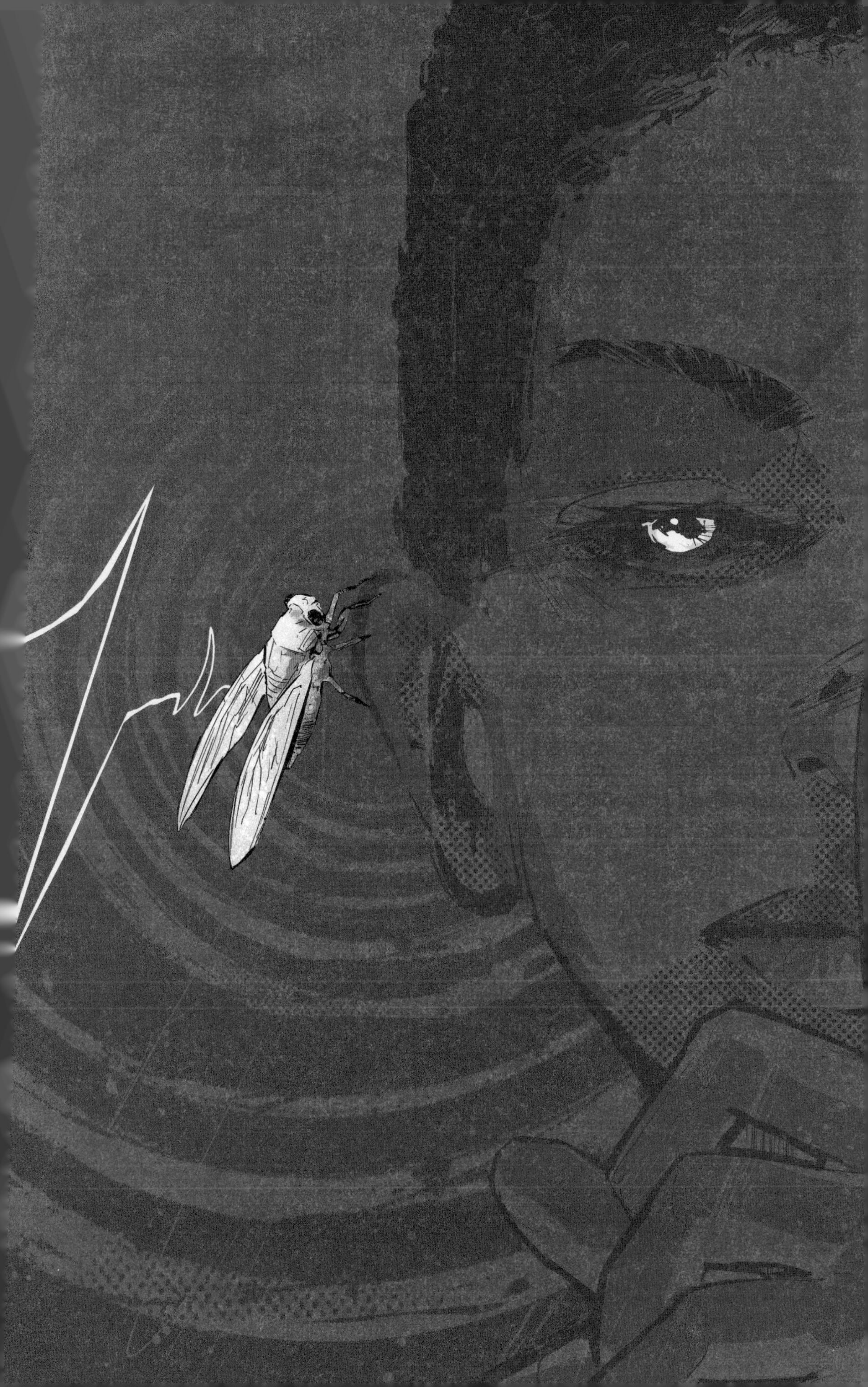

CHAPTER SEVEN

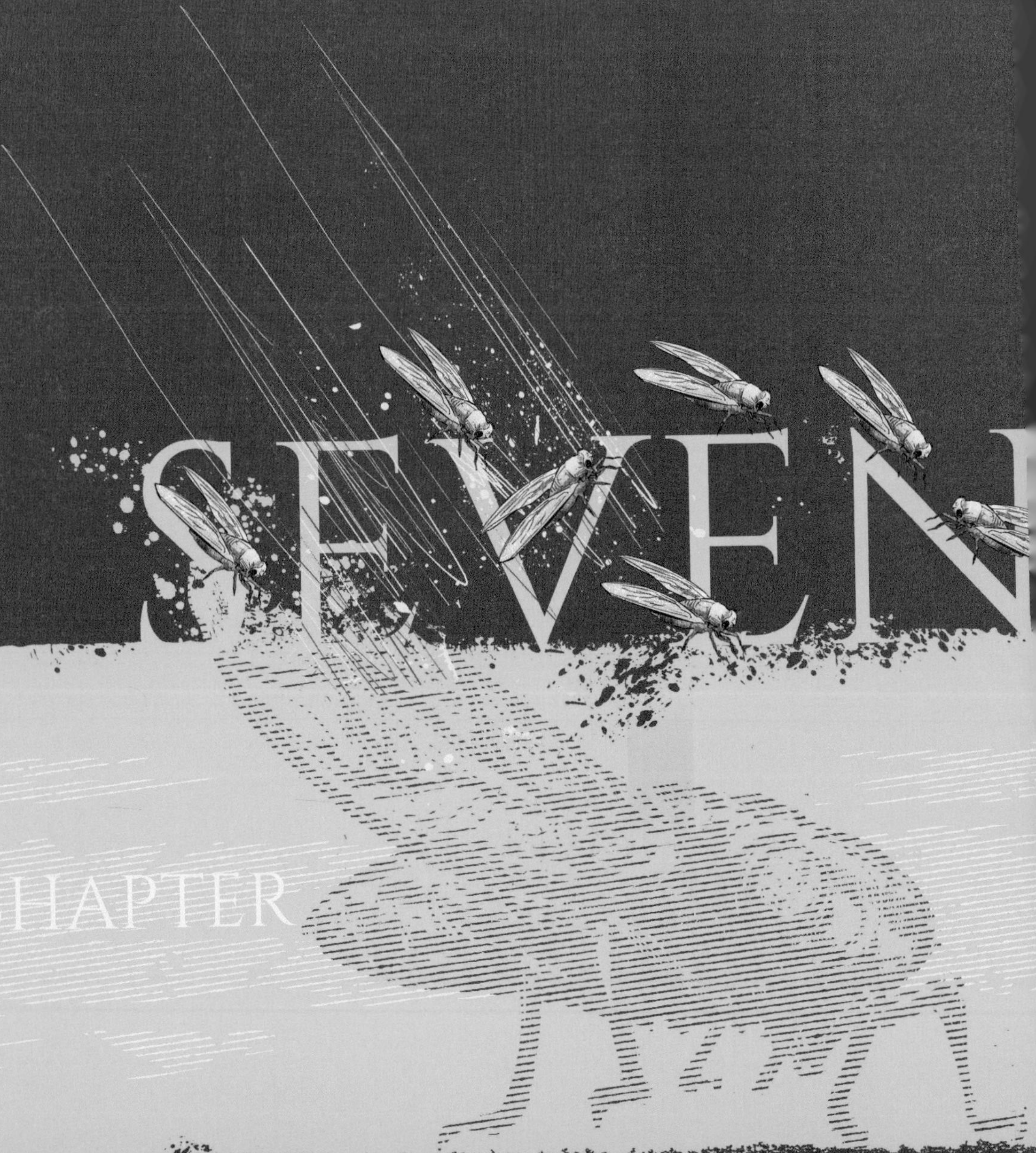

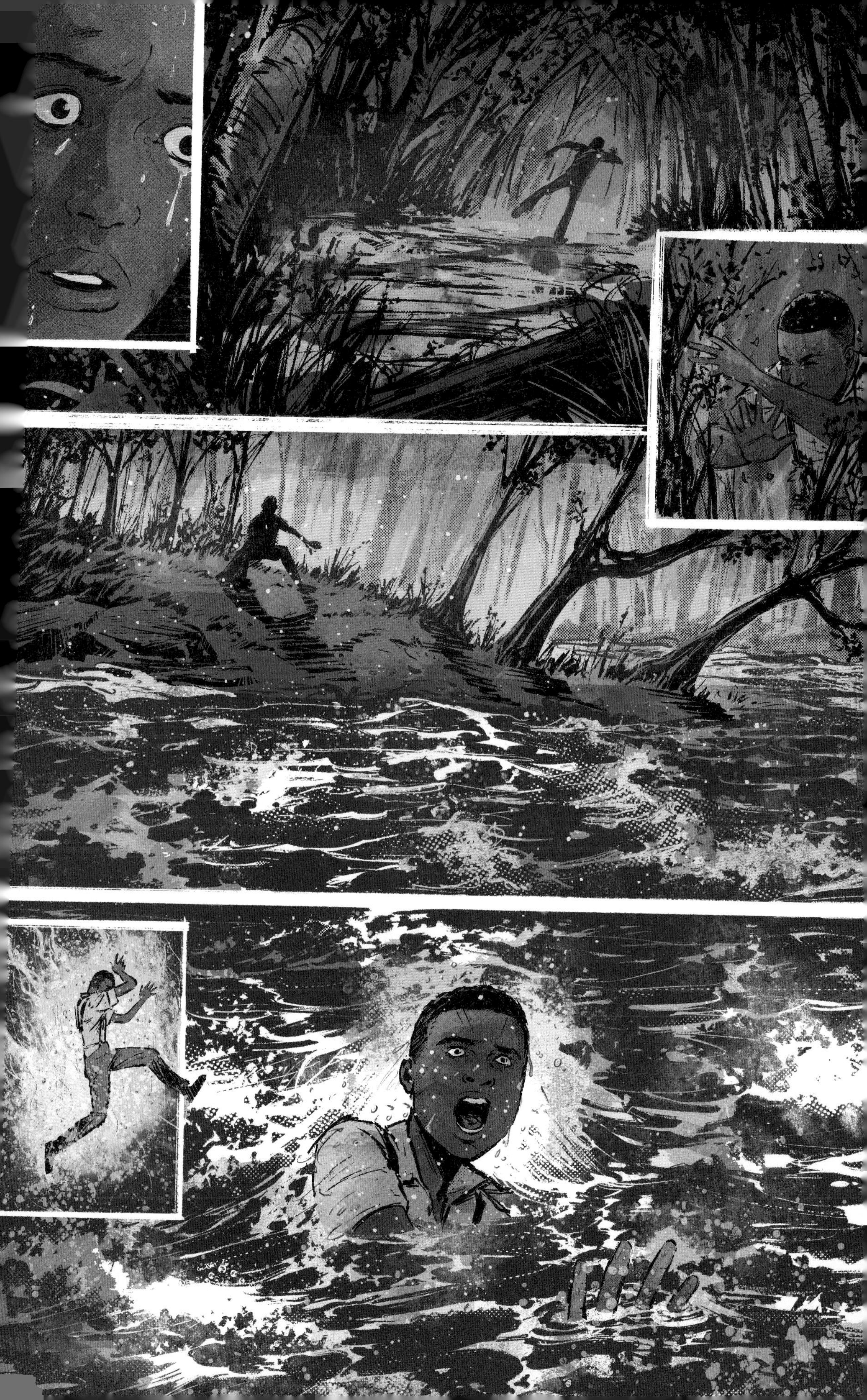

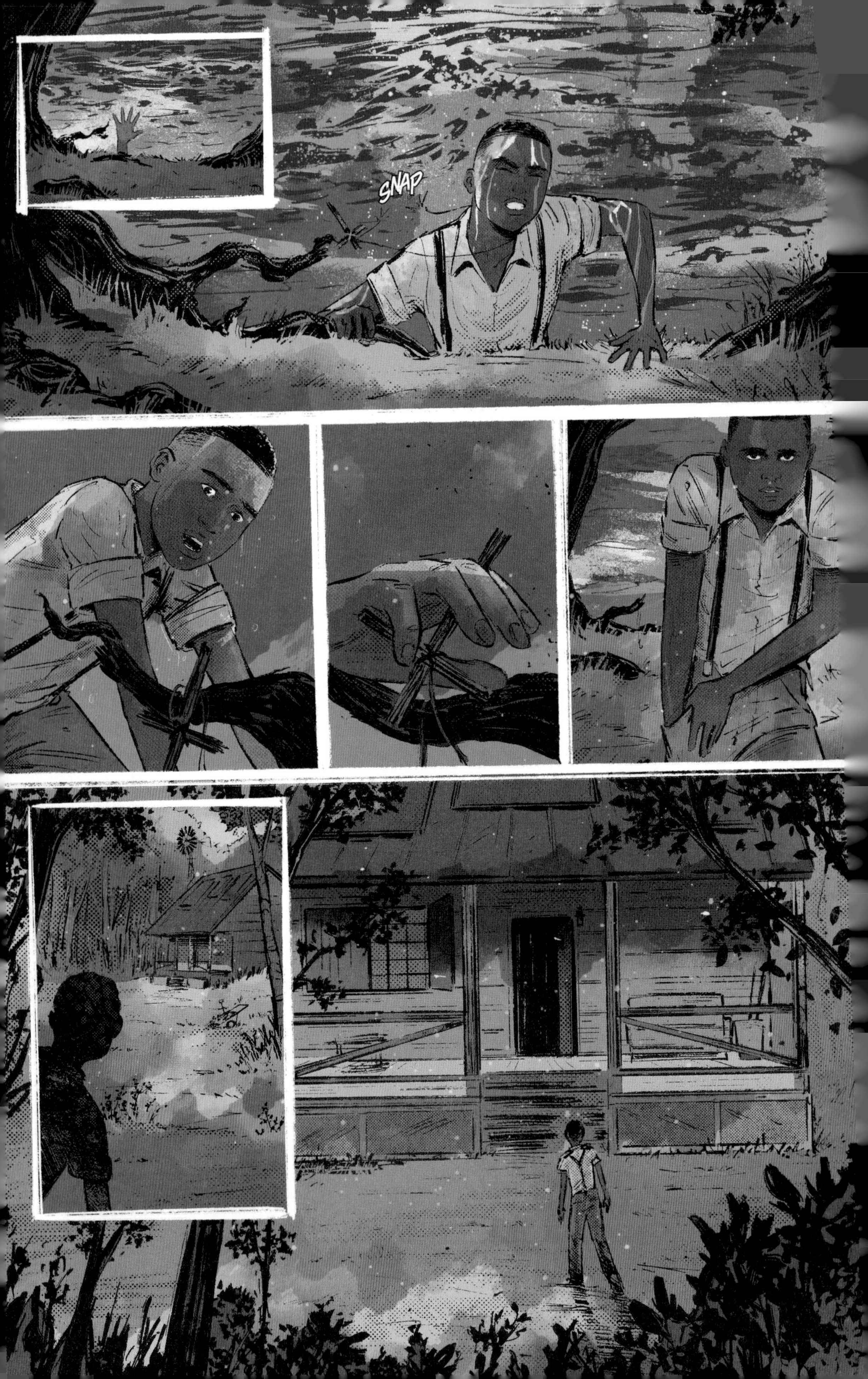
SNAP

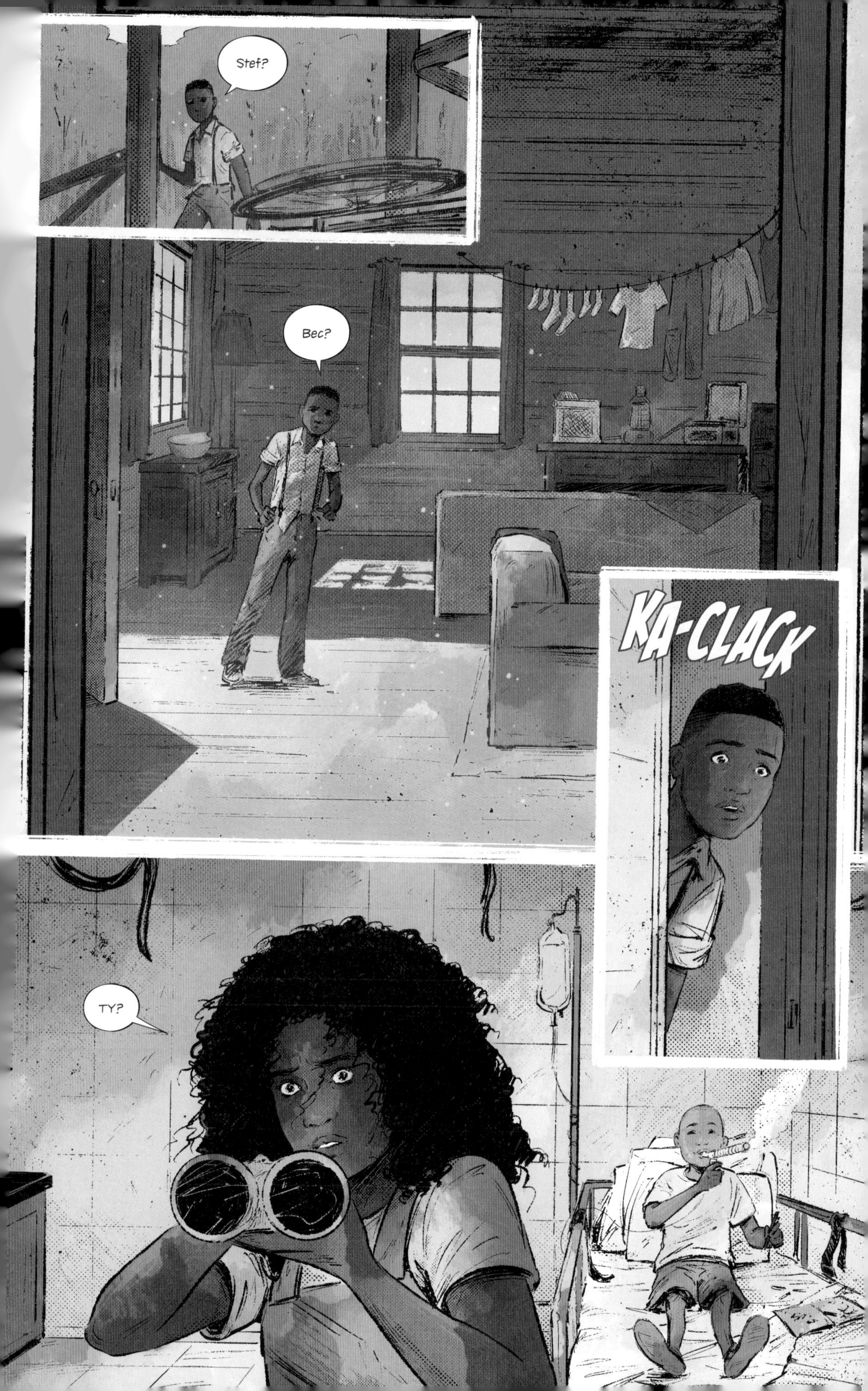
Stef?
Bec?
KA-CLACK
TY?

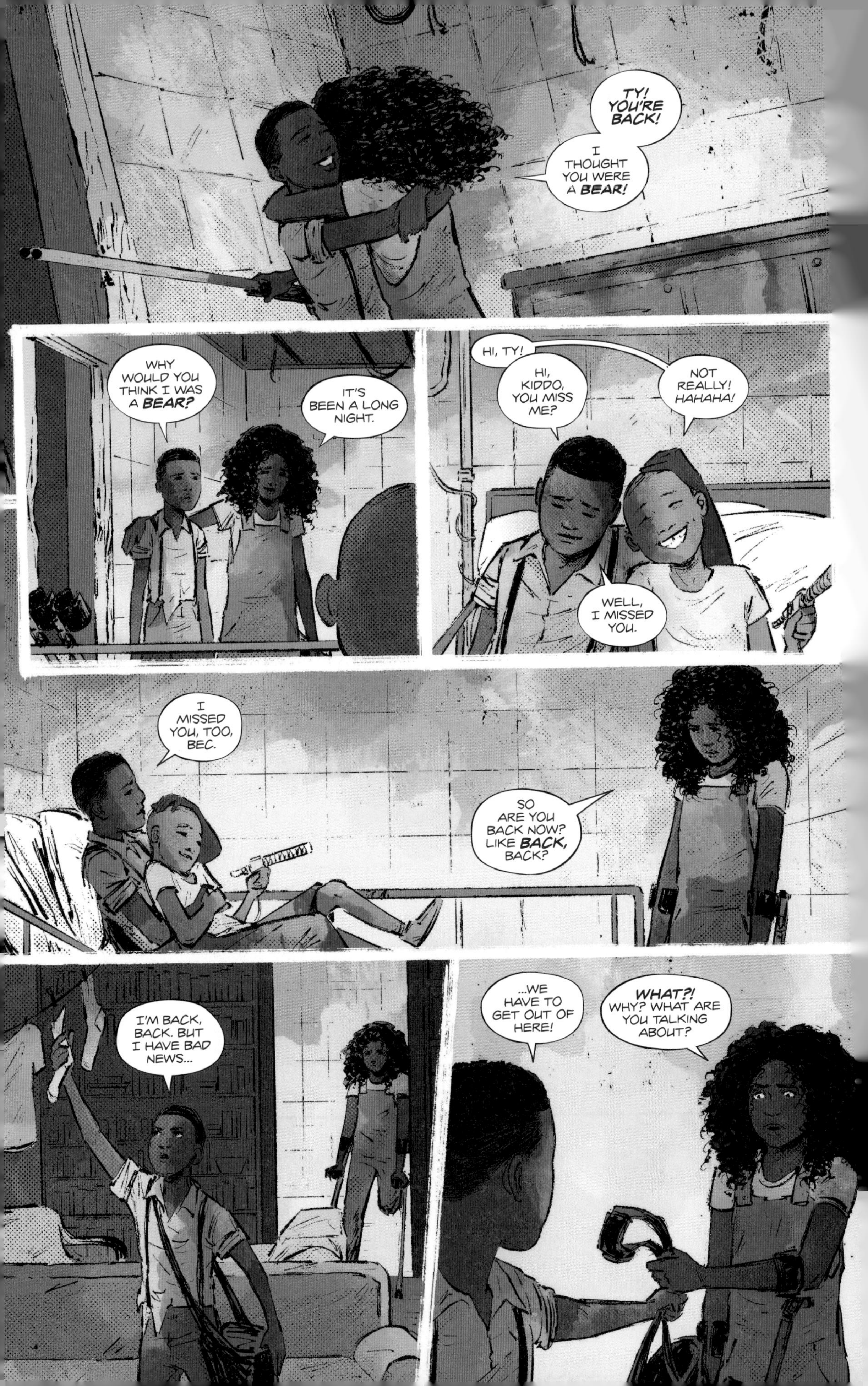
TY! YOU'RE BACK!
I THOUGHT YOU WERE A BEAR!
WHY WOULD YOU THINK I WAS A BEAR?
IT'S BEEN A LONG NIGHT.
HI, TY!
HI, KIDDO, YOU MISS ME?
NOT REALLY! HAHAHA!
WELL, I MISSED YOU.
I MISSED YOU, TOO, BEC.
SO ARE YOU BACK NOW? LIKE BACK, BACK?
I'M BACK, BACK. BUT I HAVE BAD NEWS...
...WE HAVE TO GET OUT OF HERE!
WHAT?! WHY? WHAT ARE YOU TALKING ABOUT?

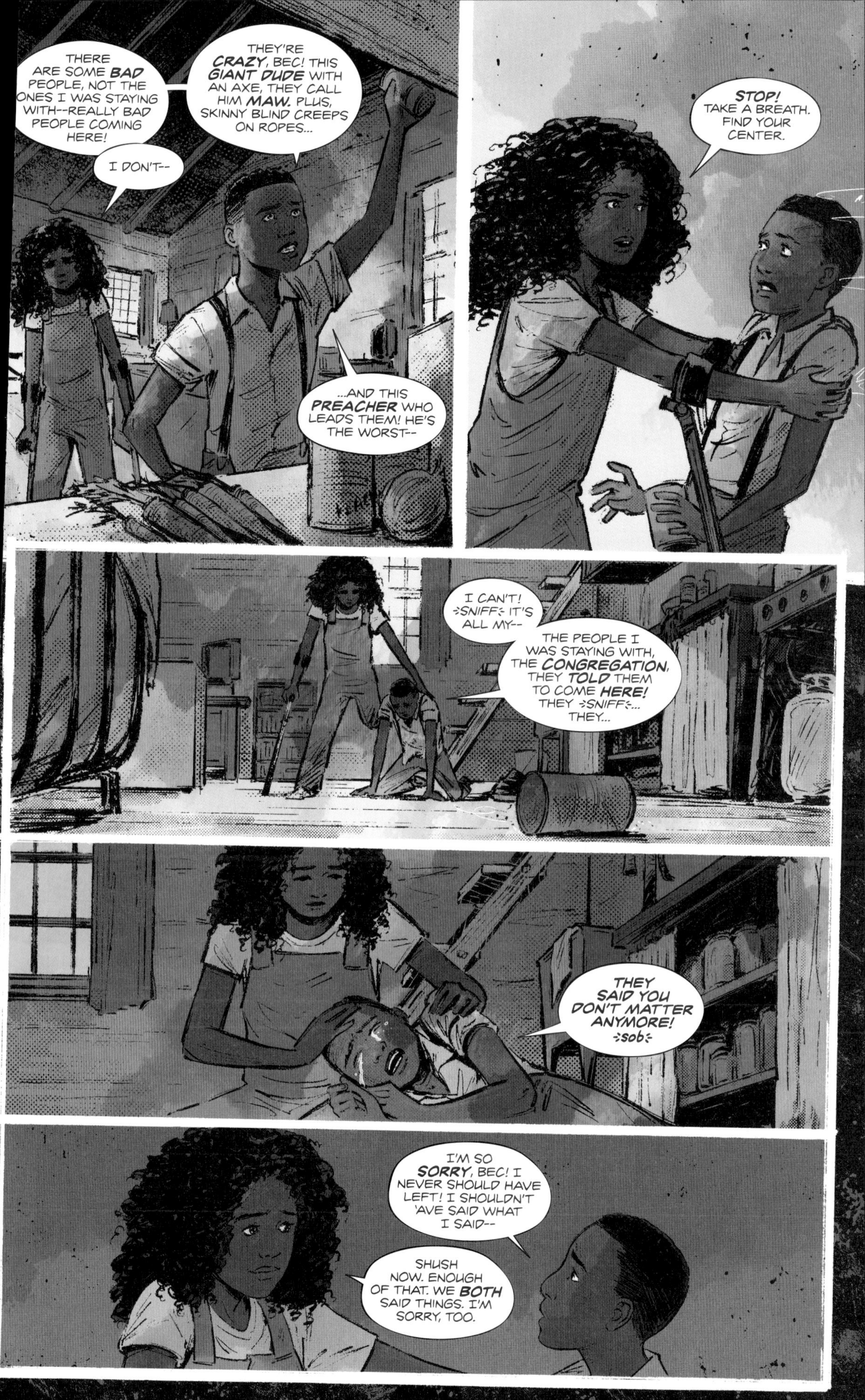
THERE ARE SOME BAD PEOPLE, NOT THE ONES I WAS STAYING WITH--REALLY BAD PEOPLE COMING HERE!
THEY'RE CRAZY, BEC! THIS GIANT DUDE WITH AN AXE, THEY CALL HIM MAW. PLUS, SKINNY BLIND CREEPS ON ROPES...
I DON'T--
...AND THIS PREACHER WHO LEADS THEM! HE'S THE WORST--
STOP! TAKE A BREATH. FIND YOUR CENTER.
I CAN'T! -SNIFF- IT'S ALL MY--
THE PEOPLE I WAS STAYING WITH, THE CONGREGATION, THEY TOLD THEM TO COME HERE! THEY -SNIFF-... THEY...
THEY SAID YOU DON'T MATTER ANYMORE! -sob-
I'M SO SORRY, BEC! I NEVER SHOULD HAVE LEFT! I SHOULDN'T 'AVE SAID WHAT I SAID--
SHUSH NOW. ENOUGH OF THAT. WE BOTH SAID THINGS. I'M SORRY, TOO.

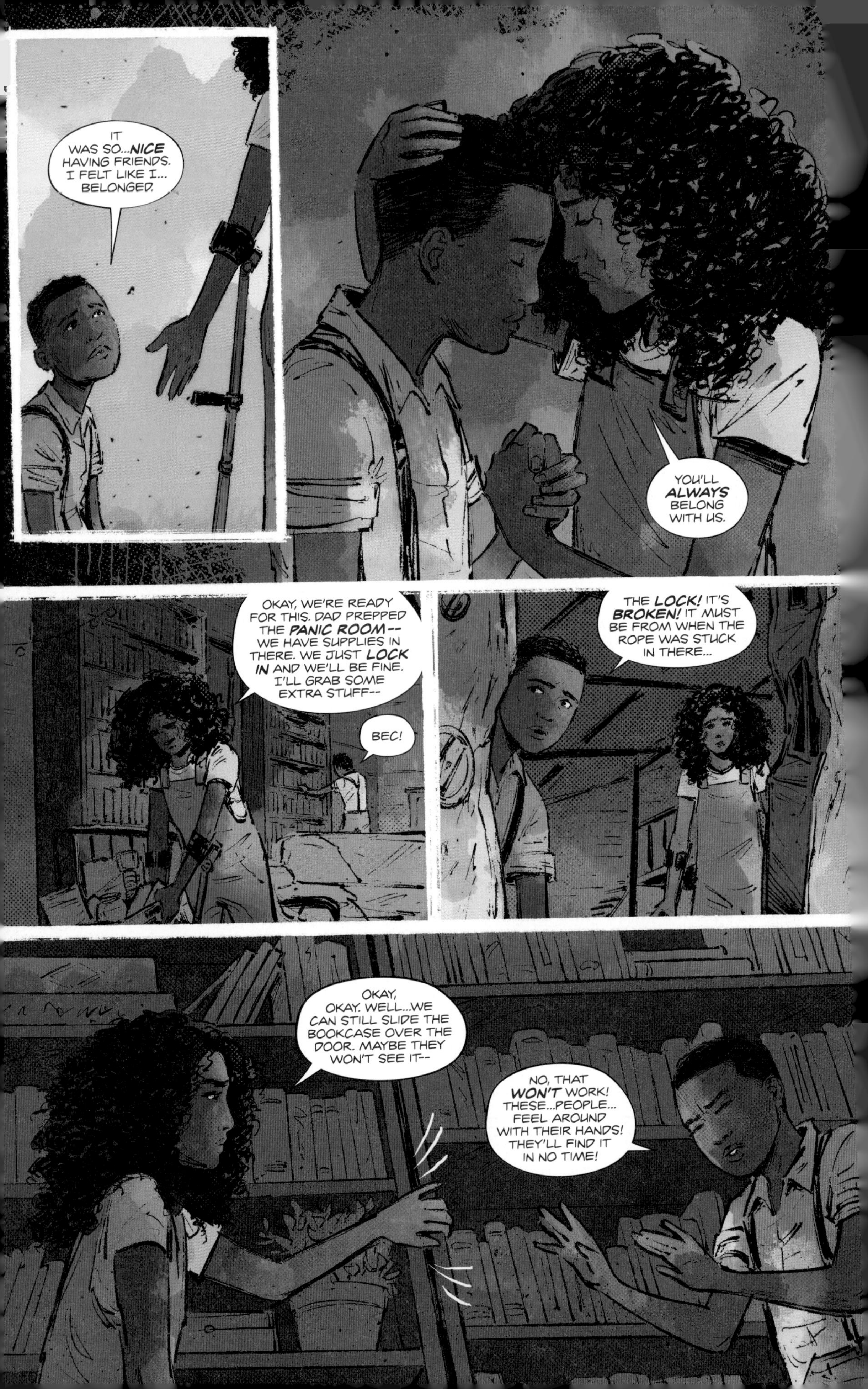
IT WAS SO...NICE HAVING FRIENDS. I FELT LIKE I... BELONGED.
YOU'LL ALWAYS BELONG WITH US.
OKAY, WE'RE READY FOR THIS. DAD PREPPED THE PANIC ROOM-- WE HAVE SUPPLIES IN THERE. WE JUST LOCK IN AND WE'LL BE FINE. I'LL GRAB SOME EXTRA STUFF--
BEC!
THE LOCK! IT'S BROKEN! IT MUST BE FROM WHEN THE ROPE WAS STUCK IN THERE...
OKAY, OKAY. WELL...WE CAN STILL SLIDE THE BOOKCASE OVER THE DOOR. MAYBE THEY WON'T SEE IT--
NO, THAT WON'T WORK! THESE...PEOPLE... FEEL AROUND WITH THEIR HANDS! THEY'LL FIND IT IN NO TIME!

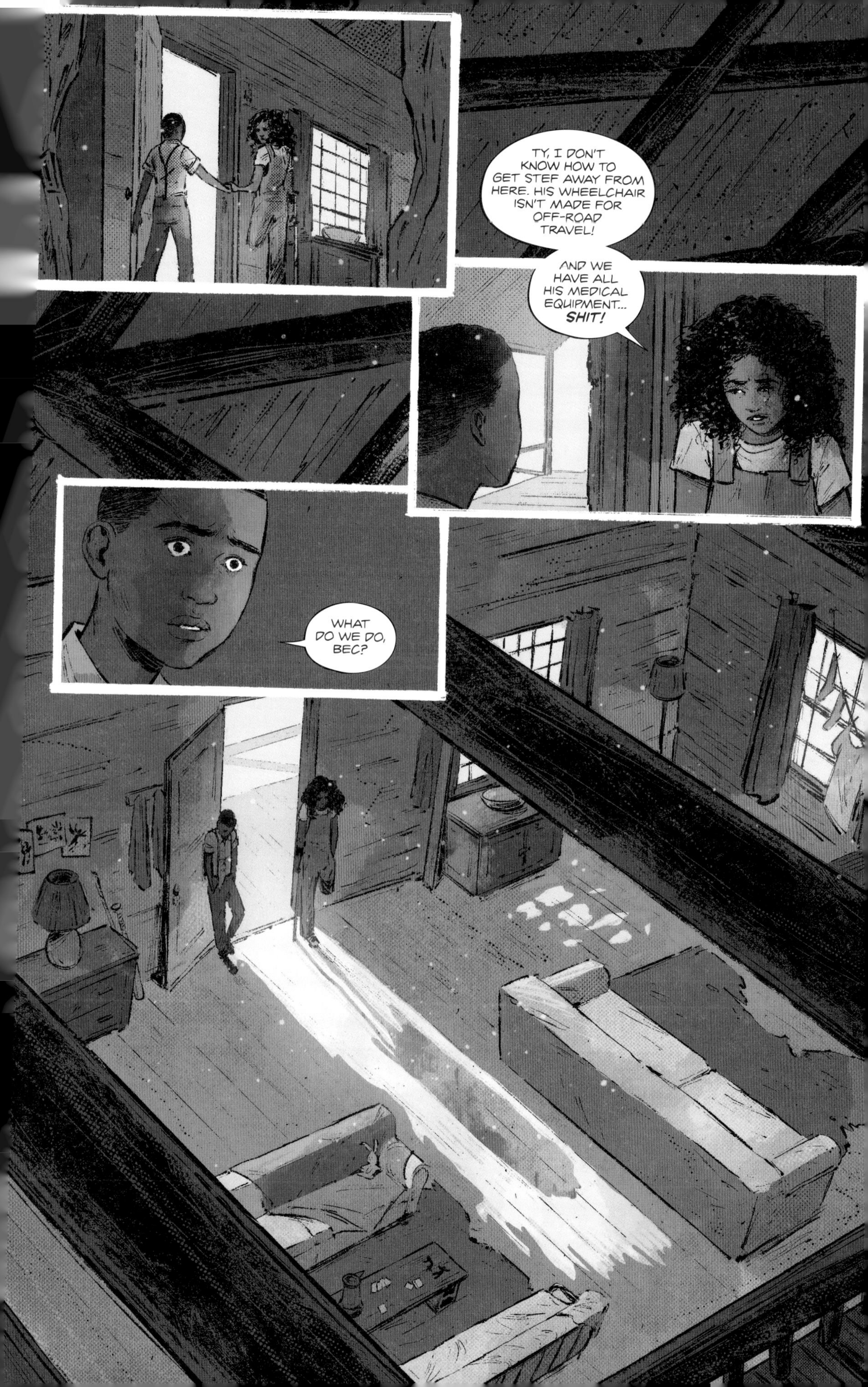
TY, I DON'T KNOW HOW TO GET STEF AWAY FROM HERE. HIS WHEELCHAIR ISN'T MADE FOR OFF-ROAD TRAVEL!
AND WE HAVE ALL HIS MEDICAL EQUIPMENT... SHIT!
WHAT DO WE DO, BEC?

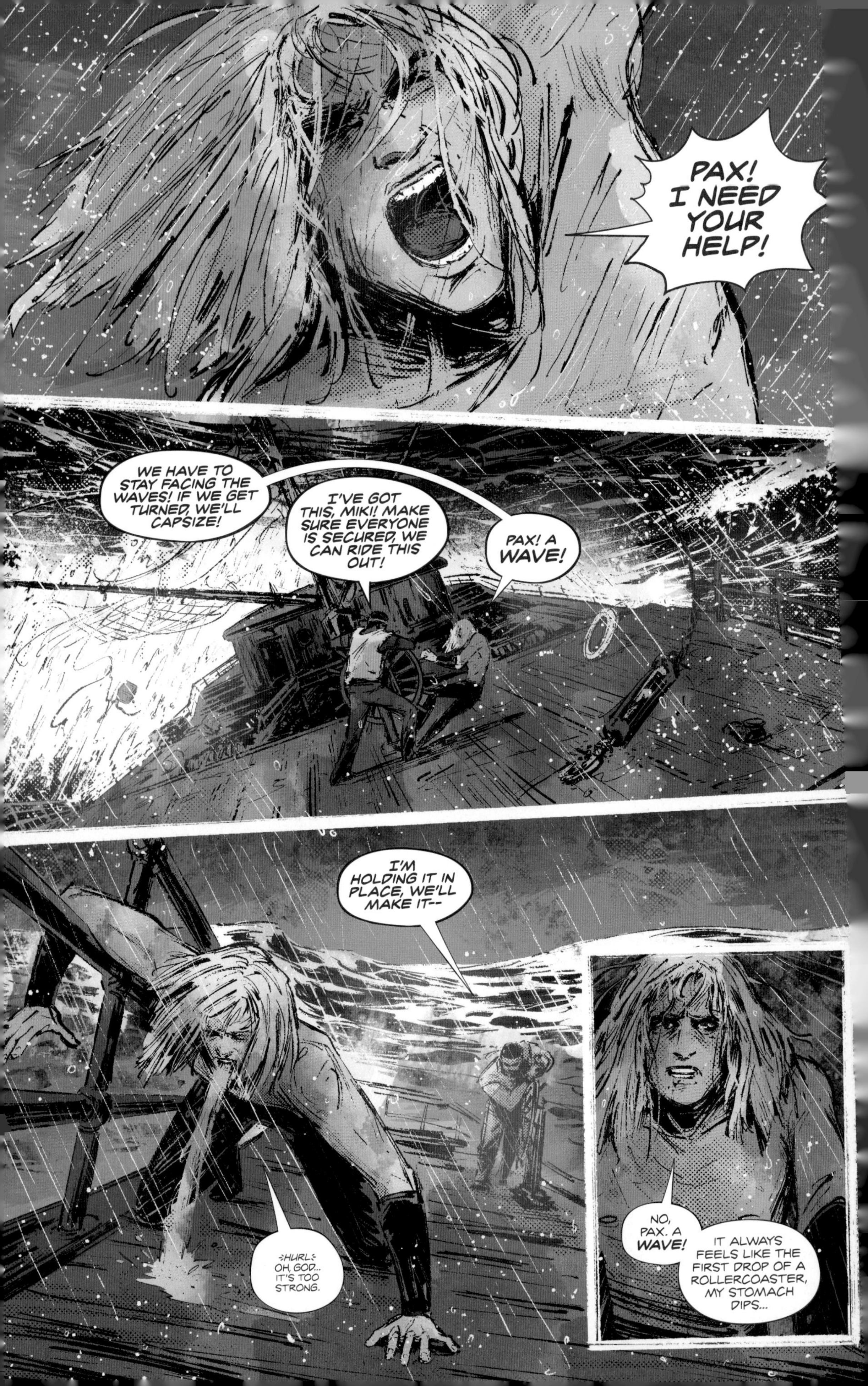
PAX! I NEED YOUR HELP!
WE HAVE TO STAY FACING THE WAVES! IF WE GET TURNED, WE'LL CAPSIZE!
I'VE GOT THIS, MIKI! MAKE SURE EVERYONE IS SECURED, WE CAN RIDE THIS OUT!
PAX! A WAVE!
I'M HOLDING IT IN PLACE, WE'LL MAKE IT--
HURL
OH, GOD... IT'S TOO STRONG.
NO, PAX. A WAVE!
IT ALWAYS FEELS LIKE THE FIRST DROP OF A ROLLERCOASTER, MY STOMACH DIPS...

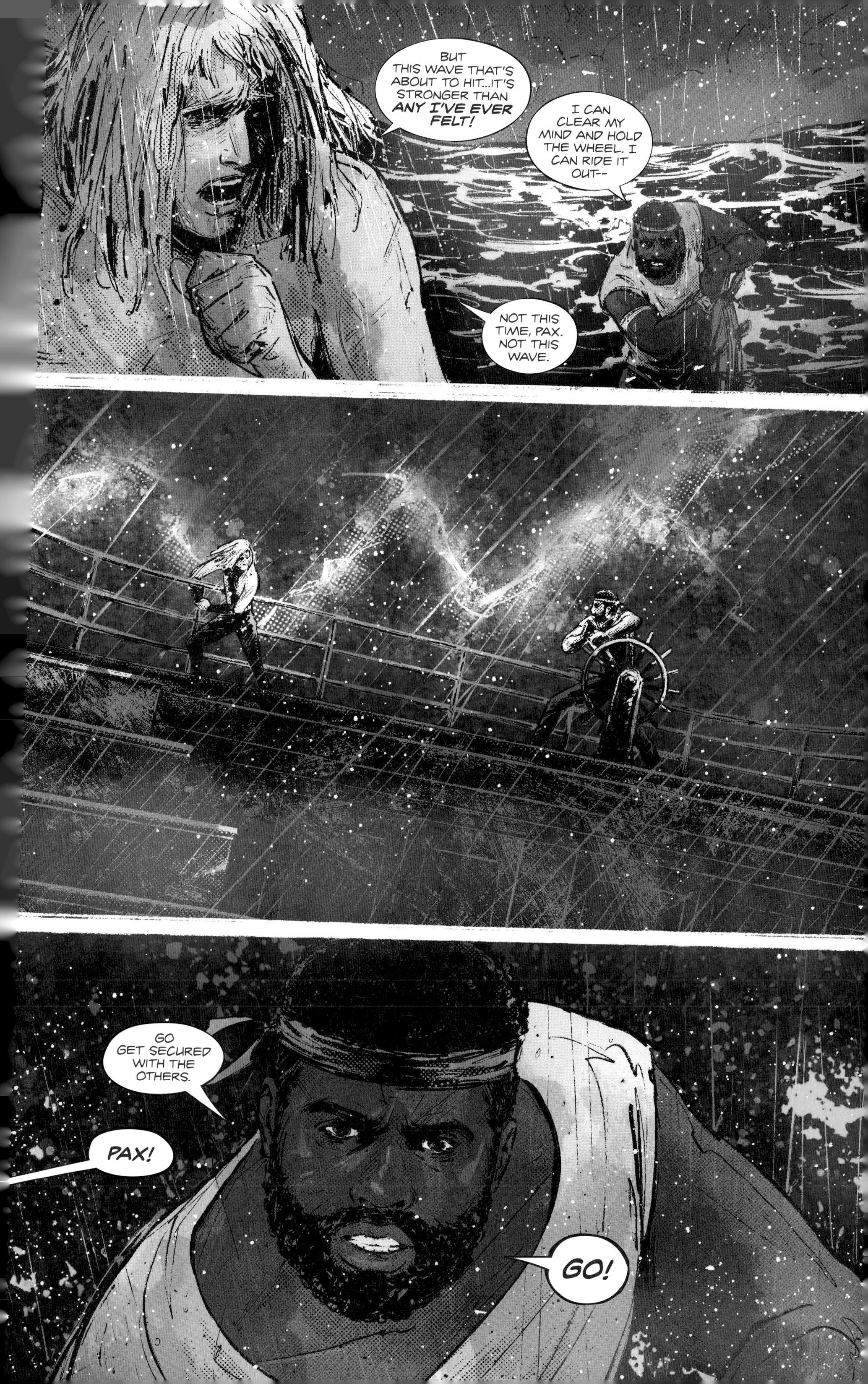
BUT THIS WAVE THAT'S ABOUT TO HIT...IT'S STRONGER THAN ANY I'VE EVER FELT!
I CAN CLEAR MY MIND AND HOLD THE WHEEL. I CAN RIDE IT OUT--
NOT THIS TIME, PAX. NOT THIS WAVE.
GO GET SECURED WITH THE OTHERS.
PAX!
GO!

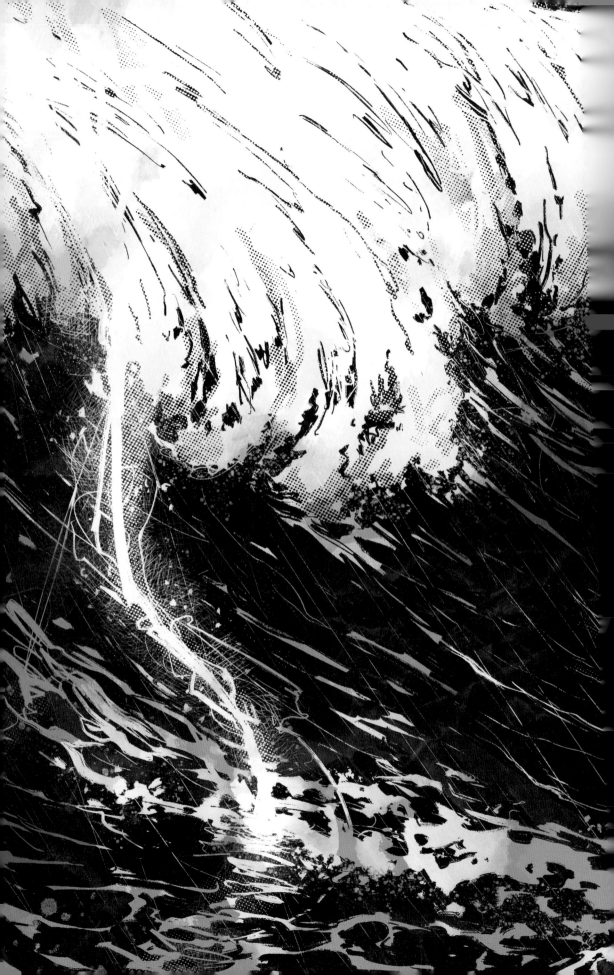

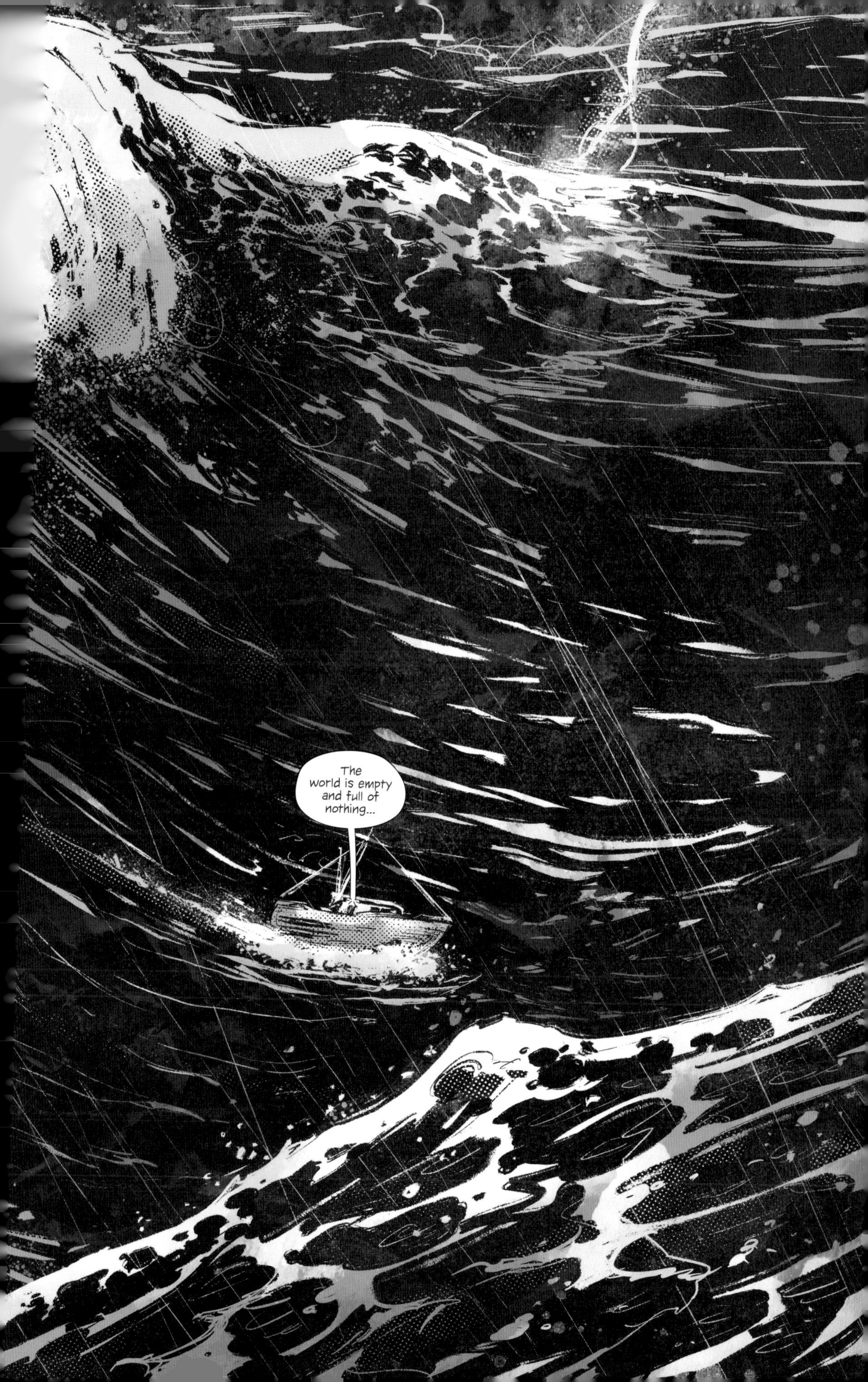
The world is empty and full of nothing...

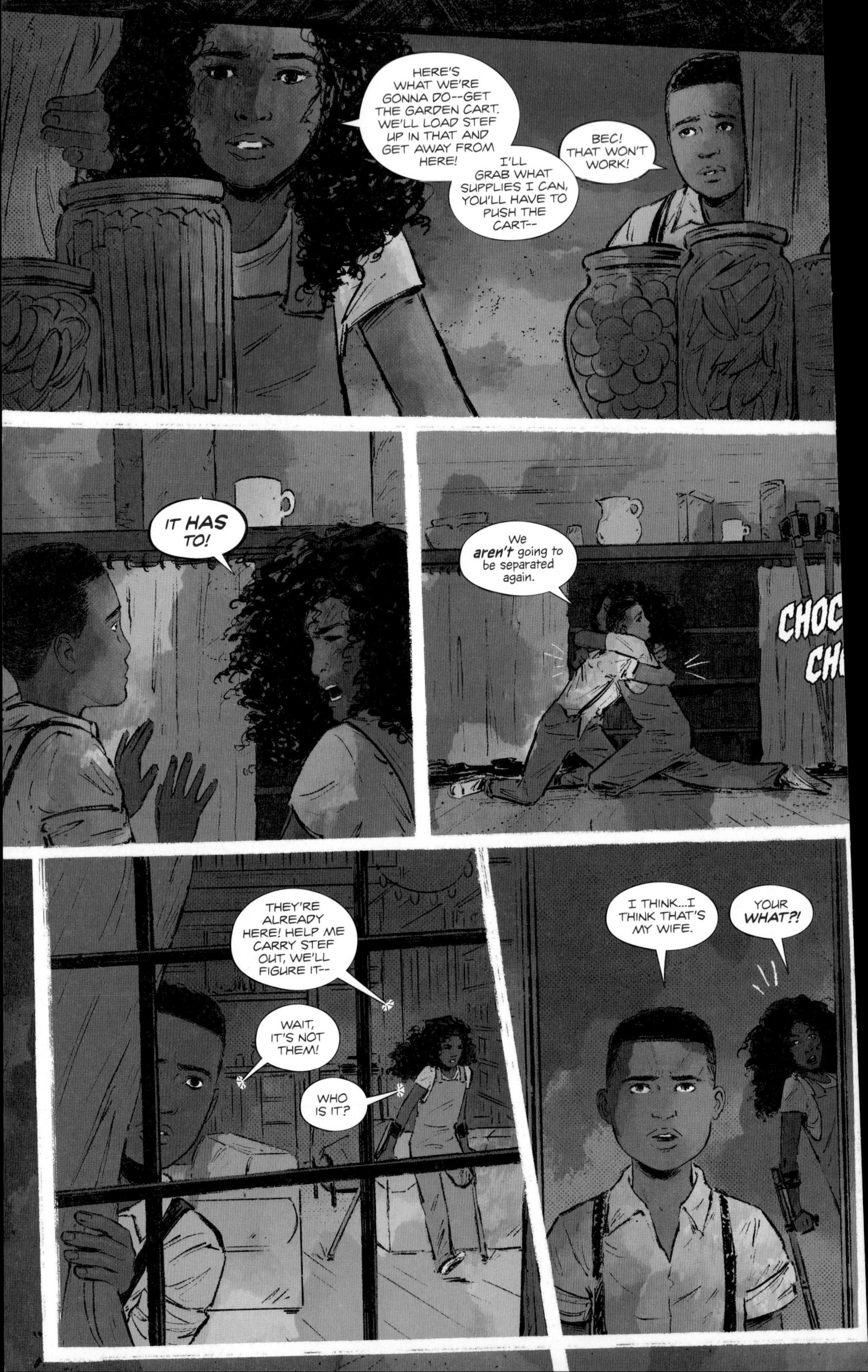
HERE'S WHAT WE'RE GONNA DO--GET THE GARDEN CART. WE'LL LOAD STEF UP IN THAT AND GET AWAY FROM HERE!
I'LL GRAB WHAT SUPPLIES I CAN, YOU'LL HAVE TO PUSH THE CART--
BEC! THAT WON'T WORK!
IT HAS TO!
We aren't going to be separated again.
CHOC
CH
THEY'RE ALREADY HERE! HELP ME CARRY STEF OUT, WE'LL FIGURE IT--
WAIT, IT'S NOT THEM!
WHO IS IT?
I THINK...I THINK THAT'S MY WIFE.
YOUR WHAT?!

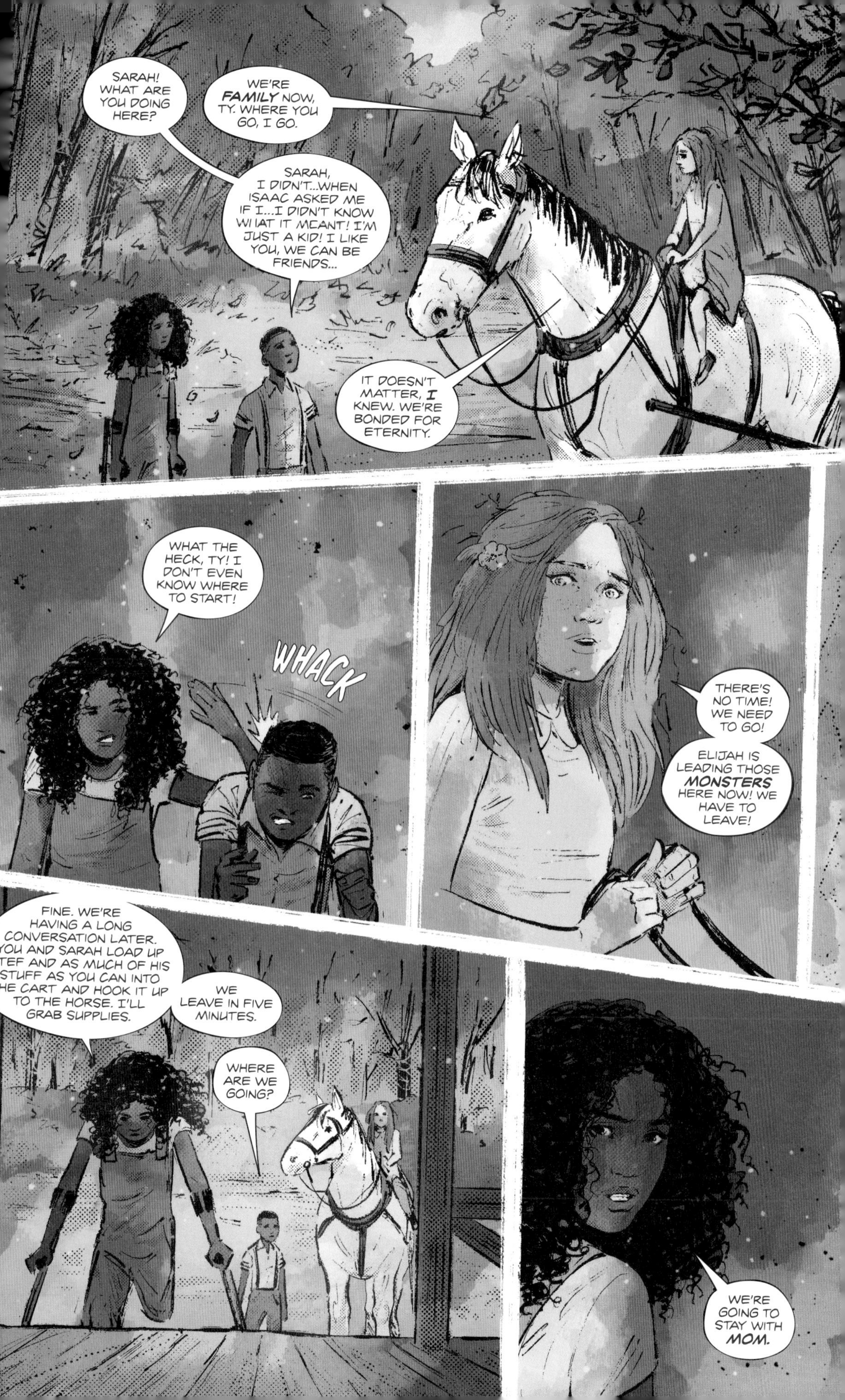
SARAH! WHAT ARE YOU DOING HERE?
WE'RE **FAMILY** NOW, TY. WHERE YOU GO, I GO.
SARAH, I DIDN'T...WHEN ISAAC ASKED ME IF I...I DIDN'T KNOW WHAT IT MEANT! I'M JUST A KID! I LIKE YOU, WE CAN BE FRIENDS...
IT DOESN'T MATTER, **I** KNEW. WE'RE BONDED FOR ETERNITY.
WHAT THE HECK, TY! I DON'T EVEN KNOW WHERE TO START!
WHACK
THERE'S NO TIME! WE NEED TO GO!
ELIJAH IS LEADING THOSE **MONSTERS** HERE NOW! WE HAVE TO LEAVE!
FINE. WE'RE HAVING A LONG CONVERSATION LATER. YOU AND SARAH LOAD UP STEF AND AS MUCH OF HIS STUFF AS YOU CAN INTO THE CART AND HOOK IT UP TO THE HORSE. I'LL GRAB SUPPLIES.
WE LEAVE IN FIVE MINUTES.
WHERE ARE WE GOING?
WE'RE GOING TO STAY WITH **MOM.**

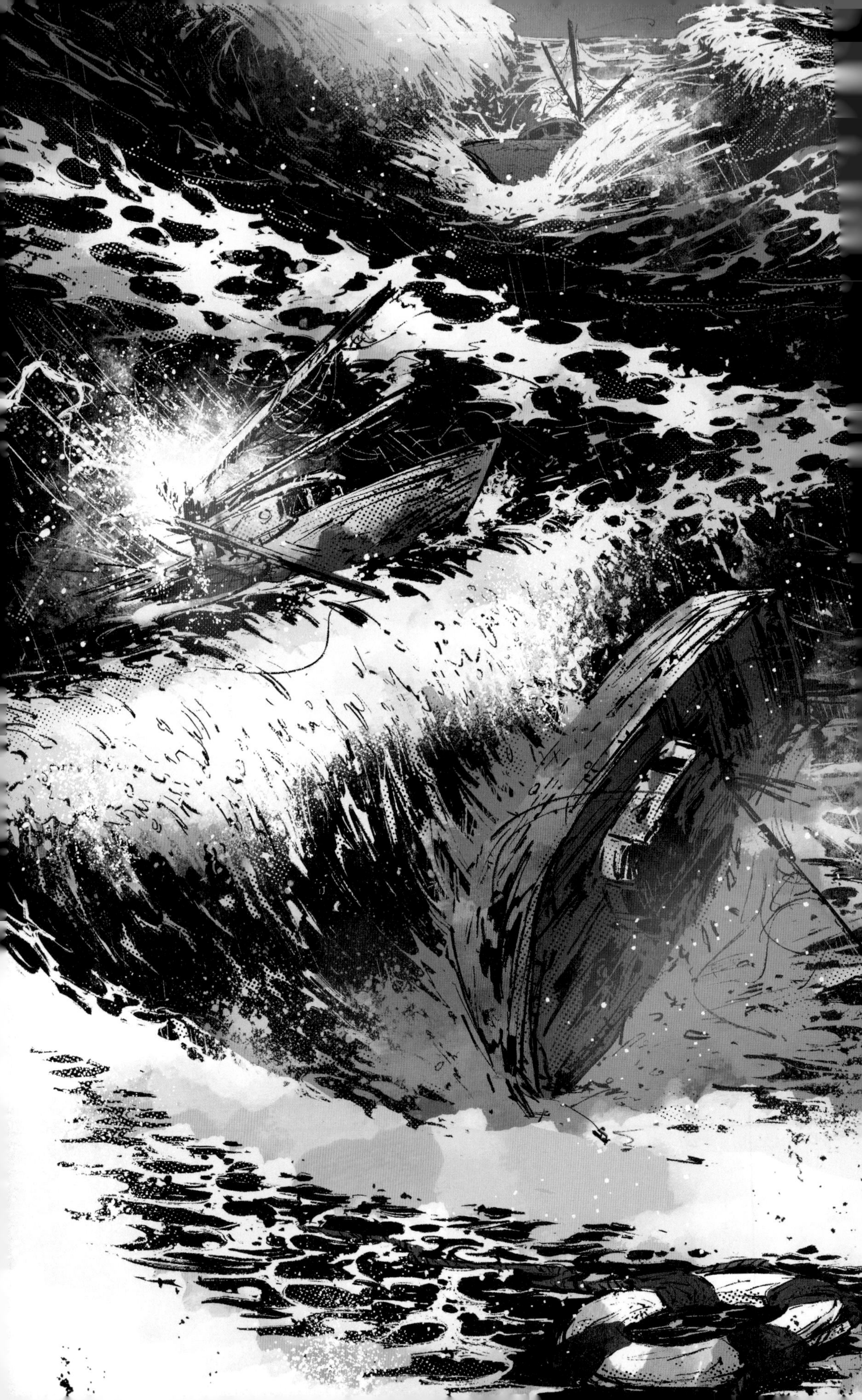

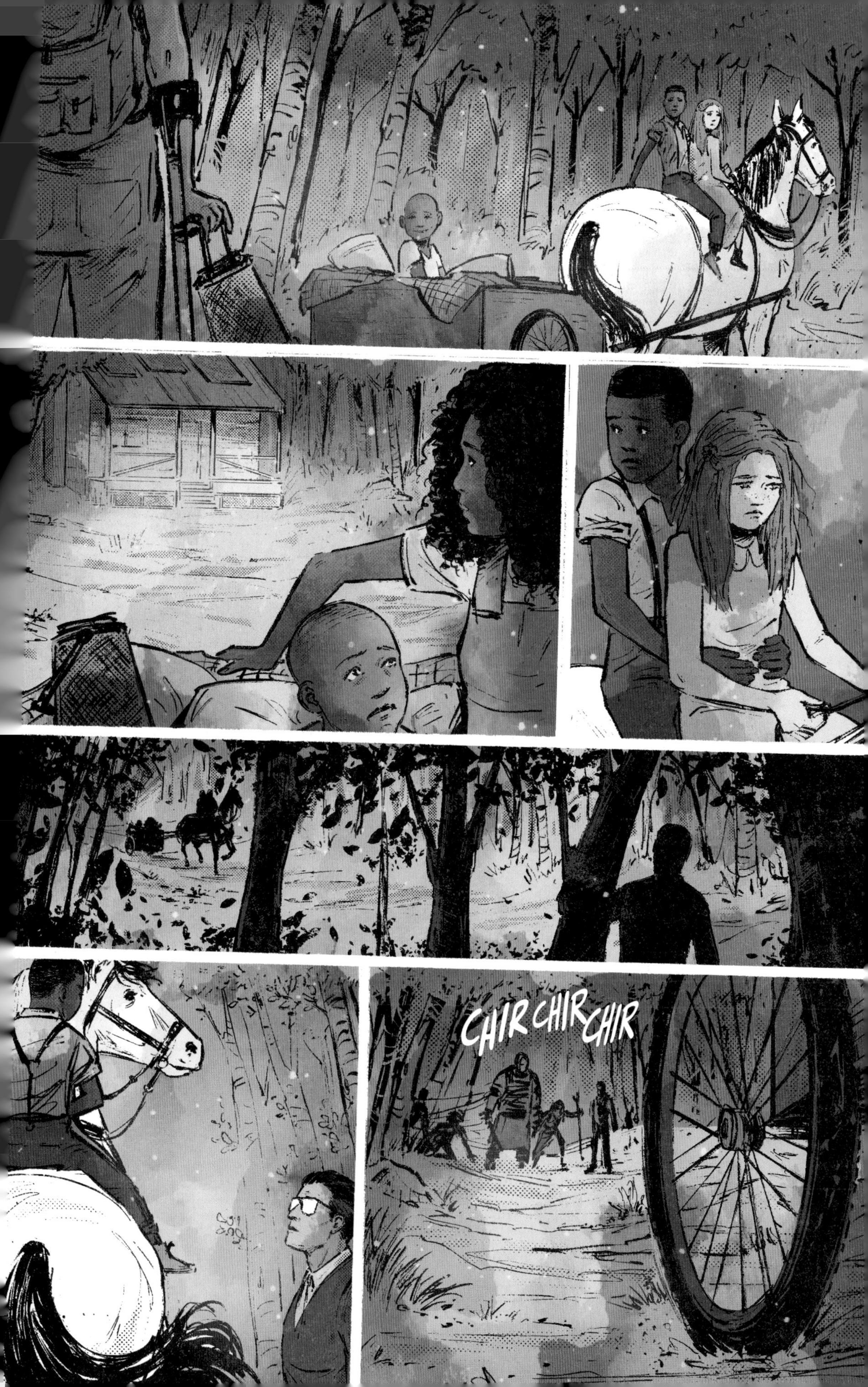
CHIR CHIR CHIR

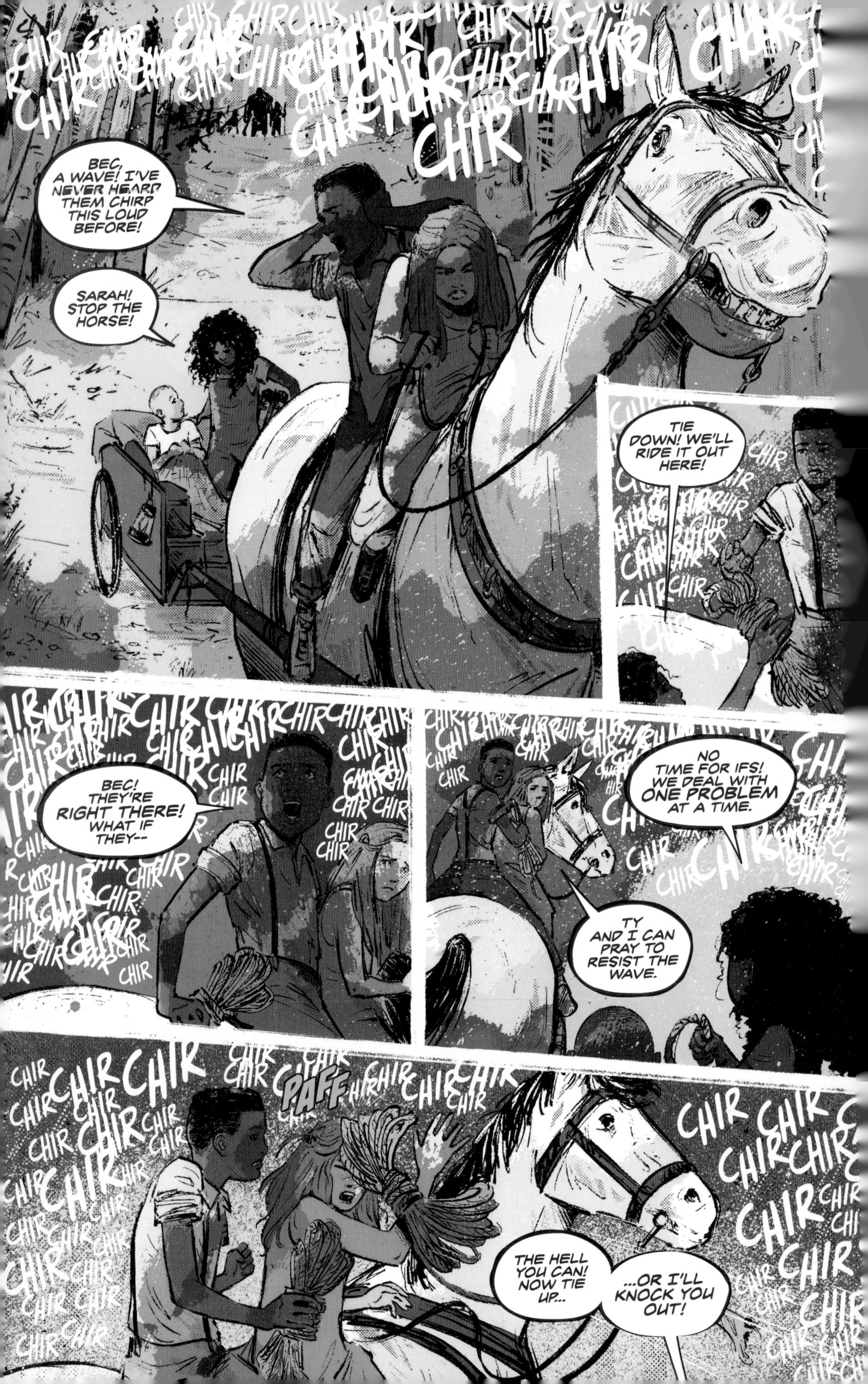

BEC, A WAVE! I'VE NEVER HEARD THEM CHIRP THIS LOUD BEFORE!
SARAH! STOP THE HORSE!
TIE DOWN! WE'LL RIDE IT OUT HERE!
BEC! THEY'RE RIGHT THERE! WHAT IF THEY--
NO TIME FOR IFS! WE DEAL WITH ONE PROBLEM AT A TIME.
TY AND I CAN PRAY TO RESIST THE WAVE.
PAFF
THE HELL YOU CAN! NOW TIE UP...
...OR I'LL KNOCK YOU OUT!

CHIR CHIR CHIR CHIR CHIR
GGRRRR!
CHIR CHIR CHIR CHIR CHIR
CHIR CHIR CHIR BRACK
CHIR CHIR CHIR
HAHAHA HAHA--
CHIR CHIR BRACK
BRACK
HURHUR HUR--
GRRR...?
URK!
CHIR
CHIR
CHIR
CHIR CHIR

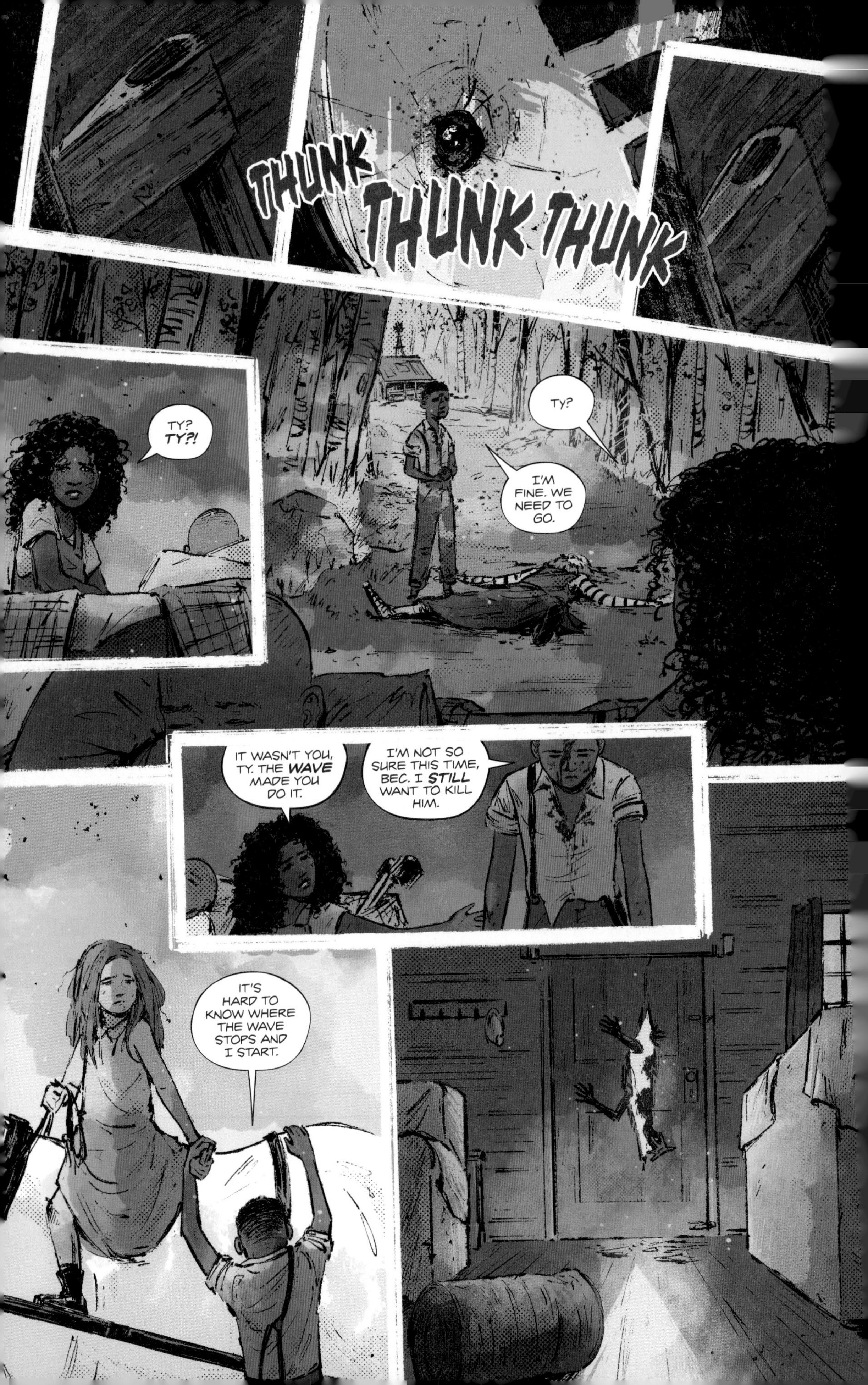
THUNK
THUNK THUNK
TY? TY?!
TY?
I'M FINE. WE NEED TO GO.
IT WASN'T YOU, TY. THE WAVE MADE YOU DO IT.
I'M NOT SO SURE THIS TIME, BEC. I STILL WANT TO KILL HIM.
IT'S HARD TO KNOW WHERE THE WAVE STOPS AND I START.

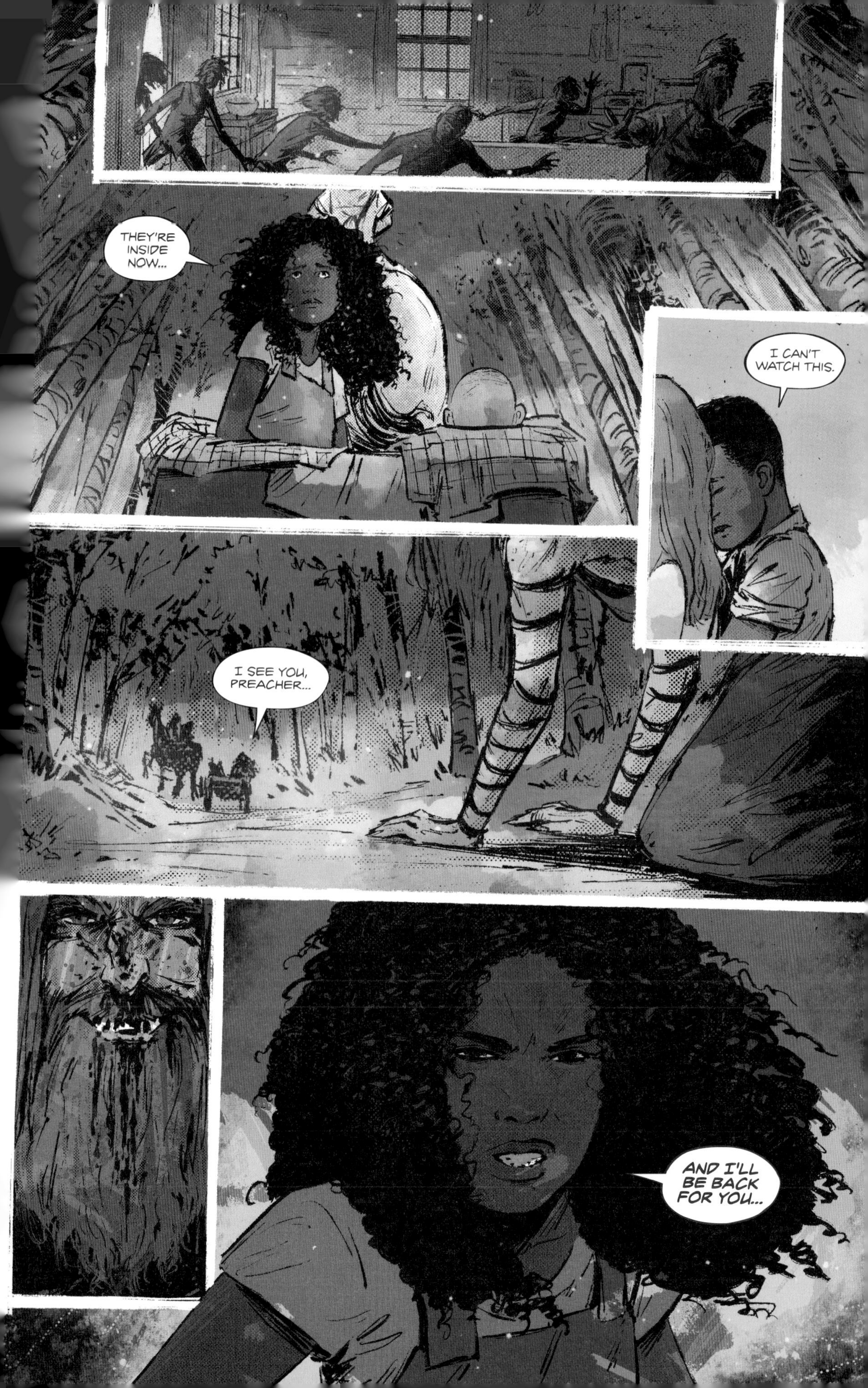
THEY'RE INSIDE NOW...
I CAN'T WATCH THIS.
I SEE YOU, PREACHER...
AND I'LL BE BACK FOR YOU...

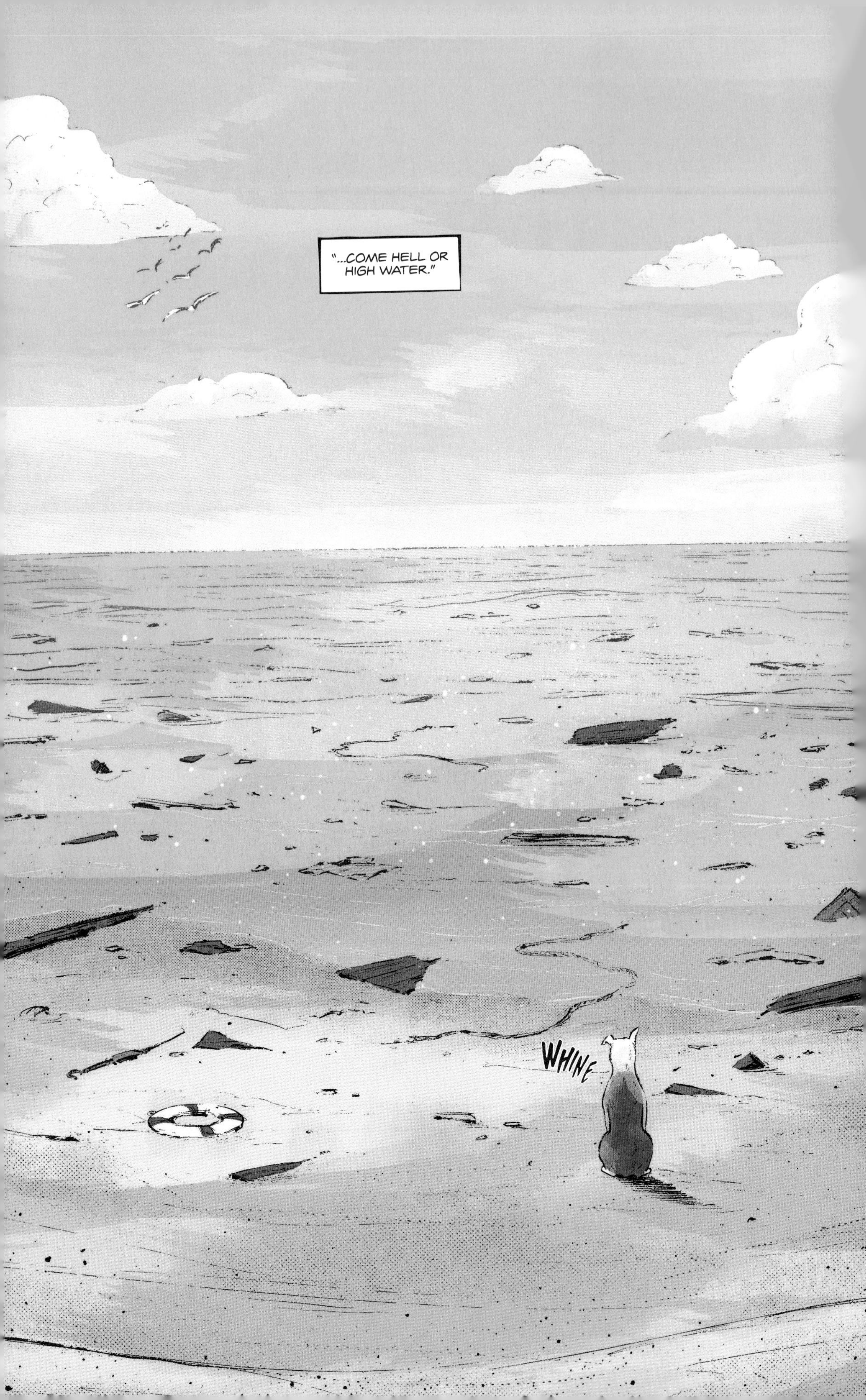
"...COME HELL OR HIGH WATER."
WHINE

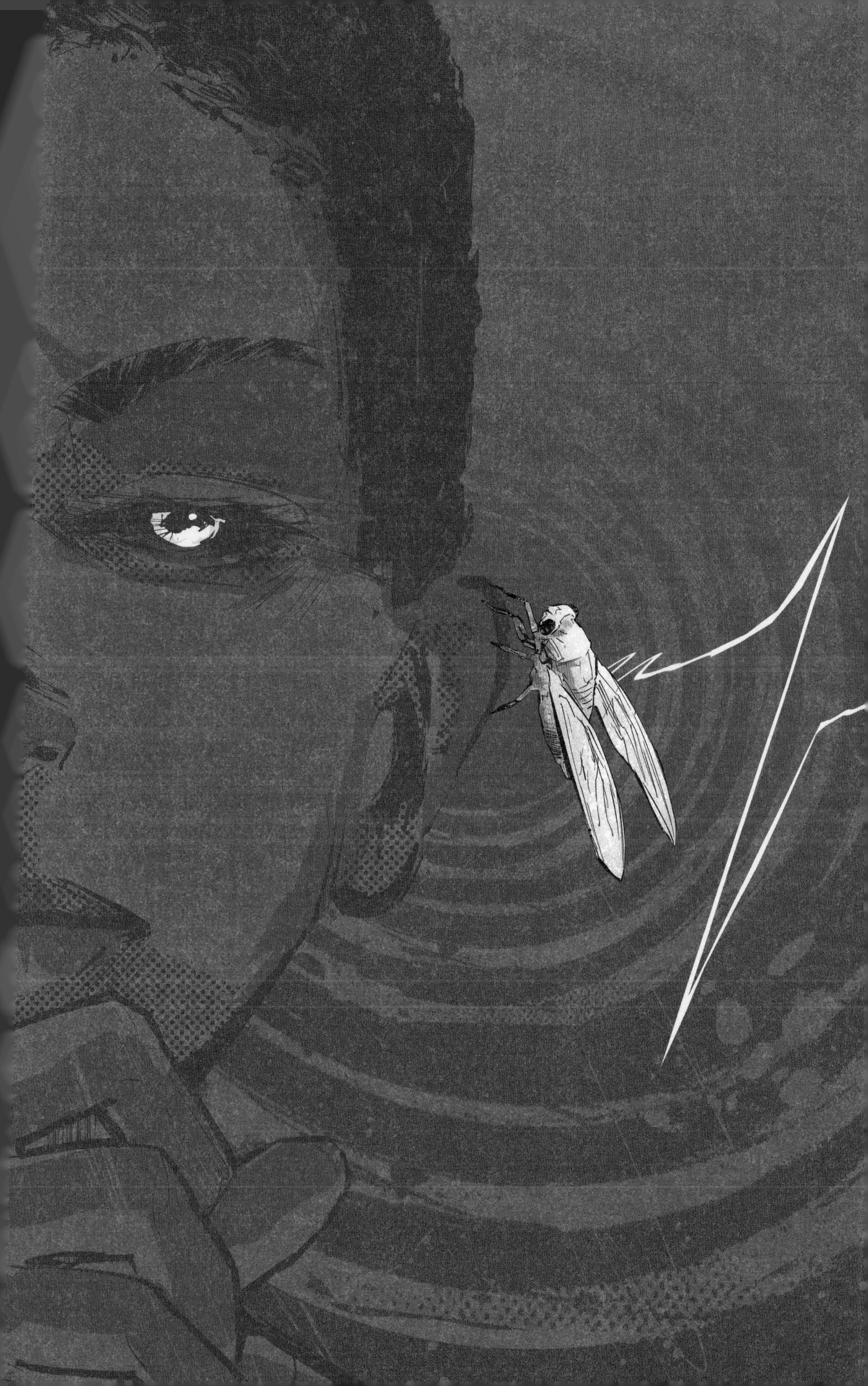

FIGHT

CHAPTER

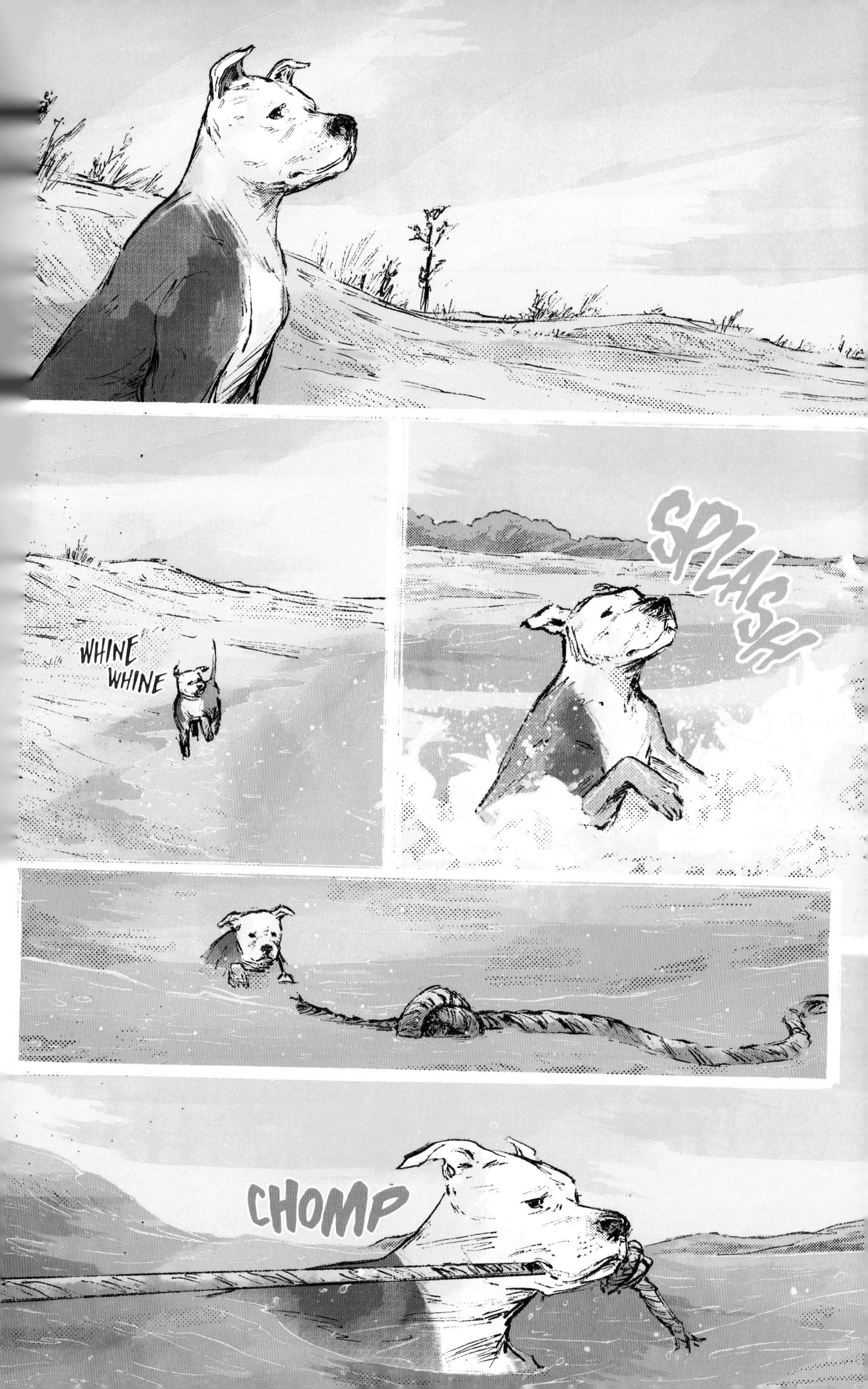
WHINE
WHINE
SPLASH
CHOMP

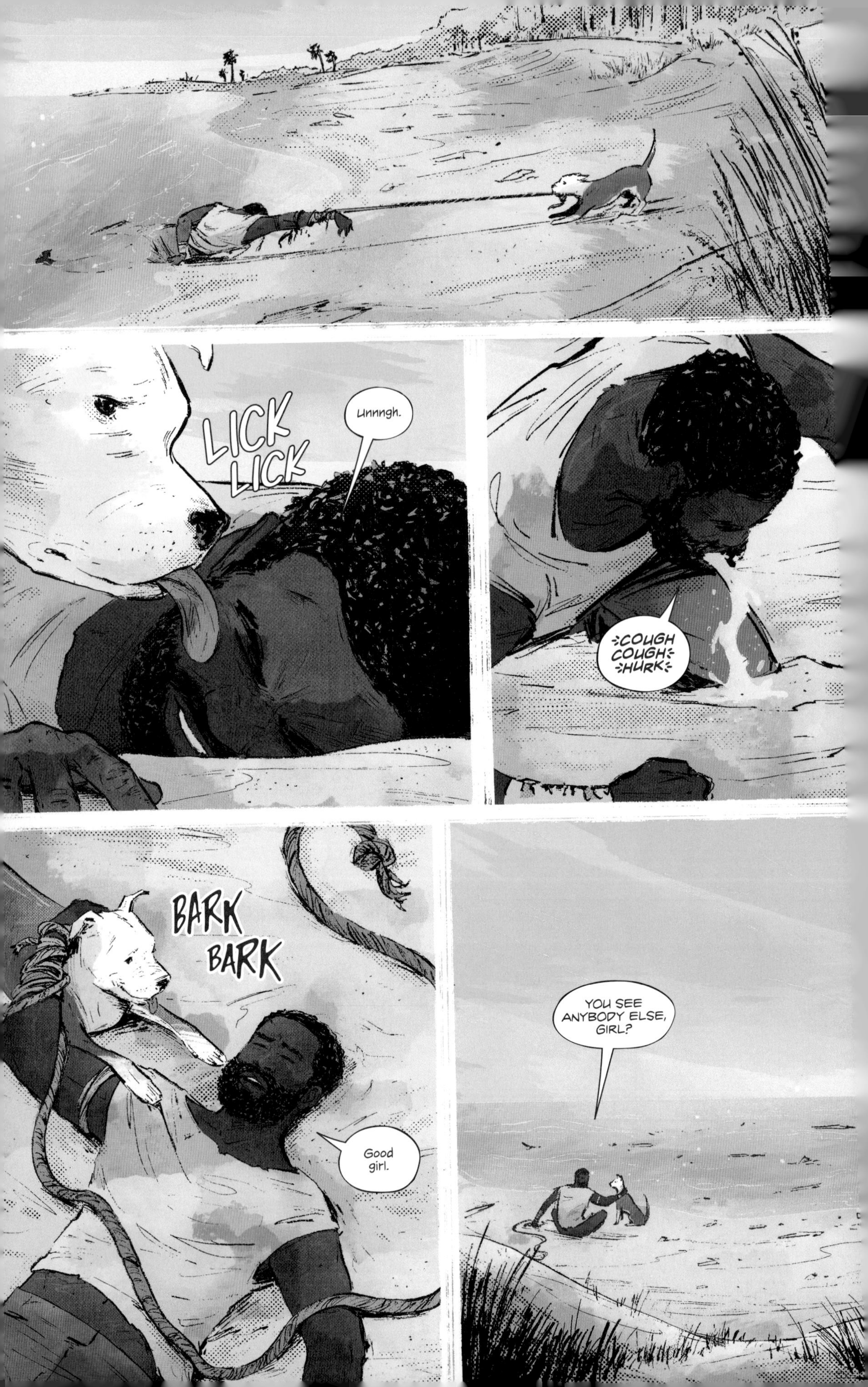
LICK LICK
Unnngh.
COUGH COUGH HURK
BARK BARK
Good girl.
YOU SEE ANYBODY ELSE, GIRL?

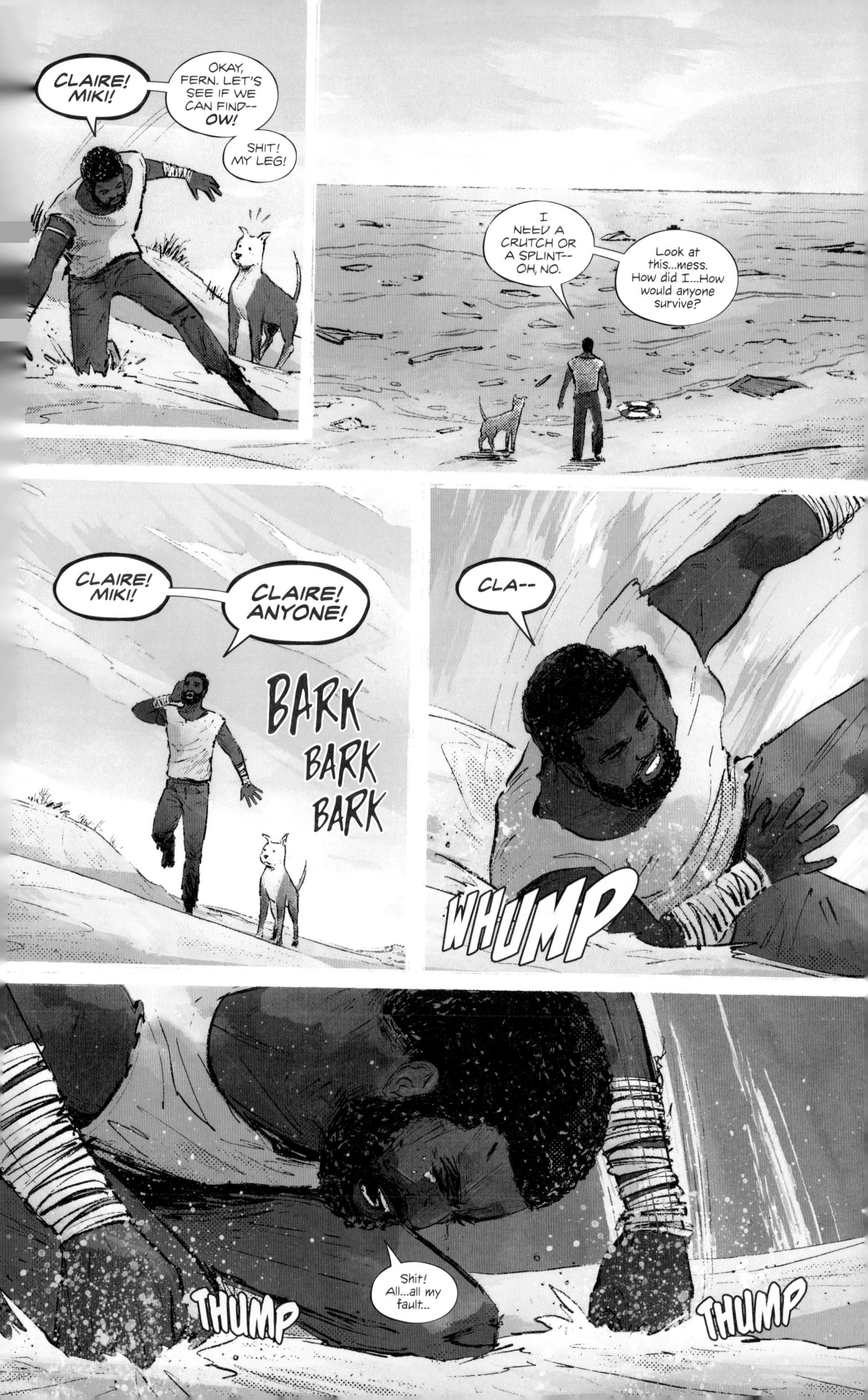
CLAIRE! MIKI!
OKAY, FERN. LET'S SEE IF WE CAN FIND-- OW!
SHIT! MY LEG!
I NEED A CRUTCH OR A SPLINT-- OH, NO.
Look at this...mess. How did I...How would anyone survive?
CLAIRE! MIKI!
CLAIRE! ANYONE!
BARK BARK BARK
CLA--
WHUMP
Shit! All...all my fault...
THUMP
THUMP

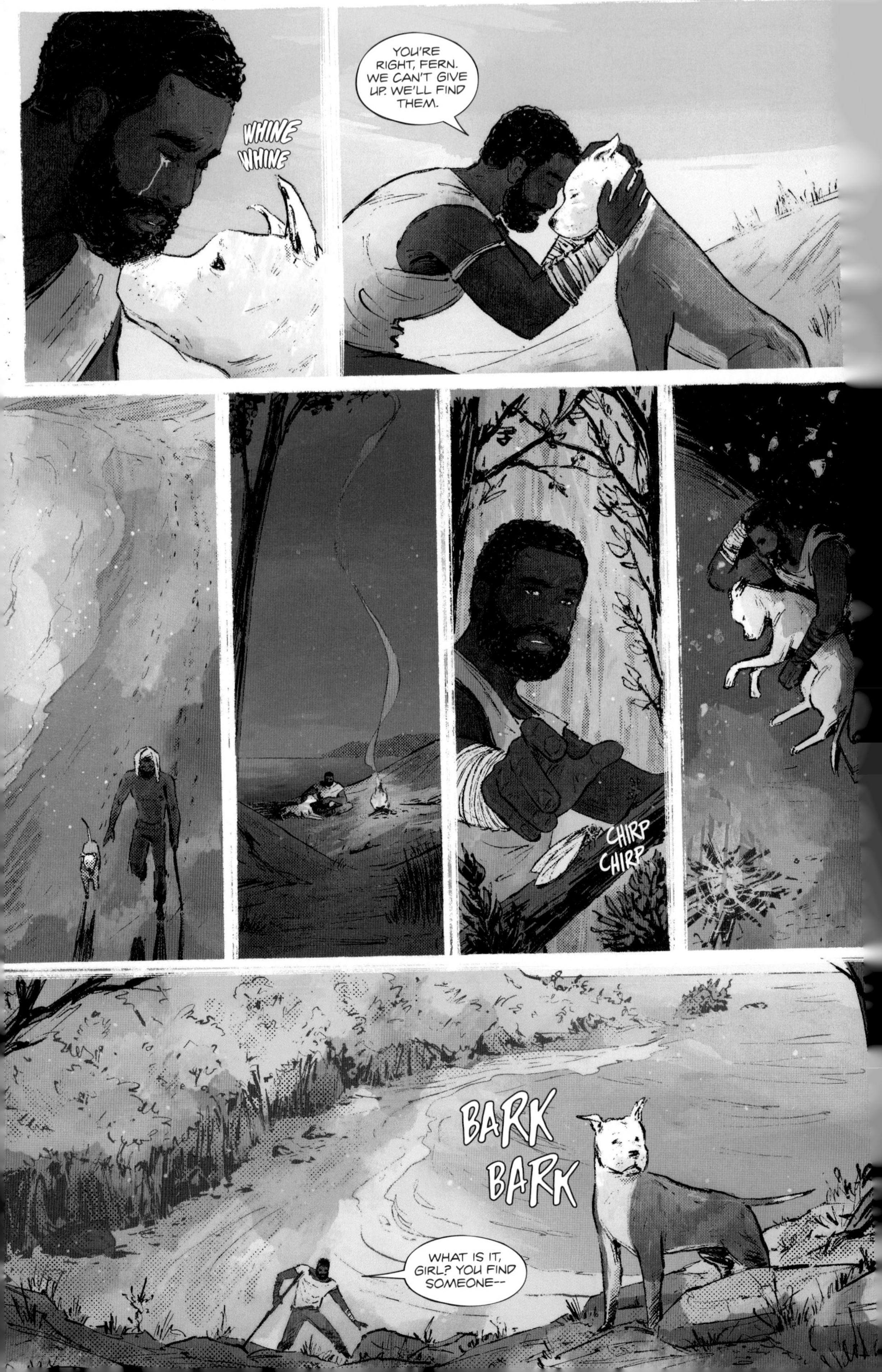
WHINE
WHINE
YOU'RE RIGHT, FERN. WE CAN'T GIVE UP. WE'LL FIND THEM.
CHIRP
CHIRP
BARK
BARK
WHAT IS IT, GIRL? YOU FIND SOMEONE--

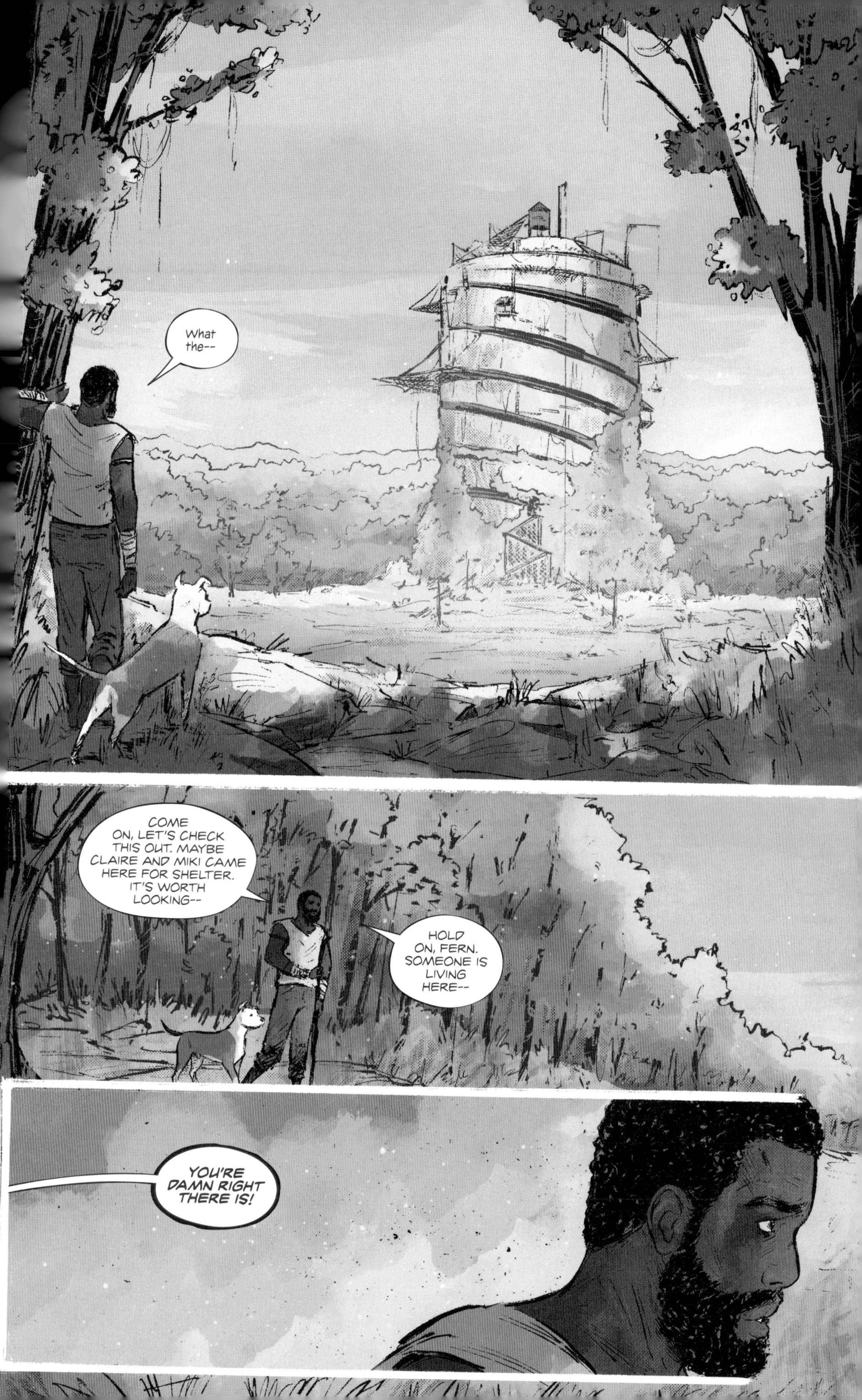
What the--
COME ON, LET'S CHECK THIS OUT. MAYBE CLAIRE AND MIKI CAME HERE FOR SHELTER. IT'S WORTH LOOKING--
HOLD ON, FERN. SOMEONE IS LIVING HERE--
YOU'RE DAMN RIGHT THERE IS!

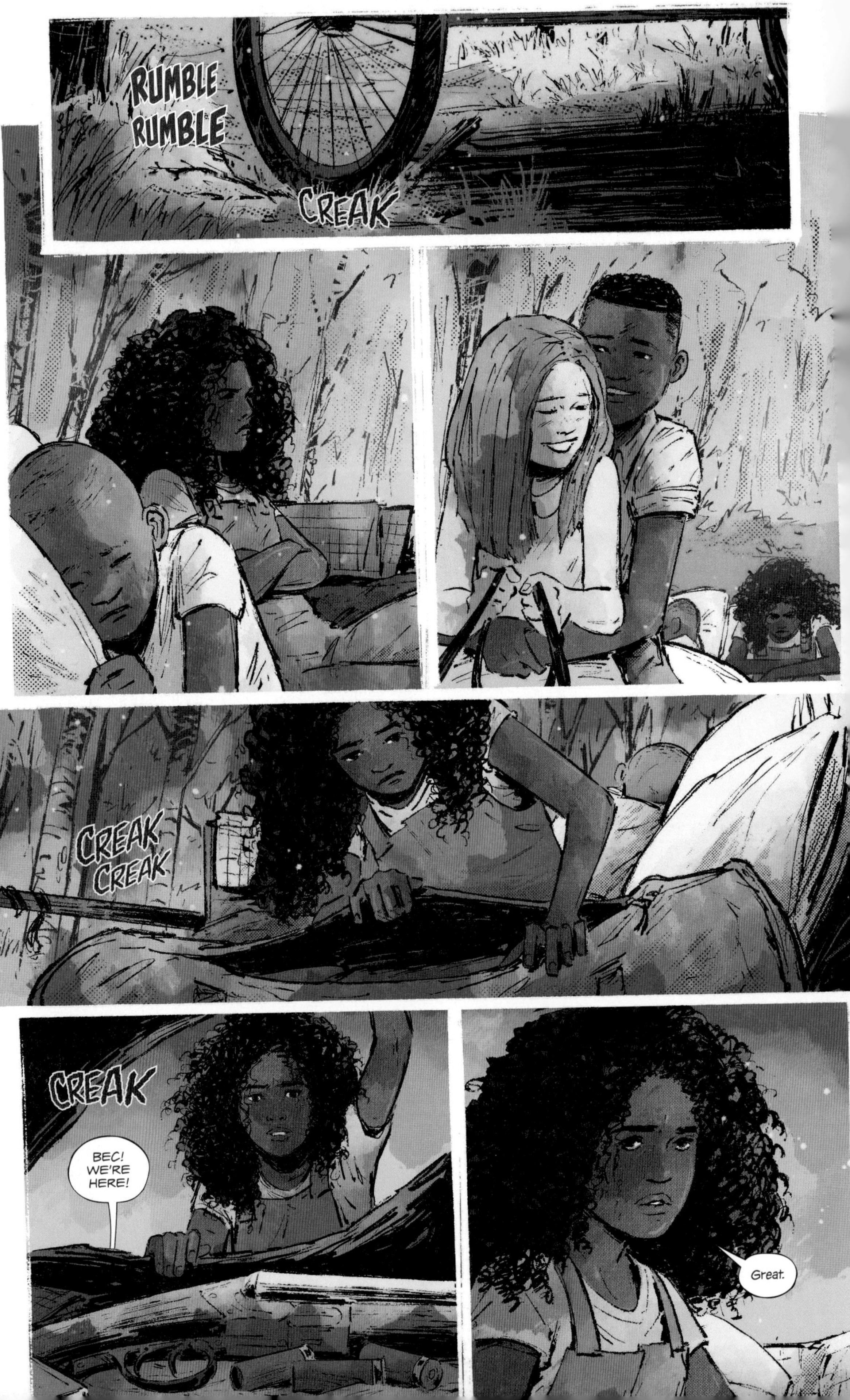
RUMBLE
RUMBLE
CREAK
CREAK
CREAK
CREAK
BEC! WE'RE HERE!
Great.

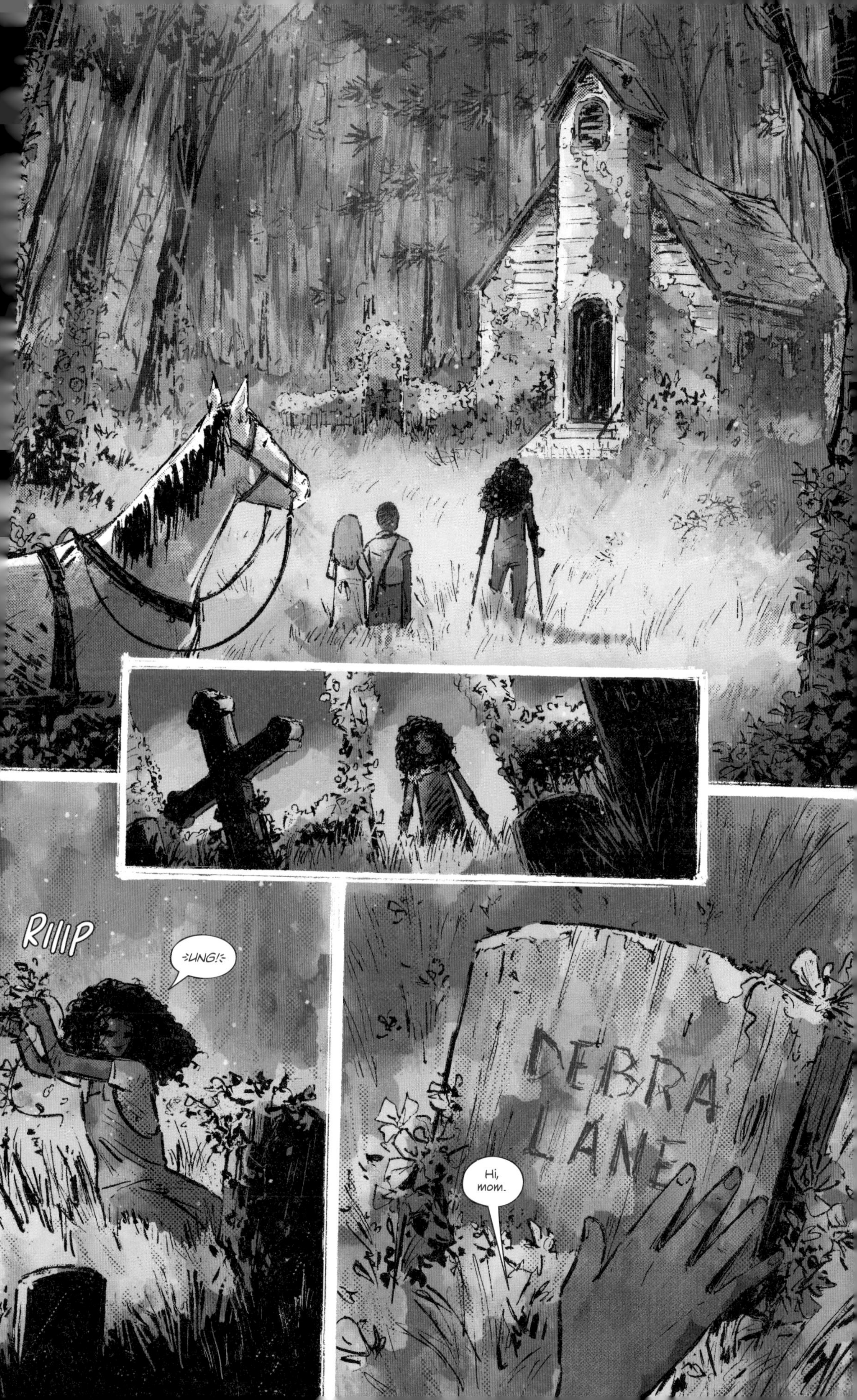
RIIIP
UNG!
DEBRA LANE
Hi, mom.

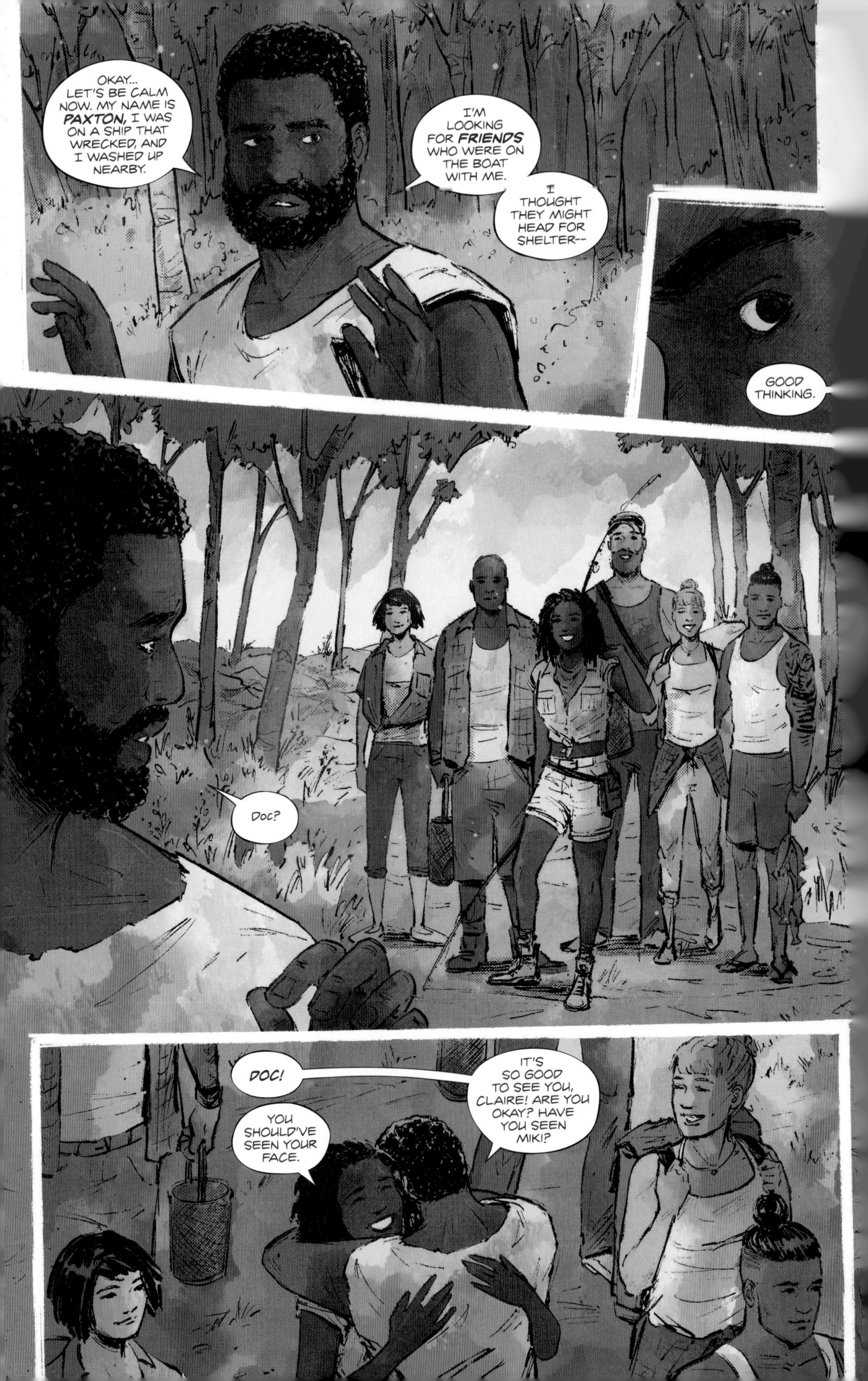
OKAY... LET'S BE CALM NOW. MY NAME IS PAXTON, I WAS ON A SHIP THAT WRECKED, AND I WASHED UP NEARBY.
I'M LOOKING FOR FRIENDS WHO WERE ON THE BOAT WITH ME.
I THOUGHT THEY MIGHT HEAD FOR SHELTER--
GOOD THINKING.
Doc?
DOC!
IT'S SO GOOD TO SEE YOU, CLAIRE! ARE YOU OKAY? HAVE YOU SEEN MIKI?
YOU SHOULD'VE SEEN YOUR FACE.

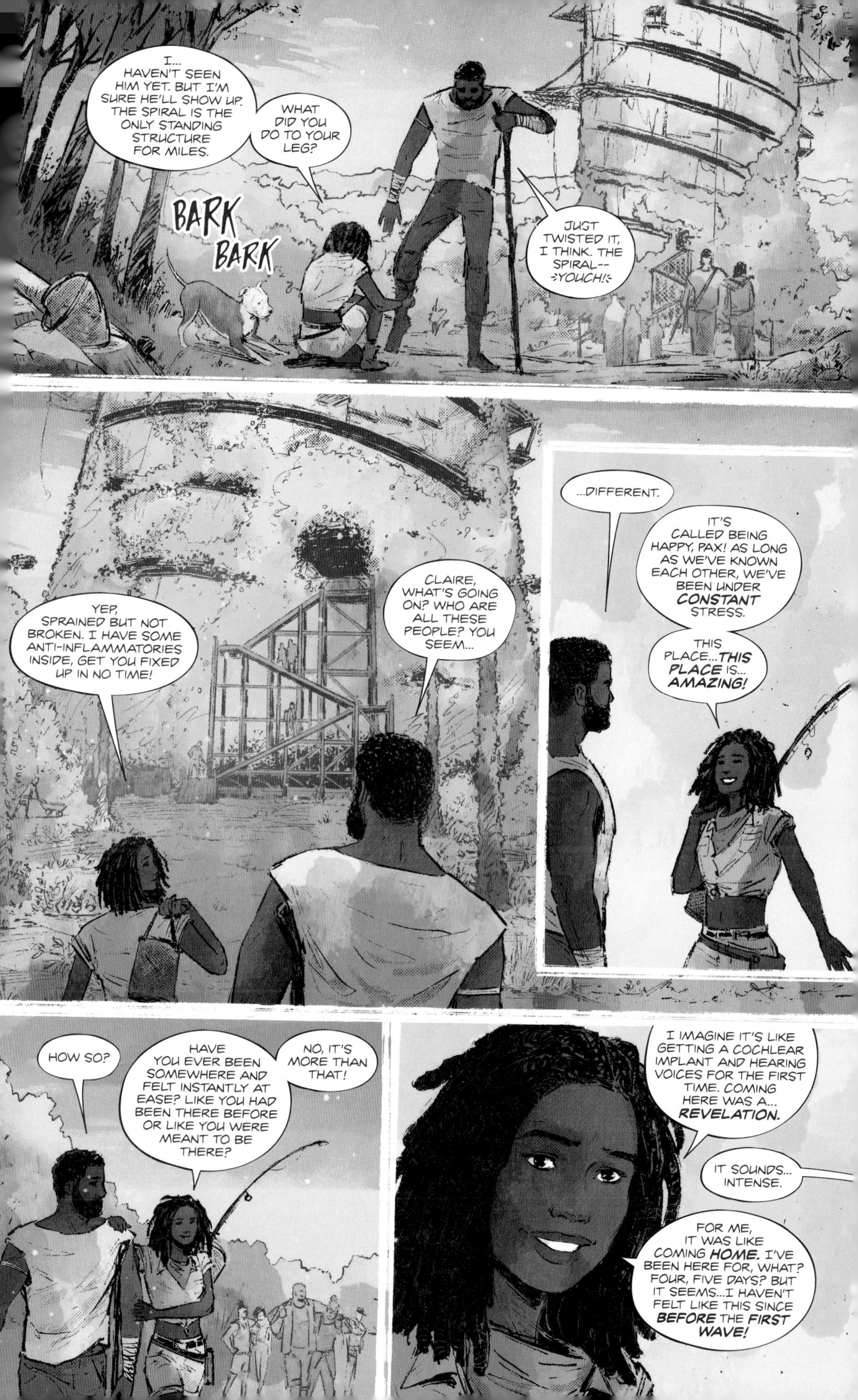
I... HAVEN'T SEEN HIM YET. BUT I'M SURE HE'LL SHOW UP. THE SPIRAL IS THE ONLY STANDING STRUCTURE FOR MILES.
WHAT DID YOU DO TO YOUR LEG?
BARK BARK
JUST TWISTED IT, I THINK. THE SPIRAL-- YOUCH!
YEP, SPRAINED BUT NOT BROKEN. I HAVE SOME ANTI-INFLAMMATORIES INSIDE, GET YOU FIXED UP IN NO TIME!
CLAIRE, WHAT'S GOING ON? WHO ARE ALL THESE PEOPLE? YOU SEEM...
...DIFFERENT.
IT'S CALLED BEING HAPPY, PAX! AS LONG AS WE'VE KNOWN EACH OTHER, WE'VE BEEN UNDER CONSTANT STRESS.
THIS PLACE...THIS PLACE IS... AMAZING!
HOW SO?
NO, IT'S MORE THAN THAT!
HAVE YOU EVER BEEN SOMEWHERE AND FELT INSTANTLY AT EASE? LIKE YOU HAD BEEN THERE BEFORE OR LIKE YOU WERE MEANT TO BE THERE?
I IMAGINE IT'S LIKE GETTING A COCHLEAR IMPLANT AND HEARING VOICES FOR THE FIRST TIME. COMING HERE WAS A... REVELATION.
IT SOUNDS... INTENSE.
FOR ME, IT WAS LIKE COMING HOME. I'VE BEEN HERE FOR, WHAT? FOUR, FIVE DAYS? BUT IT SEEMS...I HAVEN'T FELT LIKE THIS SINCE BEFORE THE FIRST WAVE!

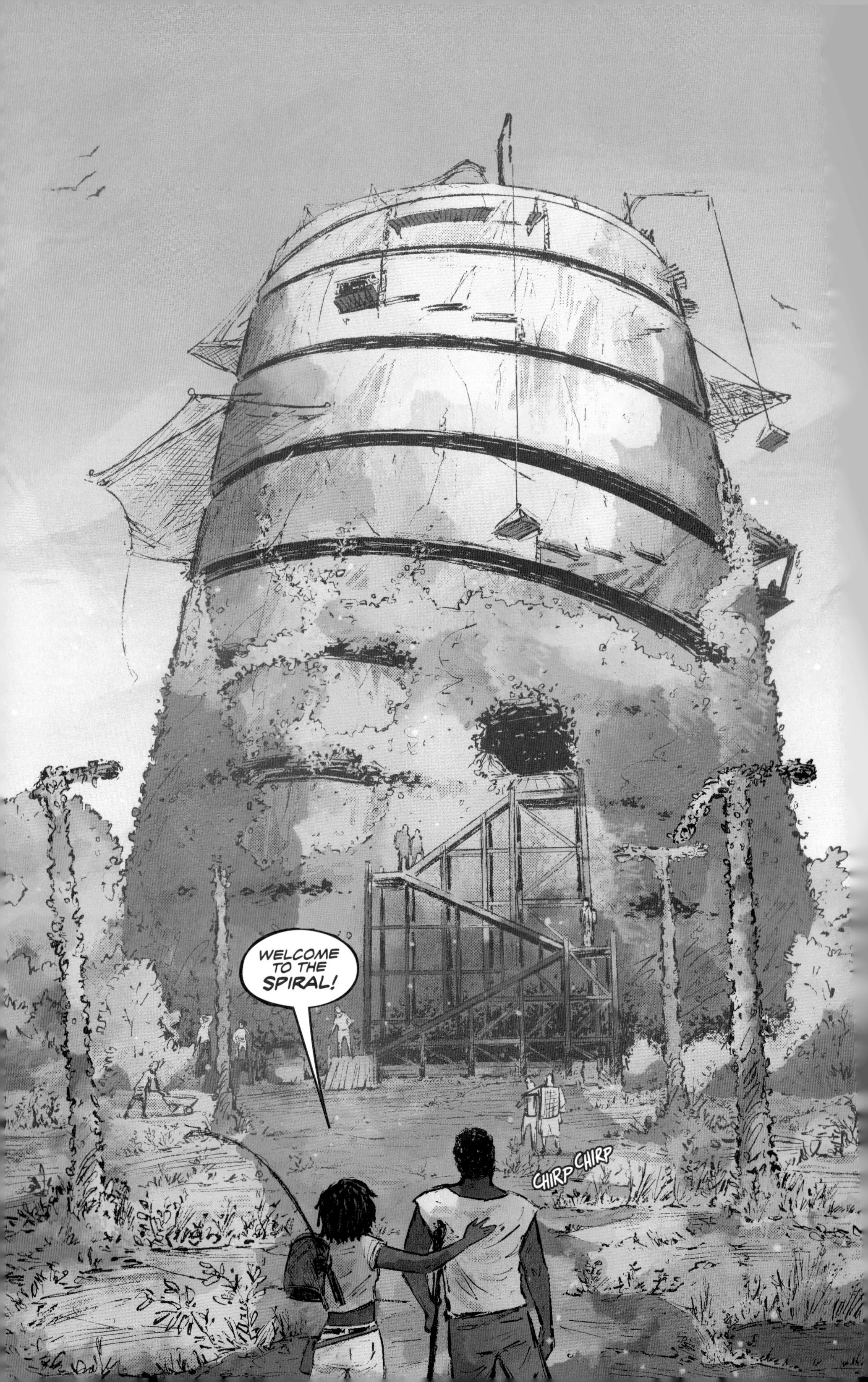
WELCOME TO THE SPIRAL!
CHIRP CHIRP

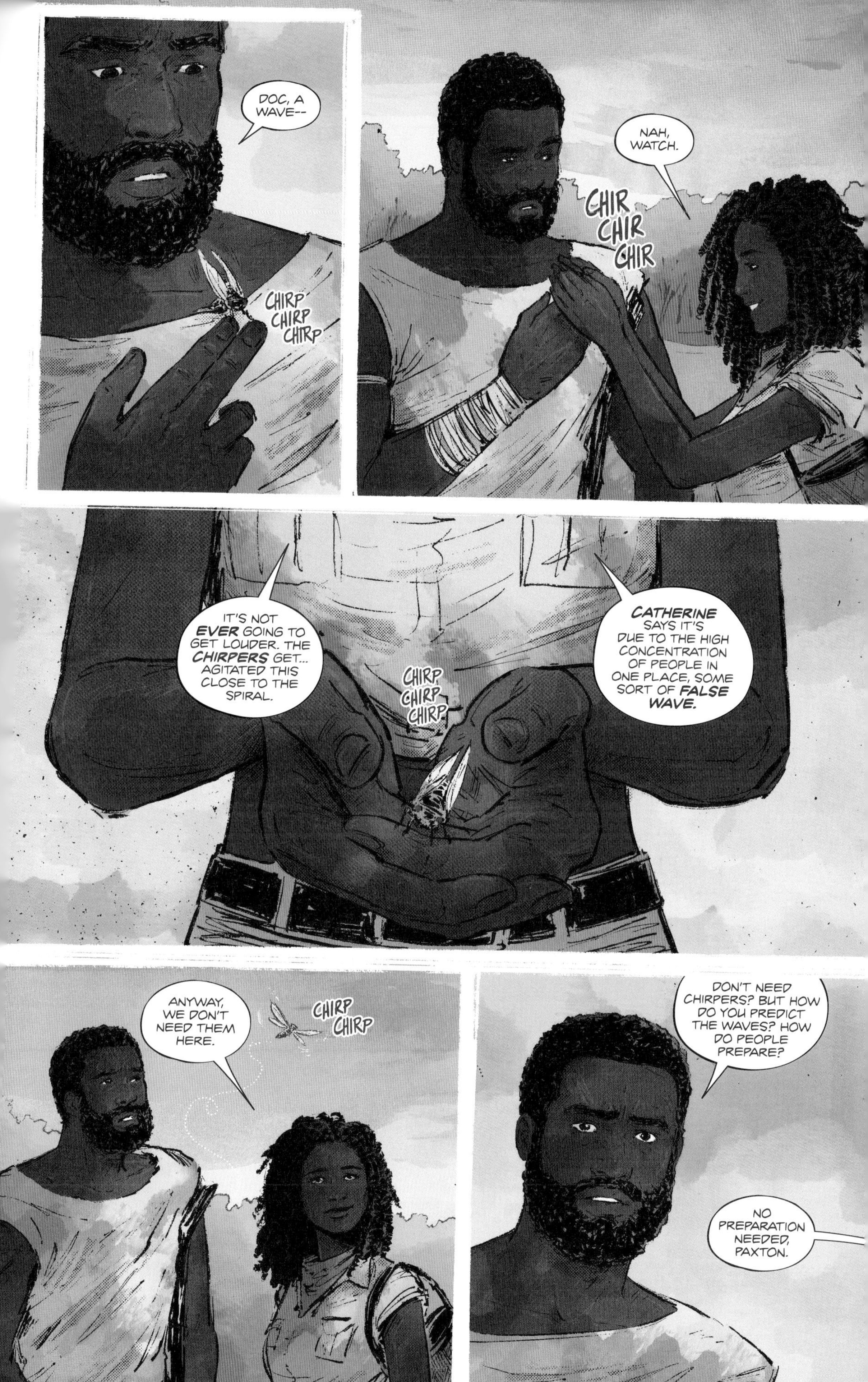
DOC, A WAVE--
CHIRP CHIRP CHIRP
NAH, WATCH.
CHIR CHIR CHIR
IT'S NOT **EVER** GOING TO GET LOUDER. THE **CHIRPERS** GET... AGITATED THIS CLOSE TO THE SPIRAL.
CHIRP CHIRP CHIRP
CATHERINE SAYS IT'S DUE TO THE HIGH CONCENTRATION OF PEOPLE IN ONE PLACE, SOME SORT OF **FALSE WAVE.**
ANYWAY, WE DON'T NEED THEM HERE.
CHIRP CHIRP
DON'T NEED CHIRPERS? BUT HOW DO YOU PREDICT THE WAVES? HOW DO PEOPLE PREPARE?
NO PREPARATION NEEDED, PAXTON.

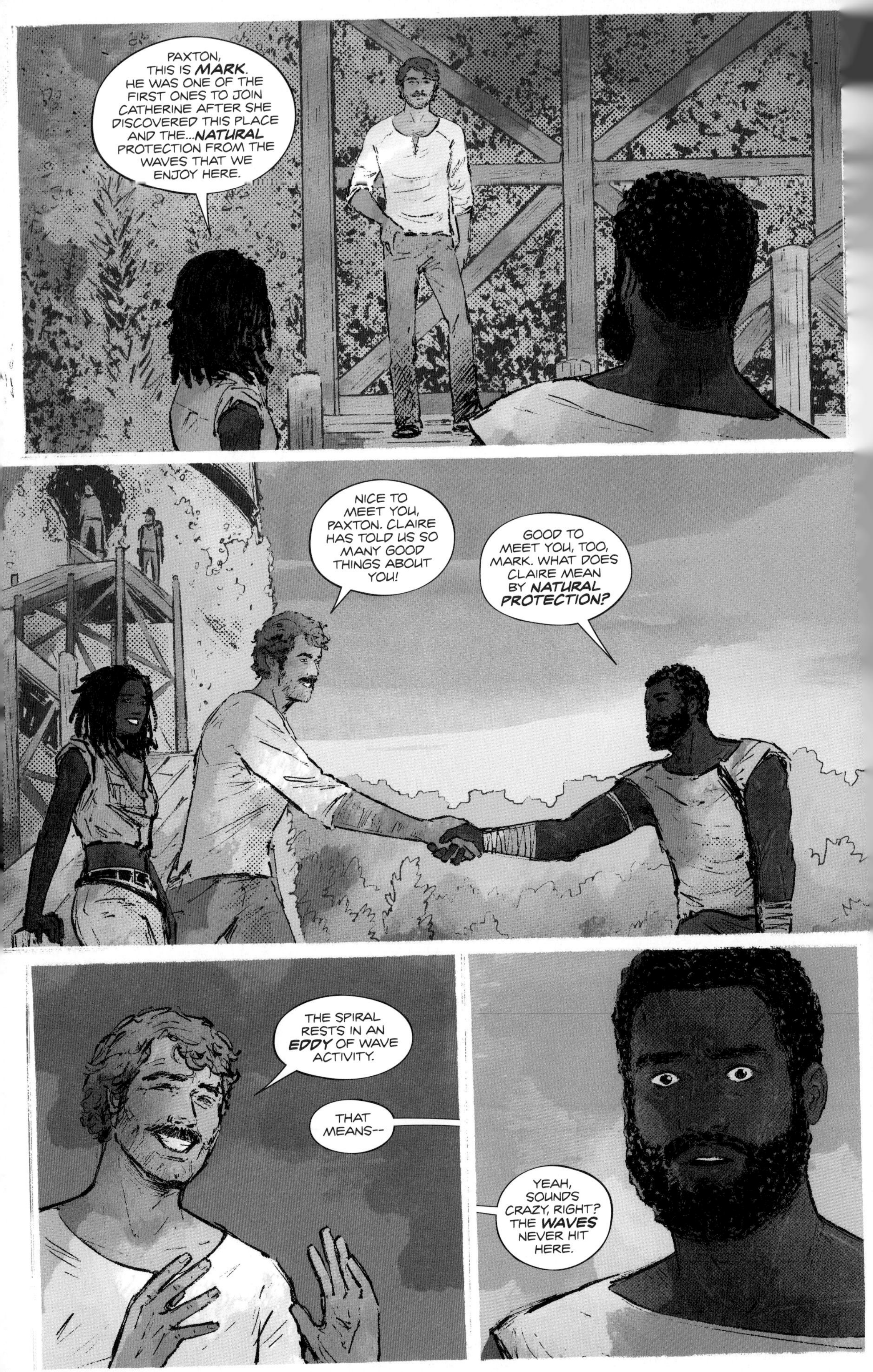
PAXTON, THIS IS MARK. HE WAS ONE OF THE FIRST ONES TO JOIN CATHERINE AFTER SHE DISCOVERED THIS PLACE AND THE...NATURAL PROTECTION FROM THE WAVES THAT WE ENJOY HERE.
NICE TO MEET YOU, PAXTON. CLAIRE HAS TOLD US SO MANY GOOD THINGS ABOUT YOU!
GOOD TO MEET YOU, TOO, MARK. WHAT DOES CLAIRE MEAN BY NATURAL PROTECTION?
THE SPIRAL RESTS IN AN EDDY OF WAVE ACTIVITY.
THAT MEANS--
YEAH, SOUNDS CRAZY, RIGHT? THE WAVES NEVER HIT HERE.

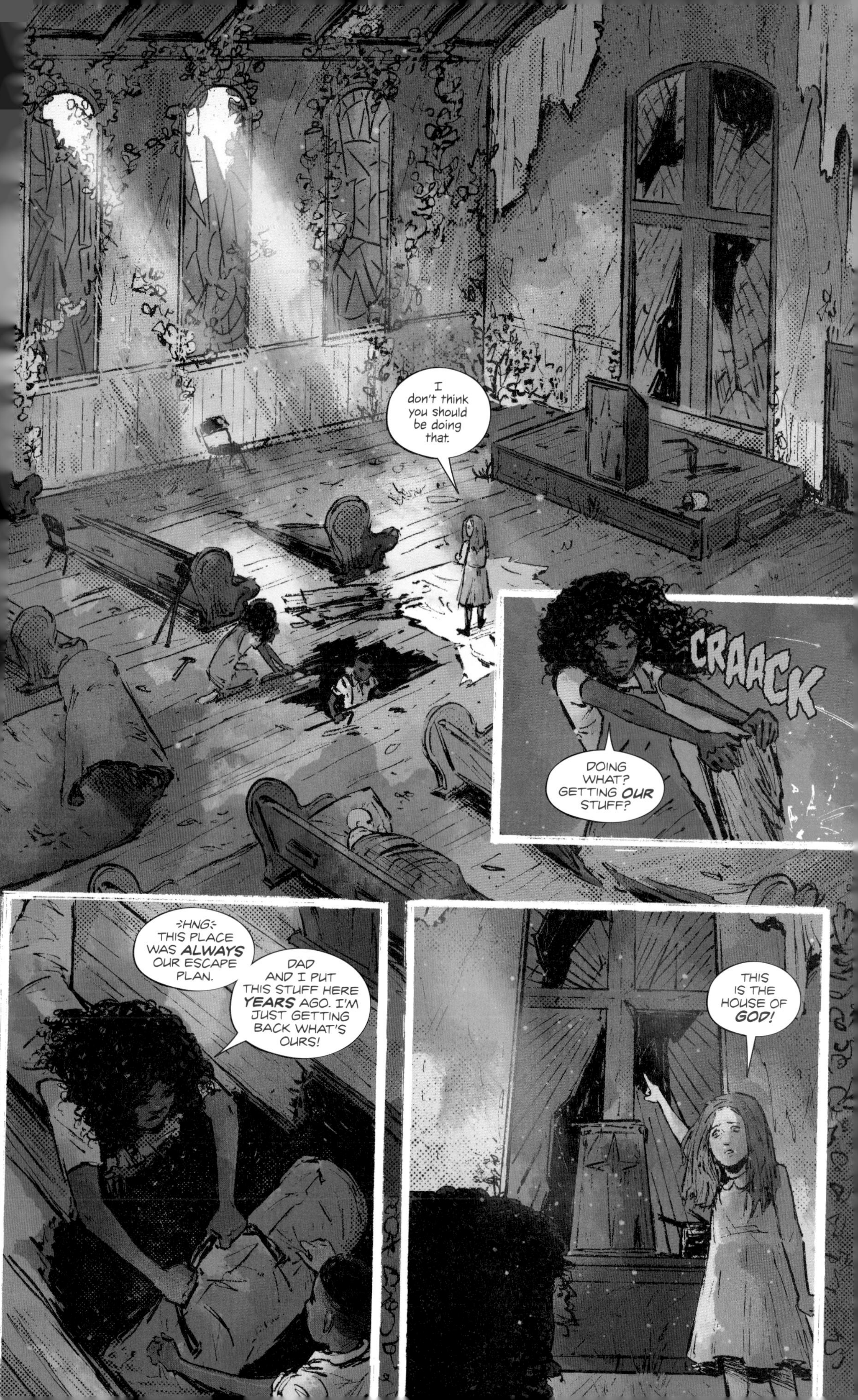
I don't think you should be doing that.
CRAACK
DOING WHAT? GETTING OUR STUFF?
≈HNG≈ THIS PLACE WAS ALWAYS OUR ESCAPE PLAN.
DAD AND I PUT THIS STUFF HERE YEARS AGO. I'M JUST GETTING BACK WHAT'S OURS!
THIS IS THE HOUSE OF GOD!

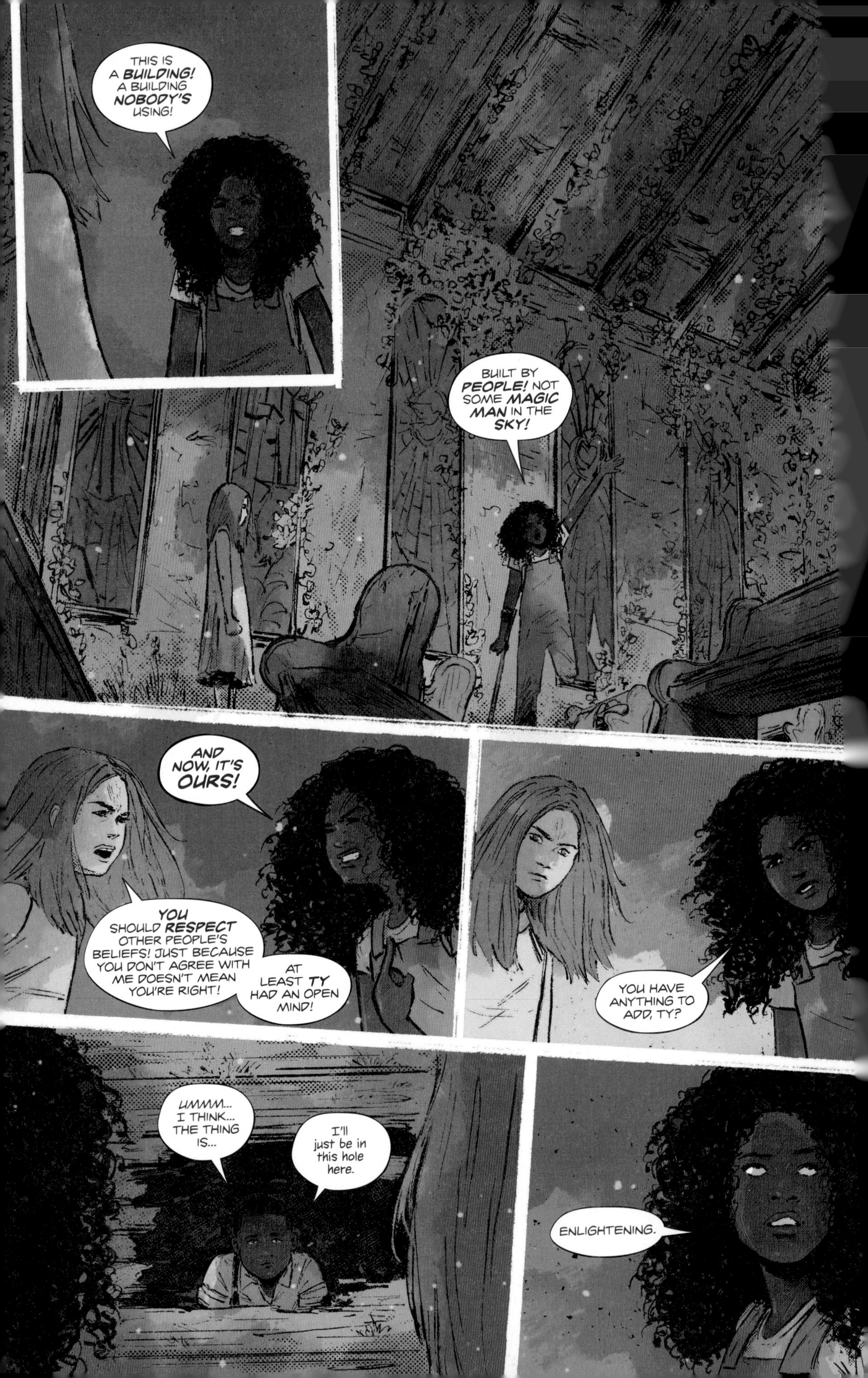
THIS IS A BUILDING! A BUILDING NOBODY'S USING!
BUILT BY PEOPLE! NOT SOME MAGIC MAN IN THE SKY!
AND NOW, IT'S OURS!
YOU SHOULD RESPECT OTHER PEOPLE'S BELIEFS! JUST BECAUSE YOU DON'T AGREE WITH ME DOESN'T MEAN YOU'RE RIGHT!
AT LEAST TY HAD AN OPEN MIND!
YOU HAVE ANYTHING TO ADD, TY?
UMMM... I THINK... THE THING IS...
I'll just be in this hole here.
ENLIGHTENING.

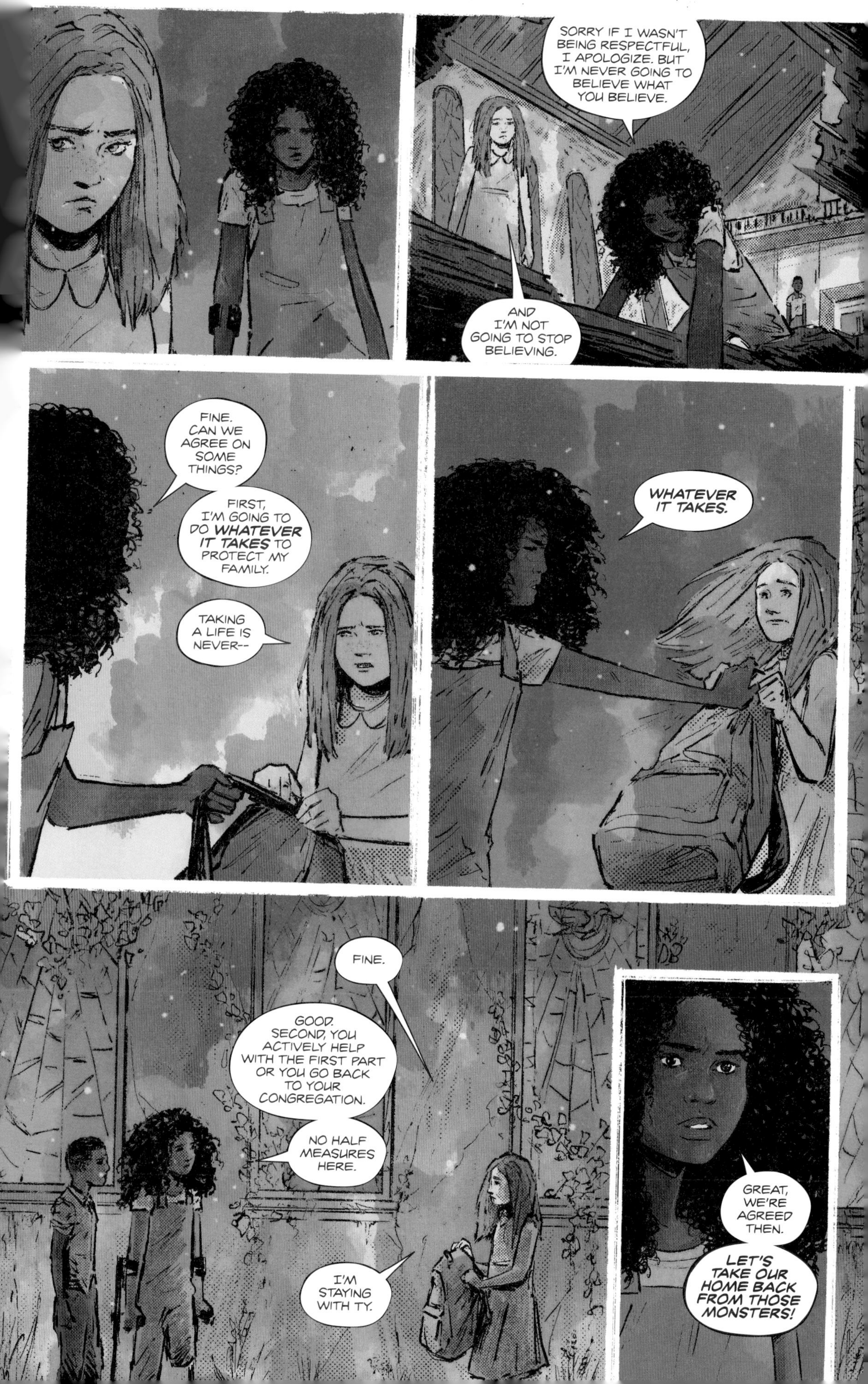
SORRY IF I WASN'T BEING RESPECTFUL, I APOLOGIZE. BUT I'M NEVER GOING TO BELIEVE WHAT YOU BELIEVE.
AND I'M NOT GOING TO STOP BELIEVING.
FINE. CAN WE AGREE ON SOME THINGS?
FIRST, I'M GOING TO DO **WHATEVER IT TAKES** TO PROTECT MY FAMILY.
TAKING A LIFE IS NEVER--
WHATEVER IT TAKES.
FINE.
GOOD. SECOND, YOU ACTIVELY HELP WITH THE FIRST PART OR YOU GO BACK TO YOUR CONGREGATION.
NO HALF MEASURES HERE.
I'M STAYING WITH TY.
GREAT, WE'RE AGREED THEN.
LET'S TAKE OUR HOME BACK FROM THOSE MONSTERS!

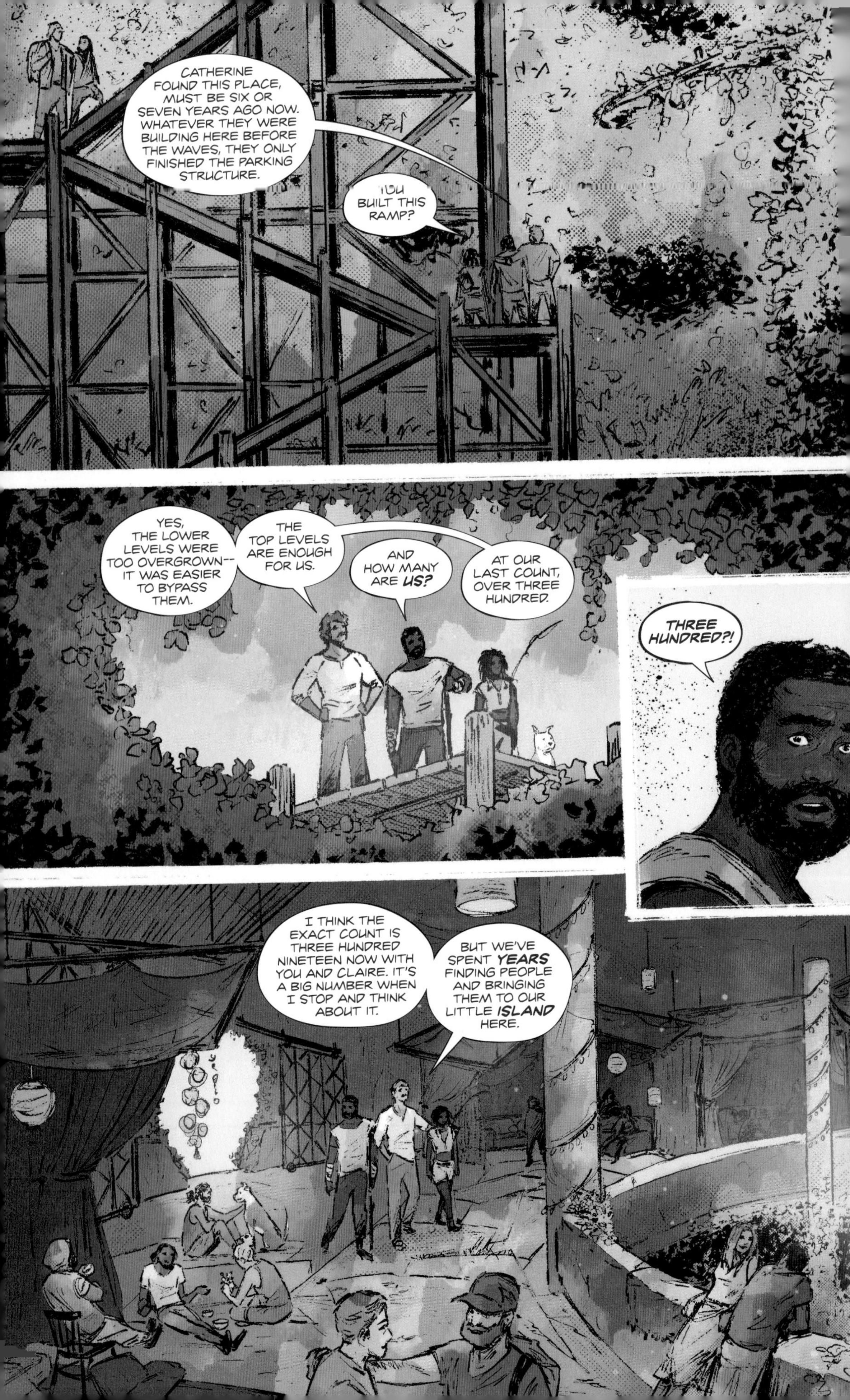
CATHERINE FOUND THIS PLACE, MUST BE SIX OR SEVEN YEARS AGO NOW. WHATEVER THEY WERE BUILDING HERE BEFORE THE WAVES, THEY ONLY FINISHED THE PARKING STRUCTURE.
YOU BUILT THIS RAMP?
YES, THE LOWER LEVELS WERE TOO OVERGROWN-- IT WAS EASIER TO BYPASS THEM.
THE TOP LEVELS ARE ENOUGH FOR US.
AND HOW MANY ARE *US?*
AT OUR LAST COUNT, OVER THREE HUNDRED.
THREE HUNDRED?!
I THINK THE EXACT COUNT IS THREE HUNDRED NINETEEN NOW WITH YOU AND CLAIRE. IT'S A BIG NUMBER WHEN I STOP AND THINK ABOUT IT.
BUT WE'VE SPENT **YEARS** FINDING PEOPLE AND BRINGING THEM TO OUR LITTLE **ISLAND** HERE.

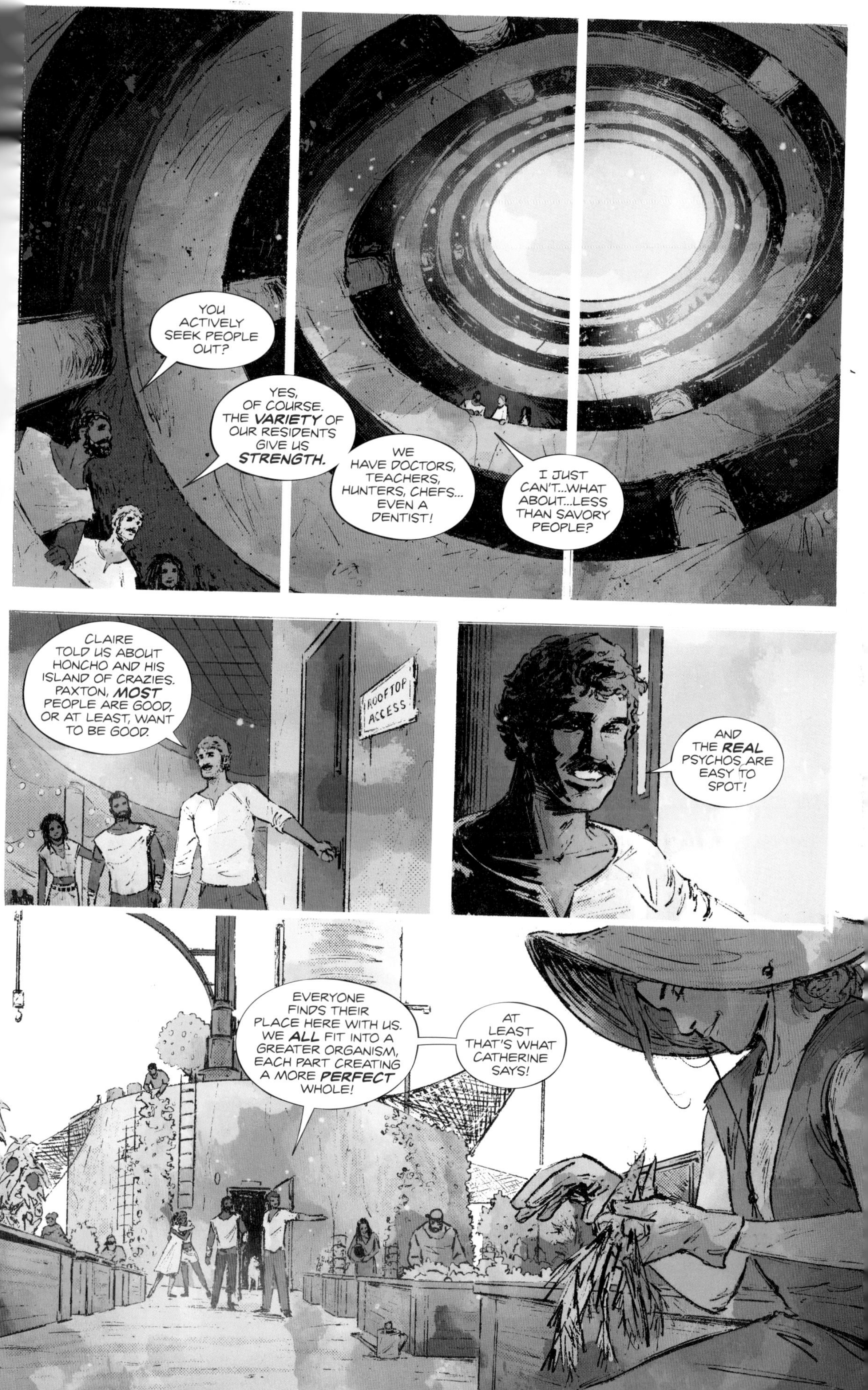
YOU ACTIVELY SEEK PEOPLE OUT?
YES, OF COURSE. THE **VARIETY** OF OUR RESIDENTS GIVE US **STRENGTH.**
WE HAVE DOCTORS, TEACHERS, HUNTERS, CHEFS... EVEN A DENTIST!
I JUST CAN'T...WHAT ABOUT...LESS THAN SAVORY PEOPLE?
CLAIRE TOLD US ABOUT HONCHO AND HIS ISLAND OF CRAZIES. PAXTON, **MOST** PEOPLE ARE GOOD, OR AT LEAST, WANT TO BE GOOD.
ROOFTOP ACCESS
AND THE **REAL** PSYCHOS ARE EASY TO SPOT!
EVERYONE FINDS THEIR PLACE HERE WITH US. WE **ALL** FIT INTO A GREATER ORGANISM, EACH PART CREATING A MORE **PERFECT** WHOLE!
AT LEAST THAT'S WHAT CATHERINE SAYS!

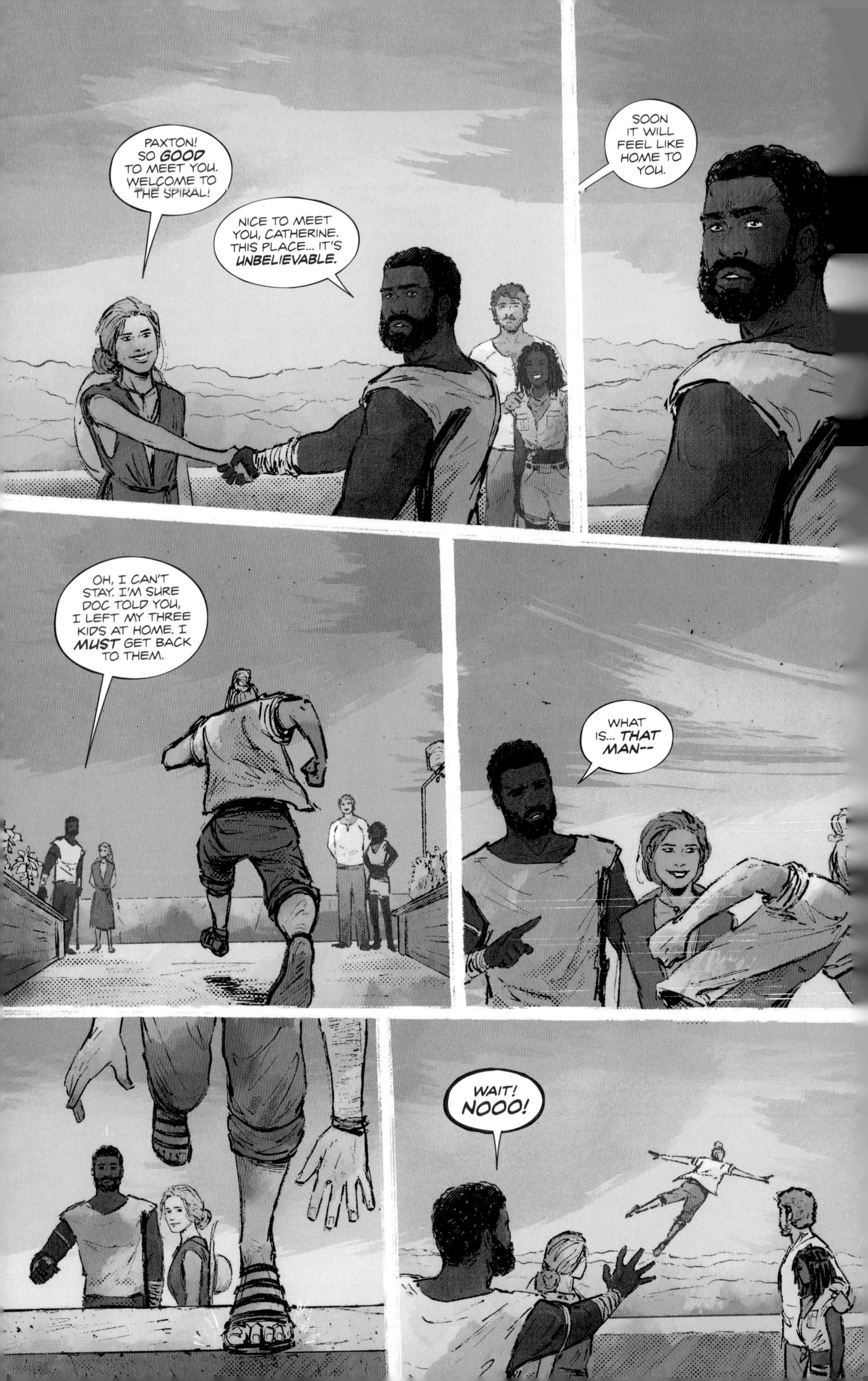
PAXTON! SO GOOD TO MEET YOU. WELCOME TO THE SPIRAL!
NICE TO MEET YOU, CATHERINE. THIS PLACE... IT'S UNBELIEVABLE.
SOON IT WILL FEEL LIKE HOME TO YOU.
OH, I CAN'T STAY. I'M SURE DOC TOLD YOU, I LEFT MY THREE KIDS AT HOME. I MUST GET BACK TO THEM.
WHAT IS... THAT MAN--
WAIT! NOOO!

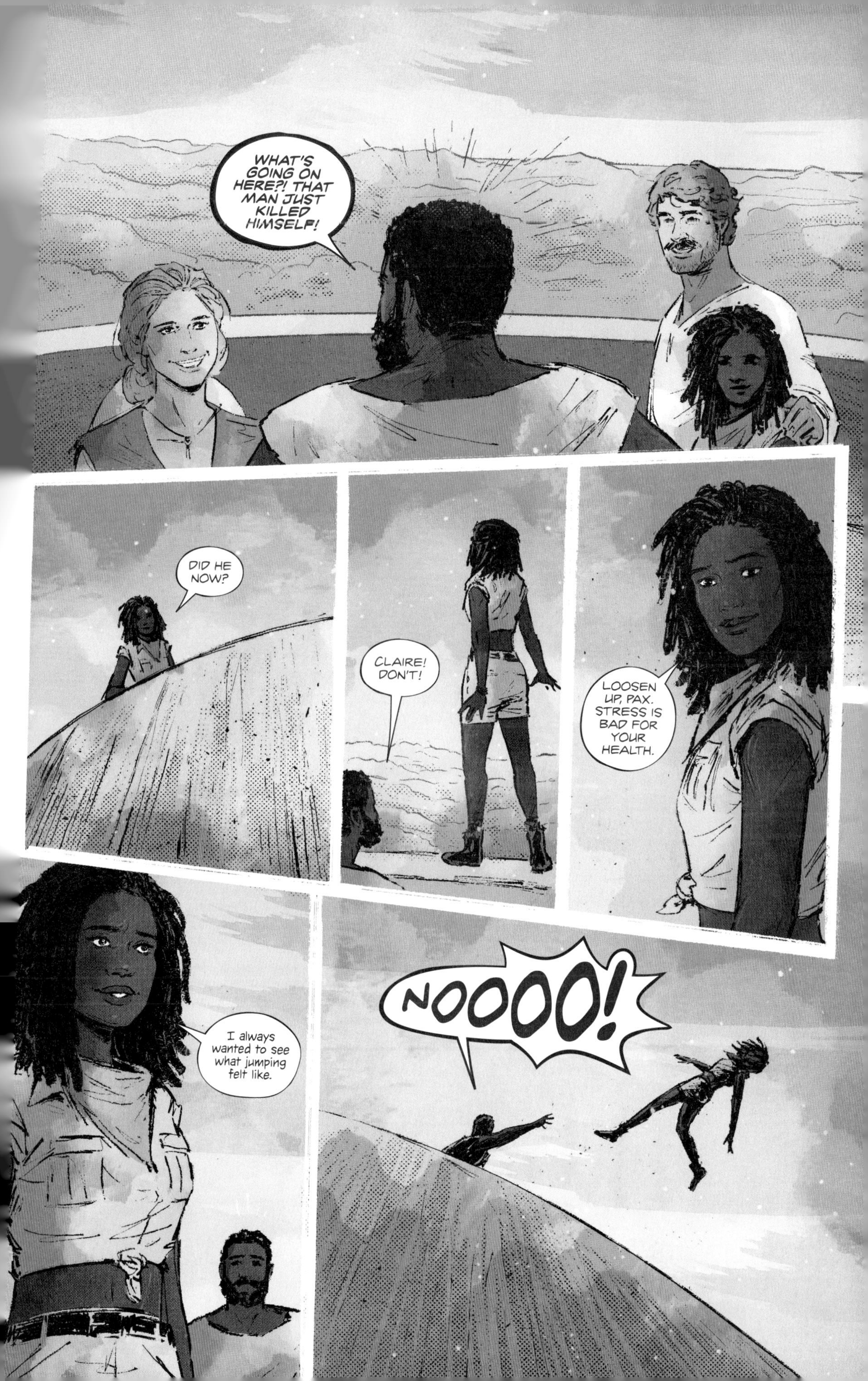
WHAT'S GOING ON HERE?! THAT MAN JUST KILLED HIMSELF!
DID HE NOW?
CLAIRE! DON'T!
LOOSEN UP, PAX. STRESS IS BAD FOR YOUR HEALTH.
I always wanted to see what jumping felt like.
NOOOO!

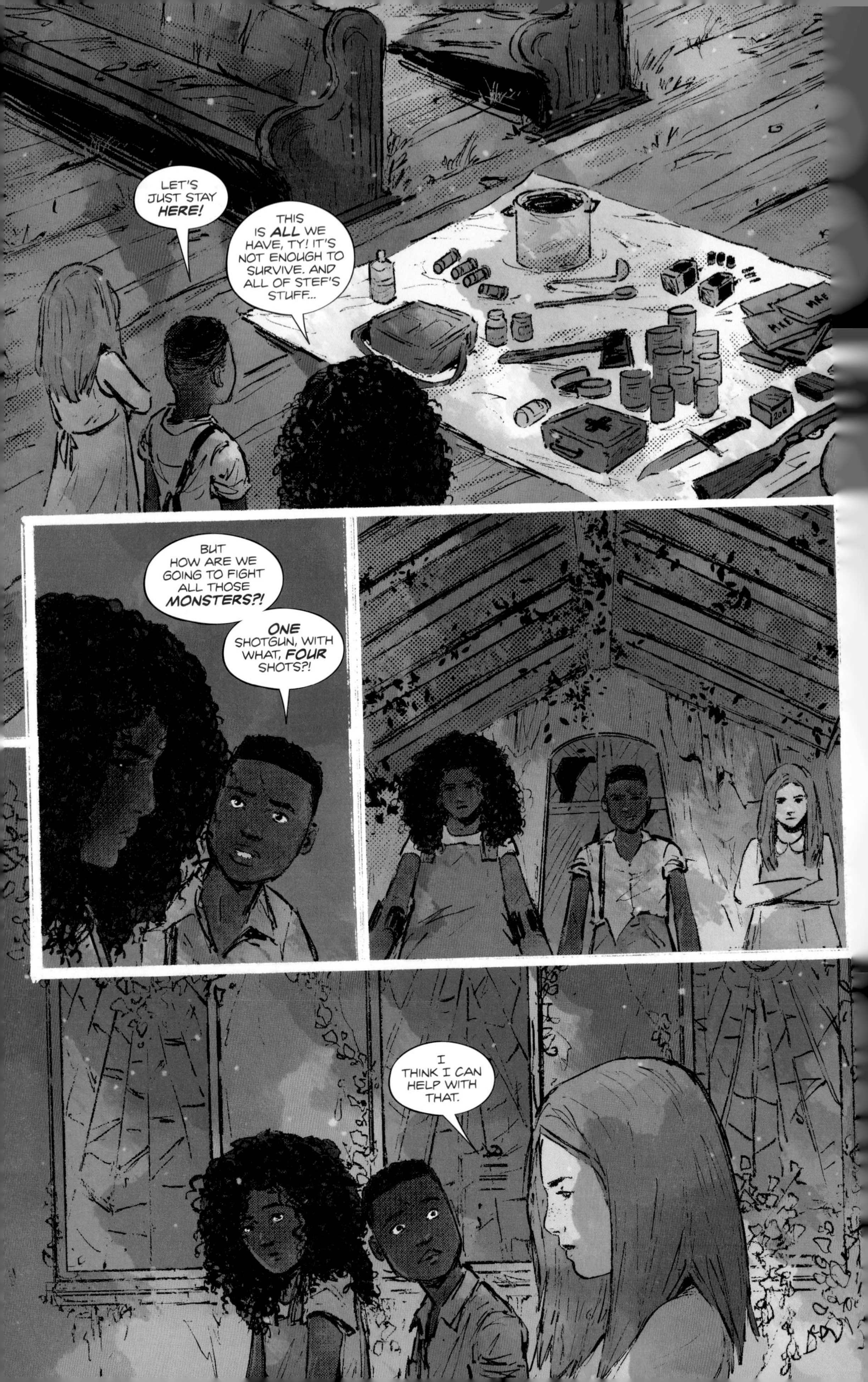
LET'S JUST STAY HERE!
THIS IS ALL WE HAVE, TY! IT'S NOT ENOUGH TO SURVIVE. AND ALL OF STEF'S STUFF...
BUT HOW ARE WE GOING TO FIGHT ALL THOSE MONSTERS?!
ONE SHOTGUN, WITH WHAT, FOUR SHOTS?!
I THINK I CAN HELP WITH THAT.

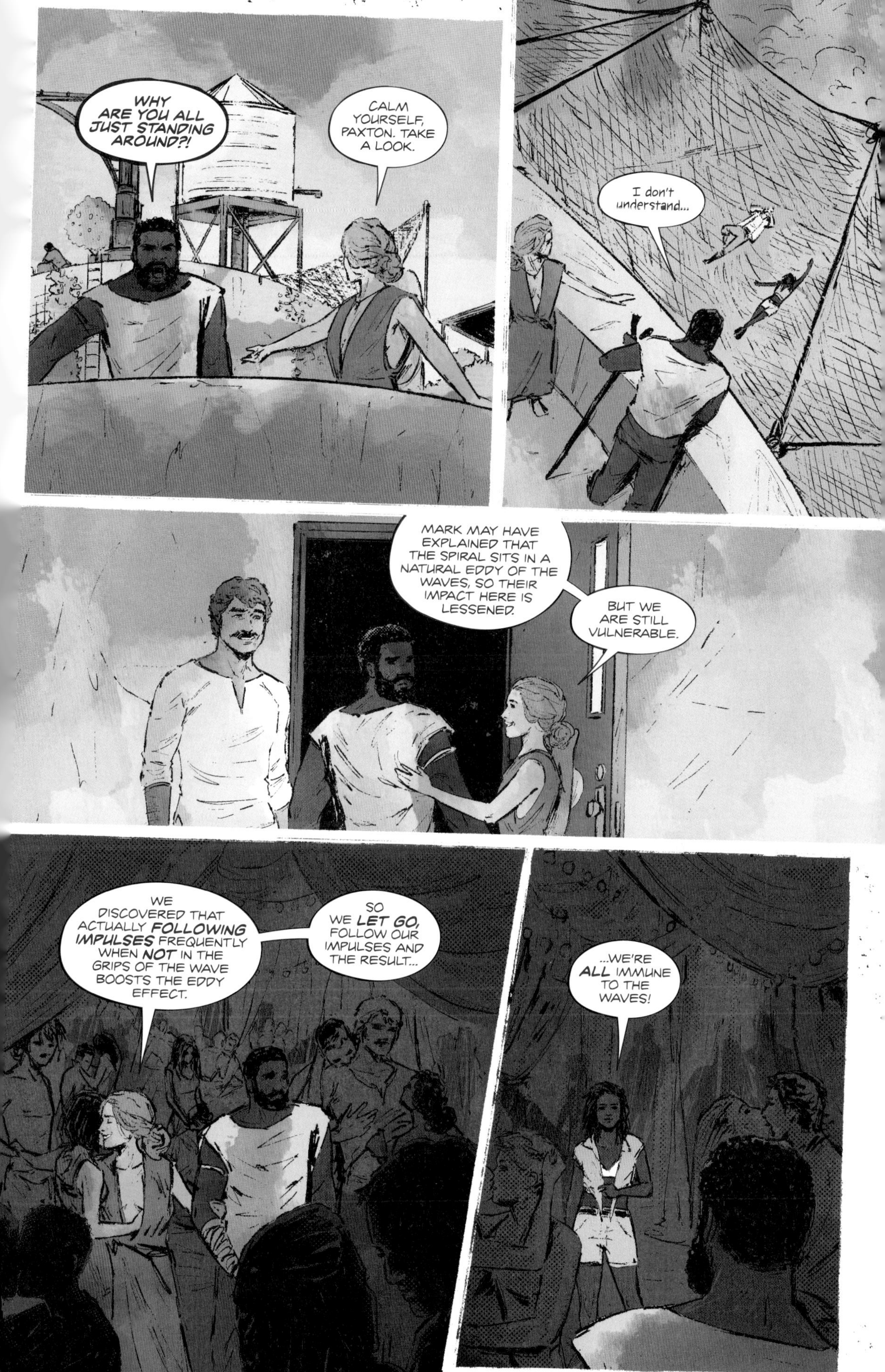
WHY ARE YOU ALL JUST STANDING AROUND?!
CALM YOURSELF, PAXTON. TAKE A LOOK.
I don't understand...
MARK MAY HAVE EXPLAINED THAT THE SPIRAL SITS IN A NATURAL EDDY OF THE WAVES, SO THEIR IMPACT HERE IS LESSENED.
BUT WE ARE STILL VULNERABLE.
WE DISCOVERED THAT ACTUALLY FOLLOWING IMPULSES FREQUENTLY WHEN NOT IN THE GRIPS OF THE WAVE BOOSTS THE EDDY EFFECT.
SO WE LET GO, FOLLOW OUR IMPULSES AND THE RESULT...
...WE'RE ALL IMMUNE TO THE WAVES!

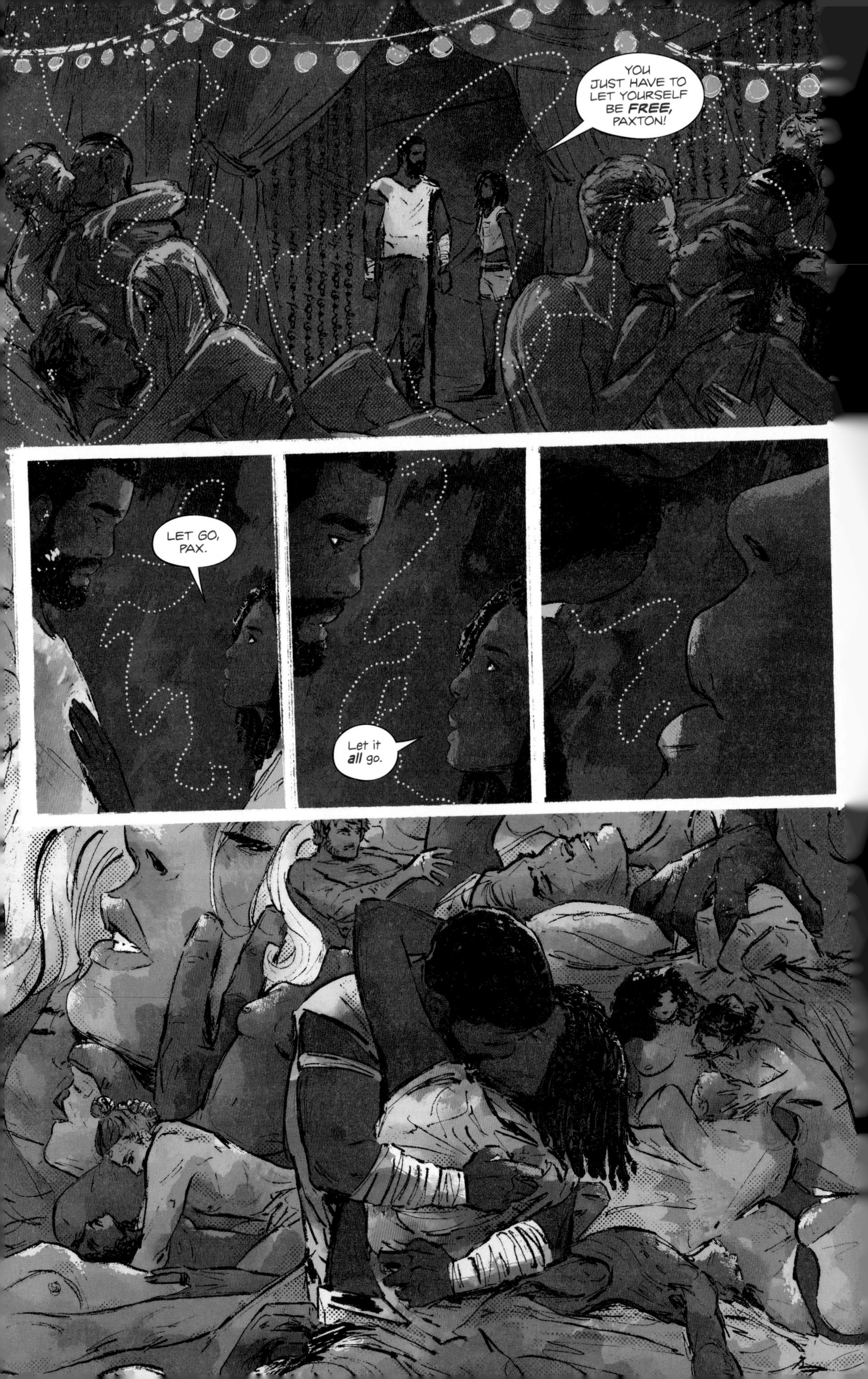
YOU JUST HAVE TO LET YOURSELF BE **FREE,** PAXTON!
LET GO, PAX.
Let it ***all*** go.

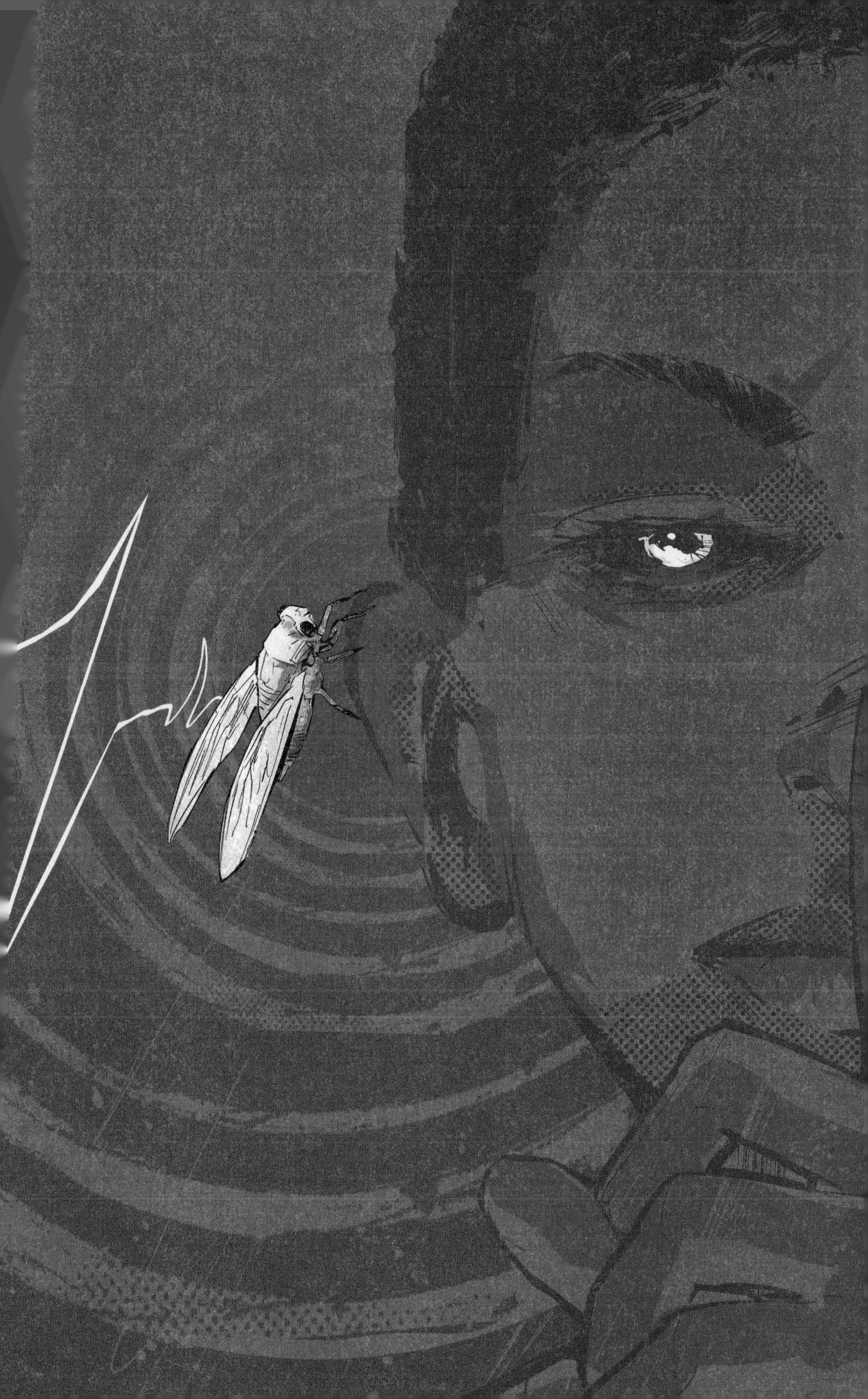

CHAPTER NINE

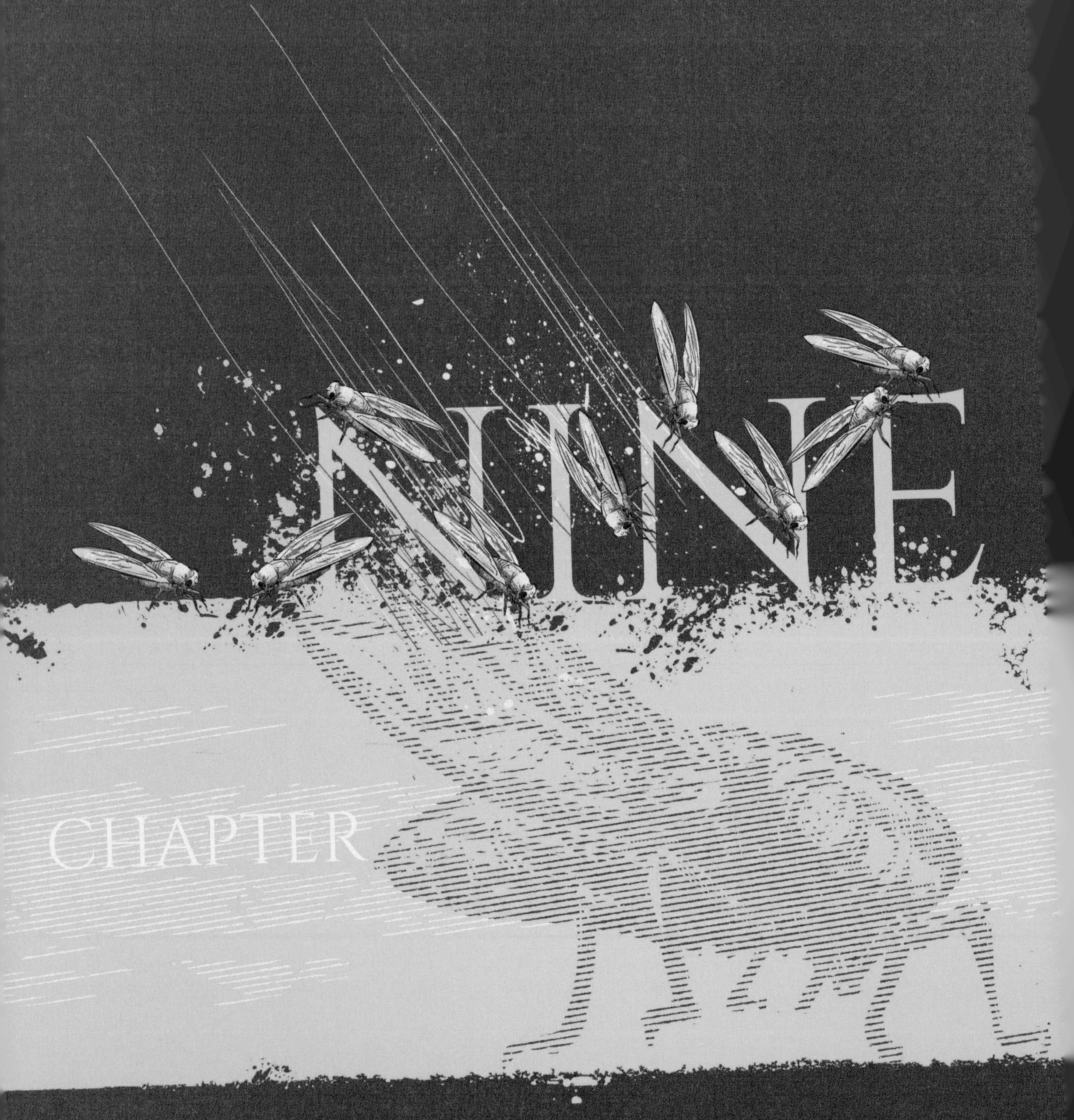

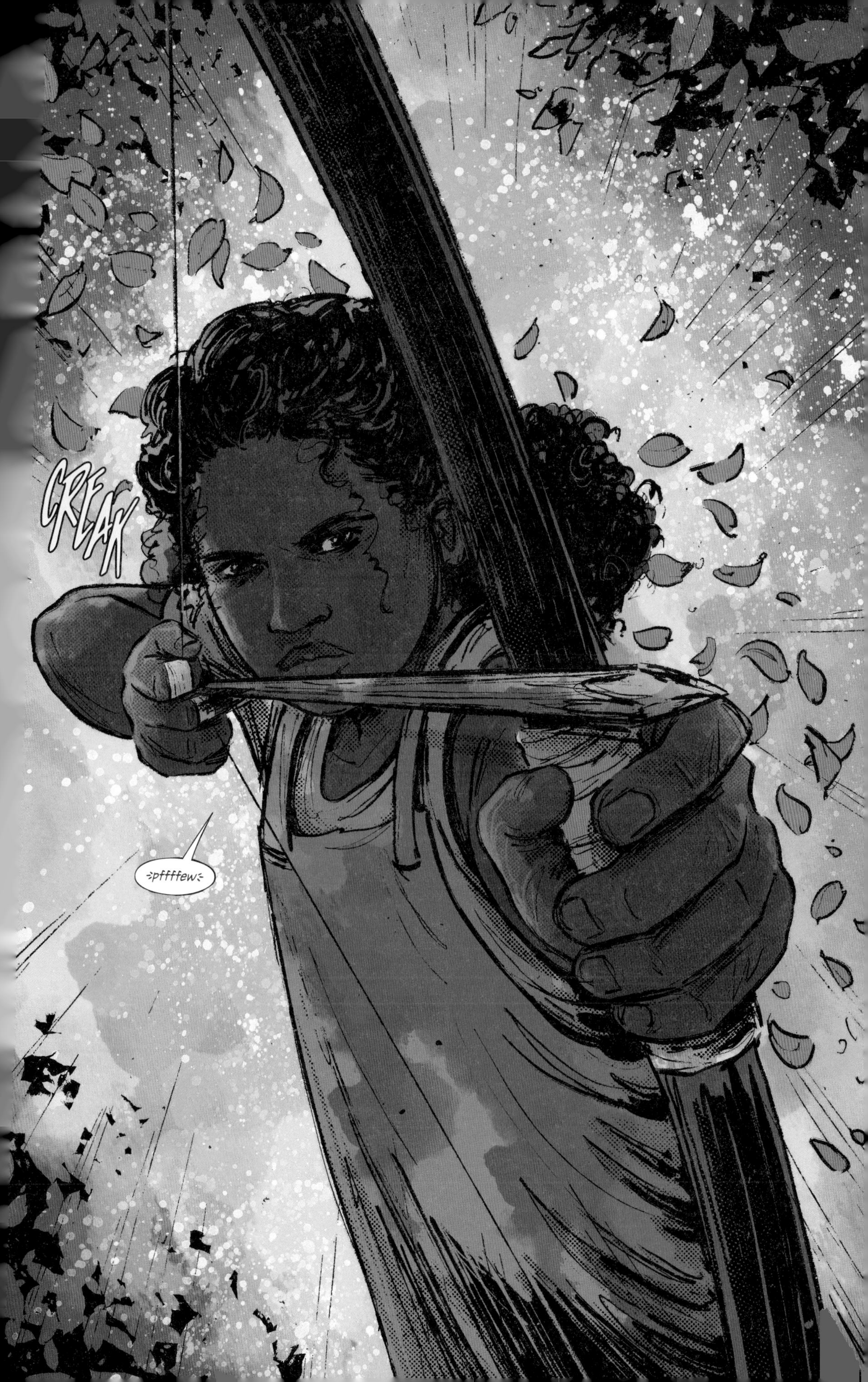
CREAK
pffffew

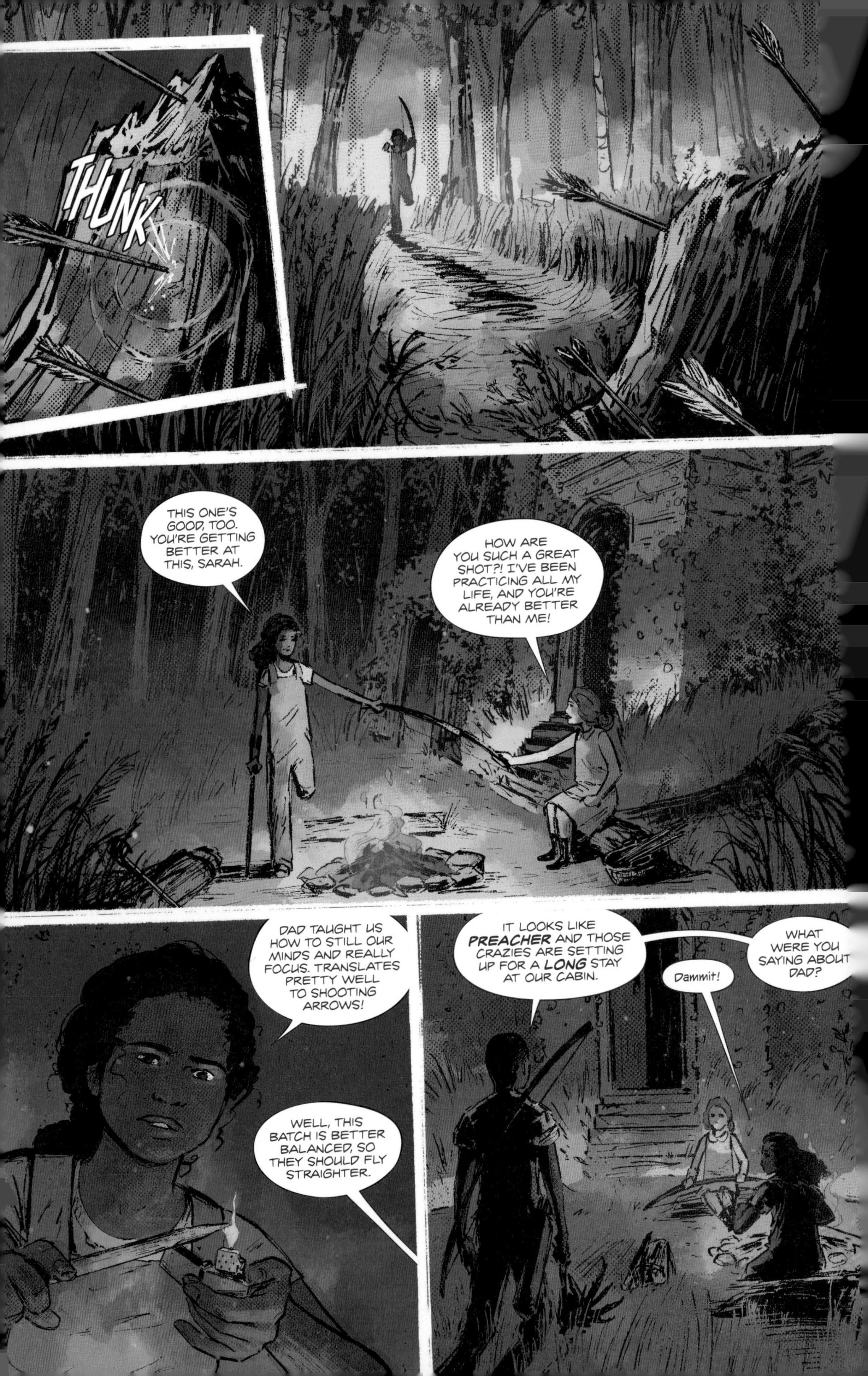

THUNK
THIS ONE'S GOOD, TOO. YOU'RE GETTING BETTER AT THIS, SARAH.
HOW ARE YOU SUCH A GREAT SHOT?! I'VE BEEN PRACTICING ALL MY LIFE, AND YOU'RE ALREADY BETTER THAN ME!
DAD TAUGHT US HOW TO STILL OUR MINDS AND REALLY FOCUS. TRANSLATES PRETTY WELL TO SHOOTING ARROWS!
WELL, THIS BATCH IS BETTER BALANCED, SO THEY SHOULD FLY STRAIGHTER.
IT LOOKS LIKE PREACHER AND THOSE CRAZIES ARE SETTING UP FOR A LONG STAY AT OUR CABIN.
Dammit!
WHAT WERE YOU SAYING ABOUT DAD?

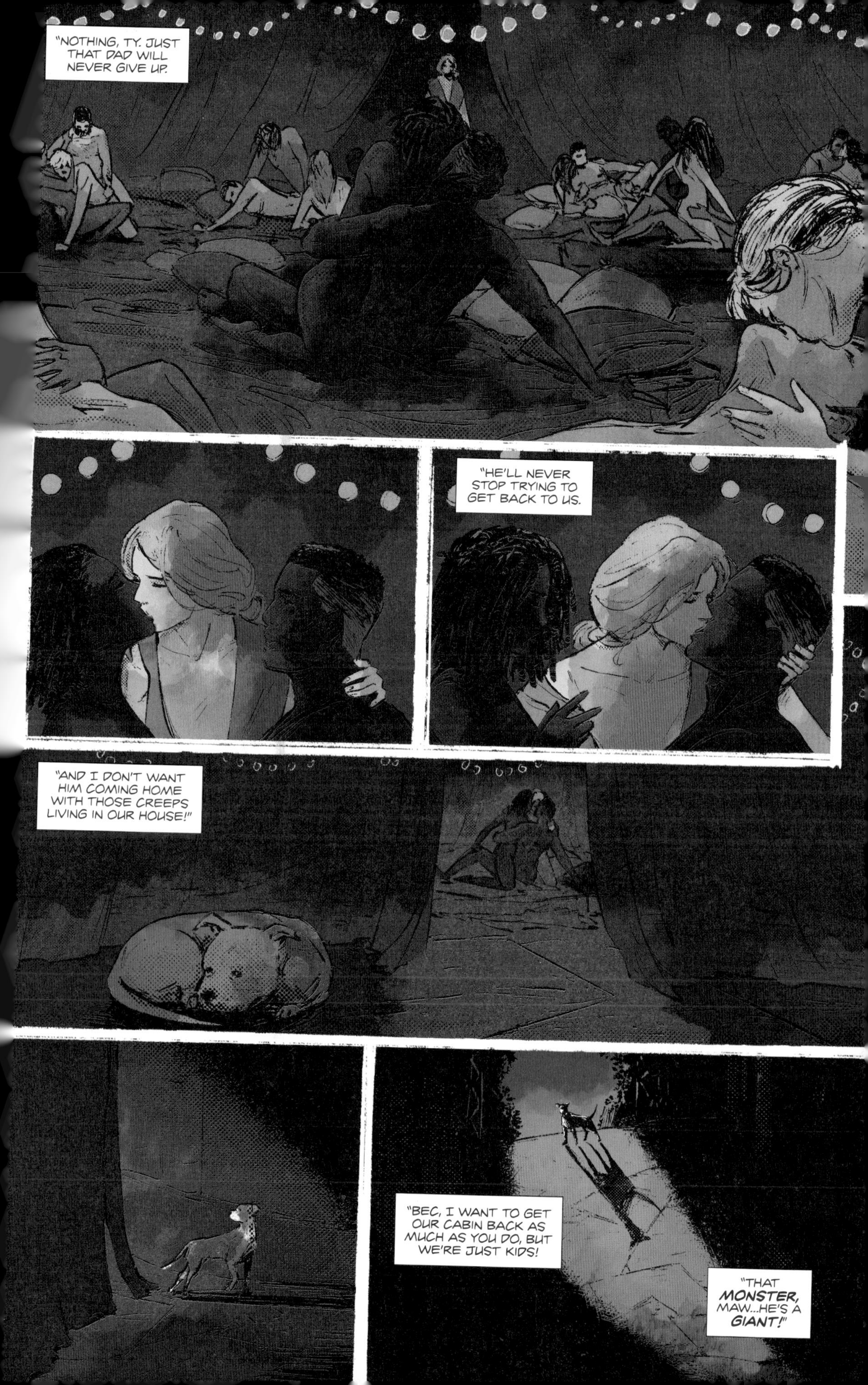
"NOTHING, TY. JUST THAT DAD WILL NEVER GIVE UP.
"HE'LL NEVER STOP TRYING TO GET BACK TO US.
"AND I DON'T WANT HIM COMING HOME WITH THOSE CREEPS LIVING IN OUR HOUSE!"
"BEC, I WANT TO GET OUR CABIN BACK AS MUCH AS YOU DO, BUT WE'RE JUST KIDS!
"THAT MONSTER, MAW...HE'S A GIANT!"

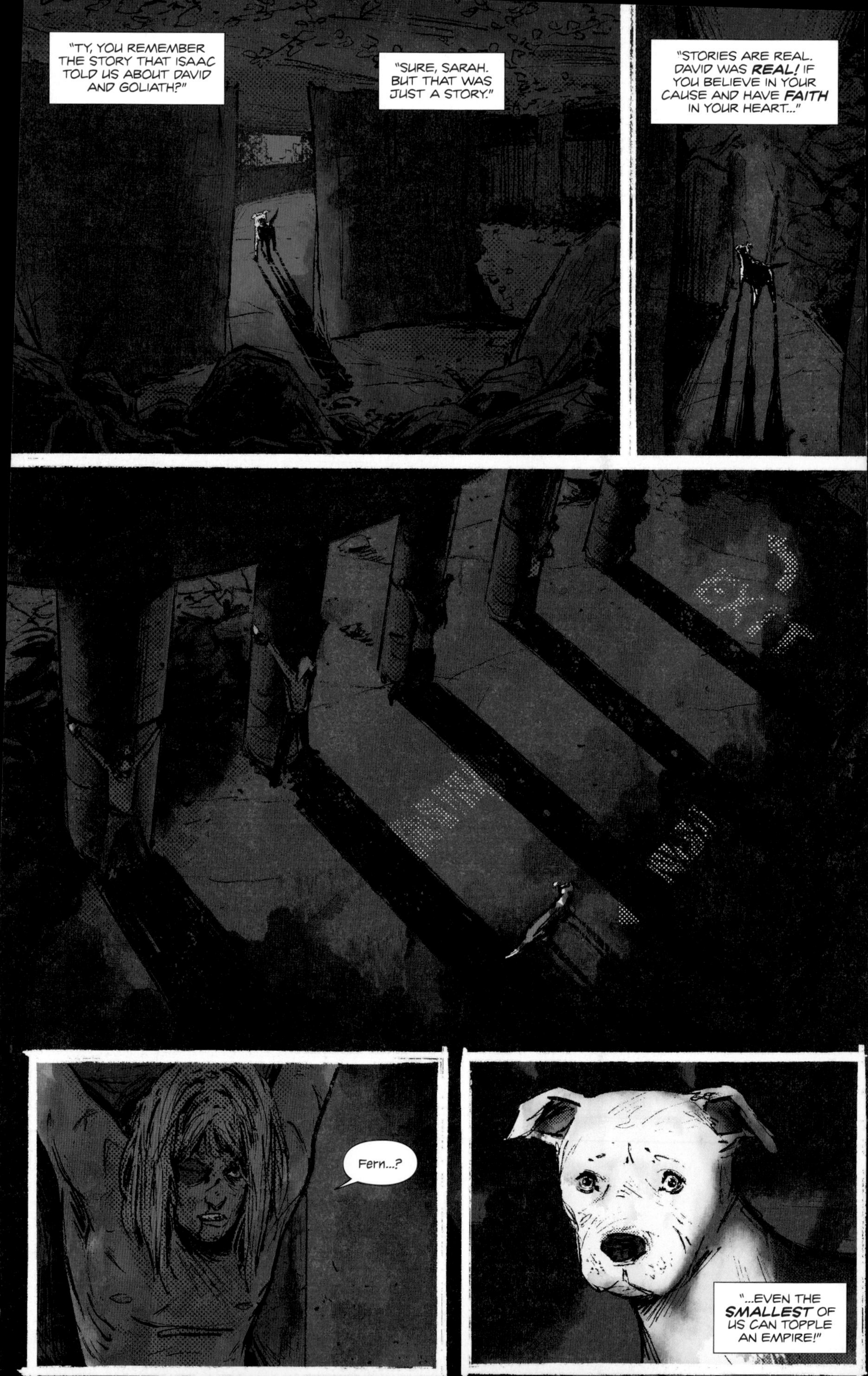
"TY, YOU REMEMBER THE STORY THAT ISAAC TOLD US ABOUT DAVID AND GOLIATH?"
"SURE, SARAH. BUT THAT WAS JUST A STORY."
"STORIES ARE REAL. DAVID WAS REAL! IF YOU BELIEVE IN YOUR CAUSE AND HAVE FAITH IN YOUR HEART..."
Fern...?
"...EVEN THE SMALLEST OF US CAN TOPPLE AN EMPIRE!"

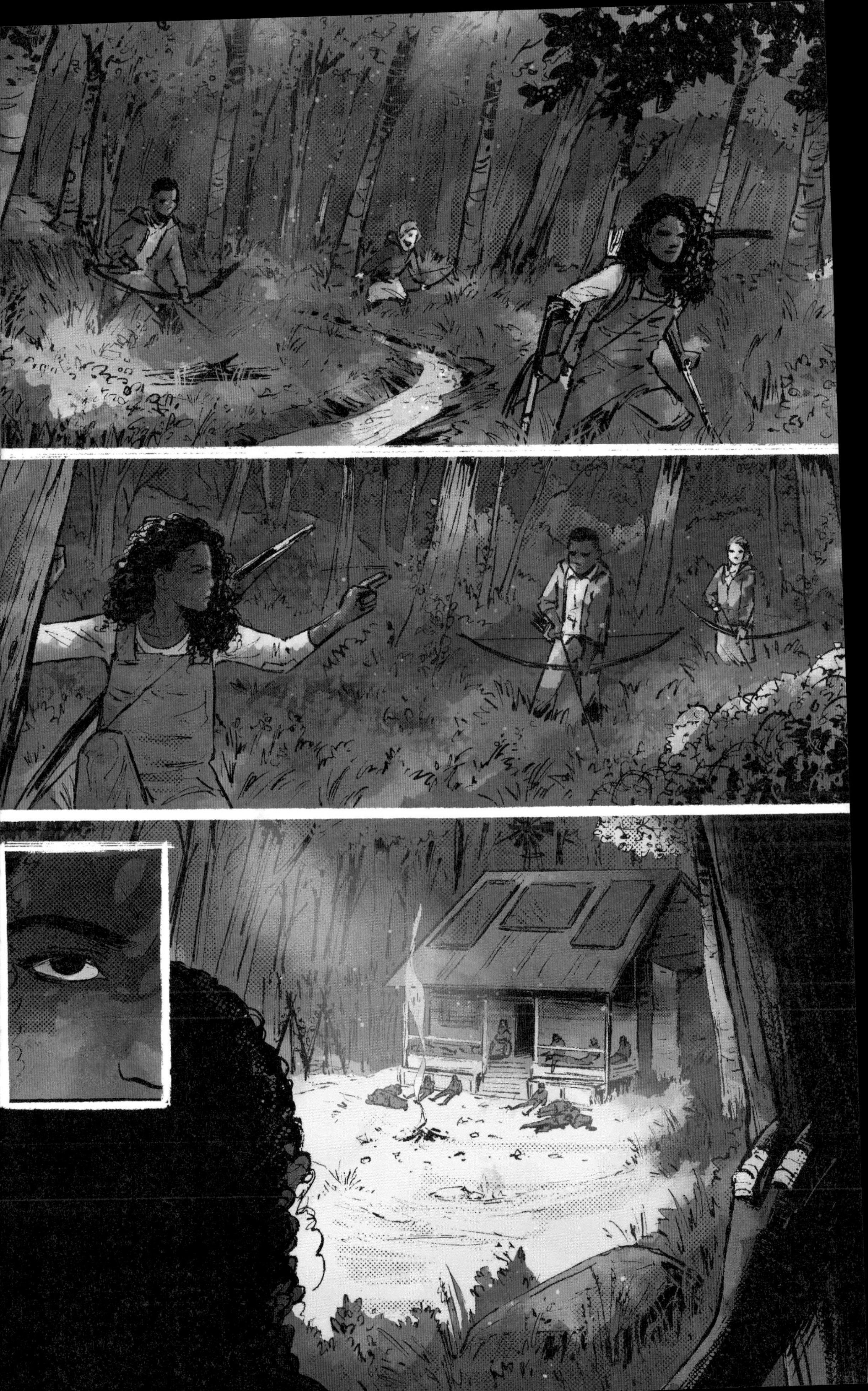

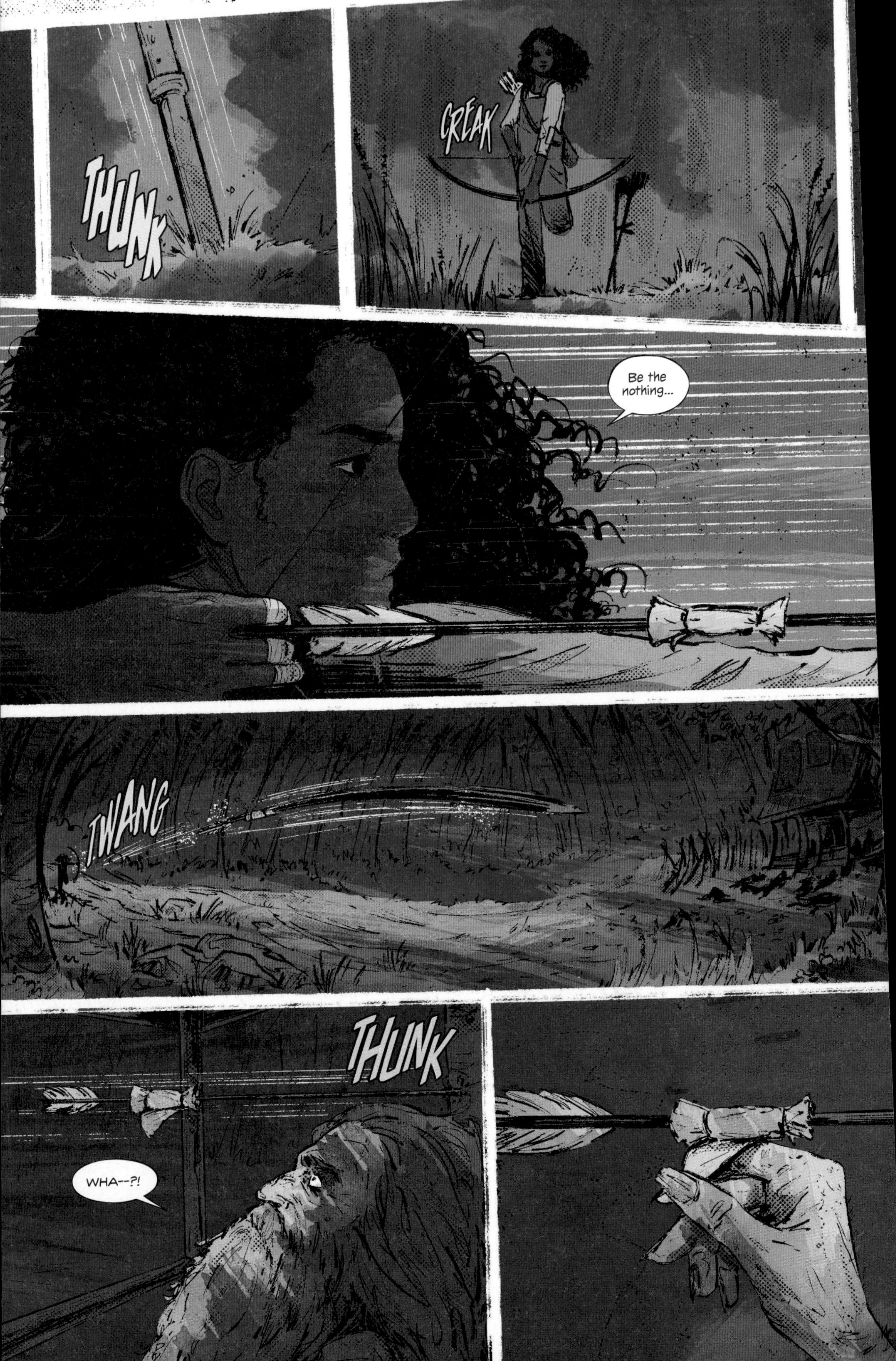
THUNK
CREAK
Be the nothing...
TWANG
THUNK
WHA--?!

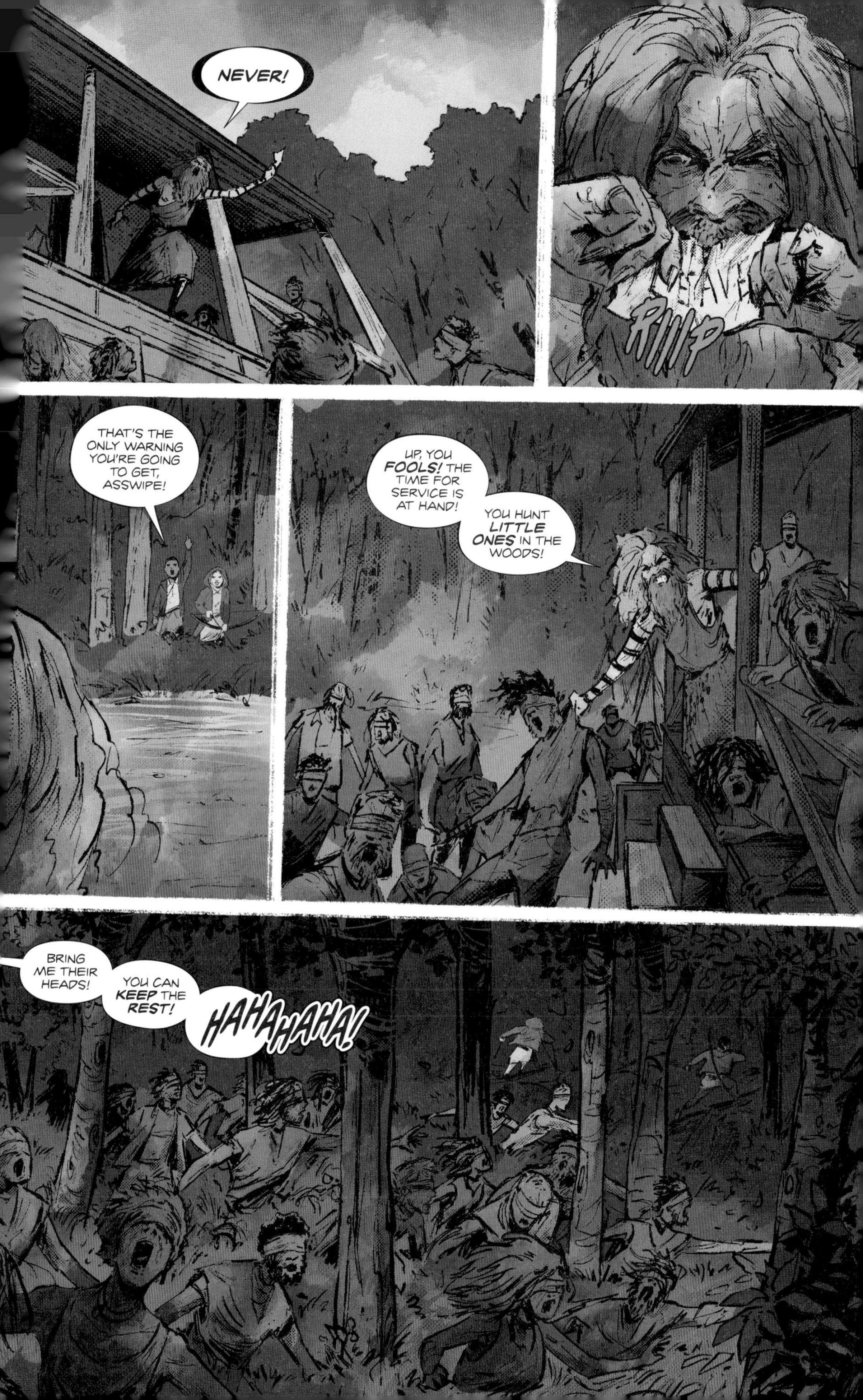
NEVER!
LEAVE
RIIIP
THAT'S THE ONLY WARNING YOU'RE GOING TO GET, ASSWIPE!
UP, YOU FOOLS! THE TIME FOR SERVICE IS AT HAND!
YOU HUNT LITTLE ONES IN THE WOODS!
BRING ME THEIR HEADS!
YOU CAN KEEP THE REST!
HAHAHAHAHA!

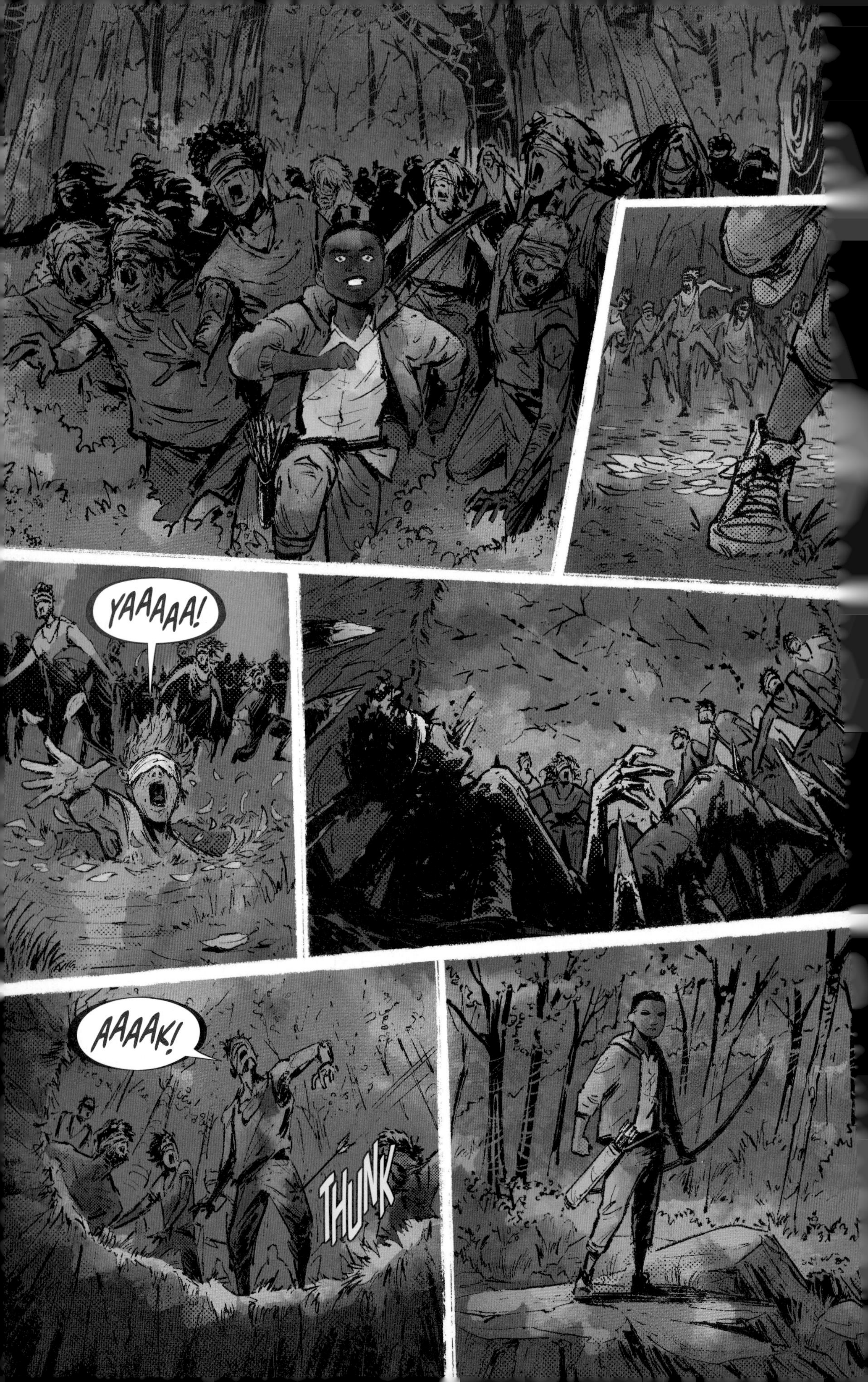
YAAAAA!
AAAAK!
THUNK

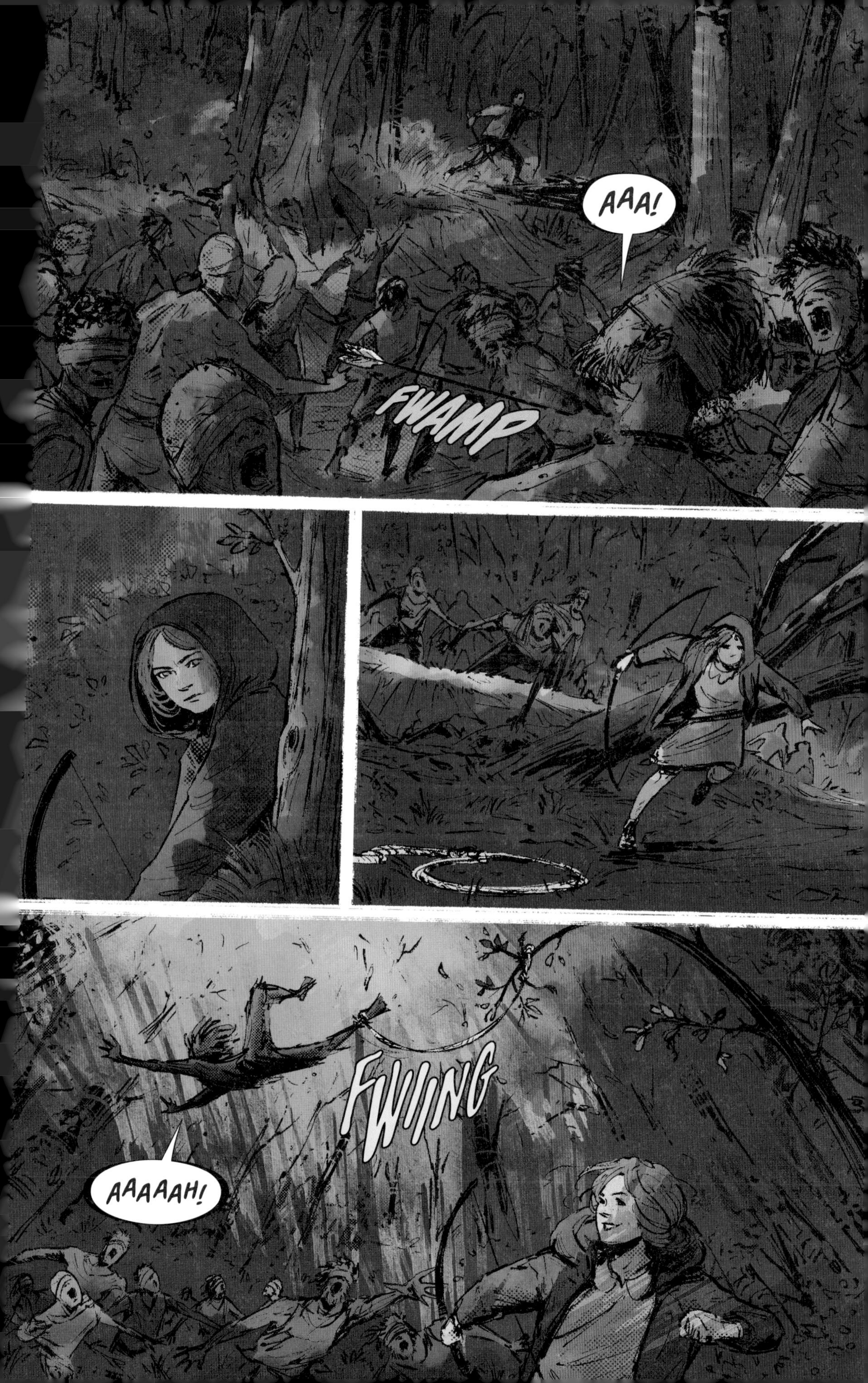
AAA!
FWAMP
FWIING
AAAAAH!

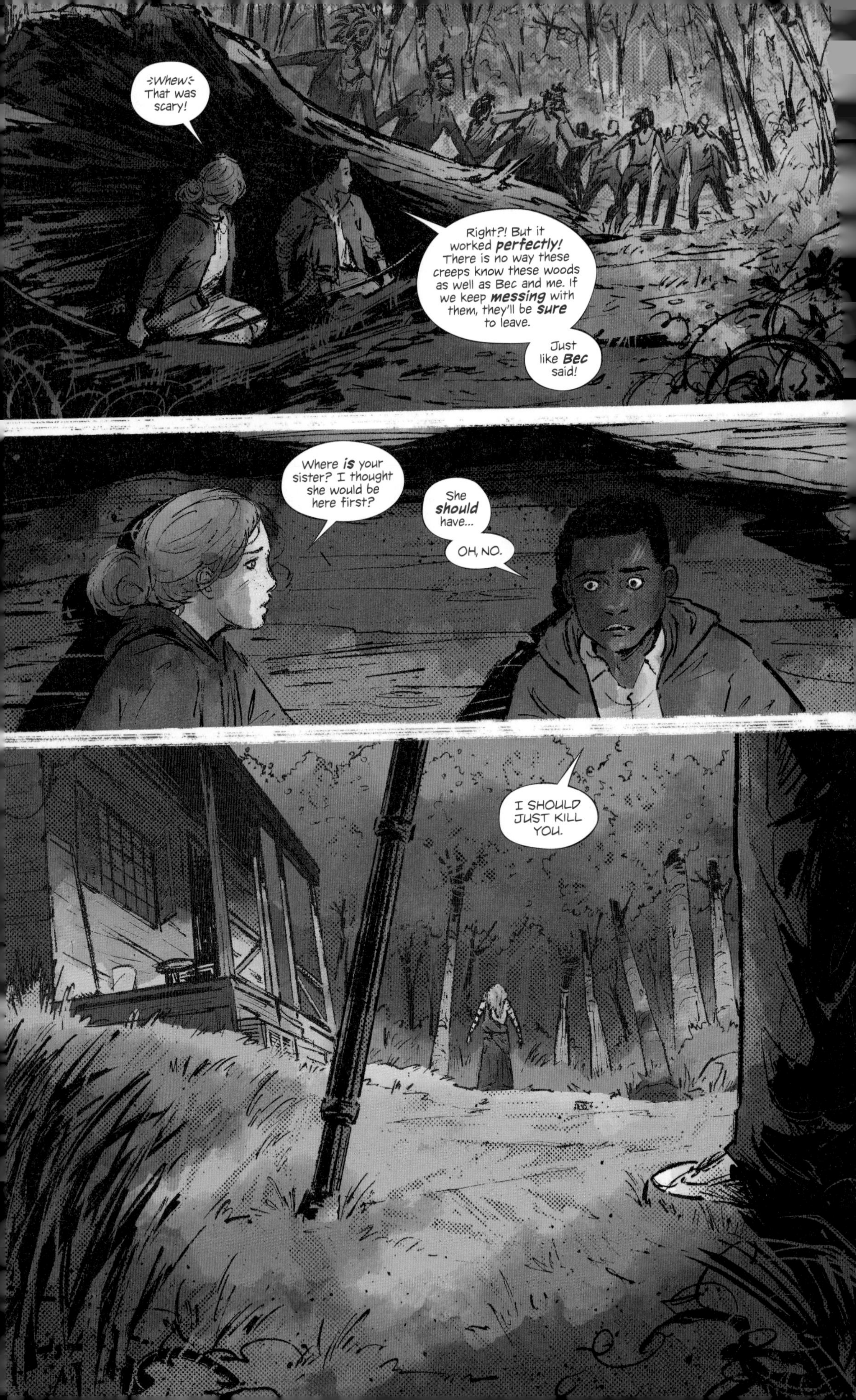

Whew
That was scary!
Right?! But it worked perfectly! There is no way these creeps know these woods as well as Bec and me. If we keep messing with them, they'll be sure to leave.
Just like Bec said!
Where is your sister? I thought she would be here first?
She should have...
OH, NO.
I SHOULD JUST KILL YOU.

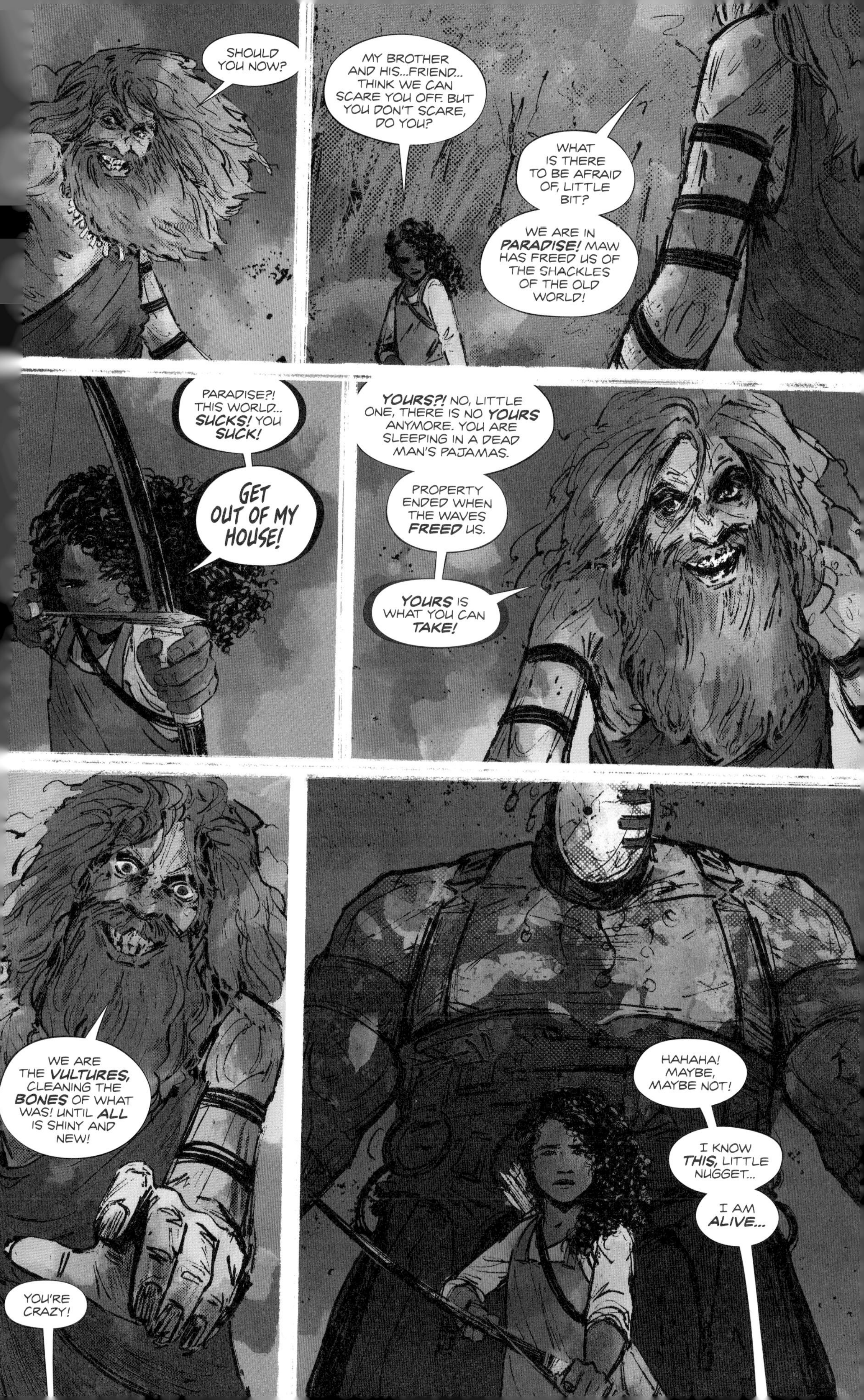
SHOULD YOU NOW?
MY BROTHER AND HIS...FRIEND... THINK WE CAN SCARE YOU OFF. BUT YOU DON'T SCARE, DO YOU?
WHAT IS THERE TO BE AFRAID OF, LITTLE BIT?
WE ARE IN PARADISE! MAW HAS FREED US OF THE SHACKLES OF THE OLD WORLD!
PARADISE?! THIS WORLD... SUCKS! YOU SUCK!
GET OUT OF MY HOUSE!
YOURS?! NO, LITTLE ONE, THERE IS NO YOURS ANYMORE. YOU ARE SLEEPING IN A DEAD MAN'S PAJAMAS.
PROPERTY ENDED WHEN THE WAVES FREED US.
YOURS IS WHAT YOU CAN TAKE!
WE ARE THE VULTURES, CLEANING THE BONES OF WHAT WAS! UNTIL ALL IS SHINY AND NEW!
YOU'RE CRAZY!
HAHAHA! MAYBE, MAYBE NOT!
I KNOW THIS, LITTLE NUGGET...
I AM ALIVE...

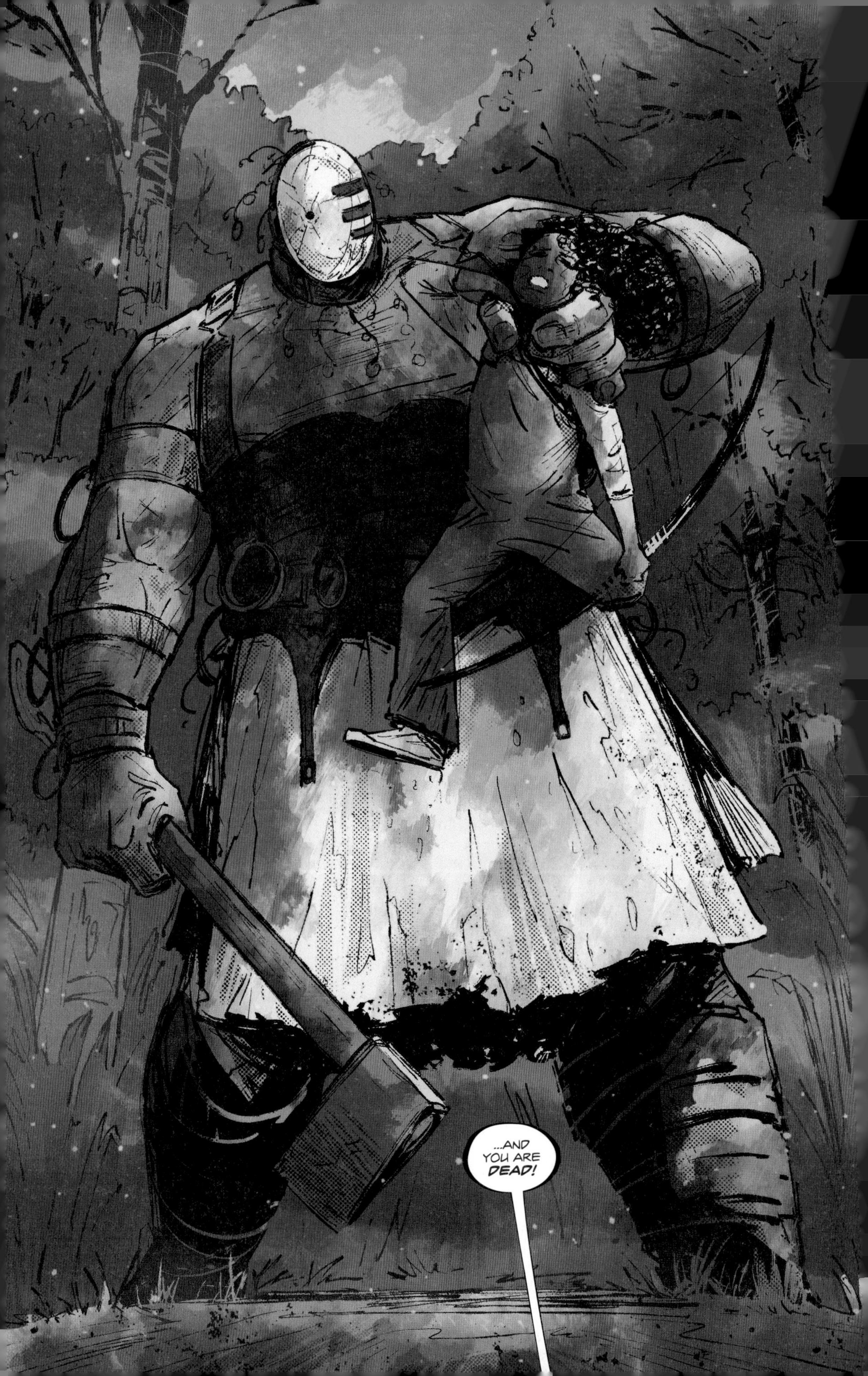
...AND YOU ARE DEAD!

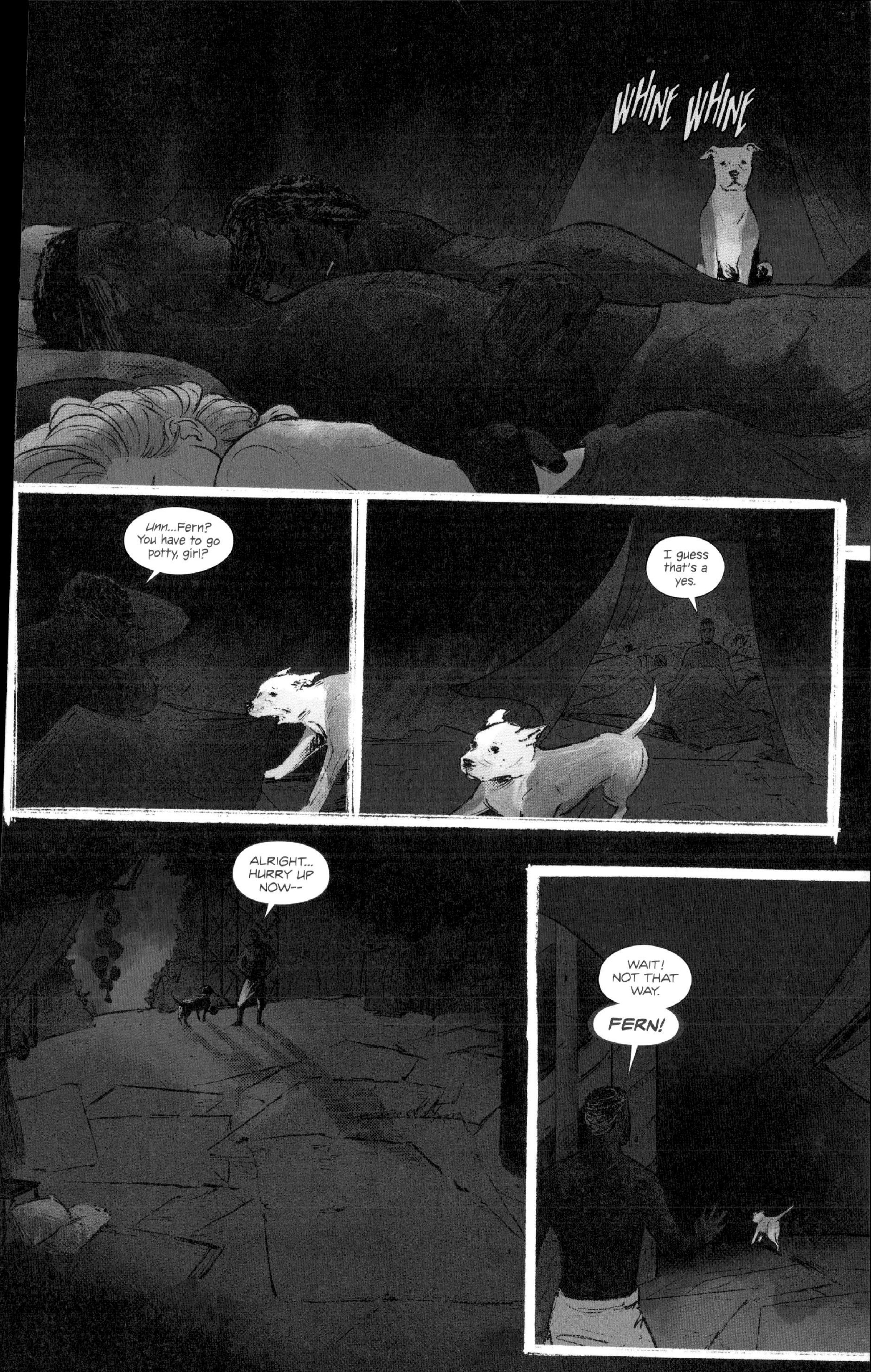

WHINE WHINE
Unn...Fern? You have to go potty, girl?
I guess that's a yes.
ALRIGHT... HURRY UP NOW--
WAIT! NOT THAT WAY.
FERN!

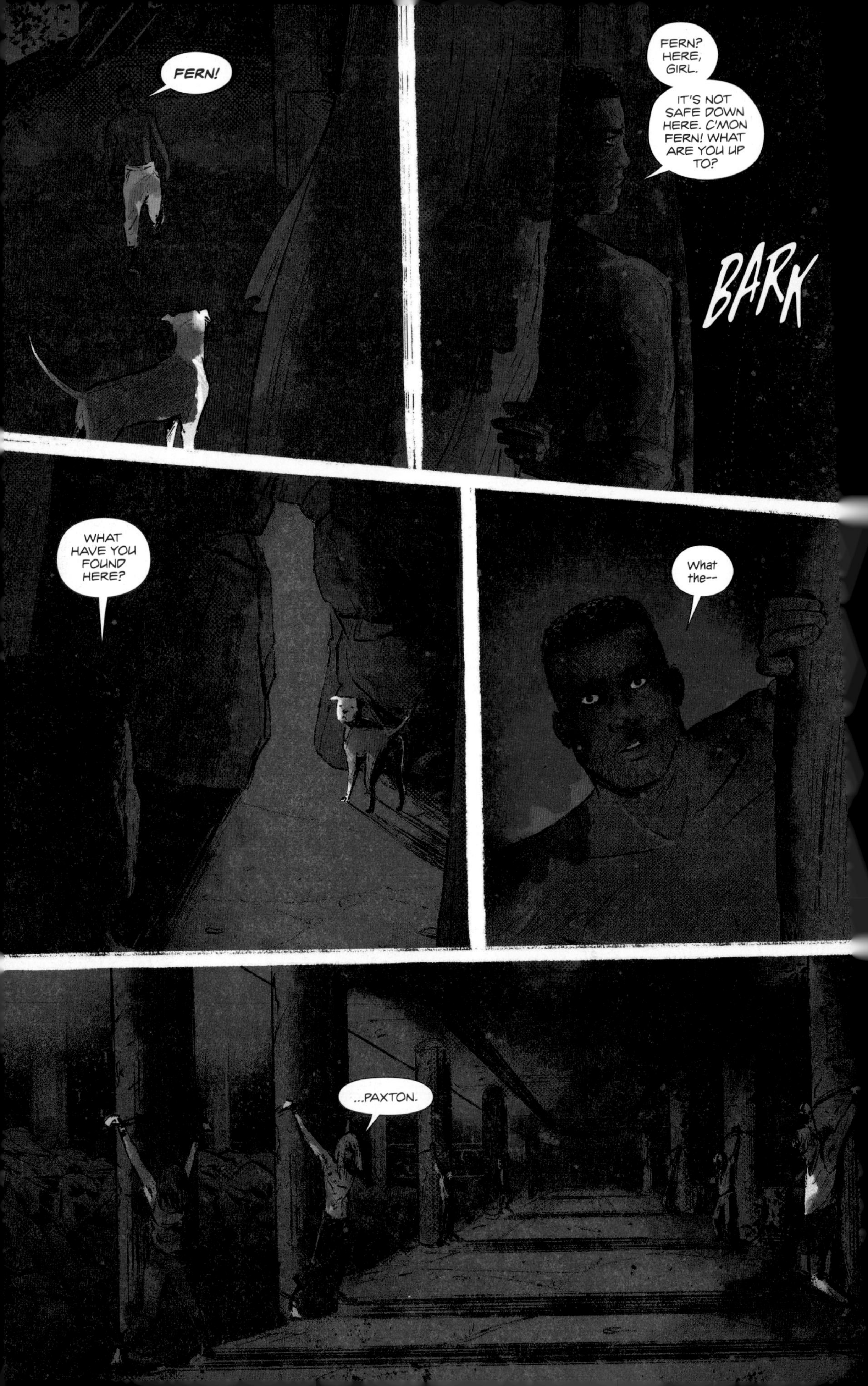
FERN!
FERN? HERE, GIRL.
IT'S NOT SAFE DOWN HERE. C'MON FERN! WHAT ARE YOU UP TO?
BARK
WHAT HAVE YOU FOUND HERE?
What the--
...PAXTON.

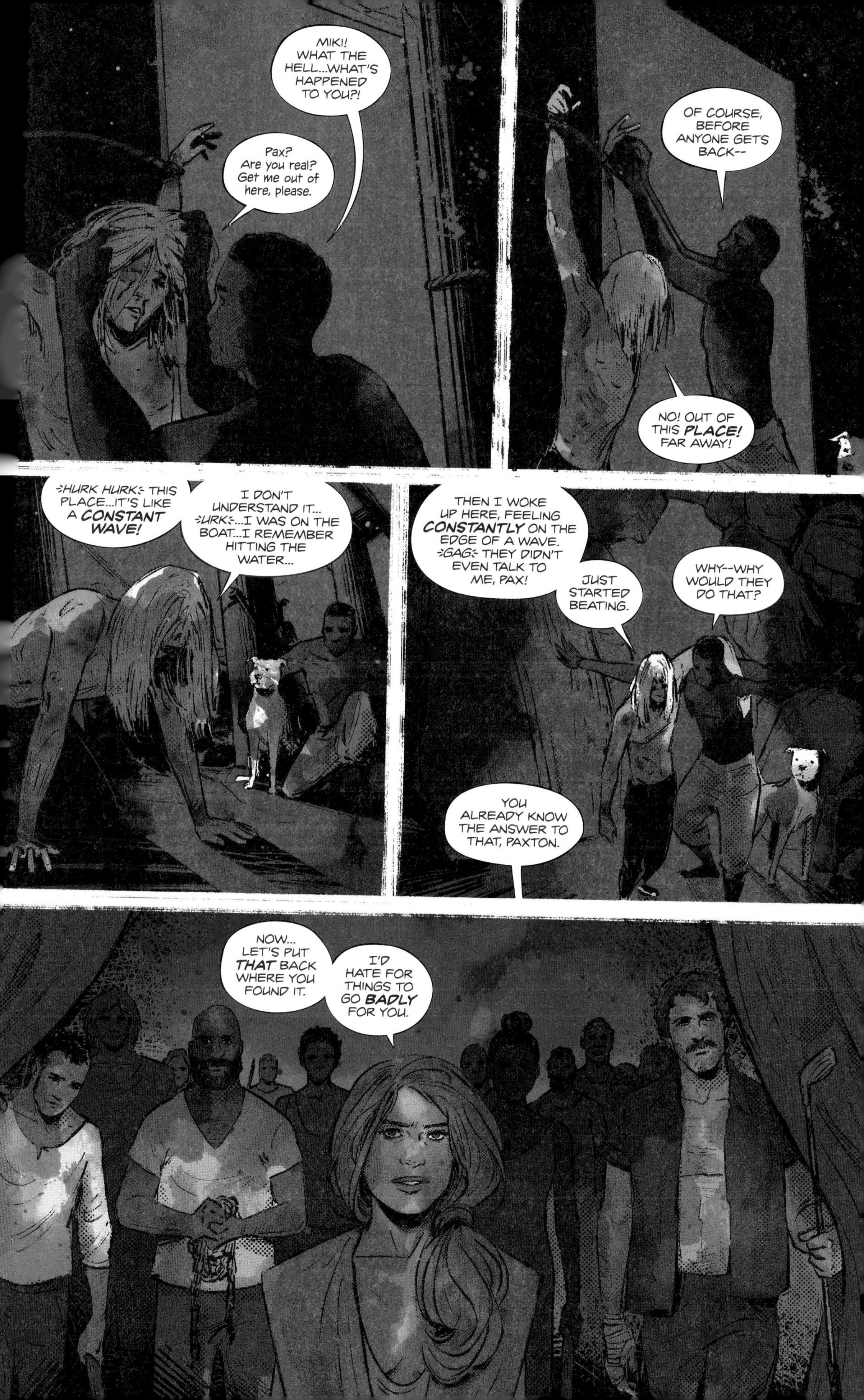

MIKI! WHAT THE HELL...WHAT'S HAPPENED TO YOU?!
Pax? Are you real? Get me out of here, please.
OF COURSE, BEFORE ANYONE GETS BACK--
NO! OUT OF THIS PLACE! FAR AWAY!
HURK HURK THIS PLACE...IT'S LIKE A CONSTANT WAVE!
I DON'T UNDERSTAND IT... URK ...I WAS ON THE BOAT...I REMEMBER HITTING THE WATER...
THEN I WOKE UP HERE, FEELING CONSTANTLY ON THE EDGE OF A WAVE. GAG THEY DIDN'T EVEN TALK TO ME, PAX!
JUST STARTED BEATING.
WHY--WHY WOULD THEY DO THAT?
YOU ALREADY KNOW THE ANSWER TO THAT, PAXTON.
NOW... LET'S PUT THAT BACK WHERE YOU FOUND IT.
I'D HATE FOR THINGS TO GO BADLY FOR YOU.

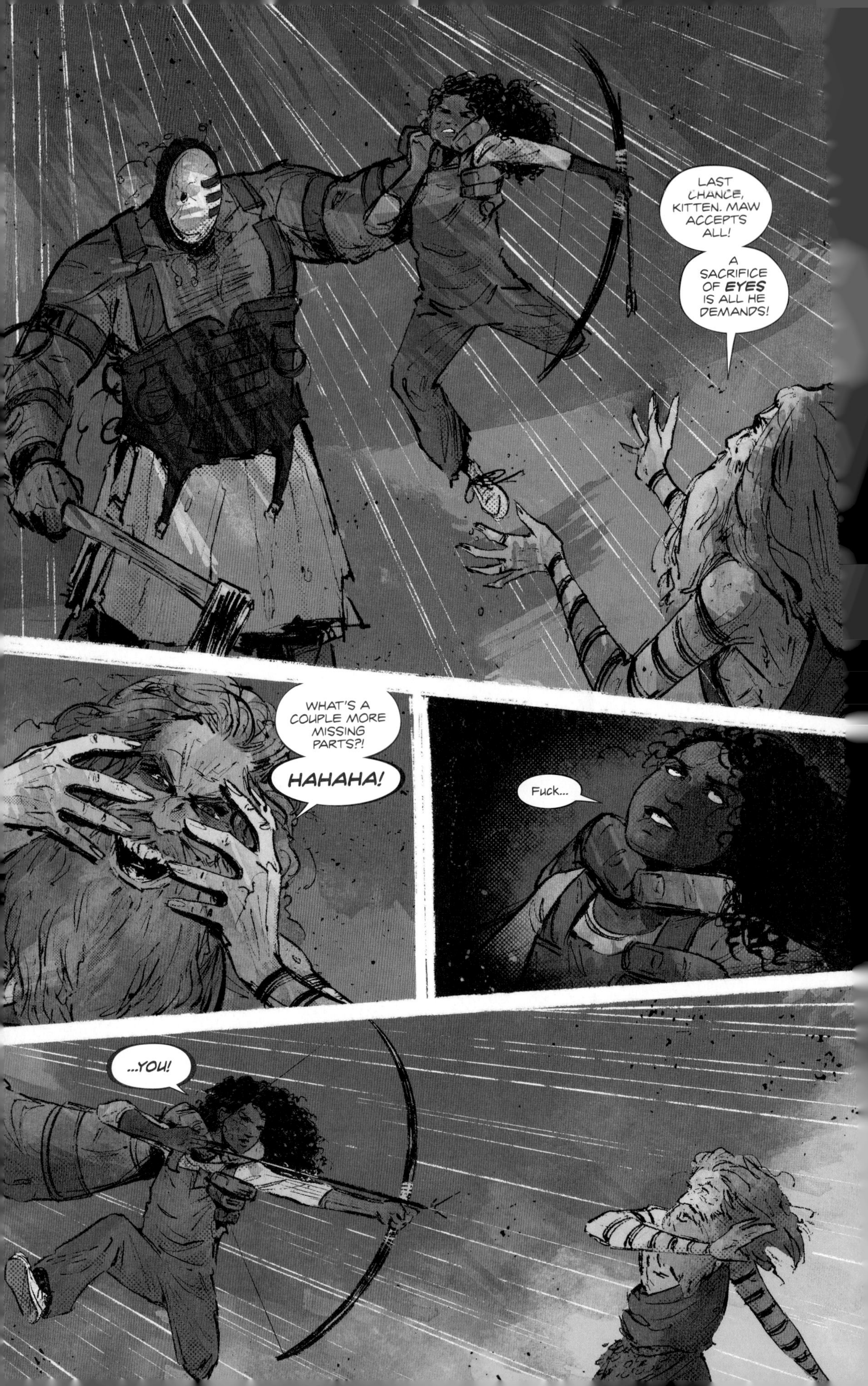
LAST CHANCE, KITTEN. MAW ACCEPTS ALL!
A SACRIFICE OF EYES IS ALL HE DEMANDS!
WHAT'S A COUPLE MORE MISSING PARTS?!
HAHAHA!
Fuck...
...YOU!

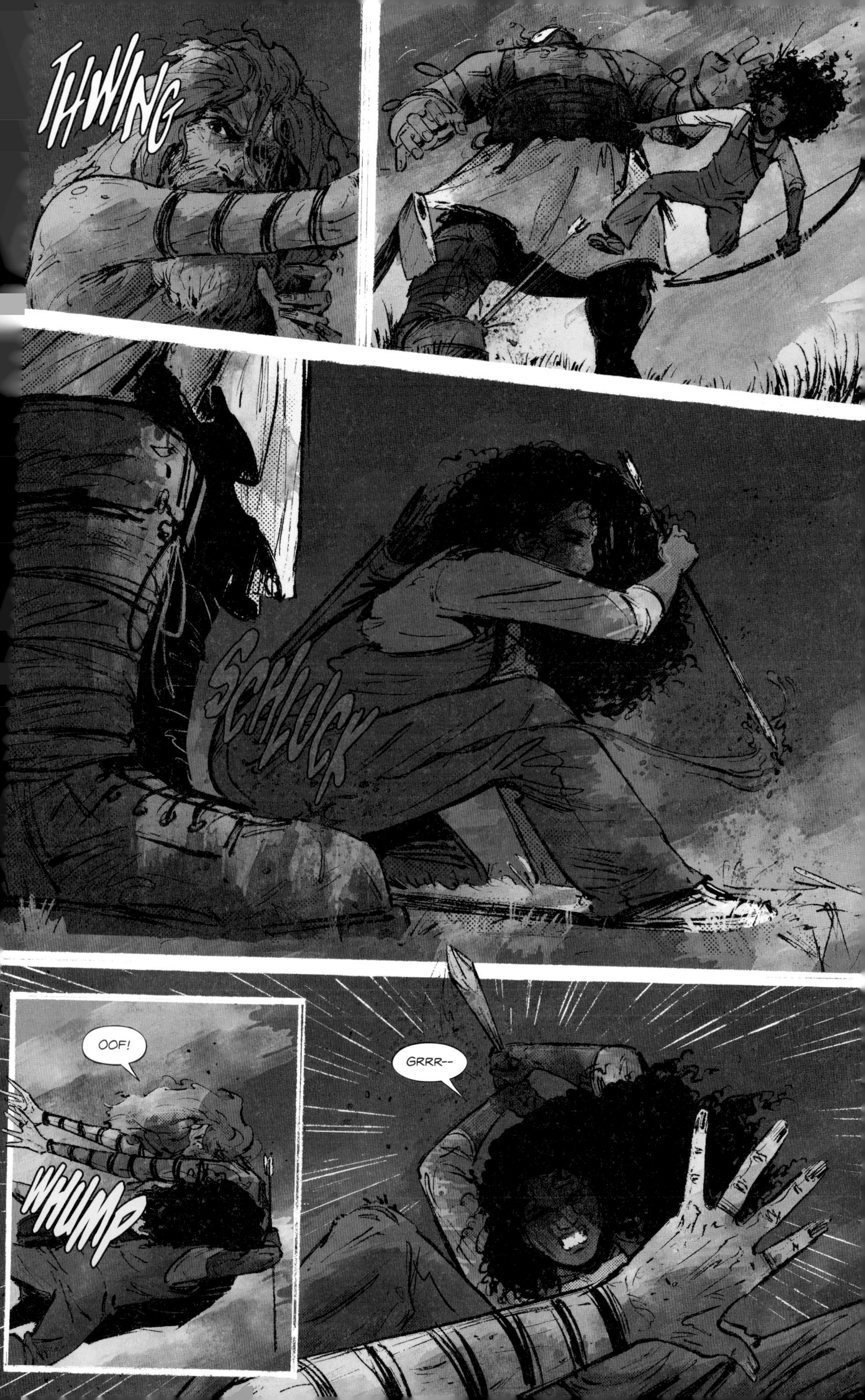
THWING
SCHLUCK
OOF!
WHUMP
GRRR--

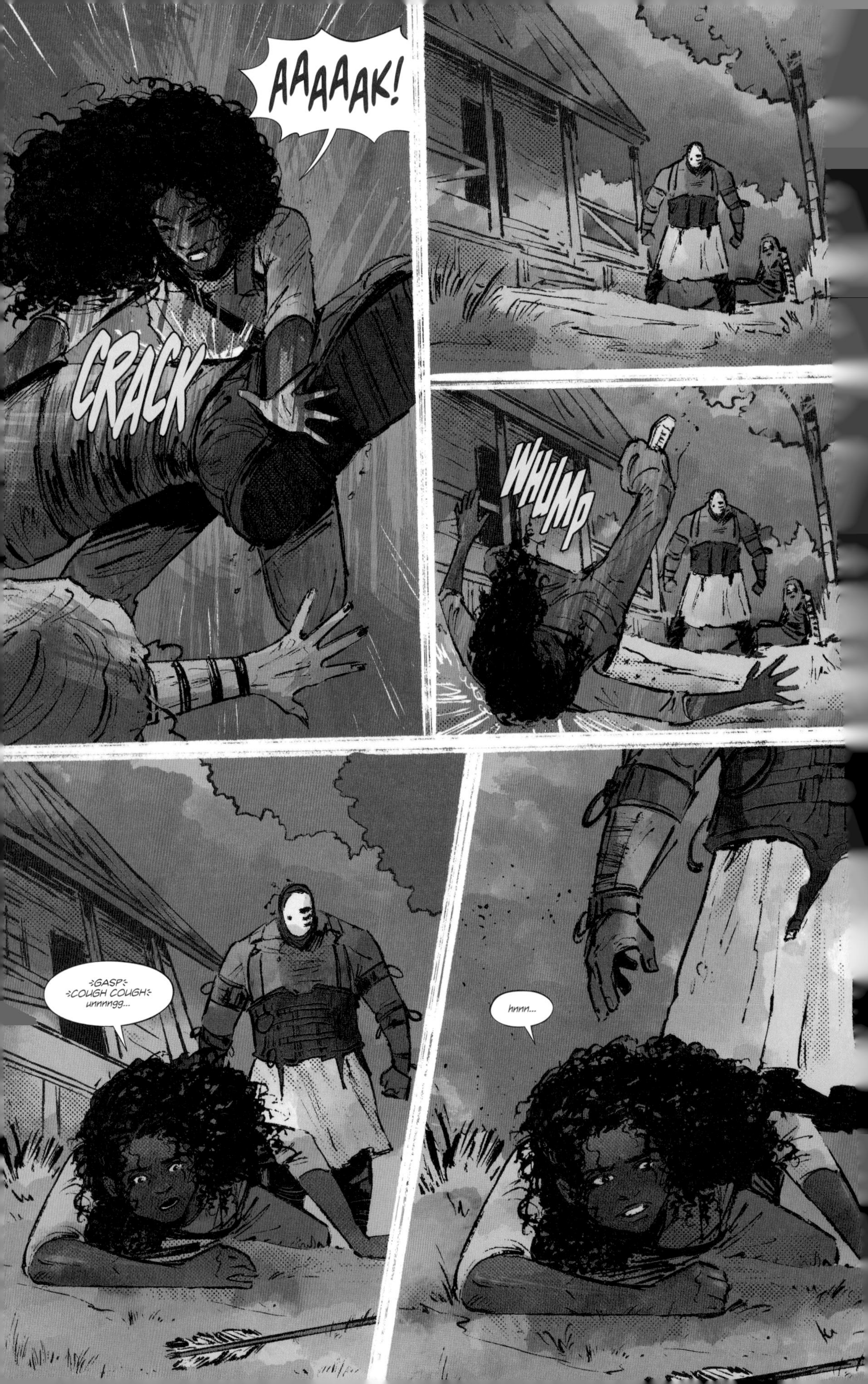
AAAAAK!
CRACK
WHUMP
GASP
COUGH COUGH
unnnngg...
hnnn...

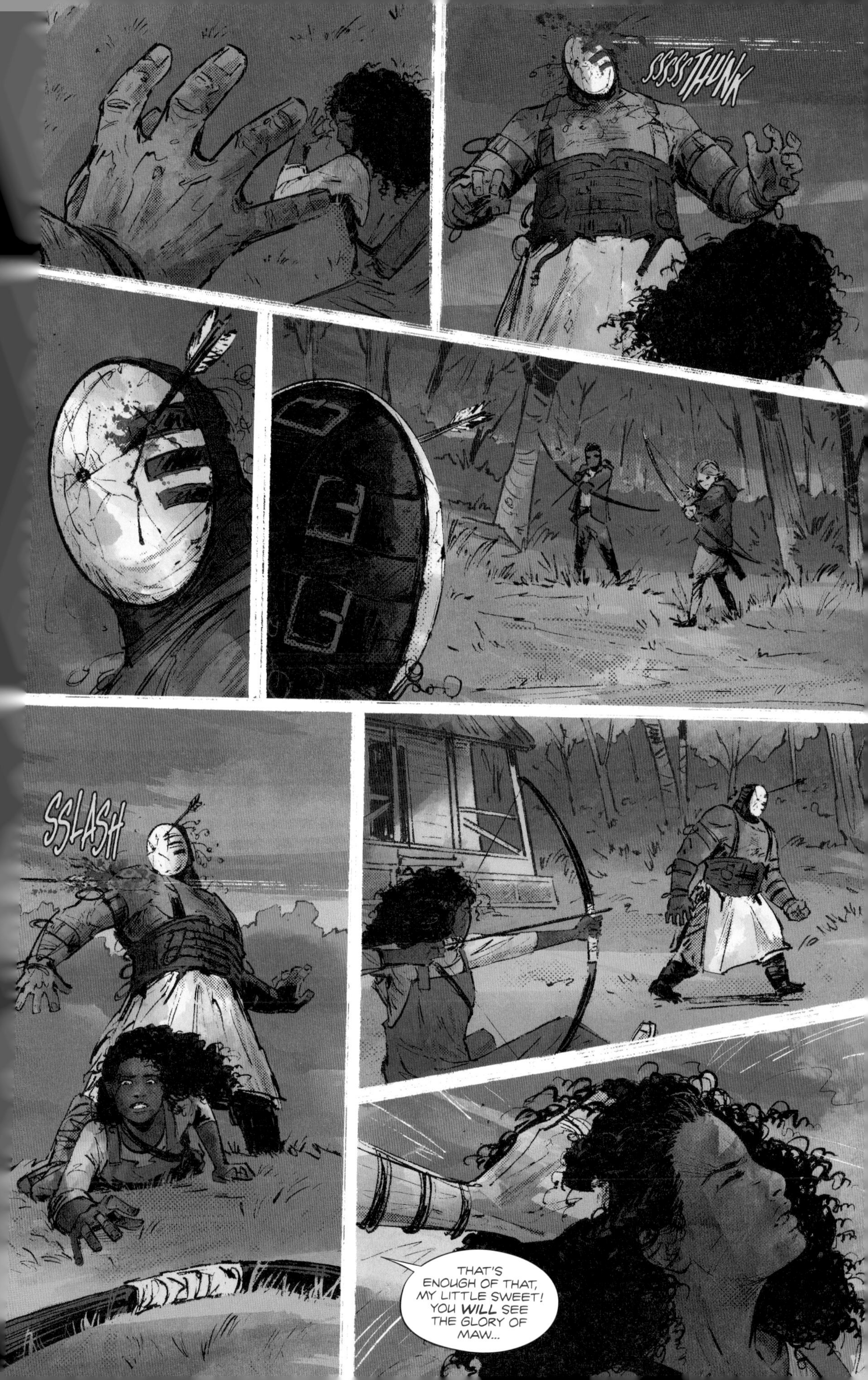
SSSSSTHUNK
SSLASH
THAT'S ENOUGH OF THAT, MY LITTLE SWEET! YOU **WILL** SEE THE GLORY OF MAW...

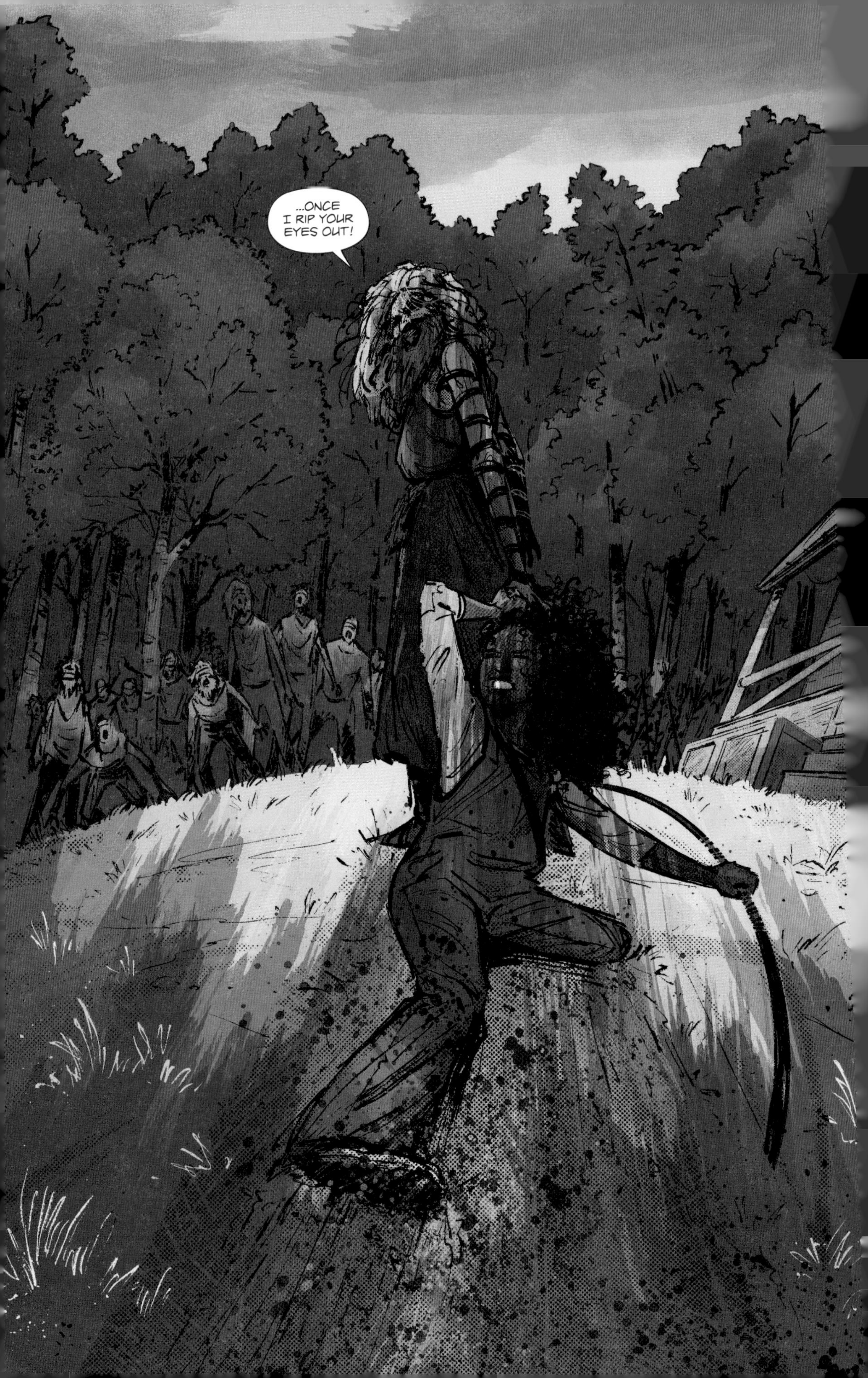
...ONCE I RIP YOUR EYES OUT!

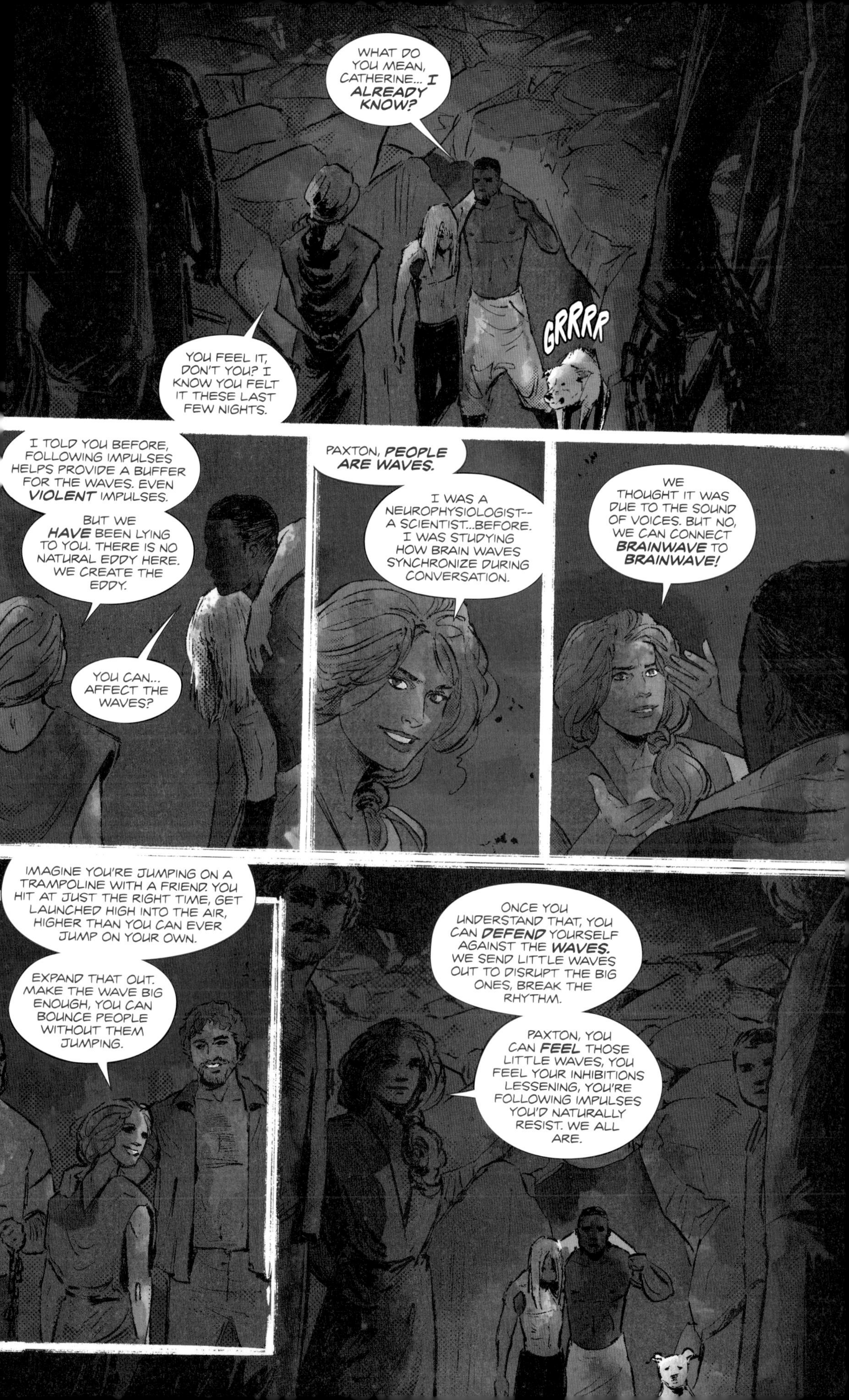
WHAT DO YOU MEAN, CATHERINE... I ALREADY KNOW?
GRRRR
YOU FEEL IT, DON'T YOU? I KNOW YOU FELT IT THESE LAST FEW NIGHTS.
I TOLD YOU BEFORE, FOLLOWING IMPULSES HELPS PROVIDE A BUFFER FOR THE WAVES. EVEN VIOLENT IMPULSES.
BUT WE HAVE BEEN LYING TO YOU. THERE IS NO NATURAL EDDY HERE. WE CREATE THE EDDY.
YOU CAN... AFFECT THE WAVES?
PAXTON, PEOPLE ARE WAVES.
I WAS A NEUROPHYSIOLOGIST--A SCIENTIST...BEFORE. I WAS STUDYING HOW BRAIN WAVES SYNCHRONIZE DURING CONVERSATION.
WE THOUGHT IT WAS DUE TO THE SOUND OF VOICES. BUT NO, WE CAN CONNECT BRAINWAVE TO BRAINWAVE!
IMAGINE YOU'RE JUMPING ON A TRAMPOLINE WITH A FRIEND. YOU HIT AT JUST THE RIGHT TIME, GET LAUNCHED HIGH INTO THE AIR, HIGHER THAN YOU CAN EVER JUMP ON YOUR OWN.
EXPAND THAT OUT. MAKE THE WAVE BIG ENOUGH, YOU CAN BOUNCE PEOPLE WITHOUT THEM JUMPING.
ONCE YOU UNDERSTAND THAT, YOU CAN DEFEND YOURSELF AGAINST THE WAVES. WE SEND LITTLE WAVES OUT TO DISRUPT THE BIG ONES, BREAK THE RHYTHM.
PAXTON, YOU CAN FEEL THOSE LITTLE WAVES, YOU FEEL YOUR INHIBITIONS LESSENING, YOU'RE FOLLOWING IMPULSES YOU'D NATURALLY RESIST. WE ALL ARE.

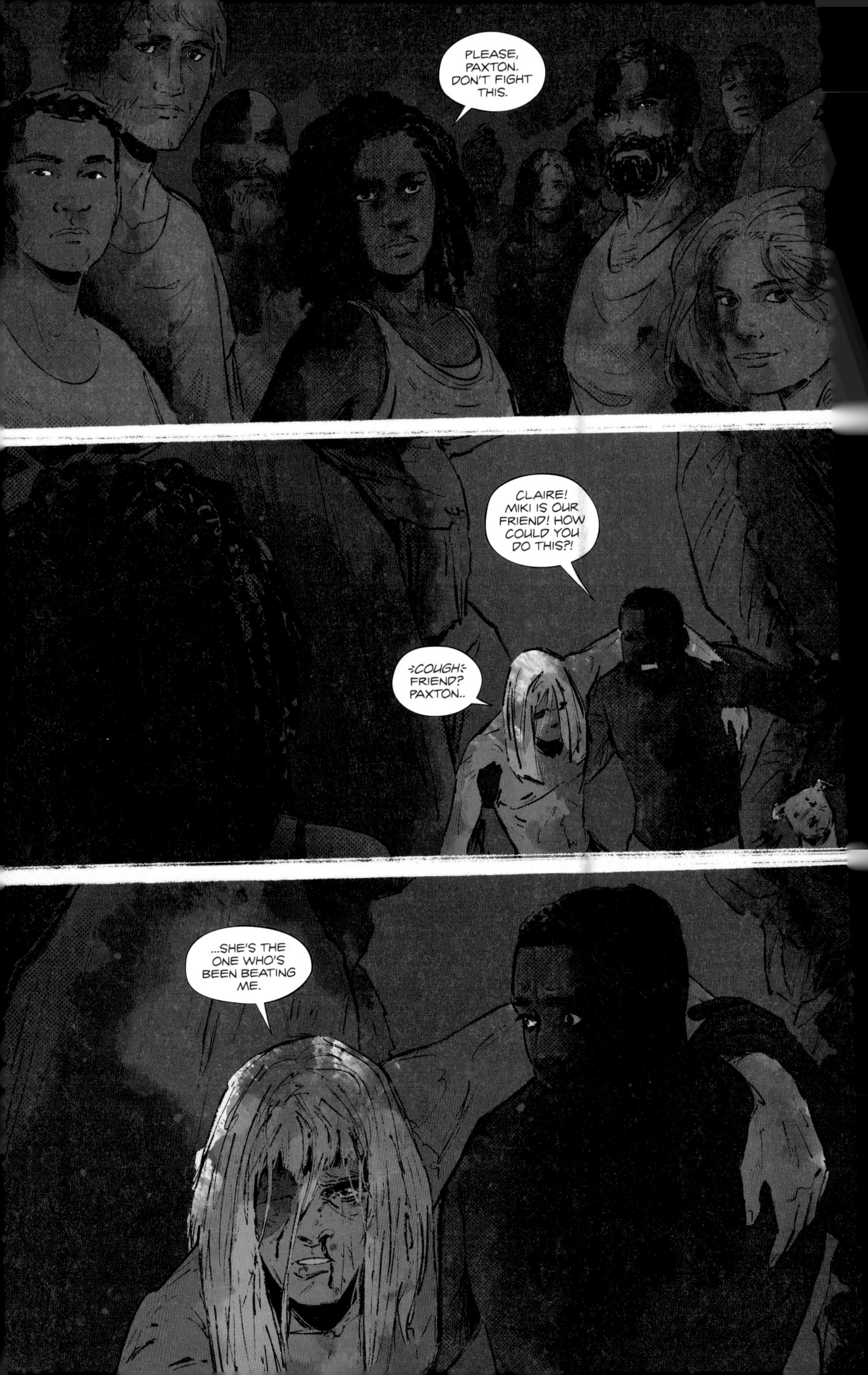
PLEASE, PAXTON. DON'T FIGHT THIS.
CLAIRE! MIKI IS OUR FRIEND! HOW COULD YOU DO THIS?!
-COUGH- FRIEND? PAXTON..
...SHE'S THE ONE WHO'S BEEN BEATING ME.

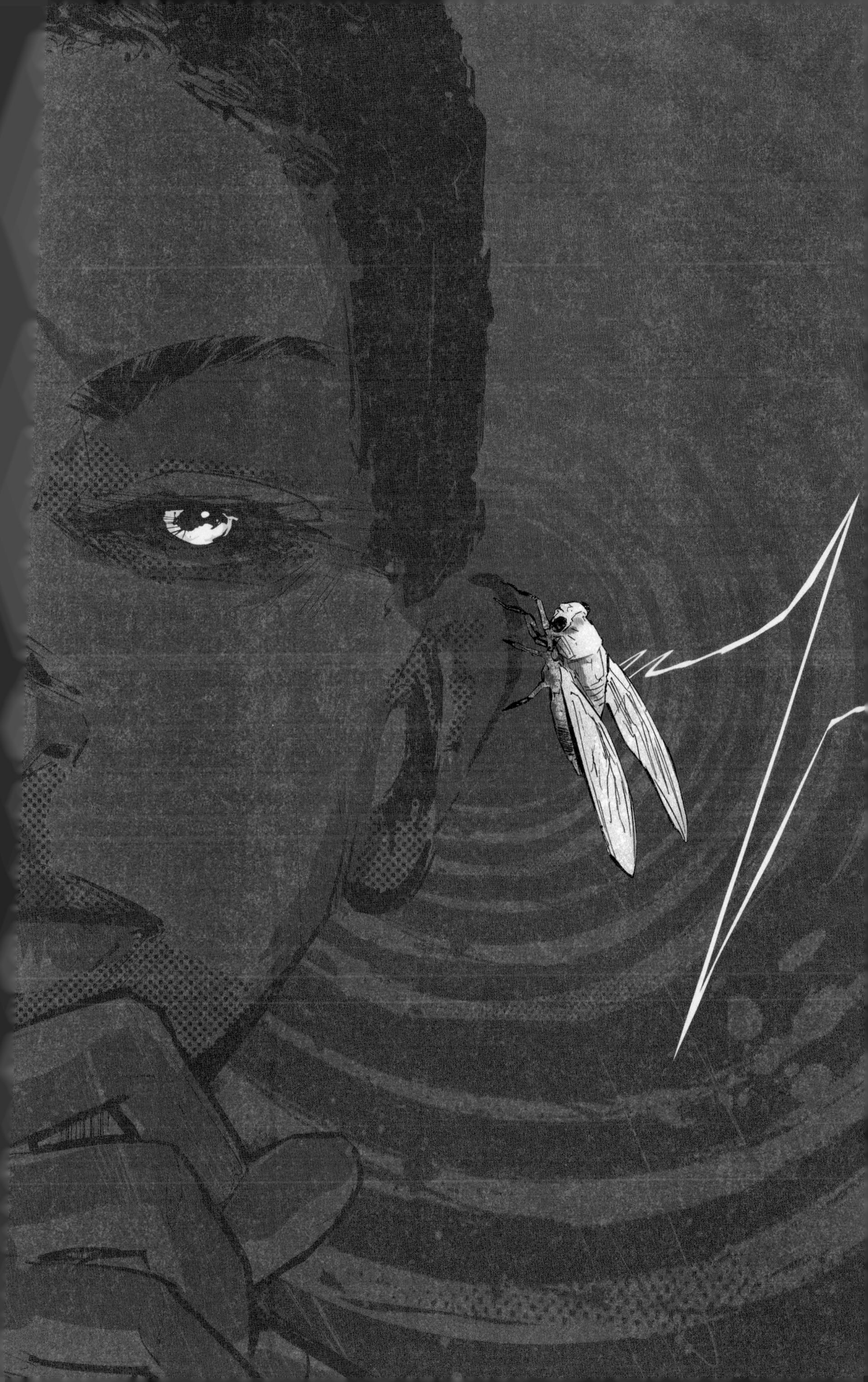

CHAPTER TEN

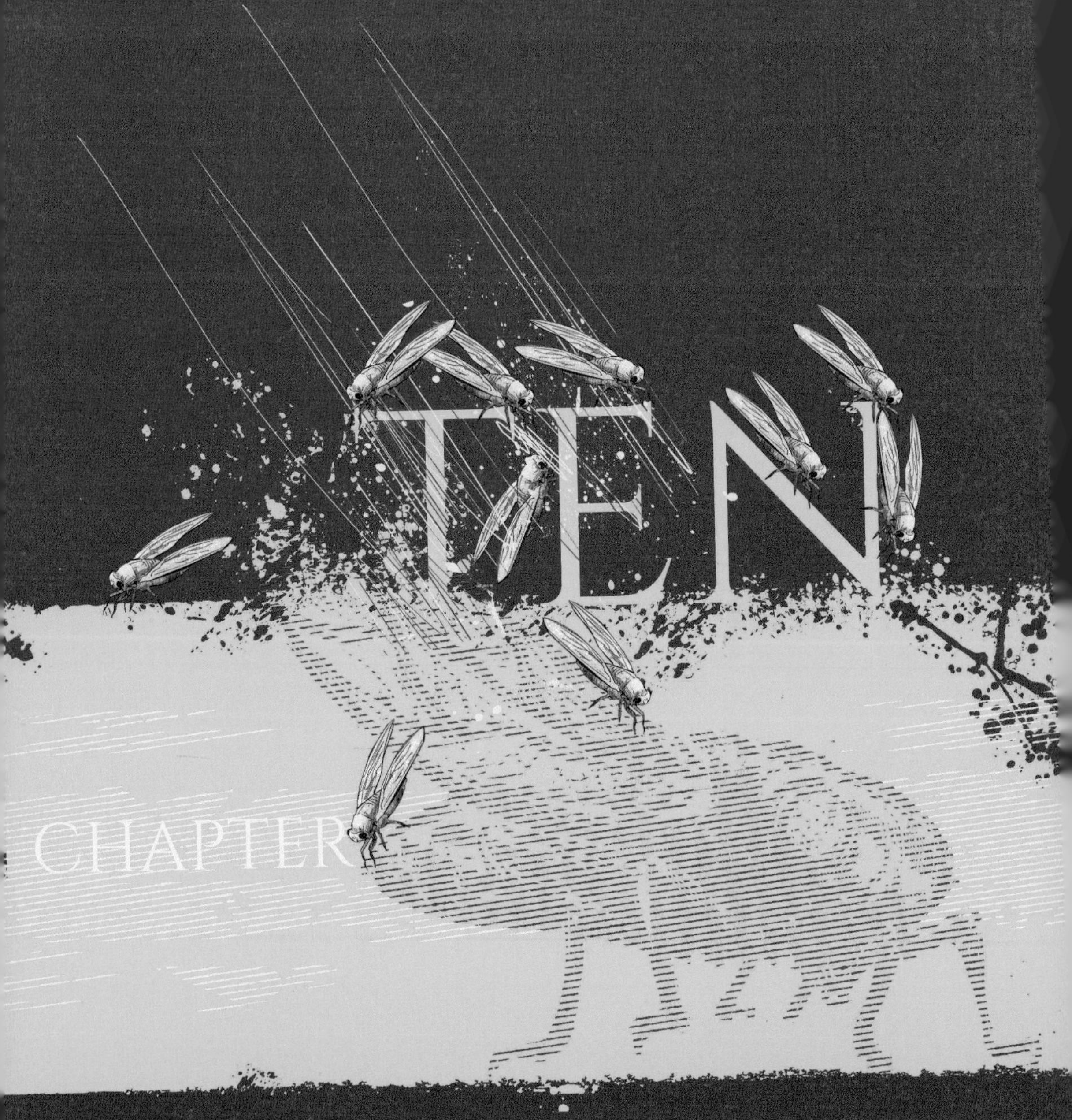

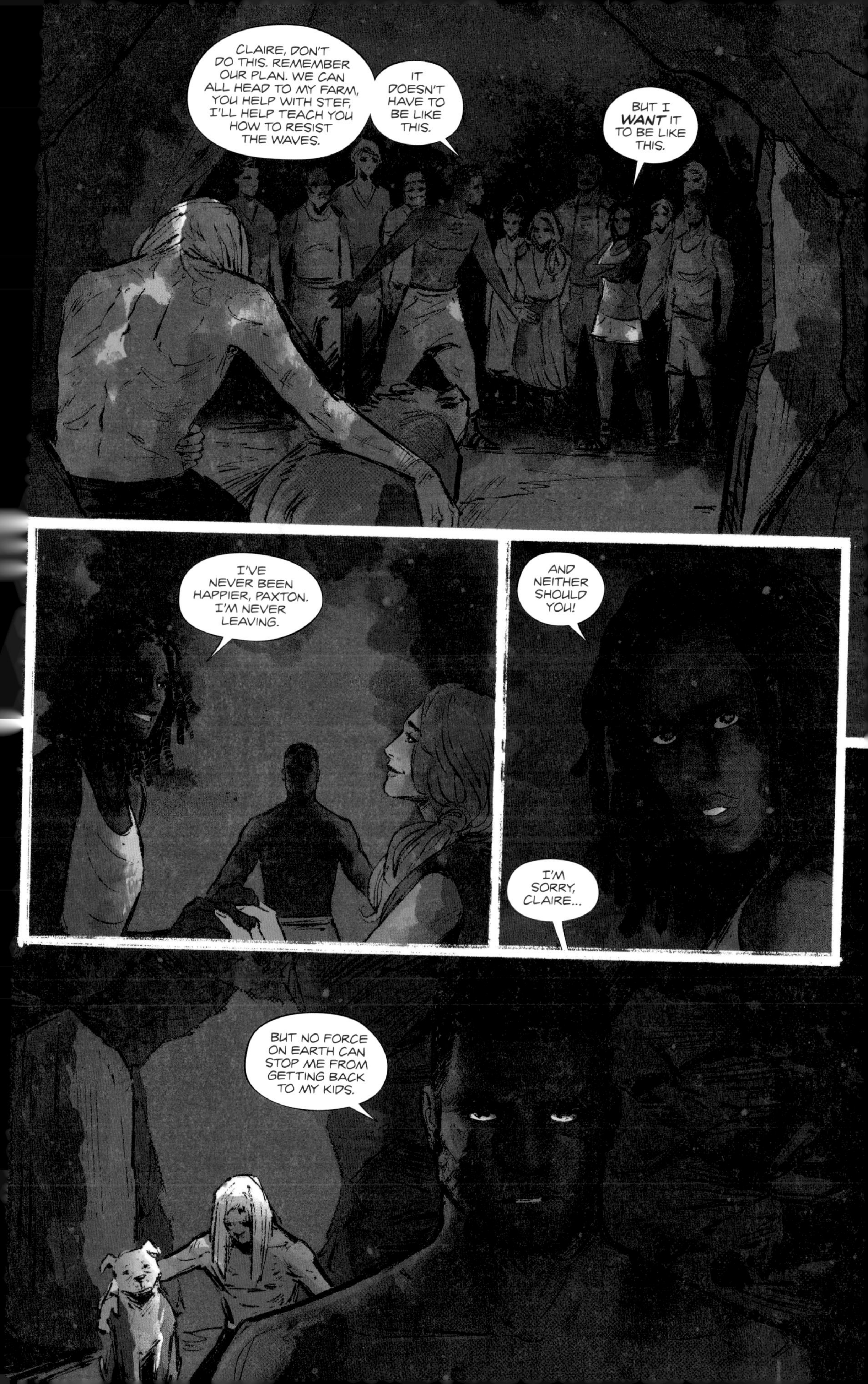
CLAIRE, DON'T DO THIS. REMEMBER OUR PLAN. WE CAN ALL HEAD TO MY FARM, YOU HELP WITH STEF, I'LL HELP TEACH YOU HOW TO RESIST THE WAVES.
IT DOESN'T HAVE TO BE LIKE THIS.
BUT I **WANT** IT TO BE LIKE THIS.
I'VE NEVER BEEN HAPPIER, PAXTON. I'M NEVER LEAVING.
AND NEITHER SHOULD YOU!
I'M SORRY, CLAIRE...
BUT NO FORCE ON EARTH CAN STOP ME FROM GETTING BACK TO MY KIDS.

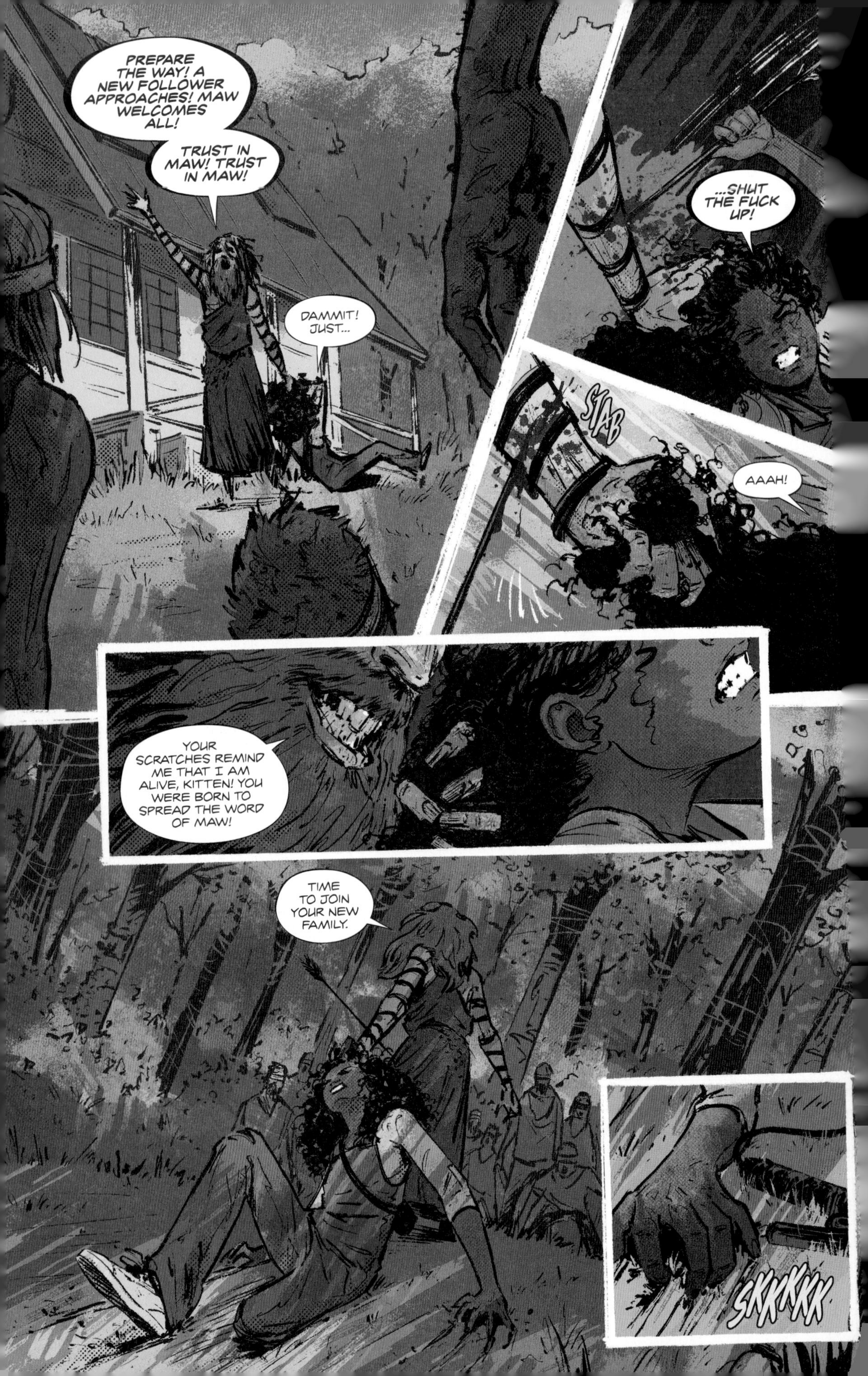
PREPARE THE WAY! A NEW FOLLOWER APPROACHES! MAW WELCOMES ALL!
TRUST IN MAW! TRUST IN MAW!
DAMMIT! JUST...
...SHUT THE FUCK UP!
STAB
AAAH!
YOUR SCRATCHES REMIND ME THAT I AM ALIVE, KITTEN! YOU WERE BORN TO SPREAD THE WORD OF MAW!
TIME TO JOIN YOUR NEW FAMILY.
SKKKKK

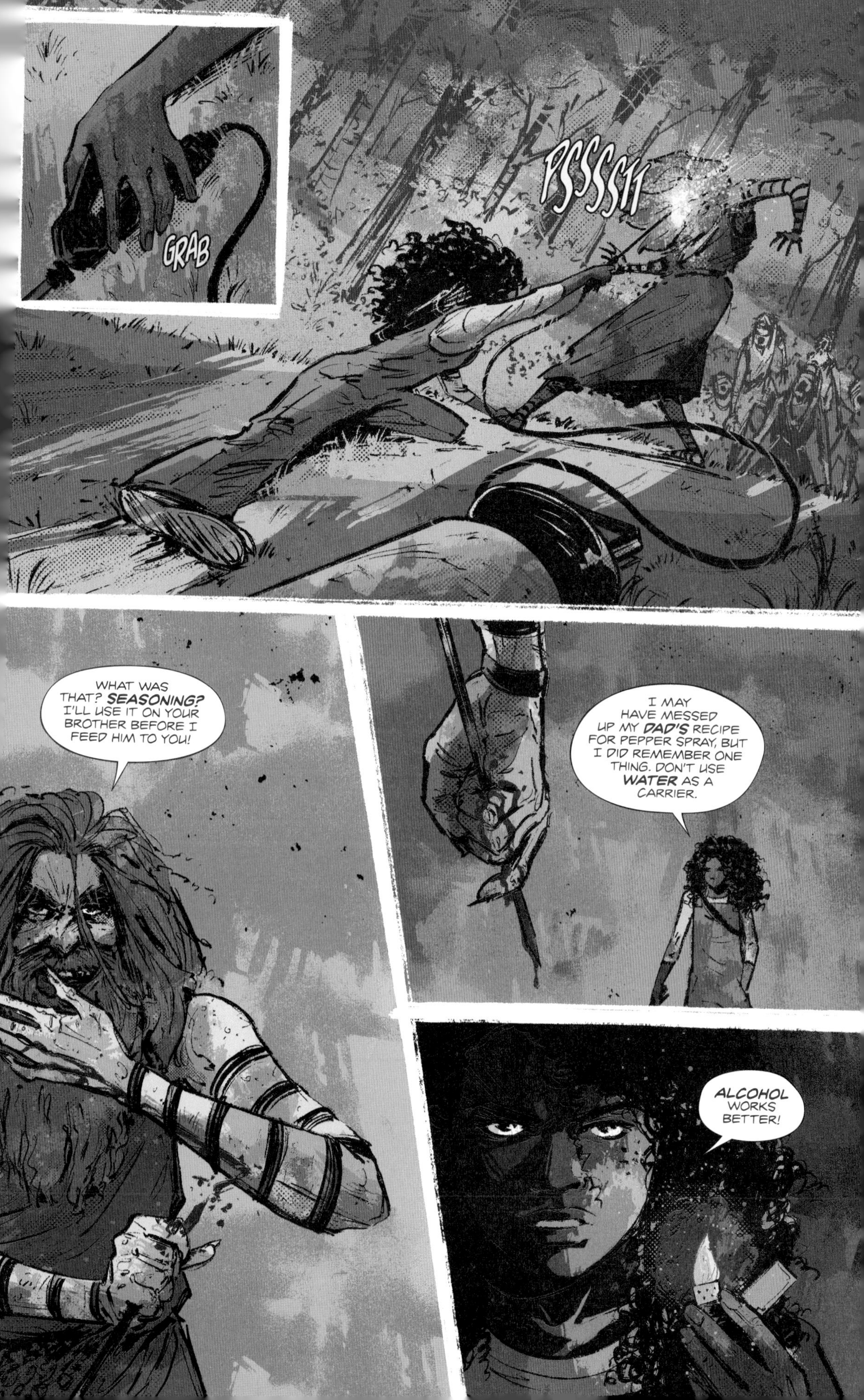
GRAB
PSSSSH
WHAT WAS THAT? SEASONING? I'LL USE IT ON YOUR BROTHER BEFORE I FEED HIM TO YOU!
I MAY HAVE MESSED UP MY DAD'S RECIPE FOR PEPPER SPRAY, BUT I DID REMEMBER ONE THING. DON'T USE WATER AS A CARRIER.
ALCOHOL WORKS BETTER!

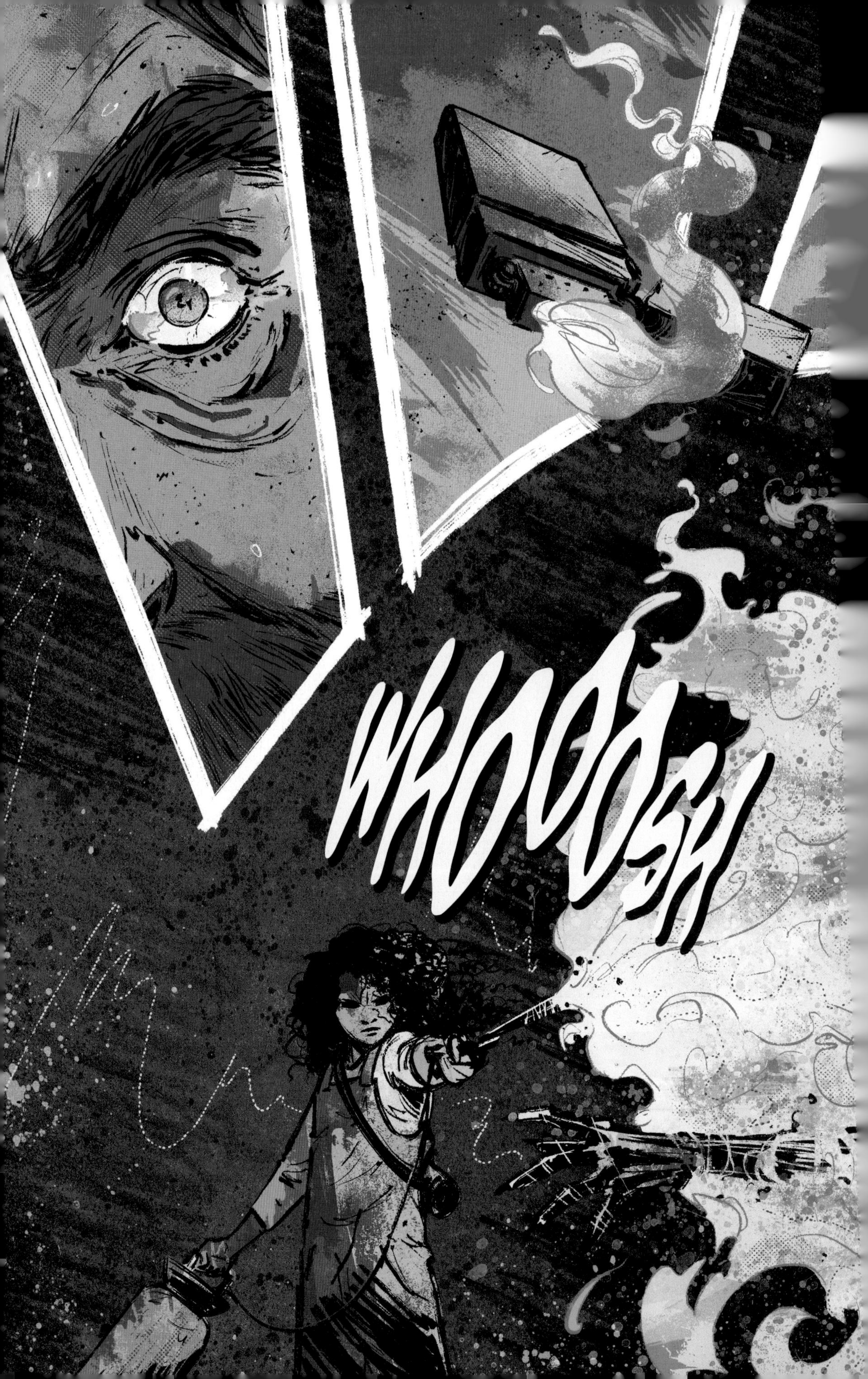
WHOOOOSH

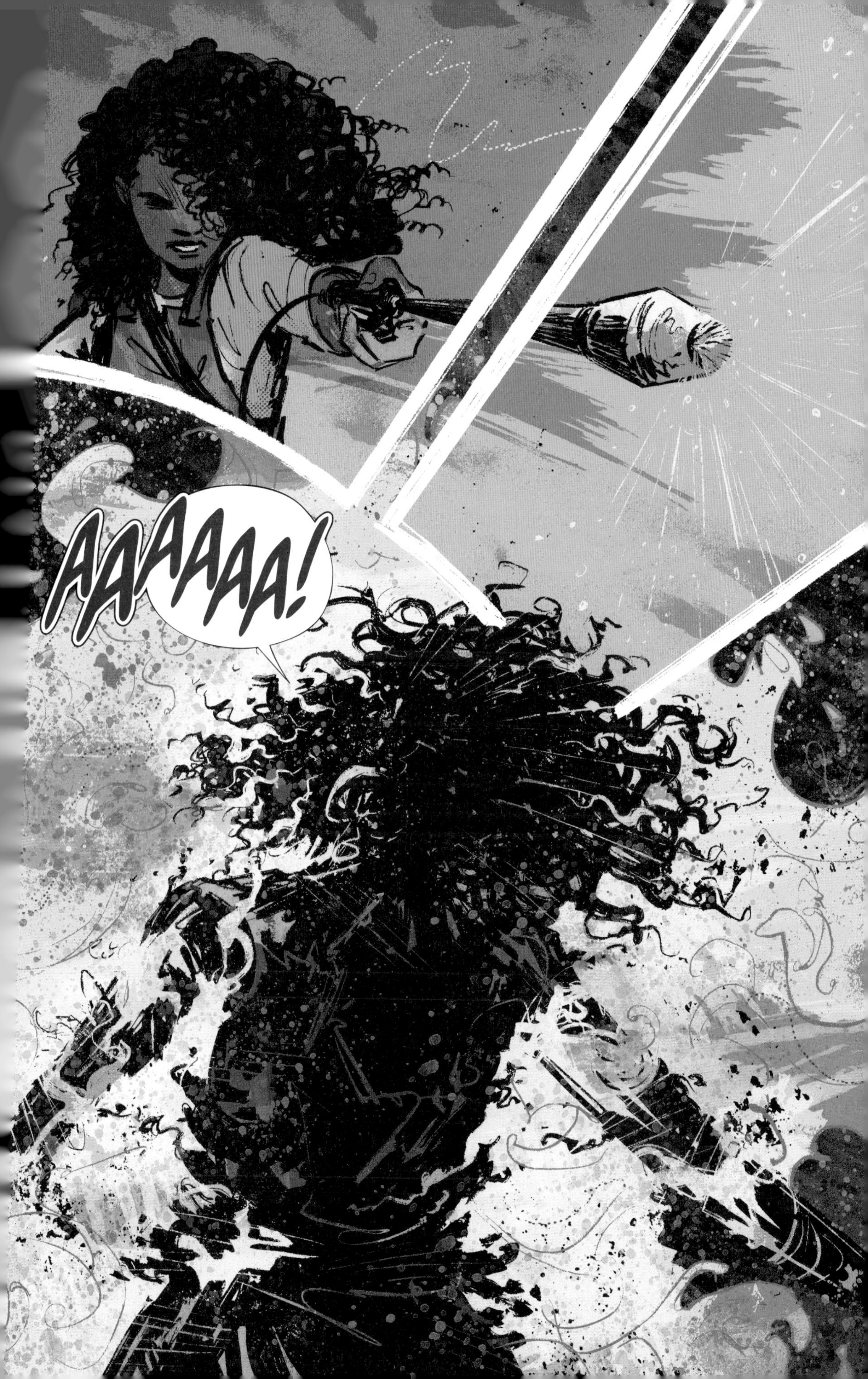
AAAAAA!

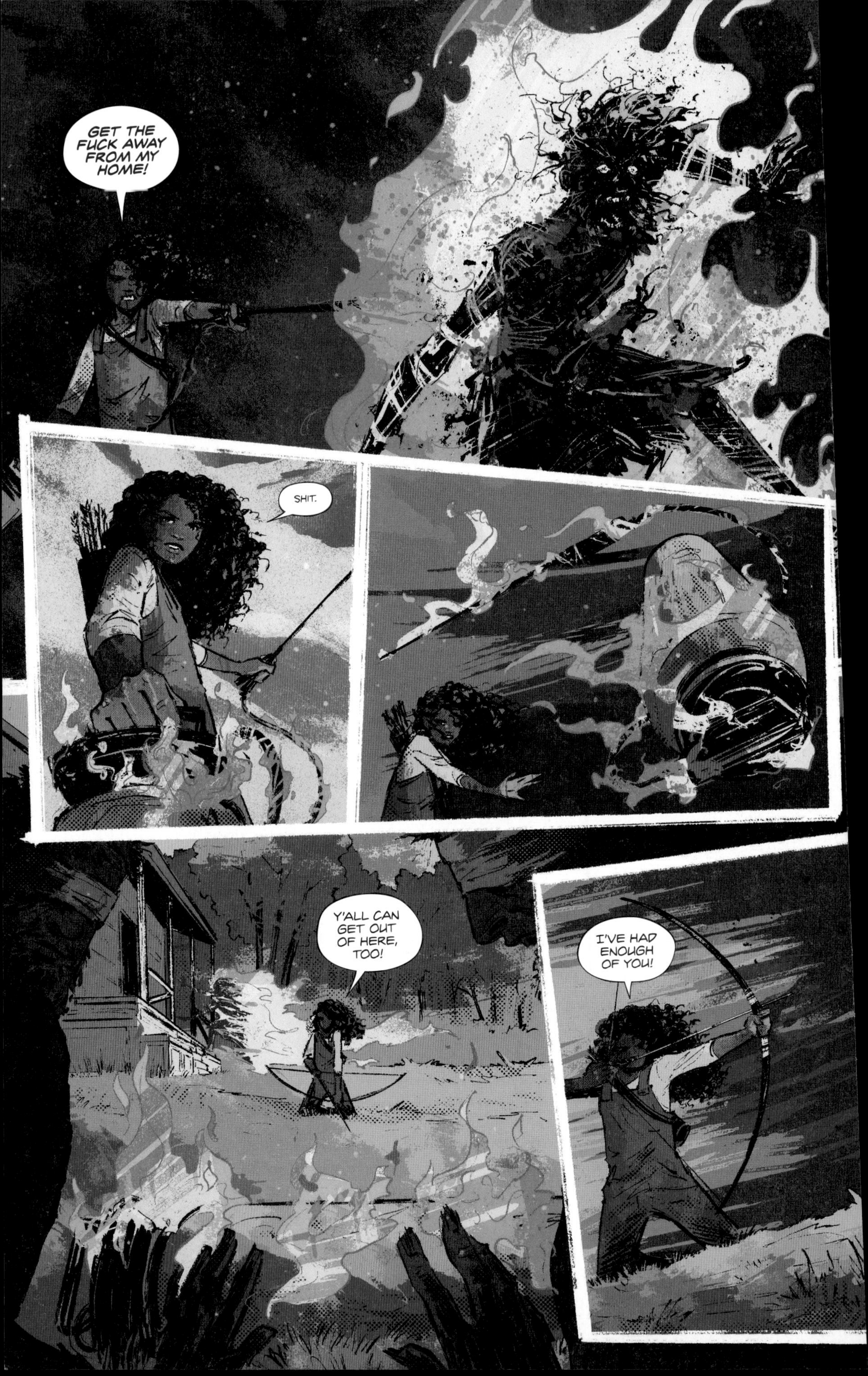
GET THE FUCK AWAY FROM MY HOME!
SHIT.
Y'ALL CAN GET OUT OF HERE, TOO!
I'VE HAD ENOUGH OF YOU!

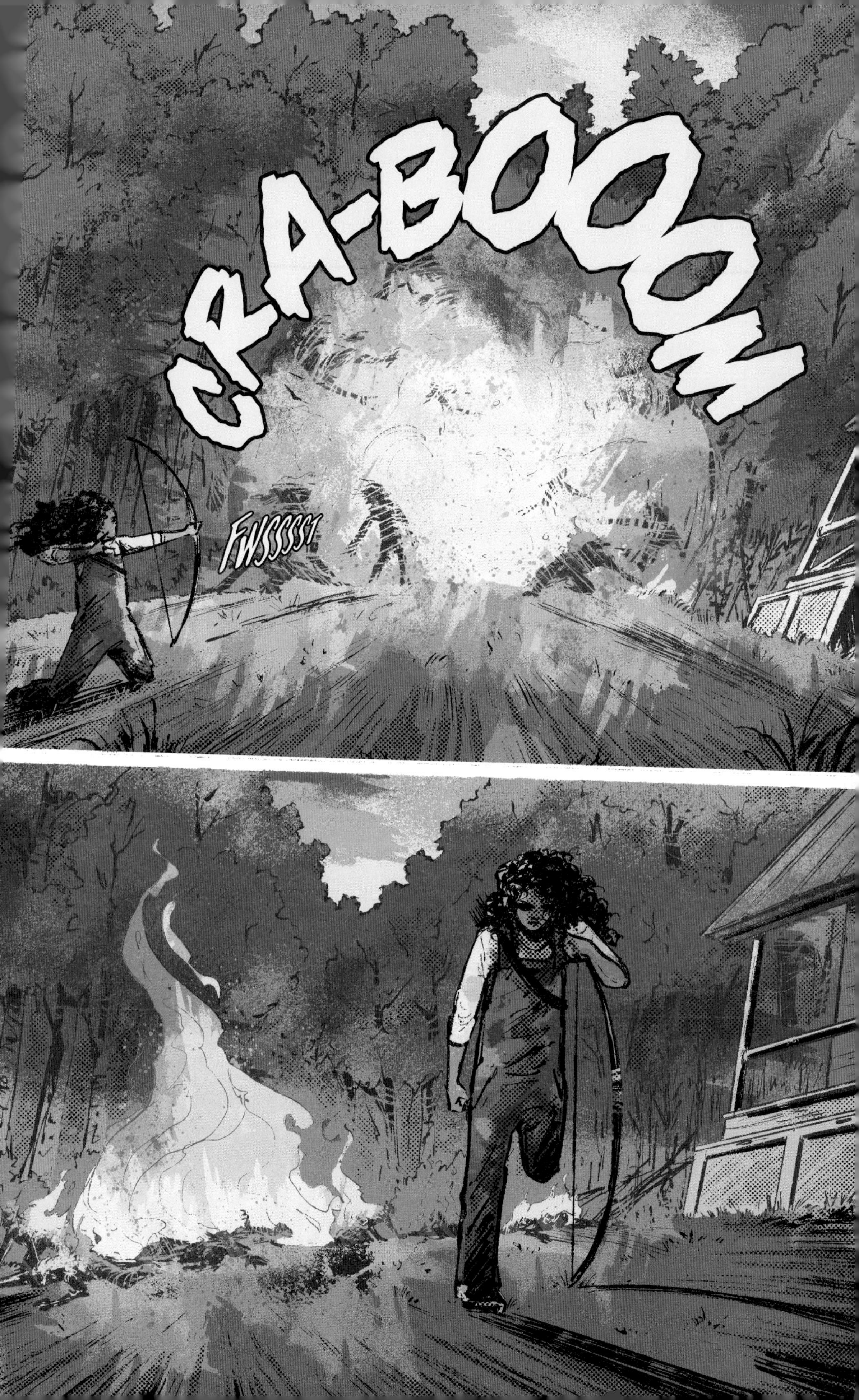
CRA-BOOOM
FWSSSST

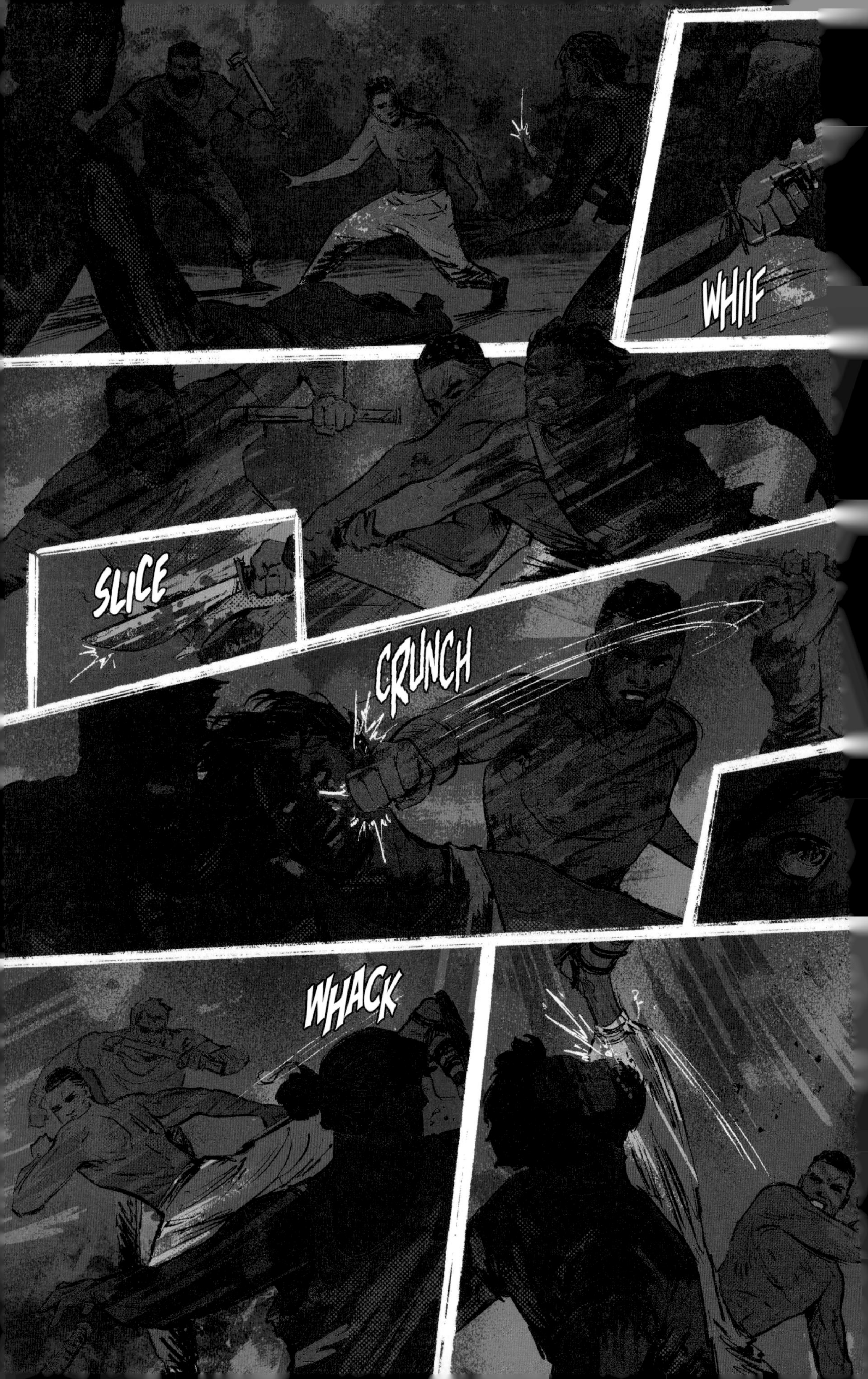
WHIIF
SLICE
CRUNCH
WHACK

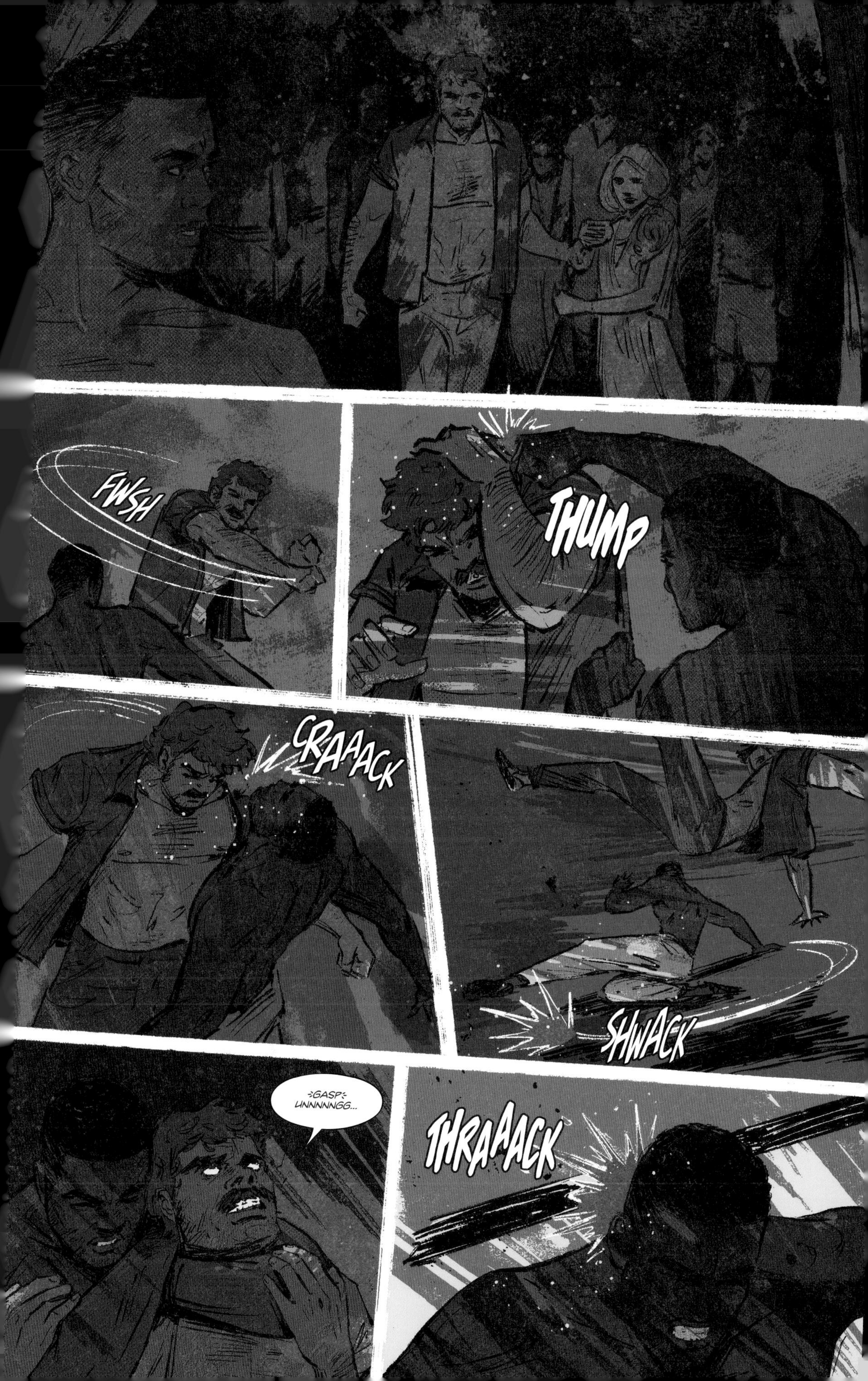
FWSH
THUMP
CRAAACK
SHWACK
:GASP:
UNNNNNGG...
THRAAACK

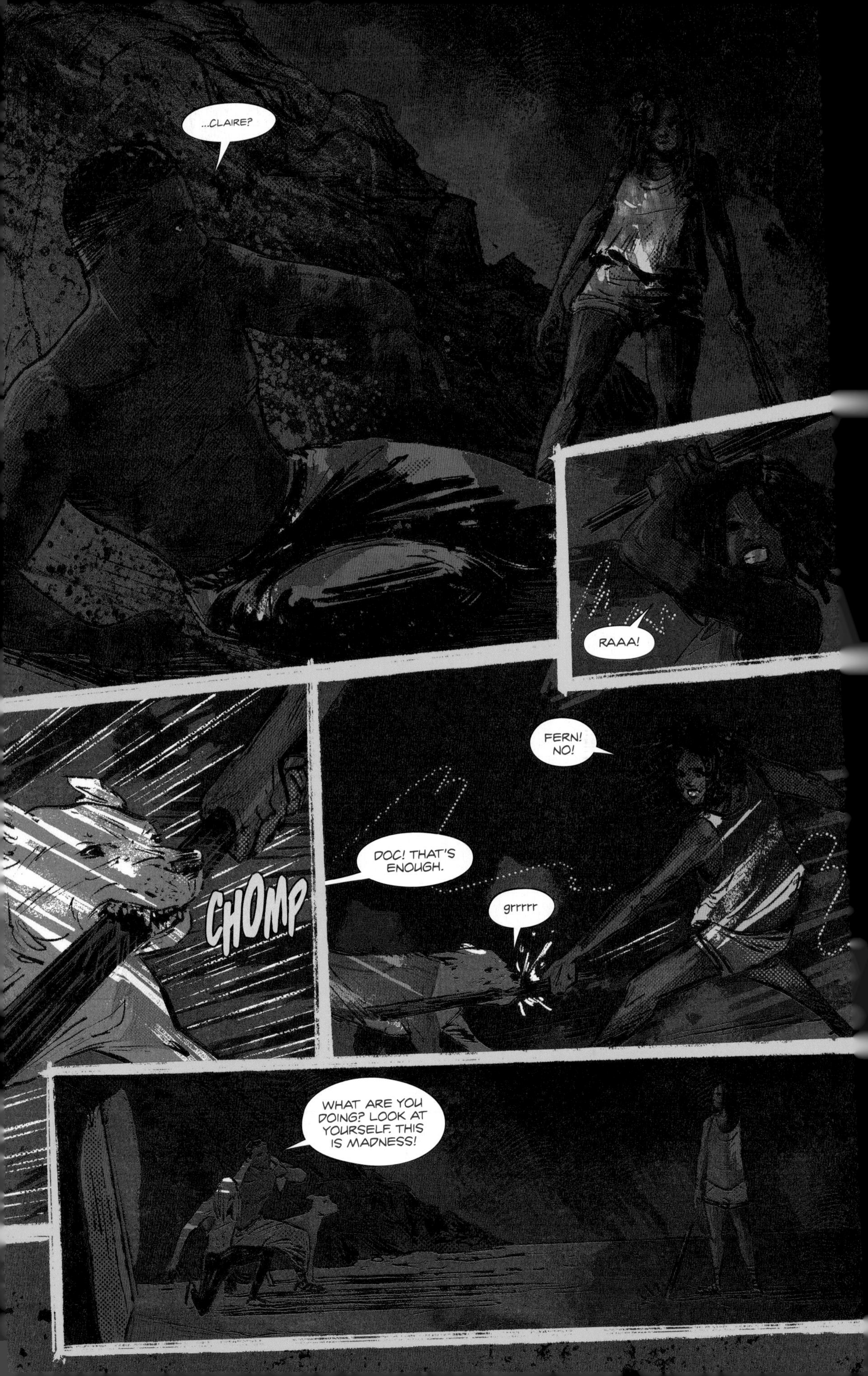
...CLAIRE?
RAAA!
CHOMP
DOC! THAT'S ENOUGH.
FERN! NO!
grrrrr
WHAT ARE YOU DOING? LOOK AT YOURSELF. THIS IS MADNESS!

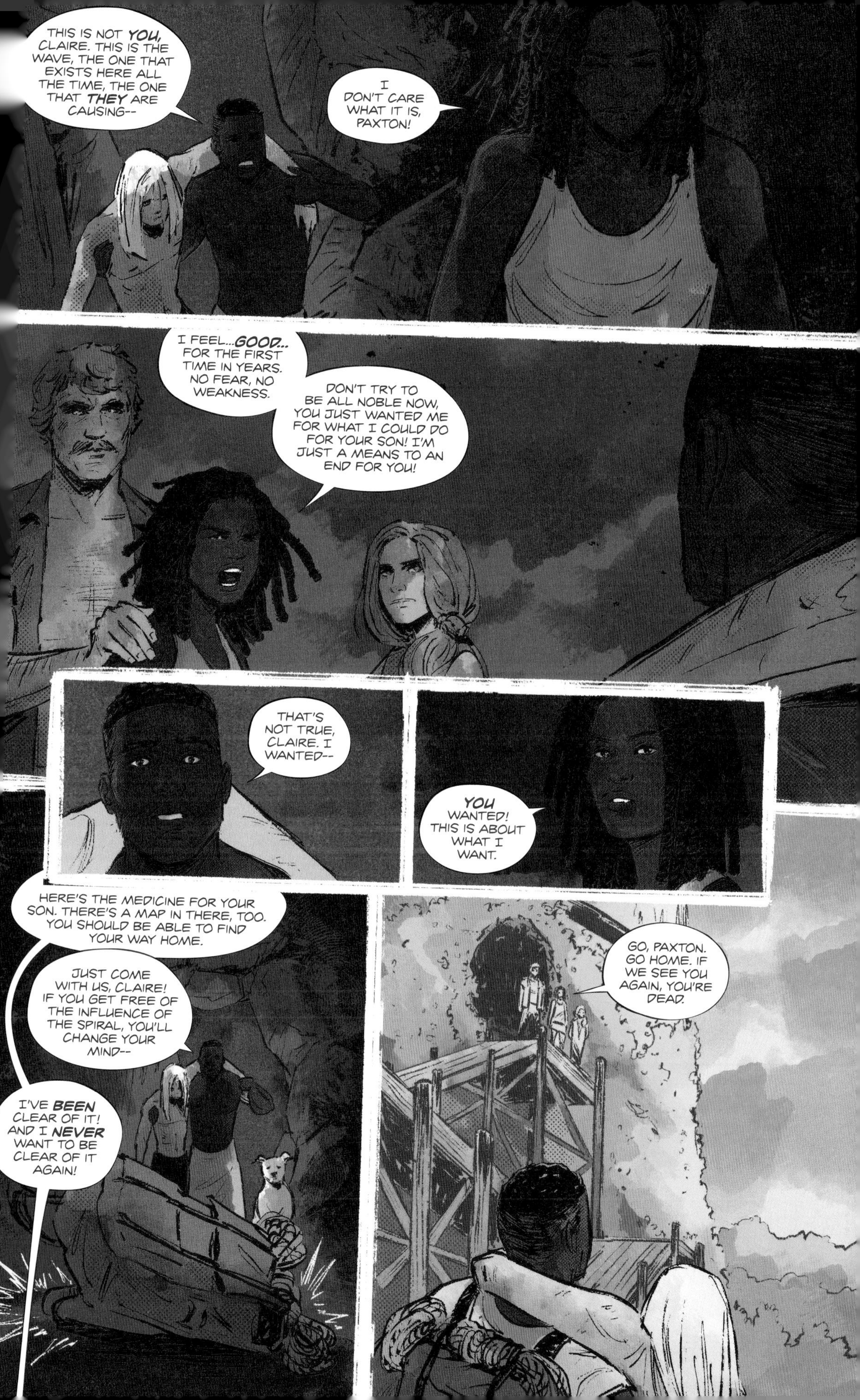
THIS IS NOT YOU, CLAIRE. THIS IS THE WAVE, THE ONE THAT EXISTS HERE ALL THE TIME, THE ONE THAT THEY ARE CAUSING--
I DON'T CARE WHAT IT IS, PAXTON!
I FEEL...GOOD... FOR THE FIRST TIME IN YEARS. NO FEAR, NO WEAKNESS.
DON'T TRY TO BE ALL NOBLE NOW, YOU JUST WANTED ME FOR WHAT I COULD DO FOR YOUR SON! I'M JUST A MEANS TO AN END FOR YOU!
THAT'S NOT TRUE, CLAIRE. I WANTED--
YOU WANTED! THIS IS ABOUT WHAT I WANT.
HERE'S THE MEDICINE FOR YOUR SON. THERE'S A MAP IN THERE, TOO. YOU SHOULD BE ABLE TO FIND YOUR WAY HOME.
JUST COME WITH US, CLAIRE! IF YOU GET FREE OF THE INFLUENCE OF THE SPIRAL, YOU'LL CHANGE YOUR MIND--
I'VE BEEN CLEAR OF IT! AND I NEVER WANT TO BE CLEAR OF IT AGAIN!
GO, PAXTON. GO HOME. IF WE SEE YOU AGAIN, YOU'RE DEAD.

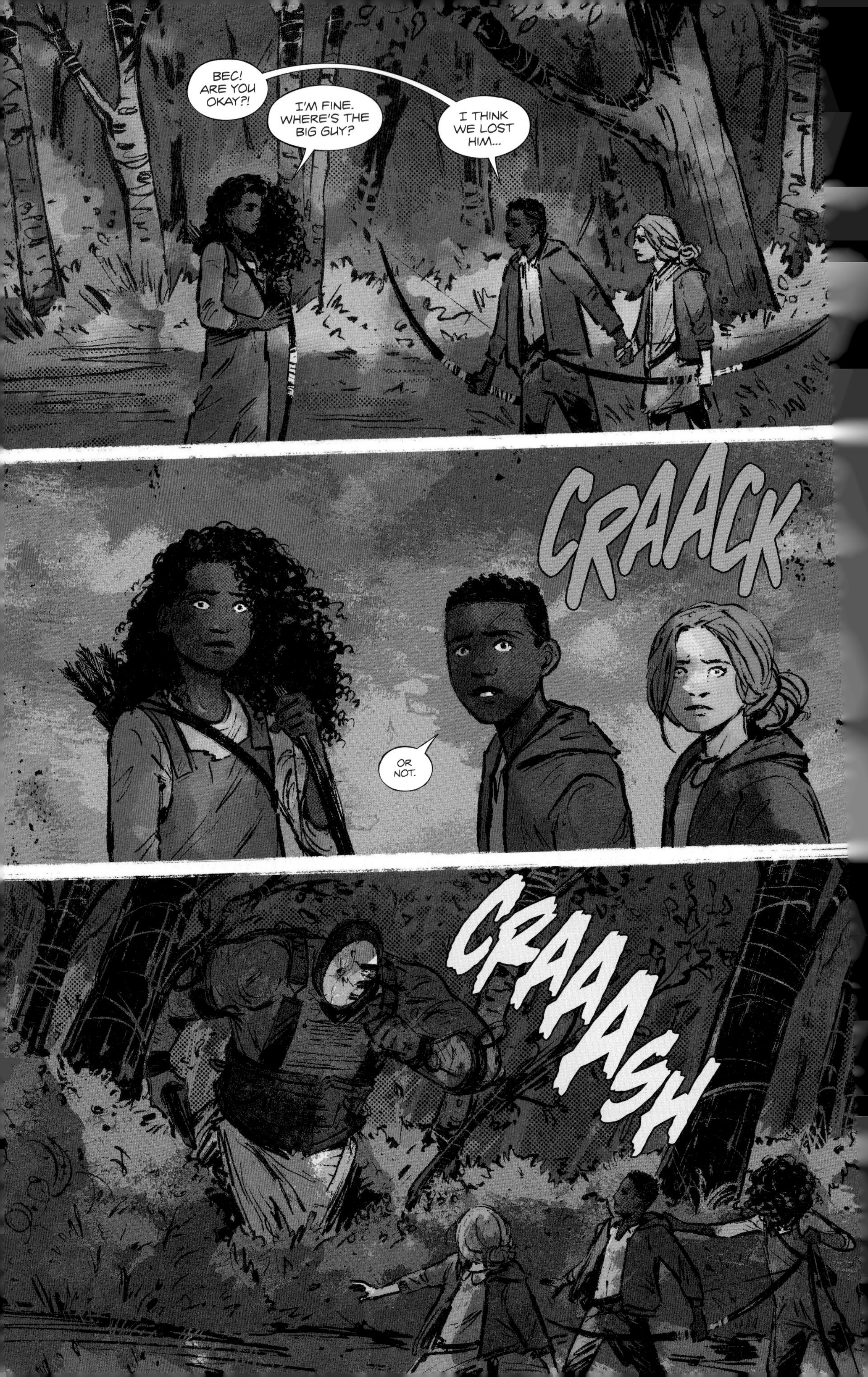
BEC! ARE YOU OKAY?!
I'M FINE. WHERE'S THE BIG GUY?
I THINK WE LOST HIM...
CRAACK
OR NOT.
CRAAAASH

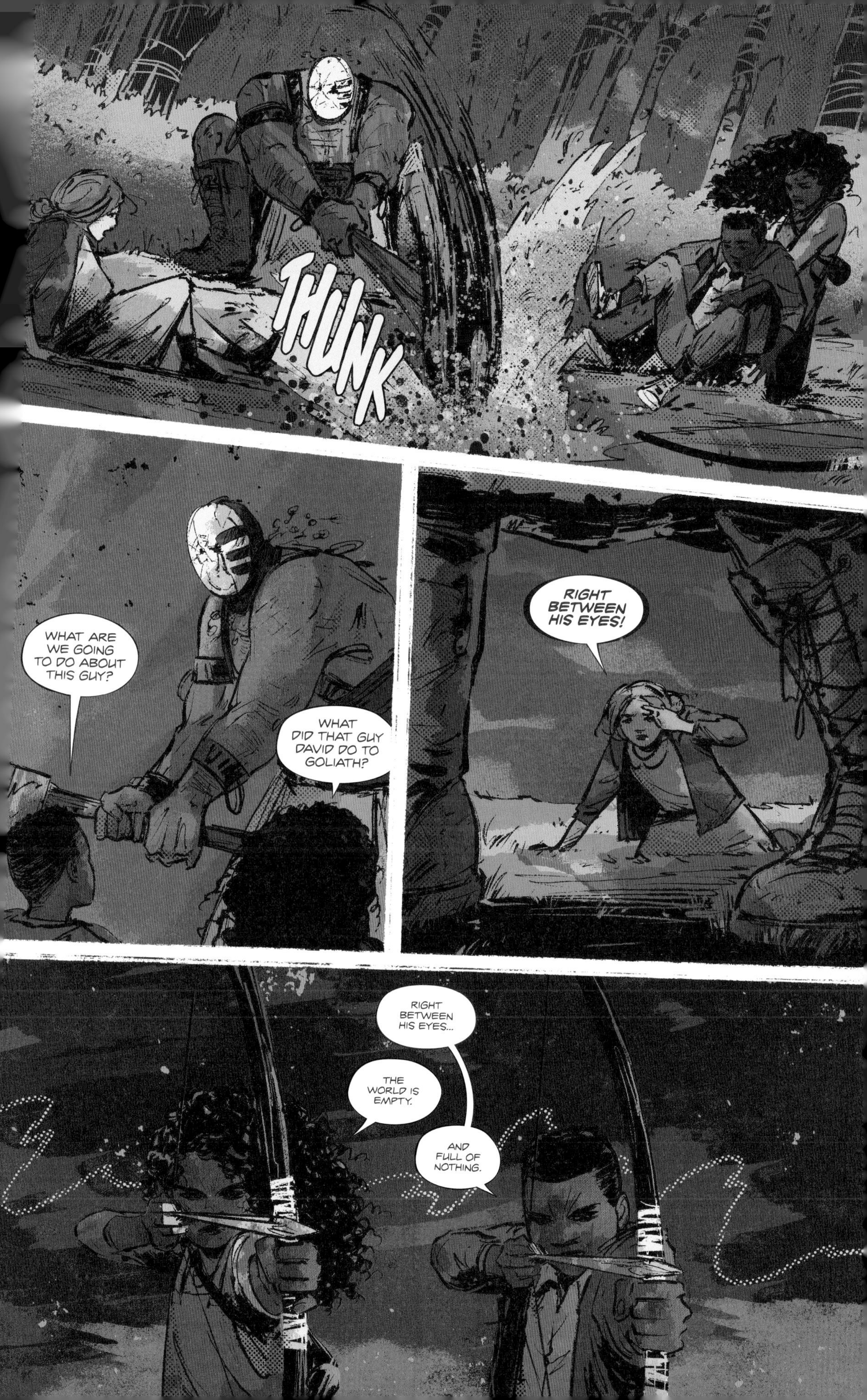
THUNK
WHAT ARE WE GOING TO DO ABOUT THIS GUY?
WHAT DID THAT GUY DAVID DO TO GOLIATH?
RIGHT BETWEEN HIS EYES!
RIGHT BETWEEN HIS EYES...
THE WORLD IS EMPTY.
AND FULL OF NOTHING.

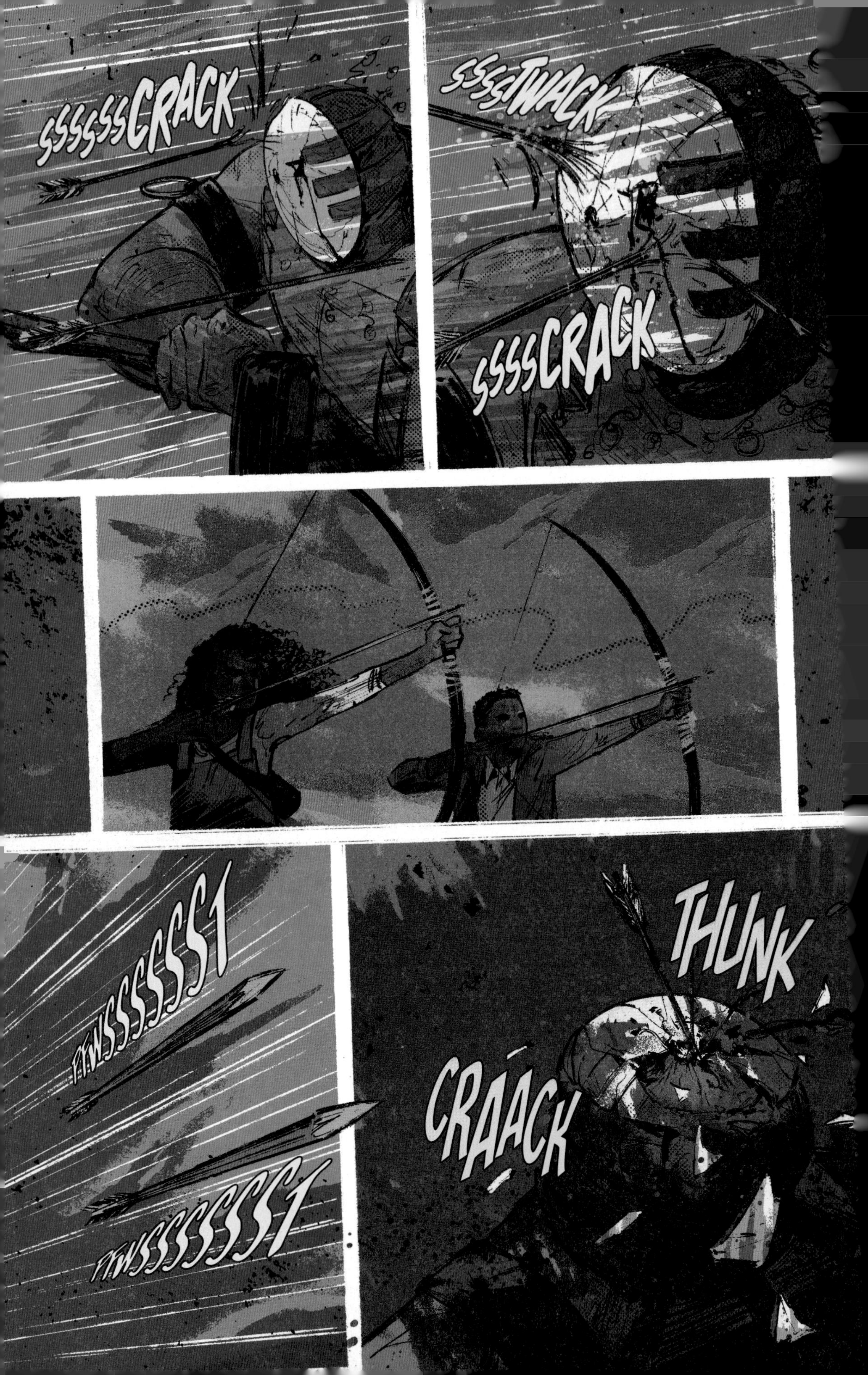
SSSSSSCRACK
SSSSTWACK
SSSSCRACK
PFWSSSSSST
PFWSSSSSSST
THUNK
CRAACK

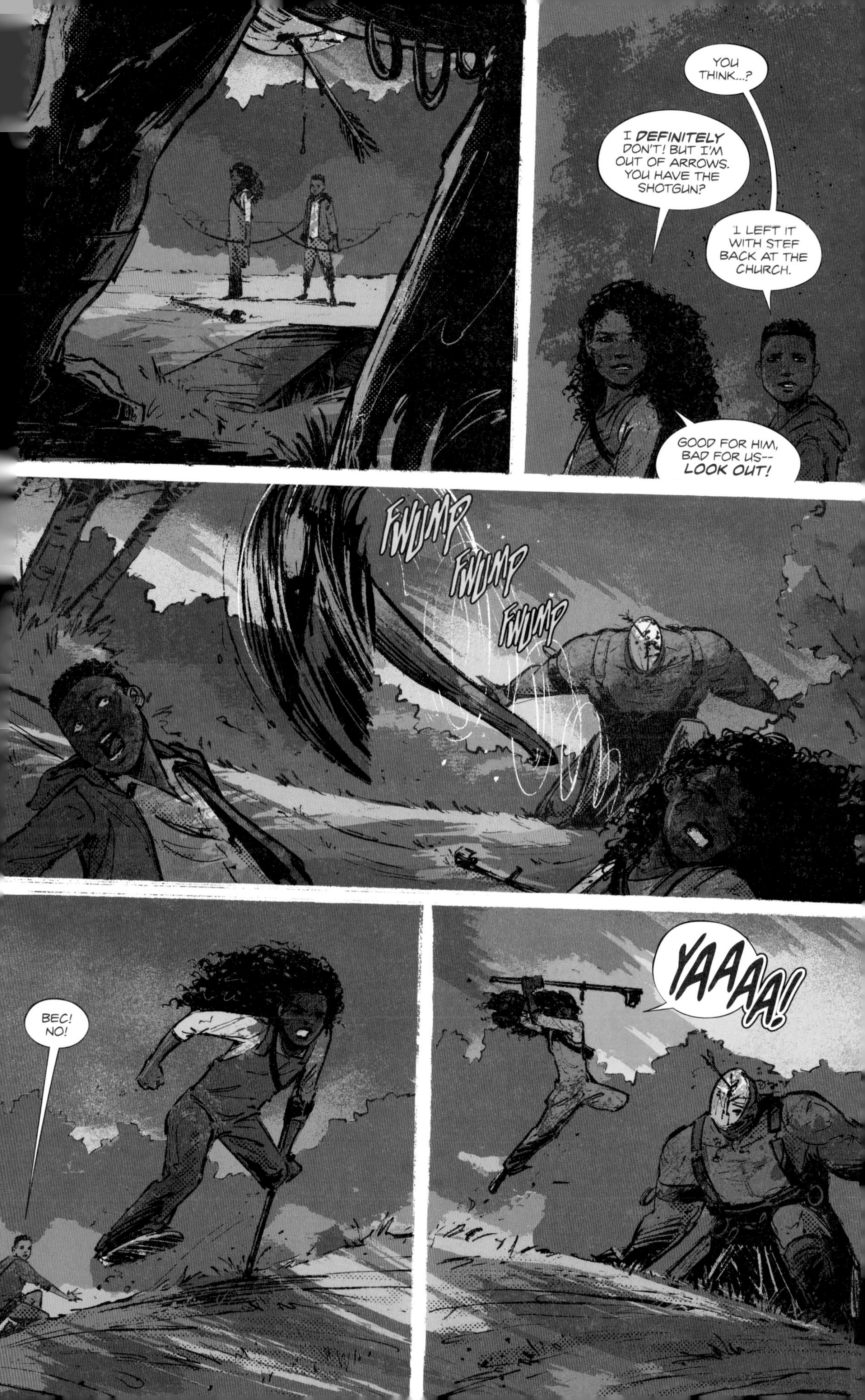
YOU THINK...?
I DEFINITELY DON'T! BUT I'M OUT OF ARROWS. YOU HAVE THE SHOTGUN?
I LEFT IT WITH STEF BACK AT THE CHURCH.
GOOD FOR HIM, BAD FOR US-- LOOK OUT!
FWUMP
FWUMP
FWUMP
BEC! NO!
YAAAA!

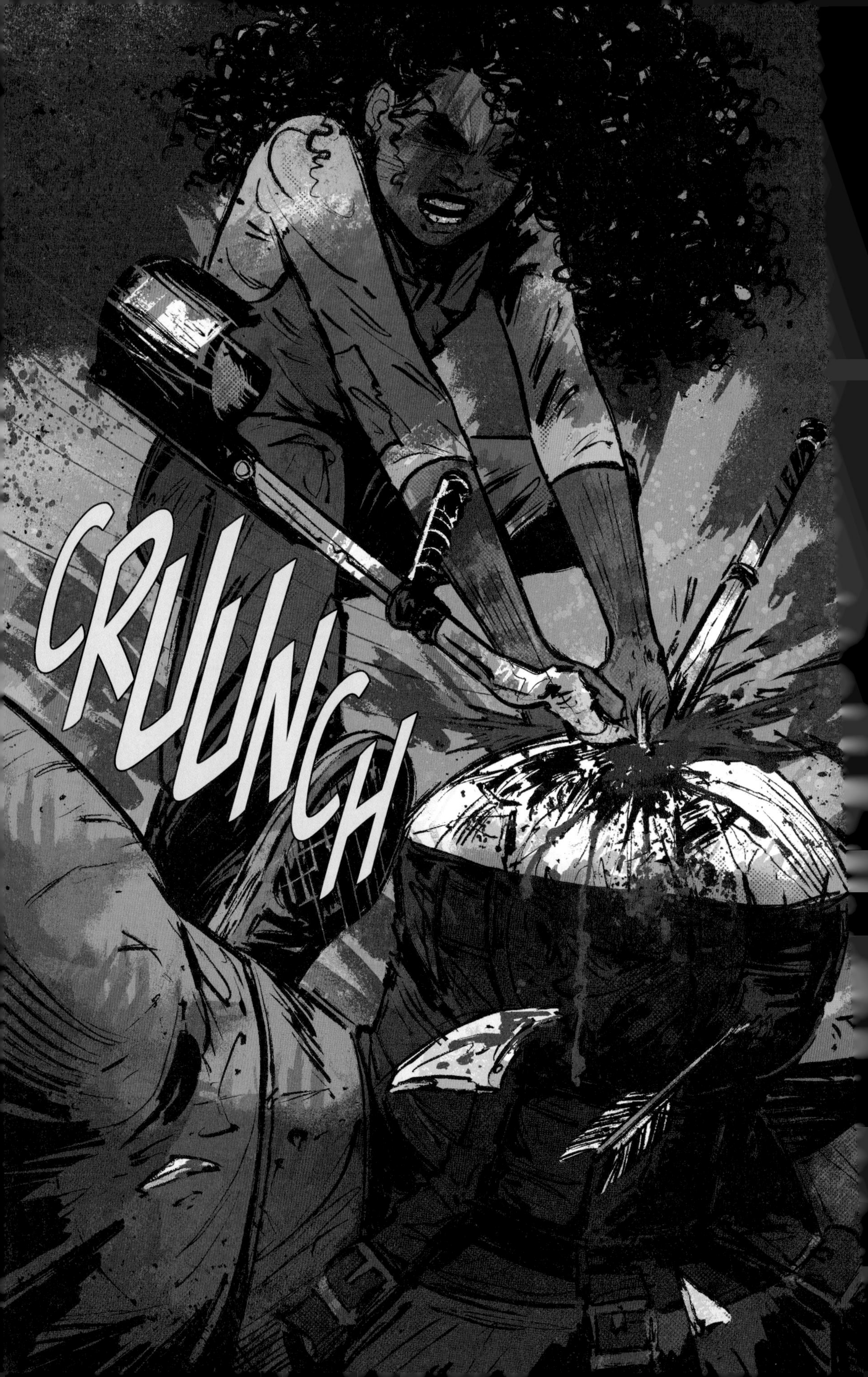
CRUUNCH

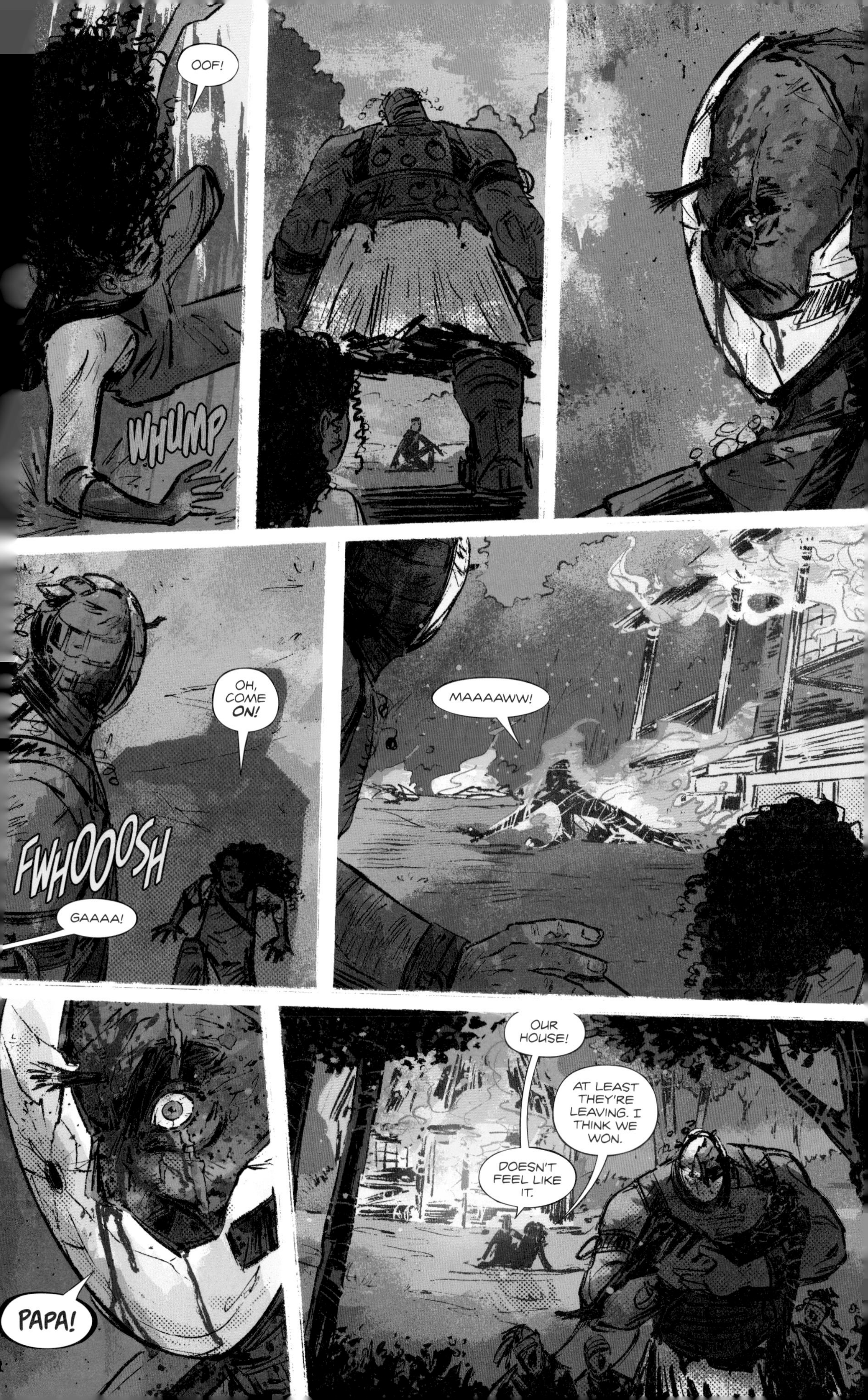
OOF!
WHUMP
OH, COME ON!
FWHOOOSH
GAAAA!
MAAAAWW!
PAPA!
OUR HOUSE!
AT LEAST THEY'RE LEAVING. I THINK WE WON.
DOESN'T FEEL LIKE IT.

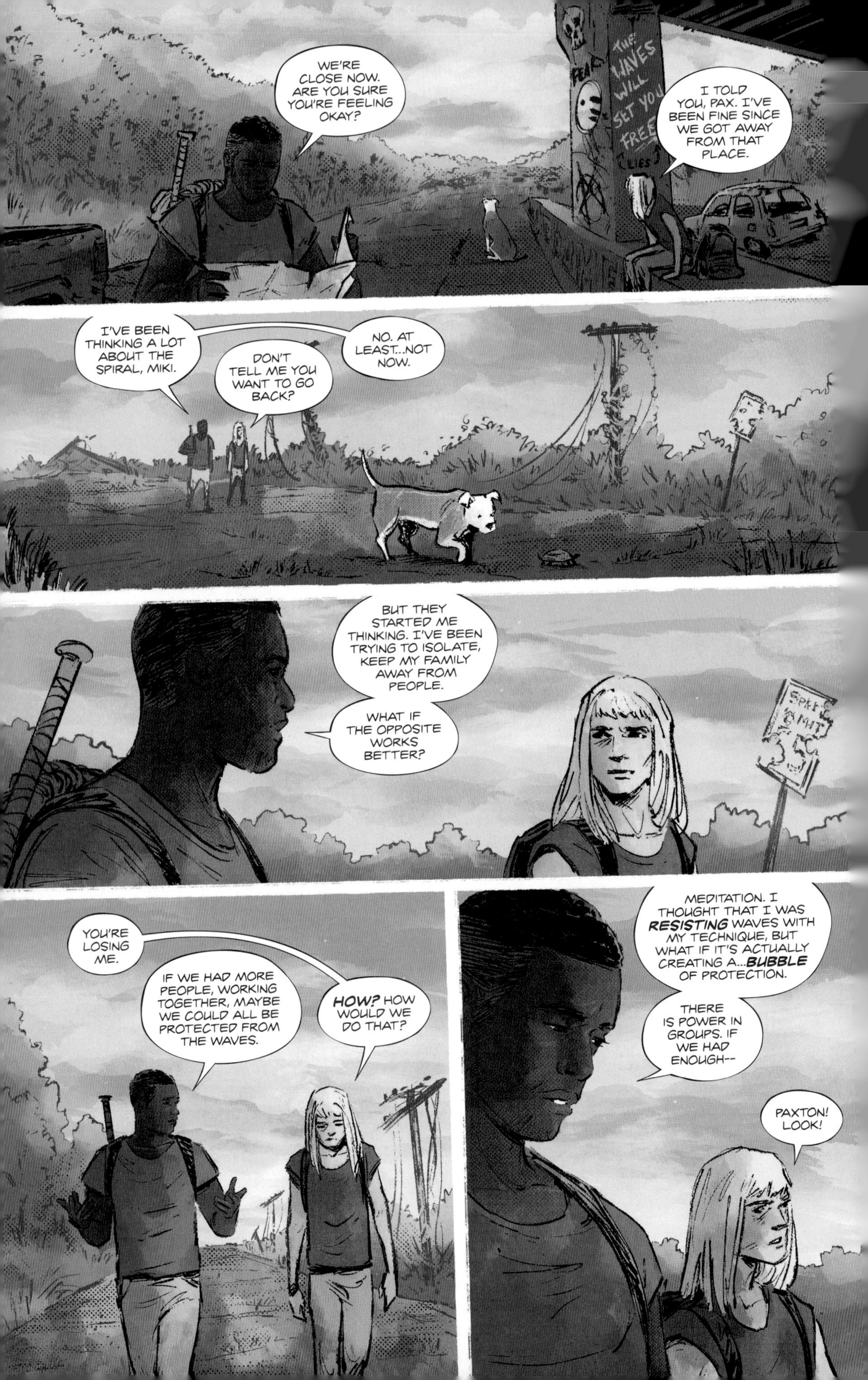

FEAR
THE WAVES WILL SET YOU FREE
LIES
WE'RE CLOSE NOW. ARE YOU SURE YOU'RE FEELING OKAY?
I TOLD YOU, PAX. I'VE BEEN FINE SINCE WE GOT AWAY FROM THAT PLACE.
I'VE BEEN THINKING A LOT ABOUT THE SPIRAL, MIKI.
DON'T TELL ME YOU WANT TO GO BACK?
NO. AT LEAST...NOT NOW.
BUT THEY STARTED ME THINKING. I'VE BEEN TRYING TO ISOLATE, KEEP MY FAMILY AWAY FROM PEOPLE.
WHAT IF THE OPPOSITE WORKS BETTER?
IF WE HAD MORE PEOPLE, WORKING TOGETHER, MAYBE WE COULD ALL BE PROTECTED FROM THE WAVES.
YOU'RE LOSING ME.
HOW? HOW WOULD WE DO THAT?
MEDITATION. I THOUGHT THAT I WAS RESISTING WAVES WITH MY TECHNIQUE, BUT WHAT IF IT'S ACTUALLY CREATING A...BUBBLE OF PROTECTION.
THERE IS POWER IN GROUPS. IF WE HAD ENOUGH--
PAXTON! LOOK!

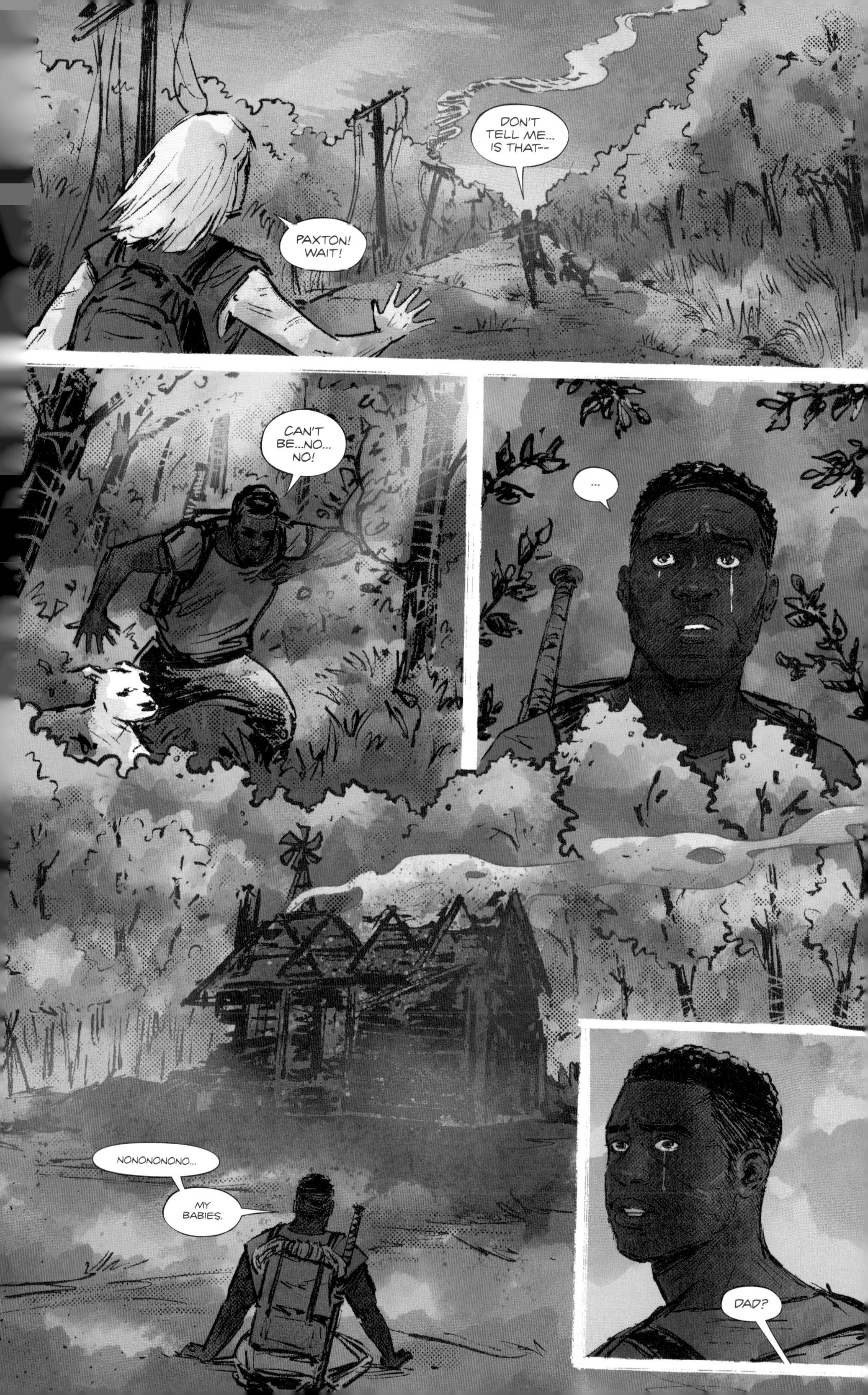
DON'T TELL ME... IS THAT--
PAXTON! WAIT!
CAN'T BE...NO... NO!
...
NONONONONO...
MY BABIES.
DAD?

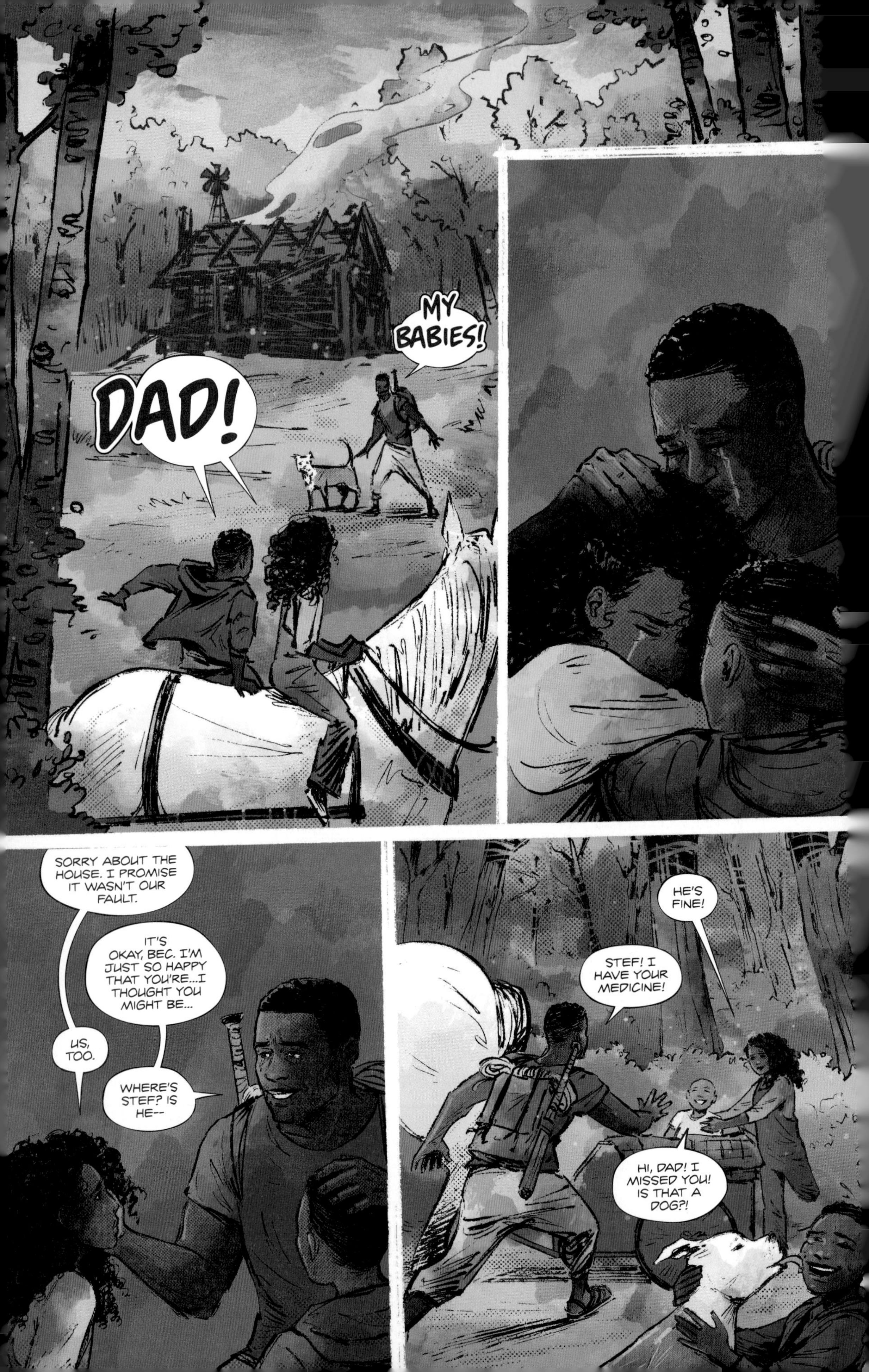
MY BABIES!
DAD!
SORRY ABOUT THE HOUSE. I PROMISE IT WASN'T OUR FAULT.
IT'S OKAY, BEC. I'M JUST SO HAPPY THAT YOU'RE...I THOUGHT YOU MIGHT BE...
US, TOO.
WHERE'S STEF? IS HE--
HE'S FINE!
STEF! I HAVE YOUR MEDICINE!
HI, DAD! I MISSED YOU! IS THAT A DOG?!

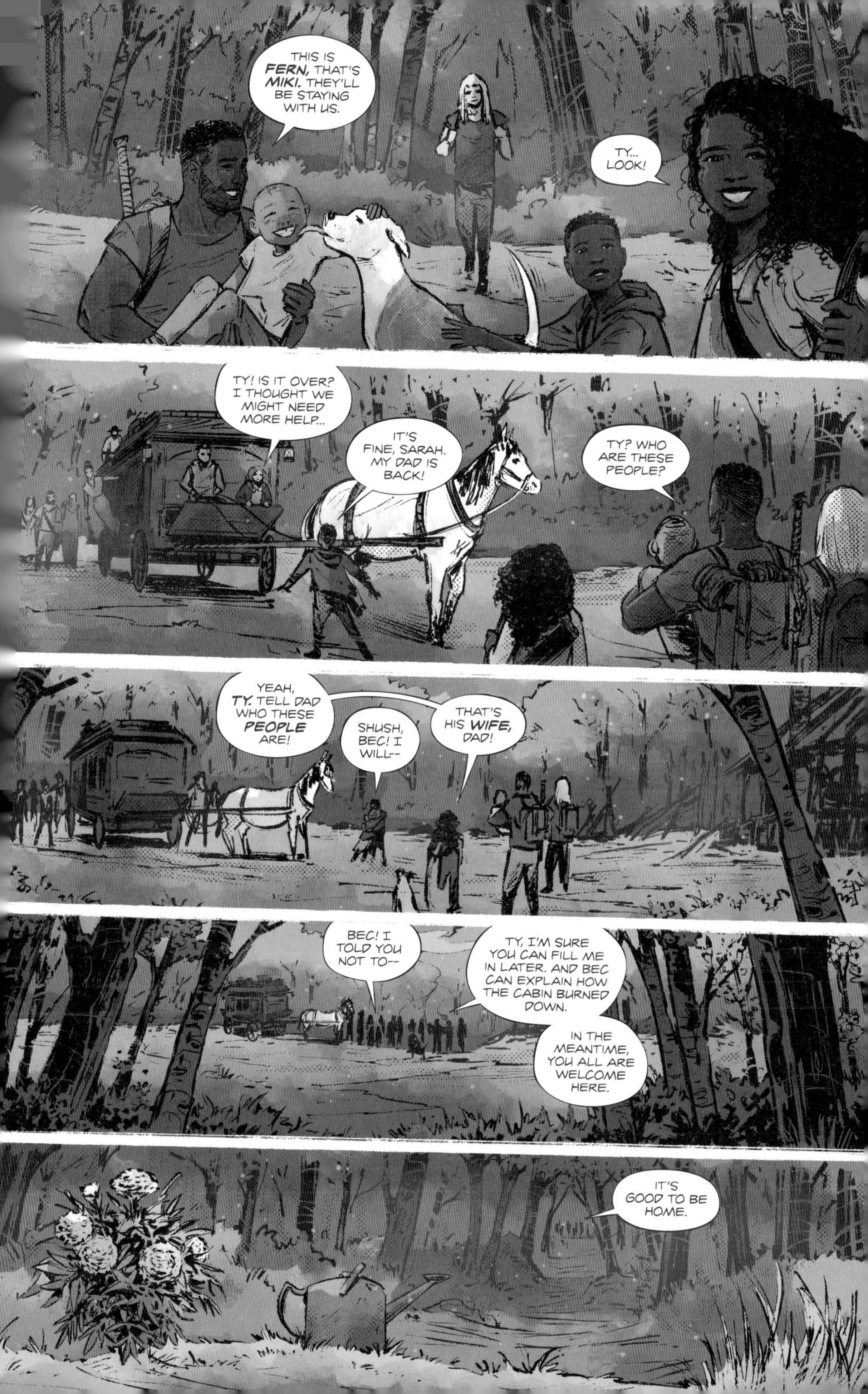
THIS IS **FERN,** THAT'S **MIKI.** THEY'LL BE STAYING WITH US.
TY... LOOK!
TY! IS IT OVER? I THOUGHT WE MIGHT NEED MORE HELP...
IT'S FINE, SARAH. MY DAD IS BACK!
TY? WHO ARE THESE PEOPLE?
YEAH, **TY.** TELL DAD WHO THESE **PEOPLE** ARE!
SHUSH, BEC! I WILL--
THAT'S HIS **WIFE,** DAD!
BEC! I TOLD YOU NOT TO--
TY, I'M SURE YOU CAN FILL ME IN LATER. AND BEC CAN EXPLAIN HOW THE CABIN BURNED DOWN.
IN THE MEANTIME, YOU ALL ARE WELCOME HERE.
IT'S GOOD TO BE HOME.

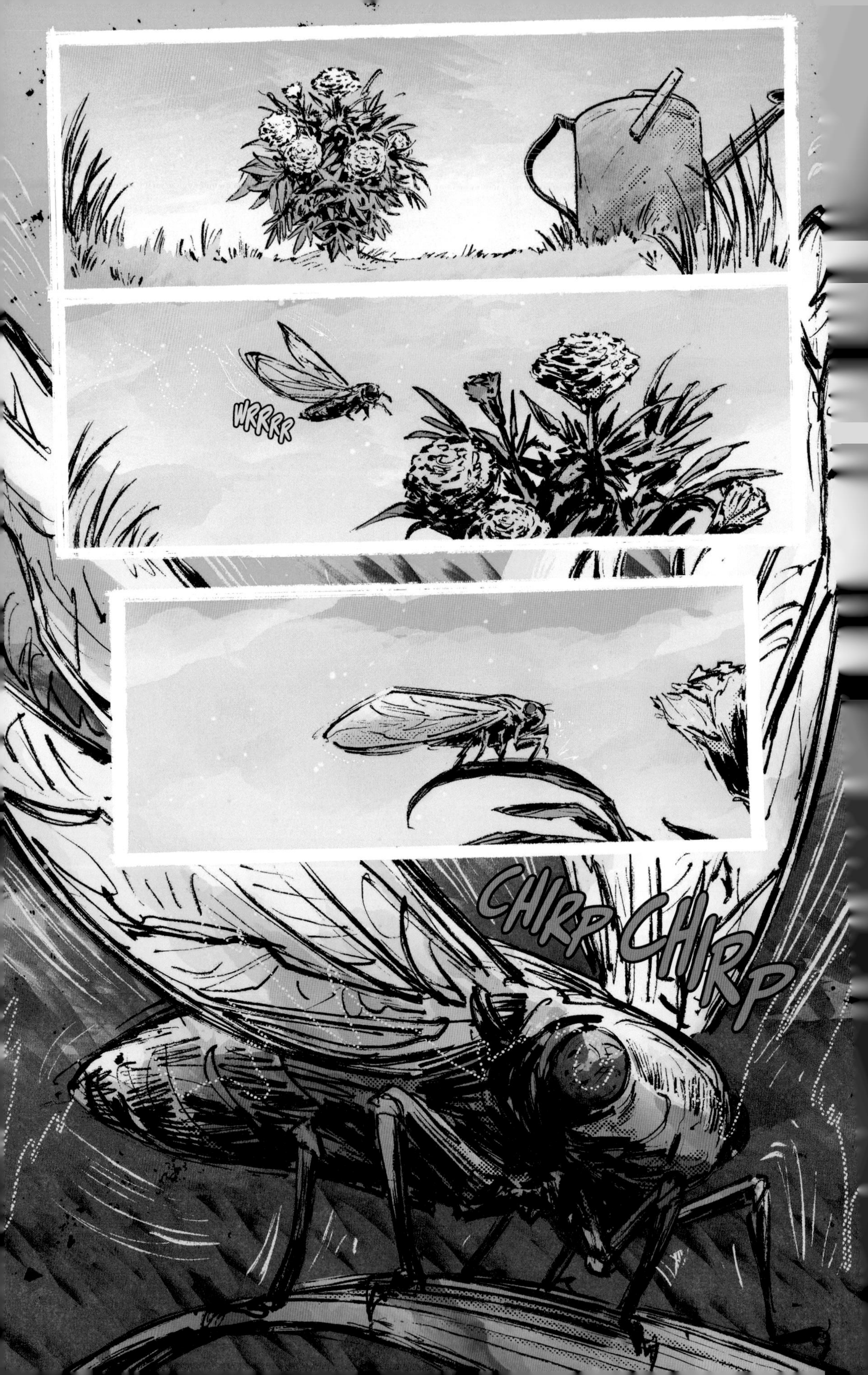
WRRRR
CHIRP CHIRP

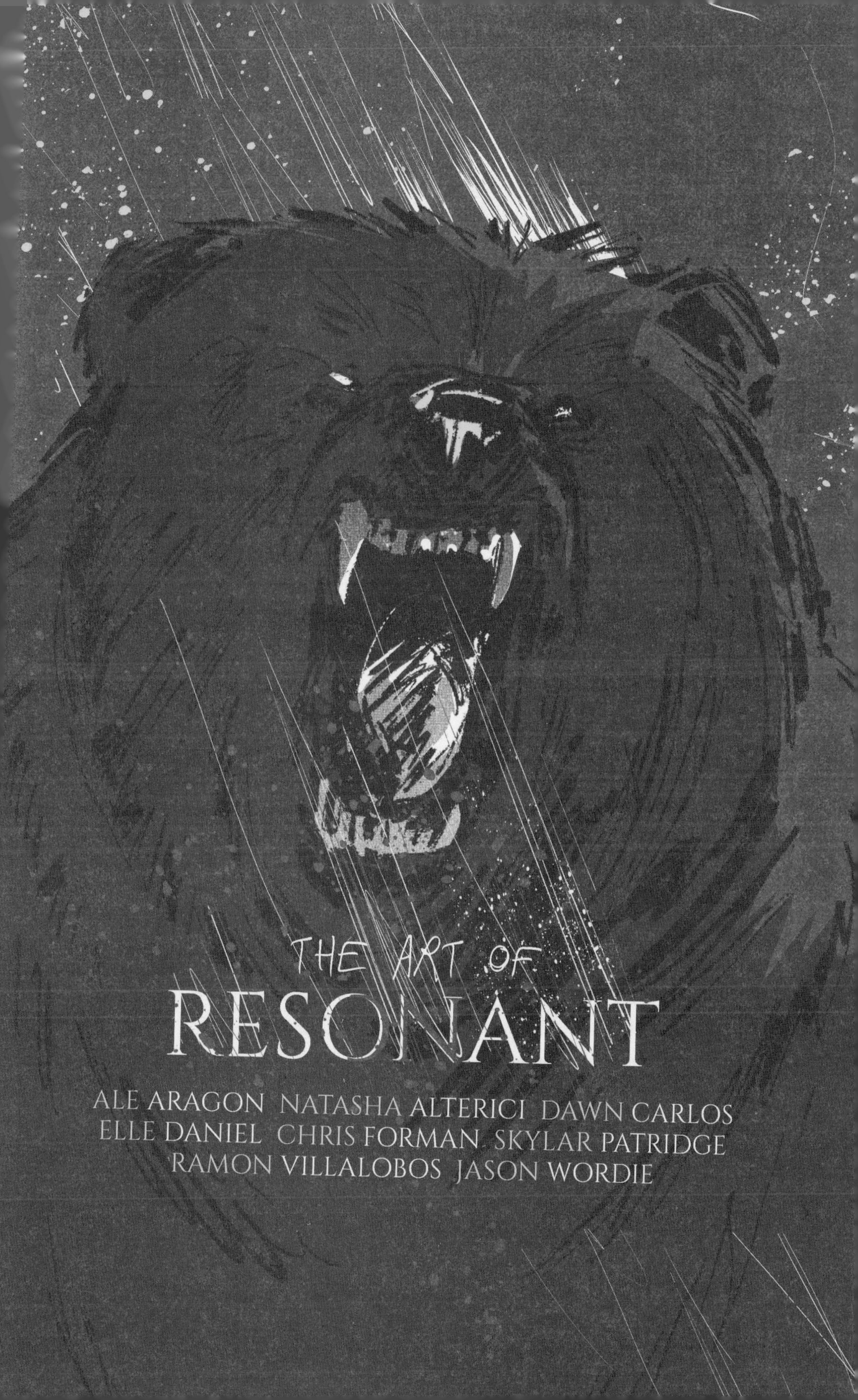
THE ART OF
RESONANT
ALE ARAGON NATASHA ALTERICI DAWN CARLOS
ELLE DANIEL CHRIS FORMAN SKYLAR PATRIDGE
RAMON VILLALOBOS JASON WORDIE

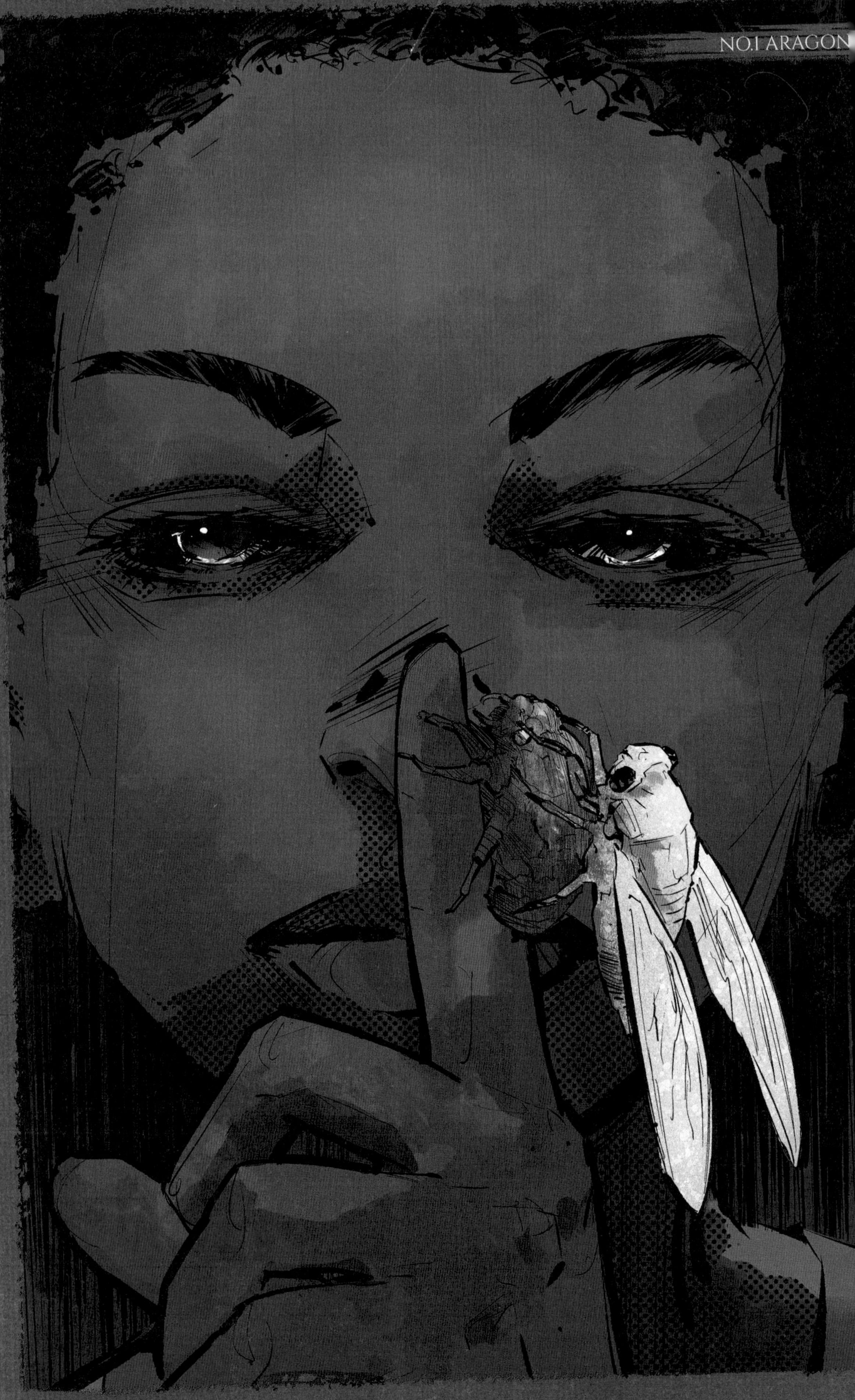

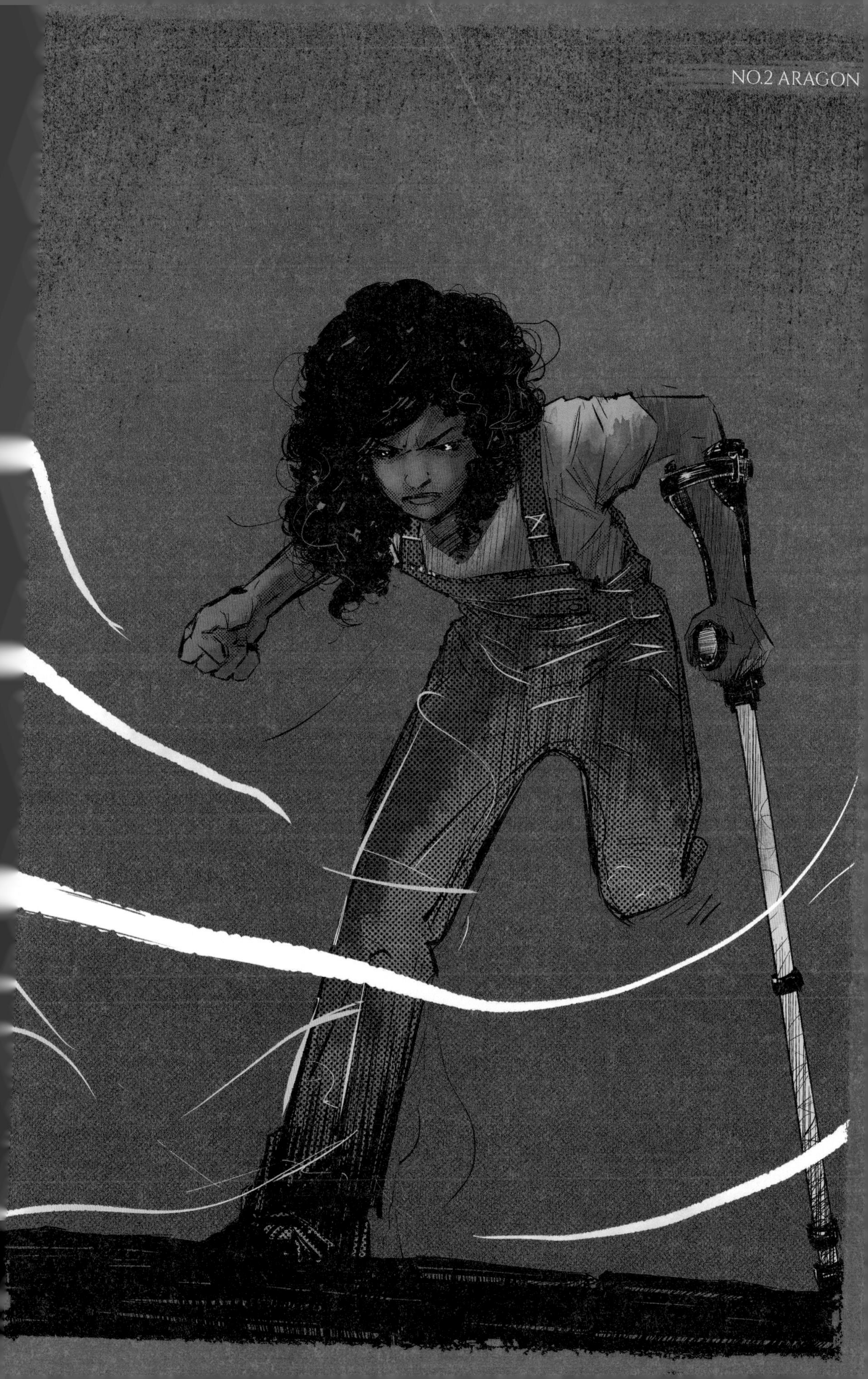

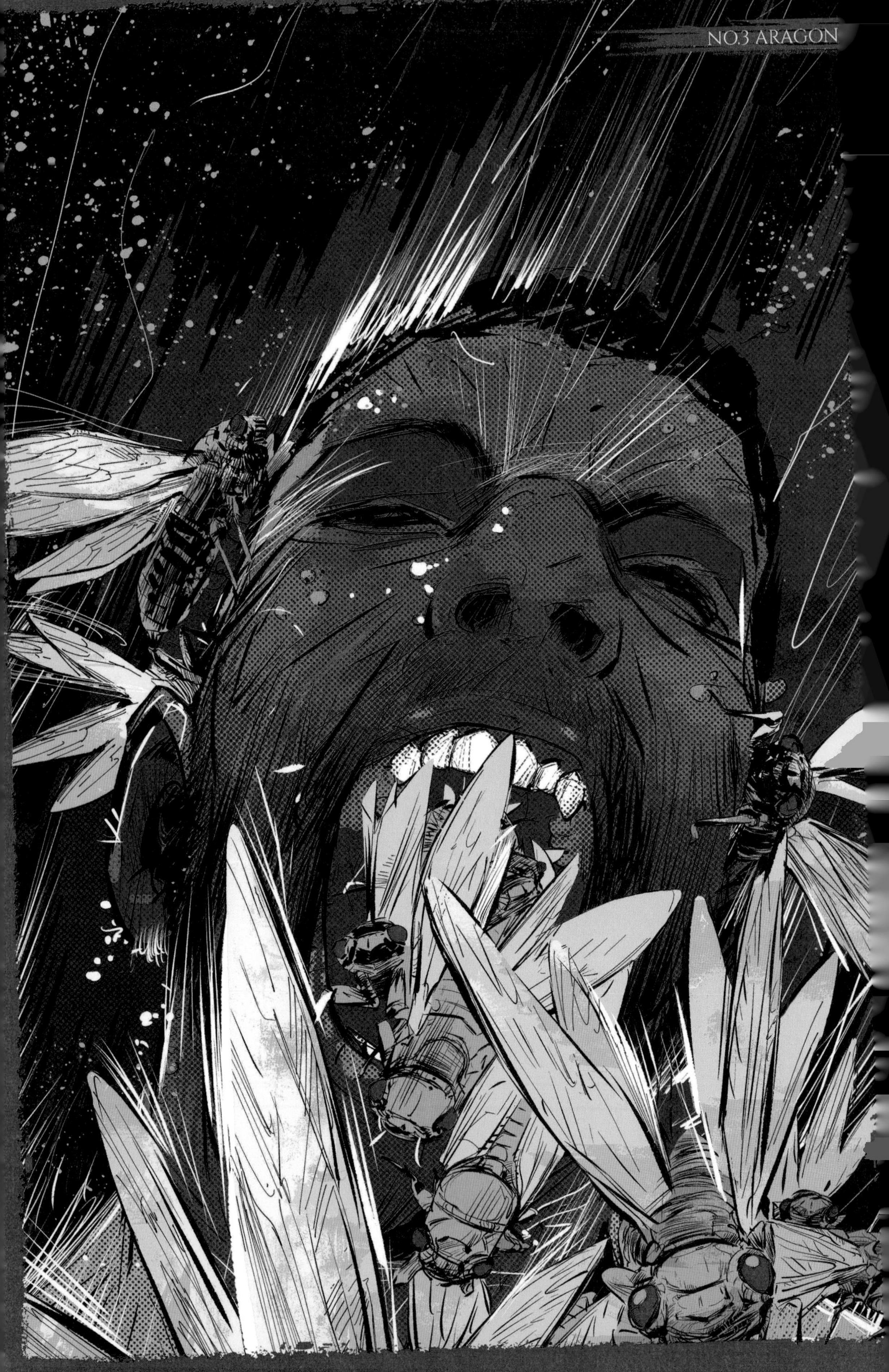

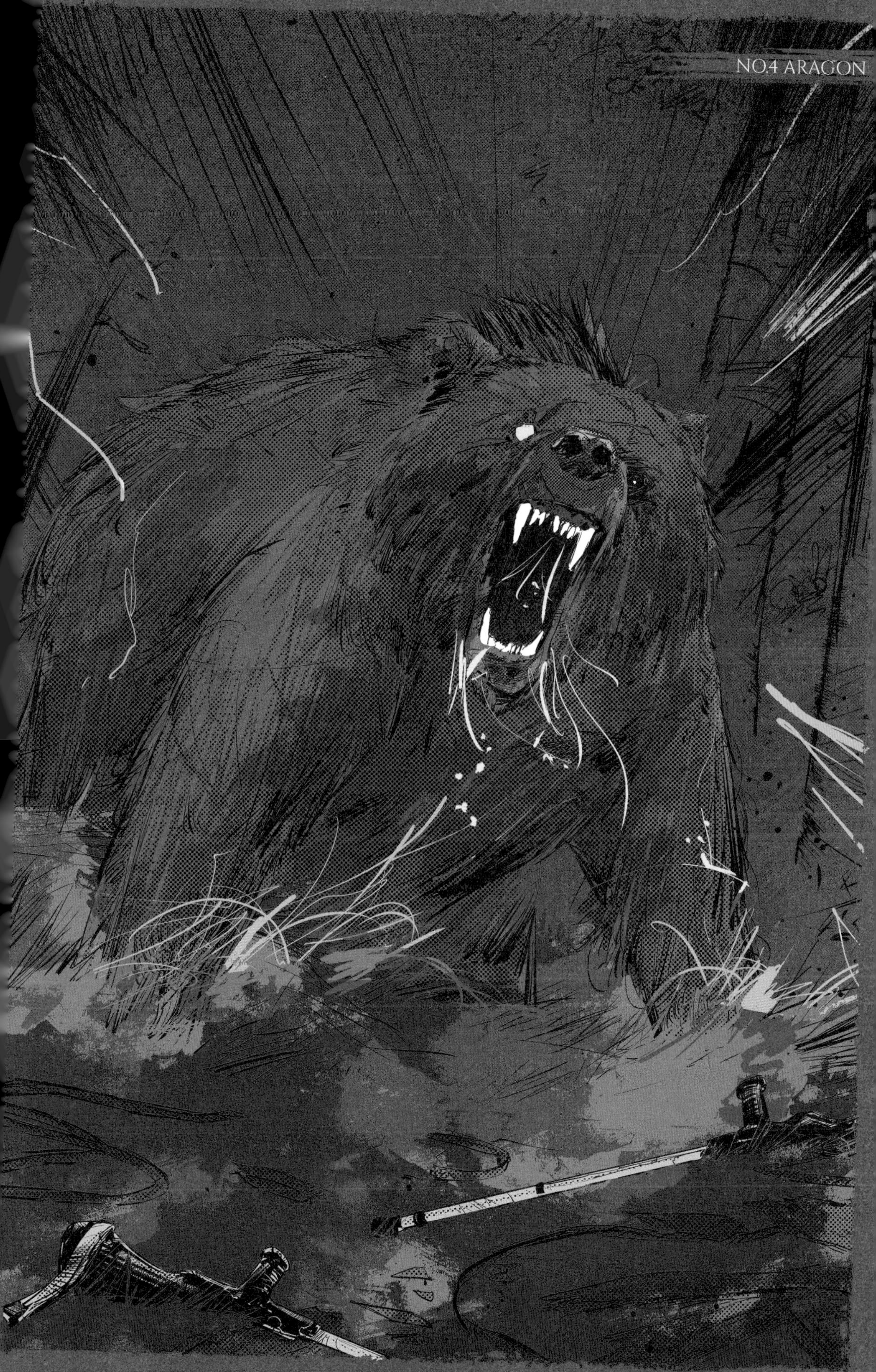

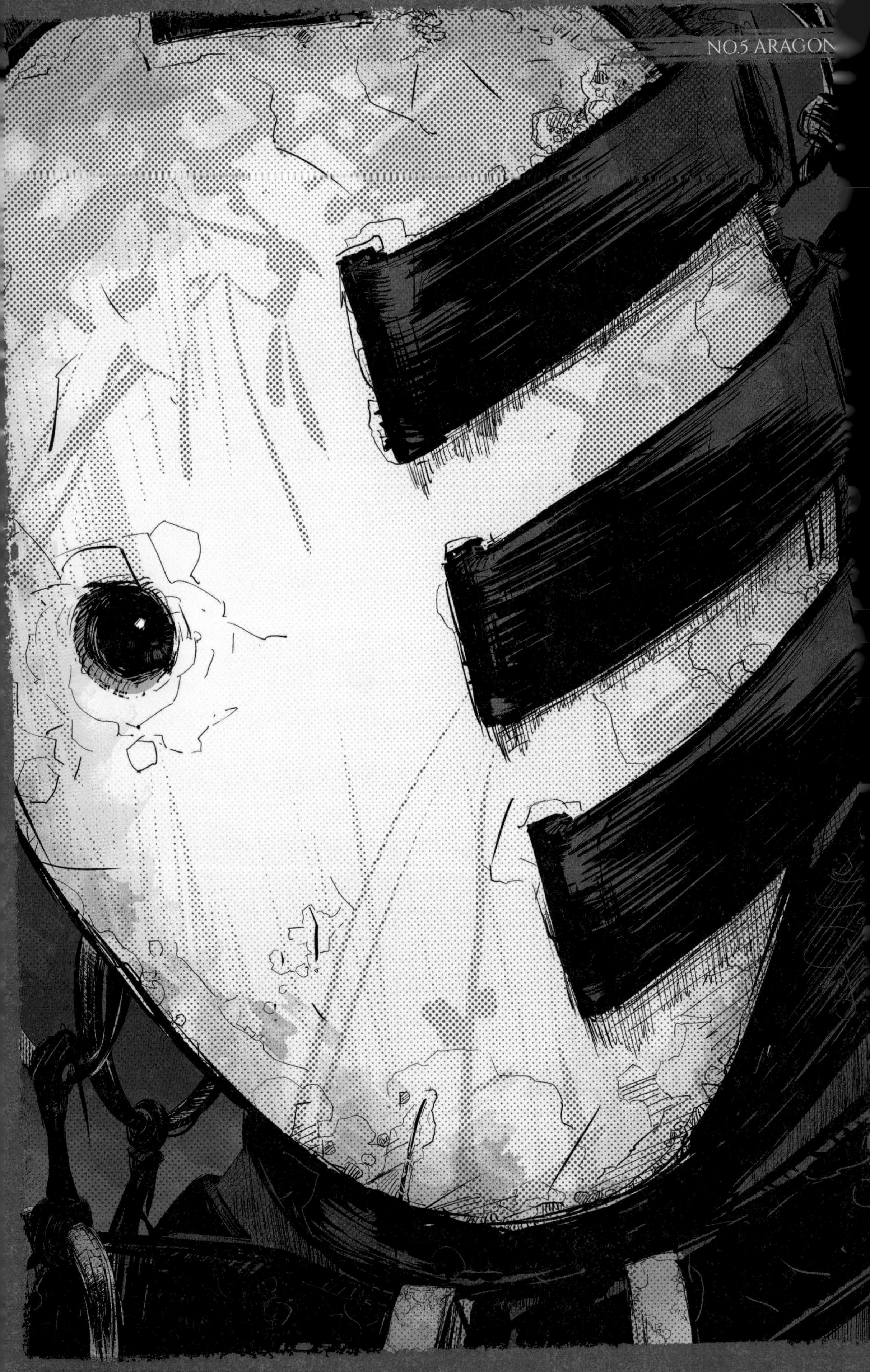

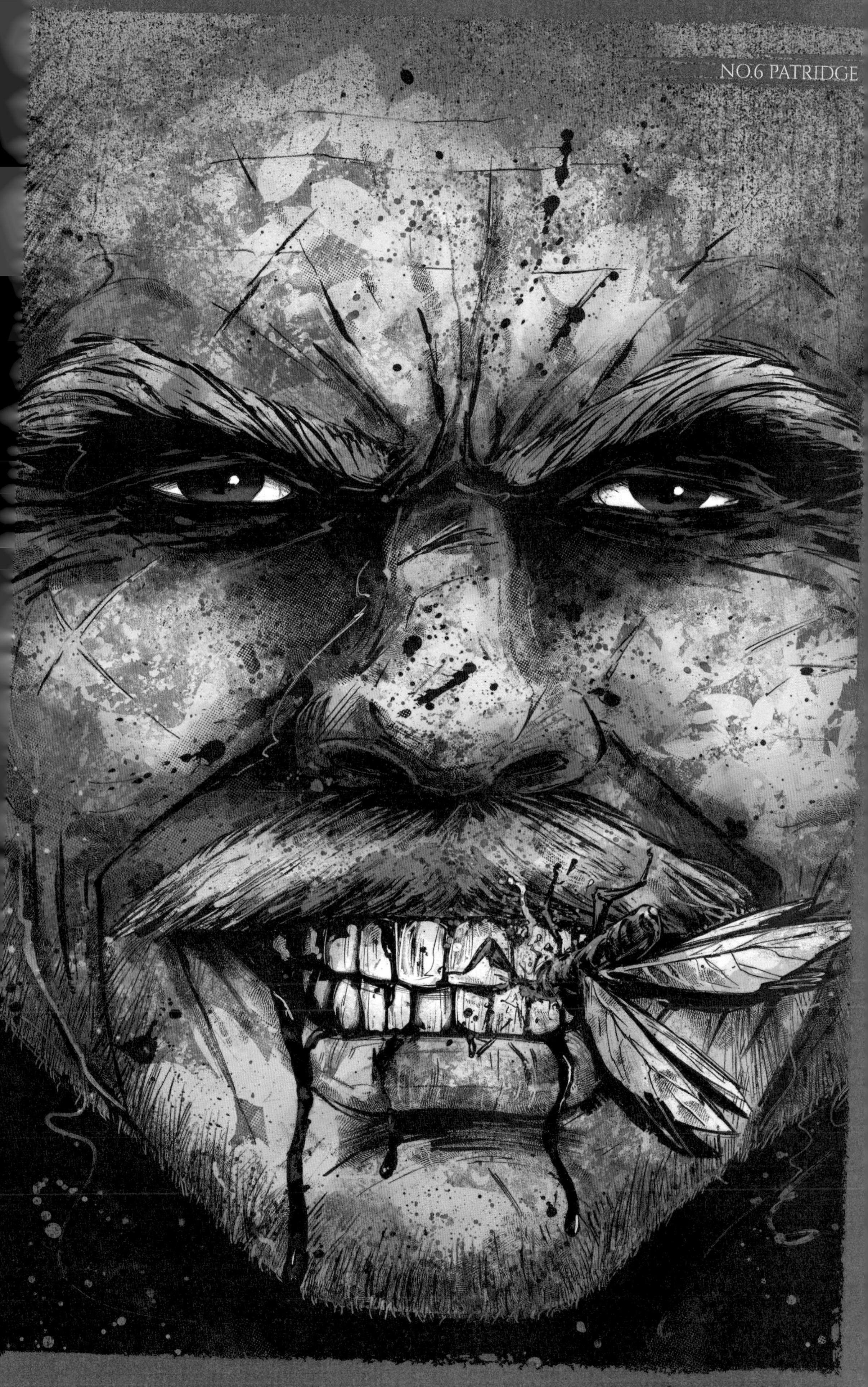
NO.6 PATRIDGE

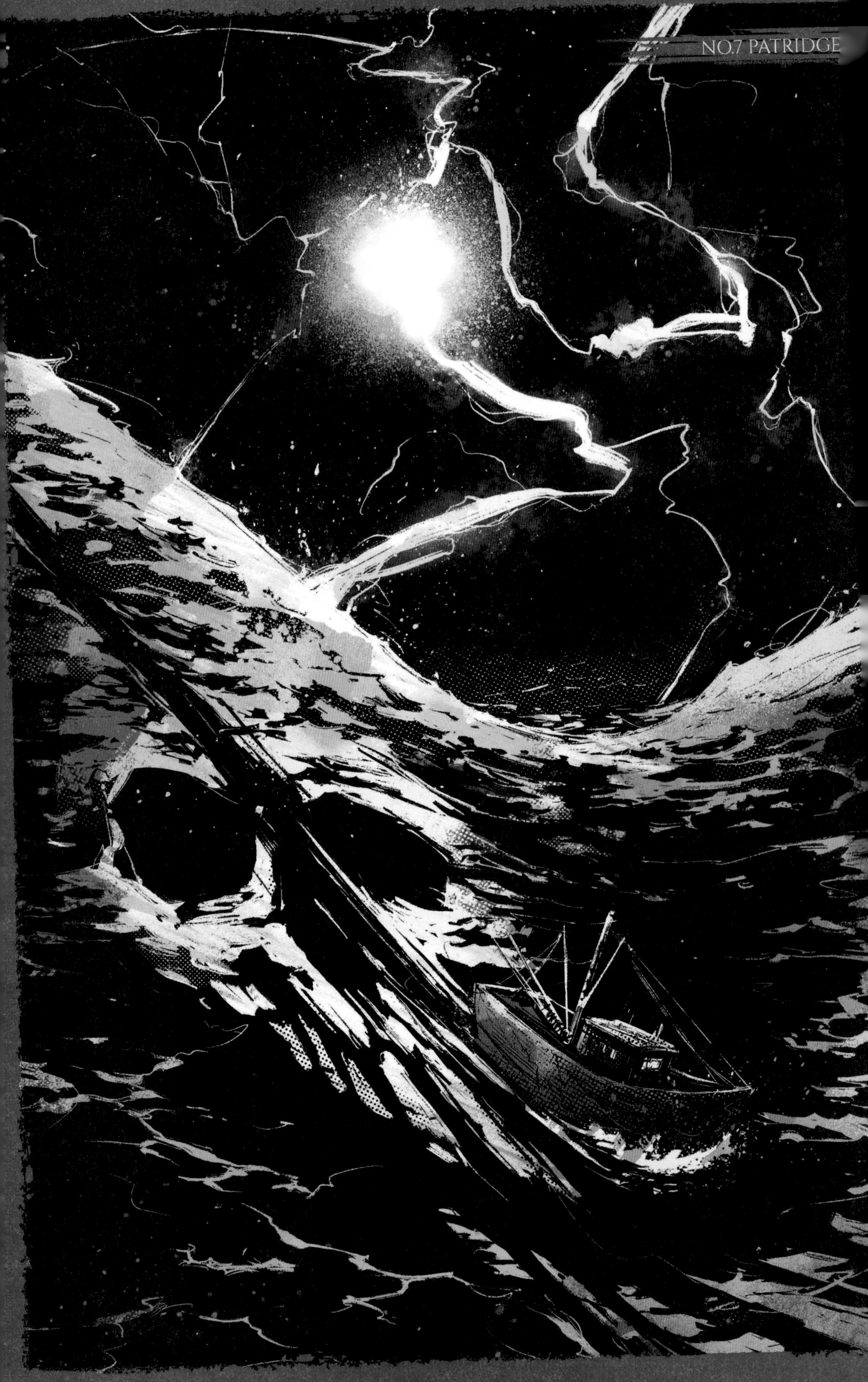

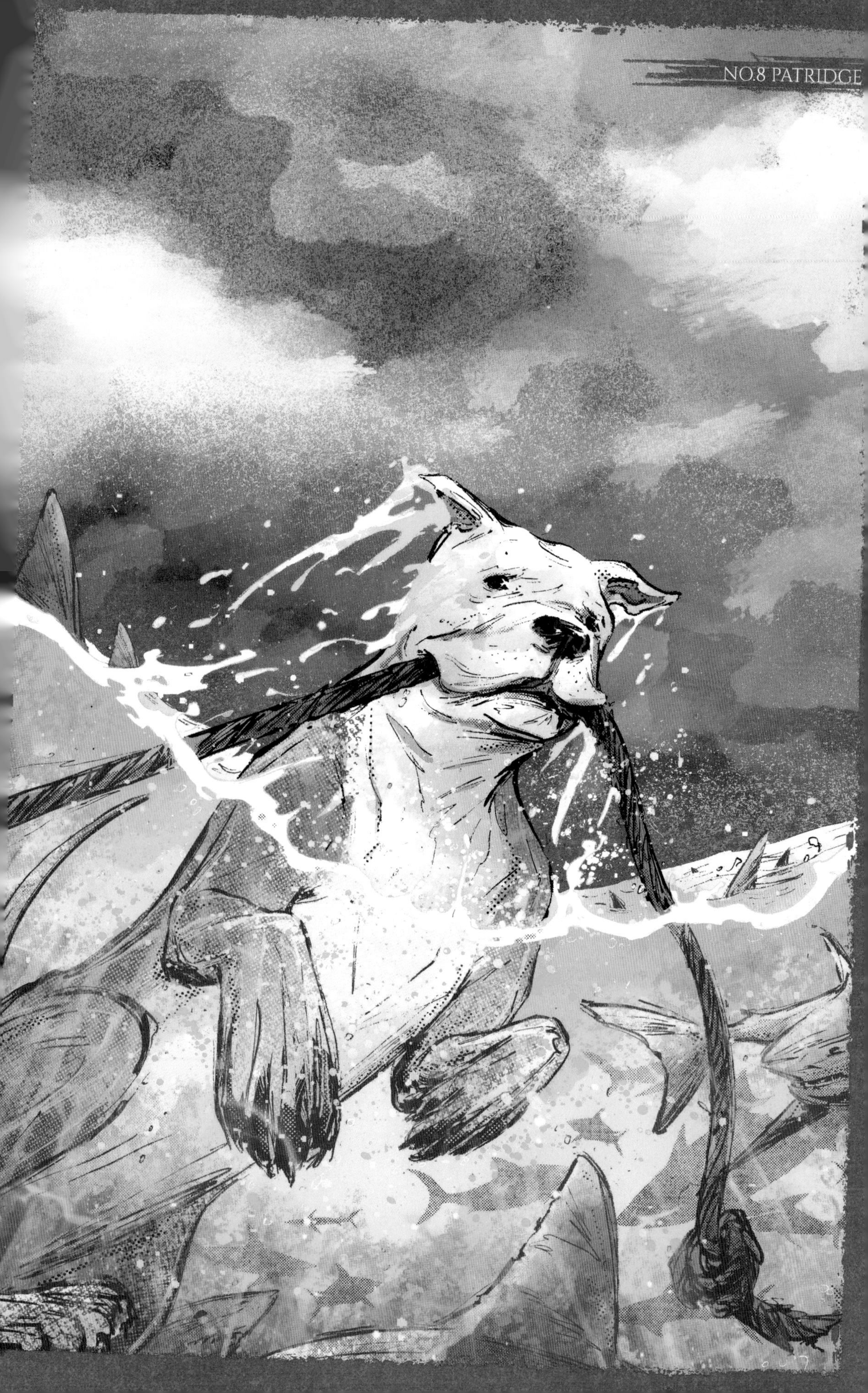
NO.8 PATRIDGE

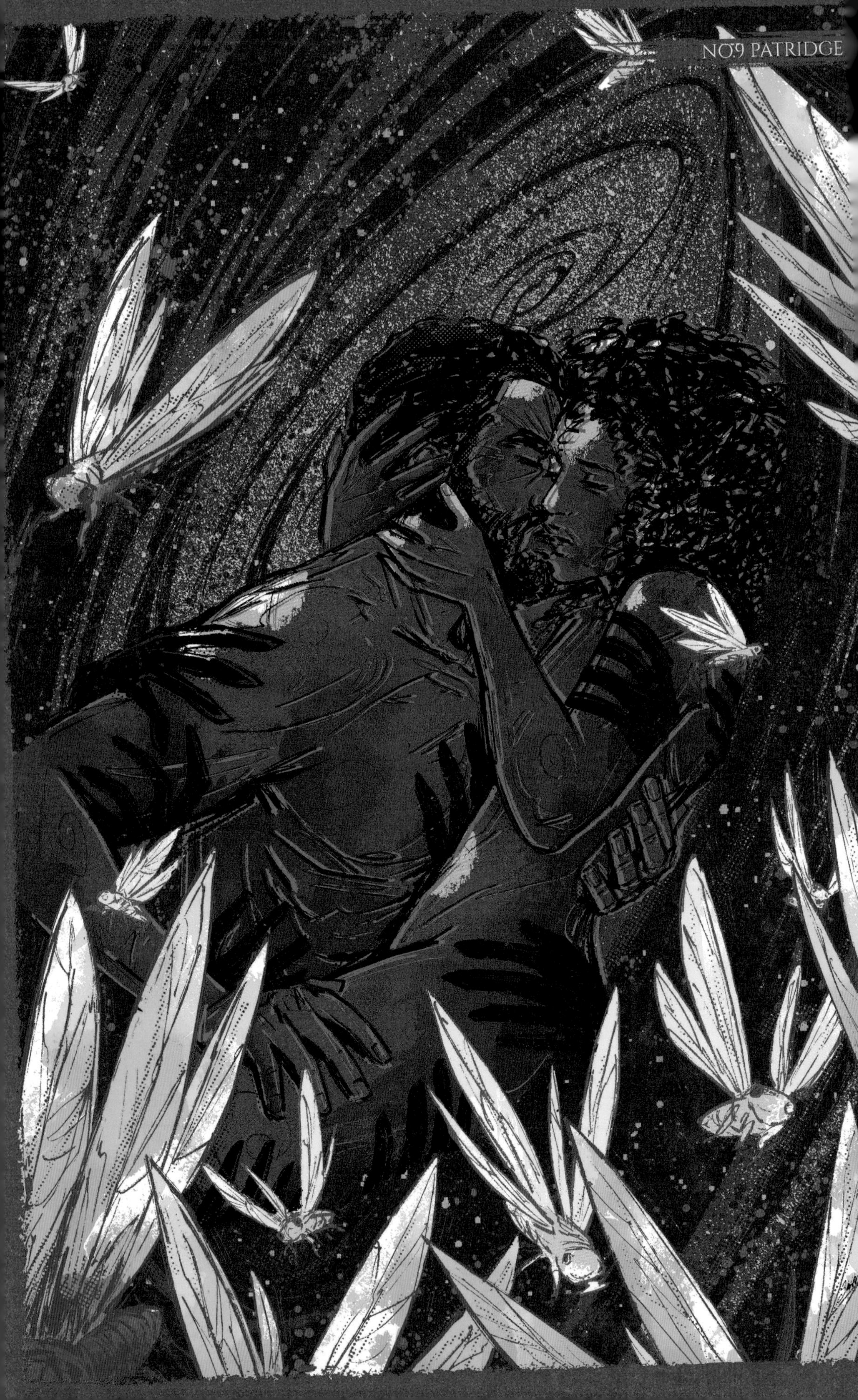
NO.9 PATRIDGE

NO.10 PATRIDGE

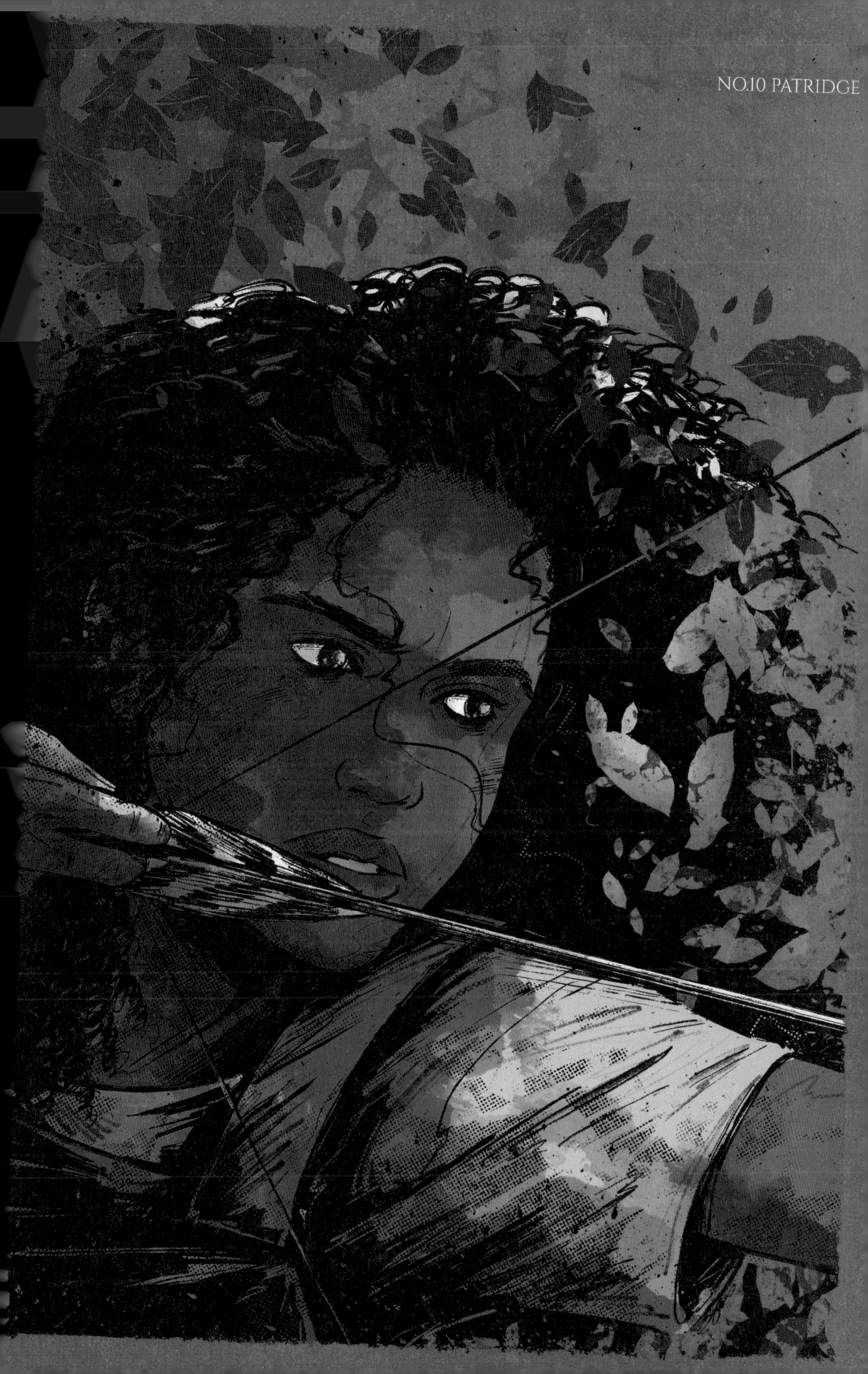

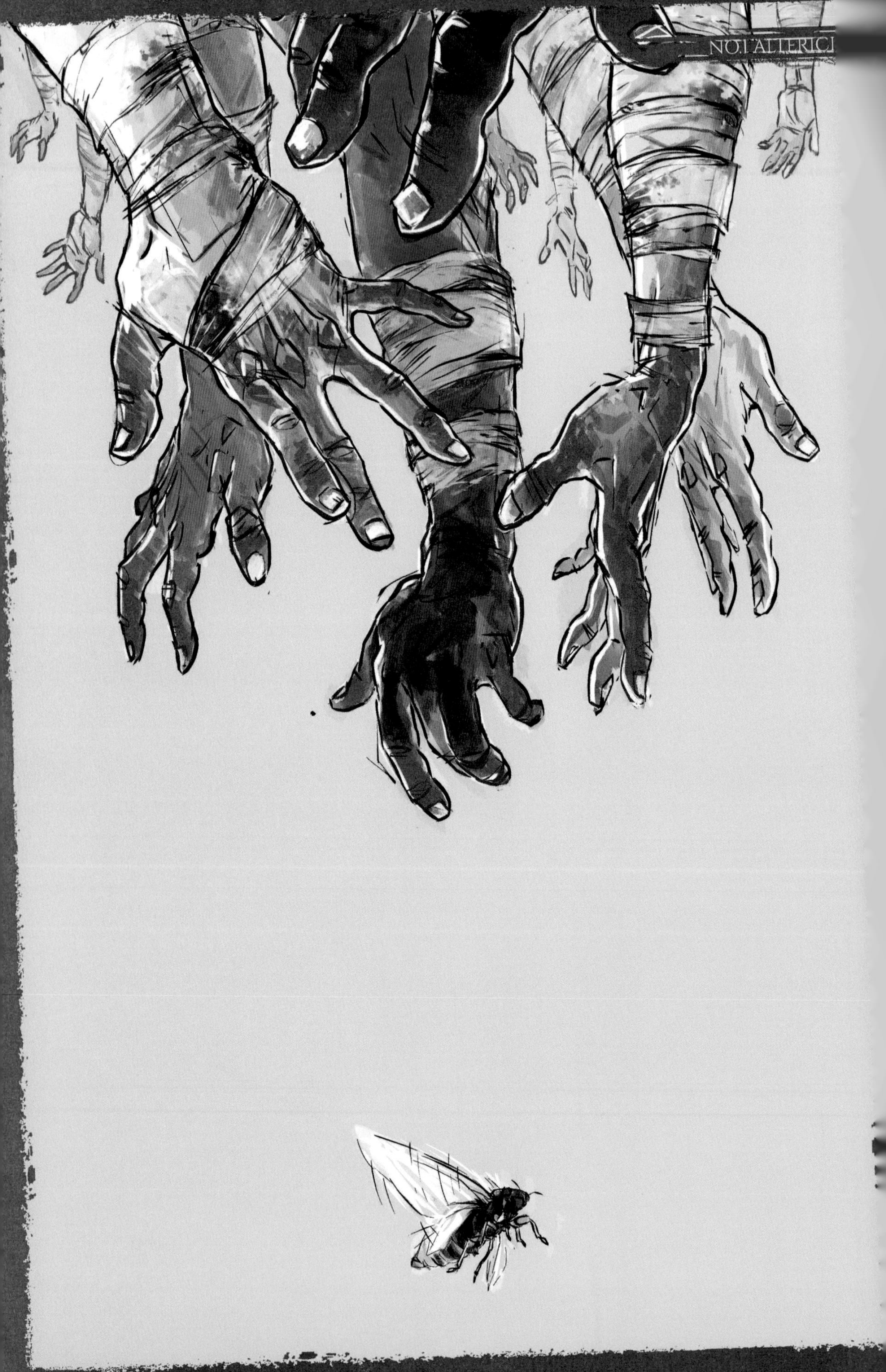
NO.I ALLERICI

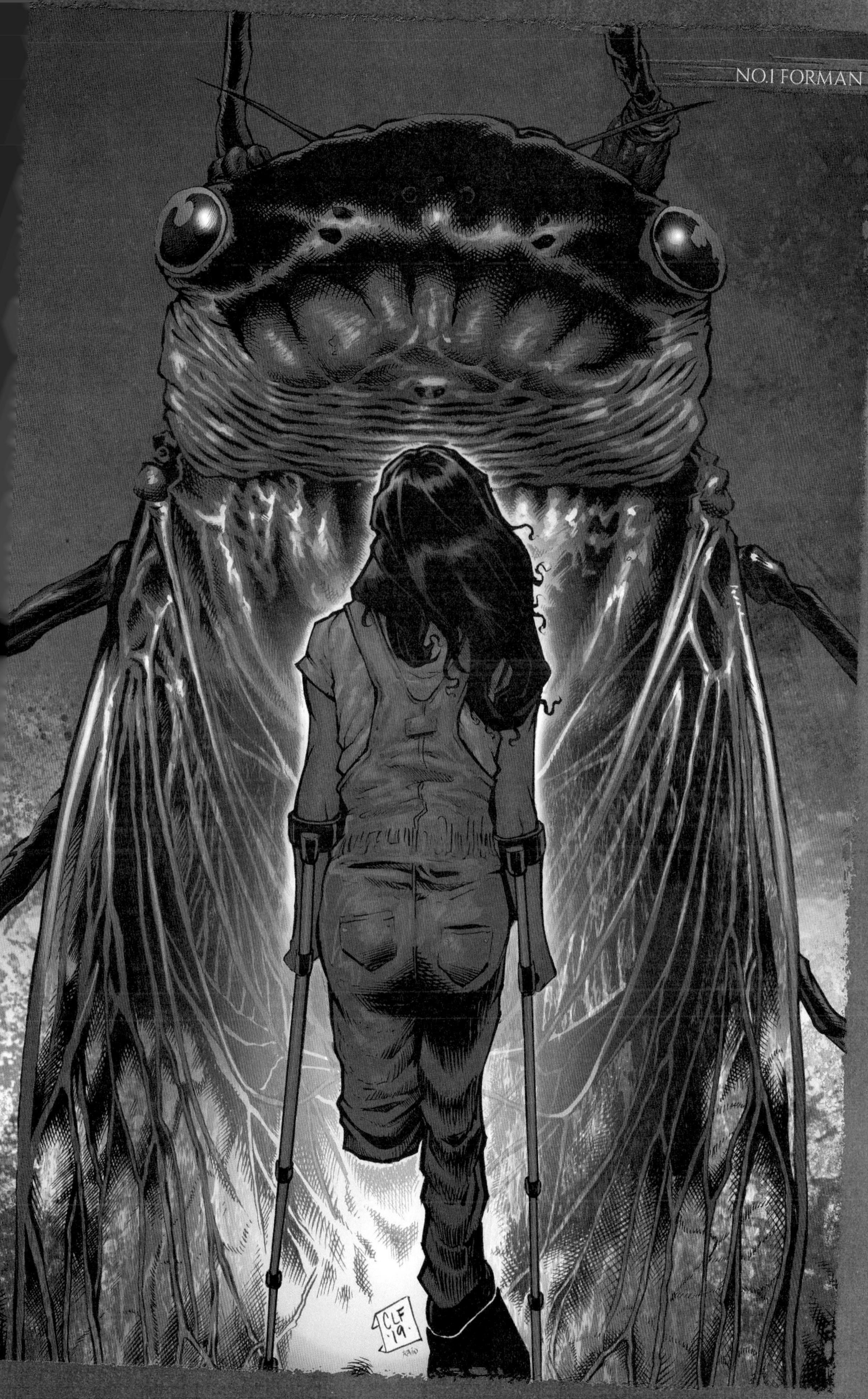
NO.1 FORMAN
CLF '19

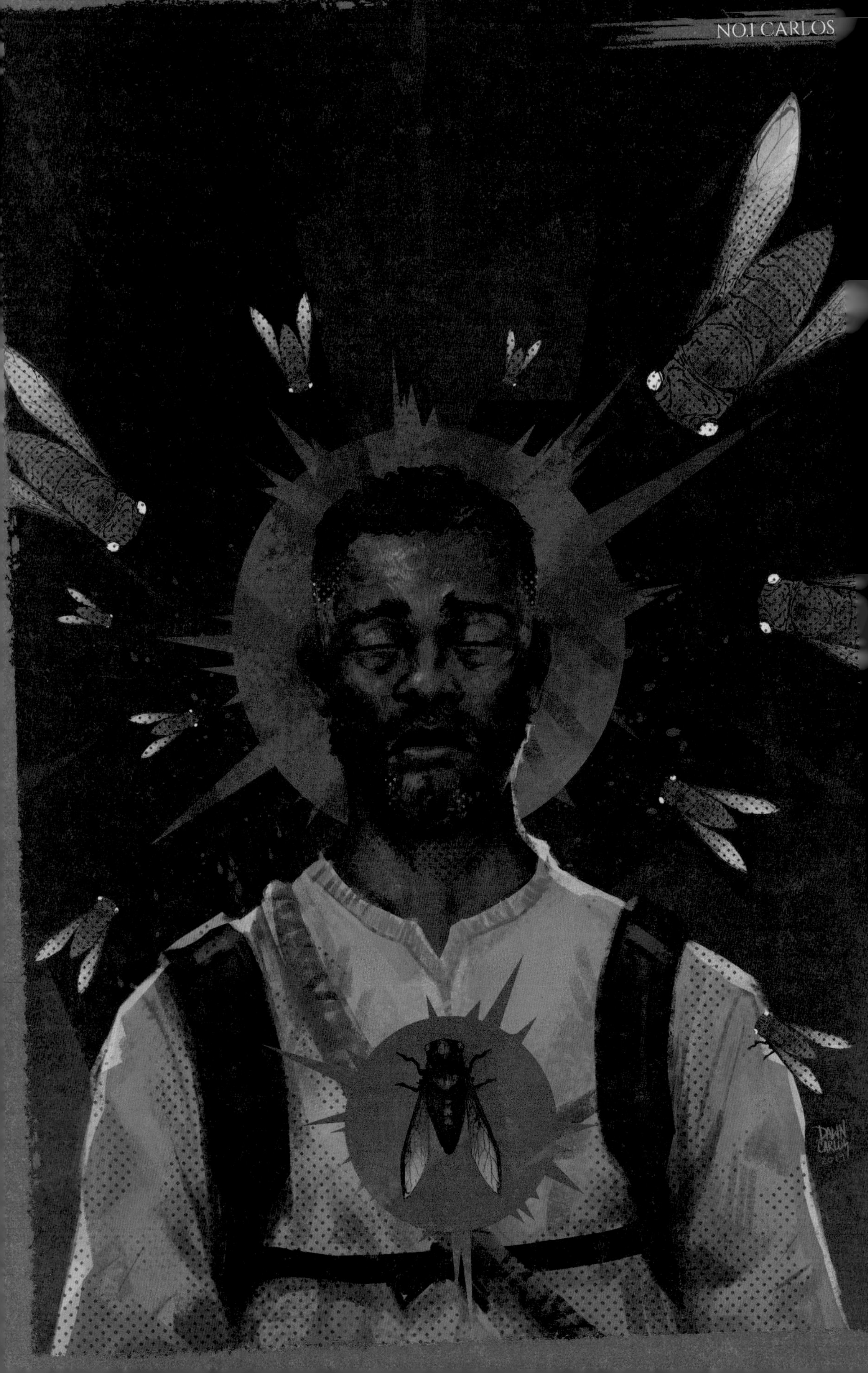
NO.1 CARLOS

NO.1 CARLOS

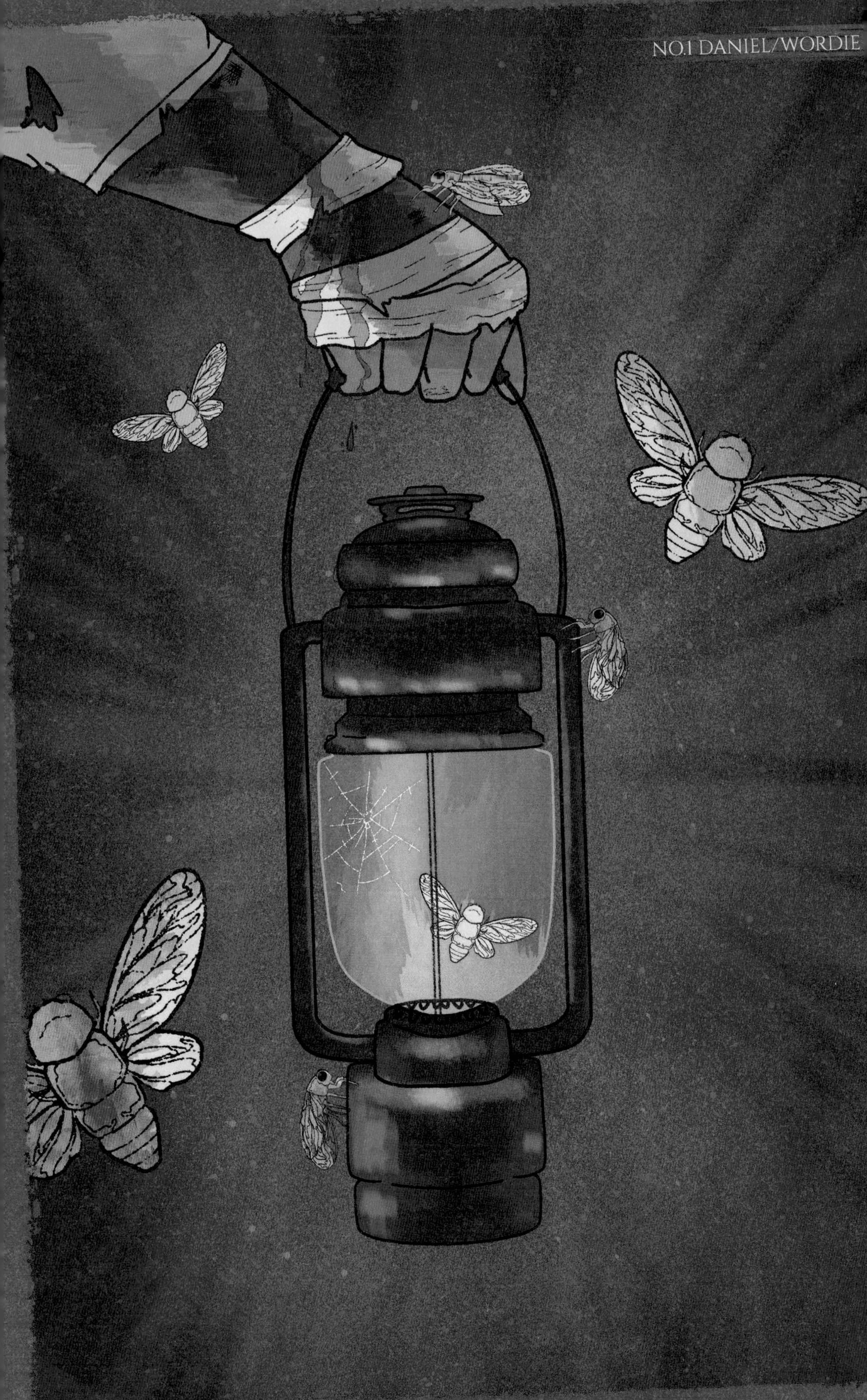

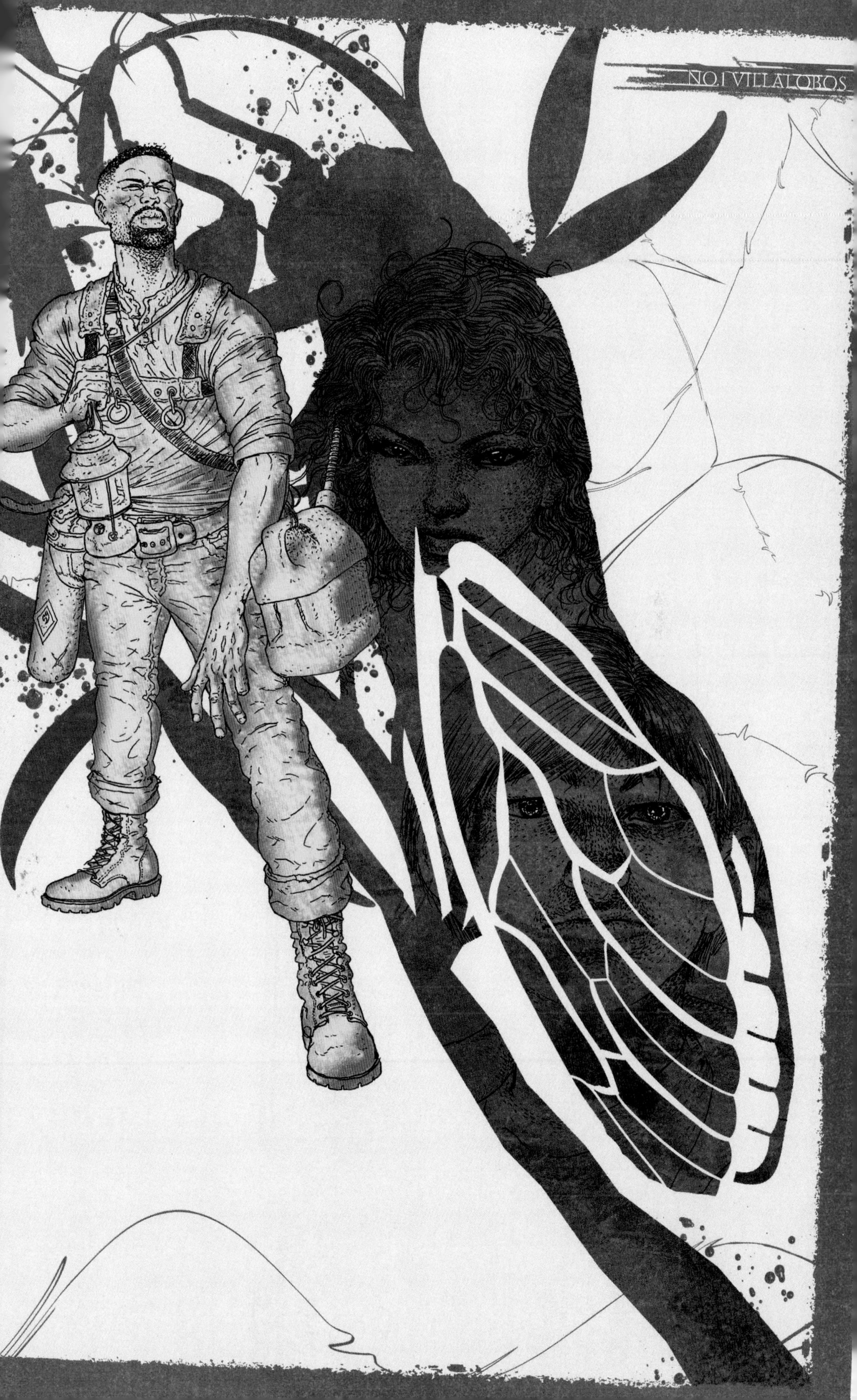
NOI VILLALOBOS

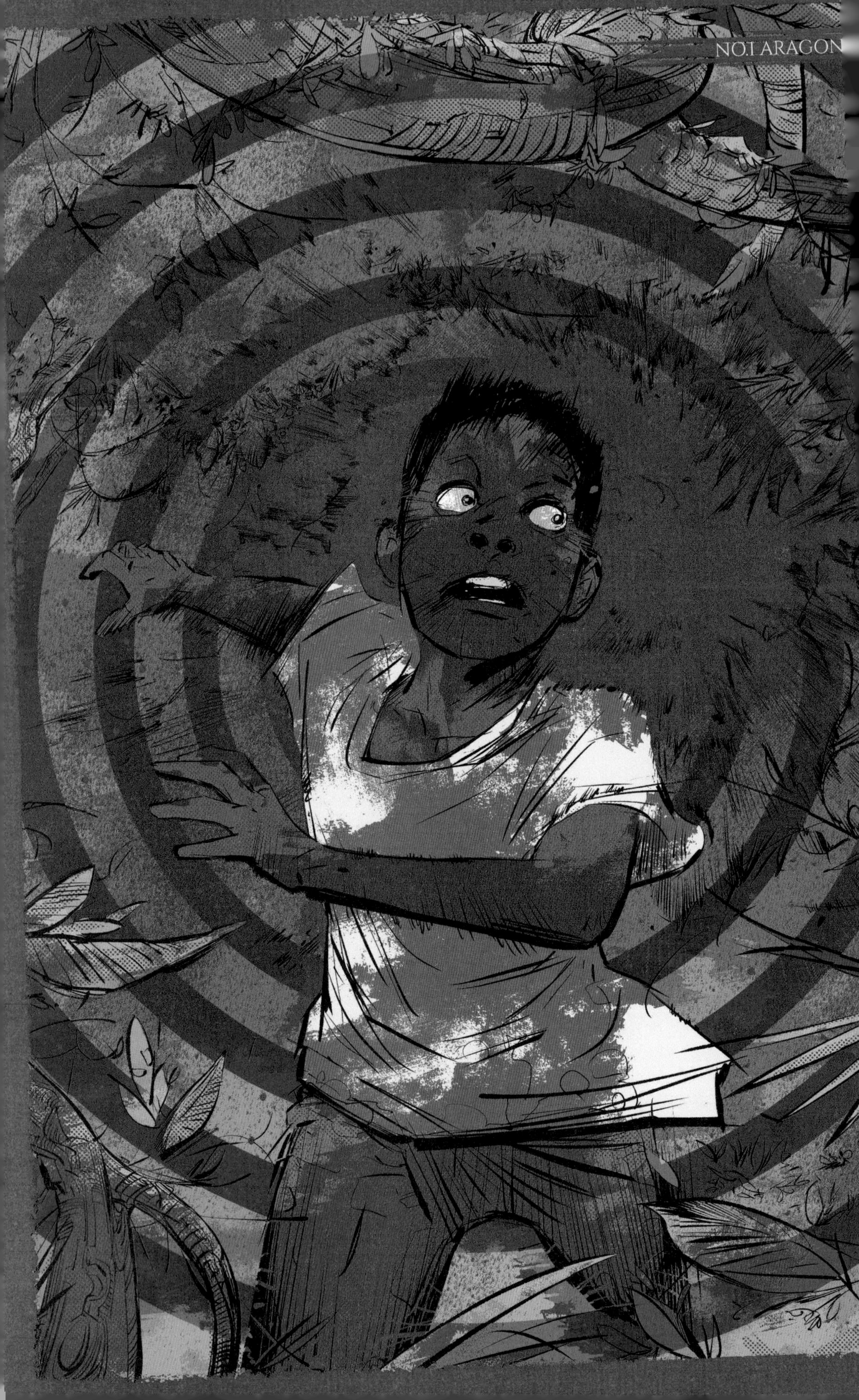

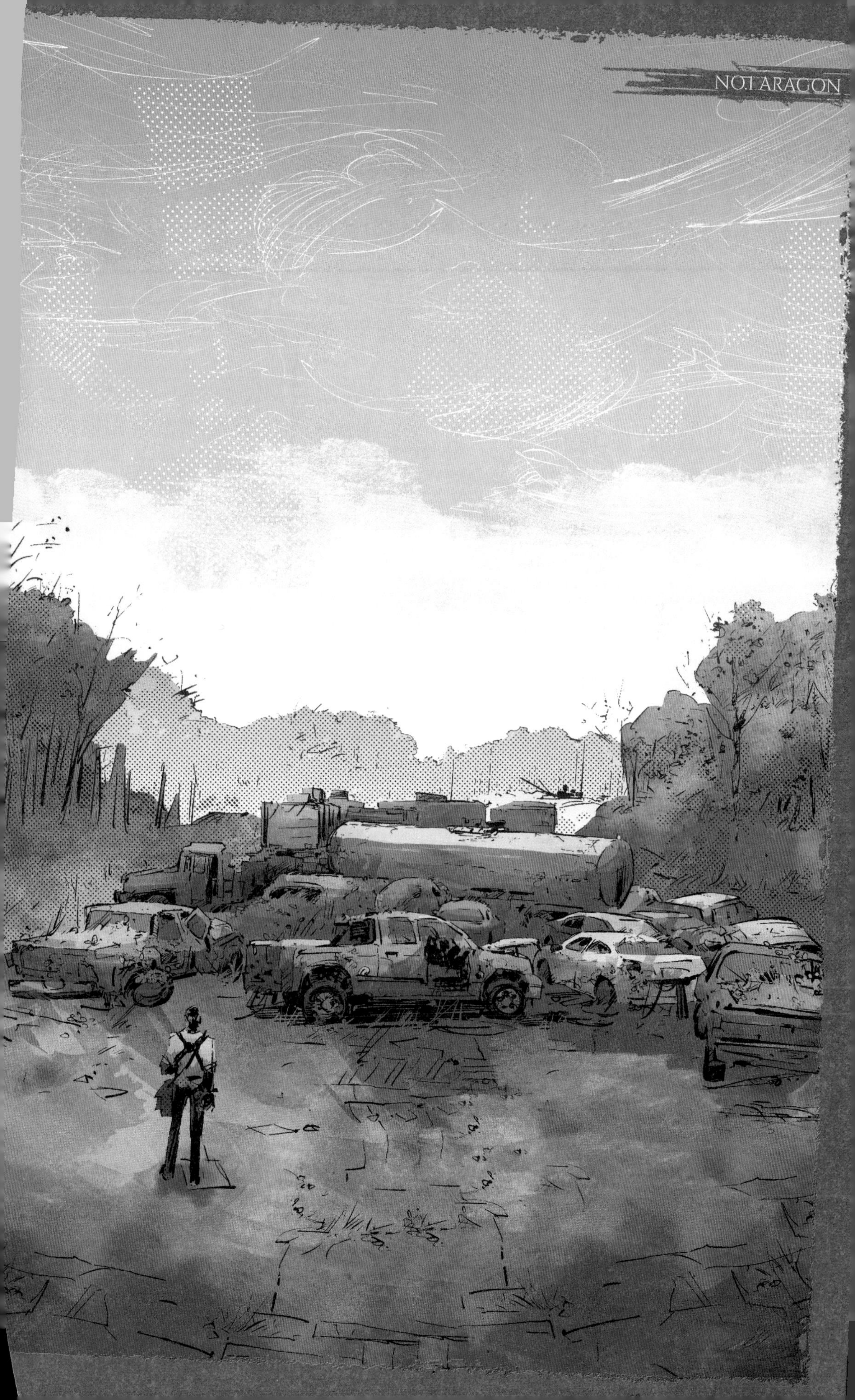
NO.1 ARAGON

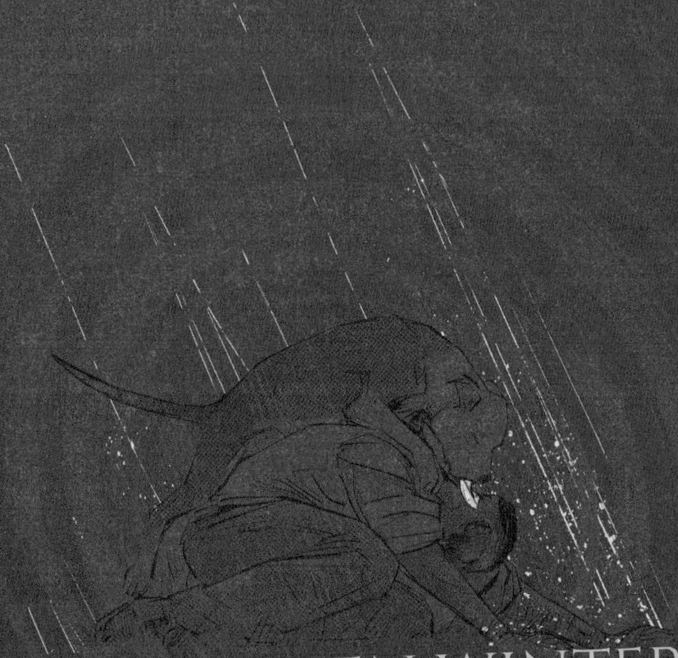

FOR LAUREN WINTERS.

EVERY GOOD IDEA I STOLE FROM YOU.